Bowhill

Bowhill

The archaeological study of a building under repair in Exeter, Devon, 1977–95

Stuart R Blaylock

with major contributions from
N W Alcock, J P Allan, B M A Ellis, C M Groves, G Edwards, J R Harrison,
A J Hopper-Bishop, R E Howard, B Knight, F P Kelly, R McNeilage, N Shiel

and illustrations by
P J F Bishop, D A Garner, T Ives, R W Parker, A Simm and others

ENGLISH HERITAGE

Published in association with Exeter Archaeology as Volume 5 in the
Exeter Archaeology Reports series

Published by English Heritage, Kemble Drive, Swindon SN2 2GZ

Copyright © English Heritage 2004

First Published 2004

ISBN 1 873592 60 4

Product Code 50095

British Library Cataloguing in Publication Data
A CIP catalogue record for this book is available from the British Library.

Brought to publication by Victoria R Trainor, Andrew McLaren and
David M Jones, Engllish Heritage Publications
Edited by Mike Ponsford
Indexed by Susan Vaughan
Designed by Val Kinsler

Printed by Arkle *Print*

Contents

10 Dendrochronology and mortar analysis

11 The development of the conservation progamme
by J R Harrison and F P Kelly

12 Concluding discussion

Appendix: the archive 344

Foreword

The story of Bowhill is that of a once rural gentry mansion that fell on hard times as the city of Exeter expanded around it. For long recognised by local antiquarians, the significance of the site was eventually acknowledged by publicly funded acquisition, study and repair. It is a story that can in outline be replicated throughout England, especially during the heritage-conscious last quarter of the 20th century, but rarely has it been told with the attention to detail that is provided here.

For twenty years Bowhill was an exciting and instructive building site. The conservation work offered many challenges. From the scaffolding in the great hall one could study at close hand the elegantly moulded roof timbers and see how the repairs were integrated within the original structure. Piles of straw and earth in the forecourt awaited their transformation into cob, a Devon building material hitherto little known to conservators of historic buildings. As work progressed there were experimental cob floors to examine, different methods of slate roofing to consider, debates on the best way to repair the window openings and discussion as to whether the evidence justified the re-creation of the pentice between hall and kitchen. There was much to learn from the process of repair, both for those involved practically and for the many visitors who were able to observe the work in progress. No less interesting, the work on Bowhill encapsulates more than one approach. This is because the philosophy of conservation evolved from the 1970s to the 1990s as a concern to retain some indication of its later history replaced the desire to return it to something approaching the authentic character of the original building.

It became increasingly clear that fundamental both to repair and interpretation was a detailed analysis of the evidence, not only of the site, the standing building, the documentary and graphic records, but also of what was done during the repair work. This account will provide the answers for those who want to know exactly what was done and why, but it also does much more. By bringing together expertise of different kinds on the variety of buildings materials, styles and techniques, it has been possible to set Bowhill within the context of related work in the area. Archaeological examination of the site and associated finds have filled in other parts of the story: of an earlier house destroyed by fire, of the sequence of construction when the house was rebuilt for Roger Holand in the early 16th century and of the parts of this building that disappeared later. The dry archaeological bones are fleshed out by documentary evidence in the form of wills and accounts, which throw light on later residents and on their possessions and furnishings. This exemplary combination of disciplines has resulted in a comprehensive record that will be of permanent value both to historians and to conservators. It cannot be the final word, for the building now, happily, has been secured for the future. The contributions of the 21st century to its history will, in time, form another chapter in the story.

Bridget Cherry

Acknowledgements

The summary nature of the present report conceals several diverse original contributions within an overview. Excavation work, above all, is necessarily reliant on teamwork and I wish to acknowledge particularly the contributions of colleagues in this aspect of the work. The individuals named on the title page as contributors can be identified as the authors of discrete sections of the text, especially in chapters 9–11. Several people, however, have made significant contributions to the work without being involved in the production of the text presented here, mainly through their involvement with fieldwork or the production of archive reports. Stephen Dunmore, Mark Hall and Peter Stead made significant contributions to the excavations covered by Chapter 4; similarly Stephen Dunmore and Beric Morley contributed to the understanding of the standing building discussed in Chapters 5–7 through their contributions to the analysis of the standing fabric during the initial phase of work in the later 1970s and early 1980s. The field survey drawings were done by Chris Gray and Bill Blake for AMDO, and by Keith Westcott, Aidan Matthews, Richard Parker and others for EMAFU.

In the course of the work on Bowhill, investigations of the documentary evidence for the building's history were commissioned by DoE/DAMHB from Mrs Norma Parfitt (1981) and by English Heritage from Ms Jean Manco (1991) and Dr N W Alcock (1998–9). The authors of Chapter 3 have drawn on the work of Mrs Parfitt and Ms Manco for some aspects of that chapter and gratefully acknowledge their contributions, although neither of the historians is responsible for the emphasis and interpretation placed on the material.

I wish to pay tribute to the role of Francis Kelly over the whole spectrum of work at Bowhill, not only as the sponsor of the work and as the co-author of Chapter 11, but also as a source of detailed observation of the fabric of the building, of many valuable ideas on its interpretation and of substantial improvements to the text of this report.

Nat Alcock, Bridget Cherry and Paul Drury acted as referees for the work; I am especially grateful to them for reading it at draft stage, and for their many valuable comments, observations and suggestions for improving the text. Nevertheless, responsibility for the final form of the text and any remaining errors or omissions, remains with the author. As a result of his comments, Nat Alcock was commissioned to carry out further research on documentary sources, greatly to the benefit of the text of Chapter 3. I am also grateful to others who have read and commented on sections of the text: John Allan, Shirley Blaylock, Stephen Dunmore, Ray Harrison and Beric Morley.

The work has been funded throughout by English Heritage as an integral part of the repair process. Many people from English Heritage were involved in the work, and contributed in various ways. I am grateful to Richard Baker, Bill Blake, Stephen Dunmore, Chris Gray, Ray Harrison, John How, Robert Locke, Arthur McCallum, Adam McKenzie, Beric Morley, Carole Owen, Harry Slade and, above all, Francis Kelly. I have also benefitted from useful discussion and cooperation from Patrick Hynes, Paul May, Harold Partridge, Mike Perrett, Roger Scobie, Charles Smith and Boysel Welham. All of these also gave valuable help with Chapter 11.

The 1977–83 DoE excavations were directed by Stephen Dunmore, assisted by Tom Loader and Jeremy Haslam (site supervisors), M Dewhurst, M Stockdale and C White Haslam. Preliminary post-excavation work was done by S L Dunmore and M Dewhurst. Other people offering help or advice at this stage were N W Alcock, C G Henderson, J M W Laithwaite, B M Morley, S E Rigold, H G Slade and J R L Thorp.

The later phases of excavation and fabric recording were carried out by EMAFU/EA staff and volunteers. Fabric recording between 1987 and 1990 was directed by Stuart Blaylock, assisted by Keith Westcott, Laura Templeton, and Aidan Matthews (1987–8) and by Aidan Matthews, Andrew Simm, Mark Hall, Jenny Norton and Neil Goodwin (1989–90). Keith Westcott supervised the initial fabric recording in 1987–8. From 1990 service recording was carried out by Aidan Matthews, Richard Parker and Stuart Blaylock.

The 1989 excavation of the parlour and service rooms (Areas 6–8) was supervised by Mark Hall (March and April 1989), assisted by Neil Goodwin and Eddie Jones. Area 2 (the screens passage) was supervised by Mark Hall and Jenny Norton (November 1989), assisted by Abigail Preston. The 1992 excavation of the eastern courtyard (Area 3) was supervised by Peter Stead, assisted by Jemima Dunkley, Neil Goodwin, Sarah Lunnon, Aidan Matthews and Paul Pearce. Post-excavation work was done by Peter Stead, Pru Manning and Stuart Blaylock. The excavation of the south and west ranges (service room and kitchen) in 1993 was supervised by Mark Hall, assisted by Neil Goodwin, Aidan Matthews, James Tovey, Jeremy Bell and Allister Clark. The excavation of the annexe in 1994 was conducted by Mark Hall and Neil Goodwin. Miscellaneous additional observations between 1993 and 1995 were done mainly by Mark Hall, Neil Goodwin and Richard Parker.

Overall direction of the work and administration of the project was by Christopher Henderson (who also directed some phases of the excavations in the author's absence). Others who provided assistance with excavation and fabric recording were John Allan and Graham Langman (finds), Graham Langman and volunteers (finds processing), David Garner and Gary Young (photography, see also below), Pam Wakeham (secretarial assistance), Clare Rance (assistance with documentary research), and Piran Bishop, Neil Goodwin, Tony Ives, Richard Parker and Andrew Simm (preliminary work on field drawings).

The line illustrations have their origins in field drawings by EMAFU and EH surveyors and illustrators mentioned above. They were originally drawn up by Andrew Simm, Tony Ives and Richard Parker; most of them have been redrawn for this report by Tony Ives, who has made a substantial contribution to the visual felicity of the line drawings. Piran Bishop drew the superb 'exploded' drawings of the roofs. Other help with illustrations has been given by John Allan and Blanche Ellis.

The photographic credits show that David Garner is responsible for the greater part of the photography used in this report and the volume (as with other Bowhill publications) is greatly enhanced by the high quality of his work. Gary Young of EMAFU/EA has done a good deal of photographic developing and printing for the volume; Paul Highnam and Jeremy Richards of the EH Photographic Department have commissioned work, and Charles Walker, Celia Sterne and Cathy Houghton organised the production of prints from the EH Photo Library. The arrangement and listing of the works photographs was carried out by Anita Travers, to whom I am grateful for much assistance with photographs.

For help with documentary, bibliographic and pictorial research, I am grateful to: Margery Rowe and John Draisey, successive Devon County Archivists, and the staff of the Devon Record Office; Ian Maxted, Devon Local Studies Librarian, and the staff of the Westcountry Studies Library; the staff of the Exeter City Reference Library (especially for repeated use of their run of *Country Life*); Peter Thomas, Librarian of Exeter Cathedral Library; Peter Thomas and Margery Rowe, respectively Librarian and Secretary of the Devon and Exeter Institution; Ian Criddle of Plymouth Local Studies Library; Christine North, Cornwall County Archivist, and the staff of the Cornwall Record Office; Caroline Dudley, Director of the Royal Cornwall Museum; the staff of the Bodleian and Ashmolean Libraries (Oxford), and the staff of the National Monuments Record (Swindon). Permission to reproduce illustrative material has been kindly granted by the Ashmolean Museum (Oxford), The Country Life Picture Library, the Devon and Exeter Institution, the National Monuments Record, the National Trust, the Public Record Office, the Royal Commission on Historical Monuments (England), the Royal Institution of Cornwall, the West Country Studies Library (Exeter), Lawrence Keefe Esq, E F Lamacraft Esq, O N W William-Powlett Esq (Cadhay), and the owner and staff of Thornbury Castle. I am also grateful to the Devonshire Association for access to Bowhill after its sale in 1997, particularly to Hugh Bodey, registrar until 1998, and Paula Ferris, administrator 1998–2000.

For help with research, general discussion, supply of information and many other forms of assistance with the work I am very grateful to the following: Rosemary Akers (Orleigh Court); John Allan, Curator of Antiquities, RAM Museum, Exeter (general discussion and help with literature on finds); Stephen Angeloni (Carew/Graves-Sawle documents in his possession); Mike Baldwin, Architect for Exeter City Council (conservation matters); Fred Barber, Parks Manager for Exeter City Council (nurserymen and the Lucombe oak, copies of his own manuscript notes, and a copy of John Harvey's notes on early nurseries of Exeter); Shirley Blaylock (West Challacombe); Stewart Brown (slates, and general architectural and archaeological discussion); Peter Child (Devon buildings); Rebecca Child (observations at Bowhill); Tony Collings (documentary and bibliographic assistance); Jannine Crocker (documentary assistance, in particular deeds); Todd Gray (pictorial and documentary sources, especially Stockdale); Cathy Groves (dendrochronology); Jane Harcourt (EH store at Salisbury and small finds, Muchelney Abbey); the late Stanley Harper (documentary research); Chris Henderson (interpretation of the excavations and standing building); Jennifer Hillam (dendrochronology); Alison Hopper-Bishop (conservation; advice on finds, textiles and X-rays of metalwork); Philip Hughes (slates and slating); Jeanne James (chapels); Sarah Johnston, Bishop of Exeter's secretary (assistance with photography); John Thorp and Jo Cox of Keystone Historic Buildings Consultants (discussion of chapels, slates, intersecting-beam ceilings, use of copy of their drawing of the roof of the Presentation of Mary Convent, and discussion and use of copy of their drawing of the roof of Traymill, Thorverton); Maryanne Kowaleski (discussion of historical material and aspects of medieval St Thomas); Hugh Meller (National Trust buildings); Steve Ottery (preparation of dendrochronological samples); Richard Parker (discussion of Exeter buildings); Peter Reeves (CEU recording procedures); Isabel Richardson (West Challacombe; vernacular architecture); Josie Ridgway (assistance with access to EH depot at Toddington, Gloucestershire); Brian Rolf (spurred pegs and building materials); Brian Selwood (identification and sources of roofing slate); Mark Stoyle (Civil War occupation of Bowhill); Sandra Turton (bibliographic and editorial advice); John Thorp (cob building techniques and roofs); Ian Tyers (dendrochronology); Angus Wainwright (nails); Robert Waterhouse (late medieval houses in the South Hams); Martin and Susan Watts (nails and nailmaking); Peter Weddell (documentary sources relating to St Thomas, Exeter); Nicky Whittenham, Plymouth University (bibliographic enquiries); Oliver William-Powlett, (access to Cadhay for photography and dendrochronology, and much useful discussion); Caroline Worthington, Curator of Fine Art, RAM Museum, Exeter (advice on 19th- and early 20th-century local artists); Cressida Whitton (wood identification).

The analysis discussed in Chapter 10 was initially funded by the Department of the Environment and subsequently by English Heritage. Cathy Groves would like to thank Stuart Blaylock, Exeter Archaeology, for providing information, a series of valuable discussions and thought-provoking comments on an earlier draft of this report, as well as arranging access to Bowhill in August 1999. Robert Howard, Nottingham University Tree-Ring Dating Laboratory, kindly provided information prior to the completion of his dendrochronological work on the other similar buildings in Exeter. Francis Kelly and Nat Alcock also participated in various useful discussions whenever we met. Nat provided additional comments and raised a number of questions following his reading of an earlier draft of this report. In addition, Cathy Groves would like to acknowledge her debt to Ian Tyers, also of Sheffield University, for providing useful discussion and comments, particularly on aspects concerning imported Baltic timbers, and for his constant encouragement, enthusiasm and patience.

Also in regard to Chapter 10, Robert Howard, Robert Laxton and Cliff Litton are very grateful to the owners and occupiers of the buildings for their permission to take samples and their tolerance of disruption. The Archdeaconry roof was sampled during the conversion of the former convent building to private residences in December 1998; the owner of the building at this time was Will Gannon; we are grateful to him and to his agent Marcus Burwood of Barclay Construction Management for access and assistance. At the Deanery we are grateful to the Dean of Exeter, The Very Reverend Keith Jones and to Mrs Jones, to Col Michael Woodcock, Chapter Clerk of Exeter Cathedral, and to Peter Bird, Surveyor to the Dean and Chapter. At nos 8–9 The Close Col Woodcock again obliged with permission for access and practical assistance; Canon Arthur Mawson and Mrs Mawson allowed a preliminary visit in a very busy week when they were moving out of the house. For access to the Law Library on a number of occasions we are very grateful to Messrs Ford Simey Daw Roberts and to their managing partner Simon Sanger-Anderson for permission to inspect and sample the roof timbers; to Maureen Greenaway and Sonia Nye for help with practical arrangements and especially to Mrs Gillian Mann for giving up a Saturday morning to assist with access for the sampling. Permission to sample in the Guildhall was granted by Anne Wilson of Exeter City Council; Michael Baldwin and Bill Olive provided advice and practical help. We are also very grateful to Mr O N W William-Powlett, the owner of Cadhay, for his assistance during the preliminary inspection visit. The programme was administered by Alex Bayliss of English Heritage; we are grateful to her, to Cathy Groves of Sheffield University, to Francis Kelly (EH Bristol) and to John Allan (RAM Museum, Exeter).

Summary

Bowhill is a late medieval country house located about a mile to the west of the centre of Exeter. The site was owned by two important county families – first the Holands in the 15th century, passing (by marriage) into the possession of the Carews in the early 16th century. It remained with their descendants until the 1930s.

The surviving house was probably built c 1500 by Roger Holand (c 1450–1506), replacing an earlier building which had been destroyed by fire. Early alterations belong to the Carew occupation in the 16th and early 17th centuries. The site was fortified during the Civil War. Some damage might have occurred then and demolition of outer structures began. The shift of the main Carew dwelling to Barley in the later 17th century ensured the preservation of the late medieval fabric of Bowhill.

From the mid-18th century the house and associated land were tenanted, notably by the Lucombe nursery from 1740 to 1794. Major alterations to the building took place c 1800 when derelict portions were demolished and the residual core repaired. By the mid-20th century suburban development had engulfed the site. A brief period of use as a restaurant from 1969 to 1976 entailed many destructive alterations and culminated in the building's rescue, by purchase, by the DoE in 1976. The subsequent phase of repair carried out under the auspices of the Directorate of Ancient Monuments and Historic Buildings and of English Heritage (from 1984), lasting almost twenty years, provided the opportunities for the study of the building that is the subject of this book.

Architecturally Bowhill is notable for its carpentry, especially its ornate roofs, and for its construction, which is largely of cob. The house represents an informative mix of vernacular techniques and materials with higher-status construction and features. The roofs, structurally similar to the jointed-cruck roofs ubiquitous in late medieval Devon, belong to a group of six highly ornate late medieval roofs characteristic of the Exeter area.

This book presents an authoritative account of the development of the site and standing building as it was recorded through many episodes of work from 1977 to 1994. It represents the combined contributions of archaeologists, building historians, documentary researchers, architects, conservators, craftsmen and many other specialists and professionals. The core of the report concentrates on the description and interpretation of the fabric of the building as it has been recorded by excavation and recording when stripped for repair, drawing equally on the buried and standing evidence. Particular attention is given to aspects of the fabric that were visible during the works, but are now obscured by renewed ground levels or re-rendered surfaces. The study also covers the history of the site and its estate, gives an account of the pictorial, cartographic and photographic sources and an assessment of the Bowhill roofs in the context of regional and national roof carpentry and domestic architecture of the late Middle Ages. A chapter on finds from the building makes important contributions to dating and to the knowledge of the original appearance of the house and its fittings. The dendrochronological study of timbers from Bowhill provides equally important contributions to the dating of the building and useful information on the procurement of materials. A parallel dendrochronological study of timber from other buildings assists in the absolute dating of other roofs in the group and in the placing of Bowhill in relation to comparable houses. The penultimate chapter gives an account of the conservation and repair process, concentrating on changing approaches to building conservation in the period spanned by the works at Bowhill and on the impact of different types of repair in various materials.

The book is extensively illustrated with several hundred photographs drawn from the large archive of material amassed on the building, while its line drawings set standards for the illustration of the archaeological study of buildings. It is intended that its integrated approach to the study of the building (which sets the building and its repairs in context and draws on the techniques of archaeology for analysis and interpretation) will appeal to architectural historians, conservators, architects and others with professional and scholarly interests in historic buildings, as well as to archaeologists.

Résumé

Bowhill est un manoir datant de la fin du moyen-âge et situé à environ 1 mile à l'ouest du centre d'Exeter. Le site a appartenu à deux familles notables du comté – d'abord aux Holand au 15ème siècle, puis il est passé (suite à un mariage) entre les mains des Carew au début du 16ème siècle. Leurs descendants en sont restés en possession jusque dans les années 1930.

La maison qui subsiste fut problablement construite vers 1500 par Roger Holand (v 1450–1506), en remplacement d'un bâtiment plus ancien qui avait été détruit par un incendie. Les premières modifications datent de l'époque où elle était occupée par les Carew, au 16ème et au début du 17ème siècles. Le site fut fortifié pendant la guerre civile. Il se peut que la propriété ait subi des dégâts à ce moment-là et qu'on ait commencé à démolir les structures qui se trouvaient le plus à l'extérieur. Le fait que la famille Carew déménagea et installa sa résidence principale à Barley vers la fin du 17ème siècle garantit à Bowhill la préservation de l'édifice de la fin du moyen-âge.

A partir du milieu du 18ème siècle, la maison et les terres qui l'accompagnaient furent louées, en particulier par le pépiniériste Lucombe, entre 1740 et 1790. D'importantes modifications furent apportées au bâtiment vers 1800, date à laquelle les parties délabrées furent démolies et la partie centrale restante fut réparée. Le milieu du 20ème siècle vit le site engouffré par l'extension de la banlieue. Pendant une brève période, entre 1969 et 1976, on l'utilisa comme restaurant, ce qui eut pour conséquence de nombreuses destructions à la suite d'aménagements et se termina par le sauvetage du bâtiment, grâce à son rachat par le département de l'environnement en 1976. La phase de réparations qui s'en suivit fut menée sous les auspices de la Direction des Monuments Anciens et des Bâtiments Historiques et d'English Heritage (à partir de 1984), ces travaux durèrent presque vingt ans, offrant de nombreuses opportunités pour l'étude du bâtiment, qui constitue le sujet de ce livre.

Sur le plan de l'architecture, Bowhil est remarquable pour sa charpente, en particulier ses toits décorés, et pour sa construction qui est en grande partie en pisé. Cette maison représente un mélange, riche en enseignement, de techniques et de matériaux vernaculaires associés à une construction et des détails d'un niveau plus élevé. Les toits, dont la structure est similaire à celle des toits en 'A' à arbalétriers assemblés qu'on trouve partout dans le Devon de la fin du Moyen-âge, appartiennent à un groupe de six toits médiévaux tardifs extrêmement décorés, caractéristiques de la région d'Exeter.

Ce livre présente un compte-rendu qui fait autorité, du développement du site et du bâtiment qui s'y dresse ainsi qu'on l'a répertorié au fur et à mesure des diverses phases des travaux entre 1977 et 1994. Il est constitué des contributions combinées d'archéologues, d'historiens, de chercheurs spécialisés dans l'étude de documents, d'architectes, de conservateurs, d'artisans et de bien d'autres spécialistes et professionnels. La majeure partie du compte-rendu se concentre sur la description et l'interprétation de la construction du bâtiment tel qu'il a été répertorié grâce aux fouilles et aux relevés pris quand il a été dépouillé pour être réparé, on y élabore également à partir des témoignages enterrés et exposés. On accorde une attention particulière aux aspects de la construction qui étaient visibles pendant les travaux, mais sont maintenant dissimulés suite au changement de niveau du sol ou au revêtement des surfaces. L'étude couvre aussi l'histoire du site et de son domaine, rend compte des sources picturales, cartographiques et photographiques et évalue les

toits de Bowhill dans le contexte de la charpente et de l'architecture domestiques régionales et nationales à la fin du moyen-âge. Un chapitre consacré aux trouvailles provenant du bâtiment apporte une contribution importante à la datation et à la connaissance de l'aspect original de la maison et de ses équipements. L'étude dendrochronologique des bois de Bowhill fournit de tout aussi importantes contributions à la datation du bâtiment et des enseignements utiles sur la provenance des matériaux. Une étude dendrochronologique parallèle de bois provenant d'autres bâtiments nous aide pour la datation absolue d'autres toits appartenant au même groupe et le positionnement relatif de Bowhill par rapport à des maisons comparables. Le pénultième chapitre relate les procédés de conservation et de réparation, il se concentre sur les changements d'approche face à la préservation des bâtiments pendant la période couvrant les travaux à Bowhill et sur l'impact de différents types de réparations avec des matériaux divers.

Ce livre est richement illustré de plusieurs centaines de photographies tirées des vastes archives de documents amassés sur ce bâtiment, tandis que ses dessins au trait devraient servir de point de référence pour les illustrations d'études archéologiques de bâtiments. C'est dans notre intention que l'approche intégrante adoptée pour l'étude de ce bâtiment (qui replace le bâtiment et ses réparations en contexte et met à profit les techniques de l'archéologie pour l'analyser et l'interpréter) attire historiens de l'architecture, conservateurs, architectes et ceux qui s'intéressent, soit pour des raisons professionnelles, soit dans le cadre de leurs études, aux bâtiments historiques, ainsi que les archéologues.

Traduction: Annie Pritchard

Zusammenfassung

Bowhill ist ein spätmittelalterliches Landhaus und befindet sich ungefähr eine Meile westlich vom Exeter-Stadtzentrum. Das Grundstück befand sich im Besitz von zwei, im diesem Gebiet ansässigen, bedeutsamen Familien – als Erstes bei den Holands im 15. Jahrhundert und ging dann im frühen 16. Jahrhundert durch Heirat in das Eigentum der Carews über. Dort verblieb es bei deren Nachfahren bis in die 1930–er Jahre.

Das heutige Haus wurde wahrscheinlich um 1500 von Roger Holand (c 1450–1506) an Stelle eines früheren Gebäudes gebaut, welches durch ein Feuer zerstört wurde. Die ersten Änderungen am Haus wurden von den Carews im 16. und frühen 17. Jahrhundert durchgeführt. Das Besitztum wurde dann während des englischen Bürgerkrieges (English Civil War) verstärkt und befestigt. Nach wahrscheinlichen im Krieg entstandenen Beschädigungen, begann der Abriss der äußeren Strukturen. Die Verlagerung des Hauptwohnsitzes der Carews nach Barley am Ende des 17. Jahrhunderts erlaubte die Erhaltung des spätmittelalterlichen Gewebes von Bowhill.

Seit der Mitte des 18. Jahrhunderts wurde das Haus mit dazugehörendem Land vermietet, unter anderem von 1740 bis 1794 an die Lucombe Nursery. Weitgehende Änderungen am Gebäude wurden um 1800 durchgeführt, wenn verfallene Teile abgerissen und vom Hauskern auf repariert wurden. Bei Mitte des 20. Jahrhunderts war das Gebäude von vorstädtischen Entwicklungen vollständig umgeben. Für eine kurze Zeit von 1969 bis 1976 wurde Bowhill als Restaurant

benutzt, in welcher Zeit viele zerstörende Änderungen vorgenommen wurden, am Ende in einem Ausmaß, welches das DoE veranlaßte, das Haus durch den Kauf des Besitzes zu retten. Die darauf folgende Phase von Reparaturarbeiten wurde unter Aufsicht vom Direktorat für Historische Stätten und Gebäude (Directorate of Ancient Monuments and Historic Buildings) und English Heritage (seit 1984) durchgeführt. Über 20 Jahre andauernd, erlaubten diese Arbeiten eine Reihe von Möglichkeiten zum Studium des Gebäudes, welche Subjekt dieses Buches ist.

Architektonisch ist Bowhill nennenswert für seine Holzarbeit, insbesondere die kunstvollen Dächer und seine Konstruktion, welche überwiegend aus Kopfstein besteht. Das Haus repräsentiert eine informative Mischung von überlieferten Bautechniken und Materialien und neueren Konstruktionen und Merkmalen. Die Dächer, strukturell den Fugendächern, allgegenwärtig im mittelalterlichen Devon, ähnlich, gehören zu einer Gruppe von sechs, sehr aufwandreich dekorierten, spätmittelalterlichen Dächern, charakteristisch für die Exetergegend.

Dieses Buch bietet eine verlässliche Wiedergabe der Entwicklung dieses Standortes und des noch stehenden Gebäudes, welche an verschiedenen Zeitpunkten der Arbeiten von 1977 bis 1994 aufgezeichnet wurde. Es repräsentiert die vereinten Zugaben von Archeologen, Gebäudehistorikern, Dokumentforschern, Architekten, Konservierern, Handwerkern sowie vielen anderen Spezialisten und Professionellen. Der Kern des Buches beschreibt und interpätiert das

Gefüge des Gebäudes, wie aufgeführt in den Zeichnungen der Ausgrabungen und Begutachtungen, durchgeführt während der Freilegungen für Reparaturarbeiten und gleichzeitig einbezogen sind sichtbare sowie vergrabene Nachweise. Insbesondere Aufwerksamkeit wird dabei den Aspekten des Gefüges gegeben, welche sichtbar waren während der Arbeiten, jetzt aber von erneuerten Grundebenen sowie überarbeiteten Oberflächen verdeckt werden. Die Studie befaßt sich auch mit der Geschichte des Gebäudes und des Besitztums und liefert eine Aufzählung der Bilder-, Karteografischen- und Fotografie-Quellen und eine Einschätzung der Bowhilldächer in deren Zusammenhang mit der regionalen und nationalen Dachholzarbeit sowie der domestischen Architektur des späten Mittelalters. Ein Kapitel über die Fünde aus dem Gebäude liefert einen wichtigen Beitrag zu dem Datieren und dem Wissen über das originale Erscheinungsbild des Hauses und dessen Ausstattung. Im gleichen Ausmaß hilft das dendrochonologische Studium der Hölzer in Bowhill beim Datieren des Gebäudes und es gibt Auskunft über die Beschaffung der Baumaterialien. Eine parallele dendrochronologische Studie von Hölzern in anderen Gebäuden macht ein absolutes Datieren anderer Dächer in der Gruppe möglich und hilft beim relativen Plazieren von Bowhill im Zusammenhang mit vergleichbaren Häusern. Das vorletzte Kapitel enthält eine Wiedergabe der Konservierungs- und Reparaturarbeiten, und konzentriert sich auf die sich ändernden Methoden von Gebäudekonservierung im Zeitraum der Arbeiten an Bowhill und auf die Auswirkung der verschiedenen Arten von Reparaturen an unterschiedlichen Materialien.

Das Buch ist reichlich mit mehreren hunderten Fotografien aus der großen Ansammlung von Bildmaterial über das Gebäude illustriert. Die Strichzeichnungen sollten einen neuen Standard für Illustrationen innerhalb archeologischer Gebäudestudien setzen. Mit seiner intergrierten Studienmethode dieses Gebäudes (welche das Gebäude und dessen Reparaturen in Zusammenhang setzt und auf Techniken der Archeologie für Analyse und Interpretation zurückgreift) wird das Buch für architektonische Historiker, Konservierer, Architekten und andere mit professionellem oder wissenschaftlichen Interesse in historische Gebäude und natürlich Archeologen sehr attraktiv sein.

Übersetzung: Norman Behrend

Abbreviations

AMDO	Ancient Monuments Drawing Office (DoE)
AML	Ancient Monuments Laboratory
ARCUS	Archaeology Research and Consultancy at the University of Sheffield
Carew-Pole	Carew-Pole manuscripts at Antony House, Cornwall
CF	Coode and French deposit (CRO)
CRO	Cornwall Record Office, Truro
DAMHB	Directorate of Ancient Monuments and Historic Buildings (DoE)
DEL	Directly Employed Labour (DoE/EH)
DoE	Department of the Environment
DRO	Devon Record Office
EA	Exeter Archaeology (formerly EMAFU)
ECA	Exeter City Archives (DRO)
ECC	Exeter City Council
EH	English Heritage
EMAFU	Exeter Museums Archaeological Field Unit (Exeter Archaeology since 1995)
HPR	Historic Property Restoration
MoLAS	Museum of London Archaeology Service
MoW	Ministry of Works
NMR	National Monuments Record
PRO	Public Record Office
RAMM	Royal Albert Memorial Museum, Exeter
RCAHMW	Royal Commission on Ancient and Historical Monuments in Wales
RCHME	Royal Commission on the Historical Monuments of England
TM	Tithe Map
WSL	Westcountry Studies Library, Exeter
WMN	Western Morning News

Throughout the book there are references to the Devonshire Association, who were the lessees of Bowhill 1997–2002. Since the text was completed the Association has withdrawn from its lease.

Preface

Summary description

Bowhill is a gentry house, built *c* 1500 by Roger Holand (*c* 1450–1506), on the site of an earlier house known from excavation. By the marriage of Thomasina Holand, Roger's daughter and co-heir, to John Carew, the house passed into the possession of the Carew family, in which it remained until the early 18th century (except for a short period 1660–1 when it reverted to the crown on the attainder of the regicide John Carew). It continued in the ownership of their Sawle and Graves-Sawle descendants, by marriage and sale, until the 1930s, although the house and associated land were tenanted and were long used as a nursery garden. The house has frequently been described as a manor, but this term only appears in the later 16th century and thus has been rejected in this account.

Plan

The present plan is a reduction, *c* 1800, from a full quadrangular plan, with buildings in outer courtyards to the east (an entrance court) and west (for agriculture, stabling and storage). The house now comprises three ranges around a central courtyard, with open spaces representing the former outer courtyards. The hall is in the east range, at right-angles to the road and the kitchen is in the surviving portion of the west range opposite. Hall and kitchen were open to the roof, but the remaining ranges were two-storeyed throughout. The south range contained the principal domestic rooms: parlour, great chamber, other chambers, as well as service rooms and stores. Vanished ranges to the south-east (further main living rooms), north and west (lodgings, lesser accommodation), completed the core of the plan. The house probably contained a chapel, possibly located above the porch (although no trace survives in the fabric). Circulation was aided by a pentice walk from hall to kitchen and by gallery access from south to west range at first-floor level (bypassing the (open) kitchen), and possibly also to the north range.

Materials

Bowhill is distinctive, in a house of this status, for employing a range of earth building materials often considered wholly vernacular. Cob was used extensively and interchangeably with stone for most walling, although stone was preferred in footings, in walls with stone windows and in some other contexts. There were structural timber-framed walls at the north end of the hall, at the junction of the south and east ranges and possibly also at the junction of the south and south-east ranges. Cob, by definition, is a local material. Stone used was local volcanic trap and breccia ('Heavitree stone'). Finer volcanic lava and limestone (from Beer) appear in details. The roofs were slated.

Features

The most important features are the roofs of the great hall and the great chamber. Structurally these are similar to the jointed-cruck roofs that form the remainder of the surviving roofs, but each is heavily embellished with additional timbers and decorative elements. The timbers of the hall roof are moulded throughout; those of the great chamber are chamfered. These roofs belong to a group of six late medieval roofs characteristic of the Exeter area, centred on the houses of the Cathedral clergy, but including a municipal building and country houses. The group is defined by common decorative features applied to a variety of basic roof types. Other carpentry includes a series of screens, an early example in an Exeter domestic context of a moulded intersecting-beam ceiling that was ceiled with planking and a range of early timber window types. Masonry features include: a variety of stone cinquefoil-headed windows in single or multiple lights (architectural fragments and pictorial evidence suggest more developed window forms in the vanished ranges); primary fireplaces in the great hall (restored), parlour, great chamber and kitchen, which have massive joggled lintels or arches, with high relieving arches and projecting moulded mantels, all characteristic of Exeter houses in the 15th and 16th centuries.

Development

The earliest evidence (phase 1) represents activity on the site in the 13th–15th centuries. An ?early 15th-century building of uncertain extent (phase 2) preceded the standing building. This was destroyed by fire, perhaps in the 1490s, then demolished and rebuilt as the surviving building (phase 3). Early alterations (phases 4–5) comprised: some re-fenestration; the removal of the ground-floor garderobe in the south range and the insertion of a fireplace and stack. The site was fortified during the Civil War. Some damage may have occurred then and demolition of outer structures began at this time (phase 6). More extensive alterations took place in the south range in the 17th century (phase 7): the parlour was enlarged by one bay and the ceiling adapted; new windows and reorganisation of the service rooms accompanied these changes. Major alterations took place *c* 1800 (phase 8), comprising the demolition of derelict portions of the building and the repair of the residual core. The south-east and north ranges were removed and the east and west ranges truncated. Later alterations (phases 9–10) involved further decline, re-fenestration and the construction of small ancillary structures. The hall declined into use as a barn. After World War II suburban development gradually engulfed the site and the nursery business. A brief period of use as a restaurant 1969–76 (phase 11) entailed many destructive alterations and culminated in purchase by the DoE in 1976.

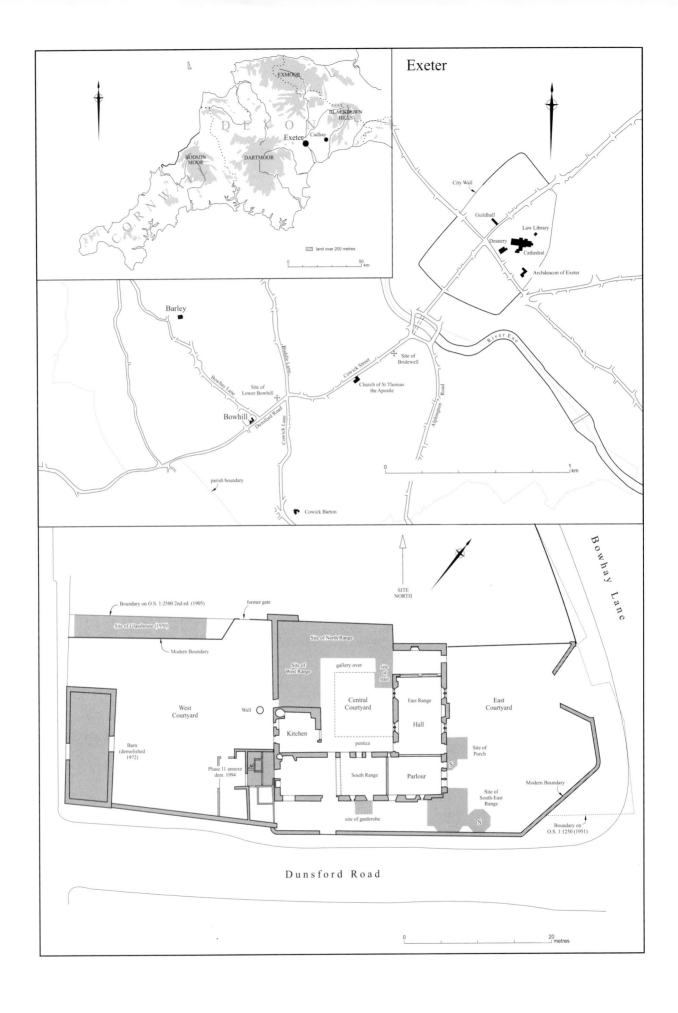

Exeter

EXMOOR

BLACKDOWN HILLS

D E V O N

Exeter • • Cadhay

C O R N W A L L

BODMIN MOOR

DARTMOOR

land over 200 metres

0   50
                     km

City Wall

Guildhall

Law Library

Deanery

Cathedral

Archdeacon of Exeter

Barley

Biddle Lane

Bowhay Lane

Site of Lower Bowhill

Bowhill

Dunsford Road

Cowick Lane

Cowick Street

Site of Bridewell

Church of St Thomas the Apostle

River Exe

Alphington Road

0   1
                                       km

parish boundary

Cowick Barton

Bowhay Lane

SITE NORTH

Boundary on O.S. 1:2500 2nd ed. (1905)

former gate

Site of Glasshouse (1950)

Modern Boundary

Site of North Range

Site of West Range

gallery over

site of stair

West Courtyard

Well

Central Courtyard

East Range

East Courtyard

Kitchen

Hall

pentice

Barn (demolished 1972)

Phase 11 annexe dem. 1994

South Range

Parlour

Site of Porch

S

Site of South-East Range

Modern Boundary

site of garderobe

S

Boundary on O.S. 1:1250 (1951)

Dunsford Road

0   20
                                       metres

1
Introduction:
background and context

The site and its setting

The parish of St Thomas formed an extra-mural suburb to the walled city of Exeter in the medieval and early modern periods. The settlement clustered at the western end of the medieval bridge across the River Exe. The first church of St Thomas of Canterbury was built close to the bridgehead in the early 13th century. This was destroyed by flooding in the early 15th century and replaced with a new building on the site of the present church (consecrated in 1412).[1] In the 15th century, the settlement was centred on the area between the new site of the church and the river[2] and did not extend very far west of the church; the 18th-century maps of Rocque (1744) and Donn (1765) show that this was still the case three centuries later.[3]

Bowhill lies towards the west of the parish on the north-west side of Dunsford Road, the old route to Moretonhampstead and the west, at NGR SX 9064 9158. The setting of the building was originally very much a rural one among fields and gardens, some 600m west-south-west of the parish church of St Thomas the Apostle and 250m uphill from the junction of Cowick Street and Dunsford Road with Cowick Lane, the ancient north–south route (Fig 1.1). The name Bowhill, meaning 'curved hill' and first recorded in 1249,[4] refers to the general area of the site, rather than specifically to the building or the land on which it stands; this extended as far as Cowick Lane/Buddle Lane to the east, was applied to another house in the 18th century ('Lower Bowhill', below) and was still used in the late 19th century.[5] Other notable medieval buildings in the parish were Cowick Priory, whose site is now occupied by Cowick Barton (*see* Fig 1.1)[6] and the Old Bridewell, a substantial late medieval house so-called from its use as a prison from the 16th to the early 19th century.[7] In the 17th and 18th centuries the outer parts of the parish were favoured for gentlemen's residences, and several substantial houses were built in the vicinity of Bowhill at this time.[8] The growth of the western suburbs of Exeter in the course of the 20th century has slowly engulfed the site, which is now confined by two suburban streets, and by residential development of the later 20th century to the north-west. The house presently occupies a plot about 72m by 28m (some 1900m²), having lost several small areas along its boundaries in the course of the 20th century (*see* Fig 1.1).

The house stands on one of the higher terraces of the Exe valley, on land that slopes gently to the east. The underlying geology consists of valley gravels overlying Permian breccia and conglomerate;[9] the soils in the vicinity are 'loamy and gravelly soils' of the Crediton series.[10] The two deposits of basalt that yielded building stone from the quarries of Barley and Pocombe lie at the top of the hill, some 800–900m to the west (*see* Fig 3.1).[11] In the recent past the water supply to the site was provided by a well in the western courtyard, probably of no great antiquity.[12] There is some evidence that water was piped into the site from a considerable distance uphill in the late Middle Ages (Chapter 3). Drainage appears to have been a recurring problem in the past; some of the earliest excavated features on the site could be interpreted as drains (Chapter 4).[13]

Early analysis of the building

Bowhill was recognised by some of the early county historians as an ancient house and one worthy of antiquarian attention. Risdon was the first historian to mention it, concentrating on the etymology of its name: 'In the reign of king Henry the sixth Roger Holland had his dwelling at the foot of the hill, whence it took its name below the hill, but at this day is called *Bow Hill*, the heir general of which name Thomazin, brought this land to John Carew of Antony, esq.'.[14] Richard Polwhele, whose *History of Devonshire* was published in 1797, described the history of the house in some detail and, quoting Sir William Pole, described Bowhill as 'in St Thomas at the end of the street westward'.[15]

Figure 1.1 (facing page) Location map and general site plan of Bowhill (scale 1:500) (line drawing by Tony Ives)

The house was largely ignored by Revd John Swete, travelling in the same year: 'Near on my approach to the suburbs of St Thomas, ... I observed Barley, a large edifice of brick thrown forward to the view by a large and gloomy plantation of old Scotch firs at its back. This with the old seat of Bowhill, more in the valley, about the time of Henry the 8th, descended from a family of the name of Holland to the Carews of Anthony [sic] in Cornwall ... ';[16] it is reasonable to conclude from this that its outward appearance was unprepossessing. Bowhill was further described by the Exeter historian Alexander Jenkins in 1806, who observed that the building ' ... bears evident marks of antiquity, and has a desecrated chapel remaining'.[17] Somewhat later, the Lysons brothers gave a reliable account of the descent of the building (including its forfeiture and retrieval by Thomas Carew, *see below*) and described the contemporary use of the site: 'There are considerable remains of an old mansion of the Carews, with the chapel. The premises have been long occupied as a nursery garden and it is said to have been the first garden of that kind in the neighbourhood of Exeter'.[18] Some time in the

early 1840s the roof of the hall was drawn by H Dudley, under the direction of the architect John Hayward. Published in 1843, these drawings recorded a number of details which have subsequently disappeared (Fig 1.2).[19]

The building was known to have been a house of the Carews. It was said to have contained a chapel, on the grounds of a misinterpretation of an entry in Bishop Lacy's register,[20] and the hall was often identified as the remains of that chapel. This knowledge formed the basis of various further accounts in the 19th and early 20th centuries.[21] The account of a visit by the Royal Archaeological Institute during its meeting at Exeter in 1913 summarised the decline of the house: 'This was a manor house of the Holands ... [which] might easily be overlooked, for it seems at first glance to be nothing more than the thatched house of a nursery gardener',[22] but added notices of the plan and of the roofs, including the connection with roofs of other local buildings.[23]

Little further notice of the history of Bowhill exists until the mid-1930s, when serious attention turned to the history of the Holand family of St Thomas and the fabric

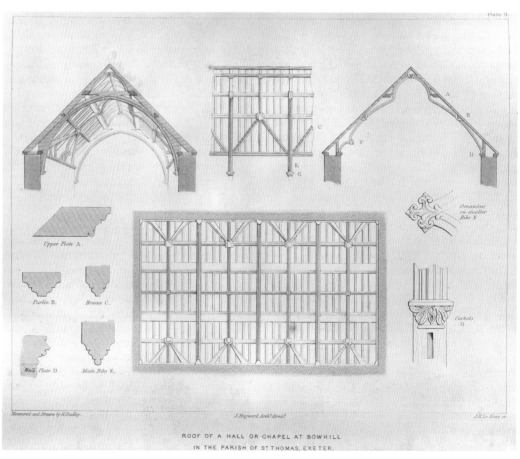

Figure 1.2
Dudley and Hayward's drawing of the hall roof (anon 1843). Note especially the details of bosses, corbels and cusp ornament, which subsequently vanished (photograph by Gary Young).

ROOF OF A HALL OR CHAPEL AT BOWHILL
IN THE PARISH OF St THOMAS, EXETER.

of the building; concise but meaty papers were published on these subjects on successive pages of *Devon and Cornwall Notes and Queries* by Ethel Lega-Weekes and A W Everett.[24] These papers laid the foundations on which recent work on the building rests. Ironically, it was just at the period when the building was receiving serious study that plans were laid for its demolition in the context of the expansion of suburban housing in St Thomas and the improvement (and widening) of roads.[25] Everett developed his analysis of the building and produced a plan and outline drawings of the roof, which saw publication in the *Archaeological Journal* for 1958,[26] doubtless in response to the Summer Meeting of the Royal Archaeological Institute which had visited Exeter again in the previous year.[27] Subsequent analysis depended fairly heavily on Everett's work since, in the absence of opportunities to strip the rendering, little more of the fabric was to be seen than had been available to him. Accounts of the building exist in published form by Portman[28] and in typescript by G W Copeland.[29] The building received attention from the press occasionally. An article and letter by Jacqueline Warren in one of the local newspapers stand out as attempting to correct errors in the published accounts of the building.[30] In the 1970s the house was visited by staff from the Archaeological Unit and RAM Museum, Exeter, and notes and photographs exist in the Unit's archive from these visits (including Figs 2.9 and 6.16 below). A guide leaflet was produced to the house in the early 1970s by Devon Carvers, the proprietors of the first restaurant and craft centre.[31]

State ownership (1976–97)

The house was purchased by the Department of the Environment (DoE) in the autumn of 1976,[32] as an addition to the portfolio of properties in state guardianship in the care of the Directorate of Ancient Monuments and Historic Buildings (DAMHB). The creation of the Historic Buildings and Monuments Commission for England (English Heritage) in 1984 and the Department of National Heritage in 1992[33] have involved nominal changes in administration and ownership. Bowhill is now Listed Grade I as 'a building of special architectural or historic interest' under the terms of the Planning (Listed Buildings and Conservation Areas) Act 1990,[34] requiring consent for any works which affect its character.

Once in state ownership, programmes of repairs and presentation works were formulated.[35] Preliminary excavations took place in 1977–8, the interior of the building was stripped in 1978–9 and the fabric examined in detail. This process led to the production of a 'Preliminary Inspectorate Report' by Beric Morley in February 1979[36] and to the first survey drawings by the Ancient Monuments Drawing Office (AMDO).[37] A 'programme for consolidation' was prepared in 1981, which has been responsible for the present appearance of much of the eastern half of the building, although many of its proposals were modified in the course of the work.[38] Repairs were commenced in 1979–80 and were carried out by a directly employed labour force (DEL) until 1993, when it became *Historic Property Restoration*, a contracting arm of English Heritage, privatised in 1996. Work on the east range (the hall) took place mainly in the period between 1979 and 1985, although the fireplace was completed in 1989. Some work on the exterior of the north elevation of the west range (kitchen) took place in 1980 and repairs to the south range between 1985 and 1993. The west range was completed in 1994, along with works to the exterior and environs from 1993 to 1995 (for further details of the works programme *see* Chapter 11). From 1987 Exeter Museums Archaeological Field Unit (EMAFU; Exeter Archaeology from 1995), as a local archaeological agency, was involved in excavation, observation and fabric survey work. In 1997 the building was sold on a 125-year lease to the Devonshire Association for use as its headquarters.

Circumstances of the work

The work reported here has taken place in the context of the lengthy programme of repairs described above. Such repair and conservation work is inevitably disruptive of the fabric of historic buildings, no matter how sensitively it is carried out. It does, however, create opportunities for the exposure and examination of the fabric and, thereby, opportunities to understand the structural history of the building. A wide range of contributions has been made over the period of the work, which is very much the product of collective effort. The factual base of the report is drawn from the results of archaeological examination (in the widest sense of the term) of the building and its surroundings. Its primary aim is to provide an account of the structural history and archaeology of the site. Other aspects of the work at Bowhill have also influenced the archaeological work, for example, by dictating areas to which access was available, or from the cross-fertilisation of ideas between the analysis of the fabric and the practical researches which were being carried out, for instance over the use of cob for repair and new building.[39]

In a case such as Bowhill, the ideal would be for a thorough examination of both below-ground archaeology and the standing fabric of a building (that is, the 'above-ground archaeology') to take place as a preliminary stage to repairs. In this way the analysis would provide an informed understanding of the building's structural history from the first and would identify areas of potential interest for further attention during conservation, as well as informing and advising the repairs themselves and providing drawings and other data for works purposes.[40] The reality, perhaps inevitably, nearly always falls short of the ideal, given the demands and expedients of works programmes, contractors' schedules and the like. In this respect Bowhill was no exception, which meant that the research objectives of the archaeological recording project had to allow for a variety of less-than-ideal circumstances. Some of these will be apparent from sections of this report. Here it is enough to mention the general constraints that bear on the results and to define the actual (as opposed to the ideal) research objectives and *modus operandi* of the archaeological examination of the site.

Various episodes of examination and recording of the standing fabric took place in the early stages of the work, but the systematic recording of the fabric was attempted to a higher level in the south and west ranges than in the east range. The final investigation of the fabric took place when the repairs to the east range were at an advanced stage and the whole building had been stripped of its modern finishes.[41] Much of the fabric recording, then, was fitted in around the works, rather than taking place in a concerted effort in advance. Excavation took place during several campaigns spread over the years 1977–94, in response to varying requirements. Although it would be fair to say that every piece of excavation work had the

investigation of the surviving archaeology as its primary motivation, each was planned separately, normally in response to the requirements of the works. Occasionally excavation work was wholly works-led, in the sense that areas of ground had to be cleared of their archaeology, prior to disturbance by the insertion of services. It is important to remember that the programme of excavation would probably have been rather different had it been planned as a concerted campaign or even as a series of staged excavations. While the results should be objective and remain unaffected by the method or timing of the excavation, the possibility that they have been influenced by this cumulative approach represents another constraint on this report. Above all, the scale of exposure is important; errors of interpretation are common in restricted exposures, while deposits which are fragmentary in a small trench become comprehensible when exposed on a wider scale.[42]

The structural analysis employs methodology derived from field archaeology, with the aim of disentangling the various builds in a given elevation and sorting them into a structural sequence (ultimately described in the numbered phases used in this report). Particular attention was paid to the relationship of builds one to another. In this there is one departure from the techniques familiar to an excavator of 'below-ground' archaeology. In the case of excavated strata it is (or should be) possible to organise a sequence of deposits into a series of absolute relationships (often termed 'primary' relationships by excavators).[43] The application of the same process to standing fabric can never hope to achieve quite so neat or absolute a sequence, since the nature of standing fabric is invariably one of a primary (original) build containing additions in the form of extensions and/or repairs. Many of the additions may have more than one possible relationship to the adjacent fabric. A sequence based on a string of 'primary' relationships thus breaks down into a series of individual builds, without necessarily having a strong absolute sequence. An analogy with excavated strata is of a site where only intrusive features survive and a sequence can only be achieved by means of occasional interrelationship of one feature to another. Other factors employed in defining or refining parts of the sequence included: the comparative dating of architectural features (such as windows or doors); the incidence or combination of building materials, which varies with time; and the comparison of mortar types, which has been particularly useful in identifying work of individual phases (Chapter 10).

Work methods and report plan

Fieldwork

Excavation work at Bowhill took place in three phases: excavations carried out in 1977–8 under the auspices of the DoE as a part of the programme of preliminary investigation of the building after its purchase; excavation carried out by EMAFU for English Heritage between 1989 and 1993 (normally in advance of or integrated with the repair process); observation and monitoring of works-led excavation for new services, improved drainage and other purposes, carried out by EMAFU for English Heritage in the final stages of the repair programme in 1993–5. Further details are given in the introduction to Chapter 4.

Recording of the standing fabric

From the beginning inspection, analysis and recording of the standing fabric took place as a parallel activity to excavation. The first phase of analysis led to the production of Morley's preliminary report in 1979.[44] Further stripping of plasters and renders in 1980 revealed much more of the fabric of the building. This was recorded in the survey drawings already begun by the AMDO, in a continuing series of record photographs and in manuscript notes and additions to the Inspectorate report.[45] The photographic archive contains a fairly full record of the fabric of the building and implicitly of the alterations in progress up to 1982–3, but is patchy in its coverage of work between 1983 and 1987. In 1987 the present author was commissioned[46] to carry out a brief analysis and assessment of the standing fabric, using the survey drawings, with a view to testing the reliability of the 'received history' of the fabric.[47] From this initial small piece of work a greater involvement developed, eventually leading to a full fabric survey, with new drawings, of the south and west ranges of the building.[48] This comprised an intensive initial phase of examination, drawing and recording in 1987–8, followed by a further, more sporadic phase of work to record areas that became accessible in the course of the repairs and a considerable amount of 'service recording', that is, the recording of observations made during works and only temporarily exposed. Towards the end of the work some drawing (especially of the roofs) was done by photogrammetry, a process that led to another type of recording – the field correction of photogrammetric surveys and the addition of detail invisible to the camera. Most of the drawings which provide the basis of the illustrations in this report, however, were constructed by hand measurement.

Processing of data

The excavations and fabric recording have led to the amassing of a large quantity of data. Little of the fine detail of the recorded data finds a place in this report, although it continually underlies and informs the presentation of the material. Inclusion of primary data would not only have lengthened the work considerably, but would also be of little interest to most of the readership of the volume. The results are presented as summary description, discussion and pictorially in a second generation of synthetic drawings. These present the major excavated evidence assembled into chronological phases, but exclude lesser detail, the multiplicity of later features and so on. The primary data are assembled in a series of archive reports, produced individually as each phase of work was completed. Copies of these are lodged with the project archive and deposited in local and national reference sources (Appendix).

The importance of drawings

Where the records of the fabric recording are concerned, the case for the full illustration of primary drawings is stronger. The building was stripped of its plaster and render during repair, but was mostly re-rendered on completion. Since much of the recorded detail is, therefore, obscured by surface finishes, the drawings play an important part in making the fabric accessible.[49] It should be emphasised that the drawings represent the building *at the time of recording*. This means that there are occasions when the drawings either show features no longer present in the building or fail to show elements that were missing at the time of recording. In the latter case, where restoration subsequently took place, it has normally been possible to add details to the drawings. Discrepancies between the recorded elevations and the final state of the building have been tolerated in order to preserve a record

5

of the structural history. For example, the long interior elevations of the south range show the scars of the original cross wall (*see* Fig 6.22, 128 and 130, and Fig 6.25, 131), including details which were subsequently obscured by the rebuilding of the wall, rather than the reconstructed wall in section. Similarly, blockings surviving at the time of recording are shown, even though doors or windows may subsequently have been re-opened (*see* Figs 5.17 and 6.25, 259), and vice versa (*see* Fig 6.25, 257). Despite occasional complications of this sort, the drawings are capable of acting as a practical (on-site) guide to the fabric of the building, which is now largely obscured.

Photography

During the initial phase of survey and recording work in the building in 1987–8, a photographic record was made with 35mm equipment; this aimed to record the state of the building at the time and significant detail as and when it was accessible. The excavations, of course, involved extensive photography as well. From 1990, allied to the cob-recording project, more and more of the photography was entrusted to a professional photographer, using medium-format equipment.[50] This has provided photographs of superior quality, although 35mm was still used for day-to-day record photography (as were small 'snapshot' cameras and colour-negative film). The photographic archive is stored with the project archive (Appendix). In order to facilitate retrieval, negative reference numbers are given in the captions of the photographs used in this report.

Post-excavation work

Although it was originally envisaged that the DoE excavations would be published separately, the new work that was developing in the late 1980s made a combination of the work increasingly sensible, because the results of the 1977–8 excavations were being supplemented and, in some cases, supplanted as more was learnt about the structural and stratigraphic history of the building. Post-excavation analysis on Stephen Dunmore's excavation archive was carried out and an archive report produced in 1990–1 following its deposition with EMAFU.[51]

For the EMAFU excavation and fabric recording, the aim of primary post-excavation work was to set down the recorded data in an accessible and ordered way and to provide syntheses and summaries of those data. To accomplish this end, approaches varied in the way most appropriate for the data. For area excavations stratigraphic contexts were divided into phases (groups) displayed in diagrammatic form on matrixes and descriptive material presented in lists of context descriptions and indexes providing cross-references to plans, sections and photographs.[52] For the report on the standing building recording, more emphasis was placed on narrative description and interpretation than on tabulated and ordered primary data; synthetic drawings also played more of a part.[53] For the observations and watching briefs the approach was deliberately more flexible, to accommodate varying levels of observation, recording and archaeological interest.[54] One rule was adhered to throughout: field drawings were drawn up into sheets of inked drawings, so that the archive reports contained versions of all of the drawn records and made this material available in a compact and ordered form.

The form of this report

Contemporary ideas on the presentation of archaeological reports tend to favour a synthesis of the material recovered and a presentation of the main results.[55] This principle has informed the planning of this report in the face of the large quantity of recorded material.[56] Coverage of the excavations has been deliberately kept short, with a minimum of stratigraphic and numerical data. Illustrations have been selected from the excavation plans and sections according to their importance or representative value for the history of the building. Chapter 4 aims to present a short description of the main findings, a discussion of their implications in relation to the standing fabric and the means to follow up material in the project archive if necessary. Much less-important material has been left in the archive reports, to which the reader is referred for details.[57] The account of the standing fabric (Chapters 5–8) is necessarily longer and more complicated, since many aspects of the building require discussion. These chapters aim to provide an account of the building, its structural history and its place in local and national architectural history, as well as a practical guide to the fabric now hidden (when used with the elevation drawings). Chapters 5 and 6 are deliberately arranged as if the reader is walking around the building, for use as a guide to the fabric. The core of the report is concluded by a general discussion designed to give an overview of the main items of interest in the building, and discussion of contentious aspects of the interpretation (Chapter 8). The presentation of the key excavated finds and collections of material from the standing building (Chapters 9 and 10), a discussion of the conservation work (Chapter 11) and an overview of the development of the site (Chapter 12) form the final chapters. Along with this introductory chapter, Chapters 3, 8 and 12 could stand alone for users of the report not wishing to consult the more detailed accounts.

The anatomy of the building

Orientation

The building is taken to be oriented north, rather than north-east, for convenience and conciseness in description. Thus the standing ranges are referred to as east, south and west, rather than (the more strictly accurate) north-east, south-east and south-west (*see* Fig 1.1). The site is divided into three general areas: an eastern court, against the eastern frontage; a central courtyard within the standing building and a western courtyard, now used as a car park.

Nomenclature

Within the building, as far as possible, location is referred to by room name or function (Fig 1.3). Conventional subdivision into *bays* is possible for the east and west ranges, but is complicated in the south range (where it would be most useful) by differing arrangements between ground-floor 'bays' (conditioned by the beams of the first floor) and first-floor bays dictated by the roof trusses. Reference to the internal long elevations (*see* Figs 6.22 and 6.25, on which ground- and first-floor bays are numbered in large arabic numerals and truss numbers in roman numerals) will show several discrepancies: there are eleven roof trusses (numbered from east to west by the carpenters' assembly marks), and eleven floor beams (again referred to as beams 1–11, although without the authority of assembly marks). The beams form bays, which are, on average, wider than those of the roof; this is most marked in the eastern rooms where bays 1–3 of the parlour are equivalent to bays 1–4 of the chamber. For the remainder

of the south range, the floor bays and the roof bays are broadly coincident, although rarely exactly so, except that two floor beams are required to support the floor on either side of the cross wall (to overcome the barrier of the wall and to accommodate a change in floor level). Thus ground-floor bays 7 and 8 fall wholly within first-floor bay 8. The floor beams will be referred to by number, the roofs by trusses and bays. Bay 1 is the space between trusses I and II and bay 10, between trusses X and XI and so on.

The east range, being largely open to the roof, can be described by the bays of the roof structure. The surviving trusses are numbered II–VI (truss I having formed the end of a missing first-floor room in the northernmost bay). The ground floor of bay 1 is now occupied by a reconstructed *hall store*, with a small first-floor *loft* above; the remainder of the east range is wholly occupied by the *hall*, with the site of the *screens passage* partly occupying the southernmost bay (bay 5). The south range is subdivided by the conventional room names on the ground floor of *parlour, service rooms* (originally two, combined to one, now restored as two), a *through passage* from the broad arched entrance to the south to the similarly broad door on the north wall in the south-western corner of the courtyard.[58] To the west of the through passage is a room of unknown function, poorly lit in its original arrangement, so here called the *west service room*. Three first-floor rooms are the *great chamber*, to the east above the parlour, the *inner chamber* and the *oriel chamber*. These names have no historical authority, but have become established in the collective vocabulary of the study of the building by common usage. The west range was originally open to the roof in its capacity as the *kitchen*. In later periods doorways gave access from the oriel chamber to an inserted first-floor room, here called the *kitchen chamber*. Modern structures abutting the west elevation of the standing building are described, collectively, as the *annexe*; this is now reduced in size and considerably modified by the restoration programme, but retains its principal recent historical function of providing access to the first floor once ancient stairs had been removed.

The rather arbitrary nature of the room names used here (for convenience of description, without accuracy as to historical function) has some justification in the case of the main living rooms. The definition of a parlour as the prime withdrawing room,

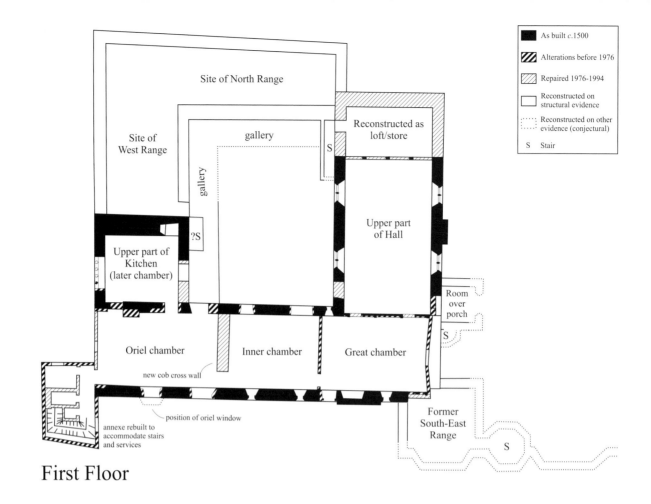

Site of North Range

Site of West Range

gallery

gallery

Reconstructed as loft/store

S

Upper part of Hall

Upper part of Kitchen (later chamber)

?S

Room over porch

S

Oriel chamber

Inner chamber

Great chamber

new cob cross wall

position of oriel window

Former South-East Range

S

annexe rebuilt to accommodate stairs and services

First Floor

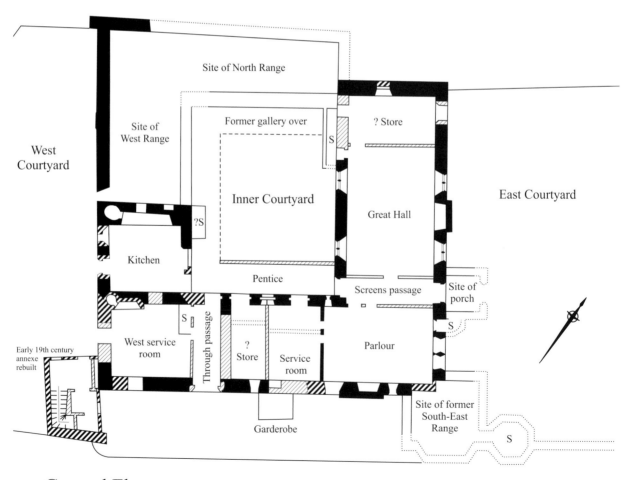

Site of North Range

West Courtyard

Site of West Range

Former gallery over

S

? Store

Inner Courtyard

Great Hall

East Courtyard

?S

Kitchen

Pentice

Screens passage

Site of porch

S

S

Through passage

West service room

? Store

Service room

Parlour

S

Early 19th century annexe rebuilt

Garderobe

Site of former South-East Range

S

Ground Floor

0   5   20
metres

where increasing privacy is the motivating factor, is widely accepted and this applies both in vernacular buildings and in gentry houses. This is refined by the suggestion that in the 16th and 17th centuries a parlour was a room furnished for sitting,[59] and that the room was generally on the ground floor, unlike a chamber, which was generally on the first floor.[60] Proximity to a garden may also have been a factor.[61] In London the term 'great chamber' originated in the third quarter of the 15th century referring to a reception and dining room, although it is recorded as early as 1380 elsewhere.[62] The suggestion that the first-floor room in the south range at Bowhill was so-called would concur with its obviously prime position and high-status decoration. The chambers beyond may then have functioned as bedchambers.

Numbering

Excavated deposits and features of and within the standing fabric are referred to by a reference number that applies to the archive record, appears on the drawings and that served to identify finds and/or samples from that fabric or feature. The series is continuous and applied similarly to all aspects of the fabric where description and identification was necessary, except the beams and roofs.

Phasing

A series of phases has been established for the site that applies equally to the excavated deposits and standing fabric (summarised in Table 3.1). On occasion it has been necessary to conflate two phases from a given part of the site, in order to avoid undue multiplication of phases across the whole site and over-complication of the sequence (for example, phase 1 in the vicinity of the south range consists of a succession of ditch cuttings that cannot have coexisted). It is not always possible, given the relative nature of much archaeological, stratigraphic and structural dating evidence, to be certain that events that are apportioned to the same phase on this basis in reality occurred simultaneously. The phases should be seen as schematic, representing a synthesis of a number of independent sequences from different parts of the site, although certain fixed points, notably the construction of the standing building (phase 3) and the major alterations of *c* 1800 (phase 8), permit events to be correlated across the whole site.

Materials

Stone

The two types used for common walling purposes were volcanic trap and Permian breccia. The volcanic trap was the predominant component in the stone walls of the building, mostly a dense, crystalline variety, purple or grey-purple in colour, frequently with prominent white veining through the stone. These characteristics are typical of the stone from the Pocombe quarry, which is also the nearest source, 750m west-south-west of the building (*see* Fig 3.1);[63] Barley quarry, slightly further north, forms another immediately local source of volcanic trap. It is thus reasonable to assume that much of the stone was obtained from one or both of these quarries. Permian breccia is a concretion of angular fragments of older rocks in a red sandstone matrix. The principal source of this stone in the later Middle Ages was the major quarries near Heavitree, just to the east of Exeter (the stone was known as Whipton or Wonford in the medieval sources,[64] but as Heavitree stone from the early 17th century).[65] Since breccia quarries at Exminster and Peamore to the west of the river provided large quantities of Exeter's building stone in the 15th and 16th centuries, it is probable that the stone used at Bowhill came from the nearer sources to the west of the river.[66] The common name for this material, 'Heavitree stone', is thus avoided here. Occasional blocks of breccia appear in the east and south ranges (where it was also used for some special purposes, *see below*). Breccia was used more frequently in the stone footings of the west range (presumably reflecting a variation in supply). Here it is of an unusual type, with distinctively fine, angular aggregate, as if the stone came from the margins of the regular deposits, rather than the uniform red colour and coarse texture of normal breccia. The breccia used for the hall chimney stack and the base of the oriel (*see* Fig 5.8, 49, and Fig 5.13) and in later contexts, is of more normal composition; the way the material is used in these contexts places it in the category of specially selected stone (described next), rather than that of common walling material.

Certain types of stone were specially selected for decorative detail. Beer stone, a fine Cretaceous limestone from the coast of East Devon, was used for the windows of the hall and for other architectural detail in the original building that has not survived (represented in the collection of excavated/salvaged architectural fragments, Chapter 9). It will be argued that much of this, otherwise unparalleled, freestone ornament derives from the vanished south-east building. For lesser detail, but where stone was still required to take a moulding or chamfer, a specific form of volcanic trap was favoured, a dense, but vesicular variety of the stone attributed to Raddon, near Thorverton.[67] This was used for the cinque-foil-headed lancet windows of the south and east elevations of the south range (see Figs 5.10 and 5.11) and the north windows of the parlour and great chamber. An intermediate type of stone, varying from vesicular to crystalline texture, was used for the doors of the screens passage (see Fig 8.30), probably for those of the through passage in the south range that have not survived and for the fireplaces of the hall, the main rooms of the south range and the kitchen. The source of this stone could have been the same as for walling (with special selection of vesicular stone).[68] It is more likely that a different quarry produced stone of the requisite quality.[69] A small quantity of stone from Raddon (near Thorverton) has been used in recent repairs, although this source was determined by present availability rather than providing a close match.[70]

Mortar

Brief mention should be made of mortars and other bonding materials, at this point. The footings, core and sometimes the interior facework of primary masonry were bonded with clay. Good-quality white lime mortar was used to point the exterior facework and for most core-work above the footings. The recipe is consistent, having a high lime content with a medium angular grit, presumably derived from a local (?riverine) source. The same composition was used for the rendering of exterior elevations (including cob), although the interior plastering employed rather finer aggregate. In later work a wide variety of mixes of lime- and earth-based mortars was employed, described in detail in Chapter 10.

Cob

The use of cob at Bowhill is an integral element in the primary construction. Stone was preferred as a material in places, but there are some positions in which cob was used interchangeably with stone throughout. There were two clear exceptions: cob was always laid over stone, with no instances of the reverse in the primary building; and roof timbers were nearly always supported by stone or timber. From this it can be inferred that cob was not expected to provide un-assisted support for major structural members (although this does happen very occasionally in the primary arrangement, and often in secondary contexts).[71] In the east range, cob was the predominant walling material of the northern bay, but was used throughout to build up the wall tops. In the south range the use of cob varied from filling of the wall tops on the south side of the inner chamber, to walling of full height (above stone footings) at the west end of the range. The vanished eastern gable of the south range was of cob above first-floor level and the west gable (like the adjacent walls) was wholly of cob, above low stone footings. The west and probably also the north ranges were built wholly of cob, on low stone footings, the only parts of the building where the conventional techniques of cob-building were applied. Here the cob was raised around the posts of the roof trusses (Chapter 7).

There was a tendency for stone to predominate in the walling of the more visible parts of the building. The variation between the south and north walls of the south range is one example: the south wall (one of the main façades of the building) was of stone to its full height in bays 1–7, while the north wall was of cob above first-floor level. Problems in roofing the building caused by differential materials will be discussed further below. This treatment illustrates the way in which the two materials were equally regarded by the builders of Bowhill. Further west, masonry in the south wall stepped down over the large entrance arch to low footings in bays 9 and 10, while the north wall was originally entirely of cob on low footings west of the cross wall (now obscured by later insertions). The obvious conclusion to this disparity is that stone was used for the more prestigious parts of the building, while cob predominated in the more utilitarian ranges to the west and north. This offers only a partial explanation of a complex relationship of materials, however, and does not account (for example) for the use of cob in the east gable in one of the most prominent elevations of the building. Nor does it account for the cob walling accommodating an oriel window whose base was certainly, and whose frame may also have been, of stone in a first-floor room of considerable status at the west end of the south range (Chapter 5). There are reasons for thinking that the exterior of the building was originally rendered (Chapter 5). Since stone and cob (and the relative incidence of the two materials) would thus have been obscured, arguments of 'prestige' for their differential use become less sustainable and the idea that structural concerns dictated the choice of material in specific areas is strengthened. An explanation which accommodates a balance between the two factors is that stone walling was used in the parts of the building in which stone window frames were intended, presumably because of the difficulty of keying stone window frames into cob walls (although even this was managed at times, as in the oriel and the east gable). This would accommodate the 'prestige' argument, while playing down the visual emphasis of stone over cob. It is probable that there was no simple, single explanation and that the choice of walling material in a given area was influenced by a number of factors.

Whatever the detail of interpretation, this account is sufficient to show that there was little difference, in terms of their status as building materials, between cob and stone. Cob and its equivalent materials (daub, mud plaster and clay flooring materials) were used throughout in screens, partitions, filling of wall tops and other cavities. The combination of materials is one of the most distinctive aspects of the fabric of Bowhill, and is a theme that will recur throughout the description of the building. The earth-based materials were presumably of very local origin (this being one of their advantages). In the early building beneath the south range, the interior of the building itself may have provided the source of subsoil for the cob and a place in which to mix it.[72] The primary cob walling of the site was largely uniform in colour and composition, although later additions showed more of a variety. This too suggests an immediately local origin.[73] The western end of the south elevation (see Fig 5.8) proved the most fruitful place for observations of cob technique. Here the cob was built up in very low stages of 4"–10" (100–250mm) in depth, although some were as deep as 20" (500mm).[74]

Timber

The primary carpentry of Bowhill was of oak throughout, with all primary joints fixed with pegs. Iron fixings were not generally used in early contexts, the only regular exceptions to this pattern being the fixing of bosses in the roofs of the hall and great chamber with iron spikes and the nailing of laths for roofing and the filling of screens. Certain items of carpentry did not survive (floorboards, for instance) but equivalent elements, such as plank filling of screens, leave little doubt that oak was used throughout. Elm was used for some additions: for example, the infilling of partitions and the frame of the replaced screen forming the west wall of the great chamber; this would fit with dates in the 17th century.[75] Deal was used for extensive repairs to the planked and moulded parlour ceiling in the late 17th century and for most new work of the 18th century and later.

Roofing materials and other evidence

No primary roof-covering materials survived on the building at the time of the survey. A small number of late medieval and 17th- to 18th-century crests (ridge tiles) had been recovered from the ridge of the oversail of the roofs of the east and south ranges, but these related to a later slate roof, that is, they themselves must have been reused (see Figs 2.9 and 2.19). Large quantities of roofing materials have been recovered in the course of the fabric analysis, showing that the early roofs were of slate pegged with oak pegs and secured by mortar bedding. Other materials recovered in some quantities from excavation or fabric recording are laths, ironwork, fragments of roof tiles, floor tiles, window glass and leadwork, as well as the architectural fragments mentioned already. These materials are discussed in Chapter 9.

The plan and circulation

In plan the main building had four ranges set around a central courtyard (see Fig 1.3). Other elements were an eastern courtyard forming the main approach to the building, with a range attached to the south-east corner of the main building (now vanished) and further structures associated with the boundary wall(s) delimiting the courtyard to the south (evidence of the Bucks' engraving, see Fig 2.1) and a western service or perhaps agricultural courtyard from which a barn survived until 1972 (Chapter 3 and see Figs 2.14, 2.15 and 3.4).

Some doubt has attached to the existence of a north range in the core of the building. No convincing interior floor levels or features were found by excavation (although their absence could be attributed to later robbing and other destructive activity) and an excavated south wall (badly robbed) failed quite to make a corner with that of the west range (see Fig 4.7).

Despite this the cumulative evidence in favour of a north range is strong, and comprises:

1. A fragment of the north wall of the west range, now forming the boundary wall of the courtyard (*see* Fig 6.45). The wall was of cob, on stone footings, much in the manner of the standing part of the west range; although it survived only for 2.75m, its alignment was continued by the modern boundary wall, showing that it formerly ran as far as the east range.
2. The northward step in the northern boundary of the site in line with the west wall of the hall (*see* Fig 1.1). This is a constant element in early plans of the building and probably perpetuates an ancient arrangement, at least of the primary structural phase of the present standing building, and potentially represents a survival from a still earlier phase (*see* discussion of this in Chapter 4). Combined with the robbed footings of the south wall, this represents a coherent structural plan.
3. The argument of access to independent lodgings within the building outlined below (Chapter 8).

The principal entrance to the house was clearly intended to be that from the east through the screens passage. There was evidence for a porch against the eastern doorway of the screens passage that was probably of two storeys. The eastern court acted as a forecourt in the main approach to the building. The original character of this area is wholly absent in the surviving building, approached as it was through an enclosed court or garden, with the ornamented south-eastern block and possibly a galleried walk around the perimeter (if the suggested reconstruction is correct, Chapter 8).

The elevation facing the road was also considered important (as the extent of stone-framed lancet windows, the oriel window and other high-grade fittings testify) and a second 'main' entrance to the central courtyard through a wide stone arch (*see* Fig 5.15 and now restored, Fig 11.36) was placed west of centre in this elevation. This entry is wider and taller than the norm for the building, but is not so large as to have been a 'cart' (or even 'carriage') entrance, as has sometimes been suggested. The inner courtyard seems to have been wholly domestic in character; stabling and storage were relegated to the western court-yard.

Two of the main rooms, the hall (occupying most of the east range) and the kitchen (in the southern bays of the west range), were open to the roof. The remainder of the extant building and probably also the vanished west, north and south-east ranges were two-storeyed from the first. The kitchen lay opposite the hall, connected to it by a pentice (vanished, but demonstrated by sockets in the cob, Chapter 5). There was probably a first-floor chamber in the northern bay of the east range reached by a stair at the north-west corner of the hall,[76] with a storeroom below, lit by unglazed mullioned windows of primitive form.

Other living rooms could have been located in the north range, but the principal living rooms lay to the south of the hall (on both floors), at the east end of the south range and in the south-east range. Evidence for stairs in the primary plan is equivocal, with probable sites of stairs: at the north-west corner of the hall; in the south-east range; in a vice against the porch (which may have led only to a room above the porch) and possible additional stairs in the parlour and the west service room through trimmed openings in the floor frame (although there is no evidence that these were permanent stairs). A door at first-floor level in the south-west corner of the courtyard gave access to a gallery along the wall of the west range to by-pass the kitchen (also represented by evidence in the roof of the west range for such an arrangement).[77]

A distinctive aspect of circulation within the building is represented by the paired doorways in screens at three points (in the north and west partitions of the parlour and the west partition of the through passage). Very little evidence of sub-partitions in ceiling timbers was recorded to give the paired doors a context in plan, nor was any evidence recovered by excavation. The paired doorways can best be explained in relation to stairs rising through one of the door-ways and to the provision of screened access from the screens passage through the parlour to the service rooms to the west (the example in the west wall of the parlour possibly also reflects a division in the service room beyond, although this has left only the slightest of traces). The absence of firm evidence in the fabric might be explained by the use of movable screens and other portable furniture.[78]

The first floor of the south range was reached by stairs in the south-east range, via the gallery in the central courtyard and possibly by the stair attached to the porch. The first-floor plan is a simple one of three rooms arranged in line. The first and third rooms (great chamber and oriel chamber) were heated, but the second room had no fireplace. This suite of chambers, communicating with the south-east range directly and with the first floor of the west (and north) range(s) via a gallery, is straightforward and can be envisaged as providing the main living and sleeping accommodation in the building. The ground-floor rooms of the south range are more varied in nature. The parlour is marked out as an important room by its ceiling of moulded beams and high level of appointment generally. It also gave access to the south-east range. Yet the room is entered directly from the screens passage at the 'lower' end of the hall. It seems best to interpret this as a product of changing priorities in the planning and arrangement of rooms at the turn of the 16th century, where innovative planning of private rooms on a large scale was tempered by the need also to provide rooms of traditional function. Thus the parlour can be seen as the first in a series of rooms, progressing from ground to first floor, of up-to-date function and furnishing, placed between the hall, still seen (if only residually) as the paramount reception room of the house, and rooms with traditionally 'lower-end' functions, here pushed further west in the ground-floor plan. A desire for the principal rooms to over-look the road may also have played a part.

The south and south-east ranges had a curious structural relationship: adjoining at a corner with the walls of the south-east range turning off from the main building some distance short of the corner; the resulting plan shows two rectangular rooms diagonally adjacent, overlapping at their corners (see Fig 12.1). Thus the parlour and chamber, on ground and first floors respectively, communicated with the rooms in the south-east range by means of a wide opening (framed by the post of the first roof truss of the south range and the post supporting the south-east corner of the parlour ceiling), which could have been filled with partitioning or could have remained open.[79] The two roofs must have been joined by valleys where they met (the Bucks' engraving gives a hint of the difficulties here).[80]

The Bucks' engraving (Chapter 2 and see Fig 2.1) shows three structural elements to the south-east range. The first is clearly that for which the wall scars survive at the corner of the building, turning at right angles to the south and east. It had a gable to the south, a two-storeyed bay window, with some sort of surface decoration between ground- and first-floor levels (perhaps a register of panelled ornament) and paired lancet windows under moulded labels at ground- and first-floor levels in its west elevation.

The second element is an octagonal turret attached to the south-east corner of the first structure, with quatrefoil windows in its

south-west-facing side, apparently at mezzanine level (when judged in relation to the windows), cruciform ?apertures in the top stage above the gable and a concave-pointed spire roof. Possible functions of this structure are: a stair turret, giving access to the roof as well as the first-floor rooms; a garderobe turret; or private closets to the ground and first-floor rooms, possibly a 'prospect room' on the third floor.[81] There is no strong evidence in favour of any one interpretation, although that of a stair turret is probably to be preferred on the grounds of the quatrefoil windows,[82] their level (which might suggest a rising stair within) and the absence of traces of a cess pit in this area when excavated (Chapter 4). Direct access via a stair from the ground to the first-floor rooms of the south-east range would support the arguments of circulation within the rooms of the south and south-east ranges presented above.

The third and last element of the structure appears to be a single wall, with a crenellated parapet and a projecting oriel/bay window at an intermediate level between ground and first floors. Little can be made of this structure that is certain.[83] It appears to have been in poor repair in the 1730s and perhaps was largely demolished. It will be suggested that this element represents a fragment of an open, galleried boundary wall to the courtyard or garden (Chapter 8).[84]

The remainder of the south range, up to the cross wall, was occupied by two rooms with simple finishes and fenestration, each entered separately from the pentice. These are interpreted as service rooms (displaced from their conventional position at the lower end of the hall by the interpolation of the parlour, as above). The cross wall provided a solid division in the ground-floor plan. Beyond the passage the rest of the south range contained one room, whose original function is uncertain. The room was unheated (a fireplace was added in the late 16th century) and probably had a door in its south-west corner and a window in the west (gable) wall. A store or additional service room seems likely.

The kitchen is the only room of known function in the west and north ranges. Lodgings or other subsidiary accommodation and storage probably occupied the remaining space. The kitchen was open to the roof and originally had no door other than that in the east wall, giving onto the pentice (the present west doorway is a later insertion). The room was probably originally lit from first-floor level, although no evidence of primary windows survived later alterations to the east and west walls.

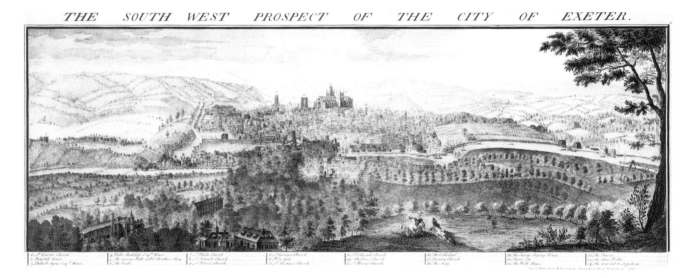

THE SOUTH WEST PROSPECT OF THE CITY OF EXETER.

Figure 2.1

The South West Prospect of the City of Exeter *by Samuel and Nathaniel Buck, dated 1736: note, in the centre, the second Bowhill House, Franklyn (= Franklin in Fig 2.2) House, and the parish church (EMAFU 1863/1); detail of Bowhill (lower left in main view) (EMAFU 1863/2) (photograph by Gary Young) (source: Exeter Archaeology, photograph © Exeter Archaeology).*

Figure 2.2 (facing page)

Hayman's map of Exeter, 1806, showing Bowhill and the other houses in the outer reaches of St Thomas parish; note also the extent of gardens (photograph by Gary Young) (photograph © Exeter Archaeology).

2
Pictorial and cartographic sources

A brief review of the key pictorial sources for the site, with commentary, will complement their presentation as illustrations. No early maps covering this area are known, but the inclusion of the building in the general view of Exeter by the Buck brothers was timely and presented a view of the building at an optimum date. Among other notable absences, the travel diaries of the Revd John Swete of Oxton, who was an indefatigable traveller and searcher after antiquities in the 1790s, show that he passed along the roads now known as Buddle Lane and Cowick Lane in the course of a journey to the west of Exeter in 1797 and thus must have passed very close to Bowhill. He mentioned Bowhill, however, only as a predecessor to Barley and failed to describe the building.[1]

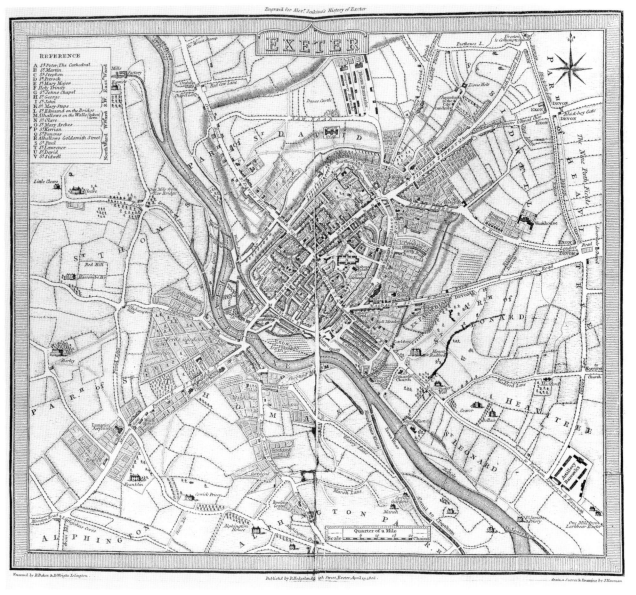

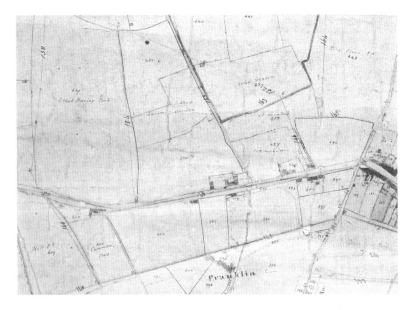

*Figure 2.3 (above)
Detail of the immediate area
of Bowhill from the PRO
copy of the tithe map dated
1839. Bowhill is just below
centre, numbered 431/431a;
note also the three fields of
'Lucombe's Garden',
numbered 430, 430a and
430b (see Fig 3.1) (reproduced courtesy of the Public
Record Office IR 30/9/407).*

*Figure 2.4 (top, right)
Mid-19th-century pencil
drawing by George Townsend
showing Bowhill from the
east (photograph by David
Garner) (reproduced cour-
tesy of the Westcountry
Studies Library, Exeter).*

*Figure 2.5 (centre, right)
Mid-19th-century pencil
drawing by F W L Stockdale,
showing the courtyard looking
south-east (photograph by
David Smart) (reproduced
courtesy of the Royal Institution of Cornwall).*

*Figure 2.6 (bottom, right)
Mid-19th-century pencil
drawing by F W L
Stockdale showing the house
from the west (photograph
by David Smart) (repro-
duced courtesy of the Royal
Institution of Cornwall).*

Buck brothers, 1736

Bowhill appears in the lower left-hand
corner of the large copper-plate engraving
entitled 'The South West Prospect of the
City of Exeter' in the series of views of
English towns and cities by Samuel and
Nathaniel Buck (Fig 2.1).[2] Considering the
fact that it forms a minor detail in a corner
of the general view of the city (albeit in the
foreground of that view), the house is
depicted with some care,[3] but the view is not
without problems of interpretation.

Chief among such problems is that none
of the rear ranges appears, although the
archaeological evidence shows that these
were still standing at the time (along with
the south-east range that is shown here).
The house is depicted as if it consisted only
of the south and south-east ranges, with
dense tree growth against the rear of this
rather shallow building.[4] Further vegetation
obscures the base of the southern wall.
Second is the strange square element on the
roof masking the junction of the roofs of the
south and south-east ranges. These problems may have arisen from the way in which
the engraving was compiled. Most of the
Bucks' town prospects were drawn from a
fixed (and often elevated) position.[5] Separate drawings were sometimes made of individual landmarks for inclusion in the
foreground and the views of the three
houses (the two Bowhills and Franklyn)
along the lower edge of the Exeter view
would be strong candidates for being
recorded in such sketches.[6] If the artist who
sketched Bowhill had done so from the road
to the south, the most obvious aspect of the
building, he might have omitted details of
the rear ranges, or merely noted their existence. The engraver (or compiler of the
draft)[7] might then have overlooked these
aspects of the sketch. The solution to the
second problem, that of the roof lines, probably lies in confusion over the structure itself
(perhaps this again reflects a tentative aspect
of the sketch). Two separately roofed structures, adjoining at the corner, must have
been roofed by means of leaded valleys, a
junction that is unusual and thus may not
have been rendered by the draughtsman in
an intelligible form. The engraver, again,
may have adopted a solution that seemed
sensible to him, but which bore no relation
to the actual arrangement.

Where the view can be tested against
surviving detail, its accuracy can be demonstrated to a remarkable level. Comparison of

Figure 2.7
Anonymous photographs,
labelled and dated 'Bowhill,
Exeter, 30.xii.1936',
possibly by A W Everett:
(left) the hall range
showing the thatched roof;
(right) detail of the screens
passage (EH B960392–3).

the detail (*see* Fig 2.1) with the south elevation of the south range as recorded in 1987 (*see* Fig 5.8) shows that every feature of the engraved view mirrors windows and doorways exactly, relieving arches where such were employed and even smaller apertures between the first-floor windows of the south range, where there are putlog holes. With this level of reliability where fabric survives, it is suggested that the features shown in the vanished parts of the building should be taken seriously as a faithful record of the south range prior to the extensive demolitions of *c* 1800 (phase 8, *see below*).[8] There is evidence in the fabric for the oriel window at the west end of the range, although in reality this was a corbelled-out structure at first-floor level only, rather than the full-height structure shown here, and for the walls of a south-east range (Chapters 5 and 8). Some of the architectural fragments recovered from the site also probably came from this building and add another dimension to the testing of this view.[9] Since the existence of the range is demonstrated by evidence in the fabric, it is suggested that the details of the Bucks' view should be accepted as the basis of a reconstruction (*see* Fig 12.5). Further discussion of the structures of the south-east range appears in Chapter 8.

Surveyor's drawing for first edition one-inch OS map, 1801

The original survey drawings for the one-inch Ordnance mapping survive at a scale of three inches to the mile.[10] Bowhill is shown in sufficient detail to demonstrate that the house had reached its present form by this

date, thereby providing useful evidence for the alterations of phase 8 having taken place prior to *c* 1800.

Hayman's map, 1806

This map (Fig 2.2) appeared as a frontispiece to the first edition of Jenkins's *History* in 1806. Prior to the publication of the Ordnance Survey in 1809, it is the only extant map of Exeter to extend beyond the core area of the walled town and the immediately extramural suburbs of the city and so to include the site of Bowhill. Other substantial houses of the vicinity, such as Franklyn, Barley and Cleave, are depicted as miniature views (presumably with some element of true representation to them), while, somewhat disappointingly, Bowhill is shown simply as a rectangular plan parallel to the street.

Figure 2.8
The east elevation in the
1950s. Note the corrugated
roof of the hall and extent
of cob walling, detectable by
smooth texture beneath
render (NMR AA
57/144).

Figure 2.9
The east elevation in 1976 (photograph by Nigel Cheffers-Heard; EMAFU 255/3)
(© Exeter Archaeology).

Figure 2.10
The south elevation in the 1950s from the opposite side of Dunsford Road. Note especially the glimpse of the cob boundary wall, which had been demolished prior to any later photographs (NMR AA 57/139).

Figure 2.11
The building from the south-east in 1969 (RCHME BB69/5012).

Lower Bowhill is shown, labelled 'Lunatic Asylum'. The Moreton turnpike is clearly shown on the downhill side of the crossroads, providing a context for Jenkins's description, quoted below (Chapter 3, n 130).

Tithe map, 1841

The map itself (on which Fig 3.1 is based) is useful for showing the local topography in the early 1840s and the attached apportionment an essential source for the field names; as will be seen, these have proved useful in some cases for identifying the land concerned in earlier property accounts and transactions. As far as the building goes, however, the map is drawn at too small a scale to show very much detail (Fig 2.3). The building is shown in plan very much as it survives, with three ranges (the eastern longer than the western) and a small structure in the position of the annexe at the south-west corner, presumably the predecessor of the surviving structure. Two key features shown in the boundaries of the site are of interest: the step northwards in line with the west wall of the hall appears here, demonstrating an early origin for this change in alignment; a similar, if slighter, step outwards is seen in the southern boundary, possibly preserving a remnant of the eastern limit of the south-east range. This was still visible on a mid-20th-century aerial photograph (*see* Fig 3.4), but was obliterated by road widening in the early 1960s.[11]

St Thomas sewer map, 1850

All of the features of interest just described for the tithe map are repeated at a slightly larger scale on a map drawn by S R Southwood in 1850 to show the water courses and sewers of the parish.[12] An additional feature shown here was a line dividing the building into two halves approximately in line with the cross wall in the south range. Since it will be suggested that the building was so divided at one of the late phases of use, this map provides one of the pieces of evidence for such a subdivision, along with the archaeological evidence (in the form of the provision of a second kitchen serving the eastern half, which is *not* shown on this map). Southwood's map also shows Lower Bowhill in its larger, extended, form.

Pencil drawings by Townsend and Stockdale, *c* 1850

Four drawings of Bowhill, all approximately mid-19th century in date, are known. Two, probably by George Townsend, are in the

Westcountry Studies Library at Exeter and the other two, by F W L Stockdale, are in the Royal Institution of Cornwall at Truro.[13] Of the Townsend drawings, one seems to be a copy of the other (and may not even have been drawn by Townsend himself); many details are repeated (such as the barrel in the foreground), but in a simpler or cruder fashion.[14] Since the second version adds nothing informative to the first, it is not illustrated here. The view (Fig 2.4) is of the east elevation and shows the building pretty much as it survived at the time of the earliest photographs, with thatch on the hall range, but the oversail and south range still slated. The porch, east gable of the south range, hall chimney stack and northern bay of the east range are all missing.

The drawings by Stockdale show different views.[15] One (Fig 2.5) shows the interior of the courtyard looking south-east. Again the hall range is thatched, with the remainder of the roofs slated and there is a large tree in the centre of the courtyard. The north gable of the east range is shown free of attached structures (although this may represent some tidying up by the artist, as derelict structures are known to have survived in this position). A chimney is shown in the roof of the south range.[16] The second drawing (Fig 2.6) shows the west elevation of the house. Here the general configuration is much as it survived in the 1970s, except that a smaller structure is shown attached to the south-west corner of the building in the position of the later 'annexe' and roofed on an east-west axis. There are windows on ground and first floors of the western gable, the first-floor window of the west range is shown blocked (although the sill is articulated) and there is no doorway through the western boundary wall into the courtyard.

Painting of 1907

One further depiction of the building has come to light; this is an oil painting, dated 1907 and signed by A D Horne.[17] The east side of the building is shown, with thatch on the hall roof, very much as in Townsend's pencil drawing, although details of glazing and window frames chart changes between the mid-19th and early 20th centuries (for example, a sash in the southern light of the parlour windows and diamond quarries are shown in the hall windows).

Figure 2.12
The south elevation in 1969 (RCHME BB69/5013).

Figure 2.13
The west elevation in 1957 (RCHME AA57/141).

Figure 2.14
The site from the west in 1969, with the barn in the foreground (RCHME BB69/5011).

Figure 2.15
The east elevation of the barn in 1969. Note the three-light window (RCHME BB69/5022).

Early photographs

The views reproduced here (Fig 2.7) are dated 30 December 1936 but are otherwise unprovenanced and represent the only pre-war views known to the author other than Fig 3.3 and the two photographs published by Everett.[18] They are useful in showing the thatched east range, the nature of the northern gable of the hall, the remnants of early ridge tiles on the junction of the roofs of the east and south ranges and the generally dilapidated condition of the building at this time (*see*, for example, the randomly glazed windows of the hall). Later photographs by the NMR/RCHME (and others) of the 1950s and 1960s provide a valuable record of the building before the destructive alterations of the restaurant period (Figs 2.8–2.28).

Figure 2.16
The west elevation in the 1950s (photograph by A W Everett; RCHME AA69/1758).

Figure 2.17
The north elevation in the 1950s (photograph by A W Everett; RCHME AA69/1759).

Figure 2.18
The north elevation of the south range in 1969. Note the 'bridge' in the corner (RCHME BB69/5015).

Figure 2.19
The west elevation of the hall in 1969 (RCHME BB69/5018).

Figure 2.20 (top, right)
The courtyard, looking west along the north wall of the south range from the hall door, that is, the site of the pentice. Note the open doorway in the first floor above, a remnant of the gallery access into the first-floor room (photograph by A W Everett; NMR AA69/1764).

Figure 2.21 (bottom, right)
The screens passage, looking east from the west doorway. Note the cobbled surface (photograph by A W Everett; NMR AA 69/1762).

Figure 2.22 (above, left) The hall in 1969, looking south-west (RCHME BB69/5025).

Figure 2.23 (above, right) The hall in 1969, looking north (RCHME BB69/5023).

Figure 2.24 The interior of the parlour in the 1950s. Note the screen in position beneath beam 5. The head of the curved post/brace that was inserted to support the south end of beam 4 on the removal of the screen from its original site is visible on the left (photograph by A W Everett; NMR AA 69/1757).

Figure 2.25 (above, left)
Detail of the parlour ceiling in the 1950s, looking west, bays 2 (in foreground) to 4. Note the detail of the mouldings of the panels. The later shallower form is otherwise recorded only in a sketch (NMR AA 57/171).

Figure 2.26 (above, right)
The parlour in 1969, looking west (RCHME BB69/5034).

Figure 2.27
The great chamber roof in 1969, looking west. Note the plaster ceiling and line of the partition on main truss III in foreground (RCHME BB69/5029).

Figure 2.28
The first floor of the south range in 1969, looking east. Note the cross wall has been removed. (RCHME BB69/5038).

3
Historical outline

by N W Alcock and S R Blaylock

The Holand family and property in the parish of St Thomas, Exeter[1]

Of the four families named Holand in 15th-century Devon, the senior were the Holands of Dartington, to whom the Holands of Weare may have been related.[2] The Holands of Cowick, or St Thomas, were descended from Thomas Holand (II) of Weare.[3] Early evidence of the family holding property in the parish comes from deeds dating to the turn of the 15th century involving John Holand, clerk (d 1419);[4] he was the younger son of Thomas Holand (I) of Weare. John's nephew, Richard Holand (c 1385–c 1452–5), was the first true 'Holand of St Thomas', inasmuch as he settled in St Thomas. The next three generations of the family provide the background to Bowhill (Tables 3.1 and 3.2). Richard Holand appears as the first witness after the vicar to the deed of consecration of the parish Church of St Thomas on its new site on 4 October 1412,[5] implying that he was one of the principal parishioners. Richard was MP for the County of Devon in 1430 and held numerous other prominent local offices thereafter.[6] On 28 May 1429 Richard and his wife Margaret were granted a licence by Bishop Edmund Lacy ' ... for divine service in the presence of either in any suitable place in their house in the parish of St Thomas in Cowykstrete'.[7] This reference has been the source of confusion as it has been interpreted as evidence for a chapel at Bowhill.[8] Richard's residence is described as a house in 'Cowykstrete', however, rather than at Bowhill. Other evidence (*see below*) indicates that the family was living in the centre of St Thomas at this period.

The position of the family in St Thomas is dramatically demonstrated by a rental of Cowick for 1451–2.[9] Richard Holand was by far the most prominent landowner in the manor, owning thirty-four properties for which he paid a total of £8 2s 7d free rent. Some fifty other tenants are listed as paying free rents and the rental also includes full details of the demesne land of the manor; Richard Holand did not lease any part of this. Most of the holdings are named from former tenants, but a number of the entries include topographical indications. One of his properties is described as 'opposite the mansion of the said Richard Holand', while another was 'at Bowehull', as was a property called Sleghes tenement held by Philip Courtney. Coklesworthy, Netherclyve, Haycombe Down, 'le Putes'[10] (surely Barley Wells) and Clyve are also named among Holand's holdings. The demesne lands included a field called 'Barle Park' and one called 'Le Parke' behind the church of St Thomas in Cowick Street. A clear inference from the 1451–2 rental is that the Holand estate in Cowick was built up by Richard Holand in the first half of the 15th century by the piecemeal acquisition of freehold land and tenements, a process still continuing at the time of the rental. The rental contains no entry for the Holand mansion and nothing in it suggests that the mansion was at Bowhill; a late tradition suggests that a Holand family mansion was on the site of the house later converted into the Bridewell, east of St Thomas' Church.[11]

Thomas Holand (c 1420–72) is believed to be the son of Richard.[12] He too owned property in St Thomas parish, being described as 'of that parish' in an entry in the Bishop's register addressed to the rector of St Thomas regarding his marriage.[13] His ownership is confirmed by an account for the proceeds of one messuage and forty acres of land in Cowick, taken into the king's hand from 2 June to 29 September 1455 because of a failure to pay over proceeds of the tax of 15ths and 10ths.[14] Thomas Holand had presumably succeeded Richard by this date, indicating a bracket of 1452 to 1455 for the latter's date of death. Thomas is also mentioned as a subtenant of one John Hacche, among the list of other tenants in 1451–2 jointly paying rent for three properties. Thomas was MP for Exeter in 1449–50, 1450–1 and 1455–6 and was described as 'of Cowyk, esq.; alias of Cowykstrete, alias late of Tiverton, Devon'.[15] In his will Thomas left ' ... all my londes & tenementis yn the pariche of Synt Thomas yn Coweke street ... ' to his wife, Elizabeth; this property is mentioned first, possibly with the implication that it was the core of the estate.[16] Among the other property willed by Thomas were lands in the adjacent areas of Exwick, Barley and Alphington.

Court rolls for Cowick

Only one run of medieval court rolls survives for Cowick, a small group for 5–6 Edward IV (1465–6).[17] The Holands are only mentioned in one series of entries, in which Thomas Holand and the bailiff of the manor were jointly amerced for not providing three named people to be jurors at the royal assizes; presumably the two men for

Table 3.1 Chronological table showing owners and tenants of Bowhill in relation to structural phases

phase	date range	owner(s)	tenants	principal/secondary events	phase
1	'medieval'	unknown? Cowick Priory? Tavistock Abbey?	unknown	pre-building ditches and gullies (several phases)	1
2	14/15C	?Holand family	unknown	construction of early building/plus occupation and destruction phases	2
3	c 1500	Roger Holand	none	construction of standing building	3
4	mid 16C/ c 1550	John/Thomasina Carew	none	alterations in garderobe area of south range service rooms	4
5	late 16C/ early 17C	Carew	none	rebuilding of stair in NE corner of courtyard/possibly other alterations, ?fireplaces	5
6	mid-17C: Civil War	John Carew, regicide; forfeit in 1660 but restored to Thomas Carew in 1661	none	defensive ditch; some damage	6
7	late 17C/ 18C	Carew to 1714; Penneck (1714–52); Sawle (1752–91); Graves-Sawle (1791– onwards)	Lucombe (1740–onwards)	enlargement of parlour, re-fenestration (pre 1736); some decay in E courtyard; filling of ditch from phase 6(?)	7
8	c 1800	Graves-Sawle	Lucombe to 1794–6	widespread demolition: W, N, and SE ranges; reorganisation; new kitchen; building split into two; new exterior surfaces (plus some interior surfaces)	8
9	19C	Sir Joseph Graves-Sawle (1841 tithe map)	Kerswill (1828–onwards)	demolition of second kitchen; garden/cultivation features throughout/minor alterations to fenestration and interior	9
10	1900–69	Graves-Sawle until 1932; Sclater until 1968	?Kerswill (until 1917); Sclater by 1919	new surfaces; partitions; annexe built (or rebuilt); increasingly suburban surroundings (1945–1960s)/ rebuilding of boundary wall	10
11	1969–76	E Showell (1968–72); R M Horden (1972–6)		'restaurant period': brutal alterations; repartitioning; demolition of cross wall in south range; insertion of stairs; demolition of barn (1972)	11
12	1976–97	Secretary of State for the Environment (National Heritage/ Culture) 1976 to date		DoE purchase (1976); first excavation 1977–8; stripping of building, c 1980; repairs mainly to E range, 1980–85; repairs to S/W ranges and environs, 1985–95; EMAFU excavations, 1989–95. Search for use, 1995–7. Sale 1997.	12

Table 3.2 Genealogical table of the families connected with Bowhill

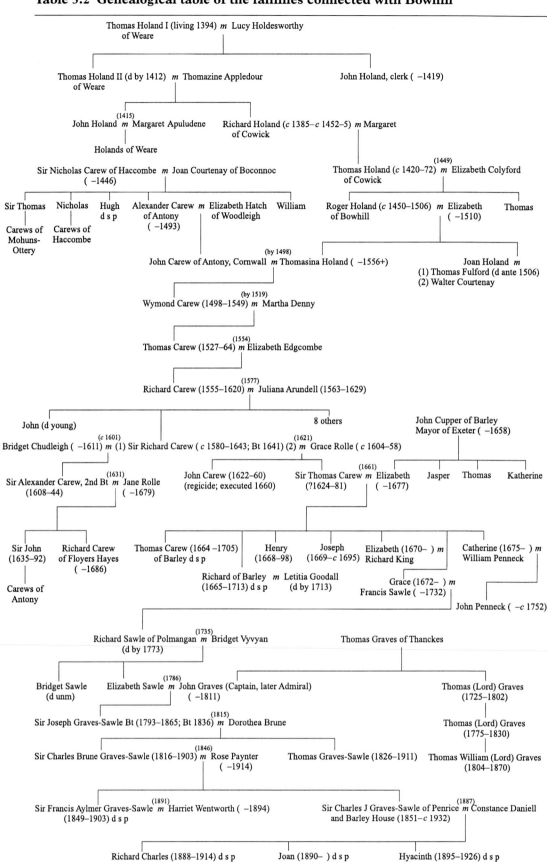

Table 3.3 Summary of the main dating evidence for the chronological sequence of Bowhill

item	description and dating	phase
1	13–14C sherds in the demolition material of the phase 2 building, which may have derived from the cob of the walls, suggest perhaps a late 14/early 15C date for its construction (context 601). Other pottery associated with the early building (pit fill 745) is in the range 1350–1450.	2
2	A silver penny of Edward IV in the fill of a post pipe relating to the early building on the site; phase 2, posthole 680 (fill 649). Dated to 1461–64 (*see* Shiel, Chapter 9), the coin was well circulated by the time of its deposition. As it must have been deposited on the removal of the post, after the fire, the coin provides a terminus post quem for the destruction of the building.	2
3	The fill of the garderobe pit of the early building, relating to its destruction, contained material dated to the late 15th/early 16thC (context 685), a similar date range to that of the construction of the standing building (*see below*).	2
4	Dendrochronological dating of timbers: one possible structural timber with a felling date of 1478+; felling-date range of 1491–*c* 1507 for the timbers of the parlour ceiling (Groves, Chapter 10).	3
5	A good group of pottery dating to *c* 1500–50, from the fill of the foundation trench of the north wall of the south range (west service room, context 1559). Although only small scraps of pottery (and therefore not illustrated here), this provides useful datable material associated with the construction (Allan, Chapter 9).	3
6	Documentary evidence for some sort of building activity in 1499–1500, in the form of a licence for Roger Holand to lay water pipes across the lands of Tavistock Abbey, plus fairly certain evidence that the building was there (and the Holands personally resident in it) by Roger Holand's death in 1506 (Chapter 3).	3
7	The late medieval character of the architecture of the standing building combined with features integral to the primary construction which indicate an advance on late 15C domestic architecture in the area. The parlour element in the plan, the oriel windows and the intersecting-beam ceiling all suggest a date after rather than before 1500.	3
8	A good group of pottery contained in the fill of the disused garderobe pit of the service room adjacent to the parlour (context 2347) indicates that this feature went out of use around 1550 (Allan, Chapter 9).	4
9	Mention of Bowhill among the sites to the west of Exeter fortified by the Parliamentary forces during the final siege of the city in 1646 (Chapter 3). The archaeological evidence for a large defensive ditch (Chapter 4) and layers within the building containing musket-balls and fragments of window came can be interpreted as deposits associated with use of the building during the Civil War, with clay tobacco pipes of 1610–50 (contexts 688, 725).	6
10	The evidence of the Bucks' engraving of 1736 shows the appearance of a part of the house at that time and provides evidence for alterations pre-1736 (coinciding with the enlargement of the parlour, dated by pottery evidence to the late 17C).	7
11	Extensive evidence for a phase of demolition of peripheral parts of the building and the consolidation of the remaining portion *c* 1800 in the following categories: common mortar types; architectural fragments interpreted as *spolia* from the south-east range; frequent incidence of Normandy floor tiles reused as scrap building materials. Dating established by the Bucks' engraving (1736) at the one end and the 19C pictorial and cartographic sources (Jenkins, tithe map etc) at the other; pottery provides a date of 1780–1820, further refined to *c* 1794–1801 by documentary and cartographic evidence.	8

whom Holand was responsible were his tenants. This entry can be interpreted as showing Holand as the most prominent man in the community, but it also suggests that he owned what was effectively a sub-manor within Cowick, though if it had had legal status this would surely have been stated.[18] One other group of entries in these court rolls is significant. The lists of those not appearing at the court (*defect of suit*) include a number of notable Devon names (Lord Bonville, Copleston, Courtenay, Tremayn). These demonstrate that the ownership of property in Cowick was useful to these major figures, although the chore of attending the court was beneath them. The Holands are not listed among these names and nor are the Carews in the 16th-century court rolls. Their absence suggests that 'suit of court' was not one of the Holands' tenure conditions, consistent with their property having semi-independent status. From this base, the Holands were able to build up the extensive property holding described in the rental and it could easily have become the sub-manor within the manor of Cowick implied in 16th-century sources.

Given what is known of the occupation of the site of Bowhill, it is quite possible that the early building on the site of the south range (Chapter 4) formed a part of the property held in the parish by Richard or Thomas Holand. The archaeological evidence certainly suggests that the site was occupied during the 15th century, perhaps also in the 14th (Table 3.3).

The site in late medieval documents

Roger Holand (c 1450–1506), the elder son of Thomas, was also a prosperous citizen of Exeter and held numerous responsible positions as a servant of the crown, the county of Devon and the city of Exeter. He sat in Parliament as the member for Totnes in 1491–2 (again in 1495 and 1497) and for Exeter in 1504.[19] He was, *inter alia*, Sheriff of Devon, JP, controller of the ports of Exeter, Dartmouth, Plymouth and Fowey, surveyor of the king's mines in Devon and Cornwall, receiver of the Duchy of Cornwall and held numerous other posts in Devon and Cornwall.[20] In addition, Roger was Recorder of Exeter in 1498.[21] Most importantly in the present context is that the same document that lists his appointments refers to 'Roger Holand Esq. *of Bowhill* in the parish of St Thomas without the walls of Exeter'.[22]

This is the first specific association of the Holand family and the place name. Although the reference is posthumous, the association of Roger with the site seems assured by this description. That the date for the construction of the standing building obtained on architectural and archaeological grounds (Chapter 12) falls within the adult life of Roger Holand ensures that he must have the strongest claim to be considered as the builder of Bowhill.

Two further documents give hints as to Roger's activities in the parish of St Thomas. The first is dated 12 September 1499 and takes the form of a licence from the Abbot of Tavistock to Roger Holand for him to lay water pipes across abbey land at Barley in their manor of Cowick.[23] The second, dated 31 March 1503, is a lease from the abbot and convent of Tavistock of two closes called Barlegh Parks in Cowyk for 20 years at £2 3s 4d per annum.[24] This must refer to the fields uphill and to the west of Bowhill, one still called 'Great Barley Park' at the time of the tithe apportionment of 1841 (Fig 3.1).[25] It is tempting to associate the licence to lay water pipes with the installation of a supply to the new house of Bowhill. This is especially relevant since the excavations in the courtyard revealed a drain or conduit that could well have accommodated a water pipe incorporated into the earliest cobbled/paved surface of the yard (Chapter 4). If this were so it would be possible to take the date of this licence as an approximate date for the construction (or at least for the fitting out) of the house.

Roger died in 1506. His will included an instruction that he was to be buried in the church of St Thomas.[26] Roger left ' ... all my silver apparell belonging to my Chapell with the best parte of the vestiments to be delyverde in suche keping as may serve for the Ile of Seint Michell in the foresaide church of seint Thomas ... '. He also left a bequest to his priest.[27] Later descriptions of this aisle as the Barley Bowhill aisle suggest that the Holand family was responsible for building it.[28] The inquisition post mortem on his estate shows that Roger held extensive property throughout the county, amounting to more than 1,200 acres, but the most concentrated holding lay in the parish of St Thomas including 224 acres in Cowick, 130 acres in Barley, 160 acres in Exwick, and 40 acres in Hayes.[29] In all, Roger's receipts from land and property amounted to just over £40 per annum. Even before the income from his official positions

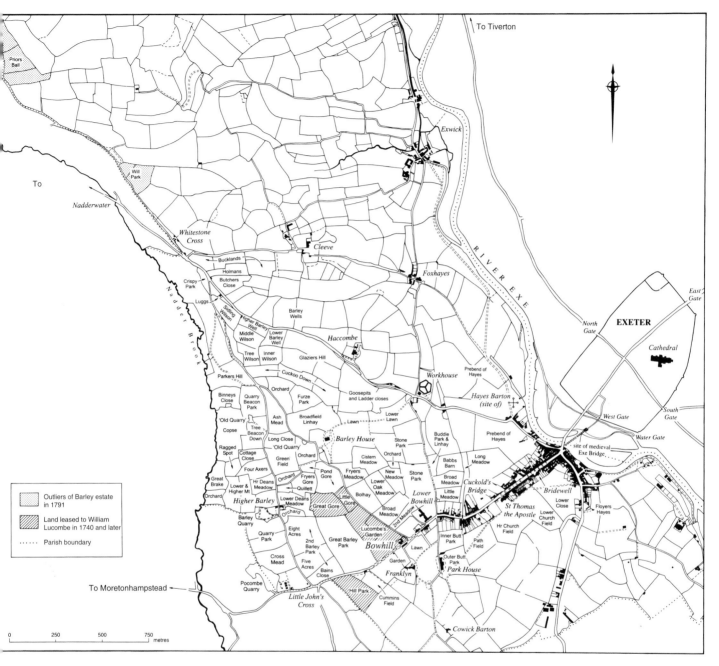

To Tiverton

Exwick

Priors Ball

Will Park

To

Nadderwater

Whitestone Cross

Cleeve

Bucklands

Holmans

Crispy Park

Butchers Close

Luggs

Sidling Wilson

Higher Barley Well

Middle Wilson

Lower Barley Well

Tree Wilson

Inner Wilson

Parkers Hill

Binneys Close

Quarry Beacon Park

Barley Wells

Haccombe

Glaziers Hill

Cuckoo Down

Orchard

Furze Park

Goosepits and Ladder closes

Workhouse

Prebend of Hayes

RIVER EXE

North Gate

East Gate

EXETER

Cathedral

West Gate

South Gate

Water Gate

Foxhayes

'Old Quarry'

Ash Mead

Broadfield Linhay

Tree Beacon Down

Copse

Long Close

'Old Quarry'

Barley House

Stone Park

Lawn

Lower Lawn

Hayes Barton (site of)

Prebend of Hayes

Ragged Spot

Cottage Close

Green Field

Orchard

Cistern Meadow

Orchard

Buddle Park & Linhay

Babbs Barn

Long Meadow

site of medieval Exe Bridge

Four Axers

Orchard

Fryers Gore

Pond Gore

Fryers Meadow

New Meadow

Stone Park

Broad Meadow

Cuckold's Bridge

Bridewell

Great Brake

Lower & Higher Mt

Hr Deans Meadow

Quillet

Little Gore

Lower Oak Meadow

Bolhay

Lower Bowhill

Little Meadow

St Thomas the Apostle

Lower Close

Floyers Hayes

Orchard

Higher Barley

Lower Deans Meadow

Orchard

Great Gore

Broad Meadow

2nd Meadow

Lower Church Field

Barley Quarry

Lucombe's Garden

Hr Church Field

Quarry Park

Eight Acres

Great Barley Park

Bowhill

Inner Butt Park

Path Field

2nd Barley Park

Garden

Lawn

Cross Mead

Five Acres

Bains Close

Franklyn

Outer Butt Park

Park House

Pocombe Quarry

To Moretonhampstead

Little John's Cross

Hill Park

Cummins Field

Cowick Barton

	Outliers of Barley estate in 1791
	Land leased to William Lucombe in 1740 and later
····	Parish boundary

0   250   500   750 metres

is taken into account, this substantial sum stands comparison with the typical income of an esquire or knight.[30]

Evidence from the chief rents paid to the manor of Cowick by the Holand family and their successors suggests that a major reorganisation of the estate took place at the end of the 15th century. The same £8 2s 7d recorded in 1451–2 is repeated in the only later *compotus* for the manor of 1488–9.[31] The next evidence comes from a full listing of the chief rents of the manor of Cowick in rentals of 1560 and 1586.[32] The former starts with a note that the 'heyres of Holland

and Courtenay' did pay £8 2s 7d but now pay £4 18s 4d, with Carew paying 49s 8d and Bret 51s 4d.[33] It is clear from the overall total that a considerable part of the chief rents as a whole had disappeared, but the largest decrease was in Roger Holand's rent. Because the two portions derived from his rent were almost equal, it is unlikely that they had been individually reduced after his death; thus the change indicates that Holand either bought out some of the chief rents between 1488 and 1506 or sold part of his property back to Tavistock Abbey (possibly that at Barley).[34] In either case, it is logical

Figure 3.1
Map showing place and field names in the Parish of St Thomas referred to in Chapter 3, based on the Ordnance Survey first edition 6" (1:10,560) map of 1890; field names from the tithe map of St Thomas Parish, 1841 (line drawing by Tony Ives).

29

to associate this change with the property rearrangement that must have taken place when the house at Bowhill was rebuilt. It is also significant that in the later rentals the payments made by the successors to Roger Holand were associated directly with Bowhill rather than relating to a large number of small freehold properties.[35] It appears from the chief rent evidence that the division of Holand's property after 1506 involved the Carew family taking Bowhill, with the land in Exwick and probably Hayes (which lay near Exwick) going to the Fulfords.

The Holand/Carew marriage

Roger Holand left two daughters as his heirs, both of whom had married into West Country gentry families – Thomasina to John Carew of Antony in Cornwall (by 1498), and Joan to Thomas Fulford.[36] The date of Joan's marriage is unknown, but by 1509, although aged only 20, she was already widowed.[37] By 1515–18, she had apparently married again, as one Walter Courtenay and Jane his wife (probably to be identified with Joan Fulford) started a case in Chancery against the feoffees of Roger Holand's property.[38] They desired the feoffees to 'make an estate to Jane of as much as of right belongs to her' of his property. The most significant deduction from this Chancery bill is that Roger's heirs had not taken over the property from the feoffees by this date. Thus, it is unlikely that the other heirs, Thomasina and John Carew, would have been in a position to build a new house at Bowhill immediately after Roger's death, even should they have wished to.

Sixteenth-century evidence

Thomasina's marriage to John Carew provides the route for the subsequent ownership of the house by that family throughout the 16th and 17th centuries. The genealogy preserved in the inscription on the grave of Richard Carew (1555–1620), the author of the *Survey of Cornwall*, in Antony church (Cornwall), outlines his descent through four generations from Thomasina Holand.[39] The marriage settlement of Richard Carew lists 'Bowell' among the properties in Devon which he was bringing to the marriage with Juliana Arundell in 1577.[40] Although few dates are known in this generation,

Thomasina Carew probably outlived her husband by a number of years. She appears on a list of the nuns of St Katherine's Priory, Polsloe (some 2 miles to the east of Exeter), who were receiving a pension after the Dissolution in 1539–40 and was still receiving payments in 1556.[41] A valuation of the Carew properties made on Richard's father's early death in 1564 had recorded this as 'properties in Bowhill in St Thomas beyond the bridge, Exeter'.[42] Bowhill was included as part of the settled lands in the marriages of Thomas Carew and Elizabeth Edgecombe in 1554 and of Richard Carew and Juliana Arundell in 1577, but not in that of Sir Richard Carew, first baronet (c 1580–1643) and Bridget Chudleigh in 1601.[43] As a result, in the settlement on Sir Richard's remarriage to Grace Rolle in 1621, following Bridget's death, which was to comprise lands to the value of £240, the manor of Bowhill could be included and was indeed the principal property mentioned.[44] The result of Sir Richard's two marriages, both with heirs, was the separation of Bowhill from Antony and the other Carew property, with Bowhill descending to John and Thomas, the children of the second marriage. The marriage settlement of Richard Carew and Juliana Arundell in 1577 contains the first description of the site as a manor.[45] The appearance of this term may well reflect a desire on the part of the Carews to enhance Bowhill's standing in their marriage settlements.

The Civil War – fortification of the site in 1645–6

The parish of St Thomas saw several phases of action during the Civil War, in which the built-up part of the parish centred on Cowick Street sustained heavy damage. Exeter was held for Parliament against the Royalists in late 1642 and early 1643, when action was concentrated on the east and south sides of the city, although Royalist troops were encamped at Ide and Alphington.[46] After the battle of Stratton on 16 May 1643, there was a lengthy period leading up to the capture of Exeter by the Royalist armies under Prince Maurice in September 1643. This involved repeated actions at the western bridgehead (held by the Parliamentarians) and bombardment of the city from positions in St Thomas.[47] Late in 1645, under the growing threat of a new Parliamentary advance, various measures were taken by the Royalist garrison of Exeter to prepare the defences of the city, including the demolition of houses in the extramural areas. In St Thomas all the houses between the church and Exe Bridge were burnt to the ground.[48] By February 1646 Fairfax's men were reported to be very near Exeter and entrenched in 'many strong forts' within a mile or so of the city.[49] One of the forts was at Bowhill, with others at Exwick Mills, Barley House and Marsh House (Marsh Barton) which formed a ring of fortifications on the western side of the river.[50] Barley seems to have been the principal element in this ring of defences.[51] The parish church was destroyed by fire on 31 January and the ruins of the church and the Bridewell were also occupied by the New Model Army.[52] A 'mansion' belonging to a Mrs Carewe (possibly a reference to Grace, who was by now the widow of Sir Richard Carew) was burnt down, as were other houses in the parish at the same time. This could refer to Bowhill (although there is no evidence of an extensive fire here), Barley, or some other Carew property altogether.[53] Nothing more is heard of Bowhill in the contemporary accounts of the siege.[54] The archaeology has provided glimpses of the building at this time, including a fragment of a large ditch, which presumably formed an element in the fortifications, and a collection of musket balls from a variety of interior and exterior contexts, which may indicate their manufacture at Bowhill.[55] The only other contemporary reference to the building relates to the period after the surrender of Exeter to Parliament on 13 April 1646, when Fairfax seems to have made efforts to repair some of the damage done to the countryside around Exeter by the army. Barley makes an unequivocal appearance in a list of sites which had been fortified and at which orders were now given ' ... for the slighting, demolishing and razing downe of the works ... at Affington [Alphington], Bootwell-house [?Bowhill], Barley House, Exwick Mills, March House [at Marsh Barton] ... and other Garrisons, which were made for the late siege of Exeter'.[56] The identification of 'Bootwell House' as Bowhill is a fair assumption, since it is mentioned immediately prior to Barley in the section on fortifications west of the river. This account provides some evidence for the clearing of the site soon after the siege, but the archaeological evidence shows not only that the ditch remained open in part for a considerable time, but also that it was not finally filled in until well into the 18th century.[57]

Later Carew ownership and residence

John, the elder of the two sons of Sir Richard Carew and Grace Rolle, was one of the judges of Charles I and a signatory to his death warrant.[58] On his attainder and execution in 1660, John's property reverted to the crown. His brother, Thomas (1624–81) petitioned the king for the return of the forfeit property, specifically 'the Manor of Bowhill, co. Devon' on the grounds that the property had been ' ... transferred to him for debt by his late brother John Carew, executed for treason against the late King'.[59] The petition was granted on 16 May 1661.[60] Thomas Carew also had a political career, including sitting as MP in 1659, 1660 and 1681. He was appointed Recorder of Exeter in 1676 and knighted in 1671.[61]

The estate was enlarged following the marriage of Thomas Carew and Elizabeth Cupper in 1661. Her father, John Cupper (d 1658), had lived at Barley just north of Bowhill and owned the four farms there, which he had bought from the Earl of Bedford in 1641. It is probably significant that Thomas and Elizabeth did not marry until after John's death as he would surely have opposed the marriage. Before John Carew's execution, Thomas was only a younger son, probably owning no property and perhaps tainted by association with his brother in the changing political climate of the late 1650s. In May 1661 his petition for restoration of his brother's estates was granted and his marriage followed in August.

John Cupper had two sons, Jasper and Thomas, but all his land was bequeathed to his eldest daughter Elizabeth.[62] He left £800 to Jasper, the elder son, but rescinded this in a codicil because of his 'many miscarriages and misbehaviours, but especially in his uglines living with her whom he now calls his wife'; Jasper did, however, confirm the Barley property (apart from that left to Thomas Cupper) to Elizabeth Carew (Cupper) in 1661.[63] Thomas Cupper was overseas (perhaps as a royalist) and was only to receive his legacy if he returned, when he would get £1,300 or could take two of the farms at Barley. He eventually returned and instituted a suit in Chancery to obtain the farms. According to the Chancery decree, although he was only to receive money in compensation, a 1753 list of estate deeds includes assignments of the two farms by Thomas Cupper to one Paul Bale in 1661

31

and by the latter's son Christopher to William Penneck in 1710. This transfer is confirmed from a schedule of tithe compositions (*c* 1665), which lists Mr Bale for Lower Barley.[64]

Thomas Carew had four sons, Thomas, Richard, Henry and Joseph, none of whom died in infancy, and so the Carew line might reasonably have been expected to continue at Bowhill. Only Richard married, however. His wife, Letitia Goodall, apparently predeceased him and they had no children. 'Captain' Thomas was so afflicted with gout that he had to retire from the infantry and was supported by his brother Henry with an annuity of £150 per annum (paid from his sinecure salary as Teller of the Exchequer) and died unmarried in 1705; Joseph died *c* 1695 and Henry in 1698.[65]

Richard left the entire Bowhill estate to his sister Catherine (married to William Penneck, a merchant), at his death in 1713. Not unnaturally, his other sisters, Elizabeth (married to Richard King, a clerk) and Grace (married to Francis Sawle, a woollen draper) and their husbands instituted a suit in Chancery attempting to show that Richard was either 'of unsound mind' or had no power to devise his estate in this way because of the previous settlements.[66] Their suit failed, however, and the estate passed to Catherine, descending to her son John Penneck. When he died without heirs in 1752, Bowhill was left to his cousin Richard Sawle. It took a considerable time for the numerous money legacies to be paid off, as they had apparently been made on the security of the estate.[67] In 1773, however, it was transferred to the latter's daughters, Bridget and Elizabeth Sawle, who immediately put the estate up for sale. Despite being described as ' ... an exceptionally good estate, replete with almost every Thing that can make an Estate valuable or desirable', it seems to have failed to attract a buyer. The sale particulars give a very detailed description of the entire estate, however.[68] In 1779, the sisters formally divided the estate and the abstract of this deed can be closely correlated with the 1774 sale description.[69] In 1791, Bridget advertised her half of the property for sale in 23 lots (207 acres) and this time was apparently successful in disposing of it all.[70] Nine of the lots, however, including Bowhill itself and 99 acres of land, were bought by Captain (later Admiral) John Graves, the husband of Elizabeth Sawle, and reunited with the other half of the estate. Their son, Sir Joseph Graves-Sawle, was the

owner of the estate in 1841, when its layout is shown on the tithe map of St Thomas. The Graves-Sawle family continued to live at Barley until the 1930s.[71]

Bowhill and Barley Houses in the 17th and early 18th centuries

Sir Thomas Carew (1624?–81) was the last member of the family to live at Bowhill, but after his marriage to Elizabeth Cupper of Barley, he was always described as 'of Barley', as were his sons Thomas (in his will) and Richard.[72] Bowhill seems to have been kept as a subsidiary residence, only used occasionally; Richard is referred to as 'of ... Bowhill, St Thomas' at a parliamentary election in 1712[73] and Polwhele, writing at the end of the 18th century, certainly thought that the family lived both at Bowhill and at Barley until the time of Penneck or later.[74]

In Sir Thomas Carew's will he instructed his executors, his son Richard and Sir John Carew of Antony, to sell his household goods and very fortunately three books of executors' accounts survive which give details of these sales. The accounts start in August 1681 and the first sales followed in October (transcribed below in the appendix to this chapter). The bulk of the contents were sold between January 1686 and the following June. The details in the accounts mainly relate to Barley rather than Bowhill; the houses seem to have been of similar size, however, both having twelve hearths and the impression of a cultivated lifestyle would be equally applicable to both.[75] The only items specifically sold from Bowhill were a table board, a little side table board, a bedstead and a furnace. By this date, part of Bowhill had been leased out (two or three people were paying rent for parts of the building in 1687)[76] and the accounts suggest that the rest of the house had been stripped when the family moved to Barley; many of the older goods there must previously have been at Bowhill.

Among his possessions Sir Thomas included gold-embroidered gloves and gold lace, silver plate and candlesticks and a gaming table and men (chess or draughts, probably). Some of the rooms were well furnished but other items, like the 'old white coverlet full of holes' and the 'litle spruce coffer all split' suggest that the furniture had not been brought up to date for a considerable time. The rooms identified are typical of the domestic accommodation in a substantial gentry house, with outer hall and great parlour (and presumably main hall and second parlour), kitchen and the Nursery, Pied (*Pide*), Green and Wrought chambers, the last three named from their decoration.

The accounts also illustrate the profitable management of the estate. Most of the fields were leased out, but a few must have been kept in hand and were clearly being used as cider orchards and for market gardening. Sales of produce included considerable quantities of cider, roses and rosebuds, mulberries, leeks, strawberries, beans, cherries, 'currence', peaskods (pods), 'hartichocks', apples and pears. Payments for maintaining both houses included paving the courtyard at Bowhill and working on the pump there, sweeping the chimneys, mending the roofs, walls and windows,[77] as well as buying arsenic and cream to kill rats.

The executors also accounted for clothes and schooling for the boys, at first in Crediton and then at Winchester and Oxford for Richard Carew, and for dancing lessons for Grace and Katherine Carew, while they also had to pay on one occasion for 'mending my ovell tabell board which my nephew Richard Carew and his companions brocke'.

The Bowhill and Barley estate

An extensive body of documentary material survives relating to the estate as a whole and to individual holdings within it, from which it is possible to examine the build-up of the estate and its composition in detail (especially for the period after 1660).[78] The earliest description of the Bowhill estate is in the inquisition post mortem of Thomas Carew (1564). It then comprised six messuages, six gardens and 200 acres in Bowhill, held from the Earl of Bedford as of the manor of Cowick, for fealty.[79] We have no evidence of any changes in Bowhill during the 16th or 17th century and it seems to have been regarded as a single unit. A brief valuation of the estate at the death of Thomas Carew, part of a summary of his debts and credits, provides a useful overview:[80]

Property	Value
Bowhill Barton in demesnes	£236 per annum
Barley Barton in demesnes	£74
Demesnes that came per my Lady; noe part of Barle Barton	£32
Demesnes held by lease by Sir Tho.	£24
High & conventionary rents	£32 9s 8d
[Total]	£398 9s 8d

The high rents were those received from property that had been granted on three life leases for a large entry fine, but paying only a small annual rent, in contrast to the rents from the demesnes that were being leased for shorter periods at rents corresponding to their full value. This list shows that the estate included a component for which we have virtually no evidence, property leased to Thomas Carew and sub-let to his tenants. A few small properties are known to have been purchased by Thomas Carew in the 17th century and by William and John Penneck after 1700.[81] Only a couple of sales are recorded as taking place before the disposal of Bridget Sawle's half of the estate in 1791.

Size of the Bowhill estate

The sizes of the various components of the Bowhill estate can be established fairly accurately, commencing with the complete descriptions given in the 1779 partition between Bridget and Elizabeth Sawle and the 1774 Sale Particulars.[82] The latter divides the estate into sections:

Manor of Bowhill	159ac	1r	6p
Great Barley	82ac	3r	23p
Higher Barley	23ac	3r	35p
Lower Barley & other demesnes	103ac	3r	20p
Total	375ac	0r	23p [as given in the particulars]
[The sum in 1779]	370ac	3r	3p [probably more accurate]

Most of the post-1660 purchases were included with Lower Barley.

The only earlier detailed description of Bowhill itself comes from an abstract of the 1688 marriage settlement between Richard Carew and Letitia Goodall.[83] It lists forty fields with their acreage, totalling 157 acres, almost identical to the 1774 figure, confirming that this is a good indication of the size of Bowhill; most of the 1688 field names can be matched with those in 1774 and identified on the tithe map (Fig 3.2).[84] It is noticeable that these original Bowhill fields are much intermingled with those of Great, Higher and Lower Barley. For the other components of the estate, the most detailed evidence comes from the 1619 survey of the Manor of Cowick (in DRO W1258/G4/49), which lists the fields held by each tenant. The relevant holdings are:

Tenement in Barley held
   by Roger Crossinge   25ac 2r 10p
Tenement in Over Barley held
   by William Brownscombe   26ac 3r 18p
Tenement at Barley held by
   John Quyshe   26ac 3r 38p
Tenement in Barley held by
   Bartholemew Berry   56ac 3r 4p
Lower and Higher Barley
   Parks   31ac 1r 34p

The Berry tenement was later leased to John Cupper. It is identified in 1641 as Middle Barley alias Great Barley and was where he lived. Brownscombe's tenement is later identified as Higher Barley and Crossinge's tenement was Lower Barley, which had lost

its house by 1773. It appears that Quyshe's tenement was combined with this and also had no house by the later 18th century.[85] Taking the Barley farms (168 acres) with Bowhill (159 acres) and the known other acquisitions (about 32 acres) gives a total of about 369 acres, very close to the 1774 and 1779 total of 371 acres. We can thus be confident that no major component of the estate remains unidentified.

Included among the estate documents are three leases of parts of Bowhill house (of 1696, 1711 and 1740);[86] each gives details of the section of the house being leased, of outbuildings and of the adjacent fields and orchards (including a requirement to maintain cider barrels). The details of the

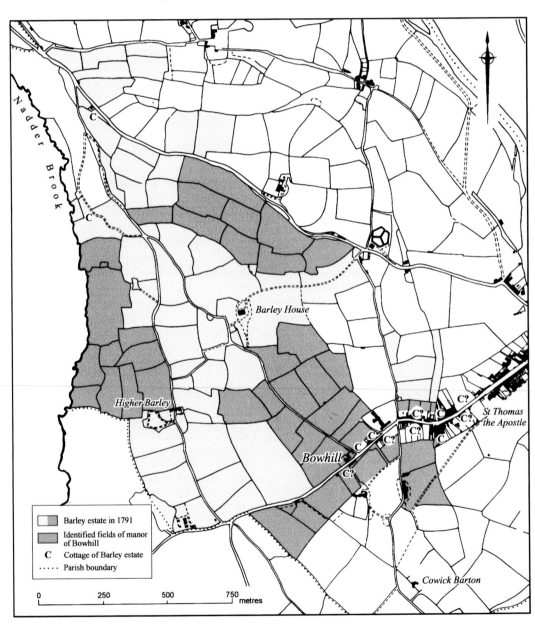

Figure 3.2
The extent of the Bowhill and Barley estate (line drawing by Tony Ives).

34

rooms in the house are particularly relevant to the house in the 17th century and are discussed in Chapter 12.

The Bowhill cottages

One of the most striking aspects of the evidence from the Bowhill leases and from the 1779 deed of partition is that the estate included a large number of cottages, many described as being part of the Manor of Bowhill.[87] The 1779 partition includes ten 'tenements and gardens' in Bridget Sawle's share and no less than twenty-two in Elizabeth's (when several had already been sold). Lot 23 of the 1791 sale comprised five cottages bought by John Graves. They lay 'north of the highway from the turnpike gate towards Little John's Cross' and so must have been very close to Bowhill itself. They may be the two blocks of cottages between Bowhill and Lower Bowhill shown on the tithe map.[88] As these were the only cottages forming part of the estate in 1841, the rest of Elizabeth's twenty-two cottages must have been sold off.

The forty-three leases relate to at least twenty distinct cottage properties (several in multiple occupancy). A couple refer to isolated cottages, one near Whitestone Cross and one nearby in the corner of The Cleaves.[89] Another lay in the corner between the highway and the way from Bowhill to Barley and all the others were apparently along the present Cowick Street/Dunsford Road, presumably towards the western end.[90]

Some of the cottage descriptions are very complex, relating to the subdivision of larger blocks. A characteristic example of 1701, granted in consideration of the surrender of a lease of 1695 and £5,[91] describes:

a tenement containing one ground room 22ft long and 17ft broad, with two chambers over, a cottage 20ft long and 20ft broad, and a herb garden 63ft long and 17ft broad, being the nearest of three dwelling houses built by William Skirrett towards the City of Exeter, part of the Manor of Bowhill.

The previous lease refers back to one of 1657 to William Skerrett (assigned in 1658),[92] which describes the property as consisting of 'those old walls' that were three houses and three gardens. It is notable that, like this example, all the earliest leases refer to the sites of houses that had to be rebuilt after being destroyed during the siege of Exeter in the Civil War.[93]

For one of the blocks of cottages some detail of the later history is available. John Penneck sold to Giles Yard in 1739 the tenements of Reed's Court, Snow's and Perkin's tenements, comprising several little tenements all lying together near Cuckold's Bridge, reserving a fee farm rent of £4 4s. After a series of transactions, by 1826 one part had been sold to Francis Southward, when it had become fourteen messuages in or near Reed's Court. It can be identified on the tithe map standing on the south side of Cowick Street at the corner east of Buddle Lane.[94]

The cottages and the Manor of Bowhill

The majority of the cottage leases identify the properties as forming part of the Manor of Bowhill, perhaps to indicate that they did not form part of the Manor of Cowick. It is reasonable to identify them with the numerous properties first recorded in 1451–2 in the tenure of Richard Holand and to suggest that the various fields with which they were originally associated later became the Bowhill estate. Certainly in the 16th and 17th centuries the occupants of the Bowhill cottages would have formed a substantial community, virtually a village within St Thomas.

Management of the estate in the 18th and 19th centuries

The numerous leases in the estate documents show the characteristic pattern of three-life/99-year leases until about 1695.[95] Thereafter, the farm lands began to be leased for between 7 and 21 years, and the cottages followed suit about 10 years later. It is very noticeable that the great majority of the leases, even in the 17th century, comprised single fields or small groups of fields; only Higher Barley was regularly leased as a complete farm. This policy presumably reflects the demand from the St Thomas residents for land, probably to be used mainly as pasture. Leases of relatively small properties for three lives would also have increased the income from entry fines. This could be substantial, for example, £110 for the lease of Barley Wells (7 acres) in 1685.[96]

Altogether exceptional in the estate management of this period was the lease of 1740 to William Lucombe of Powderham, gardener, for his life, of part of Bowhill house together with four adjacent fields.[97]

This measure may have been agreed because of the investment needed to convert the land to market gardening. Lucombe was a market gardener and nurseryman, the first in the neighbourhood of Exeter according to Lysons;[98] by the time of the tithe map in 1841, the parish contained many nurseries and gardens, some purely horticultural in function and some supplying Exeter with fresh food. The Lucombe lease was clearly a considerable embarrassment to the estate, as William lived for an extraordinarily long time, dying only in 1794 at the age of 98.[99] In 1791 the property was described as (Lot 1) 'Bowhill House, Pound-house, Court-lage, Outhouses and walled Gardens, with the Appurtenances, containing 12 A[cres]. 2 R[ods]. 6 P[erches]. in the Tenure of Mr. William Lucombe, subject to his Leasehold Interest therein for his Life (now upwards of 90) and two Years after his Death'. Lots 2 and 3 comprised the adjacent fields, also leased to Lucombe.[100]

The Lucombe nursery, although not perhaps as eminent or well known as the slightly later firm of Veitch,[101] was a respected nursery business in 18th- and 19th-century Exeter.[102] One of the better-known products of the nursery was the Lucombe Oak (*Quercus* x *hispanica* Lucombeana), a cross between the Turkey oak and cork oak, that was raised at the nursery in the 18th century.[103] John Lucombe, William's son, continued the nursery business, which was rapidly established at new premises on the Alphington Road after William's death.[104]

The firm continued into the 19th century; in the course of time family alliances caused a change of name to Lucombe Pince and Co. The nursery was also known as the 'Exeter Nursery'.[105] By the 1830s the main premises of the nursery had grown substantially on the extensive grounds between Alphington Road, Cowick Street and Cowick Lane.[106] From 1827 street directories and other sources show a John Kerswill operating as a gardener and later as a nurseryman and florist from premises in 'Moreton Road'.[107] The tithe apportionment of 1841 shows that Bowhill was let off in two residential units and that the eastern half was occupied by John Kerswill.[108] Occupation of the house and adjacent land by the Kerswill family lasted through the remainder of the 19th century.

The building, as will be seen, underwent a number of alterations and modifications during this period. There was one phase of widespread demolition and associated alterations that was probably caused by the need to remove derelict portions and make a smaller residual core habitable and more comfortable. Some re-fenestration, with early 19th-century-type glazing-bar sash windows took place at the same time. Since a date of *c* 1800 is suggested by the style of the alterations, the most likely context would be in the years immediately after the long tenancy of William Lucombe 1795–1800 (Chapter 4).

Twentieth-century ownership and occupation

The nursery business run by Kerswill continued through several generations of this family, until just after the First World War.[109] The premises were advertised for letting in 1917[110] and soon after the house (and nursery business) was in the occupation of R J Sclater, a member of another long-established family of Exeter nurserymen (Fig 3.3).[111] The Graves-Sawle family continued as the owners of Bowhill and the adjacent land. Both Barley House and the lands forming the rump of its estate (in which Bowhill was included) were sold in the course of the 1930s, in the aftermath of the death of Sir Charles Graves-Sawle, fourth baronet, in 1932.[112] The nursery grounds themselves came increasingly under pressure from the development of residential suburbs in St Thomas. There was even an attempt to get Bowhill demolished in the late 1930s, in order to clear space for road widening and development.[113] An aerial photograph taken by the RAF in September 1945 (Fig 3.4), shows much of the nursery lands immediately north of the site still

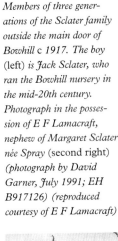

Figure 3.3
Members of three generations of the Sclater family outside the main door of Bowhill c 1917. The boy (left) is Jack Sclater, who ran the Bowhill nursery in the mid-20th century. Photograph in the possession of E F Lamacraft, nephew of Margaret Sclater née Spray (second right) (photograph by David Garner, July 1991; EH B917126) (reproduced courtesy of E F Lamacraft)

devoted to that purpose, although the suburban development had reached Bowhay Lane to the east and encroachment had begun to the west of the site.[114]

Further suburbanisation took place in the 1960s with the construction of housing on the remainder of the nursery land contiguous to Bowhill, to the west of Bowhay Lane.[115] Soon after this the house and remaining nursery land appeared on the market.[116] A sale took place in 1968 to Mr E Showell who lived in the house.[117] Soon after planning permission was granted for change of use to a restaurant[118] and this seems to have gone ahead since the building was in use as a restaurant in 1969.[119] There was a further change of ownership in 1972, which involved conversion to another restaurant by the new owner, R M Horden. Planning permission was granted for the demolition of the barn at the western limit of the site which, although it had a new roof and rebuilt southern gable, was probably medieval (see Figs 2.14 and 2.15).[120] A newspaper article of the time stated that the barn was pulled down to make the house 'more visible from the road'.[121] This second restaurant was also short-lived and by 1976 the house was on the market again.[122] It was purchased by the Secretary of State for the Environment in November 1976.[123]

The second Bowhill House (Lower Bowhill)

The 'South-West Prospect ...' of the Buck brothers of 1736 (see Fig 2.1) shows the next house to the east of Bowhill, identified as 'Chilcott Syms Esquire's House', standing on a plot of land on the corner of Dunsford Road and Buddle Lane. This was also frequently called Bowhill House (occasionally Lower Bowhill, the title used here). The simultaneous existence of two houses bearing the same name means that extreme caution is required in the interpretation of documentary references from this date onwards. By the early 1740s the confusion is evident. In the accounts of the overseer of the poor for St Thomas parish in 1741 John Penneck was rated for, among other properties, 'Bowhill Barley'. A little later Chilcott Syms Esq appeared, rated for 'Bowhill'.[124] Forty years later the Land Tax assessments for St Thomas parish maintained the same distinction, the Misses Sawle being assessed

for 'Bowhill Barley' and Chi[l]cot Syms Esqr for 'Bowhill'.[125] Syms appears to have been dead by 1782,[126] and was succeeded by Richard Chichester. In 1791 Bowhill House and other property formerly belonging to Richard Chichester was advertised for sale[127] and described as: 'A Freehold Dwelling House, Bowhill House, now lett to William Augustus Gordon Esq., and fields named: Stone Park, Lower Stone Park, Close Park, Second Close Park, Buddle Park, Lower Buddle Park, Well Park, Lower Well Park and 14 cottages contiguous to the house'.[128] The description and the ownership identify this indisputably as Lower Bowhill. John Graves of Barley bought Lot 2 in the sale – Stone Park and Lower Stone Park, Close Park and Lower Close Park; Lot 1, 'Lower Bowhill' itself, had been purchased by Richard Collett, gentleman, but was added to the Bowhill estate before 1841.[129]

In 1800 Lower Bowhill was converted to a lunatic asylum.[130] The building soon proved inadequate and a substantial addition was begun on the site in 1803.[131] The asylum or hospital was moved to Wonford in 1869 and the St Thomas buildings were demolished;[132] the site then reverted to garden and nursery use and was illustrated as such (although still called 'Bowhill') on a plan for a sale in 1887.[133] One of the more durable of the myths that have grown up around Bowhill is that the building was used as a lunatic asylum, but this is directly attributable to confusion between two houses of the same name.[134]

Appendix: the executors' accounts for Sir Thomas Carew

These volumes contain receipts and disbursements on behalf of the executors of the will of Sir Thomas Carew of Barley:

1. August 1681 to July 1685 (in private hands)
2. September 1685 to December 1686 (Carew-Pole CW/H/23)[135]
3. January 1687 to August 1688 (Carew-Pole CA/H/1).

The first book was kept by Richard Carew of Floyers Hayes, the second apparently by John Hodges (although the hands and accounting style are virtually identical) and the third by Henry Stephens (who received a salary of £15 per annum from the estate).[136] All three list payments and receipts on opposite sides of each opening, although 1 has receipts to left and payments to right, while 2 and 3 are reversed. The bulk of the accounts comprise receipts for rent and the sale of some farm and garden produce, with payments for household expenses, the childrens' upbringing and other general expenses. The most significant entries, relating to the sale of household goods, seem to have been completed before the end of 1686, and did not extend into the third account book.

The entries transcribed here relate to:

a. money received for household goods sold
b. selected other receipts
c. payments of relevance to domestic activities.

Those dated before September 1685 are from book 1, those between September 1686 and December 1686 are from book 2, and the remainder from book 3. Dates are converted to new style. The repeated 'Received' and 'Paid' are omitted.

Household goods

			£	s	d
1681					
Oct 19	Received of Geo Chudleigh esq for 8 turkey work chares at 7s per peece		2	16	0
Oct 24	For goods sold att the last survay [auction] at Barley held 10 October 1681		6	9	1
	Of Henry Stephens for a silver poringer weighing 6½ oz @ 5s 10d		1	13	0
Oct 28	Of Sir Copleston Bampfeild, Bart for the three statues in the Greate Parlour		1	1	6
Oct 29	For a wheelbarrow			4	10
Oct 30	Of John Curtenaye esq for the two coach guildings		21	0	0
1682					
April 18	For burnt silver lace 7¼ oz @ 5s		1	18	9
Oct 18	Of Sir John Carew for 12 plates, two candlestickes and one hand candlestick,				
	all of silver, wt 278 ounces at 5s 1d		70	13	2
	Of Mr Robert Davis for 22 peeces of gold little and greate		16	0	0
Dec 15	For greate and smale rings without stones		20	17	6
	For peices of silver			17	6
1683					
Jan 31	For a buntinge hutch			19	0
March 3	Of Mr Pitman for one tabell board and a little side tabell board at Bowhill		1	0	0
March 7	For a beedsteed at Bowhill			10	0
Nov 3	Of John Elley for the furnace at Bohill		7	10	0
1684					
May	For a paire of crookes			4	6
1685					
Jan 5	For a naget [agate] hearted knife and forke tipt with silver			5	0
	For a blackhorn harted knife tipt with silver			1	6
1686					
Jan 14	Received of Mr Pitman for one knife				6
	Of Richard Carew esq. for 2 knives				6
	Of Richard Carew esq. for a paire of gold Frenche gloves		1	0	0
	Of Sir John Carew for a paire of tables and table men			10	0
Jan 15	Of Richard Carew esq. for a pair of candle snuffers, snuff dish and tobacco tongs			1	6
	Of Richard Carew esq. for a suttle in the Outer Hall			5	0
	Of the same person for the side table in the same Hall			1	6
	Of the same person for two turky stooles in the same roome			2	0
	Of the same person for a red rugg in the Great Parlor			3	0
	Of the same person for one leather carpett in the Parlor			1	0

Household goods (*cont'd*)

1686		£	s	d
	Of the same person for two joint stooles in the Kitchin		1	6
	Of the same person for six paire of chimney crookes, a hangerby and three pott hangers		8	0
	Of the same person for the Jack and chain & weights thereto belonging ['Kitchen' in margin]		10	0
	Of the same person for one old bedsteed, featherbed, 2 feather boulsters, curtains with rods & metts, three old blankett & thrum coverlett in the Nursery Chamber	2	10	0
Jan 15	Of Captain Carew [Thomas] for one old feather bed, a feather boulster & a feather pillow, the bedsteed, curtains and vallens with rods & metts, one old blankett & thrum coverlett in the Pide Chamber	3	10	0
	Of the same person for one high imbroydered chaire, six low chaires covered with red serge, silk fringe & the leather chaire – Pide Chamber	1	6	6
	Of the same person for 2 sheets there		5	0
	Of the same person for a looking glass in the Staires		6	0
Jan 16	Of Gilbert Packer for a white rugg		4	0
Jan 27	Of Richard Carew esq for a paire of cofe grates & a safe iron & an iron horse	1	0	0
	For two fire pokes, a fire tongs, a grate pan, one old flesh pike and two three-legged stooles		6	0
	More of him for 31 yards of new course diaper at 9½d per yard	1	4	6
	More of him for a little side bord and a red carpett		7	0
	For one stiller and a frame of an old stool		2	0
	For two old turky stooles sold		2	0
	For a bunter armery, a bord & six cords, two stillers, both together containe 9 foot in length, and a sleeper		3	0
	One butter stander		2	0
	R Crossin [tenant of one of the Barley farms] for 2 feather beds old & rotten	1	0	0
	Of Homer Loggett for one old white coverlett full of holes		3	0
	For Mr Pittmans green rugg		1	6
	['CC' in margin, for Captain Carew?] For one feather bed boulster & pillow	1	10	0
	For one canvas sheet, one dowlas sheet & 2 blanketts belonging to the truckle bed in the Green Chamber		15	0
	For one close stool in the same chamber		6	0
	For a paire of billowes, a paire of fire tongs and a fire pan in the same room		5	0
	For a paire of pistolls and holsters & fore pattern to the same belonging and the bays covering	1	10	0
	Of Richard Crossing for one old litle spruce coffer all split		2	6
	['CC' in margin] For a little sidebord in the Green Chamber, standing next the fire		4	0
	['CC' in margin] for a grinding stone and iron qurner & timber thereto belonging		2	0
	For an old thart [athwart = cross-cut?] saaw		2	0
	One feather bed, feather boulster, 4 feather pillowes, one canvas quilt for the bed, one white rugg and 2 blanckets in the Green Chamber	4	17	0
	of Mr Pitman for a paire of dung pott		2	0
	[base of page] And the close stoole allowed out			
Feb 11	['CC' in margin] For a paire of large blancket in the Wrought Chamber	1	0	0
	['CC' in margin] For one little side table and two standers to hold a bason of water in the Wrought Chamber		5	0
	['CC' in margin] For six chaires & green coverings in the Little Parlor		16	0
	['CC' in margin] for a paire of barrell cribbs		2	0
May 1	Alexander for silver lace	1	0	0
	Alexander for gold and silver lace which he sold		10	0
June 15	Of Samuel Walkey for a zoul, yoke & chaines		12	0

Other receipts (selected)

1685		£	s	d
Sept	Sales of rosebuds, strawberries, beans, cheries, currence, peaskods, hartichocks and apples (probably taking place during the summer)			

1683				
	Extensive sales of wood took place			

1686				
March 9	Of Gilbert Packer for making cyder	5	13	0
May 1	Of Alexander Randle 4 hogsheads of cyder which he sold	7	0	0
June 1	For roses sold		2	0

Other receipts (selected) (*cont'd*)

			£	s	d
1686					
June 15	For mulberrys & strawberrys			1	1½
	For roses, mulberryes & strawberyes			2	1½
	For artichocks			1	5
June 22	For strawburyes and mulberrys				10
June 30	For mulberyes, hartychockes & roses			2	4
	For mulberyes				9
July 8	For beans			2	11¾
	Of Gilbert Parker for cherries			5	0
July 26	For Beans, gasberys & mulberys			3	4
Sept 29	For 300 of leekes sold Mr Jifford			1	6
1687					
May 23	Of Charles Bennett in part [payment] for 6 fatt bullocks & a hay rick sold him	13	0	0
July 2	Of Charles Bennett in part [payment] for the bullocks and hay rick	10	0	0
July 12	Of Gilbert Parker for the cherrys at Barley	1	16	0
Aug 15	More of Cha. Bennett in part [payment] for the bullocks and hay rick	2	10	0
Sept 17	More of Chas. Bennett for the bullocks and hay rick	10	0	0
Sept 26	Of Gilbert Parker in part [payment] of his bond of £13 for the apples and nutts at Barly	6	10	0
Oct 22	Of Gilbert Parker in full for making of cyder att Bowhill pound house for the year	17	8	0
Dec 26	Of [Gilbert Parker] for two heifers he sold at St Nicholas fair	7	10	6
Dec. 28	Of John Harkerson for a quarters rent of Barly House due midsomer last	4	0	0
1688					
Feb 3	Of Cha. Bennett for 10 sheep sold in October last £5 15s, also for a heifer sold, £3, in all	8	15	0
Feb 24	Of Gilbert Parker for a cow he sold	3	2	6
	Of Gilbert Parker in part [payment] of £6 10s, being his last payment for the apples at Barly	4	10	0
April 6	Of John Hay being the first payment of his bond due lady day last for the furze wood in the Cleeves	20	0	0
May 7	Of Goody Parker . . . for the cherries and wallnutts at Barly	2	0	0
June 11	Of John Way in full of his bond for the furzewood in the Cleeves	6	7	0
	Of John Way for 2 dozen & a [third?] of wood at 15s the dozen	2	0	0

Payments (selected)

			£	s	d
1685					
Oct 24	A years dyett & schooling for Mr Henry & Mr Joseph Carew	24	0	0
	Costs laid out when they wear sick	6	11	8
	A years schooling to their writing master	2	13	9
1686					
March 13	Seeds & half a bushell of beanes		2	2
March 20	Arseneck & cream etc. to kill ratts		1	0
April 5	For labourers about the fire & for watering afterwards		10	6
	To John Bond & John Roles who brought out bucketts by Mr Dalby's order		3	2
April 10	A new key to the back gate			6
April 19	Mary Wheaton for mending the bucketts and tubbs used about the fire		5	0
April 26	William Halce for labour & loss at the fire		2	0
May 11	Hearth money for Bowhill [12 hearths at 1s per half year]		12	0
	Hearth money for Barly		12	0
June 19	Paid Peter West the glazier his year's sallery for mending the glass at Barly House and the Isle [St Thomas' Church aisle?]		16	0
July 23	The dancing master his entrance money for Mistress Grace and Mistress Katherine Carew	1	0	0
Oct 21	Sweeping 12 chimneys		6	0
Oct 25	Box and sucker for the pump at Bowhill		5	0
Dec 3	The cryer for crying Barly House to be sett		1	0
1687					
Jan 29	Mr Richard Carew in old gold and silver	3	0	0
	Mr Pearse the Taylours for lodging & dyett of the Mistresses Grace and Kath. Carew	13	0	0
Feb 3	For coach hire for Mistresses Grace and Kath. Carew to Salisbury	2	0	0

Payments (selected) (cont'd)

		£	s	d
1687				
Feb 18	For a beaver hat, gold hatband & case for James Pittman	3	1	0
Feb 25	The hostler at New Inne for a man and horse to carry			
	Mr Richard Carew's portmantle after the coach to Honiton		5	6
Feb 28	Mrs Sarah Arundell for things for Miss Grace and Miss Kath. Carew		5	3
March 19	John Low the hellier in part for healinge boards [work?] upon			
	Bowhill & Barly houses	1	0	0
March 29	John Low the hellier in full for healing worke done upon Bowhill			
	& Barly houses	2	2	0
April 16	The glazier in part for mending the windows of the eysle in the church	1	0	0
April 20	Mrs Ewing's note for linen for Misses Grace & Kath. Carew when			
	they went to Salisbury	3	2	6
	Mrs Foxwell for 2 pare of stocking for them		4	6
	Mrs Stafford's note for Misses Grace & Kath. Carew as per receipt appears	2	3	6
	Mr Edward Cotton the apothecary for physick for Misses Grace			
	& Kath. Carew	1	11	0
	Mr Tooslows for Holland & lace for Misses Grace & Kath. Carew...	1	4	0
	White the dancing master for teaching Misses Grace & Kath. Carew			
	to dance	2	10	0
May 26	A half year of chimney rate for Bowhill and Barly due Lady day last	1	4	0
July 12	Parker in full of a note for mowing and making the hay at Barly	2	19	3
	For two heifers to feed	5	16	0
	For a heifer & calfe	2	18	6
Aug 20	Will. Woodhall for 9 days of thatching at Bowhill & Barly,			
	2s 6d a day for him & his man and also for thatching the hay			
	rick in Moores Mead	1	4	6
Aug 22	For my sallery being a half year due at Lamas last past	7	10	0
Nov 22	Gilbert Parker for 10 weeks work at Bowhill poundhouse at 6s per week	3	10	0
	More paid him for money he disbursed for wages to others as per 2 notes			
	pinned together	1	7	6
Dec 12	The Waye Warden for a half year of rate to the Wayes of			
	St Thomas Parish £1 8s 0d, sum allows for 128 seames of quarry			
	stones at 1d per seame, 10s 8d; also allowed for rypping them, 2s 4d.		15	0
Dec 26	Gilbert Parker for 33 dozen of faggott birdge	1	2	0
	More paid him in full towards the furze brake & making of furze			
	faggots in the Cleeve as p. his note	2	11	6
1688				
Feb 24	For tobacco when the tenants dined at Barly		1	6
March 1	For my half year's sallery due candlemas last past	7	10	0
April 6	John Lobb the saddler by Mr Richard Carew's order	3	3	0
May 21	Mr Walrond a barber for a periwigg for Mrs Carew		16	0
June 11	To Mr Richard Carew to carry to Chuddleigh fair to buy bullocks	8	7	0
	More paid his man John Tucker to carry there	4	0	0
July 5	Richard Parker towards mowing and making the hay at Barly			
	at 6s p. [acre?]	1	10	0
July 21	Richard Parker for mowing and making the hay at Barly at			
	6s per. acre[?] by agreement	5	10	0
July 23	Edward Arthur (a mason) for making 65 yards of cobb			
	wall against Bowhill orchard, 10d p. yd.	2	14	0
Aug 25	For my half year's sallary due Lammas last	7	10	0

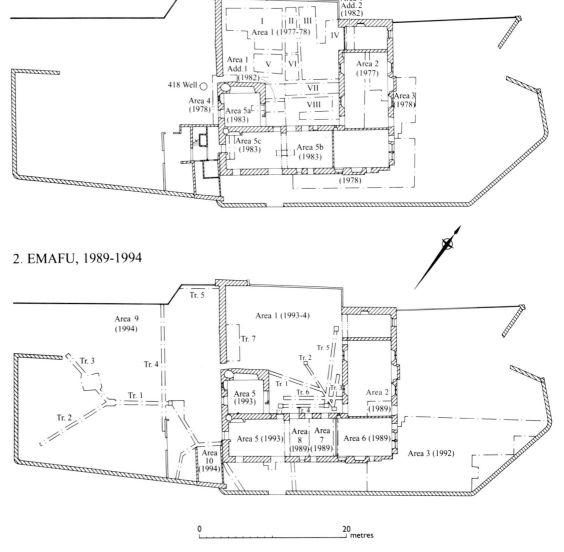

1. DoE, 1977-1983

Area 1 Add. 2 (1982)

Area 1 (1977-78)

I   II   III   IV

Area 1 Add. 1 (1982)

V   VI

VII

VIII

Area 2 (1977)

Area 3 (1978)

418 Well

Area 4 (1978)

Area 5a (1983)

Area 5c (1983)

Area 5b (1983)

(1978)

2. EMAFU, 1989-1994

Tr. 5

Area 9 (1994)

Area 1 (1993-4)

Tr. 7

Tr. 5

Tr. 3

Tr. 4

Tr. 2

Tr. 1

Tr. 1

Tr. 6

Tr. 3

Area 5 (1993)

Area 2 (1989)

Tr. 2

Area 10 (1994)

Area 5 (1993)

Area 8 (1989)

Area 7 (1989)

Area 6 (1989)

Area 3 (1992)

0   20 metres

Figure 4.1
Key to areas excavated 1977–94 (scale 1:500) (line drawing by Tony Ives).

Key for plan and section drawings in chapter 4

Edge of excavation

Edge of later intrusive feature

Top edge

Reduced top edge

Bottom edge

} of intrusive feature

Edge of surface

Standing wall

Standing wall (pre-building phases)

⑧ Section terminal and number (plan), with arrow showing direction of view

Section terminal (Figs 4.17 and 4.18)

4
The excavations

Sequence of excavations

The DoE excavations of 1977–81

These excavations occupied two major summer seasons in 1977 and 1978; some additional small trenches were excavated in 1982–3. Excavations were initiated by the Inspectorate of Ancient Monuments soon after the building's purchase, as part of the initial study of the site, to provide information on the structural history of the building, to aid the interpretation of the standing fabric and to provide guidance in the development of proposals for the restoration and display of the site. The excavations were directed by Stephen Dunmore, then an Assistant Inspector of Ancient Monuments, with a small team of excavators and volunteers. Some primary post-excavation work was carried out in the following years by the director and M Dewhurst; further post-excavation analysis, leading to the completion of the drawings and the compilation of an archive report, was carried out by EMAFU in 1990–1.[2]

In 1977 work concentrated on the central courtyard (Fig 4.1; Area 1), and the interior of the hall, including the western half of the screens passage (Area 2). In 1978 work continued in Area 1 and in an L-shaped area along the east and south sides of the standing building (Area 3), plus a smaller L-shaped area along the north and west walls of the kitchen (Area 4). Small-scale trenches were examined in the central courtyard in 1982 ('Area 1 additional 1'; 'Area 1 additional 2') and three trenches were dug inside the south and west ranges in 1983 ('Area 5, trenches a–c'), with the aim of locating original floor levels and/or wall footings.

The excavation was recorded using the system then employed by the Central Excavation Unit of the DoE.[3] Drawn records were initially inked up onto plastic drawing film from the pencilled field drawings. As the phasing of the site was established and clarified during post-excavation work, the plans were assembled phase by phase and drawn as a series of 'archive plans' that formed the principal illustrations of the archive report.[4] These, in turn, were combined with plans of the other areas to form the illustrations presented here (*see* Figs 4.3, 4.4, 4.7, 4.15, 4.19 and 4.23).[5]

EMAFU excavations I: the area excavations of 1989–93

After the excavations of 1977–8 and the stripping and fabric analysis of the standing building in 1979–80, little further close analysis was devoted to the archaeology of the building until 1987. By 1989 information about ancient floor levels was needed for the planning of the reinstatement. The need for an accurate archaeological framework with which to inform the proposals led to a series of excavations of the interiors of the building, as well as further work on the outside areas not examined in 1977–8: in the parlour (*see* Fig 4.1, Area 6), the eastern half of the screens passage (Area 2) and the service rooms adjoining to the west (Areas 7 and 8) in 1989; the eastern courtyard (Area 3) in 1992; the west end of the south range and the west range (kitchen) in 1993 (Area 5). The main purposes of the work were: to carry out the examination of modern floors by archaeological excavation (as a prelude to reinstatement); to search for and retrieve any surviving evidence for the treatment and finishes of early floors; and to examine and record sub-floor archaeological deposits prior to the digging of trenches for the installation of services.

In the case of the eastern courtyard, an additional research, or investigative, element played a part. The preliminary sample of the deposits obtained in Area 3 in 1978, immediately against walls of the standing building, showed that survival of ancient deposits was poor and that no footings or other structural remains of the porch or south-east range survived in Area 3. The poor survival was attributed to the high level of disturbance by drains and service trenches immediately against the walls. There was a chance of recovering structural traces of the demolished south-east range, as attested by the Buck brothers' engraving and by the evidence in the standing fabric, by excavating a larger area of the eastern court-yard. The opportunity to do this arose in 1992 when the completion of roofing work on the south range freed the area of scaf-folding for the first time in several years. The aims here were three-fold: to establish if any evidence survived for the extent and nature of the south-east range, either as wall footings, or as intrusive features indicating the extent of the plan;[6] to establish if the remains of the early features of phase 1 and structures of phase 2, found in 1989 inside the south range, extended beyond the limit of the standing building; and to examine areas of the eastern courtyard which were to be disrupted by the excavation of service trenches and to clear such areas as a prelude to the works.

In 1989 work concentrated on the parlour and the area of the service rooms to the west, a total of some 64m². Although this was divided into two rooms at the time of excavation, it was subsequently subdivided into three, restoring the original medieval arrangement. Consequently the rooms were numbered separately as areas 6, 7 and 8. The eastern half of the screens passage in the hall (Area 2) was also excavated in 1989 (a further area of 6.5m²), in an area limited to the north by the new cob floor of the hall (laid in 1987) and to the west by the 1977 excavation (although some features were followed into this area at the lowest levels).[7] In 1992 an area of *c* 150m² was selected to cover the various eventuali-ties of plan of the south-east range, within the area thought to be undisturbed.[8] Part of the 1978 excavations was included in the area in order to relocate the position of the trench with precision. When it was realised that much of the area was covered with intrusive features of a late date, this area was reduced by abandoning an area of 27m² in the north-central part of the area (*see* Fig 4.23). In 1993 the excavation of Area 5 comprised the passage through the centre of the south range, the west service room and the kitchen in the west range, a total area of slightly over 60m². Much of the floor of the kitchen was found to retain a well-preserved cobbled floor (of late 18th- or 19th-century date), which was left undisturbed, and the sub-floor deposits examined only within later intrusions.

A grid was established within the building in such a way that it could subse-quently be extended to any area of the site which was excavated in the future.[9] Excav-ation was done in open areas. Excavated contexts were numbered in a sequence continuous with those used in the recording of the standing fabric of the building (1–599 being used in the standing building, 600 onwards in the excavations). Each recorded context (in excavation or fabric) was described on a printed form; drawn records were compiled on A4 sheets in the first instance, the illustrations in the Archive Reports represent full collated versions of the site drawings (plans and sections).[10]

EMAFU excavations II: miscellaneous excavations and observations of 1993–5

As the repair programme drew to a close, many trenches were excavated for services, drainage, the insertion of ducting for cables and the footings for the new pentice (Fig 4.2). Thus, between November 1993 and March 1995, the work concentrated on the recording of archaeological strata exposed by the works programme: the observation of drainage trenches in the western courtyard (*see* Fig 4.1; Area 9); the excavation of an area within the building footprint of the annexe at the south-west corner of the building when it was rebuilt in July 1994 (Area 10); further observations of service and foundation trenches in the central courtyard (Area 1) at various dates between November 1993 and October 1994; and observation of trenches dug for new drainage in the area to the south of the south range (Area 3). In the central courtyard the main aim was to record information in section which had remained unexcavated in 1977–8, where the new trenches cut through the baulks of the earlier excavation. This work also provided the opportunity to review the results of the earlier work in the light of subsequent developments.

Chronology of site periods

Period I: medieval ?agricultural use

Phase 1

Early activity on the site consisted only of features cut into the underlying subsoil; no surfaces or occupation layers were certainly attributable to phase 1. Intrusive features were apportioned to phase 1 where they were stratified beneath deposits associated with the later building and the evidence of finds suggested an early date, or where they were simply the earliest deposit in the sequence in a given area. There is a marked concentration of linear features beneath the south range of the later building. To the north, beneath the central courtyard and the east range, there are fewer features of phase 1.

The standing building: the south range (Areas 5–8)
The earliest features in the interior beneath the south range were ditches cut into the natural subsoil (Fig 4.3). To the south, a series on both sides of the wall of the standing building (613, 621, 773, 781, 1561, 1619, 1620, 2386 and 2398), perhaps represented two or more phases of ditches and remnants of a further ditch against the north wall of the building (779, 1572). The better preserved southern ditches were interrupted by later features to the west. A rounded terminal represented the western end of one phase of ditch in the west service room, although which one is unclear (1561, 1620). In the central part of the room two further intrusive features were recorded, the larger (an irregular scoop some 0.25m deep) containing nine stakeholes along its northern edge (1522).[11]

One length of V-shaped ditch lay wholly outside the south wall of the standing building (2386 and 2398); the wall footings were built over its northern edge and cut into its fill. The feature had a square terminal to the east, and may have been connected with the terminal excavated separately in a later year to the west

(1561, 1620).[12] The ditch clearly forms a part of the series of early features on the site, although its alignment is at variance with 773/821 and 779 to the north; it may, thus, belong to a separate sub-phase. The fills of the ditch produced six sherds of medieval pottery which yield a date after 1250, but which, in practice, can be no more precise than generally 'late medieval'.[13]

The hall, Area 2
Something of the configuration of the pre-building ground surface can be seen in the levels of natural subsoil revealed in the excavation of the great hall. Levels were highest in the north-west quadrant of the hall, sloping away by up to 0.4m to the south of the northern window. A shallow gully was detected cutting into the slope at this point (see Fig 4.3, 2045). Over the rest of the area levels were reasonably constant, showing a gentle slope from west to east (consistent with the gradients observed elsewhere) and a slight rise towards the south. As the levels were still rather lower than equivalents in the south range, it is possible that the construction of this part of the building in phase 3 involved some lowering of the ground surface and thereby the loss of deposits equivalent to those in the south range (where remains of an earlier building survived).

Pre-building activity in the screens passage at the south end of the hall comprised a series of soil levels accumulating on natural subsoil, most or all of which could be of natural origin (see Fig 4.18, section 13, 870, 872, 876, 886, 890). These were cut by a network of shallow gullies representing drainage or erosion over open ground and which are associated by function with similar early features in other areas of the site, although they shared no common form or orientation (see Fig 4.3, 873, 881 and 2244). Then, in turn, this level was cut by another ditch (or gully) on a slightly different alignment (869).[14] The whole sequence contained little material derived from human activity, although charcoal traces were not infrequent in the soil filling the features and the fill of the ditch 2244 contained a single roof slate.

The annexe, Area 10
Traces of an early feature pre-dating the standing building that may have represented a pit of phase 1 or 2 were planned but not fully excavated in Area 10 in 1994

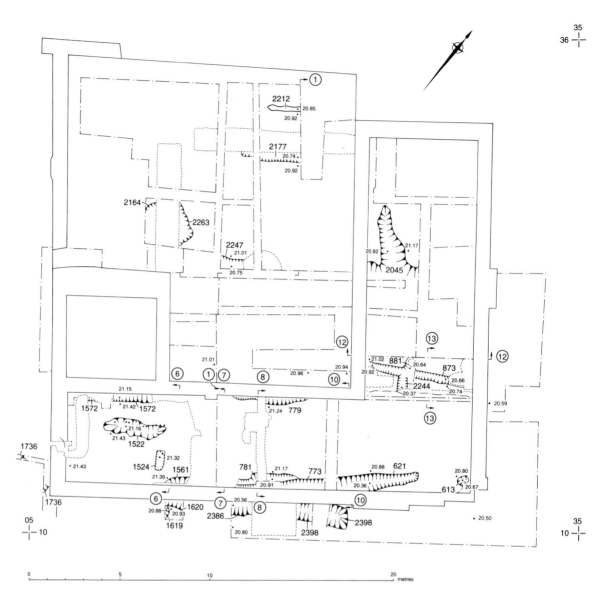

Figure 4.3
Excavated features of phase 1, pre-building; standing walls shown in outline (scale 1:200) (line drawing by Tony Ives).

(*see* Fig 4.3, 1736); no datable material was recovered from the fills, although they contained quantities of building materials (slate and mortar).

The central courtyard

Several features were excavated in the central courtyard whose fills were certainly overlain by the pebbled surfaces associated with the construction and/or earliest use of the standing building. Their use must relate to one of the early, pre-building phases (*see* Fig 4.3). Three lengths of linear ditches (2177, 2212, 2247) have been assigned to phase 1, on the grounds of their affinity with those beneath the south range. It is also possible that they could have represented traces of the phase 2 building, although no structural traces were recorded in this area.

Discussion

The nature and purpose of the collection of ditches of this phase are unclear. It is possible that the features represented or were related to the north and south limits of a structure (perhaps as eaves-drip trenches, although they seem very deep for this purpose) of which other traces did not survive the construction activities of phases 2 and 3 described below. The broad correlation of the ditches and the north and south limits of the succeeding buildings of phases 2 and 3 might favour this interpretation over the alternatives. Equally the ditches could have been related to drainage of the site or were the remnants of a crude enclosure. In these cases the features would presumably have been agricultural in purpose and pre-date any occupation of the site.

Although the ditch fills were predominantly of clean and naturally derived materials, traces of charcoal were ubiquitous and a number of the fill layers contained traces of building materials, most notably slate fragments.[15] This shows that there was building activity in the vicinity at the time that they were filled. The small sherds of medieval pottery retrieved from the fills of ditches 621 (one sherd, layer 622) and 2386/2398 (six sherds), reveal little more than could be deduced from the stratigraphic sequence – that the ditches were medieval and probably pre-date the 15th century (the date assigned to phase 2).

Comparison of the levels on the natural subsoil between the interior of the south range and the area excavated in the eastern courtyard shows that the ambient levels outside the building are some 0.25–40m lower than those on the interior. The truncation was presumably caused by the construction of the standing building and further exaggerated by later terracing and digging of cultivation trenches in phase 9 in the east courtyard.[16] The reduction in level was sufficient to remove not only the footings of the buildings, but also the slighter (if lower) traces of wall and floors and the intrusive features of still earlier remains of phases 1 and 2.

Period II: gentry houses, phases 2–7

Phase 2: earlier building beneath the south range, 14th to 15th century

Parlour/service rooms (Areas 6–8)
Deposits of phase 2 were represented by the truncated remains of an earlier building on the site of the later south range (Fig 4.4; seen under excavation in Figs 4.5 and 4.6). The walls had been built directly onto the ground surface and the floors had been cut down below the level of the wall bases; the faces of the walls were thus preserved as shallow plinths (up to 0.2m high) in the natural subsoil. The wall bases, along with the corresponding floor deposits and the fills of the rooms from the destruction of the building, had been truncated by later activity.

The surviving plan comprised a three-roomed building. Two rooms to the east were clear in plan, 9.6 × 4.7m internally. The western room survived only in a vestigial form with a possible threshold beyond the cross wall excavated in Area 5 (1553/1560, *below*). The main building was of similar span to the later (standing) building and of only slightly variant orientation (*see* Fig 4.4). The south, east and north wall lines were nearly coincident with those of the later parlour. The base of the west wall (784) was, therefore, the only wall to be seen in full, measuring 1.20m wide. The central and eastern rooms were divided by a narrow partition wall (636). The eastern room was floored with an earth floor, containing ash and charcoal (604); in its north-eastern corner a square raised area (645, *c* 0.10m above the general floor level) may represent the position of a fitting within the room, or the position of an entrance (*see* Fig 4.5, foreground). Adjacent to the west was an area of mortared stone, slightly within the line of the inner face of the wall that may represent the threshold of a doorway in the north wall (*see* Fig 4.4; 653). The vertical faces of the wall bases retained traces of burnt plaster in most places. Three small post- or stakeholes along the wall face, between the threshold and the partition (662, 664, 666), may have supported a fixture against the wall. A number of larger postholes along the inner faces of the south and east walls of the room (648, 619, 617, 615 and 609) may have supported structures, but here the interpretation is complicated by the fact that only one (648) appears to have held a post (from the post pipe of which came a coin, Chapter 9). The remainder of the holes contained burnt fills and appeared to have been open at the time the building was destroyed by fire. This might suggest that the room had a boarded floor laid on the earth layer and that these features were hidden beneath it.

The central room contained a stone-lined cess pit for a garderobe in its north-eastern corner (684), presumably contained by a closet above floor level. The form of the base of the partition, the east face of which narrowed in the area spanned by the pit (656), suggests that the closet was entered from the eastern room of the building. The cess pit was 1.5m deep and lined with clay-bonded volcanic stone. Sockets for two floor joists running north–south were preserved in the clay packing at the top of the lining (764, 766, 768 and 770). The central room had a trampled floor of clay onto natural subsoil, again incorporating ash and charcoal (637/694). No trace of fireplaces or hearths was seen in either room.

The western room of the building was represented by traces of the base of the west wall (786) and a group of features consisting

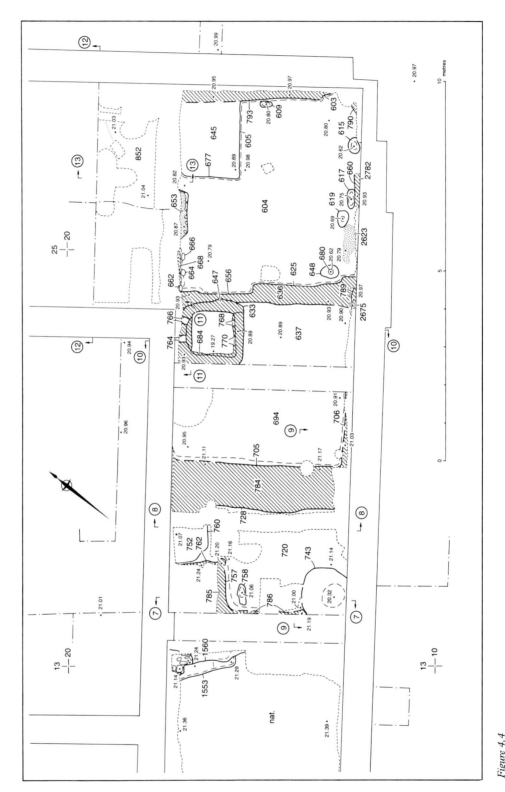

Figure 4.4
Plan of the phase 2 building (pre-dating the standing building); standing walls shown in outline (scale 1:100) (line drawing by Tony Ives).

of a rectangular raised area in the north-west corner (785; similar to that in the east room, possibly representing a threshold or partitioned area), an area of metalling to the east (752), and a stone-filled trench to the west (Area 5, 1553/1560). The interior surface was of similar composition to those of the main rooms (720). In view of the thickness of the wall to the east (suggesting an exterior wall), it would seem possible that this room was either a subsidiary outbuilding or an addition to the original plan of the building (or both?). The western room appears to have gone out of use before the main building, since a pit was dug into the south-western corner of the room, cutting both the walls and the floor (743). This feature was itself filled in before the demolition of the building (whose debris overlay the fill of the pit: *see* Fig 4.18, section 7, 719); the fill contained four sherds dated to the period 1350–1450 (Chapter 9, context 745).

Related deposits in Area 5
Little trace of the building extended beyond the cross wall separating areas 5 and 8; in the north-east corner of the (later) room an area was cut out in two steps (*see* Fig 4.4, 1553 and 1560) and filled with clay-bonded volcanic stone.[17] The feature probably represented the western limit of a cobbled stone external threshold, stepping down to a doorway in the west wall of the building and otherwise removed by the footings of the later cross wall. The upstand of natural subsoil in the corner of the west room (785) would thus have represented its internal counterpart.

Related deposits in the central courtyard
One pebbled surface which was cut by the foundation trench for the east wall of the west range may have represented a surface of phase 1 or 2, but could as well have belonged to phase 3 and represented an early stage in the construction process. This is discussed with the main sequence of courtyard surfaces in the context of phase 3, *see* p 56.

Possibly related deposits in the screens passage (Area 2)
In the screens passage a further accumulation of soil above the phase 1 features was cut by intrusive features which were still earlier than the construction of the standing building and were, therefore, assigned to phase 2 (*see* Fig 4.4, 852 and cut-out areas,[18] and Fig 4.18, section 13). Layer 852

Figure 4.5
The early building beneath the parlour (phase 2) under excavation in 1989, looking west. Note the wall bases and the garderobe pit at rear right. The vestigial nature of the structures is shown by the height of the wall bases (photograph by Stuart Blaylock; EMAFU 1581/11).

Figure 4.6
The phase 2 building beneath the service rooms, looking east (photograph by Stuart Blaylock; EMAFU 1589/31).

contained building materials (mortar fragments, slate chippings and stone). Two medieval potsherds support the broadly medieval date given to the pre-building phases elsewhere.[19] Fragments of medieval ridge tile and slates demonstrate a properly finished roof (whether the construction or destruction is not known). The deposits in this area may relate to the phase 2 building, although no structural traces had survived in the hall of the standing building and their general character differs from those of area 6. It is also possible that they belonged to the construction phases of the standing building.

Discussion

Slight survival of phase 2
The surviving deposit of the early building of phase 2 was very shallow. Aside from the intrusive features, postholes and the garderobe pit, the whole deposit was little more than 150–200mm in depth. The truncation caused first by the construction of the standing building and second by cutting away for modern floors within that building had caused the removal of most of the footings of the early building. This emphasises the fragile nature of the evidence and that survival was a matter of chance – another 100–150mm terraced into the site would have destroyed much of the coherent surviving deposits.

Building techniques

The technique of lowered floors has been observed in a number of excavated medieval and later houses in Exeter. The best example to date was seen in a mid-16th century house on the frontage of Cowick Street, St Thomas, belonging to a bronze foundry that was excavated in 1984.[20] Here the building had cob walls built directly onto the ground surface. The floor terrace perhaps represented the source of the raw material for the cob, and the place in which it was mixed.[21] The construction of cob walls without footings has been seen in other excavated buildings.[22] Although a number of examples are known in surviving standing buildings in Devon, it is rare in recorded buildings, perhaps for the obvious reason that cob walling without stone footings is very prone to decay and therefore has a more limited lifespan than cob on stone footings. The Bowhill building retained only the wall bases in natural subsoil and so there is no firm evidence that this building was constructed without stone footings. The width of the walls (as represented by the one seen in full, *see above*), at 1.2m, certainly suggests that the building was of cob; as does the demolition deposit (*see below*). In the later building most of the walls (whether of stone or cob or both) are in the region of 0.75–0.80m thick. Only the gable wall of the kitchen is substantially thicker at 1.4m and this is because it accommodates the large kitchen fireplace and its flue. The material filling the rooms, above the destruction debris (*see below*), was composed of stony clay, with plaster and fragments of other building materials, consistent with a derivation from the collapse or demolition of cob walling. This confirms that the bulk of the structure was of this material.

Character and extent of the building

Interpretation is hampered by the lack of definitive knowledge of the plan; the terracing activities to the north and east (and to a lesser extent the south)[23] mean that the possibility of further rooms in these directions cannot be excluded. The square projecting element in one corner occurs in all three rooms (in one form or another), although this distinctive aspect of the plan is of uncertain significance. The east room possessed a series of postholes along its south wall that may have been related to fittings within the building.

Taking the plan as it survives (as essentially a two-roomed building, with some other accommodation as outbuildings, but not necessarily a first floor and with unknown provision for heating) the building looks primitive. There is no sign of a cross passage[24] and as a two-roomed plan it follows the example from Cowick Street closely and is of very similar dimensions (the Cowick Street house measures 8.4 × 4.8m internally and 10.2 × 6.4m externally). Yet the garderobe pit indicates a higher level of sophistication than might be expected in a simple two-roomed house and finds of building materials contribute to the identification of a building of higher quality than might be apparent from the surviving plan. Three sherds of window glass were found in the destruction deposit of the building (Chapter 9), while slate and ridge-tile fragments in the destruction deposits in the cess pit and the room fills[25] imply a slate roof that identifies the building as more than just a vernacular cob house, at a date when most such houses would have been thatched. Roofing slate was imported from some distance away (Chapter 9).

Thus it is probable that the plan was originally more extensive and that other rooms, if not ranges, have failed to survive. In view of the similarity in plan between this building and the later south range, it is possible that there was a hall range to the north of the surviving plan, as in the rebuilt version of phase 3, and that the surviving plan represents a solar or service wing adjoining that hall range. This raises the possibility that the earlier building influenced the form and extent of its successor, a question discussed further below (*see* pp 57–8).

Destruction of the building

All three rooms of the building contained evidence of destruction by fire. All the upstanding wall faces and much of the floor area were heavily scorched. Several large sections of charred timber, presumably ceiling beams or rafters, were recovered from the fills of the cess pit,[26] and deposits of mixed burnt material were found spread over much of the floor area. Above the fire debris the remainder of the surviving depth within the walls was filled with mixed clay deposits, including fragments of building materials that derive from the demolition of the cob walls of the building.

No evidence was detected for a prolonged lapse of time between the destruction of the building and its reconstruction in the shape of the larger building that survives today. Some evidence, such as traces of further occupation or the development of soil or turf lines, could have been lost in the levelling activities that preceded the construction of the present building. The foundation trenches for the standing walls were cut into the fills of the earlier rooms, providing a clear stratigraphic separation between the two structures and removing any possibility of elements of one being associated with the other. Nevertheless the coincidence of position and alignment between the walls of the two buildings suggests that sufficient physical remains of the one were extant to influence the siting of the other, notwithstanding the differences of size and status.[27]

Dating
The very vague dating of phase 1, really no more refined than 'medieval', provides a lower limit to the dating of phase 2; as has been seen, this is unlikely to be later than the early 15th century and could be substantially earlier. The upper limit is more precise, in that the probable date of the construction of the standing building is fairly well established at *c* 1500. Thus the widest interpretation of the evidence provides a range of the 14th and 15th centuries for the construction and occupation of the phase 2 building. Further refinement depends on:

1. A collection of sherds with a collective dating of 'late 13th to early 14th century' (eastern room, Chapter 9, Appendix 1, phase 2, 601) and 'broadly 1250–1400' (western room, 719) from the demolition deposit filling the rooms that probably derived from the cob of the walls.
2. A silver penny of Edward IV found in the fill of the post pipe of a posthole in the eastern room of the building (*see* Fig 4.4, 649, fill; 680, post-pipe; 648, posthole: *see* Shiel's report, Chapter 9).
3. Late 15th- to early 16th-century floor tile fragments from the fill of the garderobe pit, which provide objective evidence that the phase 2 building was in use until very close to the proposed date of the rebuilding and thereby the destruction of phase 2 (from the pit fill, 685, Chapter 9, Appendix 1).

The sherds within the cob debris of the room fills could all be derived from deposits associated with the construction of the building of phase 2, rather than its demolition, which provides the most reliable guide

that the structure might be late 14th or early 15th century in date. The material from the garderobe pit is more certainly associated with the destruction of the building on the basis that the feature probably continued in use until the destruction of the building and that the demolition and other materials in the fill are consistent with a tidying-up operation after a fire (the charred timbers and similar debris). This is consistent with the suggested date for the construction of the standing building and would tend to support the suggestion that the two events followed closely one on the other.

Phase 3: construction of the standing building, *c* 1500

Nature of foundations/wall footings
In general, the walls of the south range were constructed in foundation trenches. These were traced in most places within the building, although the wall footings often so completely filled the trench that a cut was difficult to distinguish in excavation (Fig 4.7, 655, 674, 703, 707, 1531). The north and east walls of the west service room had foundation trenches that were wider than usual (1543, 1558). The projecting offsets in them lay somewhat below the probable floor levels. The fill of the foundation trench of the north wall contained one of the most useful groups of sherds for the dating of the construction of the standing building.[28] Possible construction surfaces were noted outside the building to the north and south of the through passage (1669, 1608). Subsidiary wall footings, such as those for screens and partitions, were also trench-built although again the masonry often completely filled the trench (for example, 726, 654/824). No foundation trenches were seen on the exterior of the south range where the wall footings appeared to rest directly on the natural subsoil. The implication here is that there was an element of terracing or reduction of ground levels to the north, south and east at the time of the construction of the building. This concurs with the levels on natural subsoil and the traces of the phase 2 building surviving only within the south range.

The footings of the east range appear to have been constructed directly on natural subsoil, without foundation trenches: no trenches were observed in 1977 and none survived in the area excavated in 1989. The west wall averaged three courses of footings (0.45m) towards the south, but only one (0.10m) at the north end, where the level of subsoil was higher. The east wall, where the footings were seen, comprised two courses (0.25m).

A deep layer of clay infill (up to 0.45m) was deposited within the hall once the wall footings had been constructed. This was lying against the footings and filling the depression in the natural ground, thus thinning out towards the north.[29] This served to make up the ground as the base for the floor. In the eastern half of the screens passage (excavated in 1989) the upper level of the phase 2 deposits became the construction surface of the building (*see* Fig 4.4, 852, and Fig 4.18, section 13). The sleeper wall for the southern partition of the hall was built in a foundation trench cut from this level (*see* Fig 4.7, 824) and there accumulated a composite deposit of trampled burnt material, burnt mortar and building debris (*see* Fig 4.18, section 13, 845) that extended over the fill of the foundation trench and the footings of the southern partition.[30] Over most of the floor of the hall the primary floor deposits had been truncated.

The footings of the demolished east wall of the west range were exposed over most of the surviving length (Fig 4.8; *see also* Fig 4.7, 2202). The wall was built in a foundation trench (2241) in which projecting footings survived towards the south end. The west face also probably represented a projecting footing, since it lies to the west of the projected line of the standing wall of

the kitchen. The footings of the north wall of the kitchen (2391) incorporated the masonry base for an oven projecting from the face of the wall (2394). Those of the west wall were built of more carefully squared blocks to form one side of a stone-lined drain along the side of the building (2364/2415).

Wall footings below ground were invariably clay bonded, the use of mortar being introduced at ground level. The main material was volcanic trap, but some Permian breccia was used in the footings of the west range (as also in the standing fabric). Larger blocks were used for facework, rubble for cores. The wall footings generally projected from both faces of the wall, interior and exterior.

The south range

Exterior

The fabric of the south wall incorporated the remains of a projecting garderobe bonded to the wall footings and comprising a stone-lined cess pit, 1.2m deep and projecting up to 1.8m from the wall face (Figs 4.9 and 4.10; *see also* Fig 4.7, 2307). The construction was of volcanic trap throughout, with large blocks squared at the face, but unworked behind. The largest blocks were seen in the chute, on the north side. The base was formed of a single block set at 45° and the sides by large quoins. The stones were clay bonded below ground; traces of mortar-bonded work survived in the topmost course, showing that, as with the walls, mortared fabric began at ground level. The base of the pit was not lined and was fairly level, showing no signs of wear from the recutting or scouring that might be expected if it had received prolonged use. Despite this it must have been regularly emptied, as the bulk of the fill related to the demolition (*see* Fig 4.17, section 5; layers 2347 and 2349 might be contemporary with the use of the garderobe). The garderobe was used for no more than 50 years; the final filling of the pit contained a good group of pottery dating to *c* 1550 (Chapter 9).

The south side of the pit lining was partially robbed and preserved no trace of the superstructure of the garderobe, which had projected from the wall by *c* 1–1.2m, to judge from the position of the chute. Two blocks of the mortar-bonded west wall of the superstructure survived at ground level. The line of the quoin was visible in the wall above and had been patched with breccia on the removal of the garderobe structure (*see* Fig 5.8, 21).

Figure 4.8
The 1977 excavations in the courtyard showing the excavated wall footings of the west range, looking south to the standing west range (EMAFU 1988/35) (source: Exeter Archaeology; © Exeter Archaeology).

Figure 4.9 (left)
The garderobe pit and the chute in Area 3 (to south of the south range), looking north, excavated in 1978 (photograph by Stephen Dunmore; EBO78/BW4/3).

Figure 4.10 (right)
As Figure 4.9, looking west (photograph by Stephen Dunmore; EBO78/BW4/11).

Interior

The parlour, Area 6

The earlier deposits were levelled off. A continuous horizon was traced across the deposits of phase 2, cutting across the fills of rooms and truncating the bases of walls. Foundation trenches were dug and footings constructed from this level (*see* Fig 4.7). A single structural feature survived in the floor, a posthole in the south-eastern corner of the room, directly underneath a mortice in the easternmost beam of the parlour ceiling (*see* Fig 4.7, 606). This position was flush with the quoin forming the return of the north wall of the south-east range. A post at this point would have provided support for the corner of the ceiling frame that was otherwise unsupported because of the wide entry into the south-east range at this corner (*see* Fig 6.2). The posthole was not sealed by later deposits and so some doubt as to its stratigraphic position and phasing remains. It is possible that it was a primary feature of phase 3, but if the end of the beam originally received support from a partition filling the opening into the south-east range, the post could have been inserted to support the ceiling after a period of decay or even on the removal and demolition of structures in this area in phase 8 (*see below*). At phase 8, however, the end of the beam received new support from the masonry blocking 253 (*see* Figs 5.8 and 6.22), and the post certainly pre-dates this.

The service rooms, Areas 7 and 8

More evidence for the original arrangement and fittings of the primary phase was preserved in the service rooms to the west. The sleeper wall of the partition dividing the two service rooms had survived (Fig 4.7, 727, and *see* Fig 4.18, sections 8 and 9, 724) dug into the subsoil and consisted of a base one course deep and *c* 0.45–50m wide, with a narrower upper course on which the sill

timber of the screen rested (*c* 0.25m wide). The east face of the sleeper wall/screen aligned with the reveal of the garderobe doorway in the south wall (*see* Fig 6.22, 36 and 724). The excavated footing was used, with the mortices in the headbeam above, as the basis for the reconstructed screen now seen in the building (*see* Figs 6.37–6.39 and Chapter 11).

A cobbled threshold 1.1m square lay immediately within the door to the pentice in the north-west corner of the west room (*see* Fig 4.7, 755) and was associated with a partition to the south, represented by a slot cut in the subsoil (753). The threshold was truncated to the east, but as a small patch of poorly preserved cobbling survived between the threshold proper and the base of the partition (734), the cobbling may have extended up to the dividing screen. The cobbled threshold probably represents an entry area or an interior porch to the west room. Communication between the two service rooms in the original arrangement is unlikely, but cannot be ruled out; if it existed, it would probably have lain in this northern area (where the headbeam had been removed by stairs of phase 11 and evidence of mortices did not survive). A small lobby would also explain the curious shared-light arrangement of the window in the north wall at this point.

Some evidence for other internal features survived in the west room. A shallow curving trench cut into underlying deposits (*see* Fig 4.7, 709) may represent the course of a water pipe, perhaps a continuation of the pipe suggested in the courtyard to the north (*see* p 56). If so the connection between the two sections, exterior and interior, remained unlocated. The feature could be secondary, but since it was sealed by deposits relating to post-medieval phases (7 and later), it belongs early in the sequence of the room.[31] In the east room the primary features comprised a slot and posthole (701 and 699), which may have formed a threshold to the garderobe entry or been associated with the functioning of the garderobe in some other way.

Flooring

Other than the volcanic-stone cobbling of the threshold, no physical traces of flooring survived in the service rooms. A peak of natural subsoil to the south of the threshold in the west room was very close to that of the threshold itself and close to the level of the timber threshold of the parlour screen, which provides another limiting factor on the original floor level.[32] The floor probably sloped slightly from west to east and could have stepped down on the line of the partition, but the level on natural subsoil gives a minimum level for the floor of 21.32m OD. For the west room, a very thin laid floor or a trampled earth surface are the most probable original finishes; a floor of earth, cob, lime or other mixture requiring a substantial thickness would have been correspondingly higher in level. The original floor level of the east room is also likely to have lain at *c* 21.30m OD.[33]

Figure 4.11
Excavation of the west service room of the south range in September 1993, looking east. Note the foundation trench to the left and the rebuilt stone cross wall in the background (photograph by David Garner; EH B934821).

West service room, Area 5
Traces of a primary clay makeup or floor layer, were recorded over approximately half of the area of the room (*see* Fig 4.7, 1508 and 1570), running directly over the fills of the foundation trenches (Fig 4.11) and up to the walls; in the north-east doorway the equivalent deposit formed a threshold of cobbles (*see* Fig 4.7, 1600 and 1674). This probably represented the bedding for a paved floor. There is also a strong possibility

that the volcanic-stone paviours that survived in the later floor of this room were reused from the primary floor (*see below*, phase 8). Despite the evidence in the standing fabric for a screen between the passage and the room, no trace of the position of the base of the screen was seen in excavation, nor was any secondary evidence for the subdivision detected, such as differential treatment of surfaces. If the extent of the clay bedding layer (1508) is reliable in indicating the nature of the floor itself, a continuous floor is suggested.

The east range

Exterior

On the east elevation of the building the main item of interest was the evidence for the structural sequence around the chimney stack. Here the wall footings, formed as elsewhere of volcanic trap (*see* Fig 5.1, 2300), stopped short of the stack. Crucially, there was a gap in the footings of 0.35m (2400) before the foundations of the stack commenced, constructed of breccia in a separate cut (2399). This evidence suggested that the building of the stack was a separate operation. Had it been part of a wholly later phase and if the wall had been in existence before the fireplace was inserted, the stone footings of the main wall would surely have continued across the gap and the stack would have been built against or on top of them.

The superstructure of the stack was also of breccia. A wide cut was visible in the masonry of the lower half of the standing elevation and a rather tidier seam in the upper half (*see* Fig 5.1 and Chapter 5); the cob of the wall top, however, ran up to the fabric of the chimney stack. Much of this (with the exception of the relationship of the cob wall top) would suggest that the stack was a later insertion in the wall were it not for the excavated evidence. The full sequence may be interpreted as follows:

1. The stack was an element in the plan from the first, but its construction took place separately from the fabric of the main wall, perhaps assigned to a different mason (the discrete incidence of breccia in some other features in the building supports the idea that it was reserved for specific purposes in phase 3).
2. The construction of the footings and superstructure of the east wall of the hall commenced first, leaving a gap for the stack.

3. When the wall had reached a height of *c* 2.5m, the stack was commenced and the gap to each side filled with mortared rubble.

4. Above this height the construction of wall and stack proceeded in parallel, although the neat, straight join with the wall at the top of the stack (*see* Fig 5.7) shows that they continued to be built as separate structures.

5. Once the masonry was complete, the roof was raised and the wall-top cob added around the trusses, running up to the masonry of the stack.[34]

The screens passage

Surviving primary flooring in the east half of the screens passage comprised a trodden clay surface and a mortar bedding layer, for a stone pavement, of which remnants survived *in situ* (Fig 4.12; *see also* Fig 4.18, section 13, 838 and 806). To the north a slot preserved in the floor layers marked the position of the screen – a rectilinear base (with some evidence of more than one position), with a square terminal, stopping 0.3m short of the central axis of the hall. This indicates that the screen possessed a central opening, although *c* 0.6m seems rather narrow. Presumably the slot represented the sleeper beam for the screen (extending partially under the central opening), rather than the superstructure of the screen itself. The floor makeup layers accumulated against the base of the sleeper beam, that is, they were deposited once the screen was in position. These layers contained late sherds and clay-pipe material (including joining sherds of a mid- to late 17th-century tin-glazed jar),[35] indicating that the floor had been disturbed, perhaps because the volcanic-stone paviours were re-laid in the late 17th or 18th century (therefore in phase 7?).

A posthole was accommodated within the offset footing immediately inside the south-west door of the hall, perhaps as a support for the screen (*see* Fig 4.7, 2226); otherwise all floor layers to the north of the screens passage belonged to later phases (*see* p 64).

The west range

Examination of early phases in the kitchen was confined to the cleaning of the sections of a late drain trench running east–west across the kitchen (*see* Fig 4.19). A discontinuous surface of irregular pebbling was observed in places on the natural subsoil.[36]

This could have been a fragment of the primary floor of the kitchen, but in view of its poor quality and discontinuous character, it is probably best interpreted as a construction surface, analogous to the early pebbled surfaces in the central courtyard (*see below*). A shallow gully packed with stone may have acted as a drain or soakaway beneath this surface (*see* Fig 4.7, 1654). The wall footings of the west range, where visible, projected from the wall faces and lay level with the cobbled floor of phase 8.

The central courtyard

Phase 3 deposits in the central courtyard fall into two groups: those associated with the construction of the standing building and those relating to the drainage, surfacing and use of the courtyard.

Figure 4.12
Excavation of the screens passage in 1989. Note two paving slabs in situ (centre) and 19th-century cobbled floor above (photograph by Jenny Norton; EMAFU 1651/14).

Structures in the central courtyard

On the north side of the courtyard the stump of a wall survived, bonded to the footings of the east range (*see* Fig 4.7, 2267), but robbed for the rest of its length.[37] This formed the south side of the north range.[38] The west end as represented by the robber trench fell short of a junction with the wall of the west range (2202). It seems that the two walls never met at the north-west corner of the courtyard. Alternatively the gap may have represented a step up in the original footings that had not survived the post-demolition phases. This represents a structural puzzle (*see* pp 57–8). No floor levels or other remains of the interior had survived later disturbance to the north.

A further structural element in the primary sub-phase was a narrow wall cutting into the natural subsoil, parallel to the wall of the east range, some 0.90–1.00m to the west (*see* Fig 4.7, 2266). The wall had a clear face to the west but none to the east. It terminated some 0.7m south of the south jamb of the inserted doorway in the north-east corner of the hall; the external pebbled surface of the yard stopped on the same line.

This represented a stair serving the northern bay of the east range, possibly of stone within the wall thickness or a timber super-structure supported on a sleeper wall. The excavated evidence supports a primary context for the structure.

Figure 4.13
The north-east corner of the courtyard looking south-west. Detail of courtyard surfaces, with phase 3 pebbled surface below and phase 8 cobbled surface within new kitchen above (photograph by Stephen Dunmore; EBO77/BW2/3).

Courtyard surfaces

Metalled surfaces were traced over most of the excavated area of Area 1, forming the primary surfaces of the courtyard. Nearly everywhere these were casually accumulated deposits of the sort which develop on exterior surfaces under conditions of hard use, perhaps with the laying of some gravel, and stone in particularly muddy places, but without consistent preparation or special materials (Fig 4.13). The lowest level of metalling was deposited directly on the natural subsoil in most places.[39] The surfaces were occasionally composed of a single layer of pebbling, but were mainly recorded as two layers, at least, separated by clay deposits or as a continuous thickness of metalling representing an accumulation through use. The natural slope of the pre-building ground surface influenced the development of surfaces in that the deposits tended to be deeper towards the south and east of the courtyard and thinner to the north and west. Poor drainage in the south-east corner may also have contributed to a greater deposition in this area (which was still prone to flooding until new drainage was inserted during the recent repairs). The process of accumulation must have begun at the construction stage, since some of the lowest metalled surfaces pre-date (in strati-graphic terms) the wall of the west range. Nevertheless the lowest surfaces elsewhere ran up to wall footings and it seems best to interpret this sequence as a continuum spanning the construction and earliest use of the building. It remains possible that some of the earliest patchy courtyard surfaces

could have been deposited in the preceding phase (phase 2), although there was no positive evidence in favour of this interpret-ation as no structural remains of phase 2 survived outside the footprint of the south range of the standing building. In one section in the south-east part of the area the clay material intervening between the two pebbled surfaces was interpreted as the detritus of cob mixing, as it was formed of cleanish clay and small stone.[40] The preparation of materials and the mixing of cob in the courtyard provides another explan-ation for the build-up of levels during construction.

Further evidence for the continuity of the surface deposits is provided by the fabric of a drain and culvert incorporated in the surface. The feature was traced over most of the courtyard. To the north it was a slight gully within the pebbled surface immedi-ately on the natural subsoil (*see* Fig 4.7, 2387, and Fig 4.17, section 3). After a gap of 4.5m, the second section ran as far as the north wall of the south range and comprised a stone-lined culvert (*see* Fig 4.7, 2150); several capping stones survived at the south end. The structure could have acted as a drain, but could also have accommodated a water pipe supplying the building.[41] Within the building, there was little trace of a south-ward continuation of the drain, but the footing projecting to the west of the stone cross wall showed a curving face which aligns with the edge of the drain to the north and suggests that the foundations of the wall could have incorporated or overlain a continuation of this culvert (1547).[42] The build-up of material in the south-east corner of the courtyard is demonstrated by the rela-tionship of the pebbled surfaces to the culvert. At the north end the stone kerbs of the feature were dug in slightly and the capping lay at an equivalent level to the lowest level of pebbling. Further south, however, later levels of metalling matched the level of the capping stones (which surely were intended to lie at, or below, the ground surface) and these, in turn, lay at the same level as the projecting footings of the west wall of the east range.[43]

No evidence for the pentice across the south side of the courtyard, attested in the standing fabric, was seen in excavation (Chapter 5). This was partly due to the intrusion of a modern drain on the probable line of a sleeper wall for the pentice.[44] No differential treatment of surfaces within the area of the pentice was observed, although later disturbance could have destroyed traces, especially ephemeral deposits such as, for example, the bedding for paving.

The excavation of service trenches in 1993–4 gave another opportunity to observe the sequence of pebbled surfaces in the southern half of the central courtyard (Fig 4.14). This confirmed that the stone-lined drain or conduit (*see* Fig 4.7, 2150) was a primary feature of the courtyard and coeval with the courtyard surfaces. Further areas of pebbled surface were recorded in trenches 4 and 5 (*see* Fig 4.1), where they had survived in the unexcavated baulks of 1977. A clean clay layer within the accumulation of pebbled surfaces was re-examined and inter-preted as the product of cob mixing.

The east courtyard

No contemporary surfaces survived to the south and east of the building. Only the foot-ings of the standing building were recorded in this phase (*see* Fig 4.7, 2300). No founda-tion trenches were seen, but they could have been removed by later activity or perhaps were eschewed in favour of construction directly onto the natural subsoil.

Discussion

Preservation
Although some information on the floor levels survived in most rooms, no room had retained its medieval floor, which provides some measure of the amount of disturbance and alteration that had gone on in the building.[45] A similar failure was evident in exterior areas, although the central court-yard had retained some of its original surfacing. Both the east and west courtyards were wholly truncated by activity in later phases – cultivation trenches of the Victor-ian and later nursery in the former, bull-dozing associated with the demolition of the barn in 1972 in the latter.

For the most part, therefore, the construction of the standing building has to be read from the wall footings and fragmen-tary remains of the surfaces. Although this was generally a problem in the archaeology of Bowhill, its effect is particularly apparent in the interpretation of this phase, *the* major phase in the development of the site (*see* p 69).

Possible influence of phase 2 structures on planning and construction of phase 3
Some of the oddities in construction are hypothetically explicable by assumptions on the possible extent of the site and standing

Figure 4.14
Service trenches dug for drains in the central court-yard, December 1993, looking east (photograph by David Garner; EH B936795).

buildings in the preceding phase 2. The unusual configuration of the north end of the hall in relation to the north boundary of the site (and thereby the relationship of the east and north ranges) could all be explained if the building was constructed within a fixed northern boundary. Had there been no constraint of this sort, a more regular arrangement of four ranges might reasonably have been expected in phase 3. The inference would be, therefore, that the boundary wall with a northward step predates the construction of phase 3 and thus was in existence in phase 2.

If some of the limits of the site had already been set during the life of the phase 2 building, then some structural continuity may also be suggested in the plan of the buildings. The possibility that further build-ings had been lost from the north and west of the excavated phase 2 building has already been discussed. If the house had attained a full quadrangular form by the time of the fire that destroyed it (or at least a part of it) towards the end of the 15th century, the rebuilt house of phase 3 may well have been influenced by aspects of the earlier building. Little trace of this was observed, but the influence of a hypothetical predecessor provides a possible explanation of some oddities in the phase 3 plan. The curious junction of the north and west ranges is one example. The failure of the walls to meet at the inner corner could be explained if there was an earlier wall in this position (perhaps wholly of cob in the form suggested for some of the excavated walls in the south range), that provided a limit for the construction of the phase 3 walls (in foundation trenches with stone footings, as has been seen), but which was then subse-quently removed.[46] Such a wall could initially have acted as a dividing wall between the west and north ranges or could have been incorporated into the east wall of a free-standing west range (if the north range came somewhat later in the building sequence of phase 3). The possibility that these ranges were constructed in sequence rather than concurrently might be supported by their different widths and by the unknown nature of the north range. It remains possible that this was a single-storey structure, because of its narrow span, although the wall footings were uniform in depth and width with two-storeyed walls elsewhere in the building. The nature of the junction of the two ranges is also uncertain, although allowing for differential preservation, the configuration here as recovered by excavation is similar to that at the junction of the south and east ranges.

The junction of the south and west ranges also provides a little evidence that the construction of phase 3 may have taken place sequentially. The building materials and styles of masonry were clearly different in the two ranges (*see* Fig 5.22, where 402 and 334 are the large blocks of volcanic trap characteristic of the south range and 323 the smaller blocks of mixed breccia and trap of the west range), but there is no evidence in the archaeology or the standing fabric that the south range stood and was used independently of the west range. A sequence is implied for the construction phase, in which the south range was completed or at least well advanced before the west range was commenced (the same is implied by the details of the roof construction, Chapter 7).

Evidence for fittings within the buildings

Knowledge of the primary layout and subdivision of the standing building was aided by the excavation of the footings for partitions in the south range and the base of the screen in the hall. Some lesser features were also traced by excavation, such as the post for the support of the south-east corner of the parlour ceiling, stone thresholds (*see* Fig 4.7).

Glimpses of late medieval decorative elements of the building

The excavations yielded finds and other materials that enhanced the interpretation of the appearance and decoration of the original building, beyond that which was visible in the surviving building (Chapter 9). The collection of excavated architectural fragments complemented masonry features surviving in the building and fragments recovered from the fabric during repairs. This provided evidence of stonework features of high quality (windows, string courses, architectural sculpture) of types that had not survived in the fabric. Many fragments of ceramic paving tiles were recovered by excavation, generally from late contexts. Again, these extended a collection observed and recorded in the standing fabric, usually in contexts associated with alterations and patching up after the demolition of phase 8. Together, these collections strongly suggest that one of the vanished portions of the building possessed tile-paved floors. A further class of material represented only in the excavated collection of finds was moulded plasterwork. Although none survived in the standing building, the few fragments from the excavation of the eastern courtyard were sufficient to show that the building must have received at least one ceiling (or conceivably an overmantel) with moulded plaster decoration in the later 16th or 17th century.

Dating

Evidence for the dating of the construction of the building is reviewed in detail elsewhere, since much of it derives from non-excavated sources. Specifically excavated dating evidence comprises groups of pottery from the foundation trenches (Chapter 9, Appendix 1) and the evidence for the terminal dating of the preceding phase (*see above*).

Phase 4: mid-16th-century alterations

Abandonment of the garderobe (Area 3)

The garderobe on the south elevation was abandoned, the pit filled and the superstructure demolished, to be replaced by a door with a small rectangular window above. Both features were of breccia. The fill of the cess pit contained reliable dating evidence suggesting that it went out of use *c* 1550 (Chapter 9). Concentrations of building materials such as plaster, mortar and slate fragments in the fill of the pit suggest that the demolition took place as the pit was filled. The homogeneous fills were semi-waterlogged and contained much organic material as well as part of the sole of a shoe (Chapter 9). Other small finds included window glass and a section of lead came (implying that the garderobe had a glazed window). The patching up of the exterior embrasure to form a doorway (with breccia blocks, *see* Fig 5.8, 21) also incorporated fragments of Normandy ceramic floor tiles (Chapter 9) reused as packing; these materials could also have been used in the finishes of the garderobe.[47] As this activity was the only alteration involving the disturbance of fabric in this phase, as far as can be traced in the surviving structure, there is a good chance that the various building materials derived from the garderobe structure itself.

No features certainly associated with this activity were discovered inside the service rooms (in Area 7). A slot immediately inside the entry to the garderobe (*see* Fig 4.7, 701), interpreted above as part of the primary phase of the building, could equally have related to the doorway of this phase. A number of otherwise unassociated postholes pre-dating phase 6 probably represent secondary activity in the eastern room and thus fall in phases 4 or 5.[48]

Phase 5: late 16th- to early 17th-century alterations

The principal excavated event in this phase was the rebuilding of the structure accommodating the stair in the north-eastern corner of the courtyard. The original stair was narrow and was contained partly within the thickness of the wall (and in view of the slight footings may have been of timber). No doubt it was inconvenient in use. The rebuilding was represented by a new wall, 2m out from the wall of the hall enclosing an area approximately 3.5 × 2m (*see* Figs 12.1 and 4.17, section 3, 2272).

The structure had an earth floor inside and a re-laid exterior surface of stony clay (*see* Fig 4.17, section 3, 2358). This sequence represented the construction of a new stair, perhaps a framed structure with an open well (rather than a room of some other function). While the northern bay of the hall remained in position, the north range was standing and a ?gallery was serving the first-floor rooms of the north and west ranges; a stair in this position was important for circulation within the building. Dating of this phase is based on initial dating of finds sealed by the new wall and in general architectural terms it would not be surprising to find stairs rebuilt on a more spacious scale in the years around 1600.[49]

Phase 6: the Civil War occupation of Bowhill, mid-17th century

Analysis of the standing fabric produced no features attributable to this phase. In this instance, therefore, the excavation provided unique physical traces of an historical event.

Service rooms in the south range
Earlier features were sealed by a widespread deposit of approximately mid-17th-century date (Fig 4.15, 688 and 725) laid to raise the floor level in the service rooms to the west of the parlour. This layer was deposited around the base of the partition dividing the two service rooms and so demonstrably pre-dates the removal of that partition and the movement of the parlour screen a bay to the

Figure 4.15
Plan of deposits associated with the Civil War period, phase 6 (scale 1:250) (line drawing by Tony Ives).

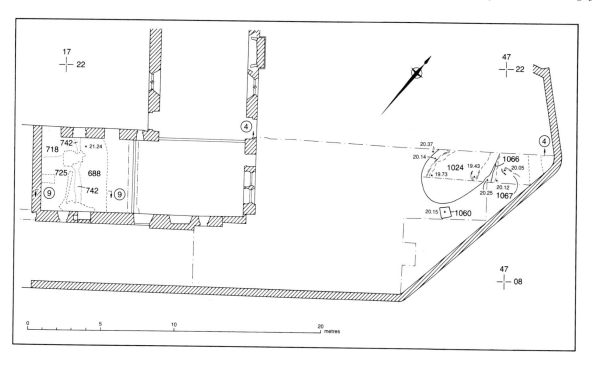

west;[50] it may, of course, belong to the same overall phase of activity. A small group of sherds and clay-pipe material dating to 1620–50 was recovered from this deposit, in addition to six lead musket balls and a quantity of lead window cames (Chapter 9). These finds help to identify a specific context for this activity in the period of the Civil War, a time when lead shot could be expected to be circulating freely on the site and was perhaps being manufactured as well. Whatever the significance of the finds of musket balls, they do surely point to a time when lead was needed for making shot and the associated cames may well have been collected for this purpose.[51]

Defensive ditch of the Civil War period in the eastern courtyard

The main discovery of the excavation in the east courtyard in 1992 was the identification of the rounded terminal of a large and shallow ditch between 11 and 16m to the east of the standing building (Fig 4.16; *see also* Fig 4.15, 1024). This provided some clues to the problems of the south-east range outlined above, as well as a new dimension to the history of the site. The ditch measured 3.5m wide and up to 0.75m surviving depth. To this should be added the depth removed by the 19th-century cultivation trenches (at least another 0.25m), plus whatever additional height/cover provided by earthworks. These substantial dimensions are similar to ditches known to belong to earthwork defences (that is, complemented by earthen ramparts) of the Civil War period. Examples of such ditches were excavated on several sites in Exeter in the late 1980s, such as Magdalen Street and the Acorn roundabout, outside the South Gate,[52] and the ABC cinema, outside the East Gate.[53] The ditch was filled with redeposited clay, plausibly the back-filled rampart material, which contained material of late 17th- to 18th-century date (Fig 4.17, section 4, 1026), and the upper fill material of 18th-century date (1028).[54]

The discovery of this ditch at Bowhill provides a glimpse of the fortification of the house as a Parliamentary fort during the final siege of Exeter in 1646.[55] The ditch also fulfilled one of the aims of the excavation, albeit in a secondary and unexpected manner, by providing a limit for the extent of the south-east range. Since it can be demonstrated that the ditch and associated earthwork ramparts did not surround the site, they are unintelligible if they did not run up to a building. Thus it can be assumed that the ditch terminal plus any associated earthworks abutted one or other of the structural elements of the south-east range, presumably the easternmost surviving element. A problem of interpretation arises from not knowing quite what form the building took at this time. The Bucks' engraving provides the strongest clues, but this view was taken 90 years after the Civil War. Further collapse or demolition of structures in this interval is more than likely.

There is some internal evidence for just this in the form of two high-quality Beer-stone architectural fragments recovered from the fill of the ditch in contexts likely to pre-date the second quarter of the 18th century (and the drawing by the Buck brothers). The lower fill of the ditch (*see* Fig 4.17, section 4, 1025) contained two large architectural fragments, both of Beer stone, which (assuming that they were from Bowhill, rather than imported from elsewhere) indicate a standard of ornament higher than any that survives *in situ* in the building (Chapter 9, catalogue nos 110 and 119). An extension of the boundary wall, with oriel windows such as the one shown by the Bucks, could provide a provenance for such fragments. The window mullion

Figure 4.16
Excavation of the eastern courtyard in 1992; the terminal of the Civil War ditch in foreground, looking west (photograph by Peter Stead; EMAFU 1988/22).

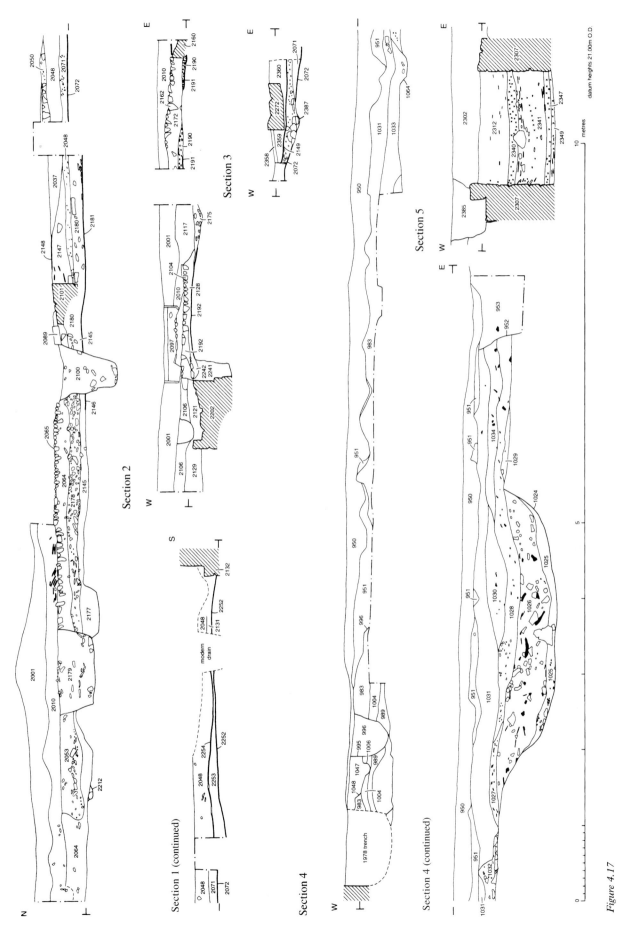

Figure 4.17 Selected sections 1–5 (scale 1:50) (line drawing by Tony Ives).

would be consistent with either the oriel or the tall bay window shown as surviving in 1736, while the shaft is the sort of fitting which ornamented the interior reveals of such structures.

A number of other Beer-stone architectural fragments were recovered from this area (Chapter 9, catalogue nos 115, 117 and 118), mostly from the foundation trench for the modern boundary wall (*see* Fig 4.23, 979). Although more modest in scale, they provide evidence for the variety of fittings of the building, including another mullion fragment with simpler mouldings and a number of small stone paviours. Given their provenance the fragments could be derived from the south-east range or a context in the standing building.

Phase 7: Enlargement of the parlour and rearrangement of the service room(s), late 17th century

The parlour was extended to the west by one bay into the area occupied by the eastern service room. This involved: the movement of the partition forming the west wall of the parlour from its original position beneath beam 4 to a new position beneath beam 5; the insertion of a pair of larger high transomed (cross) windows, characteristic of the late 17th century, in the south wall; and the blocking of a primary doorway leading into the pentice in the north wall, which clashed with the new position of the screen (Chapters 5 and 6). This area subsequently received the same treatment as the parlour itself and so suffered the loss of contemporary deposits (*see above*). The bay to the west retained a little stratigraphic evidence for the removal of the partition. This took the form of a demolition layer filling the channel resulting from the removal of the sleeper wall of the central partition of the service rooms (Fig 4.18, section 9; *see also* Fig 4.15, 742) and the cut for the parlour screen in its new position (Fig 4.19, 829). The deposit associated with the removal of the screen (742) was distinctive, containing a high proportion of crushed plaster fragments. The cut (829) was not well preserved where it was seen in excavation, as it had been modified and damaged when the screen had been removed from this position, *c* 1985, to be reset further east. This phase is dated by its stratigraphic relationship to the deposits of phase 6 and by the nature of the parlour windows (in position by the time of the 1736 engraving).

Period III: decline and contraction of the house, phases 8–11

Phase 8: demolition and rebuilding, *c* 1800

The widespread phase of demolition, alteration and retrenchment at the end of the 18th century (here called phase 8) represented a distinctive horizon in both the standing building and the excavated deposits. The widespread distribution of features associated with this phase, the laying of new cobbled surfaces, the ubiquity of the building materials used, the common incidence of reused building materials derived from the demolition and the fact that the house achieved something close to its surviving form at this phase combine to make phase 8 an important and easily defined horizon in the relative and the absolute chronologies of the site.

Dating evidence
Extensive finds of pottery in deposits of this phase yield a date range of *c* 1780–1820, although there is little possibility of further refinement within this bracket.[56] Historical and cartographic materials help to narrow the range. It is known that the Lucombe family occupied the house until just after the death of William Lucombe in 1794 and the end of their long period of tenure (from 1740) provides the most probable context for such a phase of work (*see* Chapter 3). The house was depicted in its reduced form, with only three ranges and the projecting structures omitted, on the large-scale surveyor's drawing for the first edition of the 1" Ordnance Survey map, dated 1801.[57] The combined evidence thus implies a date range for the main period of alteration of *c* 1795–1801.

The south range
The parlour
Few later features survived in the parlour. The floor level was reduced on the construction of a ventilated suspended floor in the ?19th century and this action had removed all traces of older floors. A posthole in the south-east corner immediately beneath the south end of beam 1 (*see* Fig 4.7, 606) has been attributed to phase 3 (*see* p 53). This could belong to any intermediate phase between phases 3 and 8, however, or be related to measures to support the beam during the demolition of the south-east range and the construction of the blocking

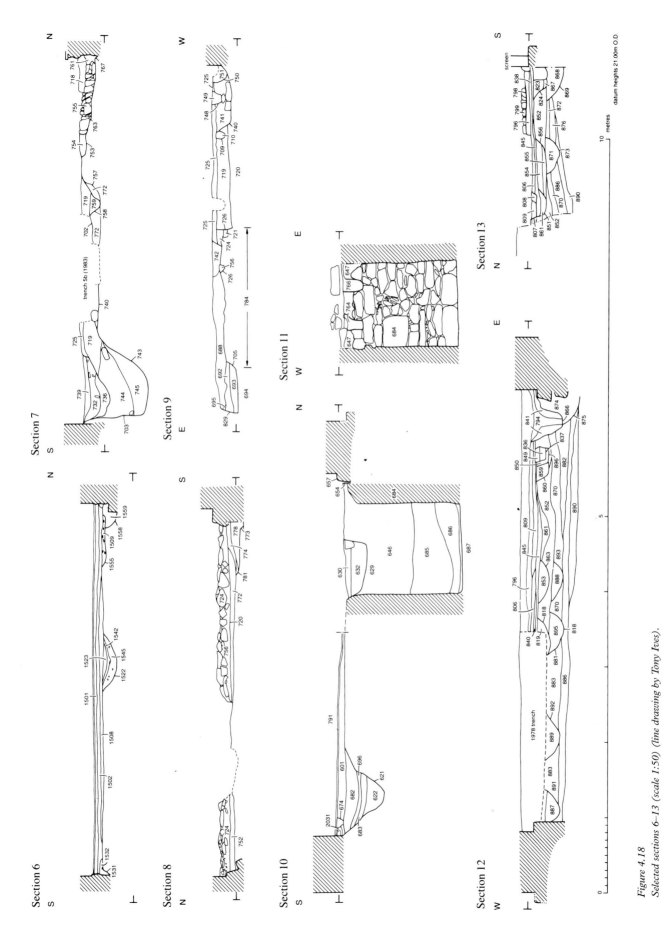

Figure 4.18

Selected sections 6–13 (scale 1:50) (line drawing by Tony Ives).

wall in phase 8 (*see* Figs 5.8 and 6.22, 253).[58] Otherwise, a short sequence of deposits survived in the fireplace. A thin mortar surface on top of the wall footings may have represented the remains of the bedding for an original hearth.[59] This was capped by the rubble base for a later hearth of broken granite slabs.[60]

The service rooms
Other small pits and postholes were recorded in Areas 7 and 8, but there is no clear dating evidence by which to assign them to a specific phase.[61] Since no function is suggested by their form or contents, no clear relationship to the standing fabric can be seen and since they occupy a late stage in the stratigraphic sequence, they can only be assigned to an indeterminate 'post-medieval' phase (that is, probably phases 8 or 9).

West service room
No trace of the insertion of the fireplace in the north-western corner of the room was detected by excavation (Chapter 6). Volcanic-stone paving within and to the south of the fireplace (*see* Fig 4.19, 1623) abutted a brick insert of *c* 1800 and was thus of that phase or later (*see* Fig 6.45), although the paviours may well have been reused from a primary floor (as suggested above). During the demolition and alteration of phase 8, the through passage was narrowed by the partial blocking of the doorways and a new partition constructed in line with the narrowed western reveals. The new reveal of the northern doorway was built on a brick footing (*see* Fig 6.25, 1596) in a shallow cut (*see* Fig 4.19, 1528). The excavation recorded a footing trench for the partition, with further slots for the base of a closet projecting to the west at the north end (1512 and 1515). A number of other small pits and intrusive features were filled with a variety of demolition materials,[62] the most significant of which was a fragment of figure sculpture (1526; *see also* Chapter 9).

The hall, Area 2
Floors and internal features
The surviving evidence for floors in the hall showed a sequence of later floors,[63] comprising:

1. A patch of cobbled floor immediately within the south-western door with a straight southern edge, where it was laid up to the north face of the screen (Fig 4.20; *see also* Fig 4.19, 2133).

2. Patches of mortar and clay flooring in the northern and central parts of the hall.

3. A rough surface of loam and mortar, with a make-up layer of red clay overlying the earlier cobbles. Another equivalent deposit had lime or mortar in its surface.

4. Isolated individual stones of a paved floor (of volcanic trap) lying on the combined makeup layers of 2 and 3 (2036).

The cobbled surface can be satisfactorily interpreted as representing a discrete and separate floor. The remainder is suggested as the bedding for a paved floor, perhaps re-laid on several occasions and finally largely removed in the 19th or 20th century. The floor probably represented a palimpsest of successive materials (cobbles, paviours and slabs), re-laid and patched on numerous occasions, while the hall was used as a barn in the post-medieval phases. The original floor of the hall probably left little trace on its removal (if it was flagged). Later replacements involved the relaying of bedding at the same level (at or slightly above the top of the projecting wall footings) and eradicated all traces of the original floor. The paviours surviving in isolation (2036) may thus represent a trace of an older (or the original) floor, if they were not brought in from another part of the site.[64]

There are difficulties in attempting to fit the sequence into the overall phasing of the site. The limited dating evidence from hall and screens passage suggested a late dating of the whole sequence.[65] The stratigraphic sequence of deposits as outlined above is clear, but bears little relation to phased work in the standing fabric. The one potential link lies in the hall fireplace, which was reduced in size and then blocked altogether. The evidence of masonry and mortar suggests that the final blocking took place in phase 8, since the mortar was of the ubiquitous red white-speckled variety and the blocking contained a moulded Beer-stone fragment (Chapter 9, catalogue no. 112, as well as other building materials) that could have been derived from the demolition works of phase 8. The narrowing of the fireplace perhaps took place in the 18th century, effectively phase 7. The stone of the blocking was associated with a pit which cut layer 2059 (not on plan, part of the surface in 2, *see above*), with the implication that the first cobbled surface (1) and possibly that succeeding make-up layer 2 could be assigned to phase 7 and the make-up layers (possibly 2 and 3–4) belonged to phases 8 and 9, that is, were broadly 19th century in date. It is also possible that the cobbled surface was laid in phase 8, in view of the ubiquity of cobbled surfaces in the reorganisation of this phase; equally the whole sequence could have taken place within phase 9. Various intrusive features, mainly in the northern half of the hall and cutting layers 2003/2023/2059 (see Fig 4.19), certainly should be assigned to phase 9 (see Fig 12.2). Many contained very late material (such as brick) and represent a phase when the hall may have been semi-derelict. Some of the postholes may have been used for the supporting struts of the inserted floor in the hall, which was constructed in phase 9.

Screens passage

The paved floor and the screen were removed in phase 8 (c 1800). A levelling layer of soil with slate and mortar fragments was spread over the whole area (see Fig 4.18, section 13, 796) to act as the bedding for a cobbled surface to the passage (see Fig 4.19, 799), with a central gap for a row of paving slabs. The cobbling of this surface was well laid and similar to the pavements in the central courtyard and the kitchen (see below). It is thus assigned to phase 8 or 9. Various postholes and other intrusive features intervened before the laying of the cobbles.[66]

West range: kitchen

A well-preserved floor of tightly laid cobbles bedded in clay survived over two-thirds of the room including the fireplace and was revealed on the removal of the modern cement floor (Fig 4.21; see also Fig 4.19, 1664).[67] The floor was of similar style and composition to the cobbled surfaces in the central courtyard and so it was assigned to phase 8. One large area of patching was noted inside the east window (see Fig 4.19, 1658), as well as other smaller repairs. Excavation was halted at this level rather than destroy the floor.

The central courtyard, Area 1

The sequence in the central courtyard can be subdivided into three: the demolition of the west (?and north) ranges (along with major demolition works elsewhere in the building); the construction of a new building in the north-east corner of the yard and the laying of a cobbled surface over much of the yard (including the site of the west range); and contemporary, or slightly later, deposits on the site of the north range.

Figure 4.20
Cobbled surface in the hall (detail) (photograph by Stephen Dunmore; EBO78/BW3/5).

Figure 4.21
The kitchen in 1993, with cobbled floor of phase 8 (photograph by David Garner; EH B934831).

Demolition

Substantial layers of clay and mixed material intervened between the primary surfaces and the cobbled surfaces belonging to phase 8. Although some of this accumulation could be attributed to processes of soil formation over a period of time, much of the deposit represented the demolition of the cob walls of the north and west ranges in the preliminary works of this phase.[68] As a result the ground level increased between 0.15 and 0.4m over the whole courtyard (see Fig 4.17, section 1, 2064, 2147 and 2048, and section 2, 2128 and 2172), with a tendency to be thicker on the north and west and to thin out towards the south and east.[69]

Figure 4.22
Courtyard, Area 1, the phase 8 cobbled surface exposed in 1977 (photograph by Stephen Dunmore; EBO77/BW1/9).

Rebuilding and new cobbled surfaces

A new building was constructed within the angle of the east and (former) north ranges, utilising for its north wall a section of the south wall of the north range (which was retained for the purpose) and abutting the west wall of the hall (*see* Fig 4.19). The building extended *c* 5.5m west and *c* 4.5m south, to the outer limits of the walls (the inner faces had not survived). It was furnished in its south wall with a large fireplace with an oven base projecting to the rear (2101 and 2213). The wall footings contained large blocks of breccia as well as volcanic stone and the hearth base was of brick (2089); the walls were dug into the underlying earth layers by only 0.1m or so, but there were no formal foundation trenches. The nature of the walls above was not clear. They could have been built of brick or they could have been timber framed, although the fireplace and chimney stack must have been of solid materials.

The new building clearly functioned as a kitchen or bakehouse. Since the original kitchen in the west range continued in use, the duplication suggests that this was the time at which the house was formally split into two dwellings.[70]

The new kitchen received a floor of neatly laid cobbles (Fig 4.22; *see also* Fig 4.19, 2065). The exterior yard surfaces were treated in the same way (*see* Fig 4.13), with pitched cobbled surfaces incorporating drainage gullies around the building and leading off to the south-east. The cobbling ran over the site of the east wall of the former west range and in part extended northwards to the boundary wall of the site. A further drainage gully ran directly south above the interior face of the former wall of the west range (*see* Fig 4.19, 2173). The cobbled surfaces were well preserved around the new kitchen and in the northern half of the courtyard, but deteriorated towards the south, where later activity had disturbed the

Figure 4.23
Plan of garden features in the eastern courtyard, phase 9 (scale 1:100) (line drawing by Tony Ives).

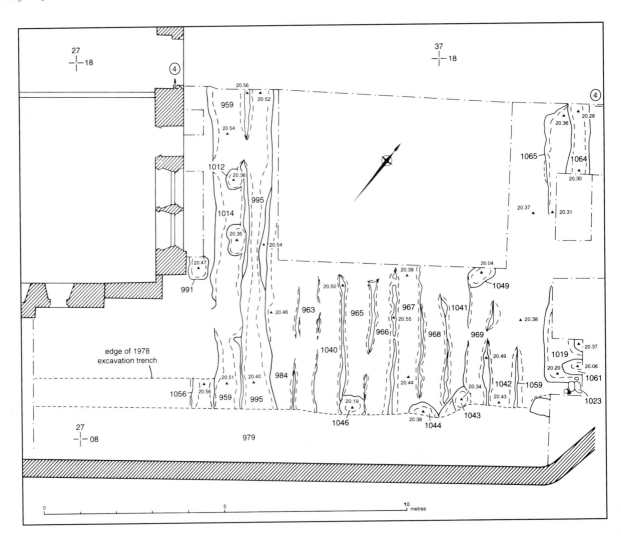

pavement.[71] Traces of the cobbling to the west (*see* Fig 4.19, 1768) show that the surface once ran up to the western boundary wall, but the site of the north range was excluded from the cobbled area (*see below*). The cobbled work was very similar to the floor in the kitchen (*see* Fig 4.21).

Site of the north range

This area was separated from the remainder of the courtyard by the partially standing wall of the former north range, now incorporated into the new kitchen. The deposits here were markedly simpler in character, being composed of layers of dark garden soil and demolition material (*see* Fig 4.17, section 1, 2053 and 2064). The upper surface contained spreads of stony material, pebbles and slate fragments (*see* Fig 4.19, 2053 and 2157). Presumably this area remained open, but without formal surfacing, at the time the cobbled yard surfaces were laid elsewhere.

Phase 9: 19th-century alterations

Excavation exposed many deposits relating to the later phases of the sequence, especially in the central and eastern courtyards. Major features appear on the small-scale phase plans (*see* Fig 12.2). The main series of features in the eastern courtyard, cultivation trenches belonging to the Bowhill nursery garden, is the only aspect of this phase to be illustrated in a detailed plan (Fig 4.23). The full sequence is described in the archive reports.

The central courtyard, Area 1
Demolition of kitchen

The kitchen of *c* 1800 appears to have lasted for less than 50 years and finds from the demolition levels suggest that it could have been demolished as early as 1820.[72] The removal of the building was associated with the robbing of the remains of the wall of the north range which had supported it (*see* Fig 4.19, 2153, 2169 and 2179) and with numerous deposits of demolition material, some directly related to the kitchen building, others representing more general spreading of demolition and makeup material over the yard. Among these was a deposit in which fragments of roof slates appeared in a heavy concentration in the centre of the area (*see* Fig 4.17, section 1, 2010).[73]

Later garden and yard deposits

A layer of makeup, debris and garden soil covered much of the area (2010). In the course of the 19th century, numerous postholes, gullies, new drains and other

Figure 4.24
Excavation of the phase 9 building on the site of the west range in October 1994, looking north-west (photograph by David Garner; EH B945339).

Figure 4.25
The eastern courtyard excavation 1992 – 19th-century cultivation trenches, looking south-east (photograph by Peter Stead; EMAFU 1988/32).

features were cut into this layer. Some of the postholes may represent an ephemeral structure on the site of the north range (*see* Fig 12.2, phase 9). Others roughly parallel to the west wall of the hall may represent a fence or similar linear structure. Some if not all of these features could as well fit into the succeeding phase (10), that is, be 20th century in date. A brick boiler house or wash house (with the brick base for a copper) was built against the west wall of the former west range (Fig 4.24; *see also* Fig 4.19, 1771/1772). This structure was still standing in 1969, but was demolished in the alterations proposed in that year.[74]

The eastern courtyard, Area 3

A series of closely spaced parallel trenches, 0.7m wide on average, were cut into the natural subsoil over much of the excavated area (Fig 4.25; *see also* Fig 4.23). They had wholly removed the earlier levels, such as wall footings or other structural traces of the south-east range, and even traces of the demolition activity of phase 8. Most of the trenches had a primary fill of white lime/lime mortar that may have been deliberately used for its value as a soil improver. The main fill of the features was garden soil.

Material recovered from the fills of the trenches indicated a 19th century or later date.[75] They are assigned to phase 9 here so that still later features can be illustrated (*see* Fig 12.2).

Figure 4.26
Excavation within the
annexe in July 1994,
looking south. Note the two
walls on different align-
ments (photograph by
David Garner; EH
B943785).

The south range
Parlour
Photographs of the building during stripping (*see*, for example, Figs 6.20, 6.21, 6.26 and 6.27) show that the latest floor in the parlour was a suspended board floor of modern character and thus of phase 9 or 10. This had truncated the sub-floor deposits by approximately 0.3m. At the same time a semicircular projecting hearth of concrete was added to the fireplace.

West service room
The phase 8 features were covered by a floor of lime mortar;[76] this survived well only in the east half of the room. Elsewhere it was removed with the 20th-century cement floor (phase 10, *see below*). The laying of the mortar floor post-dated the removal of the staircase within the passage (Chapter 6) and may have occurred as a late sub-phase of phase 9 or just conceivably in the early years of the 20th century.

The annexe, Area 10
This area (*see* Fig 4.1) was the subject of a small excavation during the repair of the annexe. The operation also revealed the west elevation of the south range for the first time (*see* Fig 5.22). Aside from a few early features, the results of Area 10 wholly related to the sequence of the annexe building in phases 9–11 (19th and 20th centuries). Two successive structures stood in this position. The building was first

constructed with wall footings of volcanic stone on an orientation square onto the Dunsford Hill frontage. This building had a cobbled interior surface (Fig 4.26; *see also* Fig 4.19, 1732 and 1723).

No dating evidence was recovered from the excavation, but the structures can be dated by cartographic and photographic sources. A structure is shown at the southwest corner of the building on the tithe map of 1841, and on the sewer map of 1850.[77] This is presumed to be the first phase which is assigned to phase 9, since it abutted repairs of phase 8.

Western courtyard
Metalled yard surfaces were seen in trenches 1, 3 and 4 of those dug for new drainage and related purposes in 1993–4 (Fig 4.27; *see also* Fig 4.1), representing the roughly paved surface of an agricultural yard of the 19th century (dating by pottery within the surfaces) and thus assigned to phase 9. The same configuration survived in 1945, as shown by the aerial photograph (*see* Fig 3.4). Trench 2, which spanned the site of the barn, contained no ancient deposits. This showed that the demolition process and the associated levelling for a car park in 1972 (phase 11) had removed all trace of structures and surfaces at this point.

Trench 5 exposed the stone footings of the former northern boundary wall, now rebuilt; these were of phase 8 or later, since they included brick fragments. The blocking of a doorway (shown on the aerial photograph, Fig 3.4, and by the OS in the 1950s, but not on later editions of the 1960s) was identified, enabling this feature to be plotted in relation to other observations (*see* Fig 1.1). The remaining trenches revealed no informative deposits, other than levels on the natural subsoil.

Figure 4.27
Service trenches dug for
drains in the western court-
yard, December 1993,
looking west (photograph
by David Garner; EH
B936794).

Phase 10: 20th-century features up to 1969

Central courtyard

The area was firstly cultivated as a garden in this phase and then became largely derelict. Paths of tarmac or concrete were laid along the east side of the yard and above the course of the former wall of the west range (*see* Fig 4.17, section 2, 2097). Drains were dug to drain the southern half of the area. A considerable depth of topsoil developed (sections 1 and 2, 2001). Two irregularly shaped hollows were probably caused by the roots of trees.[78]

Eastern courtyard

After further deposition of garden soils, traces of a further sequence of parallel cultivation trenches were excavated at a higher level (*see* Fig 4.18, section 12).[79] These may be a part of the system of planting visible on the 1945 aerial photograph (*see* Fig 3.4). Later still, and therefore belonging to phases 11 and 12, were features relating to the most recent courtyard surfaces and the rebuilding of the boundary wall in 1985. A single trench running along the east wall of the east range may have represented this phase or some other phase of ditch digging. This has been (rather arbitrarily) allocated to phase 10 here. Other late features included a collection of small pits and postholes, very slight traces of a cobbled surface or path to the south of the south range and various modern drains.[80]

Interior

Concrete floors were laid in the west service room and kitchen at the west end of the building in phase 10 (dated to the period 1957–69 by photographs)[81] and in the service rooms of the south range in the restaurant period, phase 11 (*see* Fig 6.36). A tarmac floor was laid in the hall and the flag and cobble surface of the screens passage was patched and repaired, both probably done in the 1950s. This was the first layer to be lifted in the excavations of 1977.

Area 10, the annexe

The annexe building was rebuilt in the later 19th or 20th century; the east and west walls of the building (and the north wall, which had not survived) were rebuilt on an alignment slightly to the west of the earlier structure and the main building (*see* the standing (hatched) walls in Fig 4.19). A longitudinal (north–south) wall on stone footings divided the building (illustrated at small scale in Fig 12.2) and probably served as the footing for a stair.

No contemporary surface had survived from this phase. Still later a fireplace was inserted in the west wall and was itself subsequently blocked. The structure appears on mid-20th-century maps and is documented in photographic coverage of the 1950s and 1960s (for example, Figs 2.13 and 2.16). This version of the annexe, in an extended plan of *c* 1969 (*see* Fig 12.2), survived to be rebuilt in 1994.[82]

Later phases, 11 and 12, 1969–1976 and post-1976

The latest phases were not examined by archaeology. The main effect on the building of phase 11 was a number of radical and destructive alterations and demolitions. These are covered in the description of the standing fabric, where relevant. The demolition of the barn is perhaps the most notable single event, although this had left virtually no archaeological trace.

General discussion of the excavations

The nature of the archaeology of the site

Attempts to interpret the nature and extent of Bowhill from its buried archaeology alone are severely constrained by limited preservation. The earliest deposits had survived only within the standing building, where they were (partially) protected from later disturbance. Late and intrusive deposits predominated over most of the external areas of the site. The severe truncation associated with the demolition work of phase 8 and the nursery gardening of phases 9 and 10, as well as the depredations of the restaurant period (phase 11), are to be regretted in that many of the losses to the archaeology of the site have occurred in relatively recent times.

Although the sequence of pre-building phases is represented in the buried archaeology, it would be impossible without the evidence of the standing fabric to reconstruct an accurate picture of the sequence of alterations to the building in the period from the construction in phase 3 to the major demolitions of phase 8. Nevertheless some aspects of the building's history were better represented in the below-ground archaeology than in the standing fabric – the Civil War fortification of the site provides a notable example (phase 6). Moreover the results of the examination of the standing fabric would have been the poorer had they not been supported and complemented by those of excavation.

The relationship between excavation and analysis of the standing fabric

The phasing and structural history of the building derived from the fabric are consistent in general with the sequence obtained by excavation, although the two are never completely coincident: it is a matter of chance whether minor structural phases are represented in both classes of evidence.[83] In fact, with the exception of phase 6 (*see above*), the main phases are represented both above and below ground.[84] An instructive approach is to identify gaps in the interpretation of the site that would exist if excavation had been carried out without fabric analysis or vice versa. The absence of surviving early floor levels and the preponderance of later interior features partly obscure the picture of early post-construction phases of alteration in the building. These phases are thus better represented in the standing fabric, although certain aspects of the mid- and late-16th-century phases are better known from excavated data (for example, the removal of the garderobe in the south range and the alterations to the stair in the north-east corner of the central courtyard). It is difficult to envisage the scale and the high quality of the fabric and fittings of the building on the basis of the excavated deposits alone. This applies especially to the carpentry of the roofs and the parlour ceiling, but also (to a lesser extent) to that of screens: the presence of screens could have been predicted in places from the sleeper walls, but the nature of their carpentry would have remained obscure, as would such matters as the paired doorways. The excavated architectural fragments and other materials would have provided a reliable guide to the presence of good-quality fenestration, although the sample was not fully representative of the extant features of the building.[85] In the interpretation of excavated structures in general, Bowhill provides a warning against underestimation of the fittings of a building on the basis of excavated remains alone. This is directly applicable to the interpretation of the excavated remains of the phase 2 building on the site.

The combined excavation and fabric survey of buildings has become relatively common in recent years, although there is still little examination of the vagaries of the different types of evidence. In practice, the opportunity to combine stripping of the standing fabric of a building with the excavation of its interior and environs also remains rare. A list of six or so 'recorded and excavated farmhouses in Devon' was compiled by Brown and Laithwaite in a recent paper.[86] This list could be extended to include other classes of standing building in Devon where excavation and fabric recording have been combined: the medieval Exe Bridge, Exeter;[87] the Quay House, Exeter;[88] Okehampton Castle;[89] Buckfast Abbey;[90] Buckland Abbey;[91] and St Katherine's Priory, Polsloe, Exeter.[92] Notable examples of similar approaches to the study of standing buildings may be quoted in published work at St Oswald's Priory, Gloucester;[93] St Mary's Church, Deerhurst, Gloucestershire;[94] Gainsborough Old Hall, Lincolnshire;[95] and All Saints' Church, Brixworth, Northamptonshire.[96] As these examples show, the application of archaeological techniques to the analysis of standing buildings has long been a standard procedure in the work of some archaeologists.[97] Although this is, however, by no means universally the case across the country, this type of work, long neglected in many places, has been the subject of a relatively recent awakening.[98]

Even though there are many benefits to be derived from the joint approach here advocated and few would choose to ignore the opportunity presented by standing fabric, purely from the point of view of the quality of excavated evidence, the presence of the standing building can sometimes impede the full recovery of evidence by excavation. The compromise solution described by Brown and Laithwaite for Northwood Farm, Christow, Devon, perhaps represents the optimum combination of recording and excavation. There the farmhouse was ruinous and had been photographically recorded some years prior to the excavation, when some of the timberwork remained in position. It was then excavated after further decay.[99]

Lessons for consideration in the excavation and recording of a standing building

Bowhill was excavated in a rather piecemeal series of trenches in the course of some 16 years. Excavations were planned according to a variety of imperatives, ranging from wholly research-motivated episodes to trenches prompted by works requirements or by the need to clear sections of the site of their archaeology prior to insertion of services and other new works. Had it been possible in 1977 to know quite how much would have been done by the time the project was completed in 1994, the many advantages of doing the work as a single programme of excavation would have been clear. No doubt this would have been spread over several campaigns, but it would have enjoyed a coordinated approach, a single numbering system and the benefits in interpretation of wide exposure. The advantages of the simultaneous exposure of excavated strata and stripped standing fabric, although clear, should also be emphasised in this context. At Bowhill the two invariably took place separately and the relationships were assembled afterwards from the paper record. This too is a conflict that could have been resolved by closer attention to programming.

Nevertheless there were some advantages in the approach actually adopted in that knowledge of the building improved in the course of the investigations of the 1980s and the later phases of excavations gave results that benefited from the refined interpretative framework available. Stratigraphic understanding of Exeter sites (and familiarity with local conditions) improved in the intervening years, as did (in some ways) the actual techniques of excavation and recording. The later excavations also benefitted from improved knowledge of pottery in Exeter (*see* Allan in Chapter 9) and the consequent greater confidence in its handling and interpretation.

The extent of drawn records of the standing building provides another key lesson. Drawings began in the early years with outline drawings that were added to progressively as the building was stripped and as more of the fabric became accessible

for survey. Given the need for drawings of some sort at an early stage and the gradual, staged programme of works, this sequential approach was inevitable, but some duplication of effort was unavoidable as a result.[100] Techniques in the recording of ancient monuments have developed greatly in recent years. Long projects such as this have few opportunities to incorporate new methods as they become available, because of the need to continue to work in ways established at the outset. Were such a project to occur again,[101] photogrammetric and computer-aided drawing methods would certainly be used to produce and store drawings for record and works purposes. The present report, in which nearly all of the drawings were done by hand, represents something of a swansong for traditional drawn records.

Archaeological implications for the future management of the site

Although much of the site has been archaeologically examined it cannot be assumed that Bowhill is now 'cleared' of its archaeology. Several areas remain almost wholly unexamined (such as parts of the east and west courtyards) or retain unexcavated baulks running across them (such as the central courtyard). Within the building several areas remain unexcavated, including most of the northernmost bay of the east range and some areas of the great hall. The extent and position of unexcavated parts of the site are summarised in Fig 4.28, from which it will be seen that unexcavated areas account for some 60 per cent of the area within the boundaries. Although this

Figure 4.28
Plan of the site showing unexcavated areas to illustrate the section on the 'Archaeological implications for the future management of the site' (scale 1:500) (line drawing by Tony Ives).

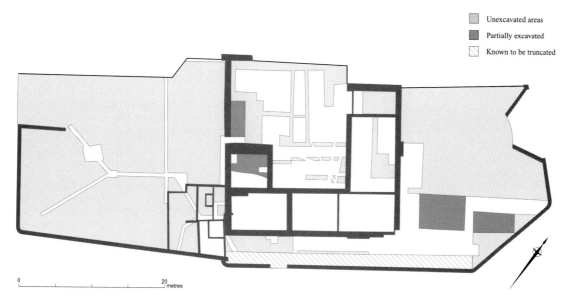

Unexcavated areas

Partially excavated

Known to be truncated

0   20
                     metres

represents a large proportion of the site, several substantial areas have been sampled by trenching and the archaeological levels have been shown (or are suspected) to be disturbed or truncated. Much of the western courtyard, although apparently unexcavated, was truncated when the barn was demolished and the car park made in 1972. Likewise much, if not all, of the eastern courtyard was probably truncated by the intrusion of 19th-century cultivation trenches. The representation on this plan of an area as 'unexcavated' means that any further disturbance of the ground should still be monitored archaeologically, although the qualifications expressed above mean that few pre-19th-century deposits are expected to survive in the outer courtyards.

Detailed matters with archaeological implications for future work at the site include the following:

1. Foundation trenches were not generally excavated, partly because they tended to be very close to the faces of the wall footings, but also because where wall footings were exposed they were not removed (unless there were works reasons for doing this). Any future disturbance will therefore have to take into account the possibility of encountering such deposits and the retrieval of finds from these features.

2. Stone footings survive below ground for the west wall of the west range, the garderobe and partition walls. Stone culverts/drains also remain below ground, where they were not cut away by service trenches.

3. In the kitchen, the 18th- to 19th-century cobbled floor was left intact and not removed by excavation; earlier deposits are known to survive beneath the northern two-thirds of this room.

4. The boundary walls of the western courtyard may contain remnants of the fabric of the barn, although they were largely rebuilt in the 1970s.

5. Immediately adjacent areas are also very sensitive archaeologically; little is known of the nature of deposits beneath the streets to west, south and east and the domestic gardens to the north.

Disturbance of any of these areas has the potential to contribute observations relevant to the ancient building and should be monitored closely.

5
The standing building: description and analysis of the exterior

East elevation

In its surviving form (Fig 5.1)[1] the general character of the elevation has lost several prominent elements: the south-east range adjoining to the south; the primary first-floor and gable wall above the east end of the south range; the projecting porch leading into the screens passage with an attached vice to the south; and the first-floor stage of the northern end of the elevation. The porch, the hall and parlour windows, and the prominent chimney stack along with the south-east range to the left suggest that this formed the principal approach and entrance to the building.[2]

The ground-floor stage of the elevation was built of coursed volcanic blocks throughout. In the centre the stone stepped up to the level of the window lintels. The upper walling was of cob, comprising the upper stages of parts of bays 2 and 5 (that is, above the screens passage and the northern-most bay of the hall), the wall top, to both sides of the chimney (repaired in stone above the head of the northern window) and the first floor of the east gable of the south range. The principal windows in the hall were of Beer stone (see Fig 5.1, 411 and 413); the doorway and the parlour windows at the south end were of vesicular or crystalline trap (80, 81 and 86). The chimney stack (2) was almost wholly of breccia, a distinctive construction discussed separately below.

The northern section of wall was heavily modified by repairs and demolition (Fig 5.2; see also Fig 2.9). Nothing survived of the first floor (which was of cob, on the evidence of surviving walling to the south) and the ground floor contained a late doorway with evidence of an earlier window with a wooden frame (Fig 5.3).[3] The present window is a reconstruction of 1985 (Chapter 11). The two 19th-century drawings of this elevation (see Chapter 2 and Fig 2.4) suggest that this area was more derelict at that time, without the lean-to roof seen in 20th-century photographs.[4]

East gable

Original work

Surviving original work comprised the masonry of the base of the wall (see Fig 5.1, 79), the return of the north wall of the south-east range (78), the parlour windows (80 and 81), and the work associated with the stair and the porch (see below). The exterior masonry was of the large, well-squared type seen throughout the stone parts of the building. When standing the north wall of the south-east range would have obscured the southern label stop of the window. The impression of the wall face survived on one of the blocks (Fig 5.4).[5]

The four-light parlour window was a developed form of the single-light, cinque-foil-headed windows of the south range. The mouldings of hood, frame and king mullion were of the same profile. Those of the subsidiary mullion(s) were more slender. The foiled heads surviving in the two northern lights were similar to those of the lancet windows, although the cusps may have been trimmed off. The internal arrangement was substantially more elaborate than other windows of the south range (although there are some similarities with the hall windows). The reveals and king mullion were formed of blocks spanning the full thickness of the wall and both were rebated for shutters and displayed an internal hollow-chamfered moulding (see Fig 6.53). The southern pair of lights was modified by the removal of cinquefoiled heads and mullion and was fitted with a sash window in the later 19th century. The original is shown in the mid-19th-century drawing (see Fig 2.4). The heads of the northern pair are now filled in and the lights fitted with fixed panes.

The gable wall

The east gable wall (seen in plan of floor timbers in Fig 6.28) was missing above the lintel of the ground-floor window. Widespread alterations in brick bonded with the

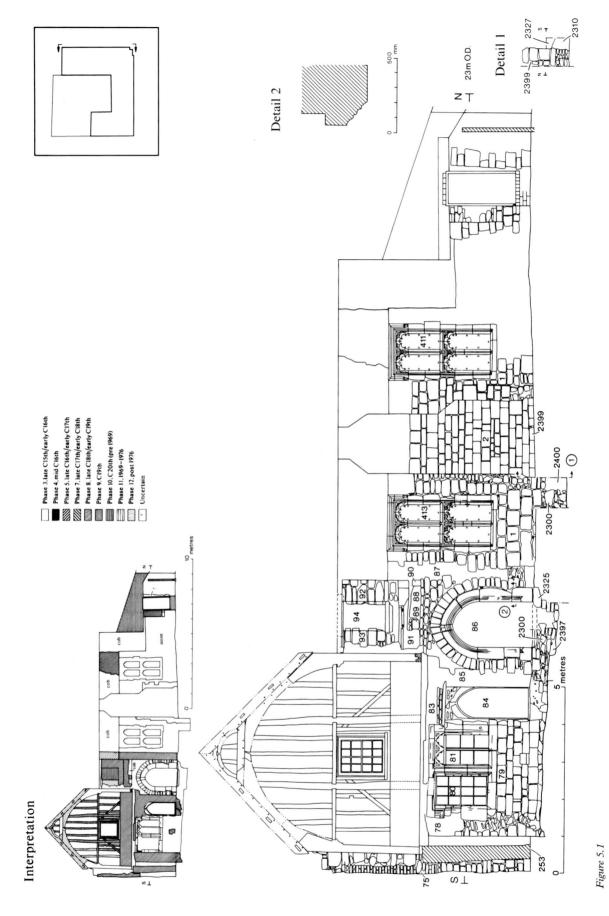

Interpretation

Phase 3. late C15th/early C16th
Phase 4. mid C16th
Phase 5. late C16th/early C17th
Phase 7. late C17th/early C18th
Phase 8. late C18th/early C19th
Phase 9. C19th
Phase 10. C20th (pre 1969)
Phase 11. 1969–1976
Phase 12. post 1976
Uncertain

Detail 2

Detail 1

23m OD.

Figure 5.1

East elevation, exterior; composite of measured survey and outline drawing (upper/north part of hall) (scale 1:100) (line drawing by Tony Ives and Andrew Simm).

distinctive mortar of phase 8 suggested that this loss occurred on the demolition of the south-east range (c 1800). Little direct evidence for the form of the gable wall had survived, but a cob gable wall can probably be inferred on the basis of the following evidence:

1. The variable level of stone walling in the east elevation – the top of stone stepped down towards the south, above the porch, on both exterior and interior. Additionally there was a fragment of primary cob walling surviving (see Fig 5.1, 88) suggesting that the wall continued to the south in this material.
2. The observation of traces of cob dust on the east face of truss I of the great chamber chamber roof.[6]
3. The failure of the gable: a cob super-structure would have been more likely to fail on the demolition of adjacent struc-tures (that is, the south-east range) than a mortared stone wall.[7]
4. The parallel example of the west gable, where evidence survived for a cob super-structure that was also demolished at this phase (see below).

Counter arguments in favour of a stone gable include the predominance of stone at this end of the building (although the use of cob for the gable would demonstrate the equality with which stone and cob were regarded) and the lack of traces of cob on the surviving wall top.[8] These do not, however, outweigh the evidence in favour of a cob wall. The gable wall probably accommodated a large window for the great chamber, possibly a four-light frame similar to that of the parlour below, or a projecting oriel like that proposed for the oriel chamber.

The replacement gable

After the demolition of the gable, a timber-framed assembly was constructed on the line of the inside face of the wall, supported on roof-truss I.[9] The frame (see Fig 5.1) was

Figure 5.2 (below) General view of the east elevation when stripped for re-rendering in May 1993 (the earliest available general shot) and thus after repairs in masonry and cob (photograph by David Garner; EH B930369).

Figure 5.3 (left) The reveal of the east window of the hall store. Note the inner splay and the chase for a timber frame, looking south-west, 1985 (EH C850070).

Figure 5.4 (right) Detail of the scar of the north wall of the south-east range. Note the conflict with the label of the window (DoE unnumbered, c 1981; EH B960399).

based on two unhewn posts of chestnut, with a horizontal rail at the springing of the arch-braces of the principals. Within this was a subdivision of studs and two braces of pine and elm infilled with lath and plaster. The offset at the base was slated over.[10]

The porch and associated fabric

The primary form of the porch

Evidence for the primary form and subsequent development of the area around the main door of the hall is complex (*see* Fig 5.1). Wall scars to north and south of the main door indicated the existence of a projecting porch. The door was set centrally within the porch, while the walls were 0.5m thick and set 0.6m out from the door jambs, giving an internal width for the porch of 2.4m (7' 10½").[11] Spandrels of finished masonry above the door arch showed that the facework was still visible here, that is, that the porch was not vaulted. The masonry terminated in a horizontal upper limit, two courses above the relieving arch. Above this the wall was of cob. Two sockets for beams survived, bearing on the top course of stone (89 and 90), with a small section of primary cob walling between them (88). This rules out a doorway in this position at first-floor level and, thereby, argues against a gallery over the screens passage in the primary arrangement (Chapter 6). To the south the walling was of later cob, but a third beam socket against the north face of the south wall of the porch would have completed a ceiling arrangement. The sockets could represent the roof of a one-storeyed porch, or the floor of a two-storeyed porch. The evidence of the adjacent stair (*see below*) supports the interpretation of a two-storeyed porch, although that of the fabric of the porch itself was poorly preserved. The scar of the south wall did not survive above first-floor level. The north wall scar survived to a height of 0.65m above the uppermost limit of surviving primary cob.[12] This would seem to rule out a return in stone and the width of the wall (0.5m) is rather narrow for a cob wall. Timber-framed first-floor stages to porches that are known in Devon farmhouses provide another possibility.[13] Whichever combination was used, this structure provides another example of the unusual but characteristic juxtaposition of materials in the building. Since there was no first-floor structure within the east range in the primary arrangement, any room above

the porch could only be entered from the vice attached to the side of the porch structure or diagonally from the north-east corner of the chamber.[14]

The stair turret doorway

Immediately to the south of the site of the porch was a narrow arched doorway set in the eastern wall of the parlour (Fig 5.5; *see also* Fig 5.1, 84) and cutting the interior facework (*see* Fig 6.2). The frame was of coarse breccia with a chamfer and simple stops set flush with the inside face of the wall; a rebate showed that the door opened outward (to the east). The embrasure was heavily disturbed and most of its superficial fabric belonged to the phase 8 alterations – principally the facing-up in brick of removed wall scars and rebuilding above the lintel after the removal of the gable, again in brick (*see* Fig 5.1, 83). Despite the disturbances the door appeared to have survived in its intended position and the large blocks of the facework and the frame of the parlour window forming the southern reveal showed signs that they had been dressed off (suggesting that originally they formed an inner quoin). The arrangement of the parlour window, squeezed into the available space between this door and the return wall of the south-east range, showed that this space was so occupied from the first.[15]

The position and orientation of the door, the constricted space and the position hard against the scar of the porch wall suggest that the door gave access into a stair vice attached to the south side of the porch. A stair turret of this sort is most likely to have been placed in the angle of two structures.[16] No evidence of the fabric of such a structure survived the removal of the porch (and the east gable) and all trace of foundations below ground had been removed by 19th-century features (Chapter 4).

If the porch and associated structures were part of the primary plan of the building, why was the door-frame inserted? A similar question arises with the door-frame of

Figure 5.5
The east elevation of the parlour, showing scars for the porch and the stair door (DoE unnumbered, c 1981?; EH B960396).

breccia in the north-west corner of the hall (*see below*), which also served a stair with a role in the primary circulation of the building and was also cut into surrounding fabric. It is possible that the supply of features in a different material (breccia) was the preserve of a separate craftsman. The primary buildings simply would not have worked without stairs in these positions. The puzzle cannot be explained by an earlier-hall theory (Chapter 8), because all the affected structures (wall of the north range, south range and porch) are bonded to the masonry of the hall. The explanation, therefore, must lie in the building process and adaptation of the plan during the work.

Later alterations

The fabric of the porch was removed, the wall scars were refaced and the sockets for the roof timbers were blocked in. The first-floor stage of the wall was rebuilt with blocks of breccia containing a window (*see* Fig 5.1, 94). This fabric incorporated as the sill of the window a large fragment of a breccia block with a hollow order on its lower edge, returning onto one end (Fig 5.6). This fragment can plausibly be interpreted as one of the corbel blocks from the base of the oriel window in the south elevation, cut down and reused here after the destruction of the oriel window (*see* pp 81–2). The other blocks of breccia used here could have been reused from this source. Mortar types suggested that the insertion of the window took place in the same programme of work as the removal of the oriel (phase 8), coinciding with the evidence of extensive alterations to the door to the stair turret at this time. The blocking of the beam sockets contained mortar of the ubiquitous and distinctive composition of phase 8. At a still later point, new cob work was laid above and to the south of the primary cob (*see* Fig 5.1, 91) and this became the base for a slated offset. The area is seen in this form, with the window open, in the mid-19th-century drawings by Townsend (*see* Fig 2.4); the window was blocked by the mid-20th century.[17]

Hall chimney stack

The exterior fabric of the stack, as well as that of the back and sides of the hearth within, was entirely of breccia, in contrast to the adjacent wall masonry.[18] A section excavated at the base of the south side of the stack in 1978 showed that the stack and adjacent walling had independent footings.

Figure 5.6
Detail of the breccia block reused as a window sill above the porch (see Fig 5.2), August 1991 (photograph by Stuart Blaylock; EMAFU 1843/15).

Figure 5.7
Detail of the hall chimney stack, showing the straight join with the hall fabric, January 1981 (DoE J11/2/81).

The same variation in material and breaks in masonry were visible in the wall to either side of the stack, approximately to the level of the transoms of the windows (2.4–2.9m above present ground level; *see* Fig 5.1). The masonry of the upper half of the stack seemed to bond with that of the adjacent wall, when examined after the works were complete in 1987. Photographs taken during the works in 1981, however, appear to suggest that the structural break continued, albeit in a tidier fashion, with the masonry of the stack butting against that of the wall (Fig 5.7). None of the courses matched from stack to adjacent wall. The impression is very much that the chimney stack (and, therefore, the fireplace within) were additions to the east range.[19]

77

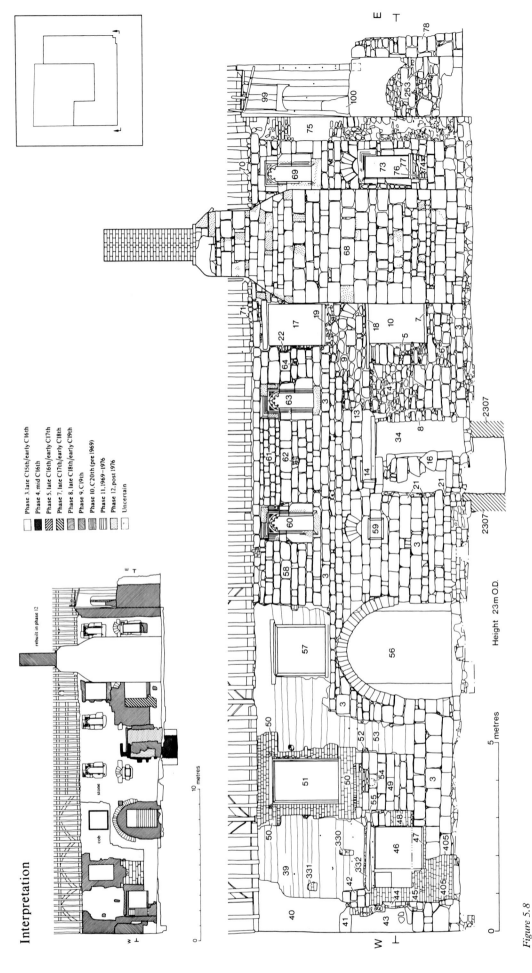

rebuilt in phase 12

cob

stone

10 metres

Phase 3. late C15th/early C16th
Phase 4. mid C16th
Phase 5. late C16th/early C17th
Phase 7. late C17th/early C18th
Phase 8. late C18th/early C19th
Phase 9. C19th
Phase 10. C20th (pre 1969)
Phase 11. 1969-1976
Phase 12. post 1976
Uncertain

Height 23m O.D.

5 metres

0

5 metres

Figure 5.8
South elevation, exterior (scale 1:100) (line drawing by Tony Ives and Andrew Simm).

The excavated evidence discussed above (*see* pp 54–5) suggested that a fireplace and chimney stack were intended from the first. A gap was left as the wall was built, into which the stack was fitted when the walls had reached a certain height. The extent of the crude seam probably represented the height that the construction of the wall had reached when that of the stack and fireplace commenced. After this, construction proceeded in tandem (hence the tidier relationship above the seam). Although much of the evidence suggested that the stack was of secondary construction, one detail confirmed that the insertion took place *during* construction – the cob of the wall top was built over and up to the masonry of the chimney stack,[20] as well as up to and around the feet of the roof trusses.[21] Since the wall-top cob here was continuous with the cob of the end bays, it follows that all the cob of the east elevation was primary work.

South elevation

General character

The elevation (Fig 5.8) was built in stone to its full height from the south-east corner to the through passage, that is as far as the point at which the interior was divided by the cross wall. Primary masonry was of uniform character, with large blocks of volcanic trap evenly coursed, although with courses of uneven depth. To the west the masonry stepped down, first to one course of blocks above the archway, then to footings level to the west of the arch, from which it continued to the west elevation. In this section the footings were at their most characteristic – three courses of large square blocks placed on an offset plinth.[22] The division between cob and masonry was clearer on the inside elevation (*see* Fig 6.22), because the exterior was interrupted by a masonry plinth for the oriel (*see below*) and by later repairs. With these exceptions, the extent of cob versus stone was the same on both sides of the wall.

Some detail of the construction of the cob was recorded in this elevation in that the gradual weathering after the removal of modern roughcast, coupled with close observation, showed the lift lines reflecting the beds in which the cob wall was built up. The surprising aspect of the lifts was their narrowness – as little as 0.15m and never more than 0.5m. It seems possible that the cob courses were built up, course-by-course,

with the masonry to the east, since the recorded bedding lines approximately corresponded to the joints in the masonry (*see* Fig 5.8).[23] Since nowhere else in the building was the cob seen in such detail over a period of time, it is not known whether this detail was typical of all cob work at Bowhill. As thin beds were also observed in an exposed section of the north wall of the south range (*see* Fig 6.47, 193) and in a section of the west wall at ground-floor level (Fig 5.9; *see also* Fig 5.22, section B), the technique may have been more general than specific observations suggest.

There was no trace of original rendering on the south elevation. Survivals elsewhere show that the cob was originally rendered in lime mortar (a sequence of renders on the north wall is described in Chapter 10). Because the building had been stripped and re-rendered more than once, the survival of original rendering depended on chance as well as on a sheltered position.[24] Where mortar render was observed it was of similar composition to the pointing and bedding mortars of the masonry. One notable detail of the pointing was incised or struck pointing in many of the mortar joints – the incision of a narrow line in the mortar of the joint to create the impression of a narrower joint. If this technique was intentional (rather than the involuntary and automatic action of masons in finishing the pointing), the illusion would only succeed if two criteria applied: the mortar pointing the joints was flush (or nearly so) to the plane of the wall face, so that the incised lines showed as the only interruption to the face; and the facework was then limewashed, but not rendered (thick coatings of the surface would obviously have obscured this pointing technique).[25]

Figure 5.9
Southern end of the surviving west gable wall of the south range, showing original stone footings and cob wall and stone refacing of exterior face (right), looking south-west (photograph by David Garner; EH B940374).

Figure 5.10
Window 73 (south-east
window of parlour) and
scar of west wall of south-
east range adjacent in April
1993. Note the tiles
employed to face up the wall
scar after demolition in
phase 8 (photograph by
David Garner; EH
B931141).

Since the cob walling must have been rendered, the render must have run out over the transition from cob to stone, to be replaced by thinner limewash on stone walling. Some evidence to suggest that the masonry was rendered was also recorded. The outer edges of the window dressings throughout were irregular and unfinished, suggesting the presence of rendering that faded out over these edges on to the dressed surfaces of the blocks. The two observations provide important, albeit incidental, evidence for the original exterior finishes of the building.[26]

Another detail observed at the west end of the south elevation was a number of small oak pegs impressed into the cob at apparently random intervals. It has been suggested that these were intended to secure daub render to the surface of the cob, although no convincing evidence of such rendering had survived.[27] In view of the evidence for the primary rendering of the building in lime mortar, this must have represented a secondary re-rendering or perhaps a patching technique.

Primary features

Quoin of the south-east range

The elevation began with the scar of the west wall of the south-east range (*see* Fig 5.8, 75) faced up after demolition with brick and numerous fragments of reused 16th-century Normandy floor tiles robbed from a pavement somewhere on the site (Fig 5.10; *see also* Chapter 9). In the side elevation of this feature (*see* Fig 5.1, 75), the facing could be seen forming an outer skin to the masonry of the quoin. Surviving fabric of the south-east range was limited to the scars of the walls, the masonry blocking the entry at ground-floor level (*see* Fig 5.8, 253) and a section of partition (99) of primary origin (comparing the details to those of the screens in hall and parlour, for example) but probably in a secondary context here. This was blocked with brickwork on the removal of the south-east range (100).

Fenestration

The south elevation preserved something of the original appearance of the building, especially through the survival of several primary, cinquefoil-headed lancet windows. Three windows on the first floor were complete, although weathered (Fig 5.11); the ground floor retained one near-complete

Figure 5.11
Two lancet windows
photographed in 1969
(RCHME BB69/5014).

window and traces of two others. Ground and first-floor windows were similar in design, but the ground-floor examples had relieving arches, with small semicircular tympana and substantial springing blocks above their heads. On the first floor, where there was only one course of masonry between the label and the eaves purlin, there was no room for relieving arches (nor were they structurally necessary). The tympana and springing blocks proved useful indicators to missing windows: a springer of a window in the east service room remained *in situ* (*see* Fig 5.8, 13); another appeared, with a tympanum block and several voussoirs, in the blocking of the successor window in the same position (4). Similar lancet windows can be reconstructed with confidence in the positions of later and larger windows lighting the western bays of parlour and chamber (10 and 17). In the case of the service rooms further west, a smaller rectangular window survived in the west service room (Fig 5.12; *see also* Fig 5.8, 59), complete with an identical relieving arch to those of the lancets to the east. The window of the east service room could have been the same type of small rectangular window or could have been a lancet.[28]

Further west, in the predominantly cob part of the elevation, the fenestration was different and the sills and lintel levels lower, even though the floor level was higher in the oriel chamber (*see* interior elevation, Fig 6.22). No evidence of fenestration survived in the ground-floor room. There may have been no primary window in the south of the western room, just the door (*see* Fig 5.8, 405), but there was evidence for a window in the west wall (*see below*), which may have given enough light to this room. At first-floor level the windows were both altered: the oriel (to the west) is described separately; the second (eastern) window (57) retained its lintels intact, although the embrasure was widened. The chamfer was crudely cut back and little evidence survived on the lintel for the original width of the embrasure. The reconstruction is uncertain since no 'typical' form of wooden-framed window survived in the building. This example cannot be compared to the timber windows of the north wall of the south range, for example, whose frames were set in chases midway within the walls (*see below*). The Bucks' engraving shows a window similar in size and shape to the stone lancets, although set lower in the wall (this concurs with the surviving levels of the lintels). A timber lancet resembling the stone windows is most likely.

The oriel window

The evidence here deserves individual description. An area of breccia ashlar in pristine condition formed an outer skin to the cob wall (Fig 5.13; *see also* Fig 5.8, 49), bearing on the volcanic stone footings (*see* Fig 5.8, 3) 1.5m wide and six courses (1.2m) high. A small circular depression on the central axis of the uppermost course

(54) represented the removal of a projecting element from the face of the block. At the top of the ashlar two further courses survived in part, preserving a stepped inner profile that could have accommodated a corbelled support for a projecting structure above, in the manner of many late medieval oriel windows (Chapter 8). A large block of breccia with a hollow chamfer on its lower edge (reused as a window sill in the east elevation; *see* Fig 5.1, 94, and above) represented part of a corbel course from this feature. Although the breccia facework was simply an outer skin to the cob (*see* Fig 5.8, 53), it was intended from the first, as the cob was built around it. Minor variations around the edge of the masonry did not penetrate to its full thickness (that is, there was no cut) and the mortar bonding was that of the primary building. The thin beds of the cob at this point also suggest that cob and stone were built up simultaneously. Above the breccia base the outline of the window was preserved in the cob (filled with the brick surround of the sash window that replaced it in phase 8). Although amorphous (representing the removal of the feature rather than any precise outline of its form), this included a broad area across the top representing a lintel or roof structure.

The primary nature of the structure was confirmed by the interior embrasure (*see* Figs 6.22 and 6.68).[29] Here a primary (that is, undisturbed) timber lintel spanned the splayed reveals of cob, running down to floor level (*see* Fig 6.22, 165 and 169), with stops in line with the reveals. A layer of primary lime plaster was noted on both reveals, as well as on the adjacent inner wall faces. In addition the southern end of roof truss X was supported on the west end of the

Figure 5.12 (above, left) Window 59 in August 1993, prior to restoration of iron bars (photograph by David Garner; EH B934806).

Figure 5.13 (above, right) Volcanic stone footings (see Fig 5.8, 3) and breccia base for oriel window (49) when first stripped c 1981 (DoE unnumbered print).

Figure 5.14
South elevation of the oriel
chamber, showing position
of the oriel (see detail in
Fig 6.69), the foot of truss
X bearing on the window
lintel and the foot of truss
XI bearing on cob. The
brick facing of phase 8 post-
dates the removal of cob
west gable (extreme right)
(photograph by David
Garner; EH B931152).

Figure 5.15
The relieving arch for the
through passage c *1981*
(DoE unnumbered print).

lintel (Fig 5.14; one of the few not carried onto stone), showing that the assembly could not have been secondary. Within the reveals the splays were cut away on both sides less than halfway through the wall. Above only the inner lintel survived (?of three). On the outside face, post-demolition brick fabric filled voids left by the removal of the oriel (*see* Fig 6.68). Inspection of the voids in the east reveal (when stripped in 1992) showed a series of cavities of varying depth within the cob, possibly formed by the moulding of cob around the tails of stone blocks. This provided some evidence that the structure of the oriel was of stone (as opposed to, say, timber).

In summary, the evidence for the oriel in the fabric comprises: an unusual form of window, with its embrasure running down to floor level; traces of a corbelled support on the exterior; an extensive area of late blocking establishing limits for the window; and a little evidence that the structure was of stone.[30] The Bucks' engraving provides additional information (although not unambiguous). The oriel is shown as a projecting 'bay' running down to ground level, although its lower stage is featureless; this must be an error.[31] The sides are canted and are blind (without windows). A four-light window is suggested in the front face of the structure and there are some similarities between the lights in the oriel and those of the bay window in the south-east range (Chapters 1 and 8).

Garderobe

The garderobe was constructed in a projection from the wall in the east service room. The associated cess pit excavated in 1978 (Chapter 4) was stone lined with a chute in the northern side of the lining (*see* Figs 4.7 and 4.17, section 5, 2307). No trace of the superstructure had survived nor is it known whether it projected as far as the pit. The position of the chute in line with the outer face of the wall perhaps suggests that the garderobe was mostly accommodated within the thickness of the wall and that the superstructure was shallow. This feature went out of use early in the life of the building, probably c 1550, and the structure of the garderobe was removed to be replaced by a door and a second small rectangular window above (*see* Fig 5.8, 21 and 14 respectively). Only the western reveal of the entry to the garderobe survived in the standing fabric (36), containing a small square niche (shown in plan on Fig 6.1; *see also* Fig 6.40).[32] No trace of other fittings to the garderobe had survived.

Arch of the through passage

The surviving arch was c 2.5m wide and represented the outer limit of a stone frame (Fig 5.15; impressions of the blocks were noted in the core).[33] The inner opening was narrower at 1.9m and spanned by a timber lintel rather than an arch (*see* Fig 6.22, 343). The grand arch was substantially larger than other arched doorways in the building at approximately 1.62m wide and 2.46m high. It was blocked and replaced by a small single doorway in the alterations of c 1800.[34]

Primary door to the west service room

The footings were cut by an opening 1.1m wide without quoins (*see* Fig 5.8, 405) that could have accommodated a primary doorway subsequently modified or could have been entirely later. The evidence was insufficiently preserved amid a complex series of later alterations (*see below*). The coursing of the large blocks of the footings did not follow across the gap, however, a discontinuity that supports a primary context for the door.

Later alterations

The garderobe area (phase 4)

The mid-16th-century alterations to the garderobe area involved the removal of the outer structure and the filling of the cess pit. The embrasure was reused to form a doorway. A few blocks of breccia represent the facing up of the broken jamb after the removal of the garderobe fabric (*see* Fig 5.8, 21). The embrasure continued to ceiling height, with a small rectangular window (14) in its head, also constructed of breccia, although similar in other respects to the adjacent primary window of volcanic stone (59). The doorway in the position of the garderobe was blocked in the 19th century and a sill constructed within the blocking for the window above.[35] At the same time or possibly later, another doorway was opened directly east of the blocking (Fig 5.16).[36] A masonry jamb (*see* Fig 5.8, 8) and lintel survived from this doorway on the exterior elevation; no trace remained on the interior. The blocking (34) was erected in 1985 when the garderobe area was reopened.

Parlour windows, late 17th century (phase 7)

The surviving arrangement was the result of the enlargement of the parlour by a bay to the west in the later 17th century and the construction of a pair of rectangular windows (*see* Fig 5.8, 4 and 10) to light the enlarged parlour (Chapter 6). This involved the enlargement of existing embrasures by the trimming down of splays and the rebuilding of quoins. The masonry between the former windows was removed and a new pier of masonry constructed to support the south end of beam 4 (which previously had received support from the screen within as well as the wall) and to act as a central division to the pair of windows (*see* Fig 6.22, 26). The relieving arches above the windows were retained at this phase, only being removed on the blocking of the western window *c* 1800.[37] The windows were probably originally fitted with high-transom cross windows in late 17th-century style. The sash was a later replacement (perhaps inserted on the blocking of the western window).[38]

Alterations of phase 8

The major phase of demolition and alteration throughout the building dated *c* 1800 saw the demolition of the south-east range, the blocking of the west parlour window,

Figure 5.16
The south range, exterior, detail of the south wall of the parlour/service rooms in August 1985, before commencement of rebuilding: pair of windows of phase 7 and blocking of phase 8, doorway of phase 9 (EH F850039/3).

the removal of the oriel window, the blocking of the possible primary doorway at the west end of the elevation and its replacement with a four-light casement window, and the rebuilding in brick of much of the south-west quoin of the building (in the aftermath of the removal of the west gable, *see below*). This work contained typical mortar and materials of this ubiquitous phase, especially the distinctive pink white-speckled mortar. Other characteristics were the incidence of Normandy tile fragments used to level courses and pack joints (Chapter 9) and of architectural fragments reused in blocking, especially the distinctively shaped components of the relieving arches of the primary south range windows.

Subsequent alterations to the south elevation (*see* Figs 5.8 and 6.22) comprised modifications to windows (mainly sashes), the insertion of doors east of the site of the garderobe and in the wide arch of the through passage and a rebuilding of the brick stack to the chimney of the parlour/chamber fireplace (phases 8–9). Later phases saw still further alterations to windows (phases 10–11).

North elevation of south range

General character

The elevation was constructed of stone to first-floor level and of cob above (Figs 5.17 and 5.18). The main timbers of the pentice roof were lodged on the top of the stone (as were the floor beams and roof trusses inside). Primary lime-mortar rendering on cob was recorded at the top of this elevation, where it had been protected by the eaves of the roof, the only instance where this was observed at Bowhill (described in Chapter 10). Here the material was a white lime mortar, very similar in appearance to the mortar seen throughout the masonry of the primary phase.

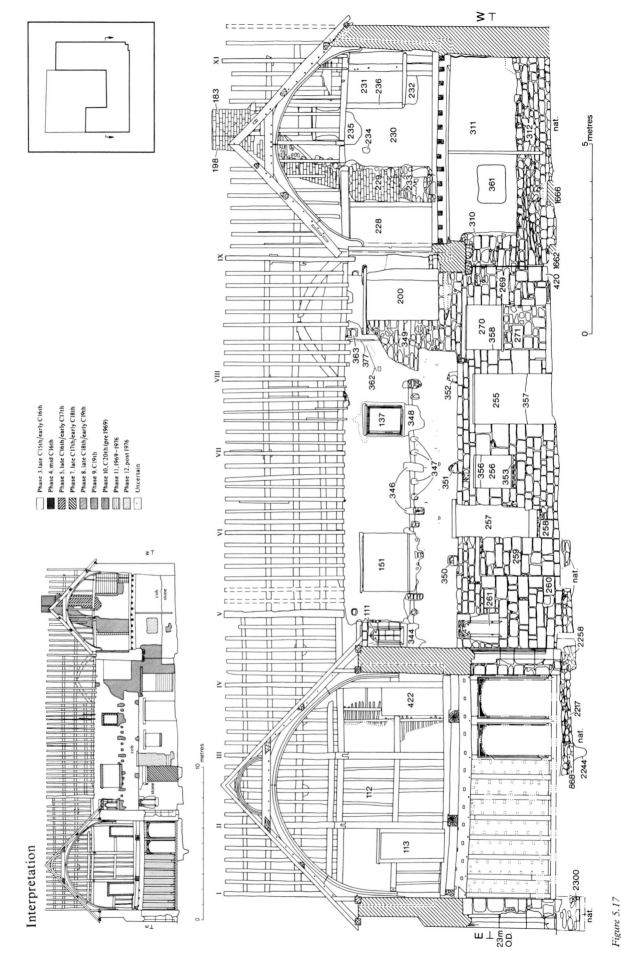

Figure 5.17

North elevation of south range, exterior, plus sections through the east and west ranges (scale 1:100) (line drawing by Tony Ives and Andrew Simm).

Interpretation

Phase 3. late C15th/early C16th
Phase 4. mid C16th
Phase 5. late C16th/early C17th
Phase 7. late C17th/early C18th
Phase 8. late C18th/early C19th
Phase 9. C19th
Phase 10. C20th (pre 1969)
Phase 11. 1969–1976
Phase 12. post 1976
Uncertain

Figure 5.18
The north elevation in 1978, after the backfilling of excavations (DoE J10/3/78).

Primary features

The pentice

Extensive evidence for a covered walkway connecting the kitchen with the hall/screens passage was recorded in the north elevation (Fig 5.19; *see also* Fig 5.17). Three components of the roof had survived: beam sockets at 'wall plate' or 'tie beam' level (regarding the roof structure here in conventional terms); a range of rafter sockets further up the wall; and a horizontal chase or weathering, perhaps for bedding of flashing for the roof.

Despite excavation in the area of the pentice walk in 1977 and further examination in the service trenches of 1993–4, no remains of the structure were traced below ground. Presumably the wall of the pentice had slight foundations, which had not survived later activity and the destructive intrusion of a modern drain in this area. A single beam socket above and to the left of the relieving arch of the hall doorway represented the seating for a plate supporting the roof on the probable line of the outer wall of the pentice (*see* Fig 5.30, 419). This established that the structure was 1.7m wide (interior) and 2m wide (exterior).[39] Three major beam sockets represented timbers bearing on the stone section of the north wall (just below first-floor level) and forming the base of the structure (*see* Fig 5.17, 350–2). The north ends of these timbers were presumably fixed to the top of the 'wall plate'. The bases of the sockets were 0.1–0.2m above the top of the 'wall plate'

socket in the east wall. The beams were placed 2.1–2.2m apart, forming three regular 'bays' east–west and a wider western bay (of 2.6m) coinciding with the exit of the through passage in the south range (a dimension which may also have reflected the width of the gallery at this point; *see below*). The beams demarcated the main bay divisions of the structure. The 'rafter' sockets above refined this into 'principal' and 'intermediate' trusses. The surviving sockets alternated between large deep slots (346), three to a 'bay' (that is, two 'principals' and central 'intermediate' sockets), with two subsidiary smaller sockets between (347) representing the common rafters of this roof. The horizontal weathering scar lay immediately above the common rafter sockets, but was interrupted by the deeper principal sockets, a reminder that the sockets represented the removal of the roof and were thus only approximate guides to the positions of timbers. The pattern to

Figure 5.19
The north elevation of the south range in February 1994, showing the wall stripped and partially repaired. Note the sockets for the roof of the pentice (cf elevation Fig 5.17, 346–7: this was the only occasion that the elevation was free of scaffolding, when any of these features were visible) (photograph by David Garner; EH B940403).

which this structure was built was clear, despite interruptions from later scars for the enlargement of the first-floor windows (344, 348 and so on). In detail the pattern failed to align precisely, especially in the matching of 'principal rafters' with the beams below. The central beam socket (351) aligned directly with the rafter above, but those to east and west, above 350 and 352, were set slightly 'inward' of their correct position.[40]

Evidence for a gallery

The timber sockets for the western bay of the pentice area were removed along with much of the cob superstructure by a large patch of late masonry infill around a door opening at first-floor level (see Fig 5.17, 349 and 200). Physical evidence for a gallery was observed in three places:

1. A chase in the north gable wall of the surviving west range stopping at first-floor level and interpreted as the southern side of a doorway in the east wall of the vanished portion of the range (see Fig 5.27) and indicating external access to this part of the range at first-floor level.
2. A door leading out of the first floor of the south range in line with the exterior of the west range (see Fig 5.17, 200). The surround of this feature was heavily altered, but the exterior lintel survived intact, with primary cob bearing upon it and the interior lintel, although reset, may have been the original (since it retained a chamfer and stops).[41] The evidence was ambiguous, in that the opening could have been interpreted as a window in its primary form and much of the fabric of the interior elevation in this area was of secondary origin (inserted lintel, surrounded by packing, crudely cut western reveal; see Figs 6.25 and 6.70). There is a strong case, however, for seeing the opening as a door from the beginning in view of the other evidence for a gallery and the continuity of function displayed by its use as a door in later phases. A socket in the cob above the east end of the exterior lintel may have supported a headbeam of the gallery wall (see Fig 5.17, 363). This was blocked after the removal of the beam in phase 8 (determinable by its distinctive mortar). Two other features related to later arrangements: a weathering scar of plaster outside the line of the gallery (362), giving a possible angle for the roof; and a vertical scar in the wall (377) representing the wall of the later diagonal bridge across the angle of the courtyard (see below).
3. An unusual configuration of purlins and common rafters at eaves level in the east side of the roof of the west range, best explained as the remains of a 'catslide' roof over a gallery. The common rafters of the roof of the west range were supported on a square-set 'plate' at the level of the cornice/lowest purlin elsewhere. On the east side there was provision in the form of peg holes in the eaves purlin for additional rafters overlapping the main common rafters, but extending outward, that is, to cover the gallery roof.[42] There were also sockets in the cob of the east wall at eaves level (see Fig 5.27, 367–75) and at two lower levels, which may have been connected with the flooring of the gallery (382–3) and the rail of a stair (379–80).

In addition to specific evidence in the fabric, there was further circumstantial evidence. First, the general argument of the need for circulation from south to west ranges to by-pass the open kitchen at first-floor level and possibly beyond. Second, that the existence of a gallery was a precondition of the solution chosen for access into the first-floor room of the west range after its removal. The diagonal-bridge arrangement (see below) was an unnecessarily complex solution had there not been a gallery and thus an original door in the appropriate position in the north wall of the oriel chamber. Mid-20th-century photographs are crucial for reconstructing the sequence (see Figs 2.17–2.18 and Fig 2.20). At this time the south-west corner of the courtyard was spanned by the remains of a short bridge leading from the door 200 (see Fig 5.17) to an entry through the east wall of the west range.[43] When the kitchen was floored over following the demolition of the northern part of the west range in phase 8 (c 1800), the only available site for a door into the new room was in the east wall, entered from the gallery. The north elevation of the oriel chamber contained no suitably central site for a doorway (because of the fireplace and the chimney flue, although one could perhaps have been squeezed in at the extreme west end of the room; see Fig 6.25). Perhaps the south end of the gallery was retained for access into the new first-floor room above the kitchen in the initial phase and at some subsequent point this remnant was removed and replaced by the bridge.

Alternatively the concept of 'gallery access' from the outside gave rise to the bridge, as seen in the photograph, without the physical survival of the gallery through the phase of demolition. Only in 1969 (phase 11) was a direct doorway cut through the north wall of the oriel chamber (*see* Fig 5.17, 228), partly destroying the primary fireplace (*see* Fig 6.25, 187) in the process.

Doorways

Primary doors gave independent access to the two service rooms from the pentice (the eastern door was 1.0m wide, but blocked [*see* Fig 5.17, 259 and 260], while the western [255] was wider at 1.3m) and to the through passage, whose original width was 1.8m, but which was narrowed in phase 8 (269) and then blocked and converted into a window in phase 10 (270). The door was reopened in its narrow, later form during the recent restoration. The lintels of the three doorways were originally placed at the same level, although that of the eastern door (260) was lowered at a stage prior to its blocking (*see* the levels on the interior elevation, Fig 6.25). The lintel of the door to the through passage was set higher, reflecting a step up in the floor level within.

The reveals of primary doors in masonry work on this side of the building showed distinctive structural details that were not encountered in the south or east elevations. The same techniques were used for windows (for example, *see* Fig 5.17, 256), probably including windows in the cob-walled areas (although no primary window survived in the cob). Timber frames were set in the middle of the walls, within a chase in the masonry.[44] The feature was seen on reveals wherever they were observed and also on surviving lintels that were generally constructed of two timbers, with a central gap to accommodate the frame. The lintel of the east window/door embrasure of the kitchen (*see* Fig 5.27 and Fig 6.47) was constructed of two timbers, with the inner edges rebated to accommodate the timber frames of the door and window (seen in section in Fig 6.47).[45] Lintels were chamfered and finished with straight stops on the outside (in the case of both door and window lintels). Inside, the stops varied according to the nature of the embrasure: splayed reveals, generally relating to windows, had splayed or diagonal-cut stops to match; unsplayed reveals, characteristic of doorways, had straight-cut stops as on the exterior.

Windows

Of three types of original window, the first, a timber window set in stone walling, conformed to the pattern of the door-frames (as above), with one example in this elevation (*see* Fig 5.17, 256). The second, stone lancets (as in the south elevation), provided two examples at the eastern extremity of the elevation lighting the north-west corners of parlour and great chamber (261 and 111 respectively).[46] That of the parlour was wholly undisturbed. The chamber window had been disturbed, showing a cut above and to the side of the stone frame, rebuilt inner reveals and sill. The window retained a primary timber lintel at the time of recording (chamfered and stopped on the exterior edge in the same manner as those of the ground floor; replaced *c* 1989) and the disturbance probably related to the repositioning of the window lower down in its embrasure, rather than to a complete replacement. A course of stone blocks filled the gap between the lintel and the head of the window. The stone windows were similar in design, layout and material to those of the south elevation, although smaller and without labels.[47] There was clearly emphasis on interior uniformity in these important rooms (as well as crucial additional lighting, Chapter 6).

The third type was a timber window frame set in cob walling. None had survived, but some traces could be recovered. The type was represented in the first-floor, wholly cob-walled and much altered embrasures lighting the inner chamber (*see* Fig 5.17, 151 and 137). The east window (151) was much enlarged in the 19th century. The interior lintel was an insertion or possibly the original repositioned. The exterior lintel survived *in situ*, albeit with the original stops cut away and the chamfer extended to span the enlarged window. Traces of the original stops (and scribing lines on the soffit of the timber) showed that the chamfer (and thus the exterior embrasure) was originally 1.17m wide. The second window (137) also retained an original lintel, although other aspects of the embrasure were modified to accommodate the 16th-century moulded frame now in this position (*see below*). On this lintel the distance between the stops was 0.80m, suggesting that the window had two lights and that to the east had three. Nothing can be recovered of the form of the primary window frames, but it is known that the frames were set centrally in the wall.

The original lintel of the west window (137) demonstrates that the frame must have been at least 150mm back from the wall face (like those in the stone wall, above).

Later alterations

Late 16th- to early 17th-century moulded window (137)

This window was unique to the building, and in its surviving form was probably a later assembly or reuse (Fig 5.20; *see also* Fig 6.53). Mortices and peg holes survived in the head and sill for two closely set mullions suggesting a three-light window, with lights between 150 and 180mm wide. There was no evidence of glazing in the mouldings, such as a rebate or sockets for glazing bars. The haphazard nature of the assembly was emphasised by the mouldings on the interior of the west jamb, where the head and east jamb had none. The reveals were certainly secondary, roughly cut

Figure 5.20
Detail of window 137 showing the inserted moulded frame and the original lintel (photograph by David Garner; EH B934812).

Figure 5.21
As Figure 5.20, with the frame removed, August 1993 (photograph by David Garner; EH B934815).

into the cob and did not retain primary plaster. The sill was replaced (with a scratch moulding and so presumably of 17th-century date), but the lintel, although cut back to its limits, was undisturbed. The sill was set in position with speckled mortar of the phase 8 type (Fig 5.21). It is proposed that the window had an origin in phase 5 and was placed in this embrasure after the removal of the pentice and associated features in phase 8. Similar windows are to be found, in undisturbed form, in alterations of the same period to the former guest hall of St Katherine's Priory, Polsloe, now in the eastern suburbs of Exeter.[48] Other examples in Exeter houses of the 16th and 17th centuries are listed by Portman.[49]

Casement window (151)

The jambs and sill of the window were cut back (to the post of roof truss VI in the case of the western jamb) and interior splays cut off in order to enlarge the embrasure. A three-light casement window was in position here by the time of Stockdale's drawing in the mid-19th century (*see* Fig 2.5).

West elevation

General character

The west gable wall of the south range was poorly preserved, but vestiges of the primary arrangement survived in footings of large volcanic stone blocks at the south end and occasional blocks north of centre (Fig 5.22, 334 and 402 respectively). To the north, the west elevation of the kitchen was better preserved (Fig 5.23) and was characterised by smaller blocks with a quantity of breccia (*see* Fig 5.22, 323). The differences suggest that the west range was built in a separate campaign and presumably came after the south range in the building sequence. In its original form the west elevation was a simple combination of stone footings and cob superstructure (here the builders followed conventional practice in building cob around standing posts of the roof trusses, a process which was possible because of the use of stone footings of a regular height).[50] At the time of recording the west gable was filled with a variety of very modern partitions and concrete-block structures, not individually recorded. The drawing shows a void in this area, spanned by truss XI of the roof of the south range. Where the elevation had survived at the south end, much of it was obscured by rendering.[51]

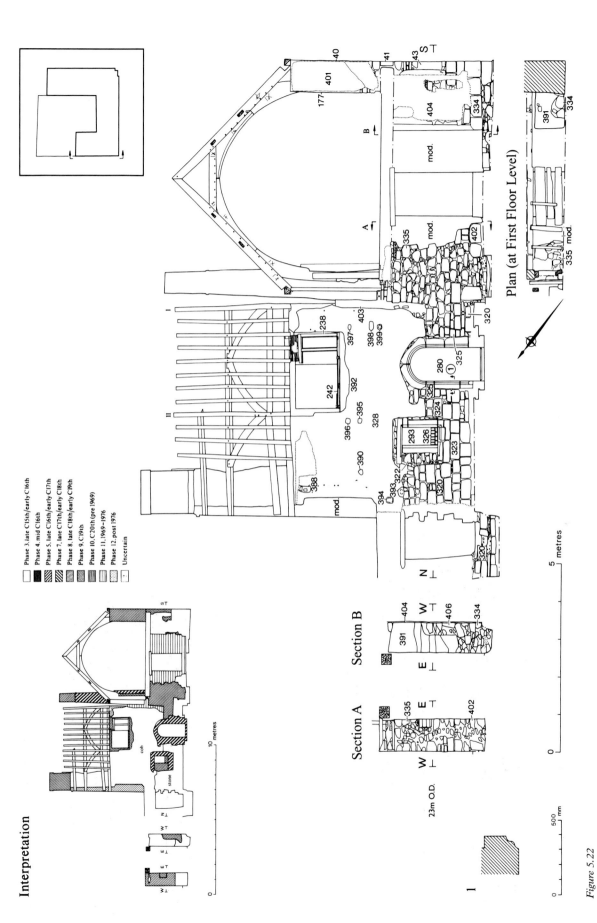

Interpretation

Phase 3. late C15th/early C16th
Phase 4. mid C16th
Phase 5. late C16th/early C17th
Phase 7. late C17th/early C18th
Phase 8. late C18th/early C19th
Phase 9. C19th
Phase 10. C20th (pre 1969)
Phase 11. 1969–1976
Phase 12. post 1976
Uncertain

Plan (at First Floor Level)

Section A

Section B

Figure 5.22
West elevation of south and west ranges, exterior (scale 1:100) (line drawing by Tony Ives and Richard Parker).

Figure 5.23
The west elevation stripped in August 1988 (photograph by Keith Westcott; EMAFU 1497/13).

Figure 5.24
The north-west corner of the courtyard in November 1994, originally the interior elevation of the west/north ranges. Note the primary cob and stone footings (photograph by David Garner; EH B945706).

The nature of the demolished part of the west range was shown by the lower stage of its west and north walls, which survived as the boundary wall of the central courtyard. Although heavily obscured by repair and later alteration, the core of this wall was of original cob (Fig 5.24; *cf* Fig 6.45, 1794) on low stone footings (Fig 6.45, 1778, 1786 and 1796), in which breccia was freely mixed with volcanic stone. This supports the observation that the west range was built in conventional cob-building fashion (*see above*). Details of the west (outside) elevation of the courtyard wall were not seen, because no

rendering was removed from this face during the repair works. One course of footings was exposed in 1995, from which it could be seen that the character of the masonry was consistent with that seen elsewhere.

Primary features

Few primary features had survived. The door and windows of the kitchen were all early additions (*see below*). They may have replaced primary equivalents, but if so, no traces remained. To the south a single original lintel survived on the internal (west gable) elevation of the south range (*see* Fig 6.45, 424). Although the supporting masonry was all later, the timber had survived in its original position through various phases of rebuilding. The lower edge of the lintel was chamfered, with a splayed stop at its northern end. This is an important detail, as it demonstrates that the opening in this position was a window with splayed reveals, rather than a door (stops of doorways elsewhere in the western end of the building were invariably straight cut). The southern end of the lintel including the stop had been cut away, but an interior width of 2.0m can be reconstructed (by assuming that the window was placed centrally in the elevation) and from this a probable exterior width of *c* 1–1.2m (?two lights). Similar windows can be suggested for the gable wall of the oriel chamber above and for an original window in the first floor of the kitchen. Lighting in this position is essential, although any trace of an original embrasure was obliterated by the 16th-century enlargement of the window (238).

Later alterations

Sixteenth-century alterations to the kitchen (phases 4 and 5)

The two principal events were the insertion of a breccia-framed arched doorway and window to the ground-floor stage of the west wall of the kitchen. On the interior, alterations were made by cutting new embrasures into the cob, inserting a lintel for the window, but leaving the internal arch of the new door as unsupported cob (*see* Fig 6.45). On the outside a square frame of breccia with a plain chamfer was fitted (*see* Fig 5.22, 293), presumably subdivided by a timber frame or mullion. The door-frame (280) was similarly of breccia, with a wave-moulded surround and convex stops (*see* Fig 8.29, no. 5).

Modifications of phase 8

The major phase of demolition and alteration of *c* 1800 saw: the rebuilding of the south-west quoin of the building; the removal of much of the western gable, since the southern and northern scars of the first-floor stage of this wall were faced up with brick of this period (*see* Fig 6.22, 177, and Fig 6.25, 179); and the refacing, in masonry, of an area of the central part of the elevation (*see* Fig 5.22, 335). The demolition of the northern bays of the west range also took place in this phase. In the west elevation of the kitchen, the ground-floor window was reduced in width. The packing contained material deriving from the demolition phase, including a section of chamfered mullion in Beer stone and mortar of the ubiquitous type. The primary first-floor window embrasure was enlarged by cutting back the reveals to fit a timber frame of four or five lights (*see* Fig 5.22, 238; discussed in Chapter 6), probably reused from elsewhere in the building (possibly the demolished ranges to the north).

Later phases

Two phases of construction were represented in the fabric of the annexe at the south-west corner of the building, both post-dating the alterations of *c* 1800 (described under the excavations in this area in Chapter 4). Still later removal of fabric and its replacement with structures of softwood and concrete are charted in the series of phased plans (*see* Figs 12.2 and 12.4).

The first-floor window of the kitchen (*see* Fig 5.22, 238) was cut down in size and fitted with a new casement in the later 19th century (242). Date-stamped bricks of 1863 were used to make up the sill of the new window and in the inclined fill above the lintel of the window (*see* Fig 6.45, 241). There were further superficial alterations to this window in 20th-century phases.

Alterations to the courtyard wall

The standing fabric of the west wall (Fig 5.25; *see also* Fig 6.45) contained many later builds post-dating the demolition of the west range in phase 8, including refacing the cob in a mixture of stone and brick and adding a doorway midway along the wall (subsequently blocked). The fabric to the north of the doorway (*see* Fig 6.45, 1782 and 1792) contained numerous fragments of the Normandy tiles familiar in contexts associated with phase 8 elsewhere (Chapter 9).

Figure 5.25
The interior elevation of the west boundary wall of the courtyard in November 1994. This was originally the interior elevation of the west range (photograph by David Garner; EH B945704).

The cutting of the present doorway against the gable of the standing building took place in phase 11 (the wall was complete on the 'as existing' architects' plans of 1969 (*see* Fig 12.2).

North elevation of west range

General character

This elevation was repaired and rendered in 1981 and was not subsequently accessible for examination. The description is based on photographs (especially Fig 5.26), an outline elevation drawing and some post-repair re-survey to establish an accurate outline (done 'through' the modern rendering, Fig 5.27). The elevation was dominated by the masonry flue of the huge

Figure 5.26
The north elevation of the west range stripped and undergoing repairs in 1981 (DoE unnumbered print; EH B960397).

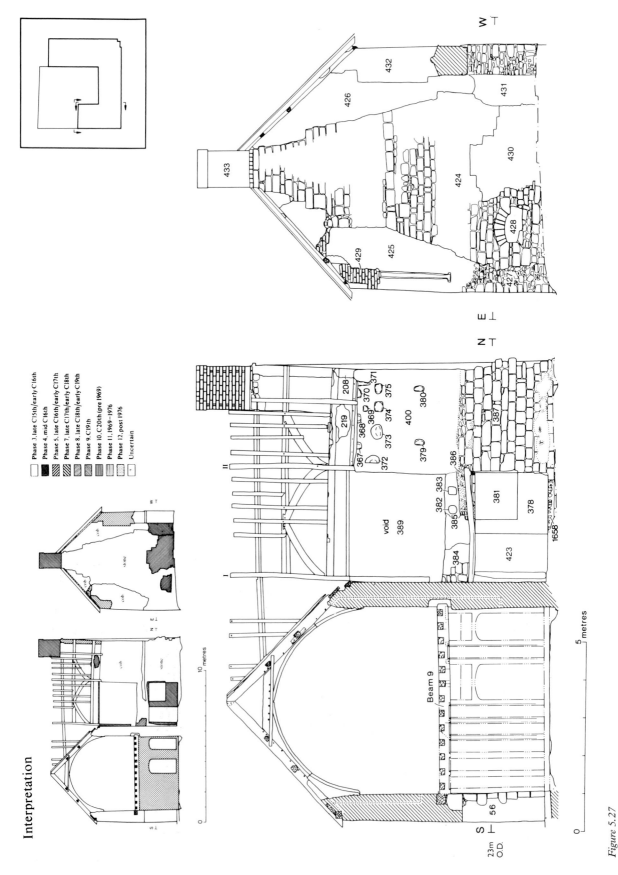

Interpretation

Phase 3. late C15th/early C16th
Phase 4. mid C16th
Phase 5. late C16th/early C17th
Phase 7. late C17th/early C18th
Phase 8. late C18th/early C19th
Phase 9. C19th
Phase 10. C20th (pre 1969)
Phase 11. 1969–1976
Phase 12. post 1976
Uncertain

Figure 5.27
North and east elevations of west range, exterior (right and centre) and section through south range on the line of truss IX (left) (scale 1:100) (line drawing by Tony Ives and Richard Parker).

kitchen fireplace (*see* Fig 5.27 and Fig 6.47) occupying the full width at the base of the wall and a tapering central area above. As far as can be judged, the flue was entirely of volcanic stone. The flanking areas, above the stone footings of the east and west walls, were composed mainly of cob walling. The cob on the east side of the chimney stack was continuous across the rear of the internal niche.[52] A vertical chase near the eastern edge of the wall marked the position of a door-frame, set midway through the wall (*see above*, the examples in the south range). A short horizontal extension at the bottom of the chase, at approximately the level of the first floor of the south range and aligning with sockets for the floor timbers of the gallery in the east wall (*see* Fig 5.27, 382 and 383), probably represented a template at threshold level. The vertical chase was about 1.8m high. At the top a wider area of blocking, now filled with brick (429), represented the removal of lintels and/or cob walling above the doorway. The western quoin was rebuilt in concrete blocks in 1981 (432).

Features within the masonry of the stack at ground level broadly corresponded to features in the back of the kitchen fireplace within. The large oven in the western side of the kitchen fireplace was accommodated in a masonry bulge projecting from the north elevation.[53] The removal of this feature above ground is reflected in the patch of brickwork hard against the east face of the stump of the west wall (*see* Fig 5.27, 431). A large area of brick blocking in the centre of the elevation (430) corresponded to the blocking of an arched ?oven opening in the back of the fireplace (*see* Fig 6.47, 297 and 298). A primary arched opening (again looking like an oven) in the north face of the wall (*see* Fig 5.27, 428), also appeared in the fireplace-back as another area of masonry blocking (*see* Fig 6.47, 302). Discussion of the siting and function of these features appears in Chapter 6.

East elevation of west range

General character

As with the north elevation of the south range (*see above*) this elevation was built of stone to just below first-floor level and of cob thereafter (*see* Fig 5.27). Thus although the stone 'footings' of the east wall stand higher than those of the west wall, for purposes of roofing the discrepancy was much less than

Figure 5.28
Composite view of the east elevation of the west range stripped c 1981:
(above) *upper half (DoE unnumbered print; EH B960398);* (below) *lower half (DoE unnumbered print; EH B960401).*

in the south range. A notable aspect of the masonry is the high incidence of breccia over volcanic stone in this elevation.[54]

Most of the southern bay lacked early fabric. On the ground floor this was because it was occupied by a broad door and window/serving hatch, under a single lintel, giving access to the pentice (Fig 5.28; *see also* Fig 6.51). In the case of the first floor, later activity had removed most of the fabric of the wall (presumably cob) in successive measures to create access into the first-floor room above the kitchen (*see* p 86). A fragment of primary cob walling survived above the ground-floor lintel among later patches of masonry (*see* Fig 5.27, 385). This contained two sockets for the support of the gallery. At a slightly lower level and extending northwards was an area of packing filling a linear ?slot at the junction of the stone facing and the cob above (386); the upper limit of this appears in photographs (*see* Fig 5.28), but was obscured by render and could not be accurately plotted. It is possible that this too related to the support of the gallery floor. A variety of other sockets was identified in the cob of the northern half of the elevation arranged in four tiers (*see* Fig 5.27). Contexts 379–80 at approximately 24.8m above OD perhaps represented the position of a rail around a stair; 372–5 at 25.95–26.00m aligned with the suggested position of the lintel of the doorway in the adjacent north elevation

Figure 5.29
Detail of window reveal
360, looking north-east and
showing the slot for the
window frame (photo-
graph by David Garner;
EH B942026).

(*see above*) and may have represented horizontal timbers in the gallery roof; 369 and 371 at 26.3m and 367–8 and 370 at 26.5m presumably related to rafters or other timbers of the roof.

The upper part of the elevation was repaired early in the works programme and later accretions were removed at that time. Some remains of stone infill above the lintel survived (*see* Fig 5.27, 384). They belong with the period after the removal of the gallery and insertion of the floor within the kitchen (phase 8) and possibly were associated with the insertion of the southern beam of the new floor. Within the opening on the ground floor, the present door and window are framed in brick (378). The post-medieval cobbles of the kitchen floor (Chapter 4) run through the opening (1658). In section (Fig 5.29; *see also* Fig 6.47) the chase for the original frame can be seen (360) in the masonry reveal, stopping some 0.5m above floor level at the level of the sill of the hatch and continuing (as a rebate) onto the timber lintel.[55]

West elevation of the east (hall) range, east side of courtyard

General character

By the time that this elevation was recorded in 1987, repairs to the east range were complete. Some repointing had been carried out, the wall of the northern cell had been largely rebuilt in new cob and the window at the south above the screens passage had been removed and blocked in.[56]

The masonry was of the standard primary type of large, squared volcanic blocks (Fig 5.30, 416); breccia was used occasionally, with Beer stone for the windows. The core of the elevation was thus of stone, but the extremities in all directions were of cob: the wall top, above the heads of the windows; the southern end (turning the corner to the north wall of the south range); and most of the northern bay (the wall of bay 1 was entirely removed by the 19th century, if the evidence of Stockdale's drawing is reliable; *see* Fig 2.5). A slim column of cob walling survived at the northern limit of the elevation. The cob of the wall top was removed and replaced with a half-thickness walling of small, semi-coursed stone in phase 8 (identified by the mortar type).[57]

A primary feature was a beam socket above and to the left (north) of the arched doorway to the screens passage (Fig 5.30, 419), with blocking bonded in mortar of phase 8. This housed a longitudinal timber of the pentice roof and provided useful evidence for the width of the pentice (*see* p 85).[58] The incised or struck style of pointing in primary mortar survives in places on this wall (and may still be seen, since the masonry remains unrendered).

Stair doorway

The door (*see* Fig 5.30, 417) gave access to a stair to the upper room in the northern bay of the hall and possibly also to the first floor of the north range. The frame was of breccia and was visibly inserted on the interior (a scar for insertion was recorded in 1979; *see* Fig 6.15). On the exterior the southern reveal survived, with brick blocking replacing the northern reveal; this too was of secondary appearance, made up by the insertion of small breccia blocks where necessary to make a straight edge (*see* Fig 5.30). Excavation of the courtyard in 1977 showed that the retaining wall associated with the stair belonged to the earliest phase of the building's use and was in place before the deposition of the earliest pebbled surface of the courtyard (*see* Fig 4.7, 2266). The evidence for the secondary nature of the door in the standing fabric suggests that the stair was an afterthought in the process of construction or possibly that the surviving breccia frame was a slightly later addition to an existing stair arrangement, perhaps coeval with the enlargement of the stair in phase 5 (represented by wall 2272 and associated deposits; *see* Fig 12.1, phase 5; *see also* Chapter 4 and Fig 4.17, section 3). The stair itself was a critical element in circulation in this part of the building and must be a primary element of the plan (Chapter 1).[59]

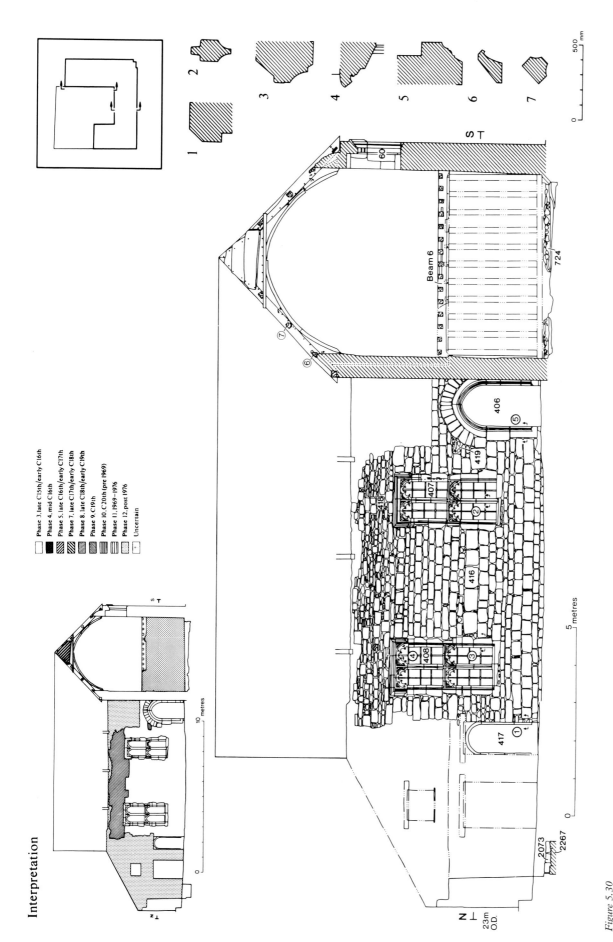

Interpretation

Phase 3. late C15th/early C16th
Phase 4. mid C16th
Phase 5. late C16th/early C17th
Phase 7. late C17th/early C18th
Phase 8. late C18th/early C19th
Phase 9. C19th
Phase 10. C20th (pre 1969)
Phase 11. 1969–1976
Phase 12. post 1976
Uncertain

1
2
3
4
5
6
7

500 mm

Figure 5.30
West elevation of east range, exterior, and section through the south range on the line of truss VII (scale 1:100) (line drawing by Tony Ives and Richard Parker).

The stair was probably constructed within a shallow lateral projection represented by the line of the footing (thus partly within the thickness of the wall). This is the type described by Margaret Wood as ' ... a union of the wall thickness and newel types'[60] whereby the main flight rises parallel to the line of the wall, with a turn at the top and the bottom.[61] An external timber stair on the stone footing as excavated is also a possibility and might explain the absence of proper wall footings at this point.

Late window over screens passage

At the south end of the elevation the masonry stepped down over the south-west door of the hall. On the exterior the gap was filled with masonry of similar composition and style to that of the wall top, forming a surround to a late window (see Fig 2.19).

On the interior, however, photographs show that the window was cut into cob walling and suggest that the gap in the masonry facework represented the original extent of cob walling at the south end of the elevation, replaced by masonry on the installation of the window in the 19th century.[62] A photograph of 1978 shows the post of the southernmost roof truss (VI) in cob walling and an inserted stone reveal on the south side of the window (see Fig 6.7). The same photograph of the interior suggests a context for this window in the partial flooring out of the hall in the 19th century (Chapter 6). The line of the floor is clearly shown by plastering which extends to the floor level, but not below it. The window was removed in the repairs of the early 1980s, along with the masonry surround. The gap was filled with new masonry c 1985 (see Fig 11.111).

6
The standing building: description and analysis of the interior

East range

The interior of the hall range measures 13.7m by 5.9m (45' × 19'4"), the widest roof-span in the building. The hall itself, occupying bays 2 to 6 of the range, is 10.25m (33'7")long. The roof trusses are numbered from the north, so that the missing (northernmost) truss I can be inferred from the numbering of the existing trusses (II–VI, Fig 6.1).

The northern bay

Bay 1 was rather wider than the bays of the hall (3.1m against an average of 2.55m) and was divided into two floors from the first. Although the first floor and roof did not survive in bay 1, a number of elements can be employed to reconstruct some of its appearance.[1]

The partition dividing the northern bay from the hall comprised a post and panel screen on the ground floor, of which only the headbeam survived (the space beneath had been underbuilt with a brick partition on a stone sleeper wall, Fig 6.2) and a large-framed partition bearing on the headbeam and filling the space up to the arch of the roof truss. The posts of the roof truss were set in cob in the lateral walls and carried down to stone at a lower level. The framing was infilled with studs sprung into grooves in the rails of the frame (Fig 6.3) and then, presumably, with lath and plaster and daub.[2] Later windows and applied timbers had also disrupted the infilling. The north face of the truss contained mortices for the longitudinal timbers of bay 1 (some still containing remains of tenons, sawn off when the roof structure of bay 1 was removed). It was unmoulded. This indicates a simpler roof than that of the hall, presumably unmoulded and without the coving and other decorative elements (and provides a parallel for the relationship of the great chamber and inner chamber roofs in the south range). The roof of bay 1 contrasts with the heavily ornamented carpentry of the reception rooms to the south of the hall and suggests that, notwithstanding its location in the traditional position of a solar or chamber, the room was not intended to provide important accommodation. An additional mortice in the north face of the western post of truss II (see Fig 6.3, bottom edge) may represent the head of a doorway in the western wall of the room at the head of the external stair.

The headbeam of the ground-floor screen provided evidence for the missing elements:[3] a run of mortices for the floor frame in its north face; a chamfer on the lower edge; and mortices on the soffit for the studs and plank filling of the partition (Fig 6.4). The south face of the beam bears interrupted chamfers on its lower edge, identifying the positions and form of the posts of the partition and showing that there was a doorway at the western end.

The east and north walls of bay 1 were stone to first-floor level and of cob above; a remnant of the cob survived (Fig 6.5). Footings of the north wall were seen in a trench dug in 1982 (see Fig 4.1), but no trace of the original floor of this room was seen. The west wall survived only as fragments in excavation (see Fig 4.7, 2273). The stone section of the walls contained evidence for two timber-framed windows. The frame of a window with very close-spaced, diagonally set square mullions was recovered from a blocked embrasure in the north wall; the window was set in the centre of the wall, with blocking in the outside half of the wall's thickness.[4] The character of the masonry and the position of the window is illustrated in Fig 6.6. The window has been replaced with a replica. The original is illustrated and described as a find (see Figs 9.23 and 9.24). In the east wall a larger embrasure, also set in the centre of the wall and with internally splayed reveals, had been disrupted by later alterations, but the southern reveal (see Fig 5.3) and part of the sill and north reveal had survived. This may have contained a similar window frame.[5]

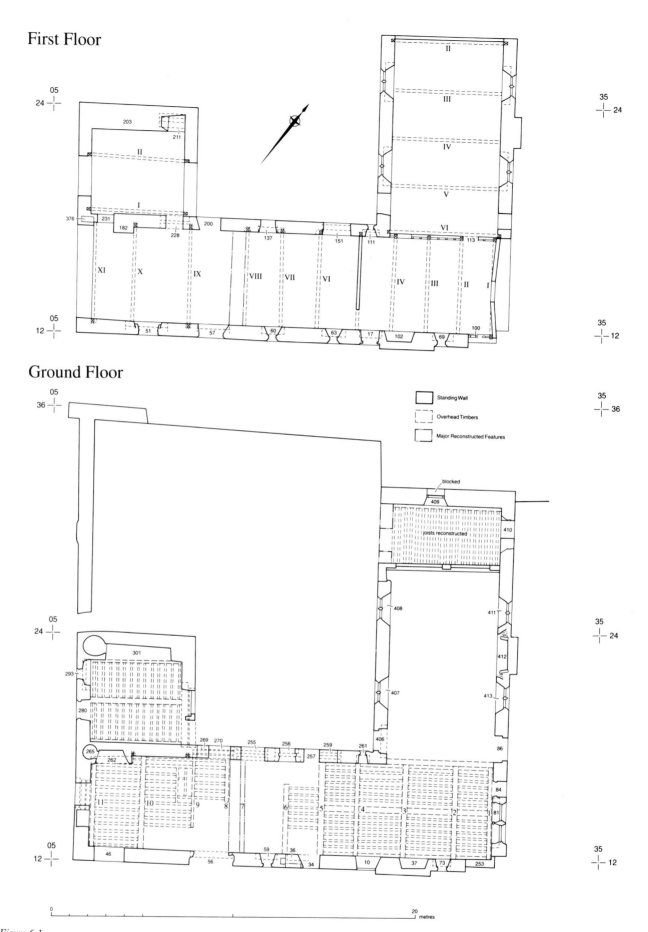

First Floor

Ground Floor

Standing Wall

Overhead Timbers

Major Reconstructed Features

Figure 6.1
Plans of the standing building, ground (below) and first (above) floors. The floor beams, joists and roof trusses are as surviving in c *1985 (scale 1:200)*
(line drawing by Tony Ives).

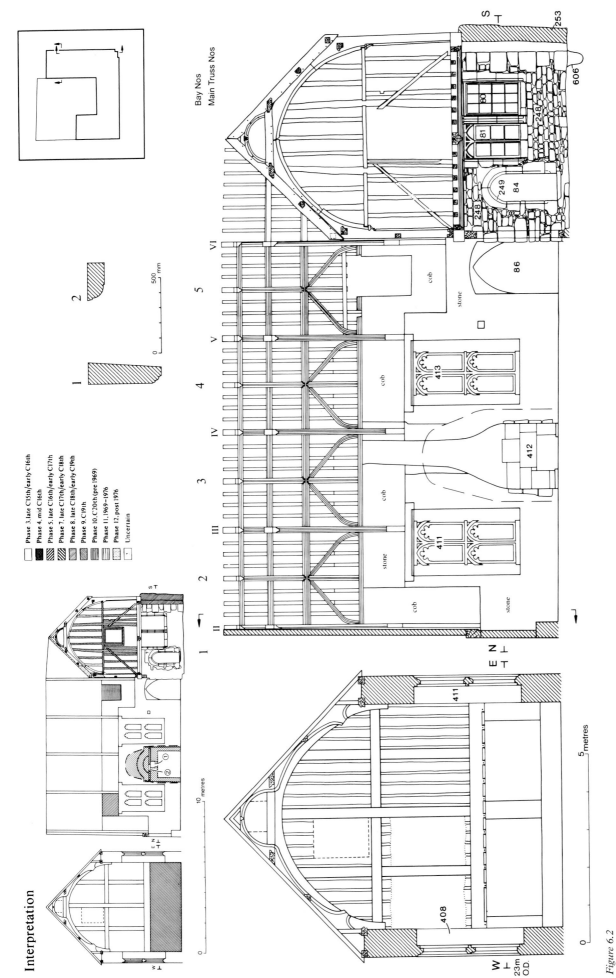

Interpretation

Phase 3, late C15th/early C16th
Phase 4, mid C16th
Phase 5, late C16th/early C17th
Phase 7, late C17th/early C18th
Phase 8, late C18th/early C19th
Phase 9, C19th
Phase 10, C20th (pre 1969)
Phase 11, 1969–1976
Phase 12, post 1976
Uncertain

Bay Nos
Main Truss Nos

Figure 6.2

Interior elevations of east range (hall), north (left) and east (centre) walls and east interior elevation of the south range (including truss 1) (scale 1:100) (line drawing by Tony Ives and Andrew Simm).

Figure 6.3
Partition at the north end of the hall in 1980, with the west post of truss II in the foreground. Note the blind rear face to the timbers, the mortices for purlins and plates of bay 1 and the studs of infill exposed (DoE J114/1/80).

The hall

The central sections of the east and west walls were constructed of stone to the heads of the windows. Stone was used to a lower level in the northernmost bay of the hall (where the headbeam of the ground-floor partition bears on the top of the stone wall) and over the relieving arches of the screens-passage doorways to the south. In these bays cob walling was substituted for the stone; cob was also used to build up the tops of the walls around the roof trusses (Figs 6.7 and 6.8). The feet of main trusses III–V bear on the top of the stone walling or on the timber lintels of the windows at a (more or less) uniform height. Those of the northern- and southernmost trusses (II and VI) have longer posts carried down onto stone at the lower level.[6] This evidence is accepted as showing that the relative distribution of cob and stone as a walling material indicates that the two materials were

Figure 6.4
The east range, interior of the storeroom, with screen at north end of hall, north side, looking south-east. Note mortices for the floor joists, November 1983 (DoE J538/7/83).

Figure 6.5 (left)
As Fig 6.4 at first-floor level with the joists restored, 1985 (EH C850070).

Figure 6.6 (right)
The north elevation of the east range in 1997 (after repair). Note the blocked window (no. 409), large quoins and uniform masonry style (photograph by David Garner; EH B970547).

regarded as interchangeable for mass walling, although there was a preference for stone around the windows. It also shows that the roof was designed for this building and is primary to it, since the timbers were in position prior to the raising of the cob walling.

The four primary windows were placed in pairs in east and west walls, constructed of Beer stone and all of the same design, with two lights divided by a transom and cinquefoil heads in upper and lower lights. The windows differ only in the form of the label stops of their external hoods: carved heads to the east (Fig 6.9a–b and Fig 6.10); moulded stops/returns to the west (Fig 6.9c–d). Evidence for glazing was observed in the upper lights of the western windows, in the shape of grooves for the glazing itself and sockets for glazing bars.[7] Pintles for the hanging of shutters were recorded in the lower but not in the upper lights of the windows.[8] From this it would appear that only the upper lights were originally glazed. This combination in some of the highest-quality windows in the building is a telling comment on the scarcity of window glass at the time.[9] At some time in the 19th century, all the lights were fitted with square-headed softwood shutters, the frames of which obscure the stone jambs from view in the photographs (Fig 6.11). Still later, round-headed softwood shutters were fitted to some of the lights of the western windows (*see* Fig 6.7).

Figure 6.7
Interior elevation of the west wall of the hall in 1978 (DoE J10/9/78).

Figure 6.8 (below)
Composite interior elevation of the east wall top of the hall prior to the removal of the roof for repair. These are important record photographs, since there is no other record of the cob (and stone patching) of the wall top, apparently butting the roof trusses (a northern half, trusses II–IV and b southern half, trusses IV–VI) (DoE J263/18/78 and J263/17/78).

a

b

Figure 6.9
Hall windows before repair
(September 1982): a south-
east (DoE J315/2/82);
b north-east (DoE
J315/3/82); c south-west
(DoE J315/1/82);
d north-west (DoE
J315/4/82).

Figure 6.10
Label stops of the east
windows of the hall:
a south window, south
(EH B960557);
b south window, north
(EH B960556);
c north window, south
(EH B960555);
d north window, north
(EH B960554) (photo-
graphs by David Garner).

a   b   c   d

Figure 6.11
East wall of the hall,
interior elevation in 1978
before the removal of the
masonry blocking the fire-
place. Note the moulded
block (catalogue no. 112)
in infill (white stone to the
left of the hole in blocking)
(DoE J10/7/78).

Figure 6.12
Detail of the fireplace in
1981 after the removal of
the blocking (DoE
J11/5/81).

The fireplace, positioned between the windows on the east wall slightly to the south of centre, had been removed and blocked (*see* Fig 6.11). The fireplace and its stack are interpreted as an insertion contemporary with the construction of the building (Chapters 4 and 5). Evidence in the fabric is less clear inside than outside, although straight joins may be discernible on a photograph of the feature once stripped of its blocking (Fig 6.12). Again the material is distinctive – breccia predominates in the large slabs of the back and sides of the fireplace. The original fireplace surround had been lost to later modifications (*see below*). One block of a joggled lintel with distinctive diagonal tooling and a section of mantelshelf with a bold ovolo moulding on its lower edge were recovered from elsewhere in the building.[10] They were used (along with the extant examples in the parlour and chamber) as the basis for the reconstruction

Figure 6.13
The fireplace in 1982 after
the construction of the new
concrete lintel and hearth
(DoE J8/2/82).

Excavation revealed traces of several later surfaces of cobbles and stone paving in the hall (Chapter 4), but no clear evidence for the nature and level of the primary flooring. Later disturbance had been so frequent and intrusive that the late deposits everywhere lay lower than the offset footings of the hall walls, which must mark the minimum level for the original floor. The nature of the original floor of the hall remains unknown, although paved, flagged, cobbled and tiled floors are all possibilities. Similarly no evidence for a dais was recorded in the standing fabric or excavated deposits, although there may have been one originally. The choice of a mud/lime material for the reconstructed floor of the hall was not based on archaeological evidence (Chapter 11).

The screens passage

Evidence for the position and form of the screen was recovered by excavation in 1989 (Chapter 4). The excavation also provided the width of the passage (c 1.75m) and showed that the screen had a single, central opening into the hall (*see* Fig 4.7). Some additional information comes from the standing fabric in the form of single sockets in the east and west walls of the hall, to the north of the doors of the screens passage (Fig 6.15; *see also* Fig 6.2), which may represent a later screen arrangement.[12] Evidence for a ceiling in the passage comprised secondary mortices for ceiling joists cut into the headbeam of the partition between screens passage and parlour (*see* Fig 5.17).[13] The mortices were smaller and set further apart than those for primary floor joists in the building. The evidence suggests a ceiling rather than a floor, although interpretation as the floor of a gallery is not entirely precluded; thus a gallery above the passage is judged to be unlikely, although possible. Traces of a second set of mortices at the eastern end of the same beam are probably related to the late inserted floor of the hall.

of 1982–9 (Figs 6.13 and 6.14; *see also* Fig 6.2). The sequence of blocking of the fireplace was observed by Dunmore:

> 1st phase – jambs and lintel removed back to rubble fill between stone window jambs and stone sides of flue. Original hearth partly survives – vitrified clay. 2nd phase – stones added on line of inside wall to accommodate new jambs for a smaller opening? – later removed – small oven on S. side. 3rd phase – blocking with red-coloured speckled clay and stones.[11]

This description suggests that the final blocking took place in the phase of alterations of *c* 1800, in which a distinctive red white-speckled bonding material appears frequently (Chapter 10, class 7). A moulded Beer-stone block reused in the blocking (*see* Fig 6.11, and catalogue no. 112, Chapter 9) is consistent with this interpretation. Many such fragments derived from the demolition of this phase found their way into new masonry of the period (Chapters 4 and 12). Traces of the second phase were revealed in the excavation of the hall (Area 2, Chapter 4).

The hall remained open until a late stage in the building's development. It appears to have been intact and unfloored in the early 1840s, the date of Hayward's drawing for the Exeter Diocesan Architectural Society (*see* Fig 1.2), but was floored in sometime later in the 19th century. Two doors were cut into the north wall of the first-floor chamber in the south range, giving access to the hall at this level. One (the eastern, *see* Fig 5.17, 113) was a reused 17th-century door-frame, but the second (the western, *see* Fig 5.19, 422 and Fig 6.59) was a 19th-century

Figure 6.14
The fireplace lintel and
relieving arch during recon-
struction in 1989. The
central voussoir and the
second block of the cornice
from the left are originals
(photograph by Stuart
Blaylock; EMAFU
1571/6).

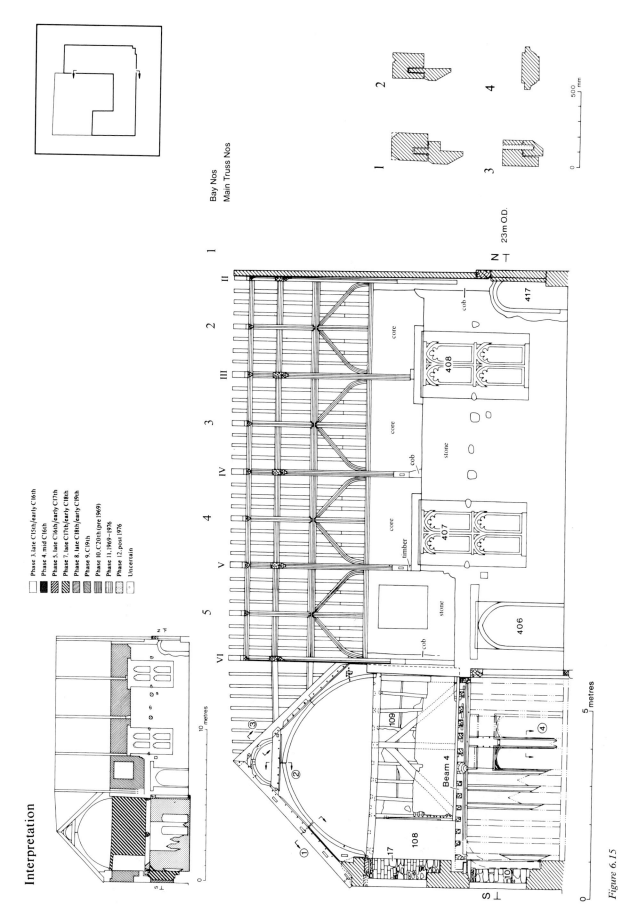

Interpretation

Phase 3. late C15th/early C16th
Phase 4. mid C16th
Phase 5. late C16th/early C17th
Phase 7. late C17th/early C18th
Phase 8. late C18th/early C19th
Phase 9. C19th
Phase 10. C20th (pre 1969)
Phase 11. 1969–1976
Phase 12. post 1976
Uncertain

Bay Nos
Main Truss Nos

23m O.D.

Figure 6.15

Interior elevations of the west end of the east range (hall) and section of the south range on the line of truss V (also showing the west partitions of the parlour and great chamber in elevation) (scale 1:100)
(line drawing by Tony Ives and Andrew Simm).

Figure 6.16
The north partition of the
hall in 1976 (photograph
by Nigel Cheffers-Heard;
EMAFU 255/1) (source:
Exeter Archaeology;
© Exeter Archaeology).

Figure 6.17 (below)
The south partition of the
hall in 1969 (RCHME
BB69/5024).

softwood door-frame. The flooring of the
hall has been assigned to the 19th century
(phase 9) and could have been still later.[14]
The floor was partly supported on beams
lodged in sockets in the walls (a number of
which were located in the west wall of the
hall, see Fig 6.15), but additional support
was given by props against the walls.[15] The
floor was removed and burnt in 1967–8.[16]
The extensive RCHME photographic
survey of July 1969 shows that the floor lay
at the height of the transoms of the windows
and that the walls were plastered and limewashed above this level (Figs 6.16 and 6.17;
see also Figs 2.22, 6.7 and 6.11).

The hall-parlour/chamber partition

The south end of the hall consisted of a
ground-floor screen of close studding
supporting the beams of the parlour ceiling
to the south. In turn, the ceiling beams
supported the sill beam of the first-floor
screen (see Fig 5.17 and Fig 6.25). The
surviving form of the ground-floor partition
was recorded in a photograph of 1969 (see
Fig 6.17). Some studs had survived in position and some had been moved and the
eastern end of the partition filled with new
brickwork. Peg holes and mortices in the
headbeam showed the original positions of
the studs and that the western end of the
screen was occupied by a pair of doorways.
One jamb of the western doorway remained
in situ and another jamb had been moved to
the far eastern end of the screen.[17] The
infilling of the screen was of an unusual
form. The sides of the studs had been drilled
with holes at regular intervals, but instead of
the holes being fitted with laths or rungs, as
is often found locally,[18] bulbous oak pegs
had been used and the cob filling packed
around them (Fig 6.18).[19] The upper stage
of the partition (Fig 6.19; see also Figs 5.17
and 6.17) consisted of a large-framed structure integral with the timbers of the roof of
the south range. The northern posts of south
range trusses I–IV formed the uprights of
the frame, with intermediate rails added
(inscribed with the relevant truss numbers)
and the cornice plates acting as the upper
rails (see Fig 7.13). The filling resembled
that of the north partition of the hall, with
studding run into grooves in the rails of the
frame and filled with lath and daub (here in
a distinctively red earth). Since no sign of
partitioning filling the tympanum of the end
truss of the hall was recorded, it must be
assumed that the void within the roof space
remained open to view (see Fig 5.17).

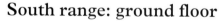

South range: ground floor

The south range measured approximately 22.1m east–west and 4.9m north–south (internally). The parlour occupied bays 1–3 (*c* 7.5m), the first service room was of two bays (4–5; 3.75m) and the second of a single bay (6; 2.5m). To the west of the cross wall (bay 7) the passage occupied bay 8 (1.9m) and the west service room bays 9–10 (5.75m).

The parlour

Doorways

The room was approached from the screens passage through one of the pair of doorways at the west end of the partition (Figs 6.20 and 6.21; *see also* Chapter 1). The west door was wider than the east and the chamfer on the headbeam (south side) of the screen spans the east doorway but does not continue above the west (*see* Fig 6.25).

No traces of partitioning or other features relating to a division have been recorded in the screens, the ceiling timbers or in the archaeology of the floor deposits. The theme of paired entries continues, however, in the post and panel screen that forms the western wall of the parlour (*see* Fig 6.15, with lower doors of equal width) and so it would seem probable that the doorways represent some sort of division in the circulation within these rooms, even though there is little surviving evidence in the fabric. The fenestration also suggests that this corner was divided off, probably as screened access to the service rooms or as a closet, since the evidence of the ceiling suggests that a stair in this position quickly went out of use (*below*).

The south-eastern corner of the parlour was effectively a wide doorway leading into the south-east range, formed by the south and east walls stopping short of the corner of the room by 1.5m and 0.3m respectively.

Figure 6.18 (above, left) The ground-floor partition at the south end of the hall after reconstruction but before infilling, 1987 (photograph by Keith Westcott; EMAFU 1398/23).

Figure 6.19 (below, left) The hall looking south in June 1990, with repairs in progress (photograph by Stuart Blaylock; EMAFU 1723/28).

Figure 6.20 (above, right) South range interior – the parlour, looking south-east, in July 1978 when first stripped. Note subdivision of the ceiling (DoE J263/2/78).

Figure 6.21 (below, right) As Fig 6.20, looking north-west, July 1978 (DoE J263/1/78).

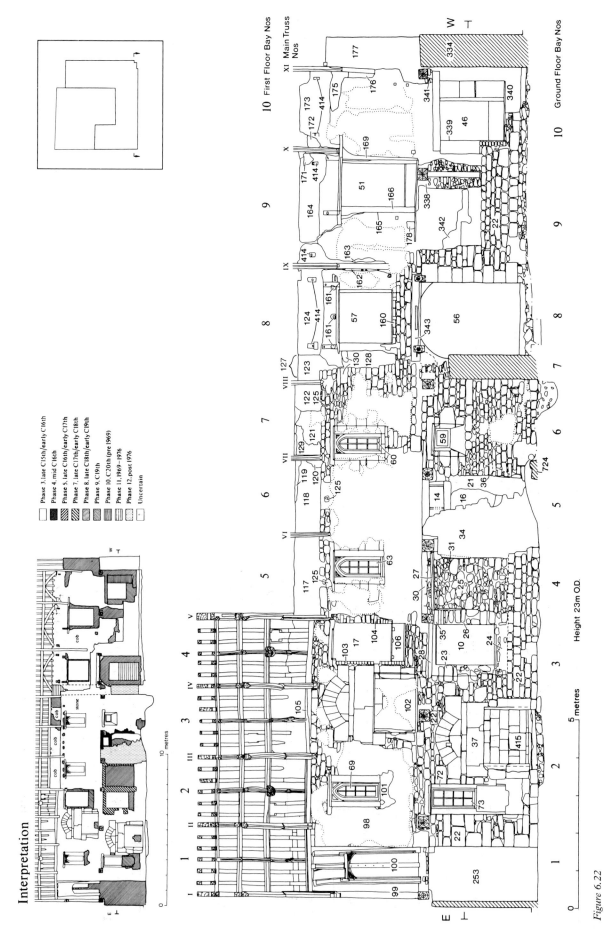

Interpretation

Phase 3. late C15th/early C16th
Phase 4. mid C16th
Phase 5. late C16th/early C17th
Phase 7. late C17th/early C18th
Phase 8. late C18th/early C19th
Phase 9. C19th
Phase 10. C20th (pre 1969)
Phase 11. 1969–1976
Phase 12. post 1976
Uncertain

Figure 6.22
Interior elevation of the south wall, south range (scale 1:100) (line drawing by Tony Ives and Andrew Simm).

Thus the corner of the ceiling, where two of the main beams joined, was not supported by solid masonry (*see below*). The opening may have been filled by a partition or framed doorway (in the manner of the equivalent position in the great chamber, above), but no trace of this had survived the construction of masonry blocking of the gap after the demolition of the south-east range (Fig 6.22, 253; *see also* Fig 6.2).

The doorway in the east wall gave access to a turret stair. The frame was repositioned within a cut in the masonry, but probably occupied this position from the first. The adjacent windows are so far off-centre that their exterior labels are built into the return walls of the south-east range and the porch stair (discussed above in Chapter 5).

Fireplace

The fireplace in the south wall (Fig 6.23; *see also* Fig 6.22, 37) was of vesicular volcanic stone, built to the same general pattern as those in the great chamber and the hall and with the same diagonal tooling marks. The moulded mantelshelf was dressed off (possibly when the walls were panelled) and quite severe damage done to the jambs and lintel by the blocking of the fireplace and the ?insertion of a smaller hearth within it in the 19th century. A patch of 19th-century mortar and breccia blocking had survived from this. The massive lintel (of three blocks with joggled joints) was unmoulded and the jambs have a very badly damaged ogee moulding (as opposed to the continuous ogee moulding on jambs and lintel of the great chamber fireplace).

Fenestration

Primary windows survived east of the fireplace (*see* Fig 6.22, 73), in the east elevation (Fig 6.24; *see also* Fig 6.2, 80 and 81) and in the north-west corner of the room (Fig 6.25, 261). Aside from modifications to the glazing and the universal removal of iron saddle bars, the principal alterations were to sills. The east window had a gently splayed sill, presumably of stone because the scars from its removal were still visible in the adjoining faces (*see* Fig 6.53). The king mullion spanned the full depth of the wall, its sides rebated for shutters (like the reveals). Foiled heads survived in the northern half of the window, although the dividing mullion was missing. To the south similar details were replaced by a sash in the later 19th century (the window was shown

Figure 6.23
Detail of the parlour fireplace (photograph by David Garner; EH B933127).

intact in its original form by Townsend's sketch, *see* Fig 2.4, but had been replaced by 1907).[20]

The south-east window showed a succession of repairs to the base of its embrasure, presumably replacing the original splayed sill. A new sill was constructed at a low level in the brick and distinctively red white-speckled mortar of phase 8, alterations were made on the exterior in the same materials and the interior reveals reduced in their angle of splay (the ghost of the original splay can still be seen on the soffit of the lintel). The cinquefoiled head of the window may also have been removed at this time.

Figure 6.24
Detail of the east windows of the parlour from within (photograph by David Garner; EH B933099).

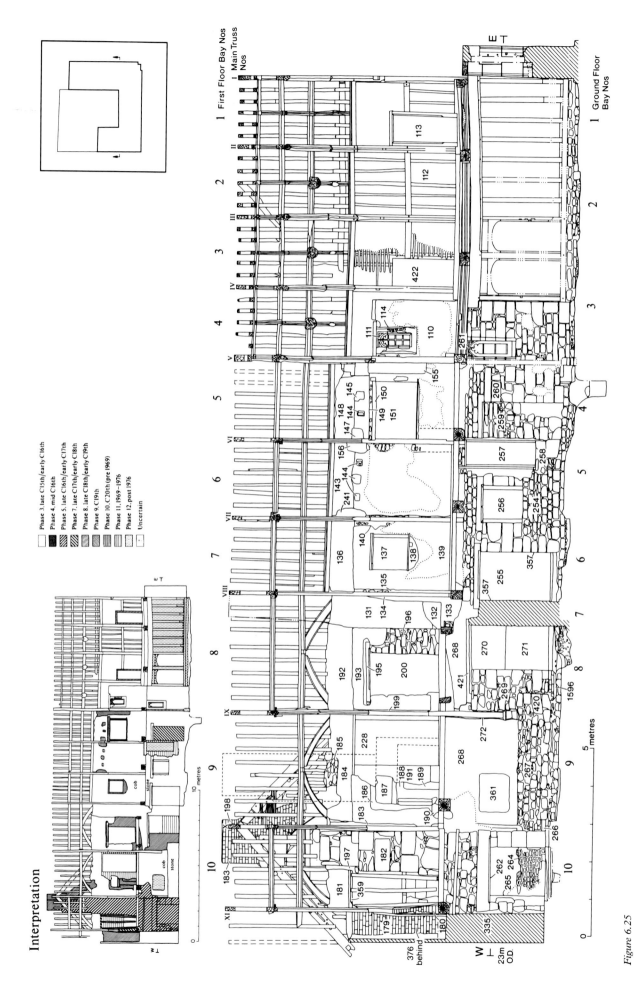

Figure 6.25
Interior elevation of the north wall, south range (scale 1:100) (line drawing by Tony Ives and Andrew Simm).

The second phase of alteration comprised more brick filling to make up the level of the sill at the rear of the niche, employing a grey lime and ashes mortar dating to some point in the 19th century. Last was a small area of blocking in the western reveal where a stove pipe had been cut through into the chimney flue. This was filled in subsequently (in the 1960s?).

The south-west parlour window has been partly described above (Chapter 5). On the interior a section of the eastern reveal was all that survived of the primary window (*see* Fig 6.22, 10 and 23). The revised embrasure was a part of the process of enlargement of the parlour in the late 17th century and thus draws in the next bay to the west, originally a part of the service room. A pair of windows was created in shallow-splayed reveals with new lintels and breccia stonework. The western screen of the parlour was removed a bay to the west at this phase. The screen had formerly given some support to the floor beam above (beam 4). The structure of the new windows was devised to provide additional support for the beam: a pier of masonry on the central axis occupied the outer two-thirds of the walls thickness (26). A timber corbel was formed at the top of the pier, spanning the full thickness of the wall (35) and on the inside a timber post with a curved head was seated on a large breccia block at the base of the pier, providing further bracing of the beam end (*see* Figs 2.24 and 6.20; position dashed on Fig 6.15).[21]

The north-west window was complete in its original embrasure (although missing glazing and ferramenta). Pintles for a shutter survived on the interior of the west side of the frame. The window was placed in the only available space for lighting in the north wall of the parlour as originally laid out. The tightness of the position is illustrated by the very shallow splay of the western reveal to bring the jamb into line with the face of the screen (*see* Figs 6.1 and 6.25, 261). The window supports the argument for the enclosure of the north-west corner of the parlour already suggested by the paired doorways, as the need for lighting from the north in the parlour is unlikely to have been sufficient in itself to justify a window in this position (especially as the available light was limited by the pentice). If this corner of the room was enclosed or subdivided by partitions or movable screens, the need for independent lighting, however limited, was increased.

Flooring

No evidence had survived for the original flooring of the parlour. A 19th-century boarded floor, its supporting joists and the disturbance associated with its construction and ventilation, had caused considerable truncation within the room. The thresholds of the screens and of the hearth within the fireplace, as well as minimum levels represented by the stone wall footings, were used to establish a level for the reconstruction of the floor.[22] The high incidence of ceramic floor tiles from the site and occasional finds of stone paviours suggest flooring of these materials somewhere in the building. The south-east range or the parlour are possible contexts for tile pavements (Chapter 9).

Screens

The screen dividing the parlour and the screens passage has been described above. The west wall of the parlour was formed by a post and panel screen whose surviving extent is well illustrated in photographs of 1979, albeit in its secondary position beneath beam 5 (Figs 6.26 and 6.27; *see also* Fig 2.24). The northern part of the screen had been completely removed. The central section was complete (comprising the southern of the two doorways, the mortice for the head of the northern door and two adjacent studs and panels of plank infill). Another large intrusion had cut away much of the remainder of the screen to the south, although the southernmost stud and some 0.6m of the intervening area at the top of the screen had survived (*see* Fig 6.15).

In the secondary position beneath beam 5, the studs were set in open mortices in a moulded headbeam added to the east face of beam 5 (*see below*, the parlour ceiling). In the original form of the screen, the studs were set in closed mortices in the soffit of beam 4, with trenches for plank infilling. The mortices allow no doubt that the screen formed the original western wall of the parlour and enabled it to be reconstructed with confidence in 1985–7. The western side of the screen was undecorated (although there were rebates to the doorframe that were filled by the reconstruction). Towards the parlour the door-frames (*cf* Fig 8.29, 6) were moulded with the combination of ogee and cavetto characteristic of all the primary work (*see* window lintels and the more complex mouldings of the ceiling) and

Figure 6.26 (left)
The interior of the parlour
after further stripping in
November 1979, southern
half looking west. The
photograph shows the
subdivision of the ceiling
removed and the surviving
extent of the west partition
(DoE J492/3/79).

Figure 6.27 (right)
As Fig 6.26, northern half
looking west, also showing
mortices for timber pegs in
the side of the post of the
screen to the hall (extreme
right) (DoE J492/4/79).

the studs were chamfered. No stops survived the reconstruction, although the early photographs gave a reliable guide for reconstruction. A curious aspect of the screen is the failure of the design to register with that of the beamed ceiling above. The lack of registration is most acute when viewed in an elevation drawing (see Fig 6.15), however, and is much less prominent when seen in the context of the room as a whole. Yet the central beam of the ceiling is just missed by the nearest post and the doors of the screen are surmounted by broad rails which then frame disproportionately small panels above. The whole composition is given an unfinished appearance by the absence of detailing which might have integrated the screen and headbeam. Further, the chamfers of the posts do not return onto the headbeam, but die into its soffit and the moulding of the headbeam precludes the removal of such a detail. Despite these infelicities, the close match between the surviving parts of the screen and the evidence of the original mortices show that it was intended to relate to the ceiling in this manner. The explanation may lie in bad planning and the failure of abstract coordination of different elements of the design that were typical of the builders of Bowhill. It also demonstrates a lack of interest in balanced design, which is typically medieval, as well as (perhaps) indicating a lack of sophistication in the client and the builder.

The parlour ceiling

The underlying structure of the ceiling was recorded by EMAFU in 1987 during reassembly after repair (Figs 6.28 and 6.29), but the boarded ceiling and associated timbers had been removed and were not reinstated. Further details are drawn from description and notes by Beric Morley and Stephen Dunmore[23] made before the ceiling was dismantled, from photographs of the room in 1957 and in 1978–9 after stripping[24] and from the examination of loose timbers removed during repair.[25]

Primary frame

Structurally the ceiling is an elaboration of the beam-and-joist assembly of the rest of the south range. The four main beams are orientated north–south, with moulded lower edges. The floor above is supported on joists running east–west. To create the decorative scheme, those along the north and south walls and on the central axis of each bay are the same depth as the main beams and are moulded to match. Thus, despite the appearance of intersecting moulded beams, the construction remains one of beams and joists.

Beam 4 (north and south terminals) and the south terminal of beam 2 are securely lodged in masonry; the north ends of beams 1–3 bear on the headbeam of the partition forming the north wall of the parlour (and in turn support the superstructure of the roof of the south range; see Fig 6.25).

The southern terminal of beam 1, at the junction of the south and south-east ranges, was originally not supported by masonry. A mortice was cut in the soffit of the beam, 530mm from its terminal, for a post that presumably served as a prop (Fig 6.30) and corresponded to a posthole directly beneath the mortice (*see* Fig 6.2, 606). The lack of support at this point is surprising, since this beam carries the full weight of the south-east corner of the roof of the south range (through the load on the post of truss 1 of the roof of the south range, *see* Figs 6.2 and 6.22). The southern terminal of beam 3 was lodged in masonry over the fireplace. Whether through lack of support, through decay or damage to the timber by heat from the chamber fireplace above, a corbel of breccia was cut into the masonry above and to the right of the relieving arch of the ground-floor fireplaces to provide extra support for the beam (*see* Fig 6.22, 22, Fig 6.20 and Fig 6.23).[26]

The main beams (2 and 3) and the central (axial) joists are approximately 300mm (12") square in section. Beams 1 and 4 are smaller, 200 × 300mm (8" × 12") and 240 × 300mm (9½" × 12") respectively. The flanking joists along the north and south walls are effectively half beams, simulating girding beams and so are smaller still (average 125 × 300mm; 5" × 12"). The standard joint (here as throughout) was the housed soffit tenon, although a greater variety was used in the north-west bay of the ceiling (below). Carpenter's assembly marks were noted on the majority of the joists, generally on the east end of the upper surface of each timber. This shows that the joists of bays 1 and 2 are more or less in their original positions, but that those of bay 3 have been disturbed.[27] A number of peg holes were recorded in the upper surfaces of some joists, perhaps for secondary fixing of floorboards (Fig 6.31; *see also* Fig 6.28). The soffits of the main beams and the axial and peripheral joists were all ornamented with the same moulding (*see* Fig 6.29). The mouldings join in mason's mitres, emphasising the beam-joist dichotomy.[28]

Surface ornamentation of the ceiling
The surfaces of the joists were left in a rough-sawn state. Had they been intended to be seen, they are likely to have been planed, if not chamfered or moulded. This, as well as the closed assembly throughout (confirming the extant joists as the originals), shows that a ceiling was intended

from the beginning. The interpretation is confirmed by evidence for successive finishes (summarised in Fig 6.29), in which three stages of construction are represented.

In stage 1, the main longitudinal (that is, east–west) timbers bear shallow grooves, *c* 20 × 20mm, cut into the vertical surfaces above the mouldings, in line with the soffits of the joists. It would seem that it was originally intended to construct a ceiling by slotting boards into these grooves. There is no evidence that such a ceiling was ever constructed, however, and the physical difficulties of construction (whereby the boards would have to be assembled with the main timbers of the frame, and slid into the grooves as the joists were attached to the main beams) may give a hint as to why this arrangement was abandoned. The grooves accommodated the trimmed opening in the north-west bay (*see below*).

In stage 2, the ceiling as actually installed comprised a boarded ceiling, with applied moulded timbers bordering and subdividing each half bay into six (that is, 2 × 3 panels in bay 1) or nine (that is, 3 × 3 panels in bays 2 and 3). Surviving timbers show that this ceiling occupied bays 1–3, but antedates the extension of the parlour into bay 4 (*see below*). The superficial detail of the ceiling survived only in bay 1 (*see* Fig 6.29).[29]

Elsewhere the boards and mouldings had been replaced by the shallower mouldings and softwood planking of stage 3. Crude applied timbers were nailed to the central and flanking beams of each half bay (in an east–west direction) and to the second and fifth joist in each bay. This provided a secondary structure to which the ceiling planks and the moulded strips were nailed.

Applied timbers survived on the axial joists in all three bays, on the south sides of the northern peripheral joists and on a number of other joists, especially in bay 1 (*see* Fig 6.28, plan). A photograph shows the northern half of bay 1 during the removal of the boards in August 1985 (Fig 6.32). From this it can be seen that the applied timbers were used for fixing the planks of the infilling (three short planks north–south in each half bay – thus four applied timbers were needed). The planks (each spanning two joists) were then nailed to the soffits of the applied timbers and the east–west subsidiary mouldings fixed over the joins in the planks. Lastly short lengths of transverse subsidiary moulding were applied on the north–south lines. The edges of the planks were fitted together in simple V-shaped

Figure 6.28
Plan of the intersecting-beam ceiling of the parlour from above, also showing details of the headbeam of the west partition and moulding sections in the parlour and great chamber (line drawing by Tony Ives and Richard Parker).

Figure 6.29 (facing page)
Details of the construction of the parlour ceiling:
(top) perspective view of bay 1, attempting to show the structure in its final form;
(centre) reconstructed sections of a single half-bay with plank ceilings as intended and as built;
(bottom) details of mouldings (line drawing by Tony Ives).

South Range: Chamber

Plan of Floor Timbers

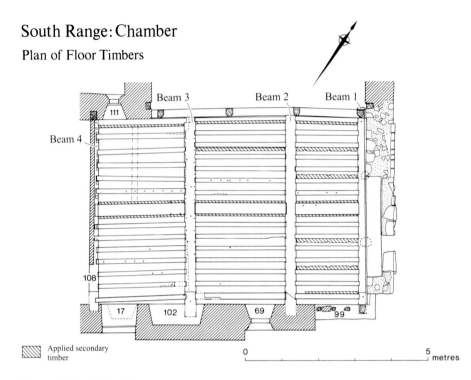

Applied secondary timber

0   5 metres

Beam 4, East Elevation

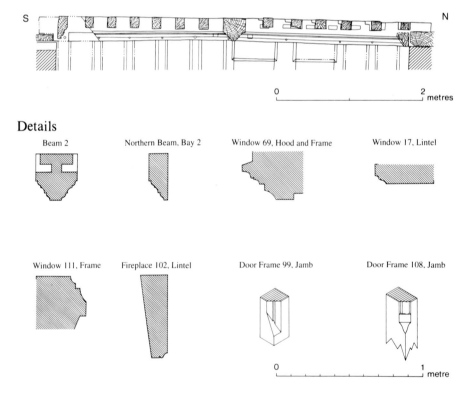

0   2 metres

Details

Beam 2   Northern Beam, Bay 2   Window 69, Hood and Frame   Window 17, Lintel

Window 111, Frame   Fireplace 102, Lintel   Door Frame 99, Jamb   Door Frame 108, Jamb

0   1 metre

Parlour ceiling, perspective drawing of Bay 1, looking north (not to scale)

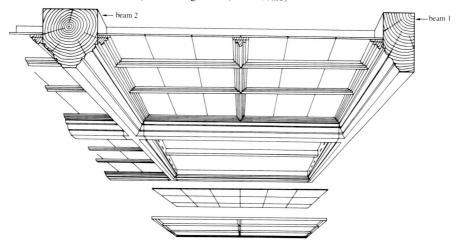

Reconstruction of intended form of ceiling, looking east

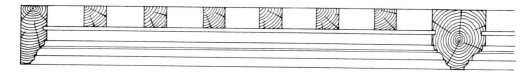

Reconstruction of ceiling as built, looking east

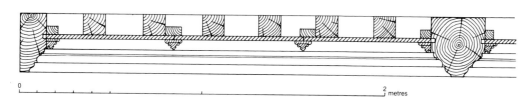

Beam 2

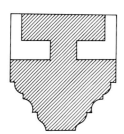

Moulded joist, Bay 3, south

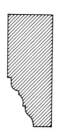

Central sub-ribs

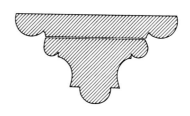

Beam 4 and additions (after Morley)

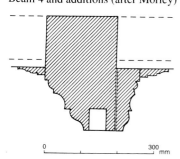

Axial beam, Bay 4

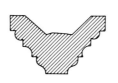

Peripheral sub-ribs

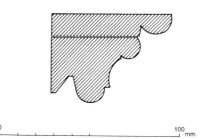

Figure 6.30 (left)
Detail of the south-eastern corner of the parlour ceiling from below during repair (with resin repair to the terminal of beam 1). Also showing is the mortice for supporting the post in line with the quoin of the wall (photograph by David Garner; EH B905040).

Figure 6.31 (right)
Vertical view from above of the frame of the parlour ceiling, bay 3 (north at the top). Note the peg holes in the upper surface of the joists, purpose unknown, and mortices on the head-beam of the western partition (extreme left) (photograph by Keith Westcott; EMAFU 1380/5).

Figure 6.32
The northern half of bay 1 of the parlour ceiling during dismantling, showing surviving ceiling boards and sub-ribs, looking east (EH F850039/11).

tongue-and-grooving (*see* Fig 10.4). In places the supporting timbers obscured the grooves of stage 1, showing that the two arrangements cannot have coexisted and forming a consistent picture of a change of plan during construction. In bay 3, the supporting timber spanned the full width of the bay across the line of the trimmed opening, showing that this feature had also been removed by the time the ceiling was installed (*see* plan, Fig 6.28).

The boards of this ceiling have provided a most valuable set of data for dendro-chronological dating (Chapter 10) and in their probable felling date range of 1491–*c* 1507 have yielded invaluable confirmation of the date of the building suggested by other evidence. The dendrochronological analysis is also of interest for the identification of the boards as Baltic oak, showing that for specialist purposes such as this, imported materials of high quality were procured for the building.

In stage 3, when the parlour was enlarged by moving the western partition a bay to the west in phase 7, extensive alterations were made to the ceiling. These comprised the addition of new timbers to imitate the main moulded beams in bay 4 (*see below*) and the renewal of the panelling and plank infill in bays 2 and 3 (as well as bay 4). The planks and mouldings of the new work were of softwood throughout and much shallower mouldings were employed in the subdividing strips. Unfortunately the subsidiary timbers were removed and discarded when the building was stripped *c* 1979 and none has survived for inspection and interpretation (although the main timbers of bay 4 were retained, *see below*). The ceiling is recorded in photographs prior to stripping (*see* Figs 2.25, 6.20 and 6.21; the form of the mouldings is shown in Fig 6.29, beam 4).[30]

The north-west bay

The north-west bay of the ceiling is now occupied by five thick joists rather than six of the normal scantling seen elsewhere. Traces of two intended earlier arrangements survive in the bay (*see* the elevation of beam 4 in Fig 6.28). The primary arrangement was intended to be the normal one of six joists fixed by housed soffit tenons in beam 3 and similar (although unhoused) joints in beam 4. This would have been a closed assembly. The joists were not actually constructed in this way, however, and the evidence for the second arrangement suggests a further change of plan during construction. A trimmer was added *c* 930mm east of beam 4 (dashed lines on the plan, Fig 6.28). The area to the east of the trimmer was floored with joists in the primary mortices, but the trimmed opening received an arrangement of five removable joists, set in open mortices on the upper edge of beam 4 (and presumably in equivalents on the missing trimmer). Grooves for primary ceiling boards (*see above*) stop on the line of the trimmer, suggesting that the opening was intended from the start. The area was certainly not ceiled at this stage, as the redundant mortices for the six original joists in beam 4 were filled with small oak implants to restore a uniform surface to the face of the beam (unnecessary had the area been ceiled; Fig 6.33). Lastly the trimmed opening was removed and the surviving arrangement of five joists was substituted. This change took place before or at the same time as the installation of the panelled ceiling (*see above*), since this filled the north-west bay as well as the rest of the ceiling.

The implication is that the trimmed opening was for a stair, ladder or simply a trap door for use in the construction of the building, but not in its primary occupation. The moulding on the lower edge of the northern half of beam 4 is an addition, having been spliced into the timber; this may represent a repair to the ceiling after the removal of the trimmed opening (perhaps resulting from damage to the original moulding by use as a construction stair/trap door). An alternative explanation is that the trimmed opening accommodated a fixed

stair from the parlour to the chamber (perhaps a service stair) and represents a primary feature that was quickly superseded. Although this makes sense of some of the other evidence, such as the twin doorways from the screens passage and especially the windows squeezed into the north wall, providing independent (if limited) lighting in this corner of the room, it does not really stand up to the dating evidence of the ceiling.

Westward extension of the parlour into bay 4

The enlargement of the parlour entailed: the removal of the western screen of the parlour from beneath beam 4 to a new position beneath beam 5; the extension of the ceiling into bay 4 (as well as the replacement of the ceiling boards and moulded strips in softwood in bays 2 and 3); and the insertion of the pair of large windows in the south wall (shown to be contemporary by the moulded lintel that formed the south side of the extended bay of the ceiling; *see above* and Fig 6.22, 27). Further evidence for the re-positioning of the screen was recovered by excavation (Chapter 4).

On the enlargement of the parlour into bay 4, the ceiling was furnished with additional timbers to imitate those of bays 1–3.[31] These comprised narrow timbers, with compressed versions of the original mouldings applied to the west face of beam 4 and the east face of beam 5 and broader timbers against the north and south walls of the bay. In the centre of the bay, a new axial joist with a direct copy of the original mouldings, rather than the compressed version of the other timbers, was inserted. Its upper surface was hollowed out to fit around an existing joist (*see* Fig 6.29, axial beam, bay 4). A softwood imitation of the earlier (oak) ceiling was erected throughout bays 2–4, probably at the same time as the extension of the parlour into bay 4. Dunmore recorded some oak planks among the softwood filling of bays 2–4.[32] This suggests that the softwood timbers were direct replacements of the earlier hardwood ceiling boards. The south flanking joist in bay 3 was also replaced with a timber with similar steep mouldings to those of bay 4 (*see* Fig 6.29, moulded joist, bay 3, south). This is identified by its thinner scantling, steep moulding profile, the absence of a groove for primary plank infill and the fact that it is placed in an *open* mortice in beam 4 to the west (Fig 6.34; *see also* Fig 6.31).

Figure 6.33
Detail of the northern half of beam 4, showing filled and redundant mortices (photograph by David Garner; EH B990722).

Figure 6.34
Detail of the south flanking joist of bay 3, showing steep mouldings (compare with the joist of bay 2 in the foreground) (photograph by David Garner; EH B990721).

The replacement of this timber was presumably linked to the enlargement of the adjacent windows. The applied moulding on beam 5 contained open mortices in its rear face to accommodate the studs of the repositioned western screen.[33] The mortices show that the screen was moved intact, that is, it had two doorways in the same place as in its original position. The removal of doorways and other alterations to the screen are thus assigned to still later phases (*see* Fig 12.2).

Painted decoration of the parlour ceiling

by Ruth McNeilage[34] and Stuart Blaylock

Selected timbers from the collection from bay 1 of the parlour ceiling were examined in July 1997, with the primary aim of establishing a sequence of paint layers and the secondary aim of recording any evidence that might help to establish a relative sequence of paint layers (and, thereby, decorative schemes). The inspection was supplemented by a site visit in November 1997 to record equivalent traces of paint on the timbers still *in situ*, the moulded beams and joists.

Both ribs and planks were painted with a red oil-based paint consisting of a mixture of red lead and iron oxide. A red lead layer has been found beneath this on the ribs. One section of rib examined (an upper member of a peripheral sub-rib, *see* Fig 6.29) appears to have been painted with only a fairly thick layer of red lead (a vivid orange-red) and no second layer containing iron oxide. This might have been part of an earlier scheme or simply a preparatory layer. The remaining pieces examined had remains of the red lead and iron oxide layer with some fragmentary evidence for a red lead layer beneath.

On the plank panels the following sequence was observed:

1. fragments of a ground layer containing chalk;
2. the red layer, a mixture of red lead and iron oxide;
3. a cream-white layer;
4. application of scrim repairs to some panels;
5. a pinkish oil layer (more brittle than 6);
6. two white oil layers;
7. wallpaper.

One panel shows significant evidence of a paint layer beneath the red layer – a thin beige layer that could be a discoloured white. This is probably a preparatory layer. The planks were clearly first painted in position, as none of the paint extends beneath the positions of the ribs.

On the ribs the stratification is similar to that of the panels, although the white layers are much more fragmentary. This is probably due to the preparation of the surface prior to later applications. The following sequence was observed on the ribs:

1. white ground;
2. red lead preparatory layer;
3. red lead and iron oxide;
4. a number of white layers;
5. very thin yellow layer;
6. very thin beige layer;
7. brown glaze (graining varnish). The graining was applied over an uneven surface composed of remains of various different white layers.

The main beams of the ceiling still *in situ* show the same sequence of paint layers as the moulded ribs, albeit in fragmentary condition.[35] They demonstrate important information about the structural sequence. Two later additions to the ceiling, the south flanking beam in bay 3 and the applied moulding on the east face of the northern half of beam 4, show traces of the full sequence of paint layers. Since both are additions to the ceiling, they suggest that the ceiling was not painted in its original form and that the first painting did not take place until these alterations were in place, perhaps in the mid- to late 16th or early 17th century (phases 4 or 5).[36]

One fragment of plank (thinner than the others in the collection) retained traces of a painted design (*see* Fig 9.27; catalogue no. 142). The piece was recovered from the infill of the later (softwood) planking of bay 4 of the enlarged parlour ceiling.[37] The polychrome painting is bound in a water-soluble size medium and has never been overpainted. If it originated in the ceiling, the piece was therefore probably removed prior to the commencement of the main sequence of paint layers.

Summary and dating of the phases of the parlour ceiling

The original intersecting-beam ceiling in a parlour of three bays was intended to have a planked ceiling which is represented by grooves on the main timbers into which the planks fitted, but was never executed. The primary frame accommodated a trimmed opening in the north-western bay (bay 3, north), which was only used during construction and was quickly superseded. The second phase, still in the primary phase of the building (phase 3, *c* 1500), probably represented an alteration during construction or the final 'fitting-out' stage of the work. This involved the erection of a modified planked ceiling with moulded subdivisions in oak, with well-defined composite mouldings (*see* Fig 6.29). The trimmed opening was removed and the area joisted and ceiled over. The felling date obtained for the boards by dendrochronology is so closely coincident with the proposed construction date for the building that it is difficult to propose much of a gap between construction and the addition of this ceiling. The third phase belongs with the enlargement of the parlour, which is dated by archaeological and structural evidence to the later part of the 17th century (phase 7). The materials employed are characteristic of this period, although it is noteworthy that this work represents a decision to copy the existing ceiling (and thereby an attempt to preserve the uniform appearance of the room) rather than replacing it in some more up-to-date style of decoration. This might argue for a fairly early date within the phase, perhaps *c* 1660, on the grounds that if refurbishment had taken place, say, 20 years (or more) later, it is more likely that the older scheme would have been replaced (for example, with a contemporary plaster ceiling).[38] Evidence for subsequent activity is confined to the successive coatings of paint on boards and ribs.

The south-east range

The appearance and functioning of this vanished range are mainly discussed elsewhere (Chapters 1 and 8). Little is certain about the interior other than that it was entered from the parlour through the aperture in the south-east corner. If left open this was a very large doorway (1.5m wide and *c* 2.7m high) spanning the angle of the room (that is, void on the east wall as well as the south). Alternatively the opening could have been filled with a timber partition similar to that in a secondary context in the equivalent opening on the first floor, although no evidence for such a partition was noted when the late masonry blocking was dismantled for repair in 1990. Nevertheless the likelihood of a division between the two rooms and the need to support the frame of the ceiling above (otherwise unsupported at this corner) both favour some sort of framed partition in this position.[39] On the basis of its appearance in the Bucks' engraving, a stair is the most likely interpretation for the attached turret (Chapter 1). It is likely that these rooms were independently heated and there is scope for fireplaces and chimneys in the north or east walls of the range.[40] Whatever the precise function of this range, it surely contained accommodation that was integral to the principal rooms of the house. Further, if the quality of the architectural fragments is a reliable guide (and they can be associated with this structure), the range probably exceeded the surviving rooms in status and level of appointments (Chapter 9).

Figure 6.35
Beam 6 seen from below, west at the top (restored to north and south), showing mortices for the posts of the partition and the slot for plank infill (photograph by David Garner; EH B933112).

Figure 6.36
Interior of the south range,
showing the service rooms
after initial stripping,
looking east in July 1978.
Note beam 6 in the fore-
ground, cut away to the
north (DoE J263/6/78).

The service rooms

Sequence of rooms

The area between the parlour and the cross wall originally formed two rooms divided by a timber partition beneath beam 6 (Fig 6.35; *see also* Fig 5.30); both were probably further subdivided. When the parlour was enlarged into bay 4 in phase 7 (*see above*), the second partition was also removed, and the remaining space (bays 5 and 6) became a single room. Later alterations entailed further subdivision, especially in relation to new stairs from ground to first floor (Fig 6.36; *see also* Fig 12.2).

Circulation

Construction of a modern stair in bays 5 and 6 in the 1970s (phase 11) entailed the removal of the northern part (*c* 1.25m) of beam 6 and associated joists to allow the stair to pass through. This removed the means to determine if there had been a door in the partition and (thereby) whether the service rooms were interconnected. No other evidence for a door was recovered. Although there are slight traces of partitions towards the north of both service rooms (*see below*), these are ambiguous in interpret-ation and need not support an intercon-necting doorway. It is probable, therefore, although not certain, that the screen was continuous. Since both rooms of the original plan had doorways in the north wall (*see* Fig 6.25, 255 and 259), independent access to each room from the pentice was possible.

East service room

Primary arrangement

The room had a window of uncertain form (Chapter 5) in the south wall of bay 4 and a garderobe in an attached projection from the wall entered from bay 5. Very little original fabric had survived successive changes to the south elevation – the western reveal of the garderobe entrance had survived in a modified form (*see* Fig 6.22, 36) and five courses of primary facework at the base of the wall in bay 4. The paired doorways in the west partition of the parlour, plus a mortice on the rear of the central post of the two doorways (not illustrated), suggest that this room was subdivided by an east–west partition in line with the two doors. The two rooms would have been unequal in size (the northern half substantially smaller than the southern), but this is a plausible arrange-ment, whether (for instance) they are inter-preted as traditional service rooms (that is, buttery and pantry) or as adjuncts to the parlour to the east.

On the north wall the original door and window had survived (*see* Fig 6.25, 256 and 260), although the door had been blocked in a later phase. The north window (Fig 6.37) is noteworthy in that its light was shared between the two service rooms. The embrasure was of the standard form for doors and windows described above (Chapter 5), with the frame set midway in the wall, a chase left for it in the masonry and lintel timbers flanking the frame over the embrasure (Fig 6.38).[41]

A groove was cut in the soffit of the inner lintel, in line with the position of the centre of the screen, to accommodate a plank to divide the window embrasure (*see* Fig 6.25). That there was clearly a need to light this area from the north, even in such an awkward manner, increases the evidence in favour of the subdivision of this space into two rooms.

Little had survived of the beam above; its sawn-off terminal was sampled for dendrochronology (Chapter 10). No trace of the original flooring had survived the cutting action associated with the enlargement of the parlour into bay 4, when the screen was moved.[42] A timber or flagged floor are possibilities. It will be seen that there is some evidence that the floor of the western room was of laid earth. Such a material is equally possible in this room.

Sixteenth-century alterations
The garderobe went out of use very early in the life of the building; the contents of the filled cess pit suggest a date of *c* 1550 (Chapter 9). It was replaced, presumably straight away, by a combined door and window (*see* Fig 5.8, 14 and 21) whose surviving fabric was in breccia.

West service room

Primary arrangement
The south wall had survived intact, with primary masonry throughout and some primary plaster. High in the wall, slightly east of centre, was a small rectangular window, with splayed reveals and a steeply splayed sill (*see* Fig 6.22, 59). The window is the only one of its type to survive in the building, although it is possible that the fragment in the south wall of the eastern service room was also of this type. As with most of the Bowhill windows, the interior lintel is chamfered and has diagonal-cut stops reflecting the splays of the reveals. The west wall of the room was formed by the stone ground-floor stage of the cross wall (now rebuilt on original footings, Fig 6.39) and probably contained no access into the passage to the west. The north wall also survived intact, with the shared window (*see* Fig 6.25, 256) and a doorway into the pentice (255).

Excavation revealed something of the original floor (Chapter 4). Inside the doorway was a paved area of pitched stone, limited to the south by a slot that may have supported a partition (*see* Fig 4.7, 753). Over the rest of the room there were small

Figure 6.37
North elevation of the service rooms in July 1993 (photograph by David Garner; EH B933570).

Figure 6.38
Detail of window 256 looking north-west, showing the chase for the frame in the reveal and lintel and the slot for a partition in the inner lintel (photograph by Keith Westcott; EMAFU 1488/28).

Figure 6.39
The western service room, looking west to the rebuilt cross wall (on original footings) in July 1993. Note the sleeper wall for the screen (photograph by David Garner; EH B933566).

areas of natural subsoil upstanding above the level of the stone pavement, suggesting that the inner threshold had been surrounded by a kerb (or perhaps by a partition, closet or inner porch) and that the floor may have been of trampled earth or thin laid earth incorporating natural clay at a high level.

Later alterations (after amalgamation)
Further alterations took place after the amalgamation of the two rooms. The eastern part of the south elevation was poorly preserved, with a complex recent structural history (Chapter 5 and *see* Fig 12.2, phases 9–12). Little remained to be seen on the interior at the time of recording, except for a panel of new masonry blocking by English Heritage of *c* 1985 (Figs 6.40 and 6.41; *cf* Fig 6.22, 34) which was constructed to fill the embrasure of the modern door (*see* Figs 2.12 and 5.16). Remarkably the plastering of the adjacent window reveal had survived the vicissitudes of successive alterations and could be seen,

until rendered over at the completion of the recent works, with the new masonry of the 1980s abutting it (*see* Fig 6.22, 31).

On the north wall the primary door (*see* Fig 6.25, 259) was blocked as a part of the late 17th-century rearrangement, when the removal of the parlour screen to its secondary position below beam 5 obstructed the west reveal. In the late 1960s a new door was cut into the wall immediately to the west of the blocked primary door, with a threshold at a very high level (*see* Fig 6.25, 257, and Figs 2.17, 5.18 and 5.19). Otherwise few alterations had an impact on the fabric. Changes in plan are charted in the phase plans (*see* Fig 12.2; two substantial internal refurbishments in the 20th century). Photographs also show that the primary doorway (as well as the adjacent north door of the through passage) was blocked and fitted with a window in 1969 (*see* Fig 2.18).[43]

The western bays

The stone cross wall provided a clear division in the plan between the main living rooms (and associated service rooms) and the passage and storeroom beyond. There was, however, no evidence for thinking that the wall marked the western limit of the house at some early phase.[44] The stone and cob of the ground- and first-floor stages respectively were firmly bonded to the north wall of the south range and were clearly of the same build. The continuous numbering of the roof trusses to either side of the cross wall supports this. Although the fabric of the cross wall did abut the south elevation (or in terms of surviving fabric the face of the south elevation ran across the line of the demolished cross wall), this can be explained in terms of the sequence of construction at the point of transition from stone to cob fabric. The cross wall survived until the 1960s, albeit with inserted doorways at two points (*see* Fig 12.2, phase 10; also on Everett's plan of 1958),[45] but was removed thereafter. Only the footings and a fragment at the northern end survived.[46]

The western bays are occupied by a passage 2.0m wide (bay 8) and the west service room in bays 9 and 10 (5.6m long). The two spaces were separated by a timber screen beneath beam 9. The mortices surviving in the soffit of the extant portion of the beam show it to have been another post and panel screen, with twin doorways towards the northern end.

Figure 6.40
The south wall of the service rooms after stripping, but before any masonry repairs in 1985 (see exterior view of the same, Fig 5.16), with window of phase 7 (for enlarged parlour), blocked in phase 8 and doorway of phase 9 (EH F850039/5).

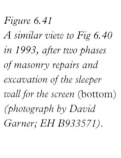

Figure 6.41
A similar view to Fig 6.40 in 1993, after two phases of masonry repairs and excavation of the sleeper wall for the screen (bottom) *(photograph by David Garner; EH B933571).*

The through passage

Primary arrangement

The south end of the passage had a large arched entrance on the exterior (removed and now reconstructed; see Fig 11.36), but a trabeate embrasure of the usual form on the interior (admittedly rather larger than normal; see Fig 6.22, 56). The stone part of the south elevation stepped down around the entrance, providing a masonry surround for the arch. This was particularly marked on the outside, where it was conditioned by the need to provide a structural context for the stone frame, but the technique was also employed on the interior. Presumably this was done to provide a masonry pier to support the west end of the lintel, the south terminal of beam 9 and the post of truss IX (see Fig 6.22), but it also served to frame the doorway. The lintel (343) is chamfered and stopped (with straight-cut stops) in line with the side walls of the passage. Evidence for a stone frame to the arch survived in the form of the impressions of the tails of the blocks in the mortar of the adjacent core. The frame was presumably rebated for a door in the same way as those of the screens passage. In view of the size of the arch this door may have been of two leaves.

The northern door also originally occupied the full width of the passage. Its interior lintel (again with straight-cut chamfer stops) survived with original cob above (see Fig 6.25, 421 and 268). The original western jamb of the door also survived in the stone footings (267 and 420) in line with the western stop of the lintel. The upper part of the jamb, it must be assumed, was originally of cob, since this material formed the wall to the west (and the foot of the nearest roof truss, IX, was carried down onto the footings, the usual configuration in cob walling). The area was subsequently filled with masonry (269, see below). The door was slightly narrower than its southern counterpart (1.85m), and trabeate inside and out. Unlike the southern doorway, therefore, it was not intended for architectural impact. Several functions converged on the area immediately outside this doorway (for example, egress from the passage, passage from the hall to the kitchen via the pentice and supporting timbers for the gallery), no doubt with potential for confusion or obstruction.

The north door had a centrally placed timber frame (as throughout the north side of the south and the west ranges, see above).

A chase was recorded in the eastern reveal, 0.21m wide. In the soffit the lintels were set 0.20m apart to accommodate the frame (see Fig 5.17, 358). The floor did not survive, since later activity had removed contemporary deposits and cut into natural subsoil (Chapter 4).[47] Six primary ceiling joists survived at the north end of the passage (see Fig 6.1), showing that the ceiling was of plain joists, as throughout the service rooms.

The screen

The mortices and chamfers in the headbeam of the western screen (beam 9) allowed a full reconstruction (see Fig 5.27 and Fig 11.118), with the qualification that the absence of upright members or an indication of floor level meant that the original height of the studs and the sill level remained uncertain. The mortices indicated two doorways separated by a plank panel at the northern end of the screen. Like those of the screens passage (see above) these were of different widths, the northern (c 0.75m) narrower than the southern (c 0.95m). The frame of the first floor in bay 9 to the west contained an original (closed assembly) trimmed opening immediately within the northern doorway (Fig 6.42). A chamfer on the lower edge of the northern side of the opening suggests that a stair rose from the northern door.[48] Although the available space was very tight, a steep ladder-like stair possibly enclosed in a closet could have been accommodated. The stair may only have been for service use as there was also access to the oriel chamber through the first-floor rooms and from the gallery.[49] The second, wider (and roughly central) doorway would have acted as a normal entry to the west service room. The remainder of the beam, up to the point 1.4m short of the south wall where it was cut off, showed mortices for three chamfered studs, with room for a further three in the missing portion. Chamfers on the headbeam were interrupted by the mitres for the posts. The plank panels

Figure 6.42
Detail of the floor frame from below, looking east, showing the soffit of beam 8, mortices for the screen (and evidence for doorways), and the trimmed opening for a stair or trap-door (note chamfer on joist to left) (photograph by David Garner; EH B940377).

were fitted into chases in the soffit of the headbeam (*see* Fig 6.42). The west (inner) side of the headbeam had a continuous chamfer, with a stepped stop at the northern end.

Later alterations

The principal alteration to the passage took place in phase 8 and involved the removal of the original doorways (north and south), the western screen and the original flooring. They were replaced by narrowed entrances of more regular size, a new partition in line with the narrowed western jambs of the doors and the construction of a stair through a secondary (that is, new at this phase) trimmed opening in the floor frame above (*see* Fig 12.2, phase 8). The fabric associated with the southern doorway was removed at an early stage of the recent repairs.[50] To the north the blocking survives, narrowing the doorway from 1.85m to 1.15m (*see* Fig 6.25, 269), coupled with the refacing of the wall, presumably in replacement of cob. The evidence for a stair was represented by a trimmed opening in the southern part of bay 8, on the east side. The surviving joists were all secured in closed mortices and there were similar closed mortices for joists continuing southward in the area of the trimmed opening. An open mortice for the trimmer (vacant) was matched by a chamfer on the lower edge of the last joist for 1.22m from the eastern edge.[51] The chamfer suggests a stair rising to the south beneath the last joist and matches the evidence of partitioning excavated in 1993 (Chapter 4 and *see* Fig 4.19). Quite extensive activity of this period was revealed by excavation, including a clay layer representing the remains of an earth floor or perhaps the bedding for a paved floor. This was associated with features containing demolition material, including a fragment of sculpture (Chapter 9).

Still later alterations comprised a lime-mortar floor (later 19th century) and additional partitioning to the west (*see* Fig 12.2). Lastly both doors were blocked and reduced to windows after the removal of the cross wall in the alterations of the restaurant period *c* 1969–70 (phase 11).

The west service room

Primary arrangement

The room had a door in the south-west corner, in the position of a complex of later windows (*see* Fig 6.22, 46 and 340) and a window in the west wall (Chapter 5). The north wall was without features. The fabric

was uniform throughout – cob walling on stone footings, ceiling beams with chamfers and stepped stops and plain joists. The mortices of bay 11 were open (presumably as this was the last bay of the floor frame to be assembled). As with the passage, no evidence for the primary flooring was observed, although scattered paviours in a later floor (*see below*) may have been reused from a primary floor.

The isolation of the room in the plan of the building, the lack of heating and limited lighting all suggest a store or service function. Easy access from the main entrance passage and proximity to the kitchen were, no doubt, also significant factors in relation to the original function of this room. Although conventional service functions have been suggested for the two rooms immediately to the west of the parlour, this room too could have performed such a function.

Early alterations, 16th to 17th century (phase 5)

The first and principal alteration to this room was the insertion of a fireplace and the construction of its associated stack in bay 10 of the north wall (Fig 6.43; *see also* Fig 6.25, 262 and 182). In the process the face of the wall was removed over the full width of the bay (although the rear face survived in the kitchen, *see* Fig 5.17). The fireplace was built against the west face of the post of truss X and underpinned beam 11 against the west wall (*see* Fig 6.25). It had reveals of large breccia blocks, spanned by a heavy timber lintel with chamfers and scroll stops. The rear was originally simply cut into the cob (part of the back is still just a cob face).

Figure 6.43
The north-west corner of the west service room during excavation in 1993, showing the fireplace (see Fig 6.25, 262) and the paving slabs forming the remnant of floor (Fig 4.19, 1623) (photograph by David Garner; EH B934824).

The lower part has been relined with brick (264). The oven in the western reveal was lined with breccia and floored with volcanic slabs (265). The facework of the stack above the lintel was of mixed volcanic and breccia masonry. From first-floor level the flue narrows and was built in a distinctive style of large face-bedded breccia slabs. A distinctive bonding material, a soft, yellow-brown mortar, was used throughout the fireplace and the stack. Similar material was used in the plastering of the wall to the east over the post of truss X, the adjacent cob walling and up to the soffit of beam 10. This was seen nowhere else in the building, although a similar (and possibly related) cob appeared in the filling of the scar of a stair in the south wall of the west service room (see below).

The excavation of 1993 revealed a number of volcanic stone paviours within and immediately around the fireplace (Chapter 4 and see Fig 4.19, 1623). Although these represented a later relaying of the floor, they might have originated in a paved floor of this phase or even in the primary floor of the room. The clay floor, found both in the passage (see above) and extending over much of the service room (see Fig 4.7, 1508 and 1570), could have been a bedding layer for such a pavement.

The fireplace probably belonged to a phase in the later 16th or early 17th century to which little else in the building could be attributed. The scroll stops of the lintel, though not a close indicator, would suggest such a date, while the distinctive materials argue for a phase not otherwise represented. The upgrading of the service room suggested by this work will still have left it with a single window (in the west wall). The inclusion of an oven suggests the provision of independent cooking facilities, possibly for a subsidiary dwelling or for a supplementary kitchen.

Early stairs

A further feature of this or another early period was a scar in the cob of the south wall of the room that had retained the outline of a stair (Fig 6.44; see also Fig 6.22, 342). The scar consisted of a well-defined lower edge in two horizontal steps separated by a possible socket. The upper edge ascended from west to east in four ill-defined steps, before disappearing against the masonry pier of the archway. The form, context and possible date of this stair were puzzling. If the upper limit of the scar is accepted as retaining the form of treads (at least roughly), then a

Figure 6.44
Cob of the south elevation showing the secondary chase for a stair (see Fig 6.22, 342) at the junction of cob and stone walling (photograph by David Garner; EH B940402).

turning stair might be expected (the lower steps to the west appear longer then the upper, as if representing the turn of a dog-leg stair). If this was so, the feature could hardly have been earlier than the late 16th century and was probably later still. The position of the stair also counted against it as a primary feature, as there was already one stair ascending to the oriel chamber (see above) and this feature was placed directly beneath the oriel window, itself a primary element of the room above. Thus the feature is assigned (rather arbitrarily) to phases 5 or 7, since it was removed in the alterations of phase 8, which saw the construction of another stair in bay 8 (see above). The scar was filled with cob of a unique, yellowish mix (Chapter 10, class 4).

Later alterations

Much of the west elevation had been removed by modern disturbances (Fig 6.45).[52] Masonry of the stone footings survived at either end and some primary cob at the south end (the construction lifts in the cob were seen in the exposed cross-section of this wall, see Fig 5.22, section B), but the remainder of the wall was a medley of 19th- and 20th-century builds. Alterations of phase 8 dominated the south wall. First a post and an area of masonry below the southern terminal of beam 10 (see Fig 6.22, 338) were inserted to support the terminal, probably associated with refurbishment in this area after the removal of the oriel above. The westernmost beam (11) may have been disturbed at this time. Signs of disturbance were noted around both terminals of the beam, possibly related to the removal of the west gable wall. Second was the construction of a window in the position of the

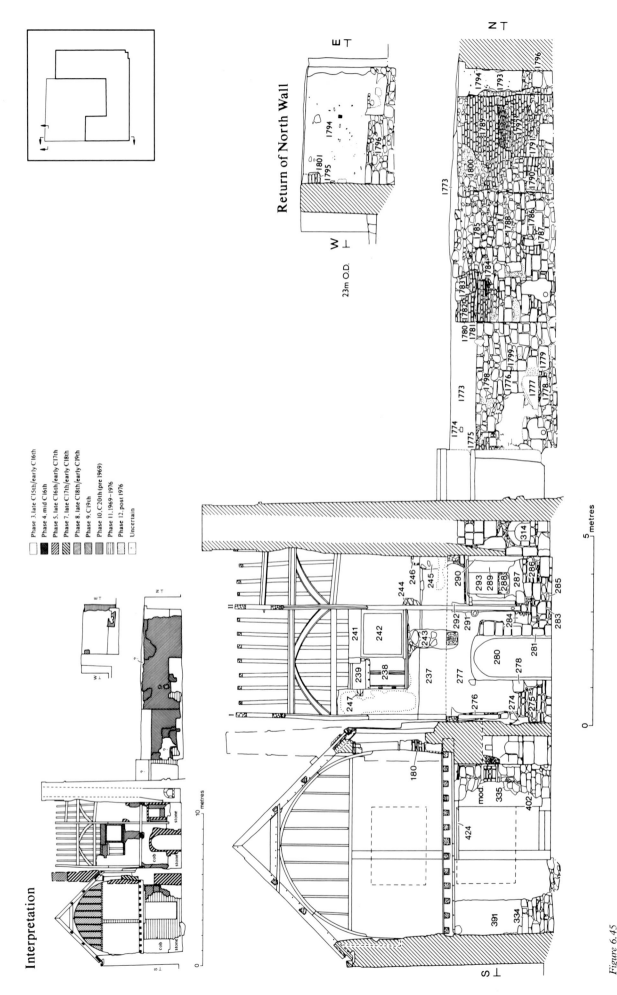

Return of North Wall

Interpretation

Phase 3. late C15th/early C16th
Phase 4. mid C16th
Phase 5. late C16th/early C17th
Phase 7. late C17th/early C18th
Phase 8. late C18th/early C19th
Phase 9. C19th
Phase 10. C20th (pre 1969)
Phase 11. 1969–1976
Phase 12. post 1976
Uncertain

Figure 6.45

West interior elevation of the south and west ranges and of west and north boundary walls of the courtyard (formerly the interior elevations of the west range) (scale 1:100) (line drawing by Tony Ives and Richard Parker).

probable primary door (46 and 340). The four-light softwood casement window of this phase was later replaced by a sash and further modified in the 1970s. The room was subdivided, first by a partition in bay 9 (*see* Fig 12.2, phase 10),[53] secondly by similar partitions in the restaurant period of the 1970s (phase 11). At the same time a hole was cut through the cob of the north wall to create a serving hatch between the west service room and the kitchen in the west range (*see* Fig 6.25, 361).

West range: the kitchen

The kitchen occupied one-and-a-half bays at the south end of the west range, separated from the rest of the range (now demolished) by a thick wall accommodating the fireplace and chimney flue. Since the room was originally open to the roof, it represented a gap in the first-floor plan. By function it was related to the rooms at the west end of the south range and was connected by the pentice to the principal living rooms to the east. Later modifications post-dating the flooring of the kitchen are described at the appropriate point on the first floor.

Original arrangement

The south and west walls had low stone footings (*c* 0.9m high) and cob superstructure above (Fig 6.46; *see also* Figs 5.17 and 6.45). The east wall was built of stone to a slightly higher level. This was probably to provide direct support for the northern end of the lintels of the wide doorway/window giving onto the pentice, since the cob begins at the level of the lintel (Fig 6.47, 303, stone, and 218, cob). The north wall contained much more stone because of the massive chimney stack for the kitchen fireplace (Fig 6.48; *see also* Figs 4.21 and 6.47, 295 and 203). Nevertheless that part of the elevation not given over to the stack was of cob. The flanking parts to east and west have primary cob bearing onto or butting up to the masonry of the stack (*see* Fig 6.47, 202, 206 and 212).

The west range was built in a more conventional method than the south range, in that the posts of the roof trusses were raised before the cob walls were erected (Chapter 7). The principal evidence of the procedure in the fabric was that the cob ran up to the posts of the roof trusses, with only minimal shrinkage gaps (Fig 6.49; *see also* Fig 6.47, 400). Both western posts originally

Figure 6.46
The ground floor of the kitchen, looking south-west. Note the relative height of cob/stone footings, the door of phase 5 (cut into cob) and the inserted floor (DoE J263/3/78).

carried down to the stone footings, although that of truss I was cut off when the floor was inserted and supported by a supplementary timber (*see* Fig 6.45, 276). The eastern posts were both originally supported on the timber lintel. Here too the insertion of the floor led to modifications to the foot of truss I and the post was cut away between the lintel and the base of the arch brace (*see* Fig 6.47).

The kitchen was dominated by the fireplace, which spans nearly the full width of the room with a segmental arch of dressed volcanic blocks with joggled joints (*see* Fig 4.21).[54] The frame of the fireplace was chamfered, the lower terminals too worn for stops to be discerned.[55] Above the head was a relieving arch of volcanic voussoirs with massive springing blocks at each end (*see* Fig 6.47, 294). The voussoirs, as well as the original blocks of the back of the fireplace (301), all bear the distinctive diagonal tooling marks also seen on the parlour and chamber fireplaces and other fine dressed stone in the building (Fig 6.50).[56] The west reveal of the fireplace contains a primary oven whose frame and lining are again of finely worked volcanic stone (*see* Fig 6.47, 314). Originally the rear of the oven was accommodated in a projecting bulge of masonry in the wall to the north, whose footings were excavated in 1978 (Chapter 4; *see* Fig 4.7, 2394). There may have been further original features in the rear wall of the fireplace in the positions of later ovens and associated fabric (*see below* and Fig 6.47, 297, 298 and 302), but no traces had survived.

The primary fenestration of the kitchen was also uncertain because of the lack of surviving evidence. The one certain primary

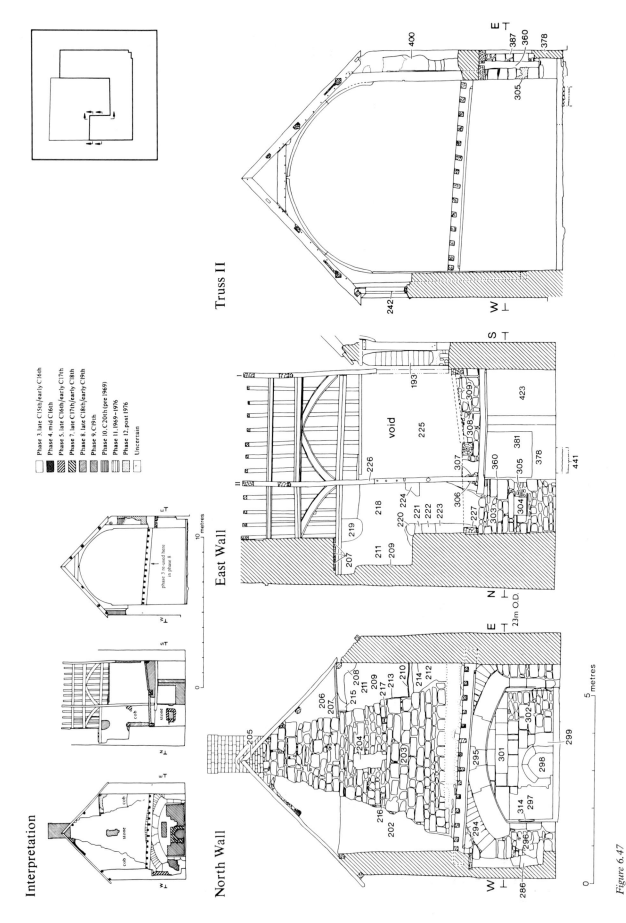

Interpretation

North Wall

East Wall

Truss II

Phase 3. late C15th/early C16th
Phase 4. mid C16th
Phase 5. late C16th/early C17th
Phase 7. late C17th/early C18th
Phase 8. late C18th/early C19th
Phase 9. C19th
Phase 10. C20th (pre 1969)
Phase 11. 1969–1976
Phase 12. post 1976
Uncertain

Figure 6.47
West range, interior elevations: north wall (left); east wall (centre); and section on the line of truss II (right) (scale 1:100) (line drawing by Tony Ives and Richard Parker).

window that was paired with the door in the double embrasure in the east wall (Fig 6.51; *see also* Fig 6.47, 360 and so on) must have been inefficient for lighting, because it was obstructed by the pentice and gallery outside and may have functioned primarily as a serving hatch. There might have been a primary first-floor window in bay 1 of the east wall, now entirely void (*see* Fig 6.47, 225), although this would have suffered from similar obstruction by the gallery. All of the extant features in the west wall were insertions, although some dated to an early phase in the life of the building (*see below*) and little trace of primary features remained. The large composite window embrasure (*see* Fig 6.45, 238 and 242) on the first floor probably marked the position of an original window smaller than its successors and thus almost entirely removed by their insertion. A filled socket to the south of the embrasure (247) represented the position of a primary lintel (since the later window seems to have had no lintel and the cob above lintel level appears to have been cut away on the insertion of the five-light window, below). The ghost of cob walling survived on the south face of roof truss II, below the lowest purlin, showing that originally there was a pier of cob to the south of the truss forming a reveal to the window and supporting the northern end of the lintel represented by socket 247. A narrow (?two-light) window is, therefore, likely in the primary arrangement. Primary-type plaster survived on the cob wall face to the south and below the sill of the window, but the reveals of the later window had no plaster, presumably because the wider reveal had cut the plastered surface away (Fig 6.52). If the ground floor of the west wall contained a window originally, it too must have been in the position of one of the later features and was obliterated by their insertion.

A further puzzle was presented by a group of features in and against the northern wall: a niche high in the wall to the east of the chimney flue (*see* Fig 6.47, 211, and Fig 6.48); and sockets, apparently representing the positions of beams in the east and west walls at the same level as the threshold of the niche, but only in the northern half bay (*see* Fig 6.45, 244 and 246 and Fig 6.47, 220 and 224). The best interpretation of these features yet offered is that they represent some form of platform or possibly a 'smokehood' linked to the storage or curing of food.[57] Uncertainties concerning the phasing of the features,

Figure 6.48
The north elevation of the kitchen at first-floor level, showing the masonry chimney flue and cob walling to each side. Note the extent of surviving plaster at this time (July 1978; DoE J263/8/78).

Figure 6.49
The east post of truss II of the roof of the west range, showing the different treatment of this roof. Here the roof trusses were raised first and the cob wall built around them; in section this view shows a narrow gap caused by the shrinkage of the cob (photograph by David Garner; EH B933511).

Figure 6.50
Detail of the kitchen fireplace, showing the distinctive diagonal tooling of volcanic trap ashlar masonry at Bowhill (photograph by David Garner; EH B990723).

Figure 6.51 (left)
The ground floor of the kitchen, looking south-east during excavation in September 1993. Note the foot of the post of the roof truss bearing on a broad lintel (extreme left) (photograph by David Garner; EH B934833).

Figure 6.52 (right)
Detail of window frame 238 and its embrasure, looking south-west (see Fig 5.2). Note the filled socket for the lintel at top centre and reveal cutting the primary plaster (photograph by David Garner; EH B943781).

Figure 6.53 (facing page) Details of windows recorded in position: 137, moulded window frame of phase 5, reused in phase 8 in the north wall of the inner chamber; 238, chamfered window frame, perhaps of phase 3 or 4 from the west wall of the kitchen (first floor) (see the comparable frames in the collection of loose timbers, Fig 9.23); 80 and 81, sill of the east windows of the parlour, with isometric view and plan of the sills (the area occupied and obscured by modern frames indicated by dashed lines) (line drawing by Richard Parker).

the structural history of the niche and the function in relation to the kitchen or to the northern rooms of the west range (if any) hamper the interpretation of the evidence. The sockets were the earliest features in a sequence of cuts into the cob, mainly associated with the insertion of the floor to the room. The northern sockets (246 and 220) were cut into by the deep slots for the insertion of the northern beam of the floor (245, 223 and so on), but this relationship alone is not sufficient to show that the sockets are primary. The niche, however, did appear to be a primary feature since the lintel timbers (*see* Fig 6.47, 207) were finished with a crude chamfer and run-out stops. They rested directly on the purlin of the roof and on the masonry of the chimney stack and the cob of the upper stage of the wall (206) bore directly upon the lintel. On the interior the upper stage of cob was isolated from primary cob below and could all have been a secondary build. Comparison with the outside elevation, however, showed that the cob was continuous across the line of the lintel within (*see* Fig 5.26). Within the niche primary plastered faces of the sides and sill (*see* Fig 6.47, 213, 214 and 210) ran behind a blocking of cob in the rear (209) and there was a remnant of the plastered rear face at the top (215), although much of this had been cut away by inserted brick blocking of *c* 1800 and 20th-century repairs (208). The total thickness of the rear of the niche including the cob blocking was only *c* 0.45–50m, and so it must have been very thin initially. The possibility that the 'niche' was a doorway into the first floor of the west range rooms beyond was considered, but was ruled out by the undisturbed nature of

the cob of the exterior elevation (*see above*) and by the failure of the lintels to penetrate to the exterior face. The sill level of the niche was substantially higher than the floor level in the vanished part of the west range (which was close to that of the south range, the two connected by the projected level of the gallery, *see* Chapter 5 and Fig 5.27).

The high kitchen open to the roof, with a fireplace spanning the full width of the room, was a familiar feature of many large late medieval houses. Comparable ranges of ovens exist in the kitchen complexes of grander houses, for example, at Thornbury Castle, Gloucestershire and Hampton Court Palace, Middlesex.[58] In Devon equivalent kitchen fireplaces of similar proportions survive at Compton Castle, Marldon,[59] Dartington Hall[60] and in various late medieval houses of the clergy in Exeter Cathedral Close discussed below (Chapter 8). The functioning of ovens in the rear walls of large fireplaces is uncertain. Either such features rely on a fire in only one part of the hearth, thus permitting access to the ovens elsewhere in the rear wall, or the ovens relate to features operated from the far side of the wall. This is certainly possible in the context of Bowhill, where the north elevation of the kitchen wall displays equivalent arched and blocked-in features (*see* Fig 5.27). The room to the north might therefore be interpreted as a back kitchen, bakehouse or other room with a function in food preparation. At a lower social and architectural level, ovens in the sides and rear faces of fireplaces are a widespread feature of farmhouse halls and kitchens. They are often of earthenware (in the post-medieval period), but are also occasionally lined and vaulted with stone, like those at Bowhill.[61]

Window 137, South Range

Exterior elevation

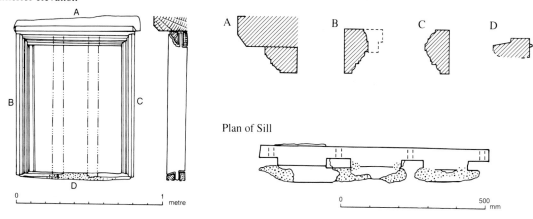

A

B

C

D

Plan of Sill

0 _____ 1 metre

0 _____ 500 mm

Window 238, West Range

Interior elevation

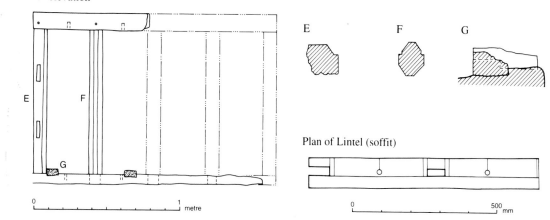

E

F

G

Plan of Lintel (soffit)

0 _____ 1 metre

0 _____ 500 mm

Windows 80,81, South Range (Parlour)

Isometric Projection of Sill

Plan of Sill

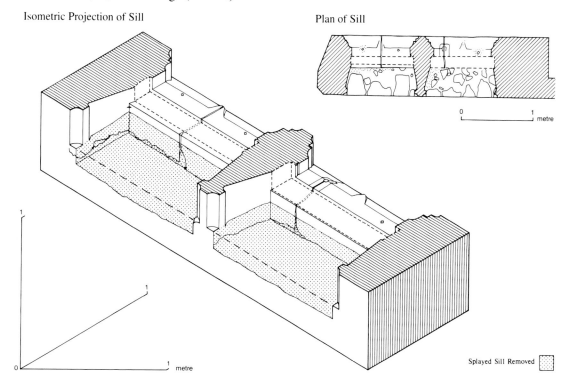

0 _____ 1 metre

0 _____ 1 metre

Splayed Sill Removed ░

Flooring

Excavations in 1993 revealed a fine cobbled pavement of post-medieval date covering the northern two-thirds of the kitchen. This appears in photographs of 1957 taken before concrete flooring was laid.[62] In the fireplace the cobbling incorporated a flagged area against the eastern reveal (*see* Fig 4.19, 1665). Rather than destroy this floor in pursuit of an earlier, but ephemeral pebbled surface,[63] the floor was left at this level (*see* Fig 4.21) and the missing areas (*see* Fig 4.19) reconstructed in 1994. The primary floor of the kitchen may well have been cobbled or paved or a combination of the two. The pebbled surface observed at the bottom of the sequence is more likely to have been a construction surface than one intended for day-to-day use in the kitchen.

Inserted door and windows in west wall

The door (*see* Fig 6.45, 280) and the ground-floor window (293) can be linked on the basis of similar building materials. They are dated to a mid- to late 16th-century or conceivably an early 17th-century phase of work on the basis of their breccia masonry and traditional if coarse and simple design. The door is formed of a breccia frame cut into the stone footings and cob superstructure. On the interior an embrasure was cut into the cob. All of the northern reveal and the lower half of the southern reveal were faced up in stone (281 and 278), but the head of the embrasure was left as naked cob without strengthening. This stands as testimony to the strength of the material, especially in view of the fact that at a later point the cob had to bear the end of an inserted floor beam (*see* Figs 6.45, 6.46 and 6.54).

The ground-floor window had a complex history. The breccia frame was clearly cut into the cob (Chapter 5) and the interior timber lintel was also clearly inserted (with small stones packing the space between the cob and the timber). It is possible that the lintel was reused from an earlier (?primary) window in the same position, repositioned to fit the requirements of the new window, since its northern end bears a straight-cut stop of the standard primary type. The southern stop was removed in a crude recutting, without leaving a trace of the original width of the inner embrasure. The traces of the first embrasure, that is, the one associated with the breccia frame in its primary form (*see* Fig 6.45, 290), comprised a crude masonry refacing of the cuts into the surrounding

walls and certainly did not look like primary work. A narrow, probably single-light, window set wholly in cob walling is the most likely reconstruction of a primary window.

The first-floor window had a timber frame of early style (Fig 6.53, 238) of the same type as two windows recovered from the barn in the 1970s (*see* Figs 2.14, 2.15 and Fig 9.23). The window was probably late 16th century in date, although reset in this position. It survived as two lights on the south side of the embrasure, cut to the north by a 20th-century window (Fig 6.54; *see also* Fig 6.45, 242, and Fig 6.52). The decayed sill timber was recovered with mortices indicating a further two lights and the placing of the window in fact suggests that it originally had five lights, occupying the space up to the south face of truss II. The frame had a simple chamfered profile, but was rebated for glazing. There were also single diagonally set vertical timber bars in each light (sockets in sills and lintels). Traces of red-lead colouring were observed on the timber. The placing of the window in this position probably occurred during the general reorganisation that took place after the demolition of the northern part of the west range and the insertion of a floor into the kitchen, *c* 1800 (phase 8). The pre-existing jambs were cut back quite substantially on the north side, in view of the evidence for the pier of cob to the south of the truss (*see above*). Short timber spurs were halved over the sill and set in the mortared outer sill, presumably to stabilise the window frame (*see* Fig 6.53, detail G). This work contained the ubiquitous red white-speckled mortar of phase 8. The window frame (along with those from the barn) may well have been reused from the demolished ranges to the north.

Figure 6.54
The west elevation of the kitchen at first-floor level, showing the broad embrasure for window 238 and the slot (243) for insertion of the floor beam, during repairs in July 1994 (photograph by David Garner; EH B943775).

Inserted floor

The central beam of the inserted floor was identical in form and decoration to the primary first-floor beams of the south range, with a chamfer and stepped stops. The north and south beams were themselves of similar form, but were otherwise unique to the building, with chamfers and diagonal-cut stops to the west, pyramid stops to the east.[64] The joists were chamfered and stopped with steep straight-cut stops in a stilted fashion that might suggest later alterations trying to fit in with an earlier idiom.[65] The three main beams all showed similar signs that they had been cut into the fabric of the kitchen, with deep slots in the cob for dropping in the northern beam (*see* Fig 6.47, 223 [E], and Fig 6.45, 245 [W]), another for the western terminal of the central beam (*see* Fig 6.45, 243, and Fig 6.54) and a slot beneath the site of the beam for swinging-up the western terminal of the southern beam (*see* Fig 6.45, 276).[66] Traces of the insertion of the eastern terminals of the beams did not survive the removal of the eastern wall of bay 1 (*see* Fig 6.47, 225), but they too were presumably dropped in from above or slid in from the outside if the flooring coincided with the removal of the wall. Everywhere this work was associated with the speckled mortar of phase 8. The obviously secondary character of this work and the difficulty of fitting beams of such large scantling into a standing structure in part explain the irregular result – the floor slopes by some 0.4m from west to east and from south to north (*see* Fig 6.47).

Because the central beam fits the span of the building so exactly, it seems probable that it was taken from one of the northern bays of the west range on its demolition and reused here. No obvious origin for the thinner north and south beams can be suggested. Perhaps they came from a demolished room elsewhere, with a similar disposition of half beams against solid dividing walls.

South range: first floor

The great chamber

As with the parlour below, the status of the great chamber was represented by a high level of fittings and comfort. The roof is described below (Chapter 7), but its level of decoration (aside from that of the hall the grandest in the building) needs emphasis here.

The room retains many original features. It was fitted with lancet windows in volcanic stone and although the eastern gable wall has vanished, similar windows to those in the eastern wall of the parlour can be suggested for this position. Further modifications were slight and reversible.

South-eastern door

Another feature shared with the parlour was direct communication through the south-east corner of the room with the lost south-east range (*see* Fig 12.3).[67] This opening spanned the corner of the room and was framed to the east by the post of roof truss I (*see* Fig 6.22). The gap was filled by a section of partition of primary type, incorporating a low and narrow doorway of the same type as those of the screens in the hall and parlour below (Fig 6.55; *see also* Fig 6.22, 99, and) and post and plank panelling above. The partition is unlikely to have been the original filling of this entrance, because although it was an authentic fragment of a primary screen typical of the building, in its

Figure 6.55
Doorway in the south-east corner of the chamber (formerly leading to the south-east range), itself secondary (?phase) and blocked in phase 8 (DoE J263/16/78).

present form its assembly is of secondary character. Presumably it was reused here from elsewhere in the primary building.[68]

The partition is too high (2.9m) for it to have had a source on the ground floor of the building (otherwise a provenance in an internal partition, perhaps in the service rooms (beneath beam 6?), would have been likely). A source on the first floor of the south, south-east or west ranges is thus most likely.

Other doorways

The great chamber may have been approached from the parlour below by the turret stair, whose primary function was to serve the room over the porch. Any evidence for the upper stage of this structure had been destroyed by the removal of the east gable wall in the alterations of *c* 1800. To the west, access from the chamber to the inner chamber by a door through the western screen is probable. There was a doorway in the surviving screen (a 17th-century replacement) and the same arrangement is presumed for the original, although no positive evidence had survived.

Fireplace

The fireplace in the south wall (*see* Fig 6.22, 102) was set west of centre against the western window, sharing the external stack with the fireplace of the parlour below (offset to the east). The fireplace was built to a very similar, although not identical, design to that of the parlour. The relieving arches and widths of the two match very closely (when the drawings are overlaid), but the joggled lintels vary in dimensions. This example also had a continuous ogee moulding to the frame (as opposed to a plain lintel). Again the moulded cornice had been removed. The fireplace was of volcanic stone throughout, with distinctive diagonal tooling on most blocks. The lintel, more massive than other examples, was composed of only two blocks, meeting at a joggled joint. Although the hearth was filled in to provide a smaller domestic fireplace in the 19th century, like that of the parlour, the detail of the original survived with much less damage than that of the parlour fireplace.

Fenestration

In addition to windows in the gable wall (now missing), there were originally three windows in the great chamber. Two flanked the fireplace (*see* Fig 6.22, 17 and 69), while the third was in the north wall in the narrow

gap between the west partition and the return of the wall of the east range (*see* Fig 6.25, 111). All three were cinquefoil-headed lancets in volcanic stone. The south windows had moulded lintels, the north a chamfered lintel. The first-floor windows differed from those of the ground floor by having flat rather than splayed sills. The south-eastern and northern windows survived in something like their original forms, both with small repairs to their embrasures (*see* Fig 6.22, 101, and Fig 6.25, 114) and were fitted with (respectively) 19th- and 20th-century casements. The north window had been reset slightly lower in its embrasure than originally (Chapter 5). The south-west window (*see* Fig 6.22, 17) had been remodelled. The lintel had survived from the original late medieval window, preserving the position of the splayed jambs (Fig 6.56). Since the moulding was the same as that of window 69 and the exterior run of windows appeared uniform, it can be assumed that this too had contained a cinquefoil-headed lancet.

North partition

The structure of this partition has already been partly described in the context of the east range (*see above*, this chapter). The large-framed panels were formed within the posts of the roof trusses, the lower bressumer (or sill beam) timbers (halved over the main beams of the parlour ceiling below), middle rails and the cornice timbers. The filling comprised oak studs tenoned into the upper rails and sprung into grooves in the lower rails of each panel. The surface was then built up in oak laths on both faces of the partition and the void between the two layers of laths filled with daub. The daub extruded onto the exterior surfaces of the partition and was worked up into a bed layer which was subsequently plastered with a skim of white lime plaster (Fig 6.57).[69]

Figure 6.56
Detail of the soffit of the lintel of window 17, south-west window of chamber. Note the moulding and outline of original splays (photograph by Stuart Blaylock; EMAFU 1704/28).

134

The posts of the roof trusses originally bore false corbels as lower terminals to the arch braces – features which only survive on the easternmost truss (*see* Fig 6.2). The positions of these features are represented on the posts of trusses II to IV by mortices at the same level.

West partition

The west wall of the chamber (*see* Figs 6.15 and 6.58) was formed by a partition of 17th-century character that had replaced an original partition in this position (whose existence is demonstrated by the rebated and blind rear face to roof truss V above the site of the screen and mortices for studs in the collar). The screen resembled the north partition of the chamber (just described) in its use of daub infill and double lathing, but its structure was clearly later in character than others in the building. Diagonal braces form the principal subdivision, with vertical studs of relatively slight scantling between. Here the headbeam, bressumer, central stud, diagonal braces and the door-frame were of oak jointed and pegged together. The remaining timbers (mainly the subdividing studs) were elm fixed with nails. The combination of materials and techniques is characteristic of the period in the mid- to late 17th century when oak was in the process of being supplanted as a structural timber by other woods, principally pine.[70] It also reflects a change in the structural emphasis, in which the studs are regarded simply as a means of subdividing the frame to support the daub filling, rather than as load-bearing elements. The headbeam was cut into the masonry of the south wall and into the timber of truss V to the north. These positions may also represent the level of the headbeam of the medieval screen, since the mortice in the north post of truss V was larger than necessary for the present timber and there was a vacant peg hole in the redundant portion. The renewal of this partition was probably also caused by the need to revise the structure to spread the load on beam 4, after the removal of the ground-floor screen at this phase (on the enlargement of the parlour; *see above*).

Laths were applied to both sides of the screen as shuttering for the filling of the core with daub and to support the surfaces finished with heavily haired earth plaster, another late feature.[71] Half of the plaster surface survived on the east face of the screen (Fig 6.58). The second stage of the

partition (above the headbeam and filling the tympanum formed by the arch of the roof truss) was filled with a variety of timbers in a flimsy partition. Mortices survived in the headbeam for original (that is, 17th-century) studs (*see* Figs 6.15 and 6.31), which may have been more substantial, although those that survived in 1978 appear to be seated in the same mortices (*see* Fig 6.58). The door at the south end of the partition had retained its jambs, but had lost its head and been fitted with a modern frame and leaf (*see* Fig 6.58).

Later alterations

After the demolition of the south-east range and the east gable wall, the south-east doorway was blocked in phase 8 with an upright post and brick infill (*see* Fig 6.22, 100, along with the masonry blocking at ground-floor level, 253). The framing of the east gable wall was of the same phase.[72]

Figure 6.57 (top)
The north elevation of the great chamber in July 1978, looking north-west, with later lath and plaster removed, showing the original plaster face and the posts of the roof trusses (DoE J263/14/78).

Figure 6.58 (bottom)
The south elevation of the great chamber in July 1978, looking south-west. Note the fireplace and studs filling the area above the inserted screen (DoE J263/15/78).

Figure 6.59 (top)
The north elevation of the great chamber when first stripped in January 1978, looking north-east, showing new wall cladding of phase 8 and cut-in doorways of phase 9 (DoE J10/15/78).

Figure 6.60 (bottom)
The south elevation of the great chamber when first stripped in January 1978, showing later blocking within the fireplace (DoE J10/14/78).

Later alterations to the north partition involved the removal of the lowest section of the arch braces (below the cornice plates), in order to accommodate a new face of heavily haired plaster (on additional studs applied to the face of the screen, Fig 6.59; *see also* Fig 6.57) and the insertion of two doorways (one a reused 17th-century frame; *see* Fig 6.25, 113). These are clearly cut into the thickened wall (*see* for instance, Fig 6.59, showing lath and plaster infill around the western of the two doors cutting into the thickened wall). The insertion of doorways belongs to the phase after the construction of the first floor in the east range in the 19th century (*see* above, east range, the screens passage). Also at some point in phase 9, the south-west window was enlarged to accommodate a sash window. The reveals were rebuilt in stone and brick to eliminate the original splays and the sill lowered, widened and rebuilt in brick (*see* Fig 6.22, 106).

In the later 19th or 20th century the chamber was divided into two rooms, with a light partition wall constructed on the line of truss III.[73] The blocking in and reduction in size of the fireplace probably formed a part of the same alterations (Fig 6.60). The partition was removed in the alterations of 1969 onwards (phase 11).[74]

The inner chamber

Primary arrangement and fenestration

The space of bays 5–7 (*see* Fig 6.1) was originally planned as a single, apparently unheated room. Although subdivided in post-medieval phases, it remained as a coherent space within the first-floor arrangement. Nowhere was the dichotomy in walling materials better demonstrated than in this room. The south wall was of masonry to the wall top and the north wall entirely of cob (Figs 6.61–6.63). The difference was manifest in the form of the windows and in the treatment of the roof trusses. The south elevation survived in its primary form largely unchanged (Fig 6.64). It contained two well-preserved lancet windows (*see* Fig 6.22, 60 and 63) of similar design to those of the chamber (externally identical and internally, with chamfered rather than moulded lintels). In the north wall there were two windows opposite the lancets of the south wall (Fig 6.65; *see also* Fig 6.63). Both were enlargements of primary windows, since original lintels survived on the interior (*see* Fig 6.25, 137, west window) and exterior (*see* Fig 5.17, 151, east window), but nothing had survived of the form of the primary windows. If a particular type of window frame had been used in primary contexts in cob walling, it had failed to survive.

The roof of the inner chamber had the same structure as that of the chamber, but was much simpler in its decoration (Chapter 7). The change in design of concern here is the repositioning of the cornice plate at a higher level to act as a purlin in bays 5–7 (*see* Fig 6.25, 156). The effect of this change was to raise the apparent top of the wall within the room (in comparison to the chamber). The space was filled with cob beam-filling on both sides of the room (that is, on stone as well as on cob walling) after the roof trusses were in position (Chapter 7). The same technique was to be used in the western bays (although here without the purlins/cornice timbers) to provide an upper limit to the wall face (*see* Fig 6.62). In section the beam-filling filled the triangular area between the wall tops, the soffit of the roof and the wall faces. When stripped, the upper surface contained the impressions of the common rafters of the roof (*see* Fig 7.4).

Much of the interior elevation was covered with primary white lime plaster, traces of which were recorded running into the window embrasures, over the cob of the wall tops (demonstrating the contemporaneity of this filling) and across the line of the cross wall at the western limit of the room. This demonstrated the existence of a door through that wall to the oriel chamber (below). Further evidence for the doorway was provided by two sockets for lintel timbers (*see* Fig 6.22, 130) cutting into masonry and cob respectively. Although these could be interpreted as secondary features, the evidence of the plaster demonstrates that the door was primary.[75]

The room had no fireplace.[76] Since all of the other principal rooms had fireplaces (including the oriel chamber to the west), the absence of heating here is noteworthy.

Subdivision of the room

At the time of the acquisition of the building the inner chamber was subdivided by a north–south partition on the line of truss VI. It was composed of an oak frame of substantial timbers incorporating a doorway with chamfered surround with diagonal stops and a four-centred head (*see* Fig 9.25). The partition may have been of primary character, although nothing else precisely like it had survived in the building. It could also, therefore, have been of later 16th-century date. The frame shared certain details of technique with the primary screens: the mortices for studding in the soffit of the headbeam; the continuous slot in the sill for the lower ends of studs (cut to a V shape) to be slid into position;[77] and the double chamfer and diagonal-cut stops of the door surround. The partition survived as a skeleton only and no studwork or infilling remained. A short length of east–west partition joined it to the west wall of the great chamber.[78] Both frames were dismantled when the building was stripped and have not been re-erected.

Collation of information from earlier 20th-century plans, principally the one published by Everett,[79] shows that there was a partition on the line of truss VII and a subsidiary partition forming a passage along

the south wall before 1969. The position below truss VI only became enclosed on the insertion of the stair in bays 6 and 7 in the restaurant period (phase 11) alterations (*see* Fig 12.4, phases 10 and 11). Although there is no direct evidence for the assumption that the pre-1969 screen below truss VII was the one placed beneath truss VI post-1969, the structure has to have come from somewhere in the building at that point. Certainly the architect's plans show that the central bays of the south range were the part of the building most heavily affected by the alterations of that time (the plans make no mention of an ancient screen in this position, but it may have been covered over and unrecognised until it was dismantled). The planks filling the apex of truss VII (Chapter 7 and *see* Fig 7.27) also suggested a partition on this line. Sockets in both north and south walls of the inner chamber showed where the headbeam had been

Figure 6.61 (top)
The inner chamber looking east after first stripping in July 1978. Note the differential walling materials and 17th-century screen beneath truss VI (DoE 263/13/78).

Figure 6.62 (bottom)
Similar view to Fig 6.61 in November 1979, after removal of the floor boards and further stripping, with truss IX in the foreground (DoE J492/2/79).

Figure 6.63
The north wall of bay 6,
showing the posts of the roof
truss running down through
the cob (partially repaired)
(photograph by David
Garner; EH B926258).

Figure 6.64
The interior elevation of the
south wall of the inner
chamber in July 1978 after
stripping. Note the height of
masonry, cob infill of wall
tops, roof trusses cut off to
fit the top of the stone wall
and the scar of the cob cross
wall west of truss VIII
(extreme right) (DoE
J263/11/78).

Figure 6.65
The interior elevation of the
north wall of the inner
chamber in July 1978 after
stripping. Note the cob
walling, the scar of the cob
cross wall west of truss VIII
(centre), the two windows
in the inner chamber
(right) and the position of
the stair of phase 11
(DoE J263/12/78).

fitted against the east face of truss VII (*see* Fig 6.22, 120, and Fig 6.25, 241). The first siting of the partition in this position has been allocated to the late 16th- to early 17th-century phase, on the evidence of the date of the timberwork itself. There is no reason, however, why it could not have been placed here at some later date, by being reused from elsewhere in the building.[80]

The longitudinal partition which divided a room on the north from a corridor along the south wall of bays 5 and 6 (after the insertion of stairs in bay 7 in the 19th century) incorporated a doorway with an ovolo-moulded frame and scroll stops.[81]

This was probably the ' … door to the adjacent bedroom … ' described by Everett as having a door-frame of *c* 1600.[82] This frame was also set within a partition. It was also removed from its position after 1979 and not replaced (*see* Fig 9.25 and Chapter 9, catalogue no. 139). Its original position is uncertain. As implied above, it may have formed the wall of the corridor in bays 5 and 6 in the 19th century, but this must have been a secondary position. Both screens could in fact have found their ways into the south range only after the phases of demolition *c* 1800; the west, north and south-east ranges provide numerous potential provenances for timberwork. It would thus be as reasonable to suggest that the inner chamber remained undivided until this late period as to accept an earlier subdivision of the room, as postulated in Fig 12.3 (*below*).

Other alterations

The north-western window has been described already (Chapter 5; Fig 5.17, 137, and Fig 6.53); it was made up of late 16th-century components, but probably not assembled in this form until a later phase. The north-eastern window (*see* Fig 6.25, 151) had a considerably enlarged embrasure and a replaced lintel (150), but retained an original external lintel. The reset internal lintel was set at the same level as those of the original lintels to either side (137 and 111), presumably reflecting the level of its predecessor. Traces of the eastern stop and the asymmetrical position of the enlarged embrasure suggest that the original window was central to bay 5 and may provide a clue to the width of an earlier embrasure. The bare cob of the widened embrasure retained traces of the very distinctive red heavily haired plaster, also seen associated with the late 17th-century partition to the east (and present throughout the inner chamber in traces over the primary plaster). This would suggest a context for the first enlargement of the embrasure in the same period as the renewed screen (phase 7?). The window is now fitted with a wide 19th-century casement.

Other alterations also related to the 19th-century room division. To the east of truss VII and the position of the headbeam already mentioned (*see* Fig 6.25, 241) was a row of sockets for ceiling timbers in bays 5 and 6 of the north wall (144, 145 and 147; 156 represents the later position of the headbeam of the screen). A similar row of sockets was seen in the south wall (*see* Fig 6.22, 125) extending into bay 7 (perhaps because the passage at the head of the stairs was also ceiled while the stair well, occupying the northern part of bay 7, remained open; *see* Fig 12.4). The north side of bay 5 contained a portion of a brick-lined flue against the west face of truss v (*see* Fig 6.25, 155), representing the provision of heating in the subdivided bedroom in the 19th century. A chimney is visible in this position in Stockdale's drawing of the courtyard (*see* Fig 2.5) and presumably served a fireplace or a free-standing stove in the corner of the room that had been removed by the time Everett came to draw his plan in the 1950s. Last in the sequence of alterations was the construction of staircases in bays 7 and 6–7. The first (phase 10)[83] rose against the west side of the partition beneath truss VII and must have entailed the removal of some floor joists in ground-floor bay 6. The depredations of the second (of 1969, phase 11) on the ground floor have been described above (*see above*, p 120), but also involved the removal of part of main beam 6 and areas of joists in ground-floor bays 5 and 6.

The cross wall

The wall was of cob above the first-floor level (the break in material occurred at the same level as in the north wall). Until it was rebuilt in 1990, the visible evidence for the wall comprised a scar in the cob of the south wall (*see* Fig 6.22, 127, and Fig 6.64), modern repairs of the scar in the cob (*see* Fig 6.22, 123), the full scar of the removed cob in the north wall (*see* Fig 6.25, 131, and Fig 6.65) and differential colouring of the timbers of the roof. The last was partly due to the staining/painting in successive layers of those parts of the timbers not concealed by the cob wall, as well as to discolouration by cob dust. This also showed that, as the wall rose into the roof, it narrowed from its full width of 0.85m to 0.6m (even less at the apex). The first-floor stage of the wall, as that of the north wall, was constructed before the addition of the roof, since its east face was cut for the insertion of the north post of truss VIII (*see* Fig 6.25, 134). The construction of the upper stage into the roof presumably post-dated the addition of the roof, and took place at the same time as the cob filling of the wall tops. The wall survived until 1969, although pierced by additional doors at ground level (*see* Fig 12.2, phase 10).[84]

The oriel chamber

Primary arrangement and fenestration

This room occupied bays 8–10 of the first floor (Figs 6.66 and 6.67). It remained without subdivision from the primary phase 3 until it was incorporated into a larger room by the removal of the cross wall in the restaurant period alterations of phase 11 (1969 and onwards). The room was predominantly cob-walled (*see* Figs 6.22, 6.25 and 6.45). Even the flue of the fireplace in the north wall was formed of cob, the only instance of this to survive in the building.[85] Roof trusses were fitted into chases in the cob and carried down onto stone (although the southern posts of trusses X and XI were supported on a window lintel and bare cob respectively). Much primary plaster survived, running over the posts of the roof timbers, over the cob infill of the wall-tops and into the oriel embrasure (below). The floor level stepped up by 0.23m from that of the inner chamber to the east, a reflection of the rising ground level to the west. The level of embellishment of the roof (windbraces and ?bosses, Chapter 7) as well as the oriel window, show that this chamber was an important room.

Figure 6.66
The north elevation of the oriel chamber when first stripped, July 1978 (DoE J263/9/78).

Figure 6.67 (below)
The south elevation of the oriel chamber when first stripped, July 1978 (DoE J263/10/78).

The awkwardness in access from the inner chamber suggests that the main route of entry to the room was from the gallery rather than from the inner chamber, emphasising that this chamber provided a separate unit of accommodation.

The south wall was furnished with windows in bays 8 and 9 (*see* Fig 6.22, 57 and 51 – the oriel). Both had primary lintels at the same level, but modified embrasures. The reveals of the eastern window (57) were cut back to enlarge the window, the sill was reformed in brick and the chamfer and stops of the lintel were widened without leaving traces of the original stops (as was sometimes the case). The window was placed directly above the arch of the large doorway of the through passage and must have represented the site of a primary window. The lintel was substantially longer than those of the stone lancets further east, suggesting a two-light window in this position. The lack of a primary timber window in cob walling as a prototype (Chapter 8) makes more precise reconstruction impossible. The oriel was placed towards the west of bay 9, perhaps to compensate in part for the absence of a window in the westernmost bay and create a more symmetrical elevation inside as well as out. The evidence for the primary phase of this structure has already been described (pp 81–2). Here it is emphasised that the window was a 'walk-in' structure with splayed reveals down to floor level whose surfaces retained primary plaster (Fig 6.68). Straight stops to the chamfer of the lintel aligned with the reveals. The lintel was extended to the west to support the post of roof truss X.

Figure 6.68
Detail of the oriel window. Note the splayed reveals with primary plaster, later brick filling behind and the foot of truss X bearing on the lintel (photograph by David Garner; EH B930204).

The west elevation had been completely removed by later activity (*see* Fig 6.45). The form of the roof to the west of truss XI (purlins extended across the width of the gable wall) suggested that the west gable wall was a full thickness of cob to its full height. There was probably a window in the west elevation, but in the absence of surviving fabric its form is unknown. The limited traces of the ground-floor window might provide a pattern (Chapter 5).

The north wall had no windows. The doorway in bay 8 (*see* Fig 6.25, 200) served the gallery, whose structural history was discussed above (Chapter 5). In its later and final form (until 1976) the doorway led into the diagonal bridge which spanned the corner of the courtyard and gave access from the south range to the inserted first floor of the west range. The present form on the interior related to this phase of adaptation, but an exterior lintel survived in position, while the original interior lintel, with chamfer and stops, was reused in the later doorway. The evidence does not preclude an interpretation in which the opening in this position was originally a window, later adapted to serve the altered circulation pattern after the demolition of the west range and the insertion of a first-floor room in the kitchen. Taking the evidence for a gallery as a whole, however, the alternative of a door onto the gallery is preferred.

Fireplace

Superficially the fireplace in the north wall of bay 9 appeared secondary, in that it was set within a cut in the cob wall (*see* Fig 6.25, 187). Indeed the preliminary interpretation consigned the fireplace to a later phase of work. Further evidence exposed during examination of the building, however, revealed a flue cut into the cob wall belonging to an earlier phase of use of the fireplace and evidence of a primary chimney stack directly above the site of the fireplace. This took the form of a pattern of decay on the south face of roof truss I of the west range. As the primary chimney stack had been built against the truss, when the protective flashing of lead or mortar failed, this had allowed water to flow against the roof timbers and caused rot against the stack (Fig 6.69). A small patch of masonry (*see* Fig 6.25, 185) may have been a remnant of the fabric of the chimney. The jambs and lintel were composed of three monolithic blocks of breccia.[86] The feature showed a long sequence of alterations (*see below*) that

had included the removal of the lower or inner edges of the stones (in order to fit an inner frame) and removed any chamfer or other ornamental devices. The back of the fireplace (*see* Fig 5.17, 229 and 233), and its surviving flue (198) also belonged to later alterations. The eastern (and greater?) half of the fireplace was only destroyed on the cutting of the door into the west range (*see* Fig 5.7, 228) in the early 1970s.[87]

Early alterations

Some alterations related to the ground-floor room, namely the chimney of the ground-floor fireplace and the possible early stairs on the south side of bay 9 (*see above*).[88] The north wall of bay 10 had little primary fabric preserved in it. Only a section of the wall-top infill of the bay had survived (*see* Fig 6.25, 181). The chimney occupied the eastern half of the bay (182; *see also* Fig 6.66). To the west the space between the face of the stack and roof truss XI was filled by a niche (now blocked). This was formed at the same time as the construction of the stack by the insertion of a lintel bearing on the chimney stack to the east and on a bracket nailed to the side of the post of the roof truss to the west (the same distinctive yellow mortar that bonded the chimney stack was seen in the packing above the lintel). The function of the niche was unclear. Utilisation of the space created by the removal of cob walling provides a prosaic explanation. The construction of the chimney led to modifications in the roof. The eastern windbrace was removed (its original existence is attested by vacant mortices), the common rafters were cut off to allow the chimney to rise through the roof and a trimmer inserted against the south face of the stack.

The dating of this phase of work within phases 5 to 7 is imprecise and uncertain. Although the details were early in character, the work cannot be assigned to the primary phase in view of the evident insertion of the stack and the awkward juxtaposition of stair and oriel.

Later alterations

From phase 8 onwards quite radical alterations took place. The west gable wall was removed (presumably to be replaced by a framed partition) and the stumps were faced up with brickwork (*see* Fig 6.22, 177; Fig 5.14 and Fig 6.25, 179).[89] In the case of the north wall (where original cob had already been largely removed) the post of the roof truss was also propped up on brick (*see* Fig 6.25, 180).[90] The oriel was removed and replaced by a sash window with a higher sill (*see* Fig 5.8, 50 and 51). The ?door to the gallery in the north wall was reformed with a replaced lintel, eastern jamb rebuilt in stone (*see* Fig 5.17, 349) and its western jamb provided with a curious outward-splaying reveal to ease the angle of the entry into the west range (Fig 6.70; *see also* Fig 6.1).[91] Quite extensive alterations to the fireplace began at the same time, probably originating in the failure of the primary chimney stack.[92]

*Figure 6.69
General view of the roof of the west range when stripped in July 1992, looking north along the east side of the roof. Note especially the weathered area on the face of truss 1 representing the extent of the primary chimney stack (centre) (photograph by David Garner; EH B924255).*

*Figure 6.70
The west reveal of door 200 formerly leading to the gallery, showing reverse splay, looking west (photograph by David Garner; EH B940400).*

141

Figure 6.71

West range, upper surface of the inserted first-floor frame, showing the rebate for a hearth slab and the extent of stone and cob (photograph by Stuart Blaylock; EMAFU 3000/3).

Figure 6.72

As Fig 6.71, showing the later (19th-century) floor above being lifted (photograph by Aidan Matthews; EMAFU 1924/17a).

Figure 6.73

The south elevation of the west range at first-floor level when first stripped in July 1978 (DoE J263/7/78).

First the frame was reset in a new cut in the cob, packed with brick fragments (*see* Fig 6.25, 186). Above, bricks of the same type were employed to form a new flue for the fireplace (*see* Fig 6.25, 198, and Fig 5.17, 229) which, instead of providing an independent chimney, fed into the ?16th- to 17th-century stack adjacent to the west. The crude curving structure of brick was supported on a wide plank lodged diagonally, with its upper end against the main stack (*see* Figs 5.17 and 6.25). Probably at this time, the edges of the breccia blocks were rebated for a new frame. Later still the fireplace was reduced in size, with bricks of a later character, and therefore 19th century in date (*see* Fig 6.25, 188); this smaller fireplace is shown on Everett's plan of 1958. Lastly the fireplace was blocked with brick in a grey mortar with Portland cement (189), representing a sub-phase of phase 10 or 11. This was itself cut away by the crude doorway of 1970–6 (228; *see also* Figs 6.66 and 7.38).[93]

The final class of alterations concerned ceilings in the oriel chamber. The evidence was all in the south elevation and comprised two levels of slight impressions in the wall-top cob (*see* Fig 6.22, 161 and 414). Both represented late (probably 20th-century) ceilings, for the evidence of plastering shows that the oriel chamber remained open to the roof in the plastering associated with the phase of *c* 1800 and, therefore, for as long as work of that phase remained unchanged.

West range: the first-floor room

This room had only a late identity, belonging to the phase of *c* 1800. The insertion of the floor and its provenance are discussed above (p 133). In the periods after the flooring out of the room, minor alterations to its fenestration and fittings were made. In the east wall the whole of the southern bay (*see* Fig 6.47, 225) was removed by successive alterations of the access from south range to gallery and later into the west range room (*see* Chapter 5, p 86). In the west wall the large five-light window (*see* Fig 6.45, 238) was blocked and a narrower casement window inserted in the northern half of the bay in the late 19th century (242; Chapter 5). The room was provided with a fireplace built against the face of the chimney stack, with a hearth let into the joists of the floor (Fig 6.71; *see also* Fig 6.47 and Fig 12.4, phase 9). The flue ran upwards against the stack to a point some 2m above floor level, where a cut in the masonry fed it into the main earlier flue

(Fig 6.72; *see also* Fig 6.47, 204). The fireplace was removed and the cut filled with brick of later 19th-century type (*see* Fig 6.48; soot staining on the wall above the gap shows that the arrangement was defective).

In the south wall the principal later features related to the fireplaces of the oriel chamber (Fig 6.73), that is, the inserted ?16th- to 17th-century stack to the west (*see* Fig 5.17, 235) and the brick back and flue of the phase 8 rearrangement of the primary fireplace (233 and 229). In the west corner a cupboard or closet was constructed in the space first employed for the niche facing into the oriel chamber (*see* p 141). The older doorway to the west of the stack (*see* Fig 6.25, 359) was blocked with studding and a new embrasure formed on the north side in brick and mortar of the phase of *c* 1800 (*see* Fig 5.17, 236 and 232). In turn a new cupboard was formed with newer studs and lath and plaster in the later 20th century.[94]

7
The standing building: description and analysis of the roofs

Introduction

The roofs at Bowhill are variations of the jointed-cruck assembly. Essentially this consists of pairs of posts whose curved heads support the principal rafters (*see* Figs 7.2–7.3). These support four sets of purlins, the lowest set plate-wise to support the common rafters at the eaves and the next in line with the inner wall face. They are thus fixed to the posts/arch braces rather than the principals. There are no ridge pieces. The rafters, between five and eight per bay, are mostly butted at the apex and pegged. The variations both structural and decorative in the roofs through the building are the subject of this chapter. The hall roof is the largest, grandest and most highly decorated and formed the prototype for the remaining roofs. Both hall and great chamber follow essentially the same structural arrangement and use the same repertoire of joints,

although the timbers of the great chamber are chamfered rather than moulded and some timbers present in the hall are omitted in the south range (*cf* Figs 7.6 and 7.13). The roofs of the oriel chamber, kitchen and inner chamber are much simpler, although each still has individually designed decorative elements. Since the roofs of the south and west ranges were studied and recorded in great detail, they necessarily form the basis of this account of the Bowhill roofs. Less attention was devoted to the recording of the hall roof and so less is known of its structural detail.

Order of assembly

In the east range trusses were numbered (and therefore assembled) from north to south. The surviving trusses were numbered from II to VI and the assembly marks inscribed on the south faces of the timbers.

Figure 7.1
The roof of the south range, trusses X and XI (showing protruding pegs) seen from the rear face (photograph by Stuart Blaylock; EMAFU 1924/1).

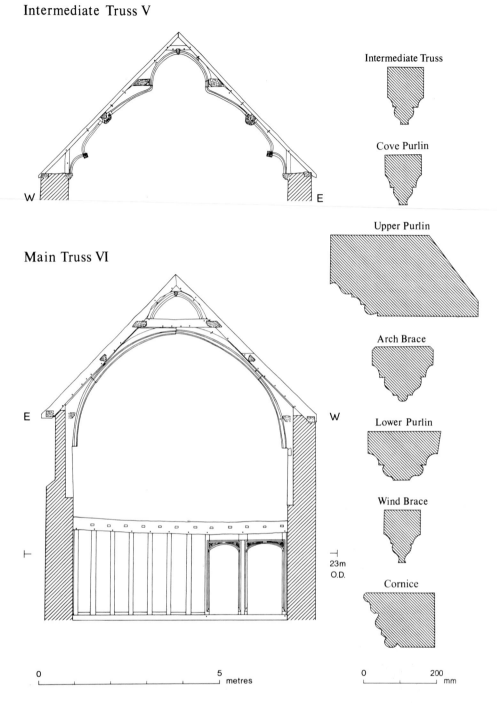

Figure 7.2

The roof of the east range (hall), specimen elevations of main and intermediate trusses (scale 1:100) and sections of timbers (line drawing by Richard Parker).

Intermediate Truss V

W   E

Intermediate Truss

Cove Purlin

Main Truss VI

E   W

23m O.D.

Upper Purlin

Arch Brace

Lower Purlin

Wind Brace

Cornice

0   5 metres

0   200 mm

The roof of the south range was assembled from east to west, following the truss numbering which survived in a consistent series (I–XI), with multiple numbering on each truss.[1] The working faces of the timbers were to the west, since setting-out lines, assembly marks and numbers are invariably found on the west face of the timbers and the pegs were inserted from that direction (Fig 7.1).[2] On longitudinal timbers the number was usually inscribed at the east end, near the point where the timber was jointed to the truss to its east. In the west range the roof trusses were assembled from south to north and numbered accordingly, with the working faces of the timbers, numbering, direction of pegging and so on to the north. Thus the roof was conceived and may have been intended to be erected in a clockwise direction from the north end of the east range (that is, east range, north to south; south range, east to west; then west range, south to north). In practice, however, the roof of the south range may have been erected first, a suggestion supported by the exceptionally odd way in which the trusses were fitted to the walls (*see below*).

Illustration

The roofs were recorded in conventional truss elevations. These appear in the main elevation drawings of the building (Chapters 5 and 6), and in two detailed elevations (Figs 7.2 and 7.3). These have been augmented with 'exploded analytical drawings' of the hall, chamber, inner chamber and oriel chamber roofs that attempt to show how the carpentry is fitted together. The west range resembles the roof of the western bays of the south range, although with some variations. With the complex carpentry of the hall and chamber roofs, details of joints and the form of the timbers were best shown with whole bays pulled away from the assembled roof (*see* Figs 7.6 and 7.13). For the inner and oriel chambers, where a key aspect is the discrepancy in height between the two sides of the roof, one side is shown assembled, the other (with the taller posts) disassembled (*see* Figs 7.27 and 7.29).

Structural aspects of the roofs

The roofs of Bowhill form an impressive display of late medieval carpentry, generally to a very high standard of design and execution. There were, however, a number of crude or bizarre aspects to the fitting (rather than construction) of the roofs, some damage as a result and incongruities in the relationship of the roof(s) to the walls. These have inspired suggestions that the roofs might be additions and of a later phase than the walls. At first sight such an argument might appear convincing, but detailed consideration of the relationship of roofs to walls will show that the roofs are original to the building.

In the hall, for example, the roof trusses do not align with the windows. The trusses bear on the top of solid masonry or on timber window lintels (*see* Figs 6.2 and 6.15), above which the walling was a mixture of lower-quality rubble masonry and cob (Chapter 6). Less-pronounced misalignments between roof bays and features within the walls were also seen in the south range (interior elevations, *see* Figs 6.22 and 6.25). The southern post of truss X bears on a window lintel and that of truss XI

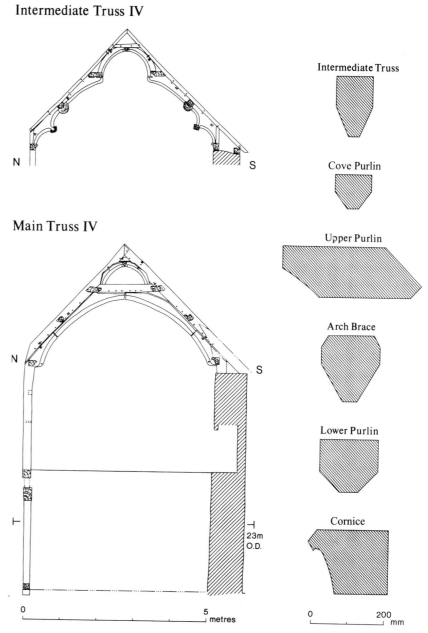

on cob walling alone. In the great chamber the spacing of the roof trusses bears little correspondence to the fireplace and the windows (*see* Fig 6.22). These factors contribute to the impression of poor correlation between the layout of the interior and the details of the roof.[3]

The trusses of the roof of the south range were constructed to a common pattern, although details of ornament varied according to position (*see below*). The trusses varied in their fitting. Although the optimum design for a jointed-cruck truss must have included two posts of equal length, this was only realised in the west range.

Figure 7.3
The roof of the south range (great chamber), specimen elevations of main and intermediate trusses (scale 1:100) and sections of timbers (line drawing by Richard Parker).

Despite the occasional lapse, the builders aimed to support each post of the roof trusses on solid footings (that is, stone walling or timber template – standard vernacular practice). The variation in walling material in the south range necessitated considerable alterations to individual trusses as they were prepared for fitting into the building. There is some evidence to suggest that the roof trusses were prepared to a standard template off-site. The trusses on the south side of the roof, which sit on stone at a high level (trusses II–VIII), have been hacked about very crudely to fit them onto the top of stone walling. Yet each was constructed to the standard pattern, which included a lower timber (the cruck 'post') morticed into the principal rafter (*see* Fig 7.13). The lower timbers on the south sides of trusses II–VIII are so truncated that little structural benefit is gained from the residual post of the jointed cruck.[4] This disjointed evidence suggests that either there was poor communication between the builders of the walls and the carpenters who were fashioning the roof timbers or poor correlation of their efforts. This then resulted in crude adjustments once the timbers had arrived on the site. The timber was clearly used green, as it had warped *in situ*. This rules out reuse, as do the excellent fit in length and width of all the roof elements and the uniform and internally consistent series of assembly marks.

The major peculiarity is the way in which the roof trusses were fitted in relation to the cob walling. The standard procedure would have been to raise the roof trusses on a stone plinth prior to the addition of the cob, as was done in the construction of the west range (shown by the narrow shrinkage cracks against the eastern post of truss I, *see* Fig 6.47, 400) and probably also in the east range.[5] In the south range, however, the cob walls were complete to wall-top level before the insertion of the posts and the erection of the roof. Every roof truss intended for the cob-walled parts of the building had a post long enough to reach the stone wall top or plinth below the cob, at whatever level that lay.[6] In every case the posts were placed in a cut or chase in the main mass of the cob wall, normally ranging from 50–250mm wide *on each side of the post*, that is, a total width of 250–600mm. At their narrowest the cut faces could have plausibly been interpreted as shrinkage of the cob, but their character argues against this. The edges were visibly trimmed rather than retaining the cast impression of the post.[7] Most of the chases were far too wide to have been caused by shrinkage, however.[8] Once the posts were in position the remaining timbers of the roof were assembled. The width of the chases may have had an associated benefit at this point, since the gaps to either side of the posts would permit the timbers to be manoeuvred to slide tenons into mortices.[9] Lastly the chases were filled with stone rubble where wide and with more cob and/or stone packing where narrower.

The next stage of construction was the filling of the wall tops (the space of triangular section between the top of the wall proper, the wall face/cornice/lowest purlin, and the soffit of the common rafters/roof – a process called beam filling [Fig 7.4]).[10] This was carried out in cob above the stone as well as the cob walling. In the great chamber the face of the beam filling lay flush with that of the ashlar pieces and, presumably, was plastered over. In elevation the beam filling abutted the roof trusses and sometimes filled the upper parts of the chases described above as well. It was clear from this sequence that the finishing of the cob walling took place after the roof timbers had been positioned. Then the walls were plastered. Everywhere the primary white lime plaster of the interior of the building was recorded running over cob (and stone) walls, posts of the roof trusses (Fig 7.5),

Figure 7.4
The roof of the south range, bay 9 (south), with common rafters and eaves purlin removed in June 1992. Note the cob beam filling on the wall top with impressions of the common rafters and brick fabric on the site of the oriel window (phase 8) (photograph by David Garner; EH B923942).

fill of the wall tops and up to the main timbers of the roof trusses. Nowhere was an earlier plaster face recorded that might have belonged to an earlier structural phase (that is, pre-dating the insertion of the present roof trusses). This point is emphasised to demonstrate that the roof was a part of the primary construction programme, despite a possible alternative interpretation that the chases were simply later cuts to accommodate a secondary roof.

Why was the roof erected in this curious way? Here the matter of walling materials is relevant again. Given the care that was taken to ensure the posts of the roof trusses received a solid footing, it is difficult to avoid the conclusion that cob was not expected to bear the thrust coming from the roof trusses. The aim was always to support the post of a truss on solid stone, whether at plinth or some higher level.[11] Had the roof trusses been erected after the stone walling but before the cob, there would have been problems in the temporary support of roof trusses of widely varying height and some instability from the lack of bracing below the wall-top timbers.[12] The trouble of fitting the roof trusses into the cob walls post-erection may thus have been preferable to coping with large-scale temporary bracing, while simultaneously trying to raise the cob walls. The interpretation is supported by the roof of the west range, which conforms to the accepted constructional sequence, with cruck posts of more equal length on the two sides of the building (see Figs 6.45 and 6.47).[13] Most likely, perhaps, is the prosaic interpretation of poor communication and late delivery which has already been hinted at. The roof was built to a common pattern, with cruck posts north and south, because

the final disposition of stone and cob had not been decided, or had not been communicated to the carpenters. The construction of the walls pressed ahead in the south range, regardless of the needs of fitting the roof. When it was delivered, the roof was subjected to savage alterations to cut the timbers to fit, the windbraces in the oriel chamber were clogged up by beam filling and carved bosses removed or omitted from the same room. It is inconceivable that the carpenters who produced the work would have tolerated such crude hacking about of their work. This suggests that they were not responsible for its fitting, but that perhaps it was done by the masons. Although speculative, the hypothesis helps to account for the various infelicities and crude alterations to the timbers. It also offers some further help with the sequence of construction, since it suggests that the construction of the south range was well advanced when the roof was delivered or added to the building and that the east and west ranges (with better and more considered relationships of roof timbers to walling) had not been commenced or were still at the stage of primary wall construction.

The east range

General description

The hall roof is the principal glory of Bowhill (Figs 7.6 and 7.7) and sets the pattern for all the other roof designs. It is structurally similar to the eastern bays of the roof of the south range (although wider at 5.90–6.05m; 19'4"–19'10"). Here the typical decorative features of the Exeter group of roofs appear in full: heavily-moulded decoration; intermediate trusses with carved cusps and bosses; upper coving on a square-set upper purlin; straight windbraces with curved feet and so on (Chapter 8).

The incised assembly marks on the main trusses of the roof are numbered II to VI, north to south, showing that the missing truss on the line of the north wall of the store was the first.[14] Further details of the assembly marks were not recorded when the roof was dismantled. As with the chamber roof, the jointed-cruck posts of the principal trusses were probably made to a uniform pattern and cut to size on site. Trusses II and VI have longer cruck posts as they were carried down onto the stone plinth at a lower level and embedded in cob walling, whereas the intervening trusses have shorter

Figure 7.5
Detail of the south post of truss IX of the roof of the south range, showing the chase for the post filled with cob (see elevation, Fig 6.22) and primary lime plaster running over both the fill of the cut and the post itself (photograph by David Garner; EH B926251).

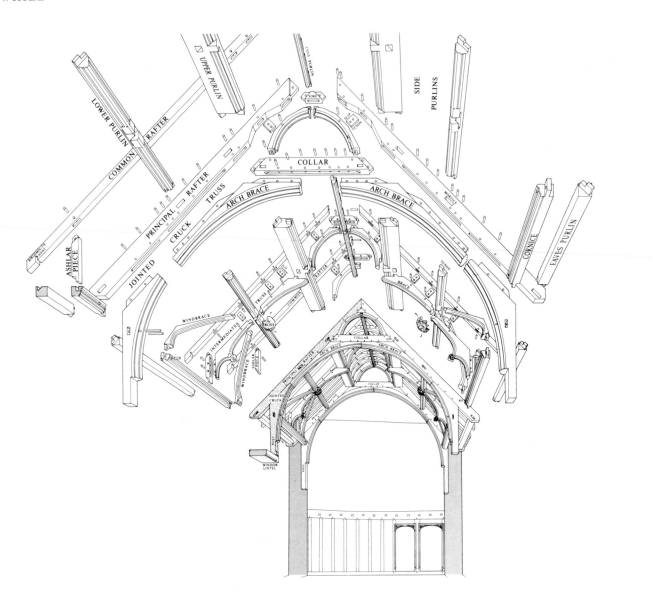

Figure 7.6
Exploded analytical drawing of the roof of the east range (hall); looking south, truss IV in the foreground (not to scale) (line drawing by Piran Bishop).

posts bearing on the stone wall top or on the lintels of windows, with the cob of the wall top built up around them (*see* Figs 6.2 and 6.15). The west posts of trusses IV and V did not sit neatly on the wall top. Truss IV, remarkably, appears to have been supported on cob, a small area of which survived under the foot of the truss (Figs 7.8 and 7.9; *see also* Fig 6.15); truss V is supported by a chock of timber.[15] In contrast to the south range, work on the walls and the roof of the hall appears to have been synchronised. Trusses II and VI are unmoulded to the north and south respectively. Thus the northern cell, in bay 1, cannot have had any significant ornament (the space to the south of truss VI was occupied by the portion of roof oversailing the south range, discussed below).

The hall roof has seven rafter trusses per bay (including the central couple embellished as the intermediate truss). The feet of the windbraces are pegged into mortices in the cornices, in the positions occupied in the other rafter trusses by ashlar pieces. At their upper ends, slim tenons are housed in mortices, forming a part of the composite joints at the junction of intermediate trusses, purlins and bosses (*see* Fig 7.6). These joints are apparently unpegged.[16] The lower terminals of the principals were ornamented with corbels as in the chamber, but here with carved foliage decoration as well as moulding. These have not survived, but are shown on Hayward's 1843 engraving of the hall roof (*see* Fig 1.2).[17] There may have been further elements that had been removed by then. The engraving shows a

Figure 7.7
The hall roof after repair,
May 1995, looking north
(photograph by David
Garner; EH B953012).

Figure 7.8 (below, left)
The foot of the west post of
truss IV of the hall roof,
supported on a remnant of
the cob wall-top filling
(unnumbered DoE photo-
graph of c *1980–1).*

Figure 7.9 (below right)
The top of the west wall of
the hall, looking north.
Truss IV is in the centre,
truss III dismantled to the
rear. Note the rubble fill of
phase 8 in the outer half of
the wall top, with cob wall
top in the background
(DoE unnumbered print).

Figure 7.10
The apex of trusses II and
III in 1978, showing the
coving and the structure
where one cove brace is
missing (right) *(DoE*
J263/22/78).

mortice beneath the detail drawing of a corbel, which could have accommodated a figured corbel or similar feature, in the manner of the Guildhall roof.[18] The same source shows bosses at the intersections of the intermediate trusses and purlins and smaller bosses or foliage carvings in the coving at the apexes of the intermediate trusses. The bosses probably survived *in situ* until the early 20th century, but they had been removed prior to Everett's interest in the building in the 1930s.[19] The photographic record of the roof made during dismantling in 1978 shows that, despite some decay, the timbers had remained clean and showed no trace that they had been ceiled, other than between the common rafters. The whole timber structure, therefore, including common rafters, was intended to be seen within any ceiling (Fig 7.10).

The junction of the east and south ranges

Photographs provide the key evidence for the arrangement prior to the dismantling of this area (Figs 7.11 and 7.12). The methods employed here are the same in most visible details as those of the equivalent area in the junction of the south and west ranges, which was studied in detail (*see below*). Unknown aspects of the construction in this area of the roof (especially the treatment at the valleys) are presumed to have resembled the west range.

The outer surface of the roof of the south range, in the space covered by the over-sailing part of the roof of the east range, was covered with closely spaced laths and a thick layer of daub (*see* Fig 7.12). The laths may either have been remnants of the general lathing of the roof (on which the slates would have been hung outside the enclosed area) or they may have been more closely spaced than was usual or necessary for ordinary slated areas. The daub plastering appears to abut the timbers supporting the jack rafters (lay boards and purlins), showing that it was added once the skeleton of the roof (at least) was in position and that this was a device for ceiling the interior of the roof void, not a remnant of a more widespread roofing technique. Short blocks of timber were nailed to the roof of the south range to support the south ends of the hall purlins (*see* Fig 7.12; *cf* the equivalents in the west range, *see* Fig 7.43). Lay boards were then laid onto the roof of the south range that, in turn, supported the jack rafters of the roof. As far as can be judged from the photographs of this section of the roof taken while it was being dismantled in 1983, the purlins and lay-board assemblies were original timber, but the rafters were modern softwood replacements (*see* Fig 7.12). It follows that the valley boards, battening and slates were also additions of a recent phase of re-roofing.[20] The roof void was apparently open to view from the hall, in that there was no evidence to suggest that the tympanum within the arch brace of truss VI had been closed by a partition nor was the rear face of the truss, although unmoulded, rebated in the manner of truss II or truss V of the roof of the south range.

The south range

The roof is of one construction, but has three separate designs and levels of ornament corresponding to the subdivisions of the first-floor plan: the embellished version in the chamber (trusses I–V, bays 1–4, a plainer version of the hall roof), with upper coving, supported on a plate, intermediate trusses, bosses and so on; a plain 'standard' version in the inner chamber (trusses V–VIII, bays 5–7); and another, partly embellished, version in the oriel chamber (trusses VIII–XI, bays 8–10), with windbraces and bosses (which were never completed or which have failed to survive).[21] Intermediate trusses in the great chamber are identified by the roman numeral of the preceding main truss, for example, intermediate truss II is between trusses II and III in bay 2. This corresponds to the original usage represented by the assembly marks. The common rafter trusses are numbered (arbitrarily) consecutively throughout the roof. Rafter trusses 1 to 16 (four per bay) occupy the great chamber, 17 to 34 (six per bay) the inner chamber and 35 to 55 (eight in bays 8 and 9 and five in bay 10) the oriel chamber. Rafter trusses 56 and 57 were over the west gable wall to the west of truss XI.

The principal trusses were probably made to a common pattern, although the first five trusses (because of the additional ornamentation of the chamber roof) are thicker – 160–180mm against *c* 100mm elsewhere (the same as the common rafters). When the trusses came to be erected, the lower timber of the jointed-cruck assembly, the post, was cut to size according to the support available (*see above*). In practice most of the posts were carried onto stone, except where they were incorporated in a timber-framed partition (trusses I–IV, north) or, exceptionally, were supported by cob (truss XI, south, and north originally) or a timber template (truss X, south).

The great chamber

Decoration

The principal timbers of the chamber roof bear chamfers, rather than the mouldings of the hall roof (Fig 7.13). There is evidence to show that the roof was originally plastered

between the common rafters, that is, that all the timbers were intended to be seen (*see below*, pp 157–8). Arch braces provide the principal visual articulation of the roof (Fig 7.14), with the main trusses below and the upper coving above. The intermediate trusses mark the centres of each bay. They form an irregular cinquefoil pattern, with foliage carvings on the pointed cusps of the lowest foils (Fig 7.15). The chamfers are carried around the underside of the upper purlins in a continuous curve onto the cove braces (*see* Fig 7.10, showing the same detail in the hall roof). Thus the coving is open within the bays and articulated by the intermediate trusses as well as the chamfered braces of the principals. The apex of the visible part of the roof was marked by an axial chamfered 'ridge' or cove purlin (Fig 7.16; *see also* Fig 7.13). Longitudinal, paired elements include the upper purlins – substantial horizontally set timbers (up to 340 × 130mm in section), whose function (both real and visual) is to support the coving, side purlins

Figure 7.11 (top)
The southern end of the hall roof, trusses V and VI, with lath and mud-plaster sealing of south range roof (beyond) (DoE J263/26/78).

Figure 7.12 (bottom)
The junction of the roofs of the east and south ranges in 1983, with truss VI dismantled. Note the purlin, lay board and mud-plaster sealing (DoE J538/8/83).

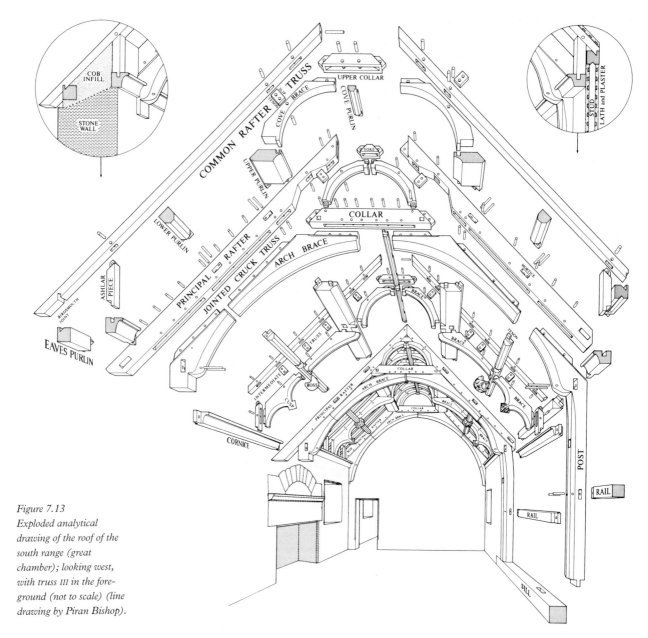

Figure 7.13
Exploded analytical
drawing of the roof of the
south range (great
chamber); looking west,
with truss III in the foreground (not to scale) (line
drawing by Piran Bishop).

with chamfers and simply moulded cornices (supporting the ashlar pieces at the wall top). The junctions of the intermediate trusses with the purlins are masked by carved bosses secured by iron spikes (one of the few uses of iron fixings in primary carpentry). The full set of bosses survives (Fig 7.17).[22] The roof had no windbraces, a detail which emphasises the simplification of the design in comparison to the hall (see above) and other roofs of the group (Chapter 8).

The lower terminals of the arch braces are cut off in a variety of crude curves. This was primarily caused by cutting to fit the stone of the wall tops (see above) but was accentuated by further trimming to

accommodate later ceilings. The end truss I (see Fig 6.2) retained the original arrangement of small moulded capitals to the shafts, supporting the lower terminals of the arch braces (Fig 7.18). Similar features must have been removed by the trimming of the remaining trusses. Mortices in the posts of trusses II to IV mark the positions of such pseudo-capitals/corbels on the north side of the room (see Fig 6.25) and these probably survived until the trimming associated with later ceilings. On the south side, however, the equivalent level lies substantially below the wall top and must have been removed when the timbers were cut to fit (see Fig 6.22). The southern terminal of truss V is

Figure 7.14
General view of the great chamber roof after repair, looking west, May 1995 (photograph by David Garner; EH A950713).

Figure 7.15
Foliage carvings on the cusps of the intermediate trusses (IT) of the great chamber roof. Since the north and south cusps bear the same carvings only one of each is illustrated:(left to right), IT I , N (EH B955479); IT II, N (EH B955480); IT III, S (EH B955484); IT IV, S (EH B955483) (photographs by David Garner).

Figure 7.16
Detail of coving in bay 1 of the great chamber roof, looking west. Note the intermediate truss in the foreground, cove braces and axial cove purlin (photograph by David Garner; EH B891245).

Figure 7.17
Bosses of the great chamber roof: (top to bottom, left to right) *Bay 1, S (EH B955470); Bay 1, N (EH B955477); Bay 2, S (EH B955471); Bay 2, N (EH B955476); Bay 3, S (EH B955472); Bay 3, N (EH B955475); Bay 4, S (EH B955473); Bay 4, N (EH B955474) (photographs by David Garner).*

treated slightly differently. The foot of the arch brace was cut to lap over the top of the stone wall (*see* Fig 6.15) and so the brace continues for *c* 0.4m below the wall top.

Structure

Much of the structure of the roof is described implicitly by the elevations and exploded drawings (*see* Figs 7.3 and 7.13). Comparison with the simpler roof structures to the west shows that the chamber roof is carried on the principal trusses alone. The intermediate trusses are almost wholly decorative, embellished versions of the common rafter trusses and add little to (if they do not detract from) the load-bearing capacity of the roof. The distinction is also seen in the joints. The principal trusses are assembled with long fixed tenons, generally side-pegged, whereas the intermediate trusses are assembled with slip tenons, reinforcing the impression that the intermediate-truss timbers are 'hung' from the central common rafter in each bay. Slip tenons otherwise are used only to fix the cove braces to principal and common rafters and are not employed at all in the simpler versions of the roof to the west.

Several complex joints are used. Most of the longitudinal timbers are secured in the principal trusses by face-halved tenons (Fig 7.19).[23] The same joint is used for the cornices, lower and upper purlins (as a part of a composite joint in the latter case) and also appears in a complex halved joint at the junction of cove purlins and cove braces/ yoke of the principals, although here it is not pegged. Other complex halved joints are used: at the junction of the lower purlins and the intermediate trusses, where the purlins are trenched to accommodate the halved terminals of the braces, a point which is masked by the bosses (fitted against a projecting block in the chamfering); and at the apex of the intermediate trusses, where tenons securing the braces to the upper collars are halved to allow the cove purlin to pass through, the purlin itself being halved to fit against another block at the apex of the coving (acting as a stop to the chamfers). This detail (both here and in the hall roof) suggests that further smaller bosses might have been fixed at the apex of each inter-mediate truss.[24] The large upper purlins are set horizontally to support the coving and are secured by composite joints comprising face-halved tenons, as described above, in unpegged mortices in the principals and subsidiary tenons (presumably for the prevention of sagging) in the adjacent collars (Fig 7.20; *see also* Fig 7.13, in which the mortices are visible).

The common rafters are secured to the eaves purlins by birds-mouth joints (employed throughout the roofs; *see* Fig 7.13, detail) and are joined at the apex in a true mitre, the joint secured (mostly) by a horizontal peg.[25] In the chamber and hall roofs common rafters are also fixed to ashlar pieces, cove braces and upper collars (*see* Fig 7.13); elsewhere they are only fixed at the two points, top and bottom. Rafters are rarely pegged to the purlins in the roof of the south range, in contrast to the west range for reasons explained below. Ashlar pieces are fitted to every common rafter and inter-mediate truss. These served to strengthen the base of the common rafter trusses and to carry the plane of the wall into the soffit of the roof above the moulded cornice.

Figure 7.18
Moulded capital at the base of the south arch brace of truss I of the great chamber roof, partly obscured by the modern east gable partition to the left (photograph by David Garner, February 2000; EH B000023).

Figure 7.19
Double-pegging of face-halved tenons, truss IX, south side (photograph by Stuart Blaylock; EMAFU 1803/18).

Figure 7.20
Detail of truss IV when the rafters of bay 4 were dismantled in April 1989, looking east. Note espe-cially the mortices for the upper purlin and cove purlin (EH B891266).

Although the plastered surface of the adja-cent walling has been reinstated so that the ashlar pieces are visible (*see* Fig 7.14), origin-ally they would have been concealed by plastering.

The usual wall-top arrangement is shown in a detail of Fig 7.13. The chamber roof is elaborated by the use of a cornice, but the eaves purlin is ubiquitous.[26] The structure is intended for a wall of average width as employed here in stone or cob. On the north side of the chamber, where the roof bears on a timber-framed partition, the wall is neces-sarily narrower and the cornice and eaves purlin are placed closer together in order to fit the narrower span (*see* detail in Fig 7.13). This has the effect of raising the eaves purlin to a higher level and truncating the principal and common rafters. The same technique occurs on the south side of bay 1 above the entrance to the south-east range. Again as the partition is thinner, the eaves purlin is brought inward and upward to accommodate the narrower span (Fig 7.21; *see also* Fig 7.13). Another exception is in bay 3, south, where the common rafters are lodged in the masonry of the chimney and the outer timber is omitted.

The four bays of the chamber roof are constructed to the same design. This section of the south range is 6.91m (22'8") east–west measuring to the east face of truss v. The four bays vary in width between 1.65m and 1.74m, but the variation is hardly significant when the amount of post-construction movement caused by the use of green oak is taken into consideration. Individual bays varied in width at different points and from one side of the roof to the other.

Figure 7.21 (top)
The north side of the roof (bays 1 and 2) during re-assembly after repairs in April 1989. Note especially the ashlar pieces, wall-top assembly and purlin/intermediate truss junction with the bosses removed (EH B891255).

Figure 7.22 (bottom)
The great chamber roof during reconstruction of the oversail of the roof of the east range in March 1990, looking south-west. Note the undecorated east face to truss I where it abutted the cob gable wall (photograph by Stuart Blaylock; EMAFU 1704/21).

The standard intended bay width was probably *c* 1.67 (or 5'6"). This is the nearest to an average measurement taken during the recording of the roof. The common rafters are spaced at an average of *c* 280mm (11") apart. The span of the roof is between 4.95 and 5.00m (16'3"–16'4").

Both posts of the first truss (I) and the north posts of the succeeding trusses (II–V) are long. The north posts of trusses I to IV are tenoned into the sill plate of the chamber partition and additionally strengthened by the rails that divide the partition. The whole assembly is numbered with carpenters' marks and is of primary, integral construction (*see* Figs 6.25 and 7.13). The rear (east) face of truss I is undecorated, as it abutted the gable wall (Fig 7.22; this provides one of the pieces of evidence in favour of a gable wall in cob).[27] The configuration is similar to those at the south and north ends of the hall and the west end of the south range, where the end trusses have long posts because they were set in cob walling. The south post of truss I bears on the unsupported terminal of beam 1 of the parlour ceiling, which was propped up by a secondary post (Chapter 6). The open arrangement at the south-east corner of the south range dictated a long post in this position because the wall returned to the east slightly short of the corner and there was nothing to support the roof truss at the corner (*see* Fig 6.1).

The rear face of truss V is unchamfered and rebated to take the infilling of the partition between the chamber and inner chamber. The whole of the truss was thus closed including the apex of the roof above the collar (*see* Fig 6.15, details 1–3). V-shaped mortices were cut in the soffit of the collar to take studded infill of the tympanum – although the mortices do not correspond with those in the headbeam of the later (17th-century) screen below. The upper surface of the collar has a groove for sprung studs (*see* Fig 6.15, detail 2). Both stages of the infilling were probably originally filled in a similar manner to the north partition of the chamber (Chapter 6), although this will have been disrupted on the renewal of the partition in the 17th century.

Assembly marks

The main and intermediate trusses had a separate system of numbering from the common rafter trusses, as all (or most) of the individual elements are inscribed with the truss number in roman numerals, a plain

number on the north side and a circular distinguishing mark (added to the last vertical stroke) on the south side. Inscribed numbers often run continuously across two or more timbers (a good example is Fig 7.23,

showing marks on intermediate truss II) or are inscribed at adjacent points on two timbers (Fig 7.24, on main truss III). Common rafter trusses have fewer marks, because they have fewer component timbers and seem to be numbered in a separate sequence. No marks are recorded on rafter trusses (RT) 1 and 2, but RTs 3 to 6 bear the Roman numerals III–VI in the correct sequence. From RT 7 onwards the numbering is confused: RT7, I; RT8, VI; RT9, V; RT10, IIII; RT11, III; RT12, II; RT13, VIIII; RT14, VIII (Fig 7.25, showing the south side of rafter trusses 14 (foreground) and 13); RT15, VII; and RT16, VI(I?). This is probably because the numbering was not adhered to in the original assembly. Although there is some evidence further west in the roof for rearrangement of rafter trusses during previous re-roofing, this is unlikely in the great chamber roof because of the large number of joints involved. In the central and western bays a muddling of the common rafters would have caused few complications, as each couple was only fixed at two points.

Evidence for ceilings

Evidence for a primary ceiling was recorded in photographs of *c* 1985 taken during the dismantling of the chamber roof (Fig 7.26),[28] which show the remains of plaster behind the laths of a later ceiling near the outer face of the ashlar pieces and common rafters. This represents important evidence for the original appearance of the chamber roof (and, thereby, that of the hall as well) in that it shows that the lesser structural timbers were intended to be visible. Evidence for a later ceiling survived in the form of nail holes and staining from lath and plaster on the soffits of some timbers. This covered the common rafters, the ashlar pieces and the braces of the coving, that is, at this stage the chamfered timbers of the main and intermediate trusses were visible, but none of the plain-surfaced timbers (*see* Fig 2.27). This secondary ceiling,

Figure 7.23 (top, left) Detail of the ashlar piece, common rafter and brace of intermediate truss II, north side. Note the assembly mark and the line of the (later) plaster ceiling (EMAFU 1423/29a).

Figure 7.24 (centre, left) Detail of the assembly mark of main truss III, south side, with the arch brace (below) *and principal rafter* (above) *(photograph by Keith Westcott; EMAFU 1404/34).*

Figure 7.25 (bottom, left) Detail of the coving of the chamber roof from above, south side, looking north-east. Note the assembly marks (rafter truss 14 in the foreground) (photograph by Keith Westcott; EMAFU 1380/16)

Figure 7.26 Montage of three views of the north side of the roof before dismantling, c 1985–6: a bay 3; b bay 2; c bay 1. These unprovenanced prints record crucial information for two phases of plastered ceilings in the great chamber towards the outer face of the common rafters and on the soffits of the common rafters. Note also the 'beam filling' with sloping face between the ashlar pieces (copy negatives, EMAFU 3908/8–12).

in common with that of the oriel chamber (*see below*), probably dated to the 18th or 19th century, although no record survives of its composition. Trusses I and III also carried the plaster lines of partitions which divided the great chamber (19th century, phases 8 and 9 respectively).

The inner chamber

Structure

The basic structure of the main trusses continues unchanged into the western part of the roof, but most of the purely decorative elements are now omitted (Fig 7.27). In consequence the roof of the inner chamber (bays 5–7; trusses V–VII) conforms more closely to the standard late medieval roof of jointed-cruck type. Again, the differential walling material (stone to the full height on the south, cob above floor level on the north) meant that the trusses on the south side were truncated and those on the north were left with long posts (Fig 7.28). The principal rafters are of the same design as those of the chamber, although the timbers are thinner and coving and yoke are omitted above the collar. The arch braces are cut to fit in the same manner as those of the great chamber, suggesting that they too originally bore pseudo-capitals or corbels as lower terminals. Again the final trimming may be related to the insertion of later ceilings, in this case the one represented by sockets in the south (*see* Fig 6.22, 125) and the north walls (*see* Fig 6.25, 144, 145, 147; Chapter 6). The common rafters are entirely plain without coving and are supported on the eaves purlin alone (plus pegs at the apexes in most cases). The three bays of this room have an average width of *c* 1.97m (slightly <6'6") and each contains six pairs of common rafters, rather than the five of the great chamber roof.

In elevation (with the longitudinal timbers) the roof changes quite substantially. There are now three levels of purlins, the upper at the same height as that of the chamber, but of standard scantling and chamfered profile. The middle purlin is at the same height as the lower purlin of the chamber and forms a direct continuation of it (*see* Fig 6.25). The third (now lower) purlin is introduced for the first time in bay 5. The moulded inner face is of the same section as the cornice of the chamber, but the tenons are set diagonally rather than vertically (*cf* Figs 7.13 and 7.27) and the

timber is positioned at a higher level. The rear/upper side of the timber is trimmed off and the common rafters bear directly on its diagonal face (*see* Fig 5.30, detail 6). This timber is now quite clearly acting as a purlin rather than a plate[29] and the cob infill on the wall top (which in the chamber had served simply to fill the interstices of wall-top purlins, common rafters and ashlar pieces) here represents a direct continuation of the wall face, sloping slightly to meet the outside edge of the lower purlin.

The southern principal of truss VI has a redundant mortice at the same level as those for the cornice of the great chamber. It is possible to suggest, therefore, that the raising of the cornice represents a change of plan. The northern principal and the trusses to the west have no equivalent mortices, and the timbers themselves were cut for the higher position, since they have the diagonal tenons characteristic of purlins, rather than the vertically set tenons of the chamber cornice. The change of plan thus took place before the erection of the roof.

Truss VII has several signs of a secondary partition fixed to it (*see* Fig 5.30) and this probably corresponds to the 16th- or 17th-century partition originally installed on this line (Chapter 6 and *see also* Fig 12.3), subsequently moved to the east and now removed.[30] A secondary timber is applied to the east face of the original collar, with mortices for studding (visible in section in truss VII on Fig 6.25). Three oak planks were nailed to the west face of the truss above the collar, filling the apex of the roof (the planks are of ancient appearance, with roughly chamfered edges and are probably 16th or 17th century in date). Softwood battens nailed at the level of the upper purlins (and shown on Fig 5.30) relate to the most recent ceiling of the roof that obscured the apex of the arch braces (visible, for instance, on pre-DoE photographs such as Fig 2.28). The west face of truss VIII is unchamfered as it was positioned against the face of the cob cross wall.

Assembly marks

The principal trusses continue the numbering established in the chamber. Bold roman numerals are incised on the west face of the main timbers. These are plain on the north side of the roof, with an additional distinguishing mark on the south side (*see* Fig 7.24).[31] Within the bays common rafters were numbered, normally

Figure 7.27
Exploded analytical
drawing of the roof of the
south range (inner
chamber), looking west,
with truss VII in the foreground (not to scale) (line
drawing by Piran Bishop).

Figure 7.28
General view of the roof of
the oriel and inner cham-
bers in May 1988, looking
east, with truss IX in the
foreground. Note especially
the differential treatment of
the feet of the trusses: those
on the right (lodged on the
stone of the south wall) are
cut off at the base of the
arch braces; those on the left
(set in the cob of the north
wall) have long posts
stretching down to floor
level (see elevation Fig
6.25) (photograph by
Stuart Blaylock; EMAFU
1449/23a).

Figure 7.29
*Exploded analytical
drawing of the roof of the
south range (oriel
chamber), looking east,
with truss IX in the foreground (not to scale) (line
drawing by Piran Bishop).*

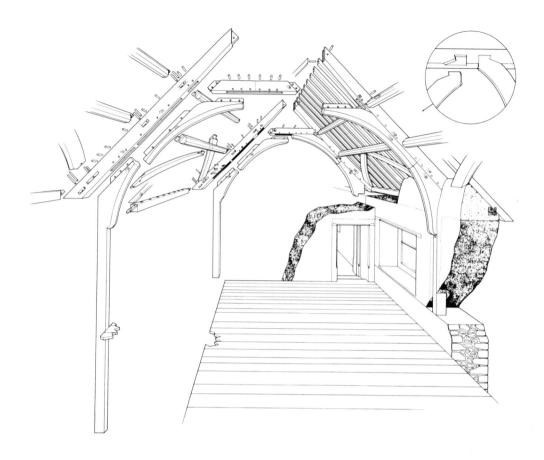

with a single mark at the apex. Here and throughout the remainder of the roof of the south range, the rafters are often out of order, presumably as a result of disturbance during an earlier phase of re-roofing. Decay has caused the loss of some marks, but the following numbers survived: in bay 5: (RT 17, missing); RT18, VIII; RT 19, VII; RT 20, IIII; (RTs 21 and 22 renewed). The significance of numbers higher than six in a bay with only that number of rafter couples is unknown. Although the numbering of common rafters in the great chamber ran through bays 1–4, there is no clear evidence of that here; in bay 6: RT 23, IIII; RT 24, III; RT 25 (rotten, one stroke survives); RT 26, II; RT 27 (rotten, one stroke survives); RT 28 (rotten, one stroke survives); in bay 7: RT 30, III; RT 32, VI; RTs 29, 31, 33 and 34 are softwood replacements.

In the numbering of the longitudinal timbers, there is evidence of yet another numbering system at work. The purlins of bays 5 and onwards are numbered bay by bay starting at I, a device which betrays some segregation of the great chamber roof from the remainder of the south range in the minds of the carpenters. Marks do not survive on every timber, but were noted on enough examples for the pattern to be clear:[32] bay 5, lower purlin, east: I; bay 6, lower and upper purlins, east: II; bay 7, lower, middle and upper purlins, east: III; the sequence continues through bays 8–10 (*see below*).

Evidence for ceilings

The common rafters and other timbers of the roof are free of nails and lath marks of ceilings, implying that this room was not ceiled in the early phases (torching between the rafters is possible, although unproven). Later 19th-century ceilings at a low level are described above from the evidence in the elevations (*see* Chapter 6, and Figs 6.22 and 6.25); these were replaced in phase 11 by a modern ceiling on the soffits of the common rafters and at the apex of the arch braces (*see* Figs 7.28 and 2.28).[33]

The oriel chamber

The roof continues through bays 8–10 in the same basic form as that of the inner chamber. Some differences were introduced. The moulded lower purlin (the continuation of the cornice of the great

hall roofs, above). The blocks have been removed in every bay, but evidence survives for their positions in the form of slight scars where the timber has been chiselled off or traces of cuts in the chamfers (Figs 7.32 and 7.33; *see also* Figs 6.25 and 7.29). It is not known whether bosses were fitted here and subsequently lost or were omitted as an alteration during construction.

Although the roof was more ornamental in character than that of the inner chamber, the finish cannot have been visually satisfactory. The lower portions of the windbraces were obscured by the cob infill of the wall tops (shown to be primary also on the evidence of primary plaster) and the wall faces lacked the articulation of the cornice/lowest purlin. The eastern braces of bay 8 (N and S) were further obscured by the cob of the cross wall as it rose into the roof. These infelicities are another example of the disparity (in planning rather than skills) between the 'wall builders' and the 'roof builders' of Bowhill (*see* pp 146–7).[34]

Form of roof over gable wall

The west face of truss XI is undecorated (*see* Fig 5.22), although the south arch brace is chamfered on its west face, which is presumably an error of construction.[35] The truss

Figure 7.30 (top, left)
Bay 10 (south) with
common rafters removed in
November 1992. Note the
wall plate with mortices for
the common rafters and the
unpegged dovetails of the
windbraces (photograph by
David Garner; EH
B926262).

Figure 7.31 (bottom, left)
Detail of the dovetail joint
of the windbraces to the
purlins, bay 8, south side
(photograph by Stuart
Blaylock; EMAFU
1947/8).

chamber) was omitted in the oriel chamber and the cob infill of the wall tops now rose into the roof to the soffits of the rafters (Fig 7.29, *see also* Figs 7.4 and 7.30). The three bays of the oriel chamber have pairs of windbraces that strengthen the angle between principals and lower purlins at the same level as the middle purlins of bays 5–7. These elements are curved planks with chamfers on the lower edges secured to the principals by long soffit tenons (pegged) and to the purlins by bare-faced dovetail joints (unpegged; Figs 7.30–7.31; *see also* Fig 7.29, detail). At the apex of the windbrace assemblies in each bay, a gap of some 100–150mm is left between the terminals, matching a block of timber left unchamfered at the centre of the purlins. These are probably the seating for bosses (*cf* the unchamfered blocks left for the bosses on the intermediate trusses of chamber and

Figure 7.32
Detail of the junction of
windbraces and purlin on
the interior, showing the
block left in the chamfers of
the purlin, presumably to
support a boss; bay 8,
north, looking north
(photograph by Stuart
Blaylock; EMAFU
1803/9).

Figure 7.33
As Figure 7.32 from the
outside, bay 8, south,
showing the gap at the apex
of the windbraces, looking
north (photograph by
Stuart Blaylock; EMAFU
1803/15).

Figure 7.34
The west face of truss XI,
south side, showing the
extended purlins and wall
plate carrying the common
rafters over the west gable
wall, September 1992.
Note also the assembly
marks and the blind rear
face to the truss (photo-
graph by Stuart Blaylock;
EMAFU 3033/1).

Figure 7.35
As Fig 7.34, detail on the
northern side of truss XI.
Here can be seen the top of
the brick blocking of phase
8, inserted after the removal
of the gable wall (bottom),
and the western post of
truss I of the west range
behind (photograph by
Stuart Blaylock; EMAFU
3025/31).

abutted the inside face of the cob gable wall. The treatment of the lower terminals of the principals and the longitudinal members displays an unusual configuration related to the continuation of the rafters over the gable wall. The eaves purlins were continued across the line of truss XI by 0.75m and the lower ends of the principal rafters were cut to fit underneath the purlin in a halved joint (Fig 7.34, south, and Fig 7.35, north; see also Fig 5.22). The purlins of bay 10 were also carried across the line of the last truss by halving the thickness (to that of the tenon alone) and threading the resulting thinner timber through the mortice. The extended timbers supported two common rafter couples to the west of truss XI, of which one survived and one (no. 57) was missing (see Fig 7.34), as well as (presumably) an eaves assembly. This arrangement is of interest in its own right, but also because it gives some indication of how the roof might have been treated over the east and north gables, where no evidence had survived.[36]

Assembly marks

The numbering system continues (Fig 7.36, detail of marks on truss IX). The marks on common rafters continue in jumbled order in bay 8: RT 35, IIII; RT 36, II; RT 37, I; RT 38, V; RT 39, III; RT 40, VI; RT 41, VIII; RT 42, VII. In bays 9 and 10 the rafters survive in sequence and thus may not have been disturbed by past re-roofing activities (or were replaced with greater care). The rafters of bay 9 run in reverse sequence, VIII to I over common rafters 43 to 50; those of bay 10 are numbered I to V, RTs 51 to 55 (although the number III is missing on RT53). No numbers were observed on the two rafter trusses beyond the limit of bay 10 covering the western gable wall. Perhaps these were not pre-fabricated.

The purlins continue the numbering established from bay 5 (described above). The numbers IIII and V are marked on the eaves purlins and upper and lower purlins of bays 8 and 9 respectively, although no equivalent numbers (VI) were seen in bay 10. The windbraces are individually numbered (at the lower terminal of the upper surface) from east to west. Thus the windbraces of bay 8 are numbered I and II; bay 9, III and IIII; and bay 10, V and VI (Fig 7.37, showing the braces numbered IIII, right, and V, to either side of truss X, south side).

Evidence for ceilings

This section of the roof preserved clear evidence for two ceilings, best exemplified on the north side of bay 9. Here the first and earlier ceiling lay near the outer face of the common rafters, allowing these timbers to be seen (as in the great chamber, *see above*). This was represented by faint impressions on the timbers, but no plaster had survived. The second ceiling lay at a lower level, on the soffits of the common rafters and level with the apex of the arch braces, that is, just below collar level. This ceiling is represented by lath nails and staining from lath and plaster on the common rafters (Fig 7.38) and by timbers applied to the principal rafters to support the laths (one is visible on truss IX in Fig 5.27). On the arch braces, principal rafters and windbraces the line of the ceiling was represented by successive layers of staining and painting of the timbers exposed below the ceiling level.[37]

The west range

General description

The general design of the roof is similar to that of the south range, although slightly wider (5–5.1m). Two bays survive (2.8m, 9'2", wide), numbered from the south (*see below*). The total number of bays of the west range (determinable had the numbering been in the opposite direction as in the east range) is therefore unknown. The third truss was positioned against the north face of the kitchen chimney stack, as the longitudinal timbers of the roof span that wall (unless the timbers were supported on the wall itself, without a truss). The roof shares many details of design and construction with that of bays 8–10 of the south range (Figs 7.39 and 7.40), but there are also significant differences. The principal variation is one of construction in that this roof retains the long timber feet of the jointed-cruck trusses throughout, although they vary in length. The cob walls adjacent to the timbers show only minimal voids against the posts. These were clearly produced by shrinkage rather than cutting action. Where the eastern post of truss II was seen in section, the cast impression of the timber was visible in the cob that had shrunk away from the faces of the timber (*see* Fig 6.47, 400, and Fig 6.49).[38] Thus it can be shown that the cob walls were raised

Figure 7.36
Detail of assembly marks on truss IX, south side, principal rafter and arch brace (photograph by Stuart Blaylock; EMAFU 1803/2).

Figure 7.37
The lower ends of wind-braces in the oriel chamber, showing assembly marks, truss X, bays 9/10, south side (photograph by Stuart Blaylock; EMAFU 1803/21).

Figure 7.38
Oblique view of the north elevation of the oriel and inner chambers, when the floors were removed in October 1985. Note the scar of the cross wall, right of centre, and traces of ceilings in oriel chamber (EH B850150/6).

Figure 7.39
General view of the interior of the roof of the west range, with truss II in the foreground, looking south. Note the protruding pegs (photograph by David Garner; EH B930166).

Figure 7.40
The east side of the roof of the west range when stripped in July 1992, with later rafters removed and surviving primary rafters in position. Note the rafters jointed into the cornice rather than the eaves purlin and the eaves purlin set diagonally (photograph by David Garner; EH B924254).

Figure 7.41
Detail of dovetails securing the windbraces to the purlins, pegged in this roof, in contrast to the roof of the south range (cf Fig 7.31) (photograph by David Garner; EH B924252).

Figure 7.42
The west side of the roof of the west range in January 1993 after further stripping and removal of rafters, showing how the roof was carried over the gable wall (modern brick facing on the outside face). Note the absence of a mortice for the second windbrace (photograph by David Garner; EH B930171).

after the roof trusses were in position – very much the normal structural sequence, but at variance with that of the south range.

The roof has windbraces of similar form to those of the oriel chamber (*see* Fig 7.39). They are fixed with the same types of joint, but the dovetails on the middle purlins are secured by pegs, a detail omitted in the previous examples (Fig 7.41). The arrangement of windbraces shows that the filling of the northern half of bay 2 was accounted for in the design of the roof, as no mortices had been cut in the purlins in the northern side of the bay, where the timbers were obscured by the chimney (Fig 7.42). This represents another sign of better integration of the construction of walls and roof in the west range than elsewhere and supports the suggestion that the west range was built in a traditional structural sequence, perhaps after the other surviving ranges.

The purlins show another variant arrangement in which the lowest internal purlin is set at the top of the wall-top infill as a cornice, in the manner of the equivalent timbers in the inner chamber (*see* Fig 7.42). The timbers are chamfered in the same way as the other purlins, but are set square rather than diagonally and thus are strictly plates rather than purlins. Each bay originally had seven common rafters. The elevations (*see* Figs 5.22 and 5.27) show those which had survived (after the removal of later softwood additions; *see also* Figs 6.69 and 7.40). The common rafters are pegged to the middle purlins (on both sides of the roof), a detail not employed in the south range and suggesting that additional strengthening was necessary in this roof. Birds-mouth joints are employed to fix the common rafters, but they are fixed to the lower purlins (cornices) on both sides of the roof instead of the eaves purlins as in the south and east ranges. On the west side of the roof the rafters continue to eaves level nonetheless, but on the east side the surviving rafters terminate (?or were cut off) at the cornice. This variation may have been determined by the need to provide for the roof of the gallery on the east side of the range.[39] Peg holes in the eaves purlin of bay 2 (east), at variance with the common rafters, may represent the positions of the extension rafters of a catslide roof over the gallery, overlapping the main common rafters (*see* Fig 5.27 and discussion of the evidence for a gallery in Chapter 5). No evidence survives in the roof of bay 1, as the eaves purlin was removed (with the rest of the fabric in this bay) on the removal of the gallery (or in one of the subsequent alterations to this area).

The wall-top infill of bay 2 was composed of cob and brick fragments displaying the red white-speckled earth mortar characteristic of phase 8, of *c* 1800 (*see* Figs 5.27 and 6.47, 219); this material contained no impressions of the common rafters nor of the extension rafters for the gallery roof. The assumption must be, therefore, that these timbers had been removed before the addition of the wall-top infill, which provides useful additional evidence for the removal of the gallery in phase 8.

Assembly marks

The principal trusses are numbered on their north faces starting from the south, indicating that the direction of erection was from south to north (this is confirmed by the pegs, which are all inserted from the north; *see* Fig 7.39). The two surviving trusses bear marks on all the main timbers (*see* Fig 7.39). The lower purlins bear the number of the bay/adjacent truss at their southern ends.[40] Some evidence of the numbering of common rafters was recorded, apparently continuous through bays 1 and 2, although the rafters were out of order (as in the south range) and some numbers were missing: RT1, IIII; RT 2, III; RT 3, VII; RT 4, II; RT 5, V; RT 6, VIII; RT 7, I; RT 8, X; RT 9, XII; RT 10 (uncertain); and RT 11, XIIII.

Evidence for ceilings

No traces of an ancient ceiling had survived, but light lath nails and staining of the main timbers represent a modern ceiling of phase 11 (the same sequence as in the inner chamber). The absence of an early ceiling is consistent with the original function of the west range as the kitchen. Archive photographs of the 1950s show bare rafters and the underside of the slates.[41]

The junction of the roofs of the west and south ranges[42]

The treatment of this area was similar to the equivalent area of the roof of the east range (*see* Fig 7.12). Here the fabric was less well preserved, although it was possible to examine and record it in detail. Laths had survived on the outer surface of the roof of the south range within the roof space. Blocks of timber with bevelled and hipped surfaces were nailed to the common rafters

on top of the laths; these served to support the south ends of the upper purlins where they met the roof of the south range (Fig 7.43) and show that the laths were applied to the roof of the south range prior to the construction of the roof of the west range (or at least the oversailing part of it).[43] Next the lay boards were positioned. The western board was halved under the eastern at the apex and both were oak planks, lengthened by simple edge-halved scarf joints.[44] Both lay boards were decayed at the eaves and the details of the treatment at this point did not survive. Evidence for the primary chimney rising through this part of the roof and abutting the unchamfered south face of truss I of the west range is discussed in Chapter 6.

The upper purlins (plain, not chamfered, timbers within the roof void) were morticed into truss I to the north and mitred to fit against the lay board to the south, supported by the nailed-on blocks described above. On the west side the purlin had been removed on the insertion of the phase 5 chimney stack in bay 10 of the south range, as this structure conflicted with the position of the timber.[45] Lower purlins (in line with the middle purlins of bays 1 and 2 of the west range) had not survived, although there were mortices and peg holes in the south face of truss I that may have accommodated such timbers.[46] Paired jack rafters completed the frame,

Figure 7.43
Detail inside the roof of the west range over the south range, showing the rafters of the roof of the south range, lath and mud-plaster covering south range, lay boards and chock for the purlin above laths (modern softwood rafters above). Note the lath nails in the common rafters (EMAFU 1984/26a).

Figure 7.44
View inside the oversail of the roof of the west range, showing lay boards and jack rafters, looking south. Note the pegged joints at the apex (EMAFU 1984/33a).

THE STANDING BUILDING: ROOFS

165

Figure 7.45
Junction of the roofs of the south and west ranges, showing the original lay board and jack rafters, east side, looking south-west (EMAFU 1987/04).

pegged at the apex (Fig 7.44) and fixed to the lay boards with nails. One rafter survived on the west side and four on the east side (Fig 7.45). Once the roof was complete, the outside of the roof of the south range within the void was plastered with daub. Later softwood purlins supported a range of later common rafters and other inserted timbers from the re-roofing in phases 8 and 9. No original valley boards or other finishing timbers had survived.

Roof coverings

The roof removed from the building as the repairs were carried out (1979–92) was largely of modern (19th- and 20th-century) slate fixed on softwood battens. One section covering most of the hall was of corrugated iron. This had replaced a thatched roof attested by photographs in the 1930s (*see* Fig 2.7). The thatched roof was itself a replacement of a ?primary slate roof, as was shown by the discovery of slates in the roof of the east range when it was dismantled in 1980.[47] A short section of ridge over the roof of the east/south range transition retained a group of mixed ridge tiles (clearly seen in Fig 2.9), reflecting the original tiling of the ridge and two phases of repair in the

17th and 18th centuries (Chapter 9). Considerable evidence of earlier roofing was recovered from the fabric as loose finds in the course of the repair programme.[48] A full description of roofing materials is given in Chapter 9. The conclusions drawn from their study are, however, summarised here.

No certain evidence for more than one roof covering antedating the modern slates has been identified in the south range. If this is so, the slate roof of Bowhill will have proved unusually durable. A recent study of traditional slating has suggested that a lifespan of more than a century is unusual in a pegged-slate roof.[49] Despite the lack of evidence, it is thus probable that the building saw at least one phase of re-roofing between *c* 1500 and *c* 1800.[50] Since most of the slate and other roofing materials recovered from the south range came from contexts associated with the major refurbishment works of phase 8, it is reasonable to suggest that the building (with the exception of the east range) was comprehensively re-roofed at this time. The nature of this phase of roofing remains elusive. Perhaps it was a poor-quality 'traditional' roof which was itself subsequently replaced by the Welsh slates removed from the building in the 1980s, probably in the later 19th or early 20th century (this roof was certainly less than 170 years old). It follows from this that the riven Devon slates recovered from the site belonged either to the original roof (perhaps removed sometime in the 17th or 18th century) or from a replacement of 17th- or 18th-century date, itself removed *c* 1800.[51] The earlier roof(s) were of peg slates laid in diminishing courses; lengths varied from 132 to 260mm (5¼"–10¾"), with an emphasis on smaller slate (*see below*). Detailed measurements show an average lap of between three and four slates. Scribing lines on the soffits of the slates indicate that the slaters were working to fixed gauges. The punching of peg holes, however, was carried out as the slates were fitted (shown by the variable position of the hole in relation to the centre of the slate). Bedding of the slates in mortar was standard. Torching of the underside of the roof was employed in some rooms, although this was not ubiquitous (*see above*, discussion of ceilings). Some slates recovered from the standing building were in very poor condition,[52] providing further evidence of the longevity of the roof and indicating that the original roof was near the end of its effective life when these slates were removed from the building.

Replacement is more often due to the failure of the pegging or other means of securing the slate than to the decay of the slate itself, which can often be reused.[53] The surviving oak pins at Bowhill are largely intact, although often fragile through rot or beetle action, a detail which argues against the general failure of the pegs as a reason for re-roofing here. Finds of numerous large wooden pegs indicate the use of many more larger slates than were recovered. A number of factors could have influenced survival: larger slates may have been more readily reusable when the roof was re-slated; they may have been carted away for some other purpose; perhaps they fell and broke more readily; or the explanation might lie in the size of the crevices, in which the surviving slates lodged that may have been too small to accommodate larger slates.

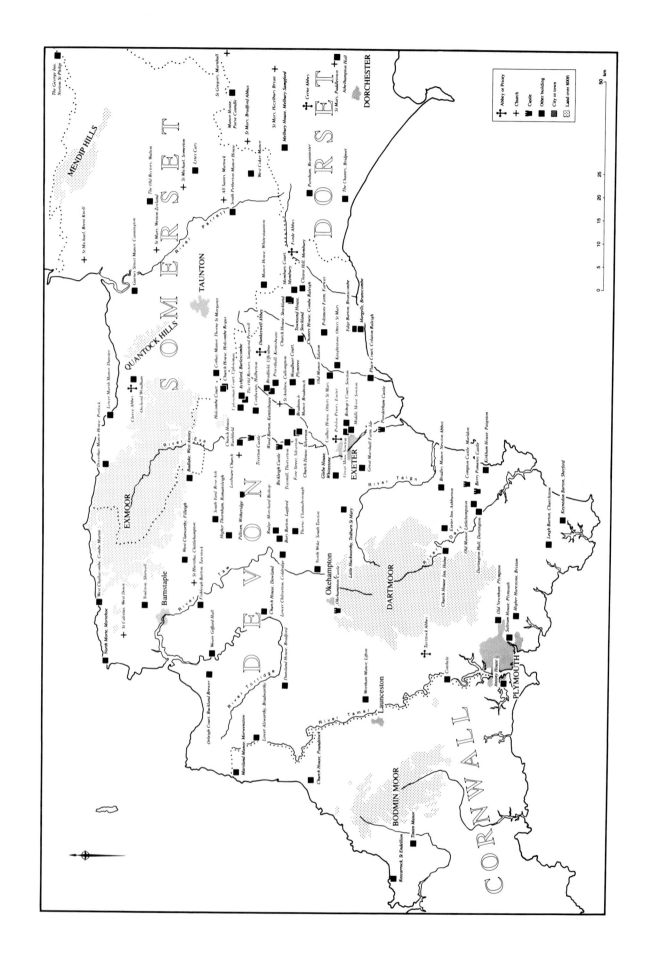

8
General discussion of the building

The plan

The plan is characteristic of a rural building. Although there were fewer constraints of space or orientation than in an urban context, pre-existing boundaries or other standing structures may have persisted to influence the plan of the new building.[1] Furthermore, the excavated evidence points to the complete demolition of the earlier building on the site before the construction of the standing building. The plan is also closely related to some larger urban house plans in Exeter and elsewhere, most notably the houses of Cathedral clergy in The Close that are also freed of some of the normal constraints of space upon urban house plans.[2] A particularly close parallel for the plan of Bowhill is the plan of no. 7 The Close as it survived in the 18th century and was recorded by John Tothill, Surveyor to the Dean and Chapter of Exeter Cathedral, in 1764.[3] Here, in a plan with major buildings on three sides of a central courtyard, the kitchen was placed in the wing opposite the hall and connected by a passage in the same way as the pentice at Bowhill. Further comparison is limited by the fitting in of subsidiary rooms within the boundaries of the plot.

Examples of a courtyard plan, with the kitchen sited in a wing opposite the hall, are not uncommon in late medieval manor houses in the West Country,[4] for example, at Berry Pomeroy Castle, Devon,[5] the Old Manor, Littlehempston, Devon,[6] Little Hackworthy, Tedburn St Mary, Devon,[7] at Scaplen's Court, Poole, Dorset,[8] and at Gurney Street Manor, Cannington, Somerset (Fig 8.1).[9] The last has the rare survival of a covered pentice walk across the centre of the courtyard, linking the kitchen and hall.[10] Although such pentice walks were once common,[11] few survive, perhaps because they were generally built of timber, lath and plaster and other non-durable materials.[12] Wood makes the important point that the former presence of a pentice is often attested by the absence of windows on a basement

(or ground-floor) wall.[13] Bowhill can show, however, that this was not always the case, as two windows (lighting three rooms) looked onto the pentice (Chapter 6), providing borrowed light for the rooms within.

A plan centred on the great hall is, of course, entirely consistent with late medieval planning conventions. The juxtaposition of hall and more private living rooms to the south is one of several features at Bowhill that associate the building with developments in architecture and interior arrangement at the turn of the 16th century. This includes the tendency for great halls to decline as larger and more private 'withdrawing' rooms developed (although many houses were still being built with large and sumptuous halls) and the parallel tendency for halls to become single storey, with other rooms above, which is suggested by the evidence of inventories.[14] The absence of conventional reception rooms at the north (that is, 'upper') end of the hall is another sign of the adaptation of the traditional arrangement to provide new types of accommodation. Parallels for this arrangement in plan are not easy to find. In Devon, parlours placed on the opposite side of the screens passage to the hall occur at Kirkham House, Paignton, and Wortham Manor, Lifton.[15] A similar arrangement is seen at Clothworkers' Hall, London.[16] The circulation from the parlour via the south-east range to further main rooms on the first floor has already been mentioned. The residents of the house would have taken their meals in the parlour (or possibly the great chamber) and the placing of this room near to the screens passage (and service rooms) is consistent with this function.[17] Although this had the effect of displacing the service rooms (conventionally in the position below the hall) further to the west, the access afforded by the pentice across the south side of the courtyard and the wide potential for the placing of lodgings and storerooms in the vanished portion of the west and north ranges provide many alternative locations for service rooms.

Figure 8.1 (facing page) Map of the West Country, showing places referred to in the text (line drawing by Tony Ives).

Galleries in the central courtyard

Gallery circulation is another notable aspect of the plan, albeit qualified by uncertainty over the details of the form of galleries at Bowhill. The evidence for galleries on the north and west sides of the central courtyard is discussed elsewhere (Chapter 5). The reconstructions presented here (*see* Figs 12.5 and 12.6) take the near-contemporary gallery at Leigh Barton, Churchstow (Kingsbridge), Devon, as a model.[18] The origin of the 'corridor gallery' in grand English houses of the 14th and 15th centuries has been briefly surveyed by Rosalys Coope, whose examples (such as Herstmonceaux Castle and the Stone Court at Knole, Kent) provide the background to the contemporary domestic galleries discussed here.[19] Local examples of gallery communication, precluding the need for internal access through rooms, are found at Kirkham House, Paignton, Devon,[20] and in first-floor galleries around three sides of an internal courtyard at Yogge's House, Finewell Street, Plymouth.[21] Other galleries in late 15th- and 16th-century domestic contexts are seen in the local urban tradition of connecting the main block of a house with a detached rear block, often containing a kitchen among other rooms, by means of a timber-framed gallery, frequently of two or more storeys.[22] Domestic examples also occur at Tretower Court, Brecnock,[23] and at Scaplen's Court, Poole, Dorset.[24] Medieval inns provide other parallel examples. The New Inn, Gloucester, has galleries on two levels around its central courtyard[25] and the George Inn, Norton St Philip, Somerset, has a first-floor gallery along one side that is perhaps more comparable to the Bowhill and Leigh Barton examples.[26] In this context the galleries were necessary to provide access to individual lodgings,[27] a function more important in an inn than in a normal domestic context. Whereas the first-floor rooms in the south range have interior access and can be interpreted as a range of interconnecting chambers perhaps for family use, gallery access in the west and north ranges suggests independent chambers or lodgings, perhaps for the use of guests or by retainers.[28]

The south-east range

The junction of two structures at the corner, as with the south and south-east ranges, is unusual and parallels are scarce. A similar arrangement is seen in plan at Cotehele in Cornwall, where the chapel is entered through the south-west corner of the hall range, but this bears little similarity to the treatment of the two Bowhill ranges in elevation, still less in their roofing.[29] Cowick Barton, also in St Thomas parish, provides an immediately local parallel, although late 16th century in date, in which two flanking wings project forward from the corners of the main range.[30]

The vanished south-east range added considerably to the grandeur and level of appointments of the main rooms of Bowhill. The exterior treatment of a projecting window spanning two floors has a local parallel in the house known as Elyott's House, in Exeter Cathedral Close (*see* p 195 and Figs 8.31 and 8.32). This house provides a good idea of the possible appearance of the front of the south-east range. A few surviving architectural fragments indicate exterior stonework of a higher quality than any seen elsewhere in the building and these may have come from the south-east range. If interior appointment can be judged by this and the function of the rooms gauged by level of ornament, then this vanished portion of the building must have contained important rooms. Without physical evidence of their precise size or specific parallels in plan, these rooms remain elusive. They are probably best interpreted as providing additional space of a semi-private nature for the parlour and great chamber, as well as a means of access via the possible turret stair from one room to the other into the 'garden gallery' to the east (*see below*) and to the roof. The rooms in the south-east range could have functioned rather in the way of the oriels projecting from some medieval halls[31] or the bay windows constructed at the dais end of halls such as Athelhampton Hall, Dorset, Gainsborough Old Hall, Lincolnshire, or Lytes Cary, Somerset.[32] An increase in privacy and/or status, with progression from one room to the next, is a well-established aspect of late medieval planning,[33] a factor that may contribute to assessing the relative status of these rooms. They may best be seen as private dining or retiring areas or perhaps as 'closets' in the sense that such rooms were described in the early 17th century at Lulworth Castle, Dorset.[34] Private closets or viewing places in the corner turret (instead of a stair) would add another tier of privacy to the circulation.[35]

Possible form of the eastern courtyard

The Bucks' engraving (*see* Fig 2.1) shows that a flanking structure survived in a fragmentary or semi-derelict condition on the south side of the eastern courtyard in the early 18th century. A minimal reconstruction of this evidence suggests that this comprised a plain, crenellated boundary wall, punctuated by one or more projecting oriel windows. Since the window spans first-floor level in the main part of the building,

a floor or raised platform within would seem to be necessary. It is possible that the fragment represented the front wall of a building, although this must have been very narrow if it was not to obstruct the east elevation. The lack of depth in the engraving, the nature of the east elevation of the standing building as an entrance front, the coincidence of the wall with the historical boundaries of the site and the resemblance to the gallery wall at Thornbury (*see below*) all suggest that this was a narrow linear structure, rather than a building of

Figure 8.2
A van den Wyngaerde's drawings of Richmond Palace, showing the galleries enclosing the Privy Garden: (above) from Richmond Green (Western Art E/DB 21); (below) detail of the view from across the River Thames (Western Art E/DB 20) (reproduced courtesy of the Ashmolean Museum, Oxford).

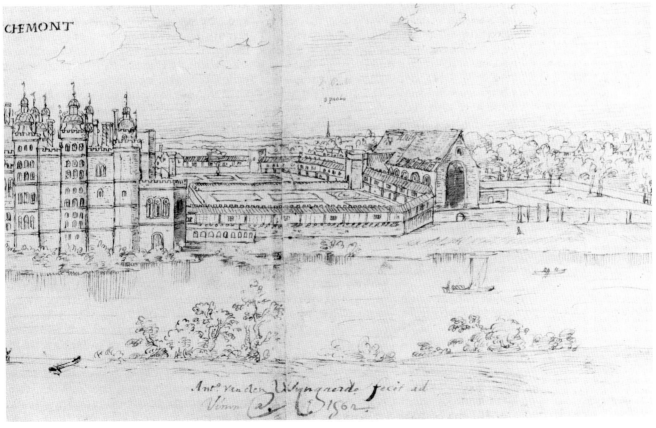

Figure 8.3
Thornbury Castle, Gloucestershire, the stone boundary wall of the gallery around the Privy Garden: (left) *west wall, interior (EA 3431/21);* (right) *detail showing the blocked doorway that gave access to the gallery (via stairs) from the first floor of the adjacent range (EA 3431/34) (photographs by Stuart Blaylock).*

any depth. Possible forms of a raised walkway to the rear include a gallery, a covered walk or an open parapet walk following the perimeter of the courtyard, reached either from the interior of the south-east range or from external steps. The interpretation must remain tentative, in view of the absence of physical evidence, but the assessment of the accuracy of the Bucks' work (Chapter 2) has shown that their view, although not without problems, deserves to be taken seriously as a record of the south elevation of the building in the 1730s. A little can be deduced of the factors which had created this remnant by 1736. The activity of the Civil War period (phase 6, Chapter 4) had involved the digging of earthwork defences around the site. This may well have caused the removal of any standing walls beyond the limit of the earthworks. Equally the earthworks could have incorporated such structures within them. Several architectural fragments from the lower fills of the ditches show that some demolition was taking place as the ditches were being filled in. Otherwise the activities of the 18th- and 19th-century nursery gardens had removed all trace of earlier structures in this area.[36]

Low boundary walls often acted in lieu of a gatehouse or closing range of buildings around courtyards. Maurice Howard has noted this in the Midlands and the south of England with the example of Stonor House, Oxfordshire, specifically noting the 'sense of self containment' which this achieved.[37] A number of manor houses in Devon and Cornwall have small-scale crenellated boundary walls, sometimes

incorporating a gatehouse, but with no interior structure other than a wall walk. These include Keynedon, Sherford, Devon,[38] Marsland Manor, Morwenstow, Cornwall,[39] and Roscarrock, St Endellion, Cornwall.[40] Examples elsewhere include Tretower Court, Brecknock,[41] and Mortham Tower and Walburn Hall, North Yorkshire, both with simple gate structures set in crenellated walls.[42] A walled forecourt is represented in a 16th-century view of Shurland on the Isle of Sheppey.[43] The punctuation of such a wall with windows at a certain level suggests that the wall supported some sort of walkway behind it. This is seen at its simplest as a raised but unroofed walk behind a boundary wall at Wilton House, Wiltshire, long vanished but recorded in a 16th-century drawing.[44] Occasionally, fenestrated pavilions are seen in such a context – for instance, in an 18th-century view of Glemham Hall, Great Glemham, Suffolk.[45]

Richmond Palace and Thornbury Castle, Gloucestershire, provide key examples. Both buildings had galleried walks around outer courtyards, a feature attributed to the Officers of the Royal Works.[46] The primary function in both cases was to aid circulation around the outer parts of the buildings, but both indubitably also functioned for pleasure and recreation.

The galleries served as covered walking places,[47] with windows for viewing the gardens from above.[48] At Richmond, galleries surrounded the Privy Garden and Privy Orchard on the south-east side of the palace.[49] These, dating to 1495–1505, are the earliest of their kind in England.[50] Wyngaerde's drawings of Richmond (Fig 8.2) show that most of the galleries were timber-framed, although the ground-floor stages of the outside walls were of brick and the view from Richmond Green shows a projecting oriel window in a gable wall which may have been of brick or stone.[51] The galleries otherwise had projecting oriel windows in the inner elevations and flush mullioned and transomed windows in the outer walls.[52] At Thornbury (Fig 8.3), dating to 1511–21, galleries surrounded the Privy Garden and also provided covered access from the principal rooms of the castle to the family pew in the parish church.[53] Crenellated stone outer walls of two storeys containing projecting oriel windows (and even fireplaces) had the galleries constructed of timber framing against them; the elevations facing into the garden were slate hung.[54] Externally (Fig 8.4) the Thornbury galleries resemble the fragment in the Bucks' representation of Bowhill. The technique of breaking up boundary walls with oriel windows could well have inspired a similar use on a smaller scale and lower down the social and architectural scale.

The south-east range was of integral construction with the remainder of the primary building, its walls bonded to the south range. This need not have been the case with the possible gallery, which could have been added to the east face of the south-east range at almost any date in the 16th or earlier 17th century. The close analogy with Thornbury (if it is correct) would suggest a date after c 1510–20. The gallery would thus represent an addition after the death of Roger Holand, presumably by one of the early Carew owners. Independent influence of royal building projects (such as Richmond), however, could have occurred earlier, in which case the structure could belong with the primary construction period of the building. Roger Holand's career included several minor royal appointments (Chapter 3). Since he would have been well placed to be aware of contemporary developments in architecture, there is perhaps a little to recommend him as the originator of this scheme.

Contemporaneity of parts of the building

The surviving elements of the building were constructed in a single building programme. The parts that are now missing also belonged to that programme or to a development of it. This fact would need no emphasis were it not for quite well-established interpretations which suggest otherwise. The present section summarises the evidence for the contemporaneity of all parts of the original building to counter suggestions that, *inter alia*, the hall is earlier than the south range,[55] the western end of the south range is an addition, that the moulded beamed ceiling of the parlour is an insertion or that the roof (of the hall, south range or both) is secondary.[56] The roof does display curious features in its fitting and mode of erection, but these, as has been shown (Chapter 7), can be explained in terms of the standing fabric without recourse to theories of replacement or addition.

Fabric exposed while the building was stripped for repairs showed the following evidence for a single, integral build:

1. The masonry of the west wall of the east range is bonded to the north wall of the south range. This was clearly visible at the inner corner (south of the west door of the screens passage), which was represented by a well-finished quoin of integral construction. The same was true of the fabric of the east wall of the east and south ranges. The masonry was

Figure 8.4
Thornbury Castle, Gloucestershire, south wall, exterior. Note the projecting oriel windows (photograph by Stuart Blaylock; EA 3397/05).

continuous and the large quoins forming the reveals of the east door of the screens passage were integral to the work. Less survived here than on the west (having been destroyed on the removal of the east gable), but the evidence of the fabric as a whole demonstrates that the two ranges were built simultaneously. At first-floor level primary cob walling is also of continuous construction around the corner.[57]

2. The scars of the north and west walls of the south-east range survived at the south-east corner of the standing building, running off east and south from the south range (see Fig 5.1, 78, and Fig 5.8, 75). The inner corners of these junctions are again finished with large quoins and the walls of the south-east building are thus, unquestionably, of the same build as those of the south range.

3. Although the remains of the stone ground-floor stage of the cross wall in the south range did not bond with the south wall, at the north end the stump of the cross wall was bonded to the masonry of the north wall. The failure to bond at the south was probably a reflection of the building sequence and of the fact that the two walls butted next to the large stone entrance arch, whose dressed-stone frame may have occupied the place of the quoin.[58]

4. The roof of the south range was the first to be constructed, since the oversailing parts of the roofs of the west and east ranges bear upon it.[59] The hall/great chamber partition is integral to the construction of the roof and this, in turn, is supported by the beams of the parlour ceiling. The parlour ceiling is thus an essential element in the support of the chamber roof, which precedes the southern end of the hall roof in the structural sequence. This sequence is important for the dating of the building, as a date much before 1500 is unlikely for the moulded beams of the parlour ceiling (see below). It also, however, reinforces the fact that the roof is dependent for its support on much of the fabric lower down. Unless it is argued that the masonry and cob shell of the building represented a primary form (which was completely stripped of its interior partitions, floors and fittings before their replacement with the present carpentry) the suggestion that the roof is secondary is not sustainable.

5. One impediment to seeing the building as a unified whole seems to have been that the hall windows are 'early' in form.[60] This is not so. Earlier examples can certainly be found, but such mullioned and transomed windows with cinquefoil heads and hollow-chamfered mouldings are not closely datable and would not appear out of context at any point in a period spanning the later 14th, 15th and early 16th centuries (see below). The hall windows should be seen in the context of other details of the building. The single lancet windows in the south range and the paired single-tier windows in the east wall of the parlour, are clearly related in form. On the evidence of the architectural fragments recovered (Chapter 9), the windows of the south-east range had more complex moulded and decorated detail and these features provide a more reliable indication of date.

The evidence for a chapel

No physical evidence for a chapel survived in the building.[61] Unless the provision for religious observance was of a purely temporary and movable nature (which is possible), it can be stated with reasonable certainty that if there was a chapel at Bowhill, it was not located in the surviving parts of the building. The many published statements that refer to a chapel in the building are based on misunderstandings of the cusp-headed windows, elaborate, vaguely wagon-type roof of the hall and on the misinterpretation of Bishop Lacy's licence to Richard Holand of 1429.[62] Nevertheless, various pieces of evidence suggest that Bowhill had a chapel. The earlier entry in the Bishop's register indicates, at least, a family history of private devotions. Although there is no later licence for a chapel, the wording of the 1429 licence is such that Roger Holand could probably have transferred his chapel to Bowhill without further licence. Roger's will shows that he was in possession of vestments and other items of valuable equipment associated with a chapel, and the bequest of 40 shillings to 'Sir Cristofere my prest' must increase the possibility that these might have been the equipment for a domestic chapel rather than, for instance, a chapel or altar maintained by Holand in the parish church.[63] The plentiful evidence of parallel buildings, which shows that some sort of domestic chapel or oratory (if only a room set aside for the purpose) was normal in late medieval houses in the West Country, also provides some support. Bowhill, in other words, would have been unusual had it not possessed a chapel.[64] Lastly the fragment of a sculpture of the Virgin and Child (Chapter 9, *see* Fig 9.10) indicates sophisticated decoration of a devotional character. While such a piece could come from a domestic context, there is a strong probability that it derives from the furnishing of a chapel.[65]

The evidence in favour of a chapel in the building is substantial. The missing parts of the building provide a number of options for its location. The south-east range can probably be eliminated because of the continuous circulation via a stair in its south-east corner from ground to first floor and from parlour to great chamber. A detached chapel is a remote possibility, although no hint of a possible location survives. Wholly detached domestic chapels are not uncommon in Devon and Cornwall.[66] Other candidates are perhaps the room to the north of the hall on the first floor (of which nothing survives) or any space in the vanished north or west ranges. One aspect of the siting of domestic chapels is clear. They were often set close to but slightly apart from the main living rooms.[67] Since at Bowhill positions such as those just named, which were some way from the main living rooms, cannot be ruled out, they may be less likely as candidates for the site of the chapel. Looking nearer to the principal rooms, the only other available space is the room above the porch. This was reached by a spiral stair from the corner of the parlour, but could also have been furnished with a squint or even with a direct entry from the great chamber. Although this space would have been tiny, perhaps about 2.5m (8ft) square,[68] the location is an established one for domestic chapels and fulfils some of the other requirements, especially in that it is set close to but slightly apart from the main rooms. Margaret Wood quotes a number of houses where the chapel is placed over the porch, for example, Congresbury Vicarage, Somerset (with the arms of Bishop Beckington of Wells, 1443–65), Lower Marsh Manor, Dunster, Somerset, Ashbury Manor, Berkshire (possible); the Chantry at Bridport, Dorset, Place Court, Colaton Raleigh, and the Chantry House, Combe Raleigh, Devon.[69] A similar location, in a block projecting from the front of the building, is seen in the 14th-century Clevedon Court, Somerset.[70] To these may be added Cothay Manor, also in Somerset, where the chapel is placed in a room above the porch. This provides a precise parallel for such an arrangement (if it existed at Bowhill), in a house of similar date and social standing. The Cothay chapel is a room no more than 2.1m square, but was so arranged that the altar could be seen from a number of adjacent rooms. The room was approached from a surviving gallery over the screens passage.[71]

Clarification of the terms involved is a useful complement to assessing the character of the chapel. The words chapel and oratory are used indiscriminately in the small literature on the subject. It should be remembered that the term chapel is used rather loosely if applied to places for domestic worship.[72] Almost all domestic chapels should strictly be termed oratories, in that they existed for the private devotions of the inhabitants and were never intended to supplant the functions of the mother church and its associated chapels, still less to jeopardise its revenues. Even in a household which maintained a priest, the oratory would have served only for private devotions and licences were often issued in the names of specified individuals and for limited periods.[73] In a paper on the medieval chapels of Cornwall, Canon J H Adams commented that domestic oratories were by far the most numerous category of chapel and that by the late Middle Ages few landowners were without oratories and chaplains. He continues: 'Anyone might build an oratory for the private devotions of a family and the saying of offices. Mass, however, could not be celebrated nor a bell set up without the Bishop's licence since the oratory was for private, not public, worship and the rights of the parish church were jealously guarded'.[74] A licence to Elizabeth Credy for a chapel at Orleigh Court, Buckland Brewer, north Devon, is explicit on the matter of protecting the existing rights of the clergy, being granted: ' ... provided that no loss accrued to the vicar of the parish, and that she attended service at the parish church on Sundays and festivals'.[75] The cumulative picture of this brief survey is that the domestic chapel would have served the household itself, but no others (especially no other parishioners), would probably have provided for the saying of one or more daily services,[76] but would emphatically not supplant any of the revenue-raising activities of the parish.

Main Truss

Intermediate Truss

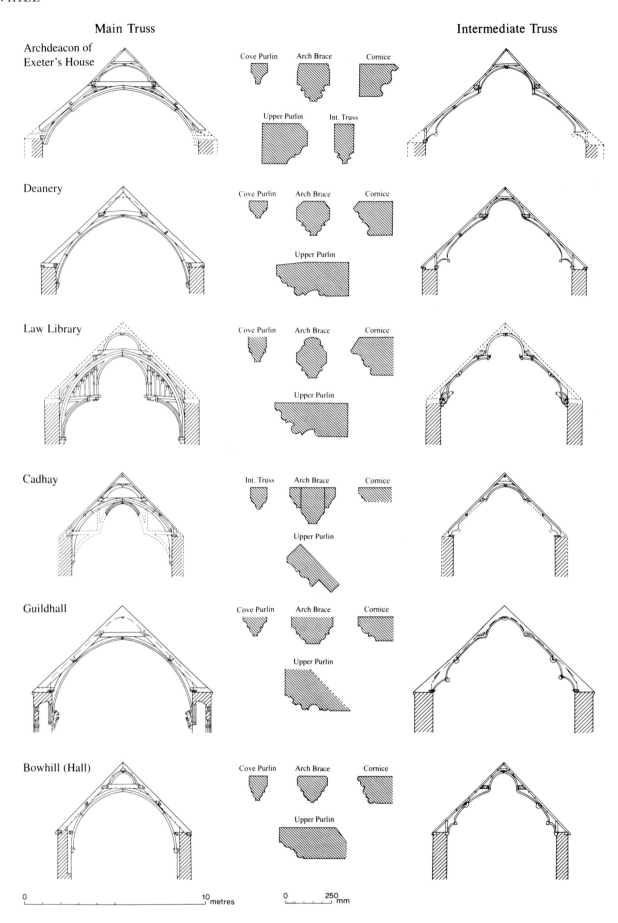

Archdeacon of
Exeter's House

Cove Purlin   Arch Brace   Cornice

Upper Purlin   Int. Truss

Deanery

Cove Purlin   Arch Brace   Cornice

Upper Purlin

Law Library

Cove Purlin   Arch Brace   Cornice

Upper Purlin

Cadhay

Int. Truss   Arch Brace   Cornice

Upper Purlin

Guildhall

Cove Purlin   Arch Brace   Cornice

Upper Purlin

Bowhill (Hall)

Cove Purlin   Arch Brace   Cornice

Upper Purlin

0   10 metres

0   250 mm

General discussion of the roofs of Bowhill

The Exeter roofs

Six surviving buildings of 15th- to early 16th-century date in Exeter and its immediate vicinity possess roofs which can be considered as a group: the hall and chamber roofs at Bowhill; the main hall of Exeter Guildhall; the main hall of no. 8 The Close, Exeter (generally known as the Law Library); the first-floor hall (or great chamber) of the Deanery, Exeter; the hall of the Archdeacon of Exeter's House (formerly the Presentation of Mary Convent, now in residential use), Palace Gate, Exeter; and the hall of Cadhay, Ottery St Mary, 17.5km east of Exeter. More probably existed originally and it is not impossible that other examples await discovery.[77] The roofs are characterised by the possession of all or most of a number of distinctive decorative features (Figs 8.5 and 8.6; Tables 8.1 and 8.2):

1. A rhythm of main and intermediate trusses through the long elevation of the roof.
2. Moulded arch braces to the principal trusses that are carried down the wall face onto corbels (or pseudo-corbels).
3. Moulded ornament of timbers throughout.
4. An irregular foiled form to the intermediate trusses (with decorated cusps and mouldings which run around the square-set upper purlins, see Fig 7.6).
5. Carved bosses covering key junctions of the intermediate trusses.
6. Straight windbraces with inward-curving feet.
7. Above all, the roofs are distinguished by a coved upper section formed of subsidiary arch braces supported on a square-set

upper purlin (thus strictly a plate rather than a purlin), elaborately moulded on its lower edge. The coving is articulated by mouldings or chamfers on the line of the main and intermediate trusses and along the crown of the coving.

Some roofs omit certain features. The Deanery, for instance, has no windbraces (see Fig 8.9) and bosses have often been lost (as in the hall at Bowhill). The distinctive character of the group is evident, however, despite departures from the standard pattern.

Several different structural types are represented in the group (see Figs 8.5–8.6). Two roofs, The Law Library and Cadhay,[78] have hammer beams giving a distinctive character to the structure of these roofs (as well as to their ornament, see below). Most of the roof structures are variations on the arch-braced structure which is the norm in late medieval domestic roofs in Devon.[79] Arch braces provide the defining characteristic of the roofs among a range of structural devices: jointed crucks at Bowhill, principal rafter trusses seated in sole pieces at the Deanery and at the Guildhall (see Figs 8.11 and 8.12) and a similar technique at the Archdeaconry, although this roof has 'short principals', whereby the principal rafters are truncated at collar level (a type of roof structure derived from base crucks; Figs 8.7 and 8.8).[80] The Archdeaconry roof has the widest span of the group (8.65m, 28'4") and the use of this technique could be related to the width in this instance.[81] Variation in technique does not appear generally to have been related to span, however, as the two examples with hammer-beam construction (which, like the base cruck, is traditionally regarded as a structural technique for the avoidance of aisle posts in the roofing of wide spans)[82] fall in the middle or narrower part of the range of widths (see Table 8.1).

Figure 8.5 (facing page) Comparative drawings of the Exeter group of roofs: elevations of main and intermediate trusses (scale 1:200) and sections of timbers (line drawing by Tony Ives).

Figure 8.6 (below) Comparative drawings of the Exeter group of roofs: bay elevations (scale 1:200) (line drawing by Tony Ives).

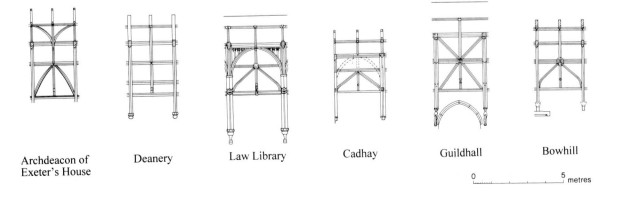

Archdeacon of Exeter's House   Deanery   Law Library   Cadhay   Guildhall   Bowhill

0   5 metres

Table 8.1 Key dimensions of the Exeter roofs and other local buildings (*italicised*) for comparison

building	no. of bays	internal span	external width
Archdeacon of Exeter's House	6	8.65m	10.1m
Exeter Guildhall	7	7.75m	9.8m
Exeter Deanery: great chamber	6	7.45m	9.12m
8 The Close, Exeter (the Law Library)	3	6.95m	8.55m
Bowhill, hall	4	6.05m	7.4m
Cadhay, Ottery St Mary	3	5.5m	7.0m
Bowhill, great chamber	4	4.95m	6.35m
Exeter: St Nicholas's Priory, frater	*8*	*7.5m*	*9.5m*
Exeter Deanery: hall	*?4*	*9.2m*	*11.0m*
Exeter: The Bishop's Palace	*3*	*14.75m*	*16.6m*

Table 8.2 Comparative table of features in late medieval roofs discussed in Chapter 8

	1	2	3	4	5	6	7	8	9	10	11	12	13	14
Bowhill, hall	✓	✓	2	✓	✓	✓	✓	✓						
Bowhill, great chamber		✓		✓	✓	✓	✓	✓						
Archdeaconry of Exeter	✓	✓	(2)	✓	✓?	✓	✓	✓						
Exeter Deanery	✓	✓		✓	✓?	✓	✓	✓						
Law Library, 8–9 The Close	✓	✓	2	✓	✓	✓	✓	✓						✓
Cadhay, Ottery St Mary	✓	✓	2	✓	✓	✓	✓	✓						✓
Exeter Guildhall	✓	✓	4	✓	✓	✓	✓	✓						
5 The Close, Exeter	✓				✓									
6 The Close, Exeter	✓	✓								4				
St Nicholas's Priory, frater										4				
Weare Giffard Hall	✓	✓							12		✓	✓	✓	✓
Orleigh Court, Buckland Brewer	✓	✓			✓				12		✓	✓	✓	✓
West Challacombe, Combe Martin	✓	✓								6	✓	✓	✓	✓
Bradfield, Uffculme	✓	✓			✓					12		✓		✓
Plymouth gin distillery	✓							✓		6				
Athelhampton Hall, Dorset	✓	✓				✓	✓			6				
Milton Abbey, Dorset	✓	✓						(✓)		16		✓		✓
Cleeve Abbey, Somerset, frater	✓	✓			✓							(✓)		✓

Key to numbered features: 1 Moulded ornament; 2 Intermediate trusses; 3 Straight windbraces with curved feet (number per bay entered); 4 Cusped terminal ornament; 5 Bosses; 6 Square-set upper purlin; 7 Upper coving; 8 Axial purlin in crown/coving; 9 Straight windbraces without curved feet (number per bay)*; 10 Curved windbraces (number per bay)*; 11 Moulded sub-principals; 12 Multiple moulded cornice(s); 13 Double ridge (/pseudo ridge); 14 Hammer beams/extended sole pieces.

✓	feature present, or good evidence for its existence.
✓?	feature probably originally present but no evidence observed.
(✓)	feature present but of unconventional form
?	uncertain

* where roofs have multiple (panelled or traceried) windbraces in each half bay, such as in Weare Giffard or Bradfield, they have been counted as two per half bay.

Figure 8.7
Archdeacon of Exeter's House: short principal, collar and arch braces. Note the traceried spandrels and sawn-off upper purlin (photograph by David Garner; EMAFU 3326/12) (source: Exeter Archaeology; © Exeter Archaeology).

Figure 8.8
Archdeacon of Exeter's House: purlins and 'vaulting' ribs (photograph by David Garner; EMAFU 3326/5) (source: Exeter Archaeology; © Exeter Archaeology).

Figure 8.9
The Deanery great chamber in August 1998, looking south-west (photograph by David Garner; EA 7058/2) (source: Exeter Archaeology; © Exeter Archaeology).

Thus the uniform elements of the group of roofs (which are mostly ornamental) are tempered by disparate structural techniques and carpentry details. This is consistent with the suggestion that the Bowhill roofs represent an embellished version of a basic roof form (timbers which are decorative in purpose are generally secured by slip tenons). Essentially the group of roofs is characterised by common decorative techniques applied to various roof designs, such as the jointed-cruck trusses of Bowhill (echoing other vernacular tendencies in the building) or the more sophisticated hammer-beam design of the Law Library.

The combination of highly competent design and manufacture with a poor attention to detail in the fitting of the roof is one of the distinctive aspects of Bowhill. Similar infelicities appear at the Guildhall (Fig 8.10), where the lack of registration between the roof and the long elevation led to awkward relationships between the corbels and windows. These are the more surprising as the whole structure appears to be of one build.[83] Similar disregard for symmetry may have occurred in other buildings in the group, although the information available is often deficient.[84] It should be emphasised that the

Figure 8.10
Exeter Guildhall: general view, looking north (photograph by David Garner; EA 7419/1) (source: Exeter Archaeology; © Exeter Archaeology).

Bowhill roofs are by far the best recorded and understood, through the opportunity to observe the roofs when stripped of their slates and individual timbers when dismantled, plus the understanding which comes from recording and drawing in detail.

Mouldings

The repertoire of mouldings at Bowhill consisted of variations on one basic profile – an ogee, a hollow moulding and a half-round moulding, the elements separated by fillets (the cornice is one exception, with a unique and complex moulding). The profile occurs in complete form on the principal timbers of the hall roof and on some other substantial carpentry in the building, such as the upper purlin of the hall roof and the main beams of the parlour ceiling.[85] Many timbers were not substantial enough to take the full profile, however, and a number of variations and simplifications are also seen (*see* Fig 7.2).[86]

Comparison of mouldings enables some connections to be identified within the group (*see* Fig 8.5). The mouldings and carved details of the Guildhall roof (Figs 8.11–8.17; *cf* Figs 7.6, 7.7 and 7.13–7.17) provide the closest similarities to the roofs of Bowhill, although they are always more slender in scantling at Bowhill than in the Guildhall. The intermediate truss, lower

Figures 8.11 and 8.12
Exeter Guildhall: (left) oblique view along the west side of the roof (bays 3–1), looking north, main truss III in foreground (EA 3620/16) (right) main truss IV, detail of wall-top assembly (EA 3620/20) (photographs by David Garner; source: Exeter Archaeology; © Exeter Archaeology).

purlins, windbraces and cove purlin all bear the same moulding (ogee-fillet-hollow) in both roofs. The arch braces/main trusses at Bowhill have an additional roll moulding on the central axis of the timber, a detail missing at the Guildhall. The cornices and upper purlins have distinctive (and more complex) mouldings that are different in each roof.[87]

Another marked similarity occurs between the mouldings of the Deanery and The Law Library, although the matter is complicated by the additional timbers found in the more complex assembly of the hammer-beam roof (with fatter and more developed mouldings; Figs 8.18–8.19). Where the members are comparable there is a good match between the two. The main arch braces of the Deanery show the same basic moulding as the subsidiary braces of the roof at the Law Library,[88] composed of an ogee and a plain chamfer separated by a prominent quirk (a feature which also occurs in the Archdeaconry, *see below*). Subsidiary timbers in both roofs employ the simpler moulding of a hollow-fillet-roll-fillet profile on intermediate trusses, cove purlins and lower purlins throughout. The similarities extend to the more complex mouldings of upper purlins and cornices. The former are identical in the two roofs, the latter different, but similar in character (*see* Fig 8.5).

The remaining two roofs, Cadhay and the Archdeacon of Exeter's House, show more singular mouldings and are less susceptible to close comparison. Some similarities can be identified. The moulding of the arch braces of the Archdeaconry is similar, though not identical to those just described for the Deanery/Law Library roofs, while the main arch braces of Cadhay share the same composite section with their counterparts at the Law Library (although they differ in detail[89]). The moulding repertoire of the Archdeaconry is curiously mixed. Other roofs of the group display a consistent use of mouldings, but in this case mouldings and chamfers are used simultaneously (in the intermediate trusses, for instance, a moulding is normally continuous throughout, but here the decoration switches from moulding to a chamfer in the coving). The mouldings of the cornice plate and the upper purlin, normally the most complex of a given roof, here are restrained. One detail also recalls the Law Library – the use of an open tracery motif in the spandrels of the main trusses (*see* Fig 8.7).[90]

Figure 8.13
Exeter Guildhall: detail of bay 1, looking west, showing the intermediate truss and windbraces (photograph by David Garner; EA 3621/01) (source: Exeter Archaeology; © Exeter Archaeology).

Figure 8.14
Exeter Guildhall: main truss, detail of the collar/arch brace/upper purlin assembly (photograph by David Garner; EA 3620/07) (source: Exeter Archaeology; © Exeter Archaeology).

Figure 8.15
Exeter Guildhall: intermediate truss, detail of the upper purlin/coving (photograph by David Garner; EA 3620/09) (source: Exeter Archaeology; © Exeter Archaeology).

Figure 8.16
Exeter Guildhall: details of
cusp carvings: (left) intermediate truss III (EA
3621/07); (right) inter-
mediate truss IV (photo-
graphs by David Garner;
EA 3621/21) (source:
Exeter Archaeology;
© Exeter Archaeology).

Figure 8.17
Exeter Guildhall: selected details of bosses: left to right (top) intermediate truss I, detail of small boss at crown of coving (EA 3623/20); bay 2, east (EA
3622/04); bay 4, west (EA 3621/14); (bottom) bay 1, east (EA 3622/10); bay 5, west (EA 3621/16); bay 5, east (EA 3622/06) (photographs by David
Garner) (source: Exeter Archaeology; © Exeter Archaeology)

On the basis of the mouldings alone, therefore, there is a case to be made for a close relationship within the group between the roofs of Bowhill and the Guildhall. The Deanery appears to be most closely related to the Law Library. Further, while the roof of the Archdeaconry shares some details with the Deanery/Law Library repertoire and is therefore linked to those roofs, it also has a distinctive and unusual character of its own. Cadhay, too, is distinctive and displays few connections with mouldings in other buildings (Figs 8.20–8.22). Assuming that the incidence of a given moulding does have some significance in making connections between roofs, it remains to examine whether the sequence can be sustained by other factors, especially the evidence for the dating, both absolute and relative, within the group.

Dating and sequence of the group

The roof structure of the Archdeacon of Exeter's house is typologically early, in the sense that the truncated principal rafters echo the base cruck roof, a form which was developed in the 13th century,[91] but it must of course belong to the broad dating limits established for the group of roofs as a whole. The roof displays some unusual features that suggest it might represent a provisional or experimental stage in the process of development. The joinery contains several uniquely complex treatments and the form of the upper coving, in which the cove braces in the rafter trusses are replaced by slender diagonal ribs, is perhaps intended to be seen as a form of vaulting (see Fig 8.11). Dendrochronological analysis has given an estimated felling date for timbers in this roof of 1415–40 (Howard, Chapter 10).

The Deanery roof belongs to a building added to the 'lower' end of the earlier hall. This structure is of two storeys and accommodated a parlour on the ground floor, with a ceiling of intersecting moulded beams with large fleurons at the intersections, and a great chamber or first-floor hall above (see Fig 8.9).[92] It is possible that this work may have been inserted into an earlier building or at least that it incorporated earlier fabric. It is, therefore, difficult to judge whether the work represents a single programme of construction or whether the various elements could have been introduced piecemeal at different dates. The dendrochronology has suggested that the floor and roof were constructed at a similar date in the early 15th century (with estimated felling-date ranges of 1400–35 for the timbers of the floor and of

1418–53 for those of the roof, Chapter 10), possibly in a single phase of work. Alternatively, they may have been constructed in two related building campaigns.

Other diagnostic features of the building suggest further work in the late 15th or early 16th century. The moulded intersecting-beam ceiling attached superficially to the soffit of the ceiling and a fireplace of the ground-floor parlour. This is ornamented with panelled reveals with quatrefoils bearing the initials of John Veysey (Dean of Exeter 1509–19, Bishop 1519–51 and 1553–4)[93] flanking a bishop's chair, presumably indicating that it was constructed after Veysey's translation to the bishopric (he could, of course, have continued to live in the Deanery as bishop). Similar decoration is recorded on a second fireplace in the building, now obscured.[94] It is presumed that the fireplaces were inserted, although

Figure 8.18
The Law Library, no. 8 The Close, Exeter: the roof looking south-east (photograph by Stuart Blaylock; author's own collection).

Figure 8.19
The Law Library: detail of coving, looking north-west (EMAFU 955/9) (source: Exeter Archaeology; © Exeter Archaeology).

Figure 8.20
Cadhay, Ottery St Mary: general view of the hall roof, looking east (photograph taken by David Garner with kind permission of O N W William-Powlett Esq; EH B960125).

Figure 8.21
Cadhay, the hall roof: bay elevations, looking southeast (photograph taken by David Garner with kind permission of O N W William-Powlett Esq; EH B960124).

Figure 8.22
Cadhay, the hall roof: detail of the coving, upper purlins and arch braces (photograph taken by David Garner with kind permission of O N W William-Powlett Esq; EH B960126).

there has been no opportunity to investigate the fabric in this area and the extent of related work is unknown. Recent investigations at the Deanery have revealed extensive alterations to the screens-passage bay of the great hall to the east in the early or mid-16th century.[95] This might provide another context for later alterations to the parlour and great chamber by Veysey.

Exeter's civic archives, principally the Receivers' accounts, suggest that the Guildhall was rebuilt in 1467–9. The roof probably (though not certainly) belongs to this campaign of work (*see* Fig 8.10).[96] The results of the dendrochronological analysis are consistent with this date bracket, suggesting a felling-date range of 1463–98 for the samples for the roof. Of the roofs that are dated with any certainty, therefore, the Guildhall is the closest in date to Bowhill (which was probably built in the last decade of the 15th or the first of the 16th century, with a possible shorter range of *c* 1500–6; *see* discussion in Chapter 12) of any building in the group. This seems to be supported by the evidence of mouldings (*see above*).

The remaining buildings can be dated within certain limits, but the dating is rather precarious. Various dates have been suggested for the Law Library in the past, on very little evidence.[97] Its connections within the group might (very tentatively) suggest a date in the mid-15th century, but the evidence is too slight for more precise dating. The dating of Cadhay has also long been a puzzle. Joan, the daughter of John Cadhay, married Hugh Grenville and their daughter, also Joan Grenville, brought the house to the Haydons on her marriage to John Haydon in 1527.[98] Haydon remodelled or rebuilt the house sometime after his marriage. Risdon said that he built a 'fair new house' at Cadhay.[99] In 1982 repairs were carried out to the Beer-stone ashlar of the north front (itself a refacing of before 1737).[100] Several blocks of stone with earlier detail on their rear faces were found to have been reused, including a block carved with a quatrefoil and a shield bearing the three clarions of the Grenville arms (with a mullet as a mark of difference) and the initials 'JH' in the lower corners of the panel.[101] Traces of letters in an upper corner might represent the initials of Joan Haydon/Grenville. The panel provides useful confirmation of building work under Haydon and gives some support to Risdon's claim. Whether Haydon's work took place in the context of his marriage in the late 1520s or in the 1540s, the period favoured by some recent commentators,[102] it appears that he retained some older fabric.[103] Several conspicuously older features are to be seen in the house, most notably a massive stone doorway at the west end of the north range (which looks like an exterior door, but whose present position at the junction of north and west ranges is firmly interior). Recent inspection of Cadhay has shown that the hall roof and one truss to the west in the screens-passage bay are of one construction, but that the remaining trusses of the north range and those of the east and west ranges belong to a later phase. It is, therefore, probable that the shell of the north range along with the ornamented hall roof were retained from an earlier house of the Cadhays or the Grenvilles by Haydon, who built the east and west ranges and re-roofed up to an existing earlier roof over the hall. The male line of the de Cadhay family, who had owned the estate from the early 14th century,[104] failed and the property was in the hands of trustees from 1483. Thus there is no obvious context for a major building project in the last decades of the century[105] and a context must be sought earlier in the 15th century, very broadly between c 1425 and c 1475. The unsuitability of the roof timbers for dendrochronology was particularly disappointing in this case, since no other definitive dating evidence appears to be available (Chapter 10).

The four buildings for which there is some dating evidence (albeit uncertain) provide fixed points and the basis of an internal sequence for the group. The Archdeacon of Exeter's house is the earliest roof in the group on typological grounds and dendrochronology now suggests that it was built c 1425–40. Then come the Deanery (perhaps in the second quarter of the 15th century), the Guildhall (probably 1467–9) and Bowhill (probably c 1500–6). In attempting to fit the undated buildings into this sequence, similarities in mouldings must be balanced against other factors (possible contexts/dating evidence, variation in form according to span and/or function and so on). Cadhay, which remains problematic, could have been built at any time between c 1425 and c 1527. The placing of the Law Library, as with its absolute dating, is also fraught with problems, but the similarity in moulding details between the Law Library and the Deanery and the more distant connections with the Archdeacon of

Exeter's house suggest that these three roofs may be close in date. Whatever the precise details of the sequence, the wide range of dating of the buildings shows that the group must be the work of more than one carpenter or carpenters and that the Exeter roofs must be seen as the product of a local workshop spanning several generations, rather than as the work of one generation of craftsmen or a single master carpenter.

Other late medieval roofs in Devon

Given that the focus of the group of roofs discussed so far is clearly on the Exeter district, can parallels be found for the Exeter group elsewhere in the county or region? The decoration of roof timbers by moulding as opposed to chamfering is very much the exception in domestic contexts and represents the apogee of the carpenter's craft. The technique is common in church roofs of the late 15th and early 16th centuries, both in the form of the wagon (or arch-braced rafter-truss) roof, which is typical of many late medieval Devon churches,[106] and in other types employing moulded timbers.[107] Despite its ubiquity in churches (and thus that carpenters were accustomed to this type of roof structure), however, the wagon roof was rarely used in domestic contexts. The question of why there was so little overlap between ecclesiastical and domestic roofing remains unanswered. Domestic medieval common-rafter roofs occur at Woodbeer Court, Plymtree, and Fishleigh Barton, Tawstock.[108] Other 'secular' rafter-truss roofs mostly turn out, on closer scrutiny, to have ecclesiastical contexts or connections, for example, Tuckers Hall, Exeter (built as a guild chapel),[109] and roofs at nos 7 and 10 The Close, Exeter (the former dubious, the latter roofing a chapel and not strictly domestic in character).[110] Outside churches and these various exceptions, the incidence of moulded timbers in open roofs is limited to the Exeter group, another group of mainly false hammer-beam roofs in the north and east of the county (see below) and occasional isolated examples elsewhere. In addition to moulded decoration, other criteria used for identifying parallel traits are the rhythm of main and intermediate trusses in the long elevation, the incidence of square-set plates or purlins at collar level and an associated trait of subsidiary arch braces in the apex of the roof related to the coving in the Exeter roofs (see Table 8.2).

Figure 8.23
Weare Giffard Hall: the
hall roof in 1915, looking
north-west (photograph
from Tipping 1915, 21, fig
8) (reproduced courtesy of
Country Life; © Country
Life).

Figure 8.24
Orleigh Court, Buckland
Brewer: the hall roof
(EH/NMR BB69/615).

Figure 8.25
West Challacombe, Combe
Martin: the hall roof,
looking west (photograph
by David Garner) (repro-
duced courtesy of The
National Trust; © The
National Trust).

The second group of late medieval roofs is exemplified by Weare Giffard Hall. This building has a roof which is unparalleled in the exuberance and extent of its decoration (Fig 8.23), but which nevertheless has connections with a number of other, less ornate roofs in north and east Devon. Weare Giffard is probably to be dated between 1485 and 1503 on the grounds of allusions in the glazing of the dais window of the hall to Henry VII and John Fortescue (d 1503).[111] This roof and those others described below should strictly be termed

false hammer-beam roofs, as the hammer beams support arch braces rather than hammer posts.[112] The distinguishing features of the roof are heavily moulded hammer beams, multiple moulded wall plates or cornices (among other timbers) and arch-braced subsidiary or intermediate trusses within the main bays of the long elevation. The rhythm of main and intermediate trusses frames the division of each bay into panels by the purlins, the (apparently double) ridge pieces, the intermediate trusses and additional moulded sub-principals placed against each face of the (unmoulded) principals (and secured to them by lateral slip tenons). The resulting panels are richly ornamented with cusped diagonal wind-braces.[113] Cusping and recusping is a feature of the principal rafters too. The only comparable example of this treatment in Devon is in Tuckers Hall, Exeter, where evidence for additional cusping survived in the form of long linear mortices in the soffits of the principals.[114] Weare Giffard also shares the detail of a double, or composite, ridge piece with Orleigh Court and West Challacombe (*see below*).[115]

Orleigh Court, Buckland Brewer, has a closely related late medieval roof in its hall. Although the ornament is generally simpler (Fig 8.24), the two roof structures share a number of decorative details, including moulded hammer beams, multiple cornice timbers and similar heraldic beasts.[116] Again each bay is divided into six panels by arch-braced intermediate trusses, purlins, double ridge pieces and moulded sub-principals. Here the panels are filled with cross braces set square and diagonally in alternate panels, with small central bosses.[117] The roof of the former open hall (now floored) at West Challacombe, Combe Martin, dated by dendrochronology to the third quarter of the 15th century,[118] has a very similar arrangement of moulded cornices and hammer beams, intermediate trusses, panelled bays with multiple windbraces (although a different pattern), double ridge pieces and moulded sub-principals (Fig 8.25).[119] The sub-principals are attached to the faces of the principal rafters by lateral slip tenons, providing a link in structural technique to Weare Giffard. A similar double ridge member to those of West Challacombe and Orleigh Court appears at South Yard, Rose Ash (although this is a single timber), in another highly decorated roof, albeit with a different emphasis and slightly earlier than the other examples (dated by dendrochronology to 1447–8).[120] Lastly the roof of the hall at Bradfield, Uffculme (near Cullompton; Fig 8.26), displays similarities in its key elements – intermediate trusses, heavily moulded hammer beams and multiple cornice plates (although other aspects of this roof appear to be rather different again).[121] One further connection, although distant, is a false hammer-beam roof at Traymill Farm, Thorverton. This is almost wholly unmoulded (only the cornice timbers are moulded, here, very curiously, morticed into the ends of the hammer beams) and it has none of the elaborate ornament seen in the other roofs.[122]

Notwithstanding the greater level of ornament at Weare Giffard, the roofs of Weare Giffard Hall, Orleigh Court and West Challacombe combine to show that there was a local school of elaborate roof carpentry in North Devon in the late 15th century to rival that of the Exeter district. These buildings have several well-defined characteristics in common, which identify them as the core of the group, and there are a number of outliers elsewhere. While general characteristics, such as the level of ornament and the use of mouldings, establish a relationship between these roofs and those of the Exeter group, this can be accounted for by the explanation of common date and function and the similar social standing and aspirations of their builders. The only specific parallel is to be found in the pattern of main and intermediate trusses and the rhythm that this imparts to the long elevations of the roofs.

In Exeter an arch-braced roof over the central range of no. 6 The Close has been inspected recently and was found to display some of the characteristics of the Exeter group (moulded arch braces, intermediate trusses formed by adding decorative braces to the central rafter truss of each bay, four (curved) windbraces per bay) without key diagnostic elements such as the coving, curved-footed windbraces and so on.[123] A fragment of roof with principal rafters bearing similar mouldings to those of the Guildhall and Bowhill was recorded in the (so-called) Norman House in King Street, Exeter, in the early 20th century.[124] Elsewhere in the county only isolated individual examples of open hall roofs with moulded decoration can be found. One of the larger and more elaborate examples is to be seen in the late 15th- or early 16th-century hall associated with Coates' gin distillery in Southside Street, Plymouth. In this roof the

Figure 8.26
Bradfield, Uffculme: the hall roof, looking south (EH/NMR CL L5096–5102) (reproduced courtesy of Country Life; © Country Life).

arch braces, one pair of purlins (out of three) and the axial collar purlin are moulded.[125] Other open roofs with moulded rather than chamfered (or undecorated) ornament are scattered across the county. Hall roofs at the Old Manor, Littlehempston,[126] Wortham Manor, Lifton,[127] and Knightstone, Ottery St Mary,[128] provide a wide distribution. No doubt, there are others. These examples are not necessarily comparable to the Bowhill and Weare Giffard groups directly. Their mouldings are relatively slight (in contrast to the elaborate mouldings of the roofs discussed hitherto) and they could all be dated earlier in the 15th century.

Chamfering was frequently preferred to moulding as a method of decoration in many late medieval roofs, even in buildings of comparable or higher status than Bowhill and its fellow buildings. The 15th-century roofs of the frater and guest hall of St Nicholas's Priory, Exeter, well exemplify this. Both are in buildings architecturally comparable to the Deanery or the Guildhall, but where simpler ornament was preferred.[129] The scarcity of moulded ornament in Devon may be partly explained by date, in that the heyday of moulded ornament coincided with the beginning of a shift away from the construction of open halls and an increase in the use of more comfortable private living rooms. One consequence of this is that, in the late 15th and 16th centuries, mouldings tended to be deployed in ceilings, screens and individual timbers, rather than roofs.[130] Date alone cannot, however, be used to explain the rarity of moulded as opposed to chamfered roof timbers. Other factors such as cost, status, the existence of separate 'secular' and 'ecclesiastical' carpentry traditions or of different schools of carpenters influenced the choice, as well as limited survival. Throughout the 15th century a love of moulded ornament is manifest in church carpentry[131] in roofs as well as in furnishings such as screens and bench ends (reaching their zenith in the early 16th century).[132]

Few parallel examples of other distinctive features of the Exeter roofs can be found elsewhere in the county. The use of bosses, while common throughout the county in church roofs, remains exceptional in wholly domestic contexts. The incidence of bosses in domestic chapels, among which those of cathedral clergy in the Deanery and possibly no. 10 The Close, Exeter, provide local examples, only serves to emphasise their absence in secular roofs.[133] The roof of a small detached former chapel at Lower Alsworthy, Bradworthy, has moulded arch braces and purlins, a collar purlin and possibly straight windbraces (plus traces of bosses, now removed).[134] There are remains of bosses at Wood Barton, Kentisbeare, a ?mid-14th century roof with base-cruck and spere trusses and square-set upper purlins with moulded faces.[135] Square-set purlins (or plates) are the logical method of supporting timbers in the upper stage of a roof, whether the rafter structure above a base-cruck roof or the arch braces of upper coving, as well as an essential component of true hammer-beam roofs. The roof of the Old Manor, Littlehempston, has square-set upper purlins, although their significance is uncertain. The same feature appears at Bury Barton, Lapford, dated to the second quarter of the 14th century[136] and in some Cornish medieval buildings.[137] The other distinctive features are equally elusive. An axial purlin in the crown of the roof of the north transept of St Calixtus's Church, West Down (with trefoil arch bracing reminiscent of the coving in the Exeter roofs, although it is *sui generis*), is analogous to the cove purlins of the Exeter group.[138] The roof of Coates' distillery in Plymouth, noted already, also possesses a central collar purlin.[139] The straight windbraces with curved feet appear nowhere else, as far as is known, nor does the upper coving (while reminiscent of the wagon roofs of churches in both appearance and in the repetitive structure of arch-braced rafter trusses) find expression in domestic roofs elsewhere in the county.

Parallels elsewhere

Limited coverage of vernacular and gentry architecture in published sources hampers the search for parallel material. Immediately east of Devon, the picture is skewed by the very full coverage of Dorset in the inventories of the RCHME and by relatively poor knowledge of equivalent material in Somerset. The relative paucity of parallels from Somerset buildings (*see* Fig 8.1) might well be augmented by further research and publication.[140] With this constraint in mind, selected buildings in adjacent counties to the east of Devon contribute useful parallel material to the study of the Bowhill roofs and their affinities.

The roof of Athelhampton Hall, Dorset, displays the now familiar rhythm of main and intermediate trusses. Here the arch braces of the main trusses are extended in extraordinary large cusps, giving the roof a trefoil section.[141] The hall was built by Sir William Martyn, beginning after 1493.[142] It is thus very close in date to Bowhill, but also post-dates some buildings of the Exeter group. Aside from the general similarities of bay arrangement and moulded decoration at Athelhampton, one detail of the treatment stands out. This roof has a square-set upper purlin or plate richly moulded on its lower edge, that supports curved (and moulded) braces to each common rafter truss (Fig 8.27).[143] Although these braces form slightly pointed arches and have no longitudinal member (cove purlin), they form a coved upper stage to the roof very similar to the Exeter roofs. One notable difference is that at Athelhampton every brace is moulded, whereas in the Exeter group only those of the main and intermediate trusses are so treated. This shows that the braces of the coving at Athelhampton were exposed to view and could support the idea that the coving at Bowhill was ceiled (Chapter 7).

Figure 8.27 Athelhampton Hall, Dorset: the hall roof, looking north-west. Note the square-set upper purlins and moulded cove braces (EH/NMR BB99/11093).

In Salisbury the hall of John Hall, built between 1455 and 1479, is particularly notable for its roof of three bays supported on main and intermediate trusses.[144] The roof is a false hammer-beam construction in which the main trusses, with moulded arch braces, are supported on moulded hammer beams or extended sole pieces and the intermediate trusses on angel brackets at the level of the moulded cornice.[145] At Milton Abbey, Milton Abbas, Dorset, the great hall of the medieval abbey which survives within Milton Abbey House was built by Abbot William Middleton in 1498.[146] As with the Salisbury building, this heavily ornamented roof is chiefly of value in comparison to Bowhill for the rhythm of main and intermediate trusses.[147] Features like the very heavily moulded wall plate and cornice, the false hammer beams which support the main and intermediate trusses and the elaborate windbracing are more closely related to those in roofs of the Weare Giffard group in Devon than to those of Bowhill and related roofs.[148] The elongated stone corbels supporting the feet of the main trusses in this roof, however, echo those of the Law Library at Exeter[149] and could provide models for the missing elements at Bowhill.

The roof of the 15th-century refectory at Cleeve Abbey, Somerset (probably built by Abbot Juyner towards the end of his reign of 1435–87),[150] provides a number of other parallels. The roof has main and intermediate trusses supported by extended sole pieces (or false hammer beams), moulded purlins, including an axial purlin, and many bosses. The elaborately moulded wall plates are reminiscent of the Weare Giffard group of roofs and the angel terminals of the sole pieces recall the same features at the Law Library in Exeter.[151] The principal trusses are ornamented with small trefoil-headed panels very similar to the unfinished decoration at South Yard, Rose Ash, Devon.[152] The axial purlins of the Exeter group of roofs find a parallel in South Wales, where collar purlins are a common feature of Glamorgan church roofs.[153]

The possible influence of major roofing projects on a national scale should also be considered. One much-discussed question is how far the design of the Law Library roof was influenced by that of Westminster Hall and its implications for the dating of the former roof. Margaret Wood, in discussing the Exeter group of roofs in

The English Mediaeval House, evidently considered that the similarities were close enough to suggest a direct copy and a close relationship in date. Indeed she suggested a context for the transfer of the design in Hugh Herland's presence at Dartington during the construction of the roof of the great hall there (thereby implicitly dating the roof to the same period as Westminster).[154] This view would not be without its supporters today, but the author would suggest that other factors should take priority in assessing the date of the Law Library roof (which still has no precise evidence for its date; *see above*, p 184 and Chapter 10). While some aspects of the Law Library roof are clearly influenced by Herland's design of Westminster Hall (the traceried spandrels and infilling of the arch braces and transverse arches, the composition of bold arches springing from low down the walls and rising to the collar and the angel terminals of the hammer beams), there is a local counter-influence at work in the shape of the distinctive features of the Exeter group (coving, curved-footed windbraces, cusped intermediate trusses and so on) which are thoroughly integrated into the design. Unless this roof is to be assigned to an outlying and substantially earlier period than the bulk of the group (*see above* on the dating evidence), the general trend of the dating of the Exeter roofs and the detailed comparison of the Law Library with other roofs in the group suggest a date at least a quarter of a century later than 1400 for the Law Library roof, most probably a date in the mid- or late 15th century (but with an outside possibility of one in the early 16th century). The details also support the case for a mid- to late 15th-century date. The mouldings (*see above*) and the angel terminals of the hammer beams and the moulded stone corbels all fit happily into the local late Perpendicular decorative repertoire.

This argument is not intended to discount the influence of Westminster Hall or, taking another rather later example, the roof of the hall at Eltham Palace, dated to 1479–80.[155] The profound influence of such major carpentry projects is undeniable. It is, however, suggesting that, rather than the Law Library roof being a direct copy of Westminster Hall, the influence was more subtle, perhaps exerted over a generation or more and filtered through a number of other building projects on a regional scale.

Other structural carpentry

Moulded, intersecting-beam ceilings

Moulded beamed ceilings were a feature of domestic decoration at the highest level in the 14th and 15th centuries. An early example in Exeter was in the parlour added to the Bishop's Palace by John Grandisson (1327–69).[156] Some of the bosses survive from this ceiling, enabling its massive scale to be gauged (the mouldings were more akin to contemporary stone mouldings than those of later timber ceilings and may have been imitating stone).[157] Another is in no. 10 The Close, where a ceiling of cusped and foiled panels divided by slender ribs is dated by the arms of Bishop Lacy (1417–55) in its decoration.[158] Another exceptional early moulded ceiling in a secular context is of substantial, close-set moulded beams in the first floor of the gatehouse tower of Tiverton Castle, Devon, dated to the mid- to late14th century by dendrochronology, although reused in a late 15th-century structure.[159]

The frequent incidence of moulded roof or ceiling ornament in churches in Devon, Somerset and Dorset represents a separate and probably slightly earlier class to domestic ceilings, although this well-established aspect of church carpentry must surely have had an influence on the development of the intersecting-beam ceiling in domestic contexts. Details with the strongest resemblance to secular moulded ceilings tend to be found in aisle roofs (presumably because they were generally shallow-pitched, whereas naves had arch-braced or wagon roofs). Most are dated to the later 15th or early 16th century. Key examples in churches include Hazelbury Bryan, Dorset (late 15th century), where the south aisle has intersecting moulded beams (slightly cranked in section), with joists set alternately in adjoining panels,[160] a feature which occurs in domestic ceilings (*see below*). The aisles at Cullompton, Devon (built *c* 1500–1546/9) have flat ceilings of intersecting beams (with reticulated joists in the panels). Only the five western bays of the north aisle are moulded. Since these also have a markedly cranked profile, it is possible that they represent work of a slightly earlier date.[161] Somerset has dated examples at Brent Knoll (north aisle, *c* 1510) and Martock (dated 1513), the latter with the higher pitched roof characteristic of the county, but still employing heavily moulded ornament.[162] Also in Dorset, the nave at Marnhull (*c* 1520) has a heavily coffered structure[163] and Hilton (rebuilt in 1569) has flat ceilings in north and south aisles with scratch-moulded joists, another very domestic-looking detail (perhaps unsurprising given its late date).[164]

Moulded beamed ceilings do not appear in domestic contexts until 1480 at the earliest[165] and are generally dated after 1500.[166] Examples in which the panels are subdivided by slender moulded ribs include several ceilings in the Master's Lodgings of Christ's College, Cambridge, largely built in the first decade of the 16th century by Margaret, Countess of Richmond (the mother of Henry VII). The state bedroom provides a particularly close parallel for the parlour of Bowhill, with each 'bay' of the ceiling divided into square panels (four-by-four to each).[167] At Baddesley Clinton, Warwickshire (probably a part of alterations of the end of the 15th century), the main bays of the 'kitchen' ceiling of intersecting beams are subdivided by subsidiary, thinner moulded strips.[168] There is a similar treatment of moulded sub-ribs over planks in the parlour at Wortham Manor, Lifton.[169] The parlour at Cothay Manor, Somerset, of *c* 1480, has an intersecting-beam ceiling, subdivided by quite substantial subsidiary timbers.[170] Holcombe Court, Holcombe Rogus, close to the Devon/Somerset border (as Cothay, a house of the Bluetts), has an early 16th-century intersecting-beam ceiling in the dining room at the upper end of the hall.[171] The ceiling (or lower roof) of the great hall at Forde Abbey, now in Dorset, is panelled with diagonal braces. This was the work of the last abbot of Forde, Thomas Chard (the adjacent porch is dated 1528).[172] The concept of moulded subdivisions is clearly related to (and perhaps derived from) the ribbed and patterned ceiling of Cardinal Wolsey's Closet at Hampton Court.[173] But more complex geometric patterning tends to be later. Examples include the intersecting stars and crosses on the ceiling of the 'White Room' at Cotehele, Cornwall, and two ceilings with geometric patterning in a now-demolished building at 25 High Street, Poole, Dorset.[174]

Most examples of domestic intersecting-beam ceilings in Exeter, where datable, appear to be early 16th century or later. The ground-floor parlour in the Deanery, Exeter, possesses a ceiling of moulded beams, whose intersections are marked by composite bosses. This probably dates to the period of Bishop Veysey's decanate or episcopate (1509 onwards).[175] Other examples in new buildings of the period are in the rear parlour of the White Hart Hotel, South Street, Exeter, which has a central boss carved with vine foliage and fruit[176] and at Larkbeare House, Holloway Street, Exeter, of the second quarter of the 16th century, perhaps c 1540.[177] The Larkbeare House ceiling is a particularly developed example, with main and subsidiary beams forming square panels in which the joists were countercharged (set in alternating directions).[178] The same technique is seen in the Old Rectory at Sampford Peverell, where the floorboards are also set alternately in adjacent bays and rebated into the main beams.[179] Alternating joists also occur at Margells, Branscombe (with floor boards rebated into the joists, so that no joins were visible when viewed from below), and at the Chantry House, Combe Raleigh, Devon.[180] A fragment of ceiling at Bishop's Clyst, with especially complex mouldings, displays another decorative device where boarding was set above the joists in herringbone pattern (that is, on the diagonal), alternating in adjacent bays.[181] Fragments of a similar ceiling, painted in bold colours and with black and white chevrons survive in a post-Dissolution context at Polsloe Priory, Exeter, showing another dimension to the interior decoration of the period.[182] These devices imply that the joists and the soffits of the boards above were exposed to view. The Bowhill ceiling, as with others quoted previously, was ceiled with planking on the soffits of the joists. The rough, unfinished appearance of the joists confirms that they were not intended to be seen.

Intersecting-beam ceilings occur occasionally in grand farmhouses. South Yard, Rose Ash, had a ceiling inserted in the mid-16th century into the older hall, again with countercharged joists.[183] There are other examples at Townsend House, Stockland, and Cleave Hill, Membury.[184] In most farmhouses and other vernacular buildings, the love of moulded decoration was expressed in simpler forms, such as the moulding of main beams in combination with plain or chamfered and occasionally moulded joists.[185] Moulded beams are often associated with the flooring in of previously open halls, a process that was taking place in the course of the 16th century according to need and the status of the building.[186] Examples can be named throughout the century from the hall ceiling at Wortham Manor, Lifton (early 16th century), in which moulded beams and joists were coupled with elaborate foliage-carved stops,[187] to Lower Chilverton, Coldridge

('into the 17th century').[188] It is possible to view some intersecting-beam ceilings (the Bowhill example included) as elaborations of the cross-beam and joist-flooring arrangement. In the Bowhill parlour the flanking timbers along the walls are simply joists of greater-than-usual depth morticed into the main beams and do not contribute to the load-bearing capacity of the floor (Chapter 6 and see Fig 6.28).[189]

Screens

The standard late medieval type of stud and panel screen is represented by two extant examples at Bowhill, the ground-floor stage of the north partition of the hall (see Fig 6.2) and the partition on the west side of the through passage in the south range (see Fig 5.27). Both were represented only by head-beams, but sufficient information survived in these to permit the reconstruction of posts and doorways. In this type of screen the chamfers of the posts return onto the lower edge of the headbeam, framing the plank panels (reconstructed examples visible in Figs 11.113 and 11.118). The lower end of the chamfers would be stopped above the sill beam, generally with simple diagonal-cut stops. Screens of this type are found in numerous houses of the period in Devon and in farmhouses spanning the whole of the 16th century.[190] Specific parallel examples can be quoted from Cordwents, Halberton, and Lower Chilverton, Coldridge.[191] Other screens are variations on the standard pattern. The west screen of the parlour (Fig 8.28i; see also Fig 6.15) displays the same chamfered posts, but has no return onto the headbeam (possibly because the headbeam was moulded and could not accommodate returning chamfers on its lower edge). The fragment of screen now filling the south-east corner of the chamber appears to be similar in this respect (see Fig 6.22). One further wholly timber screen dividing the two service rooms appears to have been still simpler, perhaps with plain, unchamfered studs (represented by mortices in the headbeam, see Fig 5.30, beam 6, and a stone sleeper wall, see Fig 4.7, 727). Other techniques are associated with the use of cob and earth plaster for the infilling of partitions. The north screen of the parlour, with cob packed around oak pegs is unique, at least in the surviving building.[192] The studs of this screen were plain timbers without chamfers and the interstices were filled with cob to the full depth of the timber, producing a flush surface (Fig 8.28ii).[193]

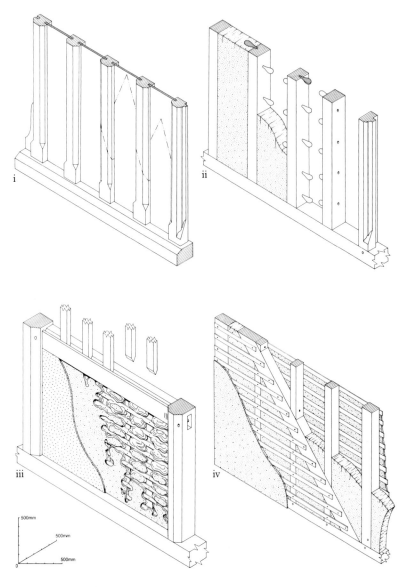

i

ii

iii

500mm

500mm

500mm

0

iv

Door-frames

Primary doorframes survived in the two parlour screens (north and west), and in the section of reused partition in the south-east corner of the chamber. They had either moulded frames (see Fig 6.15, detail) or a double chamfer (see Fig 6.28, detail), with carved leaf ornament in the spandrels. The slightly later door in the loose screen from the inner chamber (see above), had a chamfered frame and plain spandrels (see Fig 9.25).

Paired doorways

Possible functions of paired doorways in three partitions at Bowhill have been discussed in the context of the plan (Chapter 1). Double (or triple) service doorways provide the most obvious and frequent parallel for paired doorways elsewhere. Two adjacent doorways in a partition on the lower side of the screens passage at the Old Manor, Littlehempston, provide a precise parallel to the equivalent area of the plan at Bowhill. One door leads to a service room, the other to a stair.[196] The same arrangement, in which one door leads to a stair, the other to the kitchen, is seen at Priesthall, Kentisbeare.[197] North Wyke, South Tawton, retains a partition with multiple doorways, two of which are paired in the same fashion as Bowhill, in a first-floor passage.[198] At Cordwents, Lower Town, Halberton, the screen on the lower side of the screens passage displayed a pair of doorways (again presumably leading to service rooms), although here one was an afterthought added during construction.[199] In another area of the country, a recently published survey of medieval houses in Kent illustrates a number of similar paired doors. This level of incidence is probably not uncommon elsewhere.[200]

Other carpentry

Lintels

Primary lintels vary in their ornament according to position. Those of the hall and the principal rooms at the east end of the south range have moulded lower edges, with the moulding returning at each end (for example, window 17, Fig 6.28). Elsewhere, where simpler elements predominate, lintels are finished with plain chamfers, stopped according to the type of embrasure. Doors generally had straight reveals (that is, at 90° to the wall face) and thus straight-cut chamfer stops. Windows had splayed reveals

Of later (or inserted) partitions in the house, one was removed during the recent repair programme and is now among the collection of loose timbers from Bowhill (see Fig 9.25). This probably originated as a dividing wall in the inner chamber in the mid- or late 16th century (Chapter 6). The second screen is the first-floor partition of mid- or later 17th-century character forming the west wall of the chamber (see Figs 6.15 and 8.28iv); this contains a door-frame with ogee-moulded surround and small scroll-and-flat stop.[194] The type of braced framing seen in this partition occurs frequently in mid- to late 17th-century buildings locally. Where it is used in new building, the partitions are usually built once the structure is floored.[195]

and diagonal-cut stops. This distinction occasionally enabled the function of an opening to be identified where only the lintel survived.

Beams

With the exception of the moulded beams of the parlour and those which act as the head-beams to stud and panel partitions (*see above*), primary floor beams had simple chamfered lower edges and stepped stops.[201] The only exceptions are the beams inserted into the kitchen that probably derived from the demolished part of the west range to the north of the kitchen (Chapter 6). Primary joists were everywhere left plain. In the parlour they were hidden by a planked ceiling, but elsewhere they were left without moulding or chamfering. Later joists in the kitchen had chamfers and steep run-out stops.

Discussion of other architectural features

Fireplaces

Two fireplaces in the south elevation of the south range (serving the parlour and chamber; *see* Fig 6.22, 37 and 102) share the following characteristics: splayed jambs and back of ashlar masonry; a massive lintel, normally a composite construction of several blocks of stone with joggled joints; a projecting mantelshelf (dressed off at a later period in both surviving examples); and a relieving arch of a distinctive style, with large springer blocks and a central tympanum.[202] The parlour fireplace bears a moulding on its jambs, but has a plain lintel. That of the chamber is moulded on jambs and lintel. All the blocks are of carefully dressed volcanic stone finished with distinctive diagonal tooling marks. The hall fireplace was of similar design. One block from a lintel and one section of a moulded mantelshelf (particularly important because this detail is missing on the extant fireplaces) were recovered from the building and informed the reconstruction (*see* Chapter 6 and Fig 6.2).

The fireplace with plain lintel was much the most common in late medieval Exeter houses.[203] Other types also occur. For instance, many of the houses of the Cathedral clergy were provided with grand fireplaces of Beer stone, with relief-carved ornament on the lintels and panelled jambs.[204] The type was not confined to later medieval contexts, but as this was the period in which it was becoming normal for houses

to be provided with fireplaces, the established local type was employed. The earliest dated example with some of the characteristic features is found at St Katherine's Priory, Polsloe (two miles east of central Exeter), in the room known as the Prioress's Chamber (of *c* 1300). This has a massive lintel with joggled joints, projecting mantelshelf and superincumbent relieving arch, although the lintel is supported by jambs with attached shafts and moulded drum bases.[205] The first-floor hall of the same building has a large inserted fireplace (still of pre-Dissolution date), with monolithic lintel, jambs and tympanum of breccia.[206] The fragment of primary fireplace of breccia in the oriel chamber at Bowhill (*see* Fig 6.25, 187) would have resembled this, although on a smaller scale (and without the relieving arch above, since it was set in a cob wall).

From many such fireplaces that survive or have been recorded prior to demolition in Exeter buildings, several provide close parallels for Bowhill. Number 166 Fore Street (*c* 1500, demolished 1958) contained two fireplaces, one with a monolithic stone lintel (in the hall), the second (heating a parlour) with a timber lintel and stone jambs and relieving arch.[207] Another of the same period was a primary feature of the hall at 38 North Street (early 16th century).[208] Inserted fireplaces of similar design were added to other rooms of this building later in the 16th century. The type remained popular later in the 16th century. The pair of houses at nos 41–2 High Street, built in 1564, show several breccia fireplaces, including hooded examples in which the lintel was supported on projecting brackets or corbels.[209] When the new front block of Exeter Guildhall was constructed in the 1590s, an exposed stone fireplace was still considered suitable,[210] even though this type of fireplace was beginning to decline in the face of the increasing ornamentation of overmantels and added wooden surrounds.[211] Nevertheless similar fireplaces continued to be constructed into the 17th century, such as those inserted during the modernisation of medieval houses in Fore Street, Silverton.[212]

Still simpler are fireplaces with stone jambs and a timber lintel without a relieving arch. The later 16th-century example in the west room of the south range at Bowhill is an example of this type (*see* Fig 6.25, 262), with a chamfer on its lower edge, but otherwise unornamented. Similar plain fireplaces were the norm elsewhere in humbler and utilitarian contexts.[213]

Figure 8.28 (facing page) Isometric drawings of typical screen-filling techniques at Bowhill: (i) stud and panel (sometimes called plank and muntin) screen, based on the parlour west partition, but also used in the hall (north) and west service room (east) partitions; (ii) pegged daub, as used in the ground floor partition between the screens passage and parlour; (iii) double laths with daub packing extruded onto surfaces and worked up into plaster, as used in the north wall of the great chamber; (iv) double laths with daub packing and discrete surface rendering of heavily haired daub, as used in the west screen of the great chamber (17th century) (line drawing by Stuart Blaylock and Tony Ives).

Figure 8.29

Moulding and chamfer stops:
1 hall/screens passage, west
door (no. 406), north stop
(volcanic stone); 2 hall/screens
passage, west door (no. 406),
south stop (volcanic stone);
3 parlour, east doorway (no.
84), south stop (breccia);
4 hall, north-west doorway
(no. 417), south stop (breccia);
5 west range, west doorway
(no. 280), north stop
(breccia); 6 screens passage,
south partition, central post of
the double doorway (timber);
7 chamfer stop of main beams,
south range (timber) (line
drawing by Tony Ives).

Large kitchen fireplaces, spanning the full width of the building, occur in a number of the larger late medieval houses of Exeter, as at Bowhill (*see* Fig 6.47, 295). Wide relieving arches for such features survive at no. 11 The Close,[214] the kitchen of St Nicholas's Priory[215] and in the kitchen of the medieval canonry in Catherine Street occupied by Canon John Stevens in the 1440s.[216] All have double rows of stone voussoirs. It is uncertain whether these arches framed inner arches of dressed stone or if they themselves formed the arch of the fireplaces. Although similar in its proportions, as well as in function, the kitchen fireplace at Bowhill is exceptional in its extensive use of volcanic stone (the local option in terms of materials here) and in its massive segmental arch with

joggled joints. This arch is an adaptation of the treatment of the lintels of the domestic fireplaces of the building. The joggled joints are strictly unnecessary in an arch.

Stone doorways

The volcanic-stone arched doorways of the screens passage have triple mouldings and plain bulbous stops (Fig 8.29, no. 1 and Fig 8.30). The south side of the west doorway has a spurred stop (*see* Fig 8.29, no. 2). The wide arched entrance in the south elevation may have accommodated a similarly moulded frame, although this had not survived.[217] Moulded doorways of this sort are uncommon locally.[218] There are examples in the screens passage at no. 10 The Close,[219] and in the west (tower) door at St Thomas' Church, Exeter.[220] The plain chamfered stair doors in the north-west corner of the hall and in the parlour have bulbous stops and each side of the arch is composed of a single block of breccia. These details are paralleled in a pair of breccia door-frames at Great Marshall Farm, Ide, near Exeter.[221] Similar breccia doorways, with plain chamfers and irregular stops, served stair turrets in an early 16th-century building at 2 Broadgate, Exeter.[222] The inserted breccia frame in the west wall of the kitchen has a wave moulding and bulbous stops (*see* Fig 8.29, no. 5).

Windows

The variation in character of the building, from very high status to the most basic vernacular, is reflected in the wide range of window types in the building in stone and in timber. The windows of the hall and of the missing south-east range, crafted in Beer stone and comparable in quality to features in other high-status buildings on a regional and national scale, are in contrast to crude timber window frames whose only known parallels occur in the simplest of vernacular contexts in the West Country and South Wales.

Stone windows

Oriel and bay windows
These features are attested by the Bucks' engraving (*see* Fig 2.1 and Chapter 2), although they have failed to survive. The probable form (and construction) of the oriel window in the south range (first floor), for which some evidence in the fabric survives, has been discussed above (Chapter 5). Whether of stone or of timber, it is likely to have looked something like the oriel windows

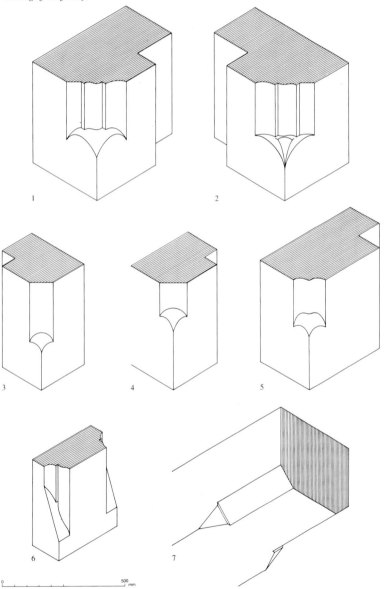

at Lytes Cary, Somerset, of 1515–20[223] or one at Purse Caundle Manor House, Dorset.[224] In Devon, Bradley Manor, Newton Abbot, has a narrow canted oriel window in its main, late 15th-century elevation.[225]

The bay window in the south elevation of the south-east range (*see* Figs 2.1 and 12.5) was a prominent feature of the main front of Bowhill. It was probably constructed of Beer stone (the surviving hall windows and the fragments recovered from excavation suggest that all the fine details of the building were of this material). The engraved view shows a bay of full height spanning the two storeys of the building, with three or four front-facing lights and single lights on the canted sides (*see* Fig 2.1). The multiple lights, the hint of blind panels below the windows (possibly with carved ornament) and the possibility of a parapet at the top are features strongly reminiscent of the Elyott window. This three-storey bay window was added to the Cathedral Close elevation of the house of Thomas Elyott at 73 High Street, Exeter, in 1500 (Fig 8.31).[226] The house was demolished, *c* 1840[227] and the window eventually reused in an adapted form in the Bishop's Palace (Fig 8.32).[228] The surviving version combined with drawings of the window in its original form constitute an accurate record, from which something of the

probable form of the Bowhill window can be reconstructed.[229] The Elyott window possessed five forward-facing lights and single lights on the sides with plain rather than foiled heads. There were registers of panels at parapet level and beneath each tier of windows (ornamented with quatrefoils and shields). Moulded drip courses or labels further articulated each storey. Each of these features can stand translation directly to the Bowhill bay window, on the evidence of the Bucks' engraving.

Multi-storeyed bay windows were frequently a feature of the upper stages of tall gatehouses or porches in the years around 1500. West Country examples can be drawn from both secular and monastic contexts: the porch tower at Holcombe Court, Devon (early 16th century, three storeys of 1+3+1 uncusped lights);[230] the porch of the Abbot's Hall at Cerne Abbey, Cerne Abbas, Dorset (1497–1509), of two storeys arranged in 1+3+1 cinquefoiled lights – this window had moulded string courses with paterae or fleurons on a deep hollow order, which compare with fragments from Bowhill that may be from this structure (*see* Fig 9.13, 104 and 105);[231] and the porch of the Abbot's lodging at Forde Abbey, Dorset, of 1528.[232] For the siting of a bay window in a gable wall, there are specific parallels at Southam Delabere, Gloucestershire (*c* 1512; in the great parlour);[233] Barnstone, Dorset;[234] South Petherton Manor House, Somerset;[235] and in the cross wing of Horham Hall, Essex (associated with a full-height bay window and crenellated parapet), built in the first decade of the 16th century.[236]

Of the structures still further to the east in the Bucks' engraving, the octagonal turret is an oddity. The typical position for a stair turret is, of course, in the angle of two structures, often against a porch. It might also project from an elevation, as at Cadhay or Wortham Manor (below). The nearly free-standing nature of this turret, attached to the corner of a building is, however, without close parallel. The small quatrefoil windows as stair-lights are reasonably common. The immediately local example in the parish church of St Thomas has been quoted above (Chapter 1, n 82) and single examples in attached stair turrets occur at Cadhay, Ottery St Mary, and Wortham Manor, Lifton.[237] The oriel window in a crenellated wall beyond is most closely matched by the galleried wall at Thornbury Castle, Gloucestershire, discussed already (*see* Figs 8.3 and 8.4).

Figure 8.30
Detail of the moulding and stop of the west door of the screens passage, north side (photograph by Stuart Blaylock; EMAFU 1834/4).

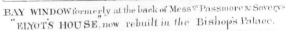

BAY WINDOW formerly at the back of Mess.ʳˢ Passmore & Saverys "ELYOT'S HOUSE", now rebuilt in the Bishop's Palace.

Cinquefoil-headed windows (of the hall)

Margaret Wood listed a number of similar two-light windows with transom. Most have cinquefoiled heads only in the upper lights, that is, they have a plain transom.[238] Bowhill and the hall of Bishop's Waltham, Hampshire, are distinguished by having foiled heads to all the lights. In Devon, aside from single-light windows with cinquefoiled heads,[239] two-light transomed windows can be seen at Bradley Manor (15th century, with some unfoiled lower lights),[240] the Old Manor, Littlehempston (late 15th century, unfoiled lower lights),[241] Weare Giffard Hall (?late 15th century, foiled lower lights and traceried spandrels)[242] and at Compton Castle (c 1520, foiled lower lights).[243] Traymill, Thorverton, has a fragment of a similar window.[244] Most of these windows have square-moulded labels. The first-floor lodgings in Wolsey's Great Quadrangle at Christ Church College, Oxford (1525–9), show the continued use of this type of window in the 1520s, albeit with a moulded rather than chamfered frame.[245] The carved head stops which distinguish the east windows of the hall at Bowhill (those of the west windows terminate in moulded returns) are widely paralleled in church architecture (although these details are invariably replaced by restoration). Sculpted label stops are employed at Bradley Manor[246] and at Weare Giffard Hall.[247]

Volcanic-stone lancet windows

Vesicular volcanic stone was used for the multiple-light east windows of the parlour, the single-light lancet windows used throughout the south side of the parlour, chamber and inner chamber, in the north-west corner of parlour and chamber and possibly also the two-light windows shown by the Buck brothers in the west-facing elevation of the south-east range. It is probably correct to say that volcanic stone was regarded as an inferior material to the Beer stone used in the hall and elsewhere. Even if the nature of the materials was obscured by limewash or rendering, the limestone would have been capable of a much finer cut and finish. The difference could well have been only marginal and partially related to the size of the intended window, as well as the status of its position. Most of the lancet windows have moulded frames (in contrast to the hollow chamfers of the hall windows in Beer stone) and thus present an appearance consistent with that suggested for the south-east range.[248] If the main elevation of the building was rendered and limewashed, there may have been little difference in appearance between features constructed of these different stones. Such lancet windows are frequent and long-lived. Local examples occur, *inter alia*, in clergy houses in The Close (nos 9 and 10).[249] Similar windows in timber can be seen in an early 16th-century timber-framed house at the corner of West Street and Stepcote Hill, Exeter, and at the Old Manor, Littlehempston.[250]

Bowhill has one surviving example of the type of small rectangular window that was widely used in medieval buildings where the need for lighting was coupled with that for security (and which was therefore often heavily barred). This was in the western of the two service rooms (*see* Fig 6.22, 59, and there was probably another in the room to the east before it was modified, Chapter 5). Similar windows appear in service rooms of the early 14th-century at Okehampton Castle, in the front range of Cothay, Somerset (after 1481), and in the kitchen of Compton Castle of *c* 1520.[251]

Timber windows

Primary timber windows
Timber windows were employed in the less-prestigious parts of the house (largely coinciding with the areas of cob walling), but no primary timber window frame survived in the residential core of the building.

One timber window is indubitably primary to the building. It was recovered from the north wall of the storeroom to the north of the hall and has a squat and heavy timber frame with diagonally and closely set square mullions, giving narrow lights no more than 50mm wide. There was no evidence for glazing or shutters (*see* Figs 9.23 and 9.24, catalogue no. 135).[252] This type may have been used elsewhere originally, but it is emphatically utilitarian in character and unlikely to have served domestic rooms or long survived improvements in fenestration. The one example presumably survived because it was blocked at an early date.

Windows of such massively crude construction were probably quite common in Devon and Cornwall, but extensive replacement of windows in the course of the 16th and later centuries (as well as a dearth of published examples) mean that few parallels for this window have been traced. Diagonally set square-mullioned windows of much lighter scantling, wider-spaced mullions and generally less massive construction are common in late medieval timber-framed buildings.[253] Comparable windows to the Bowhill example seem to be a western phenomenon, however, with a distribution focused on South Wales and the Welsh Marches. Many examples were recorded by Sir Cyril Fox and Lord Raglan in Monmouthshire, where the type is particularly characteristic of sub-medieval houses.[254] Further examples are recorded by the Royal Commission on Ancient and Historical Monuments in Wales in neighbouring Glamorgan (with a concentration near the Monmouthshire border).[255] The most recently published distribution map reinforces this distribution, with the addition of a thin spread in Brecon and Radnor, immediately to the north and west.[256] Many of the Monmouthshire windows resemble the Bowhill window in their scantling and proportions.[257] Perhaps the closest parallel is one from a one-roomed house at Little Llwygy, Lower Cwmyoy, which is described as 'exceptionally massive' in its construction.[258] The proportions of the window (low in relation to its width), the substantial lintel and sill chamfered on the outside and the spacing of the mullions closely resemble the Bowhill window. The low status of this building (and the crudity of the window form) fit happily into the context of small vernacular buildings in Monmouthshire, but the occurrence of such a window at Bowhill looks exceptional, notwithstanding the

Figure 8.31 (facing page, left)
The Elyott window, Exeter Cathedral Close, in its original position in the rear elevation of a house near St Petrock's Church in a contemporary watercolour by Edward Ashworth (undated but probably 1840s) (photograph by David Garner; EH B990728) (© The Devon and Exeter Institution, Exeter).

Figure 8.32 (facing page, right)
The Elyott window as reconstructed at the Bishop's Palace, Exeter, in a photograph by M Tomlinson of September 1942 (NMR B42/4002). As the window is now obscured by shrubs planted against the walls of the palace, it can no longer be photographed so clearly.

vernacular tendencies in the building. It is unlikely that many of the missing primary timber windows at Bowhill were ever of this type.

A number of late 15th- to early 16th-century timber windows illustrate the possible range of window types available for the original fenestration of Bowhill. In addition to timber versions of the stone lancet windows of the building (which are paralleled, for instance, at The Old Manor, Littlehempston, or Knightstone, Ottery St Mary),[259] another class of early timber window occurs in several variations in local contexts, with two, three or four narrow lancet lights, normally with trefoil heads and chamfered mullions. There is little evidence to suggest that the surviving examples were glazed, although they were generally shuttered. A very simple two-light timber window, with pointed arched heads and plain, square (unchamfered) mullions was recorded in no. 198 High Street, Exeter, in 1975.[260] Examples of the windows with trefoiled heads have been found at West Challacombe, Combe Martin (three lights),[261] the Glebe House, Whitestone (four lights),[262] Little Hackworthy, Tedburn St Mary (four lights)[263] and Priesthall, Kentisbeare (four lights).[264] More ornate versions are seen at Badlake, West Anstey (four lights, with cinquefoil heads, intersecting arches and open spandrels)[265] and reused in a barn at Yelland near Barnstaple (four lights, with king mullion).[266]

Secondary timber windows
Three examples of another type of timber window frame survived, two as loose windows (reused in the medieval barn in the western courtyard and preserved on the demolition of that structure in 1972), the third in a secondary context in the first floor of the west wall of the kitchen. The windows share the same form in design and section of timbers, but vary in size. Of the loose examples, catalogue no. 136 is of two lights and is 750mm high and no. 137 is of three lights and is 910mm high (*see* Fig 9.23). The window still in position in the west range (*see* Fig 6.53, 238) is still larger, being 1.12m high and four or five lights in width (Chapter 6). Common features are chamfered jambs and mullions, sockets for a single vertical saddle bar (of iron or timber?) in the centre of each light, flat sills and

lintels with exterior chamfers and remains of pintles on the inside for shutters. Each light is rebated outside the position of the saddle bar, a feature that suggests that the windows were glazed from the beginning. This feature casts doubt on the primary status of this type of window. If only the upper lights of the hall windows were glazed (Chapter 6), then lower-status windows such as these are unlikely to have been glazed in the first phase of the building. These windows, therefore, probably represent a phase of re-fenestration later in the 16th century, a time when any work of improvement is likely to have included re-fenestration, given the great increase in the availability (and decrease in the price) of window glass in the last quarter of the century.[267]

Such chamfered timber windows are of the plainest character, and must once have been widespread in 16th-century buildings. (The assumption here is that this type with plain chamfers precedes the ovolo-moulded window frames of the later 16th and 17th centuries and perhaps takes the place of simple types with sunk (or reserved) chamfers known elsewhere in the country.)[268] Of the few examples which have been published, the closest similarities occur in three windows at Bury Barton, Lapford, in an early 16th-century range of farm buildings,[269] at Great Moor and Middle Moor farms, Sowton[270] and in the rear wing at Poltimore Farm, Farway (which otherwise has ovolo-moulded windows).[271] Similar windows occur in a number of church houses in Devon (presumably explained by the fact that church houses represent a large class of well-preserved late medieval buildings rather than by any aspect of their function in particular) at Silverton, Stockland, and Washfield[272] and in at least one similar example in east Cornwall, at Poundstock.[273] Unpublished parallels exist at the Old Manor, Talaton, at the Church House, Holcombe Rogus, and at Hele Manor, Tawstock.[274] Something of a hybrid of the chamfered-mullion and foiled-head types described earlier is found in the windows of the church house at Dowland, where the construction is analogous to the rectangular windows, but the windows have round heads with small sunken spandrels and are closer in proportion to the narrower lancet windows. This possibly indicates an earlier date than the rectangular windows.[275]

9
The finds

The following standard abbreviations are used in descriptions: Av average; D diameter; De depth; L length; H height; Max maximum; Min minimum; Th thickness; W width.[1]

The pottery

by John Allan[2]

Introduction

The excavations conducted in Exeter since 1970 have assembled one of the finest series of late medieval and post-medieval ceramics in Britain. In such a context a good sequence of pottery from Bowhill might have allowed a revealing comparison to be made between the ceramics of the city's households and those used in a neighbouring rural house of fairly high social status. The excavations at Bowhill have recovered 3,912 sherds of which about 2,000 are pre-industrial wares (that is, before the late 18th century). Most of these, however, are late in date, the bulk of the collection belonging to types dating after 1700, and even the 18th-century material is largely residual in 19th-century or later deposits. There are a mere 158 small sherds of medieval pottery and even the 16th- and 17th-century finds are few, apart from the garderobe group described below; the buildings and their immediate surroundings must have been kept clean well into the 18th century. The bulk of the collection, therefore, does not merit detailed description and illustration, but has been tabulated (Table 9.1).

Method of study and publication

The pottery from each pre-1800 context has been identified macroscopically and listed by fabric type, following the Exeter type-series of fabrics and forms.[3] Quantified listings of the numbers of sherds, minimum numbers of vessels and vessel forms in each context, with estimates of context date, are deposited in the site archive.[4] These form the basis of Tables 9.1 and 9.2. In view of the poorly dated or unstratified nature of so much of the collection, only the individually interesting vessels have been drawn, apart from the pit group 2307.

Roman pottery

Although no Roman features were identified, eight residual Roman sherds were found in post-medieval deposits. All (samian, Dressel 20 amphora, flagons and BB1) are late 1st- or 2nd-century in date. They presumably reflect some form of Roman occupation in the vicinity. In the last 150 years various finds of Roman coins have been recorded in St Thomas.[5]

The medieval wares

The medieval pottery comprises 97 stratified sherds scattered among 35 medieval contexts, with 61 further residual fragments in post-medieval deposits (*see* Table 9.1). Such a collection does not allow extensive analysis, but offers at least some indication of the date range of the occupation preceding the standing buildings. There must have been some form of occupation on the site at least by the early 13th century, judging by the residual sherds of imported Rouen pottery (c 1180–1260), Dorset hand-made sandy ware (characteristic of the early and mid-13th century in the Exeter market)[6] and the probable tripod pitcher sherd. The coarseware bodysherds (fabrics 20 and 23), which form the bulk of the ceramics before the late 14th century could be earlier still, but in the absence of diagnostic finds can only be very broadly dated c 1000–1350. The series of late 14th- to 15th-century sherds amounts to about 50 fragments.

The pit group 2307

The one really worthwhile group is that from pit 2307, which is datable to the middle of the 16th century (Table 9.2; *see also* Fig 9.1). Various comparable groups of this period from Exeter have already been published,[7] but the Bowhill group is better-preserved than most of them, with a useful series of complete vessel profiles.

Table 9.1 Total potsherds from contexts other than pit 2307

		sherds	min no. vessels	forms/types vessel
medieval				
Rouen yellow-glazed, 13C		1	1	? jug
Saintonge green-glazed		1	1	"
unclass French white ware, glazed green		4	3	"
coarseware fabric 20		46	*c* 20	? cooking pots
coarseware fabric 22		12	3	"
coarseware fabric 23		14	9	"
fabric 40		17	8	? jugs
fabric 42		19	12	? jugs; costrel
fabric 43		4	3	? jugs
Totnes-type		2	2	jug
N Devon med. coarseware		5	2	
Dorset-type sandy ware		1	1	
Cornish micaceous		1	1	
fabric 62		1	1	? tripod pitcher
unclass English jug		12	9	
unclass coarsewares		18	7	
	TOTAL	158	83	
late 15th century/16th century wares				
Merida-type ware		7	2	1 small lid★; 1 ?standing costrel★
Beauvais green-glazed		1	1	drinking jug
Tudor Green		2	1	
unglazed Saintonge		2	2	
Raeren stoneware, L15C/E16C		2	2	drinking jugs
Cologne stoneware, E16C		1	1	drinking jug with applied rosette
S Somerset 15/16C		37	19	lobed cup★
Coarse Sandy Ware		10	?7	
	TOTAL	62	35	
17th century/18th century imports				
18C Chinese porcelain: blue and white		28	8+	1 large bowl, 2 saucer-dishes, 1 cup
18C Chinese porcelain: *famille rose/vert*		13	6+	1 teacup, 1 dish, 1 footed cup, 1 saucer-dish
Seville olive jar		5	2	
North Holland slipware		1	1	bowl – prob cockerel bowl★
Cologne/Frechen stoneware		2	2	
Westerwald stoneware		35	6+	3 jugs (2★), 1 chamber pot, 18C, + vessel 27★
	TOTAL	84	25+	
Delftwares				
Continental		1	1	? cup★
English/Dutch, 17C		3	3	
Dutch, *c* 1670–1710		3	2	
18C, prob mainly English		103	29+	
	TOTAL	110	35+	
17th–19th century English wares				
N Devon sgraffito		5	3	1 jug, 3 dishes
N Devon white ware		2	1	ointment pot
N Devon gravel-tempered		211	25++	12 bowls, 2 jugs, 2 chamber pots, 3 storage jars
S Somerset – all types		1305	197+	details in archive
plant pots, 18C and later		289	30++	
Staffordshire-type yellow slipwares, creamwares, pearlware, transfer print, stonewares and so on		1493	?200++	details in archive
	TOTAL	3305	456	
	SUM TOTAL	3719	634	
TOTAL COLLECTION (INCLUDING CONTEXT 2307; TABLE 9.2)		3912	681	

Drawn sherds★

Table 9.2 Contents of pit 2307, mid-16th century

	sherds	min no. vessels	vessel forms
Valencian lustreware	1	1	dish*
Saintonge	1	1	plain unglazed sherd
Martincamp Type 1	1	1	flask*
Martincamp Type 2	1	1	flask
Beauvais	3	2	bodysherds from yellow-glazed drinking jugs
Raeren stoneware	2	1	drinking jug*
Frechen stoneware	2	1	drinking jug*
North Devon calcareous	29	4	2 jars*, 1 ? jug*
North Devon gravel-free	2	1	
North Devon gravel-tempered	2	2	
North Devon (?) Micaceous	12	5	1 bowl*, 1 cistern*
South Somerset	3	3	1 jug*, 1 bowl*
Coarse Sandy Ware	128	19+	9 type 1A bowls (5*); 1 type 1B bowl*; 1 type 1E bowl; 5 closed forms, unclass
Unclassified coarsewares	6	5	
TOTAL	193	47	

Drawn sherds*

Although, therefore, the group was included by the writer in the tabulations of dated fabrics and vessel types in the Exeter finds volume,[8] it has been published fully here. The minimum vessel count of 47 vessels (Table 9.2) must be quite close to the actual number of vessels represented, since most sherds can be attributed to specific vessels. Obviously this is not a large sample, but the proportion of imports – eight imported vessels forming *c* 16 per cent of all vessels – is not noticeably rich. In the city's three monastic assemblages of this date at Exeter imports formed 25 per cent or more of sherds and in two major collections from urban tenements they exceed 20 per cent. In groups which are believed to represent the urban poor, the proportion is about 10 per cent.[9] Among the coarsewares, the Exeter series offers close parallels to the range of Coarse Sandy Ware and South Somerset bowls. Published examples of North Devon wares of this date, however, are not numerous. In the Bowhill group these are well represented (nos 5–9). As in groups of this period excavated elsewhere (for example, Launceston Castle,[10] Plymouth[11] and Exeter[12]), the most common North Devon form is the globular jar.

The other post-medieval wares

Since most of the collection dates after *c* 1720, the imports are restricted largely to the Chinese export porcelain and Westerwald stonewares which formed the last bulk imports of foreign ceramics into Britain (*see* Table 9.1). As is typical of collections of this late date, Westerwald stonewares are much more common than Frechen stonewares. Among the coarsewares the proportion of North Devon wares compared to South Somerset products is fairly typical of the 18th century in Exeter, as is the very small number of North Devon sgraffito sherds.[13]

Catalogue

Standard descriptions of the fabrics and glaze colours of the common classes of imports will be found in Hurst *et al* 1986 and will not be repeated here. Brown and Vince's thin-section analysis of selected sherds will be found below.

Pit Group 2307

The following group comes from the stone-lined cess pit 2307 (Fig 9.1; *see also* Fig 4.17, section 5). Layers 2349 and perhaps 2347 appear to have accumulated while the pit was in use. Layers 2341, 2340, 2312 and 2344 (the last not visible in the section) were successive layers of backfill post-dating the use of the garderobe after its outer walls had been demolished. They appear to represent a single event. All the imports and most of the coarsewares are in these upper layers. It is possible that the few finds in the primary fill, including no. 14, are somewhat earlier in date. The full contents of the group, quantified by sherd count, minimum number of vessels and forms will be found in Table 9.2. Two glass vessel fragments and much crushed plain window glass (*see below*, p 216) are associated.

1. Sherd of a Late Valencian Lustreware dish. Typical pink-buff fabric with buff margins under dull matt white tin glaze. On the upper surface is the faint ghost of copper lustre – a cross-hatched band at right-angles to the throwing marks (that is, radiating from the dish centre) flanked by spirals and dots. On the back even more faint lustre of simple lines, oblique to the throwing. The spirals and cross-hatched bands are typical elements of Late Valencian Lustreware painting,[14] which is datable to the years *c* 1475–1550.[15] Previously published by Allan and Hurst, although the faint decoration on the back was missed.[16]

    While Late Valencian Lustreware is far from common on sites in Britain (Gerrard *et al*[17] list a total of only nineteen sites in the entire British Isles where such vessels have been recorded, most of them represented by a single sherd), six such finds are now known from the Exeter area, with others from Totnes and Plymouth.[18] These luxury products must, therefore, have circulated in some numbers in the local market. Layer not recorded.[19]

2. Neck of a Martincamp Type 1 flask with typical pale cream fabric. Layer 2344.

3. Shoulder of a Raeren stoneware drinking jug. Layer 2344.

4. Sherds of a Frechen stoneware drinking jug with sand tempering.[20] Layer 2340.

5. North Devon type 14 jar,[21] with calcareous fabric and internal glaze. A fragment of a slate setter, used in separating pots during firing, is embedded in the glaze on the rim top. Layers 2312 and 2344.

6. As 5 but the fabric with rounded water-worn sands and black mica. When the present writer identified this distinctive fabric in the early 1980s, it seemed likely that its origin was a south Devon kiln using clays from Dartmoor.[22] In recent years, however, various vessels of this type have been excavated in Barnstaple, where they must surely be local products. They will be described henceforth as 'North Devon Micaceous Ware'. There is a characteristic patch of slip under the glaze on the rim. Layer 2341.

7. North Devon ?jug, the fabric with scatter of calcareous inclusions; dark reduced green internal glaze. Layer 2344.

8. North Devon Micaceous Ware, as no. 6. Cistern, type 15,[23] with external dull green glaze. Layer 2344. Thin-sectioned.

9. North Devon Micaceous Ware bowl, glazed internally, heavily sooted externally. The sooting extends over the rim top, running in a regular band of lighter sooting *c* 10mm wide on the edge of its upper face. This might indicate that it was covered by a lid which sat within the rim when in use. Layer 2341. Thin-sectioned.

10–14. Coarse Sandy Ware bowls of type 1A;[24] 10 sooted, layers 2312 and 2341, thin-sectioned; 11 heavily sooted, layers 2341 and 2344, thin-sectioned; 12 blistered, unsooted, layer 2341; 13 sooted, layers 2341 and 2344; 14 heavily sooted, layers 2347 and 2349.

15. Coarse Sandy Ware bowl, type 1B, heavily sooted externally. Layer 2344.

16. Sherd from the neck of a South Somerset sgraffito jug with usual iron oxide fragments in fabric; thin slip and combing under a green-brown glaze. Good examples of the type are published from Exeter.[25] Such vessels were certainly made at Donyatt site 3, and site 13[26] and probably also in other kilns working in the same tradition. Layer 2344.

17. Rim of a South Somerset bowl with internal green glaze. Possible traces of very light external sooting. Layer 2341.

Dating

The combination of Raeren and Frechen drinking jugs points to a date soon after 1550, when Frechen quickly supplanted Raeren in the production of this vessel form.[27] Other imports represented here are typical of the first half of the century: late Valencian Lustreware, Beauvais Medallion drinking jugs and Martincamp Type 1 flasks are all believed to disappear from the English market *c* 1550.[28] The common coarseware forms span the entire 16th century, but the predominance of Coarse Sandy Ware types 1A and 1B in the local market is very characteristic of the early and mid-16th century.[29] Mid-16th century.

Sherds in other contexts

The following are illustrated in Figures 9.1 and 9.2.

18. Sherds of an Exeter fabric 43 jug,[30] the body with sub-angular grey stone inclusions. Mid-green glaze over combing. Plain fabric 43 jugs are typical of the late 14th and 15th centuries.[31] Context 1609.

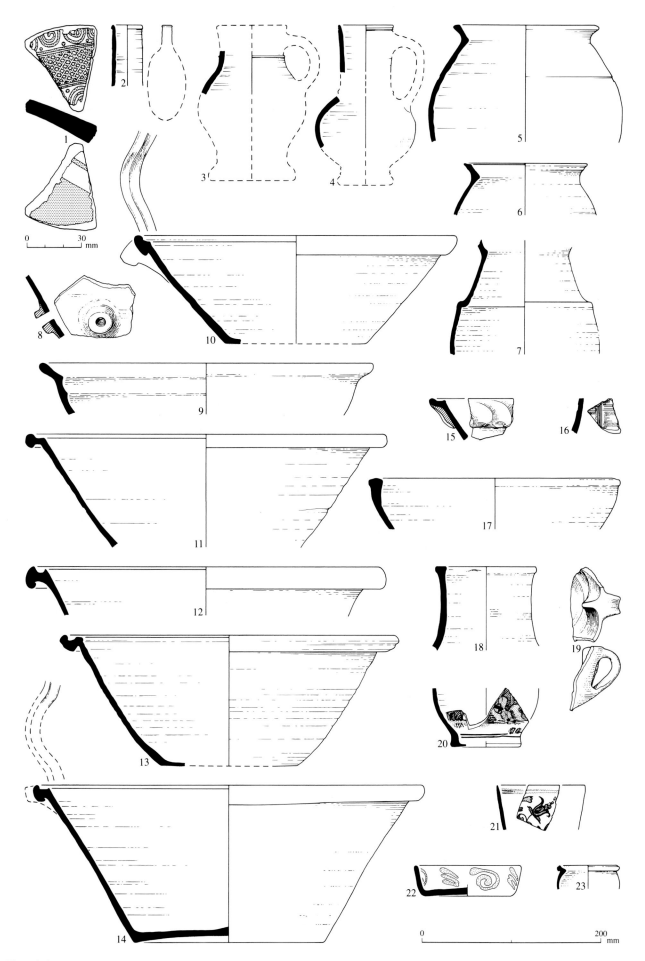

Figure 9.1
Pottery from pit group 2307 (nos 1–17) and other contexts (18–23); scale 1:4 (except no. 1 – 1:2) (line drawing by Piran Bishop).

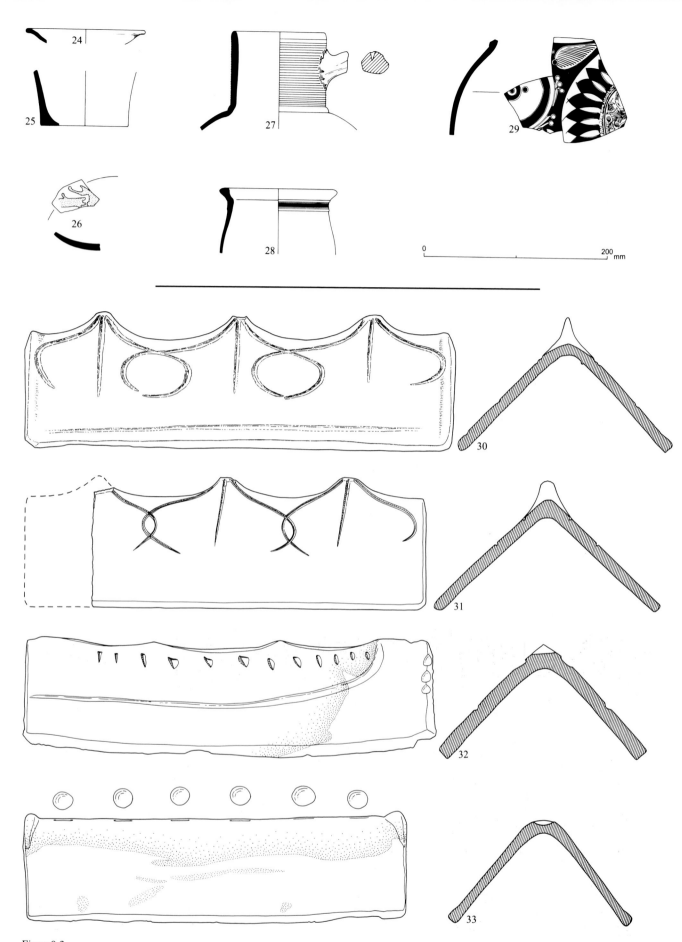

Figure 9.2
Pottery from miscellaneous undated contexts (24–9) and ridge tiles from the roof bridging the hall and great chamber (30–3); scale 1:4 (line drawing by Piran Bishop).

19. South Somerset lobed cup with granular brick-red fabric, thinly applied slip and copper-green glaze. The type is known to have been produced at Donyatt in the early 16th century[32] and probably in the late 15th century.[33] Context 756.

20. Sherds of a delftware bottle or tall mug with pale and mid-blue painting and glossy white internal and external glaze.[34] The decoration is of an oriental landscape with the lower part of a 'Chinaman' (left). The foot-rim of the more common wine bottles is more pronounced.[35] This painting style was popular, both in England and in the Netherlands, in the last quarter of the 17th century.[36] Probably Dutch, in view of the very glossy glaze. Contexts 843 and 864.

21. Sherd of a tin-glazed cup with buff fabric, pale and dark blue painting under a dull and crazed tin glaze showing a lively flower pattern. There is a slight thickening of the sherd to the right of the flower – presumably the edge of a handle attachment. Continental, ?17th century. Context 736.

22. Complete South Somerset plant pot stand. Alternating trailed slip spirals and groups of three diagonal dashes – four of each. Dark greenish-brown glaze. Context 2107, with mixed 18th- and 19th-century sherds.

23. Surrey-Hampshire Border ware jar, glazed yellow externally.[37] Context 718.

24. Unglazed Merida-type rim or lid. The form has a raised central boss and it is quite common locally in late 15th- and 16th-century contexts.[38] Unstratified.

25. Unglazed Merida-type base, perhaps from a standing costrel. Unstratified.

26. North Holland Slipware bowl sherd with typical thick slip. Unstratified.

27. Large Westerwald stoneware jug neck, with purple glaze, c 1720–50. Unstratified.

28. Westerwald stoneware. This is an unusual form of 18th-century import. It is closely comparable to a vessel from Norwich[39] and another from Exeter,[40] both of which have a loop handle rising above the rim. Jennings[41] suggests that the Norwich vessel may have been a hanging flowerpot; it has also been suggested that they served as urinals. Context 2107, with transfer-printed wares, after c 1780.

29. Westerwald stoneware jug sherds with edge of applied medallion and incised and blue-painted surround. The complete medallion shows a crowned GR monogram flanked by birds,[42] c 1720–50. Context 2064, with true white Staffordshire salt-glazed stoneware, c 1730–60.

Appendix 1: summary of the dating evidence

Phase 1: from early contexts in the parlour/service rooms

622 One sherd fabric 20; after AD 1000.
646 Three sherds fabric 20; after AD 1000.
693 Three sherds fabric 20; after AD 1000.
852 Two sherds fabric 23; probably 12th or 13th century, that is, all these could be 11th to 14th century.
2386 Ditch fill; two sherds fabric 23, one of fabric 42; broadly 1250–1400 (residual?).
2398 Ditch fill; four sherds including fabric 40; broadly 1250–1400 (residual?).

Phase 2: from demolished early building

601 Demolition deposit of early building; presumably from the cob of the walls, small group of fabric 20, 22 and 42; late 13th to early 14th century.
685 One Normandy floor tile from the fill of garderobe pit of the early building, preceding the standing building. The stratified examples of such tiles elsewhere in the city belong entirely to the early 16th century[43] and that appears to be their date elsewhere. If the writer's presumption that they are to be equated with the Normandy tiles listed in the Exeter customs accounts is accepted, such tiles arrived in bulk in the years 1490–1540. The earliest reference known to the writer is in 1490;[44] it would, however, be unsurprising if earlier references do turn up in accounts of the 1470s or 1480s. The importation of these tiles seems to have been an aspect of the rise in miscellaneous household goods from Normandy which is a striking feature of the city customs accounts after c 1475. While it is quite possible that such plain tiles had been produced in Normandy well before that date, the Bowhill find probably dates at least after c 1475 and probably after 1490.
719 Fill of western room, early building, possibly redeposited cob wall; seven sherds, broadly 1250–1400 (residual?).
745 Pit cutting early building and preceding standing building; four medieval sherds of which the latest is fabric 25, typical of the late 14th or early 15th century (all residual?).

Phase 3: from construction of earliest standing buildings

823 Foundation trench for screen footings of hall/parlour screen; fabric 43, after c 1300, residual.

1559 Group from the foundation trench of the standing building. The key find is the Coarse Sandy Ware sherd since this fabric is absent from groups of the end of the 15th century; the fabric comes into use *c* 1500. (The fabric was introduced after the deposit of group 1582–3 at Polsloe Priory with its South Netherlands maiolica, Beauvais drinking jug, Raeren stonewares and Martincamp flask, which most students would regard as dating to *c* 1500 or later.)[45] Other sherds are broadly late 15th to early 16th century.

2145 Extension of stair in 16th or early 17th century; Coarse Sandy Ware sherd. Dunmore's note states this equals 2359, however, which has one 18th-century coarseware sherd, post-1690–1700.

Phase 6: Civil War and mid-17th-century events

688 Small group with clay pipes of 1620–50 and early 17th-century coarsewares.

725 Very small group, only broadly datable to the 17th century.

1026 Filling of the Civil War ditch. Sadly the pottery is unspecific; five coarseware sherds of long-lived 17th- to 18th-century types (and three residual medieval).

1028 Top fill of ditch; sherds of post-1700 South Somerset slipware.

Phase 8: screens passage area

805 Post-dates removal of screen; English white earthenware, after *c* 1800.

808 Said to be the foundation trench for the screen; one clay pipe stem, after *c* 1600, intrusive/error.

864/843 Pit cutting site of screen; English/ Dutch tin-glazed jar sherds, probably mid- to late 17th century.

Western end of building

1527 In addition to the sculpture fragment, contains brick fragment (probably after *c* 1580 although a few early 16th-century finds are known) and ridge tile, probably 17th or even 18th century.

Late kitchen

2064 From cobbled floor; Westerwald stoneware, *c* 1720–50 and Staffordshire true white salt-glazed stoneware, *c* 1730–60.

2065 Transfer-printed white earthenware, after 1780.

2141 Small group of *c* 1730–1770.

2147 Staffordshire true white salt-glazed stoneware *c* 1730–60.

The ridge tiles

by John Allan

Prior to the repair programme conducted by English Heritage, Bowhill was one of the dwindling number of Devon buildings which still retained at least some of their ancient ridge tiles. Such tiles, known locally as creases or crests, must once have been virtually universal in the larger Devon towns, where slate roofs were obligatory and the use of crest tiles had been the normal means of providing a watertight roof ridge since the late 13th century.[46] Considerable numbers of such tiles were still to be seen in Exeter in the late 19th and early 20th centuries, as is evident from early photographs of the city (for example, Fig 9.3), but to this writer's knowledge the last Exeter examples were removed to the city museum when nos 42–4 Magdalen Street were demolished in 1977. In publishing this series of tiles the author has taken the opportunity to offer some general discussion of ridge tiles in Devon and to review the local documentary evidence relating to their use, which is in fact quite extensive. As John Cherry has recently pointed out,[47] there is a need for regional studies of the subject in many areas of Britain; the recovery in recent years of tile fragments from a number of major buildings of known date in the county now allows some progress in understanding the distribution, typology and dating of various types of ridge tile.

Six traditional ridge tiles stood on the roof that bridges the junction of the great hall and the great chamber (*see* Figs 2.9 and 2.19).

Figure 9.3

Old roofs at the rear of 76–81 Fore Street, Exeter, in 1893 (reproduced courtesy of the Westcountry Studies Library, Exeter).

These were salvaged by English Heritage works staff and are now deposited in Exeter City Museums. They are in three different styles and fabrics. Four are in Totnes-type ware with tall moulded ridges, one in North Devon gravel-tempered ware and one in a ?South Somerset/Honiton/Exeter fabric (see catalogue). Clearly they are of different dates and must reflect the replacement of parts of the house's original ridges on at least two occasions. This mixing of different types of crest on a roof has been noted elsewhere. The Magdalen Street roof mentioned above displayed three different types of crest, as did that of the west range of Polsloe Priory. Michael Laithwaite has noted the same mix of types among the crests formerly to be seen on the roof of 17 Highweek Street, Newton Abbot (demolished in 1975),[48] and the good series which until 1998 survived on the ridge of the hall range of Bull Hill, Pilton, north Devon, again had three traditional types.[49] In fact many roofs must have displayed a motley collection of ridge tiles of different styles and dates. This is unsurprising when the remarkably frequent replacements of ridge tiles recorded in building accounts or churchwardens' accounts is considered. For example, the Ashburton churchwardens' accounts published by Hanham[50] record the expenses of maintaining its large church and church house in the century 1479–1580. During the first 50 of those years they record purchases of ridge tiles in no fewer than 21 separate years. Many of these are for just two, three or four tiles; the two largest purchases were each for a dozen tiles. Similarly the Dartmouth churchwardens' accounts of 1495–1538 record nine different purchases of crests, the quantities bought varying from a single tile to eighteen.[51] Such continual expenditure was by no means unusual, as many other churchwardens' accounts and the endless repairs to Exeter Guildhall's roof[52] also show. This Devon evidence corresponds to the picture presented by Salzman, based on records from other parts of England, showing that other types of medieval roof were likewise the subject of continual repair.[53] Not only were crests frequently replaced (and presumably re-set), but a further complication could arise when old ridge tiles were salvaged from an old building to be reused elsewhere. That appears to be the explanation of the payment of 2s made in 1620 to the Plymouth Corporation by John Creaze (who had been working on the town's Guildhall and hospital) for twenty-six old crests at 2s,

while new crests were being bought by the Corporation at 1½d or 2d per foot and 3d each.[54] By contrast, records of fresh replacements of all the crests are rare; the instance might be quoted of the payment in 1597 of 350 feet (106.7m) of new crests for Hartland church at 3s 4d per hundred, recorded in the Hartland churchwardens' accounts,[55] an entry followed by payment of 20d for 200 hatch nails for fastening the crests upon the church.

Tile sizes and prices

Purchases of ridge tiles were most usually by number of tiles, but quite commonly by the foot, as in the Plymouth, Hartland and Ashburton accounts quoted above. This had been a medieval practice, as illustrated by Exeter's early 14th-century cathedral fabric rolls[56] and the early 15th-century accounts recording the costs of building cottages at Bishop's Clyst, published by Alcock.[57] The cathedral rolls record purchases for various ancillary buildings with slate roofs – the plumbery, the gates of The Close, the house in which fodder for horses was stored and the masons' lodge – as well as the Cathedral with its leaded roof. Payments by the foot are recorded, for example, in 1316–17, 1318–19 and 1323–4. Prices generally vary from 1d per 3 feet (0.91m) to 1d per 4 feet (1.22m) although there are occasional purchases at higher prices.[58] By the early 15th century prices had often risen to about 1d per foot. At Bishop's Clyst, 40 feet (12.19m) of tile were bought at 3s 4d in 1411 and 10 feet (3.05m) of tile at 12d.[59] It might, therefore, be expected that tiles would have been made in foot (305mm) or 18-inch (458mm) lengths. The intact tiles from Bowhill are 475mm (no. 28), 448mm (no. 30) and 423mm (no. 31) long and the examples at Exeter City Museums from other local sites measure 440mm,[60] 435mm,[61] 425mm,[62] 455mm[63] and 436mm.[64] They were probably intended to be 18 inches (458mm) long but varied somewhat with differential shrinkage upon firing – in many instances the potters had not allowed sufficiently for shrinkage. The lack of uniformity of size must have created problems when only a few were being replaced, leaving gaps or requiring tiles to be trimmed to fit. Such problems presumably lie behind efforts at standardisation of sizes, such as the act of 1477 quoted by Salzman, which stated that ridge tiles should be 13½ inches (343mm) long and 6¼ inches (159mm) deep.[65]

Tile typology

Typological studies of tiles elsewhere in England have shown the same general pattern of development. First come those tiles whose peaks are triangular in form, the edges of the peaks being knife-cut, then those with high moulded peaks made without knife-cutting, and later lower moulded peaks – the 'debased type'.[66] While the chronology of this sequence may vary from region to region – even from kiln group to kiln group – this same broad sequence almost certainly obtained in the south-west; however, the separate chronologies for the different production centres need to be established if the types are to be distinguished accurately. In Devon the following can be used to provide a chronological framework:

1. Several buildings excavated in recent years were constructed in the years *c* 1300–30 and dissolved or dismantled at the Dissolution in the 1530s, or *c* 1540. These are: Exeter Greyfriars;[67] Buckfast Abbey guest hall;[68] Polsloe Priory refectory range; and Okehampton Castle great hall, kitchen and bakehouse.[69]
2. Buildings belonging to the end of the 14th century or *c* 1400: the major building programme at Dartington Hall[70] and the small lodging added at Okehampton Castle.[71]
3. The main building programme at Bowhill *c* 1500.
4. The mid-16th-century and *c* 1600 building phases at Berry Pomeroy Castle.[72]
5. There are also large quantities of stratified tile debris from excavated contexts in Exeter, Plymouth and Barnstaple with lesser groups from Totnes, Newton Abbot, Crediton, Dartmouth and other places.

Examples of the earliest type with knife-cut peaks (Type A, below), like those from Exeter[73] are not common and are not represented at Bowhill, nor indeed on any of the major 14th- and 15th-century buildings described above. They probably belong to the late 13th and early 14th centuries.

The Totnes-type tiles

Among the Bowhill tiles, the four that should be typologically earliest are those in Totnes-type ware (*see* Fig 9.2, nos 30–1).

The potteries that produced tiles in this fabric were almost certainly at Bridgetown Pomeroy.[74] They made barely any impact on any of the other branches of the ceramics market of the Exeter area. Their products form about 1 per cent of the total domestic ceramics of the 16th-century city, less in the 17th. Their ridge tiles are rather more common since they form 2.5 per cent of a sample of 684 tile fragments from eighteen 16th- and early 17th-century contexts in the city. The Exeter finds form part of a widespread distribution of these tiles. Further examples have been found at Berry Pomeroy Castle,[75] Dartington Hall,[76] Leigh Barton, Churchstow,[77] Polsloe Priory,[78] Newton Abbot,[79] Buckfast Abbey,[80] Okehampton Castle[81] and Dartmouth.[82] The greater popularity of the ridge tiles may simply reflect the greater success of the Bridgetown potters in competing at the coarsest end of the ceramics market, but could be linked to the marketing of roofing slates from the Totnes and Dartmouth area. The excavated tiles in Totnes-type ware may be grouped into the following types:

Type A, with knife-cut peaks (not illustrated).
Type B, with very high moulded peaks.
Type C, with crests of the form represented at Bowhill.
Type D, with very close-set peaks.
Type E, with very low and widely spaced residual peaks.

The dating evidence is presented in Figure 9.4.

The Totnes-type tiles include not only conventional ridge tiles, but also examples with horse-and-rider finials of the sort discussed by Gerald Dunning.[83] The equestrian tile from Totnes, now in Totnes Museum, is in this fabric and that on Ashburton church roof is possibly of this type.[84]

The North Devon tiles

Ridge tiles with knife-cut peaks had been produced in North Devon in the Middle Ages (probably late 13th and 14th centuries), as the finds from Pilton churchyard illustrate.[85] Large numbers of medieval and post-medieval ridge tiles have been recovered from excavations in Barnstaple. It will only be possible to offer a typology and dating evidence after much work has been conducted on the excavation site archives.

site name	context	construction date of building	date of deposit	types present A	B	C	D	E
Totnes Castle	bailey	? 13C	? early 16C		XX			
Buckfast Abbey, Southgate	601,634	—	late 14/early 15C		XX			
Exe Bridge, Exeter	505	after 1200	c mid 15C		XX			
Polsloe Priorys ranges	various	c 1300–20	1538		X			
Buckfast Abbey, Guesthouse	various	c 1300 +	1539		XX			
St Nicholas' Priory, Exeter	church robbing	—	c 1536–1550		XX	X		
Okehampton Castle	lodging west of chapel	c 1400	c 1540				XX	
Goldsmith St, Exeter	L16–19, F33–8	—	1550–80		XX	X		
39 Fore St, Totnes	34 & 42	—	c 1600			XX		
Queen St, Exeter	314	—	c 1600			X		
Trichay St, Exeter	316	—	c 1660			X		
Berry Pomeroy Castle	inner courtyard	mid 16C +	c 1700					XXX
Berry Pomeroy Castle	north range & kitchens	1590–1630	c 1700					XX
Friars Gate, Exeter	103	—	?early 18C			XX		
Bowhill, Exeter	standing building	c 1500	c 1985			XX		
17 Highweek St, Newton Abbot	standing building	early 16C	1975			X		
Kingston House, Staverton	garden walls (?reused)	?mid- to late 18C	standing		?X	XXX		XXX

X = Present XX = Two to ten examples XXX = More than ten examples

Figure 9.4 Totnes-type ridge tiles. Tiles are shown at 1:8 scale; no examples of Type A have been noted (line drawings by John Allan, Piran Bishop and Mike Rouillard).

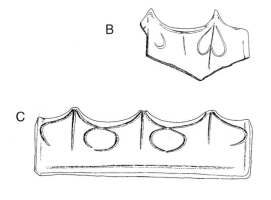

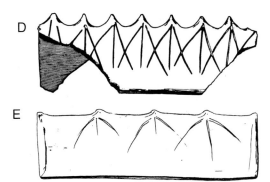

Catalogue

The following are illustrated in Figure 9.2.

30– One intact tile and a second in the same
 31. fabric and style which has subsequently been trimmed to fit. Totnes-type ware[86] with usual reduced dark grey sandy fabric; moulded peaks and incised 'crow's foot' decoration. The glaze has almost been lost through decay. Perhaps the primary tiles of *c* 1500.

32. North Devon gravel-tempered ware with very low peaks, knife-stabbing to aid firing, shallow incised line, shallow stabbing below peaks and mid-green glaze over most of length of tile (shown stippled). Tiles of this style are present in the late 17th-century kiln waste from Potters Lane, Barnstaple, and are known in a context of *c* 1690–1720 from Exeter.[87]

33. Brick-red fabric with few inclusions (?Honiton, ?South Somerset, ?Exeter brickworks), shallow thumb-impressions on top surface, orange-brown glaze over top half (shown stippled). 18th century?[88]

Appendix 2: the petrology of the Bowhill pottery and ridge tiles

by Duncan H Brown and Alan Vince

Six Bowhill samples were thin-sectioned and examined under a binocular microscope in 1983 as part of the programme of examining the petrology of the fabric types represented at Exeter.[89] Three comparative samples of ridge tiles – from Berry Pomeroy, Exeter and Leigh Barton – were also examined. The purpose of the exercise was to characterise more precisely the components of three distinctive fabrics, to compare these in thin-section with fabrics previously examined elsewhere in the south-west and, if possible, make progress in isolating the sources of these wares.

Fabric A: Coarse Sandy Ware

Samples were taken from the illustrated mid-16th-century vessels 10 (sample 1) and 11 (sample 2). A general macroscopic description of this commonplace 16th-century coarseware has been published,[90] but no petrological work to establish its source has been undertaken. The fabric is characterised by abundant sub-angular to rounded well-sorted quartz 0.2mm across with some fragments up to 0.4mm. There is also moderate rounded red iron ore, possibly altered glauconite, up to 0.6mm in size, sparse black iron ore, muscovite up to 0.2mm and rare fine-grained sandstone in an amorphous brown matrix up to 0.4mm across. The clay matrix is anisotropic and has sparse to moderate angular quartz and muscovite.

Fabric B: North Devon Micaceous Ware

Two samples were examined – sample 3 from vessel 8 and sample 4 from vessel 9. Both contain abundant angular to sub-angular quartz up to 0.2mm across, sparse to moderate biotite up to 1mm, sparse tourmaline up to 0.1mm and moderate plagioclase and orthoclase felspar up to 1mm. Sparse sub-angular chert up to 0.5mm in size was also identified in sample 3. Sparse altered limestone was visible in sample 4. Both have an anisotropic matrix, with abundant angular quartz (up to 1mm), muscovite and biotite.

Fabric C: 'Totnes-type ware' ridge tiles

Sample 5 was taken from a tile in context 2115 (not drawn) and sample 6 from a complete ridge tile (no. 30). Further examples of ridge tiles from other sites, identified macroscopically by John Allan as being in the same fabric, were examined from Berry Pomeroy Castle (sample 7), Goldsmith Street, Exeter (sample 8), and Leigh Barton, Churchstow, South Devon (sample 9). The samples indeed match and a common source may be presumed. The samples are also petrologically similar to Okehampton Castle Fabric 9.[91] In each case the fabric contains moderate quantities of sub-angular to angular quartz, plagioclase and orthoclase felspar, angular tourmaline and muscovite, all between 0.5 and 1mm in size. There is also sparse biotite (similarly sized) and sometimes fragments of igneous and metamorphic rocks and also a sandstone, possibly a greywacke. The matrix contains abundant angular quartz and occasional mica. The dense clay of the matrix is comparable to that of Fabric B here, but the nature of the temper makes comparison difficult as it can be so variable.

Petrological descriptions of each sample have been deposited in the site archive.

The floor tiles

by John Allan

In total some seventy-three fragments of plain floor tile were recovered from the excavations. Most were in contexts postdating *c* 1750, many of them certainly after *c* 1780. A single worn tile of the same type was found, however, in a context preceding the construction of the south range, showing that tiles of this type must have been brought to Bowhill before the construction of the standing buildings (Chapter 4). At least seventy further fragments of the same type were recorded incorporated in the standing fabric. Most of these had been reused in the repairs of the end of the 18th century, principally in the wall scars. One was noted in the mid-16th-century re-facing of the door jamb of the demolished garderobe, however (*see* Fig 5.8, 21). No evidence was found to indicate the room which they had floored, but it seems probable that they come from a structure modified or demolished in the late 18th century, most probably from one or more of the rooms in the south-east range, where lay the best rooms demolished at that time.

The tiles have a very distinctive sandy white or pink fabric, often with streaks of red or white clay. Among the excavated examples, only four tiles preserved one or more intact face. Each was between 159 and 163mm long; the tiles were certainly square. The glaze colours represented were as follows:

Copper-green-glazed	53 fragments
Plain yellow lead-glazed	11 fragments
Glaze colour lost	9 fragments

They belong to a series scattered along the south coast of England, for example, at Southampton, Winchester and Bishop's Waltham (Hants), Dorchester and Poole (Dorset), Plymouth and numerous sites in Exeter.[92] Such tiles are especially numerous in South Devon and Cornwall. The finest intact pavement is that in the chapel of Cotehele House, Cornwall. Fragmentary tiles have also been recovered from Polsloe Priory, Plympton Priory, Haccombe church, Torre Abbey, Fore Street, Totnes, and two sites in Exmouth, as well as those in Exeter.[93] There are also a few finds in eastern England and South Wales. It was argued in the Exeter finds volume[94] that such tiles were probably made in Normandy and are examples of the floor tiles recorded in the Exeter customs accounts of the years 1490–1540 which were imported in considerable numbers in ships of Rouen and le Havre. In his study of the Winchester Cathedral tile pavements, Dr Christopher Norton draws attention to tiles of similar fabric and glaze in a house in Rouen.[95] This appears to strengthen their attribution to Normandy. A programme of thin-sectioning, organised in 1990 by David Watkins of Poole Museums Service and undertaken by Dr D F Williams of the Ceramic Petrology Project, University of Southampton, found no clear evidence of their origins and did not preclude a source in the Saintonge.

The clay tobacco pipes

by John Allan

A total of some 356 fragments, including fifty-three bowls and bowl fragments, was recovered. There are no usefully stratified groups and nearly all these finds come from layers of 18th- to 19th-century date containing much residual material. The identifications of the thirty recognisable bowls are listed in the site archive.

A single unusual bowl (Fig 9.5) was submitted to David Higgins, who comments:

34. The fragment [from context 2327] is part of a Dutch pipe of *c* 1690–1740 with a small funnel-shaped bowl. The bowl surface has been finely burnished and it has a stem bore of 6/64". The heel is stamped with a crowned bucket mark surrounded by a fine beaded border. Symbol marks were quite commonly used by the Dutch makers; a bucket mark was registered at Gouda from *c* 1710–62, but not a crowned bucket mark. This is a useful addition to the group of Dutch pipes recorded from the south-west.

The remaining bowls are all local products belonging to types already published from Exeter.[96] They reflect the scarcity of pre-*c* 1700 material (only five bowls) and the relative abundance of post-*c* 1720 finds (twelve bowls).

Ironwork

The following are illustrated in Figure 9.5.

35. Rectangular plate with four rivet holes, three with rivets of ?lead surviving *in situ* and one with the rivet missing and the hole just detectable on the X-ray photograph.[97] Flat in cross section; curved in long section. The short ends possibly broken or cut, that is, the object is a part of a longer strip. W 40–42mm; L 92mm; Th 2–3mm. Head of rivets circular, flat, D 9mm. From context 2341, small find no. 388; the mid-16th-century fill of the medieval garderobe pit (*see* Fig 4.17, section 5).

36. Holdfast, or possibly a pintle for a strap hinge; heavily corroded, but the X-ray photograph shows a right-angled bend.[98] Tapering shank, rectangular in section; upright conceivably square or circular in section. Dimensions (with corrosion): max L 100mm; max H 63mm; shank (where visible) *c* 5 × 12mm. From context 601, the demolition deposit of the phase 2 building beneath the parlour, possibly representing the cob of the walls of that building (*see* Fig 4.18, section 10; Chapter 4).

37. Long rectangular plate of gently tapering form, with a loop or open feature at one end; possibly a handle. The X-ray photograph shows four rivet holes in a line, positioned off-centre.[99] L 152mm; W 24–32mm; min Th 7mm, although expanded. From context 736, small find no. 520; fill of pit 731 (*see* Fig 4.18, section 7), possibly of phase 5, late 16th to early 17th century.

38. Large staple; U-shaped form, arms tapering to points that are turned slightly outward. Probably rounded-square in section. Moderately corroded, but form is clear in X-ray photograph.[100] Max L 184mm; max W 90mm; max Th 43mm. From context 1026, small find no. 1111; the primary fill of ditch 1024 (*see* plan, Fig 4.15; Fig 4.17, section 4); deposit of phase 7 or 8 (late 17th to 18th century), although the object itself is presumably earlier.

39. Knife fragment, broken at both ends, but comprising a section of blade (tapering section), a bolster of circular section and the stump of a circular tang of narrower diameter (to which a handle of wood or bone was attached).[101] Total L 90mm; W of blade 11mm; Th of blade 2–3mm; D of bolster 9–10.5mm; D of tang 5–6mm. From context 1026 (as no. 38, above), small find no. 1110.

Non-ferrous metals

The most common non-ferrous metal find was the copper-alloy 'dressmaker's' pin. A total of fifty-three was recorded: thirteen from one deposit in the 1977–8 excavations; a further forty from the EMAFU excavations of 1989–94. Five pins are from indubitably medieval contexts (601, 745, 852) and twenty-five are from post-medieval contexts belonging to phases 5 and 6 (16th and 17th centuries). The remaining twenty-three are from 19th-century and later contexts. Despite the wide chronological spread little variation in form is seen in the

collection, possibly because the examples from later contexts were largely residual; equally it could reflect production methods which remained unchanged until the 19th century.[102] Pins from stratified contexts of phases 2 and 3 (that is, of undoubted medieval date) display both spherical and wound-wire heads, as well as traces of white-metal (?tin) plating. Thus the tinning of copper-alloy pins may have been normal at an earlier date than suggested elsewhere.[103] The complete pins in the collection range from 21mm to 40mm in length, but the majority (thirteen out of twenty-seven measured examples) are very close to 28mm.

Of some twenty-one other excavated objects of non-ferrous metals,[104] the following merit individual description and illustration (*see* Fig 9.5):

40. Copper-alloy mount, possibly a fragment of a strap or buckle fitting or similar attachment. Traces of gilding on surviving surfaces. L 35mm; max W 13mm; Th 1mm. From context 983, small find no. 1100; a widespread topsoil layer in the eastern courtyard (*see* Fig 4.17, section 4), phase 9 or 10.

41. Copper-alloy thimble, straight sided with a marked break in angle at the shoulder.[105] The rim is solid, indicating a cast thimble, and is thus probably earlier than *c* 1780.[106] The indentations are arranged in horizontal rows on the side, but in a diagonal stamped pattern on the top. The thimble is substantially smaller than the published examples from Exeter.[107] H 15mm; D (bottom) 14mm; D (top) 10mm. From context 1502, small find no. 115; the lime-mortar floor of the west room of the south range, phase 9 (*see* Fig 4.18, section 6).

Two spurs from Bowhill

by Blanche M A Ellis[108]

42. Rowel spur in copper alloy, with iron rowel, studs and buckle pin (Fig 9.5; *see also* Fig 9.6). Traces of non-ferrous coating. From context 2057 (small find no. 58).[109] Typologically the spur dates to *c* 1700.

The thickest part of the spur is the junction of the D-section sides which taper forward towards their small, evenly set figure-8 terminals. The oval-sectioned neck rises into a graceful slight curve, then swells horizontally and smoothly into wide rowel

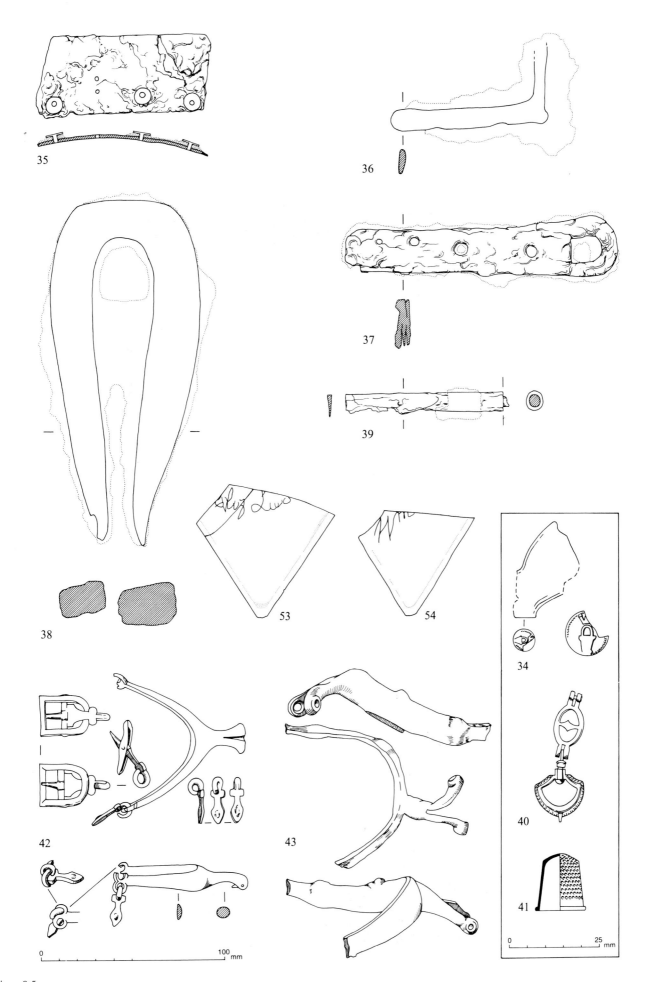

Figure 9.5

Small finds of iron, copper alloy and window glass: catalogue nos 34–43; scale 1:2 (except nos 34, 40, 41 – 1:1) (line drawing by Tony Ives and Blanche Ellis [nos 42–3]).

Figure 9.6
Copper-alloy spur, cata-
logue no. 42 (photograph
by David Garner; EH
B960388).

bosses which hold the rowel pin. Only two points of a small iron rowel survive and they are rusted into the rowel box. Three rings of the spur terminals are damaged. The unbroken one holds a copper alloy attach-ment of slender lozenge shape, with two small bulges flanking the base of its ring. A rust patch shows that the missing stud that would have been pressed through a slit in the spur leather was iron. Two more stud attachments that are now detached but accompany the spur are of similar form and condition, one of them still held by the broken part of one spur terminal. The copper alloy buckle, now separate, has a D-shaped frame with central bar and an iron buckle pin. The rod within the bar also appears to be iron. The buckle plate is waisted with two projections flanking the base of its ring as on the attachments for the leathers. Those parts of the buckle frame and spur sides that are not covered in corro-sion are very smooth, but traces of thin non-ferrous coating survive, especially on the buckle. L (overall, measured along neck to midway between terminals): 70mm; L (neck): *c* 22mm; span (between terminals): 67mm; buckle frame: 25 × 21mm; L (attachments) 22 and 23mm.

The spur may have been made for a youth, but despite its small size it could have been worn by an adult. A small spur of this type is worn on the narrow part of the ankle above the heel in the painting of *King William Landing at Brixham, Torbay*, by Jan Wyck and dated 1688.[110] A pair of spurs of the same basic form are hallmarked 'London 1729'. They are silver with steel rowels.[111] The addition of iron parts to non-ferrous spurs was a fairly common practice.

43. Fragment of a rowel spur of iron, severely rusted and covered in soil accretions (*see* Fig 9.5). From context 1527 (small find no. 1120).[112]

The broken sides are deep and of flat or possibly originally of flattened D-section. They arc around the back of the wearer's heel tapering as they project forward and very slightly downward. Both have lost their front ends. The longest one is stepped as it changes to a much shallower depth, just before its break. The short remnant of that front part now rises slightly. The top edge of this side may have extended into a small decorative scallop about one-third of the way forward from the junction with the neck, but in its present condition it is no longer possible to know whether this was a decorative feature or merely a build-up of rust and soil. The short and relatively slender neck of the spur projects from the centre of the deep junction of its sides. This down-curved neck consists mainly of the rowel box which has D-section sides and conical rowel bosses. One of these is now splayed open so that the rowel and its pin are lost. Overall L (measured forwards from the end of the neck) 100mm; L (neck) 31mm; L (rowel box) 25mm.

The spur's typological date is post-medieval, probably 16th century. Two iron spur fragments, each with a complete side of deep section around the wearer's heel, but changing to shallow section towards the front end, are nos IW 25 and IW 26 from Somerby, Lincolnshire. These are associated with a smith's workshop of mid-15th- to mid-16th-century date.[113] It is also of interest to compare a complete iron rowel spur excavated from a 16th-century deposit at the Manor of Tretire, Herefordshire. This spur has a decorative feature halfway along each of its sides but, as far as one can tell, its general form is otherwise similar to what remains of the fragment under discussion.[114]

Lead musket balls

Seven lead musket balls were found in the excavations; six (nos 44–9) from deposits either side of the screen dividing the two service rooms of the south range (*see* Fig 4.15, 688 and 725), which contained clay-pipe material of 1620–50 (Chapter 4) and were cut by features associated with the reorganisation of the parlour and service rooms in phase 7. They are attributed here to phase 6. The seventh (no. 50) was from the fill of the large ditch of phase 6 whose terminal was located in the eastern court-yard (*see* Fig 4.15, 1024 and 1026, fill and Fig 4.17, section 4). The excavated finds are illustrated as a group in Fig 9.7. Data on

one further, unprovenanced, find from the standing building are added below, no. 51 (not included in the photograph).

These finds have been mentioned already in the context of the Civil War fortification of the site (Chapter 3). While the temptation to make too much of them must be resisted, the concentration of musket balls in layers of this phase is significant. The many deposits of other post-medieval phases produced no such finds. Musket balls are equally uncommon as archaeological finds on other sites in Exeter (with the exception of Hayes Barton, where some forty balls were deposited, probably as a result of a Parliamentary attack in July 1643)[115] and no other site excavated in Exeter has yielded any finds of lead shot. It is against this background that the finds from Bowhill should be interpreted. If the optimum diameter was *c* 18mm and weight was 32g (as in nos 45–49) a specification of fourteen balls per pound is suggested as the average of the lead shot from Bowhill, perhaps slightly smaller than the twelve-to-the-pound specification which appears to be the norm for musket balls, although there is considerable variation in detail.[116] Several associated finds of scrap lead were found in the same contexts (window came fragments, other scrap, below), implying that raw material had been assembled for the production of shot on site. Although there is evidence that shot was supplied centrally and to standard specifications, it is also probable that irregular supplies ensured that local and individual production was often necessary.[117]

44. Max D 17–19mm; weight 30g. Prominent seam, forming a 2mm flange. From context 688 (small find no. 508).
45. Max D 18mm; weight 32g. From context 688 (small find no. 510).
46. Max D 17.5mm; weight 32g. Clear seam; cut or gouge 11mm long; corrosion on one side. From context 688 (small find no. 513).
47. Max D 18mm; weight 32g. Corrosion on one side. From context 688 (small find no. 517).

48. Max D 18.5mm; weight 32g. Deep gouge from one side; distorted at this point to max D 20mm. From context 725 (small find no. 511).
49. Max D 18mm; weight 32g. From context 725 (small find no. 518).
50. Max D 17mm; weight 28g. Pockmarked surface. From context 1026 (small find no. 1107).
51. Max D 15–17mm; weight 26g. Feint seam, and mark of casting (pontil); various flattened planes on surface. Unprovenanced.

Leather shoe fragment
(not illustrated)

by Glynis Edwards[118]

A damaged and worn middle-sole from a shoe of welted construction was recovered from the south range cess pit. This method of making shoes was introduced about 1500.[119] The surviving length is *c* 230mm but the forepart and outside joint are missing. Most of the edges are gone but a flesh/grain seam (stitch length *c* 5–6mm) survives at the waist extending to the inside joint. There are also some detached fragments of this seam. It is compressed at the seat and worn at the tread. Two holes in the tread may be damage or traces of nailing. It is probably calf/cattle by the thickness of the skin, *c* 4mm. From context 2349 (within cess pit 2307), mid-16th century; small find no. 350; Ancient Monuments Laboratory no. 782205.

Textile fragments *(not illustrated)*

by Alison Hopper-Bishop[120]

A small bundle of carbonised textile fragments was recovered from the fill of the phase 2 garderobe pit, context 685 (*see* Fig 4.4); small find no. 504. The main group of fragments was bunched around a small, heavily corroded iron nail or pin, 30mm long; there were also eleven individual fragments detached from the bundle. The charred textile was extremely frail and brittle. Some areas were also encrusted with iron corrosion products. It was not possible to open out the largest group of fragments for detailed examination, since the threads shattered and fibres powdered at a touch. The layers were also fused together in places by the corrosion products. The textile's relationship to the iron was not clearly established by X-radiography; it might be coincidental.

Figure 9.7
Lead musket balls, catalogue nos 44–50 (photograph by David Garner; EH B960391).

215

The detached fragments could be more closely examined. All threads are Z twist, unplied, plain tabby weave, warp and weft direction not identified. A trace of a self-patterned, floating warp and weft stripe was identified, 18 × 9mm, on the main bundle of fragments. In addition one other small fragment had a few floating warp and weft threads, apparently in the form of a small diamond. Although the fibres were not positively identified, it is possible that they are flax: 'The fact that the threads have preserved their form when burnt suggests they were a vegetable fibre and not wool which is highly combustible'.[121]

Dimensions of the main bundle: 100 × 92mm max; the eleven detached fragments varied in size from 57 × 55mm to 15 × 10mm. Thread count: 1.4 per mm in both directions. No selvedges or borders and no finishing or other evidence of use were found.

The coins *(not illustrated)*

by Norman Shiel [122]

One ancient coin was found in a useful stratigraphic context (649; small find no. 502).[123] This is a late medieval silver penny, which is somewhat clipped and worn, and this does not facilitate totally accurate attribution. The mint is certainly Durham and the legible letters combine to suggest the attribution given. Given the state of the coin, it would seem likely to have been in circulation for some time prior to loss.

52. English silver penny; Edward IV First Reign, 1461–70; heavy coinage 1461–4. Durham mint *R*): CIVI [TAS DUN] OLIN, no additional marks visible (North 1543).[124]

Three modern coins were found in late contexts in the 1977–8 excavations.[125]

Window glass

by John Allan and Stuart Blaylock

Excavated window glass
(not illustrated)

Three very small and decayed sherds of window glass were found in the destruction deposit of the phase 2 building (*see* Fig 4.18, section 10, context 601). The presence of window glass in this early building, albeit in very small quantities, is another indication that the building may have been of higher status than it appeared from its excavated plan (Chapter 4). A mass of crushed fragments of plain, thin (less than 1mm thick) window glass with iridescent opaque weathering were contained in context 2347, one of the fill layers in the garderobe pit 2307 (*see* Fig 4.17, section 5 and assigned to phase 4 (mid-16th century). These are likely to represent the original glazing of the building and are typical of the domestic glass imported into Exeter in the late 15th and throughout the 16th century. Much of it evidently came from Normandy, a little also came from the Rhineland and an uncertain amount was English.[126] These fragments, therefore, may well be imports from Normandy.

Nine sherds of the same type came from the layer that also yielded several lead musket balls and fragments of lead cames (context 688; below, lead nos 1 and 2). If, as suggested (Chapter 4), this was deposited during the Civil War, the sherds of window glass and came fragments may indicate the removal of glazed windows (perhaps as a source of lead) at that time. Ten further fragments were retrieved from late contexts outside the east wall of the hall, and may indicate damage to the hall windows in the 19th or early 20th century. Eight came from context 2333/2304 (a late ditch along the east wall; not illustrated);[127] two were sufficiently large to show that they came from diamond-shaped quarries with cut edges. Two further scraps were retrieved from 2330, one of the linear cultivation trenches in the eastern courtyard (also numbered 1014; *see* Fig 4.23); also 19th century.

Glass recovered from the standing building *(not illustrated)*

A large quantity of broken window glass was recovered from context 376, the dump of demolition material at the north end of the west gable of the south range (Chapter 6; location in Fig 6.1, first floor). The deposit also included slates and window cames (*see below*). The structural context confirmed that the material had been deposited as the major demolition work of phase 8 was under way and supports the picture derived from other parts of the building, that re-roofing and re-fenestration formed major elements in the phase 8 alterations.

The collection comprises about 180 sherds, weighing 962g. There are no complete quarries and few fragments possess more than two surviving original faces. Most of the glass is greenish in colour, but occasional sherds have a blue colouration; thicknesses vary substantially within the range 0.5–2.0mm and there is considerable variation in surface texture. Five fragments represent square or rectangular panes (with two faces at right angles) up to 150 × 73mm; a further eight are fragments of diamond quarries, with a variety of shapes. Two retain traces of four faces, making reconstruction possible: 137 × 97mm and 158 × 118mm, with lower angles of 73° and 79° respectively. The remaining quarries (with only two surviving faces), show a variety of angles, mostly between 65° and 70°, and represent a reasonably consistent set of shapes, perhaps from the glazing of one window or group of windows. The diamond and rectangular quarries probably derived from separate windows, since the evidence of the cames from this deposit showed only diamond-shaped glazing.

Much of the glass is similar in appearance to that recovered from the mid-16th century garderobe pit (*see above*) and, even though the quarry fragments display a mixture of grozed and diamond-cut edges, suggesting a mixture of 15th- to 16th-century and later glass in the collection,[128] they probably belonged to an early phase of the building. The cames suggest some repairs, re-glazing and re-leading in the 18th century (below). It seems very unlikely that new glazing of this date would have employed diamond quarries (or even leaded rectangular panes) and thus it is preferable to see the 18th-century work represented by the cames as the repair and/or re-glazing of earlier windows, perhaps in association with re-fenestration elsewhere in the building.

Window glass with graffiti

Two of the diamond quarries bear legible graffiti (*see* Fig 9.5). The first (no. 53) reads 'Eliz. Luc ... ' (break). The second pane (no. 54) is more fragmentary, but reads 'Wm ... ' (break). Both graffiti are in the form of signatures and in rather shaky hands, probably from the difficulty of writing in an unaccustomed position with a diamond.[129] There is little doubt that the first is the signature of Elizabeth Lucombe, who was in occupation of Bowhill, probably from 1740 until after William's death in 1794 (Chapter 3). It is thus reasonable to identify the second signature as that of William Lucombe himself. These fragments represent unique physical evidence of the Lucombes' tenure of Bowhill and help to link the documented sequence of occupation and the physical fabric. Five further sherds of glass also bear graffiti too small or random to be legible.

Lead window cames

by Barry Knight[130]

Only three small fragments of window lead were recovered in the excavations. Of these, two are unmodified cast lead of the type produced throughout the Middle Ages until about the middle of the 16th century, while one fragment used as a tie to attach a glazed panel to the window bars has been trimmed to remove the casting flash and could be later 16th or 17th century. The small quantity of lead found does not necessarily indicate that the windows were not glazed in the Middle Ages, but merely that the vast majority of lead was recycled.

A larger quantity of twisted cames was discovered in two tangled masses in context 376 (nos 4 and 6–8, *see below*), together with a quantity of loose glass described above. After unfolding, these two masses of cames proved to be substantial parts of (probably) two windows with diamond-shaped quarries. The minimum dimensions of these windows are approximately 300 × 500mm. The lead is typical of the mid- to late 18th century. One small detached fragment (possibly a repair) is inscribed ?'GD 1770'. Small pieces of glass retained in the cames were also typical of the 18th century, being thin (*c* 1.5mm), very pale green and diamond cut.

Since other glass fragments found in the same deposit appeared to be of earlier date (thicker, greener, more uneven, with grozed edges as above), it is possible that earlier glazing was re-leaded in the latter part of the 18th century and pieces of new glass incorporated into the windows.

Catalogue of lead fragments
(not illustrated)

1. Small fragment; type C, medieval cast lead.[131] L approx 90mm; W 4mm. From context 688, ?mid-17th century; small find no. 504.
2. Twisted fragment, used as a tie; could be type D, post-medieval. Used to attach a glazed panel to the window bars. From context 688, as no. 1; small find no. 512.

3. Small fragment, probably type C, medieval cast lead. L approx 35mm; W 4mm. From context 1004, fill above 19th-century cultivation trenches in east courtyard; small find no. 1104.

4. Melted fragments; either these are just dribbles of melted lead which have solidified and taken up the shape of whatever they were lying on, or it is lead which has been poured around a masonry cramp or similar to hold it in place. From context 376 (*see below* no. 6).

5. Fragment, probably one side of a diamond-shaped quarry. Milled lead, type G, 18th century; 5 teeth to 20mm. L 140mm; W 9.5mm. From the roof of the south range, bay 11, SW corner.

6. Part of a window, W approx 10mm; surviving area of window approx 300 × 500mm, with fragments of thin (*c* 1.5mm) pale green glass, diamond cut (not grozed) diamond-shaped quarries. Quarry size approx 90 × 95mm, angles 80°, 100°. Eighteenth-century milled lead, five teeth to 20mm. One fragment, L approx 15mm; W 9.5mm; four teeth to 20mm, inscribed ?'GD 1770' in the heart. The letters have been flattened by the edges of the glass, and are not clear. Cames marked 'GD 1760' are known from Battle Abbey[132] and marked 'GD' with '1742', '1743' or '1746' from London,[133] but these need not be (and probably are not) made by the same person as this piece. From context 376 (a deep deposit of demolition debris that had accumulated behind brick blocking at the north-west corner of the oriel chamber – sample 1).

7. Piece from the edge of a window, plus long strip from edge, *c* 350mm, plus some glass fragments. One complete triangular quarry from edge: 66 × 65 × 58mm; angles approx 65°, 63°, and 54°. Same lead as no. 6. From context 376 (sample 2).

8. Large piece from window, at least 350 × 500mm, with two straight edges. One tie for glazing bar made of split lead soldered to joint. Rather smaller quarries than sample 1, about 75 × 75mm, but appears to be the same lead. From context 376 (sample 2).

Architectural ironwork

Of the iron architectural fittings recovered from the standing building, six merit description and illustration (Fig 9.8).

55. Pintle (the lower of two) from the east doorway of the great hall, removed when new fittings were inserted in 1991 (*see* Fig 6.2, 86). Complete, although in two fragments (the shank broken on extraction). Rectangular shank, with down-turned section at the inner end, presumably intended to improve stability,[134] partially encased in lead. The shank is heavily worn at the outer end by the action of the hinge and is fractured at its narrowest point; circular pin, worn on outer edge. Shank 40 × 20mm; downturn at end 43 × 17mm max D of pin: 36mm (max); 31mm (min); overall L: *c* 230mm; overall H: 80mm. Overall dimensions in section with lead setting in position: max H: *c* 75mm; max W: *c* 86mm. One of the original pintles, thus *c* 1500.

56. Pintle, unprovenanced, but from its size probably for a door; perhaps an addition to one of the main doorways. Rectangular tapering shank, circular pin worn smooth on the shaft, and around the base. Shank: 26 × 22mm, tapering to 12 × 9mm; D of pin: 19mm; overall L: 189mm; overall H: 94mm.

57. Pintle, unprovenanced; smaller than 55 and 56, possibly for a window/shutter or smaller door.[135] Shank splayed in plan, encased in lead and the full shape not visible; surface corroded and exfoliated. Shank: 14 × 16mm; D of pin: 15–16mm; overall L: 135mm; overall H: 48mm. Overall dimensions in section with lead setting in position: *c* 65 × 65mm.

58. Holdfast or hook,[136] unprovenanced.[137] L 132mm; H 42mm.

59. Holdfast or hook,[138] unprovenanced (as no. 58). L 107mm; H 45mm.

60. Holdfast or hook, unprovenanced (as no. 58). L 97mm; H 24mm.

61. Pintle, a much smaller example, probably from a later window or shutter, 'found in the great hall, behind fireplace' in 1989. Shank square in section; tapering to point; pin circular. L 115mm; H 61mm.

Further iron finds from the standing building (*not illustrated*)

1. Pintle (the lower of two) from the west doorway of the great hall, removed in 1991. The rear section of the shank survives, with a tapered point partly encased in lead; the front was cut off. Total L 113mm; max W 35mm; max H 33mm (both expanded by corrosion); dimensions including lead setting 47 × 47mm.

2. Mason's pointing trowel found in the great hall roof in 1980 (complete, with wooden handle); probably 19th century. Blade 131 × 68mm; handle: L 101mm; D 36mm.

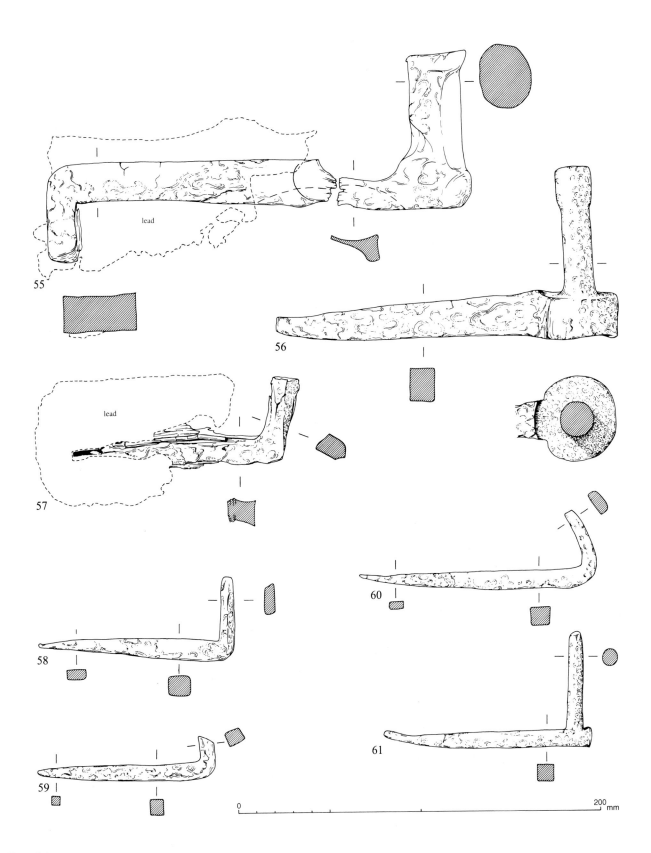

Figure 9.8
Architectural ironwork, catalogue nos 55–61; scale 1:2 (line drawing by Tony Ives).

*Figure 9.9 (facing page)
Nails from excavated
contexts (catalogue nos
62–78) and from the
standing building (nos
79–102): type A: 79–84;
type B: 85–92; type C:
93–7; type D: 98 and 99;
type E: 100–2; scale 1:2
(line drawing by Tony
Ives).*

3. Blade of an iron spade, found above the kitchen doorway (*see* Fig 2.20, 423), in 1991. Modern, 19th or 20th century.
4. Iron strip, probably a fragment of a hinge strap; from packing above the lintel of window 46 in the south elevation of the south range (*see* Fig 5.8, 332). Tapering form, one end flattened and splayed; phase 8, *c* 1800.

Nails

The surviving fabric shows that iron nails were used sparingly, and for specific purposes, in the primary building. The bosses of the great chamber roof were secured by iron spikes, as presumably were those of the hall roof that had not survived. Laths for roof covering and plastering of partitions were secured by nails and the many small-sized nails recovered from the site, especially from the roof, can be identified as primary lath nails with some confidence. Nails were also used for some exceptional purposes in roofing, for instance, the wood blocks against which the ends of the purlins were lodged in the junction of the roofs of the south and west ranges (*see* Fig 7.43, in which many lath nails are also visible) and to secure the jack rafters to the lay boards in the same area. No primary flooring survived in the building, but it is likely that the boarded (that is, first-floor level) floors were originally secured by nails. Since few other examples of nails are clearly associated with the early phases of the building, it is probable that most of the primary carpentry of the building of *c* 1500 was assembled without nails. The large quantity of hand-made nails recovered from the building during the works probably belongs mostly to later phases of activity.

The nails illustrated here have been chosen as a representative selection from a sample of 268 nails, made up of twenty-five examples from excavated contexts and 243 recovered from the standing building (Fig 9.9).[139] Most of the nails were associated with the roof, although some were observed in structural carpentry elsewhere.[140] Nails recovered from datable excavated contexts provide a means of identifying early types; one particularly useful group was recovered from the destruction deposits of the phase 2 building, dated at the latest to the late 15th century and possibly somewhat earlier. These nails form a good group for comparison with the later specimens found elsewhere in the building. Ten nails (or

fragments) are illustrated from a group of twelve examples from the fill of the garderobe of the phase 2 building (685; Fig 9.9, nos 65–74) and there are two other examples from contexts associated with the same building (nos 62 and 75). The collection includes a range of small nails comparable to the lath nails described as type A, below (nos 62–9), and several larger nails, possibly similar to type B (below). One large nail was recovered from the fill of a foundation trench for the standing building (phase 3, 1615; Fig 9.9, no. 77). The remainder come from later contexts, but are included because they provide useful parallel examples for the collection from the standing building. This includes one large square-headed nail, similar in type to those of type C, below (no. 76);[141] two further small nails of type A (nos 63–4)[142] and a large round-headed nail, possibly related to type B (no. 78).[143]

The much larger collection of nails from the standing building displays a more consistent range of types. This is tempered by the possibility of error, however, since few were recovered from sealed or uncontaminated deposits. Such hand-made nails could be as late as the 18th century in date, although the majority are probably 16th or 17th century.[144] Even in the 19th century, once wholly industrialised production of cut nails was established, blacksmith-made, hand-forged nails were still required for some purposes, although in this case the context of most of the nails would rule out such a late date. One large group of sixty-five nails of broadly the same sort, although somewhat more standardised, was recovered from the framing of the east gable wall of the south range (not illustrated). This structure was constructed after the demolition of the south-east range and porch in phase 8 and demonstrates the continued use of hand-made nails in the 19th century at Bowhill.

The total of 243 nails divides into five classes (types A–E), excluding obviously modern nails. Three encompass the majority of the ancient hand-forged nails; a further two categories (plus miscellaneous, one-off types) cover later nails of distinctive type or associations.

Type A (nos 79–84): small hand-forged, round-headed nails, generally square in section (occasionally rectangular) and tapering in two planes (that is, all four faces tapering). Total sample: forty-five nails; size range from 21–26mm in length, most averaging 23–25mm, so these are 1" nails. Many other examples observed *in situ* in common

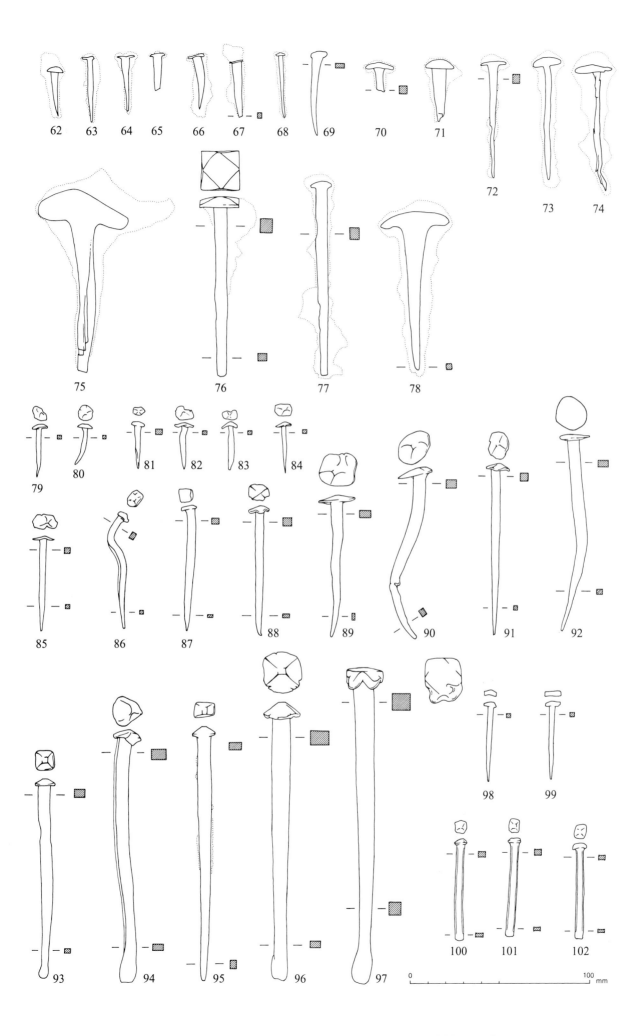

62 63 64 65 66 67 68 69 70 71 72 73 74

75 76 77 78

79 80 81 82 83 84 85 86 87 88 89 90 91 92

93 94 95 96 97 98 99 100 101 102

0 100 mm

rafters and in riven oak laths show that this type is the primary lath nail of the building, used in roofing and in partitions.

Type B (nos 85–92): larger hand-forged, round-headed nails, similar in specification to type A, but occurring in a variety of larger sizes, up to 104mm ($4^1/_8$"). Square or rectangular in section, the heads are widely variable in size and shape. Total sample: twenty-six nails. Lengths of the illustrated examples show a range with no clear imperial increments: 51mm (2"), 62mm ($2^1/_2$"), 69mm ($2^3/_4$"), 75mm (3"), 91mm ($3^1/_2$"), 95mm ($3^3/_4$") and 104mm ($4^1/_8$"). Specimens of this type (of which one is illustrated, Fig 9.9, no. 89) were recovered from the partition in the south-east corner of the great chamber (a secondary partition, but probably belonging to an early phase). This use, combined with the similarity in form and method of manufacture to the primary nails of type A, gives grounds for thinking that this type too may belong to the early phases of the building. The examples with fairly small heads (such as nos 86 and 87) could conceivably be 'board' nails, that is, the type which, *inter alia*, may have been used for flooring;[145] those with larger heads are clearly unsuitable for this purpose, and must have been used for general carpentry.

Type C (nos 93–7): large or very large nails with square or rectangular section, square, often facetted head[146] and a tendency for the point to be slightly flattened.[147] Tapering in two planes, but often more in one than the other. Total sample: twenty-nine nails. Extant examples range in size from 105mm ($4^1/_8$") to 169mm ($6^5/_8$"). One large group of this type (ten in all) came from the roof of the west range (represented here by no. 97), others were distributed through the south range. These nails may have been used for repairs in the roof or for fixing something to the roof timbers. Their size might suggest that they were some variety of 'spike' or 'spikenail'. The group of ten nails from the west range would fall within the range for this type of nail as described by Salzman, perhaps averaging 5–6 inches (127–152mm) long, and weighing between 64 and 120g apiece.[148]

Type D (nos 98–9): small nails with a flat profile, and two-dimensional T-shaped head. Tapering to point in one plane only. Possibly a cut nail, certainly manufactured by a method approaching mass-production and therefore late in date.[149] Total sample: five nails. Several examples of this type occurred in the roof.

Type E (nos 100–2): flat nail, rectangular in section and tapering in one plane; round head; cut by shears, flanges are occasionally visible on the edges of the nails from this process. This type is invariably 50–54mm (2") in length; occasional examples are longer, up to 60mm ($2^3/_8$"). This type of cut nail is ubiquitous in the secondary roof of the building and was probably used for securing the battens of the phase 8 roof. Many examples were recovered from the rafters of the roof of the south range during the repairs; many more were recovered loose. Three examples from the total sample of forty-seven nails are illustrated here. These nails may have been associated with the few examples of cast nails (perhaps used for fixing the slates in the roof of this phase, not illustrated).

Catalogue of illustrated nails

The nails are illustrated in Figure 9.9.

Excavated nails

62. Round-headed nail; L *c* 30mm. Context 638, small find no. 506, X-ray ref CX 204. From a demolition deposit of the phase 2 building, thus late 15th- to early 16th century.

63. L *c* 36mm. Context 688, small find no. 507, X-ray ref CX 204. From an occupation layer containing material of 1620–50, possibly associated with the use of the site during the Civil War (Chapter 4); phase 6; mid-17th century.

64. L 32mm; shaft *c* 5 × 4mm. Context as no. 63, small find no. 507, X-ray ref CX 204.

65. Max L 20mm. Context 685, small find no. 505 (1/12); from the fill of the stone-lined garderobe pit of the phase 2 building, late 15th or early 16th century.

66. Max L 36mm; probable L *c* 30mm. Context as no. 65 (2/12).

67. Max L *c* 30mm; section near tip 3 × 2.5mm. Context as no. 65 (3/12).

68. L *c* 35mm. Context as no. 65 (4/12).

69. L 44mm; shaft 5 × 3mm. Context as no. 65 (5/12).

70. Surviving L 17mm; shaft 6 × 7mm; max D (head) 19mm. Context as no. 65 (6/12).

71. Surviving L 34mm; shaft *c* 7 × 8mm; max D (head) 15mm. Context as no. 65 (7/12).

72. L 63mm; shaft 5 × 4mm; max D (head) 18mm. Context as no. 65 (8/12).

73. Max L 72mm; approx D (head) 18mm. Context as no. 65 (9/12).

74. Max L 72mm; actual length *c* 67mm. Context as no. 65 (10/12).

75. Max L 100mm; shaft *c* 12 × 12mm; approx D (head) 50mm. Context 745, small find no. 516. From the fill of a pit associated with the phase 2 building (*see* Fig 4.4, 743); 14th- to 15th century?

76. L 94mm; shaft 8 × 8mm; max D (head) 23mm. Context 741, small find no. 515. From the fill of a pit of phase 5 or 6 (not illustrated); 16th or 17th century.

77. L *c* 104mm; shaft *c* 5.5 × 6.5mm; D (head) *c* 11mm. Context 1615, small find no. 1122. From the fill of the external foundation trench for the construction of the primary south wall of the south range (not illustrated); phase 3; *c* 1500.

78. Max L *c* 84mm; D (shaft) *c* 10mm; D (head) *c* 36mm. Context 1028, small find no. 1112. From the upper fill of the large Civil War period ditch (of phase 6; *see also* Fig 4.15, 1024 and Fig 4.17, section 4); phase 7 or 8, late 18th century.

Nails recovered from the standing building

Type A

79. Lath nail (1/10). L 27mm; shaft 3 × 3mm; max D (head) 8mm. Roof of south range, bays 5/6.

80. Lath nail (2/10). L 21mm; shaft 2.5 × 2.5mm; max D (head) 8mm. Roof of south range, bays 5/6.

81. Lath nail (1/17). L 24.5mm; shaft 3.5 × 3mm; max D (head) 7mm. Roof of south range, bay 8S.

82. Lath nail (2/17). L 24.5mm; shaft 2 × 3mm; max D (head) 10mm. Roof of south range, bay 8S.

83. Lath nail (3/17). L 25mm; shaft 2.5 × 2mm; max D (head) 8mm. Roof of south range, bay 8S.

84. Lath nail. L 26mm; shaft 3 × 3mm; max D (head) 10mm. Roof of south range, bay 8N.

Type B

85. Hand-made nail. L 50mm; shaft 3.5 × 4mm; max D (head) 13mm. Roof of south range, bay 5N.

86. Hand-made nail. From the valley board at the junction of the roofs of the south and west ranges, west side. L 61mm; shaft 5 × 4.5mm; max D (head) 9mm.

87. Hand-made nail. L 67mm; shaft 5.5 × 4mm; max D (head) 8mm. Roof of south range, bays 5/6.

88. Hand-made nail. L 68mm; shaft 4.5 × 5mm; max D (head) 11.5mm. Roof of south range, bay 5N.

89. Hand-made nail. L 74mm; shaft 5 × 7mm; max D (head) 24mm. South range (from partition no. 99, *see* Fig 6.22, one of four similar nails).

90. Hand-made nail. Provenance as no. 86. L 89mm; shaft 6 × 7mm; max D (head) 19mm.

91. Hand-made nail. L 91mm; shaft 5 × 5mm; max D (head) 15mm. Roof of south range, bay 5N.

92. Hand-made nail. L 104mm; shaft 6 × 7.5mm; max D (head) 18mm. Roof of west range.

Type C

93. Hand-made nail. L 105mm; shaft 6 × 7mm; max D (head) 11.5mm. Valley junction, N/W?, board nails.

94. Hand-made nail. L 133mm; shaft 9 × 7mm; max D (head) 16mm. Roof of south range, bays 5/6.

95. Hand-made nail. L 133mm; shaft 8 × 6.5mm. South range, bay 5N (1991), flue 155 (*see* Fig 6.25).

96. Hand-made nail. L 143mm; shaft 9 × 10.5mm; max D (head) 22.5mm. South range, first floor, otherwise unprovenanced.

97. Hand-made nail. L 167mm; shaft 11 × 11.5mm; max D (head) 23mm. West range.

Type D

98. ?Cut nail with T head. L 42mm; shaft 3 × 3mm. roof of south range, bay 5N, flue 155 (*see* Fig 6.25).

99. ?Cut nail, with T head; One of four examples of this type. L 40mm; shaft 3 × 2mm; max D (head) 8mm. West range, kitchen door (*see* Fig 5.27, no. 423, *see also* Fig 2.20).

Type E

100. Cut nail (1/10). L 53mm; shaft 5 × 3mm; max D (head) 7mm. West range, kitchen door (no. 423, *see* Fig 5.27).

101. Cut nail (1/17; 2" cut nails, presumably used for nailing battens to the roof in the re-roofing of phase 8). L 52mm; shaft 3.5 × 5mm; max D (head) 8mm. Roof of south range, bay 8S.

102. Cut nail. L 51mm; shaft 5 × 4mm; max D (head) 8mm. Roof of south range bays 5/6.

A fragment of architectural sculpture

103. Fragment of Beer-stone figure sculpture. The surviving detail comprises a small human figure, the head and feet missing, holding a bird (Fig 9.10). This in turn is held by the right (dexter) hand of a larger figure, represented only by a fragment of the forearm clothed in a sleeve. Broken away to the rear (clean break) and to the right-hand side;

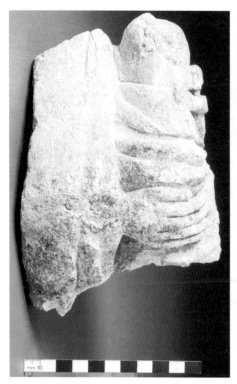  

Figure 9.10
Fragment of sculpture,
catalogue no. 103:(left)
side view (EH B960378);
(centre) *front view (EH*
B960380); (right) *side*
view (EH B960379)
(photo-graph by David
Garner).

angled breaks to upper right and lower right. Where the carved surface survives the detail is well preserved, although there are minor patches of damage to the upper torso, the upper right arm and the arrises of the draperies of the small figure, and to the fingers of the large figure. The piece displays some very fine carving, notably in the treatment of the bird. Although this is only 84mm in length the head and feathers are carved in great detail, with feathers of the wings and tail treated in a different style to those of the body (Fig 9.10, *right*). Traces of polychrome survive in crevices and folds of the draperies, most notably a patch of bright red pigment in a fold of the large figure's sleeve and some traces of gilding on both the small figure and the bird. A dowel hole (D 9mm; De 19mm) in the upper surface of the small figure suggests that the head was attached separately (or that it had been replaced). Context 1527, fill of pit 1526 (*see* Fig 4.19), of phase 8 (found with other demolition debris, brick fragments and mortar). Max H 185mm; H (small figure) 158mm; max W 99mm; max Th 123mm.

Iconography

The fragment probably formed part of a Virgin and Child group, the surviving portion representing the Child with the hand of the Virgin holding Him; the bird, a common attribute in medieval and later painting, probably represents a goldfinch. This species was very commonly included in pictures of the Virgin and Child because of the legend that the red patch on its face originated from a drop of Christ's blood which splashed onto the bird as it drew a thorn from His brow on the road to Calvary.[150] The bird thus symbolises Christ's Passion.[151] Treatments of this subject are plentiful in European painting of the 15th and 16th centuries (as many as 80 per cent of birds identifiable to species level in paintings are goldfinches, according to Friedmann).[152] The widespread incidence of the theme in Italian painting may be derived from French Gothic carvings. Carvings of the Virgin and Child with a small bird were produced in 'enormous numbers' in later 13th- and early 14th-century France.[153] The subject appears in English manuscript paintings in this period[154] and is common in late medieval English alabaster carvings: the collection of the Victoria and Albert Museum has several figures of the Virgin and Child.[155] The pose of the figures and composition in general (although not, apparently, the detail of the goldfinch) are paralleled in a figure of *c* 1470–90 from Winchester Cathedral.[156] Of the many Virgin and Child groups on roof bosses quoted by Cave, none appears to include a bird.[157]

The Bowhill piece is closely paralleled in several West Country sources. The first, conceivably a product of the same workshop (*see below*), is a carving of the Virgin and Child, holding a bird (Fig 9.11), on the west end of the canopy of the tomb of Margaret Beaufort, Countess of Devon (d after 1449), in St Andrew's Church, Colyton, Devon.[158] This is of similar size to the Bowhill fragment (*c* 200mm high, but 155mm without the head, which is remodelled in plaster) and may give a clue to its composition when complete. The second local parallel is a fragment of figure sculpture from Muchelney Abbey, Somerset, also of Beer stone, extraordinarily similar both in composition and extent of survival (Fig 9.12).[159] The accounts of its discovery, probably in the vicinity of the north choir aisle, suggest that more of the piece was present on first discovery than now survives and there is now little trace of the polychrome and gilding then described.[160] Little information is available on the context and date of the Muchelney piece, other than a vague suggestion of a 14th-century date (on the grounds of proximity to a tomb of that date);[161] it could be of almost any later medieval date. The subject also appears in 15th-century exterior sculpture on a number of east Devon church towers. Virgin and Child with bird groups appear at Clyst St Lawrence and Talaton, but at Plymtree no bird has survived, although the sculpture is heavily weathered.

Identification as a representation of the Holy Trinity is an alternative possibility, in which the hand of the large figure is a fragment of God the Father, the small figure represents God the Son and the bird the Holy Spirit (thus a dove rather than a goldfinch). Indeed the subject of the fragment from Muchelney Abbey quoted above, was originally identified as the Trinity.[162] Although this is a persuasive explanation of the fragment in some ways, it is not supported by any convincing iconographic parallels. The Trinity was often represented as a large figure of God the Father, with the figure of the Son either crucified at his feet, or as a smaller figure carrying a cross (the Holy Spirit represented by a dove above or elsewhere in the composition or sometimes omitted altogether and thus more strictly 'God the Father with the crucified Christ').[163] Late medieval alabaster carvings provide frequent examples of this.[164] There are sculptural parallels on roof bosses in the Lady Chapel at Chester and the choir at Lichfield[165] and similar treatments on monumental brasses.[166] Alternatively the

Figure 9.11
Carving of the Virgin and Child (heads restored) on the tomb of Margaret Beaufort, Countess of Devon (d after 1449), Church of St Andrew Colyton, Devon (photograph by Stuart Blaylock; author's own collection).

Figure 9.12
Fragment of figure sculpture of the Virgin and Child from Muchelney Abbey, Somerset (photograph by David Garner; EH B990727).

Trinity could be represented as three figures of uniform size and status (as in the stained glass of St Michael, Doddiscombsleigh, Devon, or on a roof boss at Norwich)[167] or with Christ as a younger (and smaller) figure as in a boss at Peterborough.[168] Exotic representations of the Trinity on roof bosses include a figural composition at St George's Chapel, Windsor[169] and a more abstract composition in the porch at St Thomas of Canterbury, Thorverton, Devon.[170] But no convincing depiction of the Trinity in which Christ is represented as a child in the arms of the Father has been located. This identification is, therefore, rejected in favour of that of the Virgin and Child, for which there are plentiful and varied precedents.

Sculptural style

The style of the piece is consistent with that of the local style of late 15th- to early 16th-century school of architectural sculpture in east and south Devon, invariably working in Beer stone. This is best represented by the two chantry chapels of the second decade of the 16th century in Exeter Cathedral, the Speke (east end of north aisle, 1518) and Oldham (east end of south aisle, c 1513–19) chapels.[171] Both chapels are heavily ornamented with sculpture, and the style of the Bowhill fragment would fit comfortably into either. Other chantries and aisles added to major parish churches in east Devon at this period include: Greenway's chapel and porch at St Peter's, Tiverton (1517); the Lane aisle at St Andrew's, Cullompton (1526–29); and the Dorset aisle at Ottery St Mary (c 1519–30).[172] Fragments of relief sculpture recovered from the chapel of St George in Exeter Guildhall (of the 1480s) are also very similar in style and execution.[173] The Kirkham chantry at Paignton (late 15th century) has been linked to the workshop that produced the Speke and Oldham Chantries,[174] while the many monumental tombs of the late 15th and early 16th centuries (such as the Beaufort tomb at Colyton mentioned above) provide other possible candidates as products of this 'workshop' in the area.

Possible purpose and location

The use of relief panels and free-standing sculptures for private devotions was well established in the late medieval period, the Virgin and Child being one of the most popular subjects for such panels.[175] If this fragment belonged to such a group it could well have been used in a private chamber of a family member at Bowhill, if not in the chapel itself. Other possible contexts might be in a niche, perhaps over a door (the porch?) or a free-standing position in a more public room. The painting by Robert Campin (1375/8–1444) of St Barbara, now in the Prado Museum, Madrid, shows an image of the Trinity in a domestic context placed above a fireplace.[176]

When complete, the piece was probably quite large: the small figure was c 200mm in height. Judging by the size of the hand of the larger figure, a full-length figure in proper proportion would have been about 500mm high, or c 350mm if a demi-figure. The similar figure at Colyton described above is 490mm high and 180mm wide. The form of the full group is most likely to have been a free-standing or high relief carving (compare Colyton again), but it could also have been a relief panel (from which the surviving portion projected). The provenance of the fragment is potentially questionable, since it could have come from another building and been brought into this site as rubble or waste material. Since there is no other indication of imported material at the site, however, the assumption that the piece derived from Bowhill would seem to be justified, not least by the other architectural fragments of high quality from equivalent archaeological deposits.

Architectural fragments

Numerous architectural fragments were recovered by excavation and by salvage from the standing building during the works. As a body of material they assist the production of a reconstruction of missing elements of the building and thereby the interpretation of the building as a whole. Thirteen fragments are illustrated (Fig 9.13). Some are presented only as a section, others (where a fuller drawing is informative) by surface views. Photographs provide additional views where necessary. A further five fragments are not illustrated, but are catalogued and described for the additional information they offer about aspects of the building. Unfortunately many of the best fragments were recovered in the early years of the conservation programme and are unprovenanced.[177]

Catalogue of architectural fragments

104. Block from a string course; Beer stone; moulded front face with carved decoration on a deep hollow order, comprising a shield (blank) and a fragment of a carving, possibly a lion's mask (note the ear in Fig 9.14) if not a leaf or a 'fleuron'. One end survives, the other is broken; the top surface has been roughly re-dressed, and the rear face limewashed, suggesting that the block was reused. Unprovenanced. L 370mm; W 265mm; Th 160–180mm.

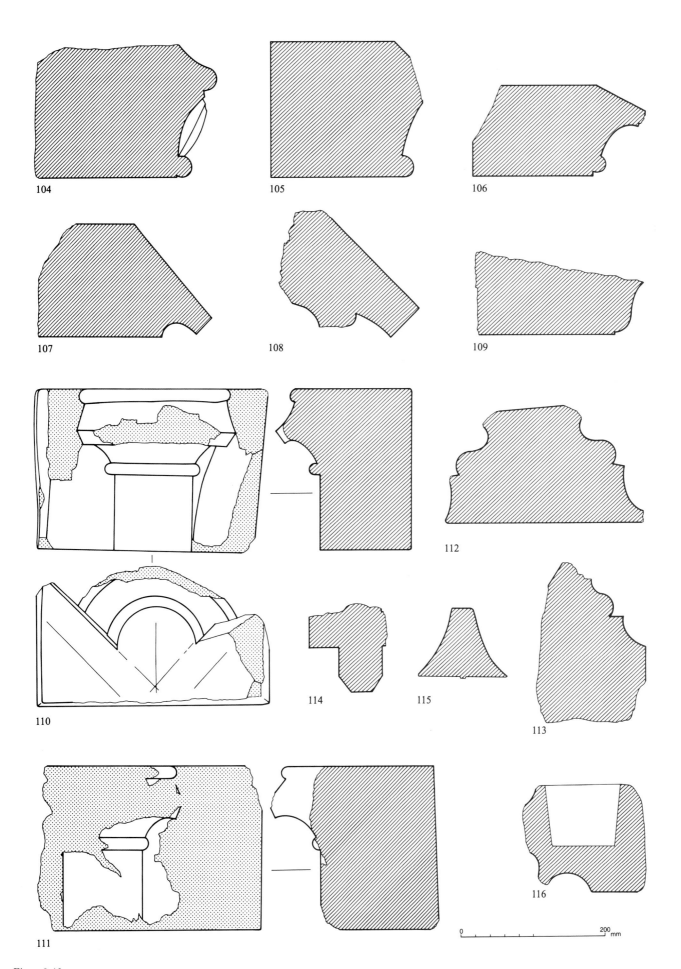

Figure 9.13
Architectural fragments, catalogue nos 104–16; scale 1:5 (line drawing by Tony Ives).

105. Block with trace of moulding, probably of the same section as 104 and thus also from a string course, but poorly preserved; Beer stone. Surfaces weathered; top surface dressed off; the block has lost the upper/outer part of the moulding; rear face limewashed, suggesting reuse. Unprovenanced. L 260mm; W 200mm; Th 180mm.

106. Fragment of Beer-stone string course or hood moulding; projecting chamfered weathering above, hollow order with bead moulding below. Unprovenanced. L 245mm (complete); W *c* 250mm (broken); Th 122mm (complete).

107. Section of string course in vesicular volcanic trap; broken at one end. Unprovenanced. L 160mm (broken); W 250mm; Th 150mm.

108. Moulded block, possibly the hood of a lancet window (as seen in the south elevation of the south range); coarse, highly vesicular purple volcanic trap; typical modern roughcast of Bowhill adhering to exterior surface in part. Unprovenanced. Max L *c* 80mm; max W 220mm; max Th 110mm.

109. Section of a fireplace lintel or reveal in two fragments; one end broken; fine, purple vesicular trap; diagonal tooling on surface. Unprovenanced. L 350mm; W 245mm; Th 85–110mm.

110. Moulded shaft section and capital (Fig 9.15); Beer stone; shaft contained within a right-angled nook or rebate, perhaps from the inner angle of a window or door reveal? Original angle of 90° widened to *c* 115° by re-cutting the right-hand face (as drawn); limewash on this face suggests that this was a structural alteration rather than reuse of the block. Setting-out lines inscribed on top and bottom surfaces (the latter illustrated in Fig 9.13). Excavated find, from context 1025, the primary fill of the phase 6 defensive ditch (1024, *see* Figs 4.15 and 4.17, section 4), thus deposited in phase 7 or 8. L 315mm; max W 180mm; H 210mm.

111. Moulded shaft section and capital (Fig 9.16); Beer stone; the same as no. 110, the upper part of a shaft from an inner angle; possibly even a pair with that block, although less well preserved. From backfill within the annexe to the south range, recovered during works in 1994, but under archaeological observation. L 300mm; W 170mm; Th 220mm.

112. Moulded rib or king mullion (Fig 9.17); Beer stone; nearly symmetrical ogee moulding; centre line inscribed on each end; cross (?mason's mark) incised on one end; two holes 50mm deep in centre of front

face; arrises of mouldings battered and worn. From the blocking of the hall fireplace (*see* Fig 6.2, 412), shown in photographs of 1969 (*see* Fig 6.11).[178] L 355mm; W 270mm; Th 150mm.

113. Fragment of a moulded block in volcanic trap; dense, red/purple trap with occasional patches of vesicular texture; moulding of a similar form to no. 112, although clearly a different feature, well cut with good tooling; this fragment has been re-dressed as a slice out of the moulding. Unprovenanced. Max L 190mm; max W 155mm; max Th 85mm.

114. Rear portion of a mullion in volcanic stone (fragment). Chamfered and rebated (for shutters), thus from a window similar in type to those of the hall (that is, of two or more lights), although in volcanic stone rather than Beer stone (*see* the section in Fig 5.30, detail 2). Possible locations for windows of this type could be the parlour east windows or from those in the west wall (or elsewhere?) of the south-east range (on the evidence of the Bucks' view). Unprovenanced. L 125mm; max W 110mm.

115. Mullion fragment in Beer stone; front element with hollow chamfers to both sides (*see* hall windows, *see* Fig 5.30, detail 2); broken at one end; rear face sawn off. Excavated find, from context 980 (fill of 979, *see* Fig 4.23), phase 12 (presumably disturbed and backfilled again at that date). L 190mm; max W 120mm; max Th 92mm.

116. Section of moulded block (Fig 9.18); Beer stone; fragmentary remains of three hollow mouldings and an edge; possibly a mullion or moulded rib if original axis is correctly interpreted, although form remains uncertain; the block was reused as a limestone trough by hollowing out the rear face. Excavated find, from context 2053, stone spread capping a pit of phase 9 (*see* Fig 4.19). L 190mm; max W 155mm; Th 150mm.

Not illustrated

117. Fragment of a plain Beer-stone block; no features. Excavated find, context 979, as no. 115, above. As a plain block, suggests ashlar Beer-stone masonry in the building (not otherwise demonstrated). L ?; W 135mm; Th 120mm.

118. Three small Beer-stone blocks; square and rectangular. Excavated finds, context 979, as no. 115, above. *a* Square and of regular thickness, all surfaces smoothly dressed, one lower edge dressed (or worn) away; a rough groove has been chiselled across the lower

face; 77 × 77mm, Th 26–27mm. *b* Long thin rectangular block, broken into two fragments; one end missing; all surfaces smoothly dressed; L 152mm (minimum, as broken); W 62mm, Th 25–26mm. *c* Roughly rectangular block, with lower surface broken away; surviving surfaces smoothly dressed; L 88mm, W 64mm; Th

Figure 9.14 (facing page, top)
Section of ornamented string course, catalogue no. 104 (photograph by David Garner; EH B960385).

Figure 9.15 (facing page, centre)
Shaft section and moulded capital, catalogue no. 110 (photograph by David Garner; EH B960383).

Figure 9.16 (facing page, below)
Shaft section and moulded capital, catalogue no. 111 (photograph by David Garner; EH B960384).

Figure 9.17
Moulded rib or king mullion, catalogue no. 112 (photograph by David Garner; EH B960381).

Figure 9.18
Moulded block, catalogue no. 116 (photograph by David Garner; EH B960382).

45mm (minimum). Blocks a and b are of similar thickness and might represent paviours from a stone pavement; the third is substantially thicker; possibly this had a different function or all three could be derived from some form of stone veneer or facing of rubble core. If the blocks can be attributed to a pavement, then they may have been used in combination with the ceramic tiles from Normandy (*see above*).

119. Large moulded Beer-stone block, probably a mullion or king mullion; the moulding – an ogee, fillet and broad hollow – is symmetrical about the axis of the block. Excavated find, from context 1025, as no. 110, above. The block is shown in position (*see* Fig 4.17, section 4). L at least 300mm; W approx 230mm; Th approx 200mm.[179] The block is of considerable interest, because of its large size and moulded form; it may represent a fragment of a large bay or oriel window, subdivided in the manner of the east window of the parlour (Chapter 5). Possible contexts are a window of the south-east range or perhaps an oriel of the boundary wall. In view of the archaeological context (which probably, though not certainly, pre-dates the demolition of the south-east range in phase 8), an origin in some part of the building already removed by the time of the Buck illustration (approximately in phase 7) is preferred.

120. Fragment of a door jamb or ?other feature; Permian breccia, coarse textured; rebate for door leaf, front (moulding or chamfer) missing. Unprovenanced. Demonstrates another door-frame of breccia somewhere in the demolished parts of the building. L 290mm; W 230mm; Th 180mm.

Roofing slates and related materials

The collection of roofing-related materials amounts to: 138 complete (or substantial fragments of) slates; 450 oak slating pegs (or 'helling pins'); 144 iron nails of various sizes and manufacture; eleven oak pegs or fragments, from the jointing of carpentry; and quantities of associated lath fragments, mortar and plaster fragments with impressions of laths and slates and various other informative traces. The largest (and most useful) single deposit of roofing materials was discovered in a cavity at first-floor level at the north end of the west gable wall (*see* Figs 6.1 and 6.25, 376). It contained debris from re-roofing, re-fenestration and other alterations to the fabric forming a deposit

some 900mm deep.[180] From the structural context it is possible to date this deposit to the major phase of alterations of *c* 1800 (phase 8). From the excavations, aside from occasional finds of odd slates such as those described below, only one significant deposit of slate was found – demolition layers of phase 9 excavated in the central courtyard contained high concentrations of slate fragments.[181] This probably represented the demolition of phase 8 buildings rather than the re-slating of the main roofs.

Fourteen roofing slates are catalogued and illustrated below, giving a representative selection of sizes, shapes and features (Figs 9.19 and 9.20). The remainder of the sample has been inspected for this general account of the slate material. Data on the collection as a whole are summarised in Table 9.3.

Geology[182]

Three types of slate are represented in the collection. Most of the material is attributable to the Gurrington Slate Formation of the Upper Devonian and to the Nordon Slate Formation of the Middle Devonian. In addition there are a few examples of material from the Kate Brook Slate Formation, again in the Upper Devonian. All three types could be derived from a relatively restricted area to the west and south of Newton Abbot and, as such, represent the most immediately local sources of roofing slate available.[183] The slate sample breaks down into three groups by provenance. Two small excavated groups of roofing slate fragments were entirely Gurrington slate,[184] the first associated with the remains of the early building of phase 2, beneath the south range (contexts 720, 769 and 775). The second came from the garderobe pit in the south elevation, filled in the mid-16th century (phase 4; contexts 2312, 2340 and 2341). Third is the large collection from the roof of the standing building, which contains all three types of slate, and may reflect a range of sources from one phase of roofing. The small excavated groups could imply that the original roof was of Gurrington slate and that the other types were introduced in one or more later phase(s) of re-roofing. Alternatively, the roof removed in phase 8 (*c* 1800), from which the bulk of the slate finds are derived, could have been itself of mixed composition or contained slates reused from an earlier roof. It could also be concluded that the excavated samples were

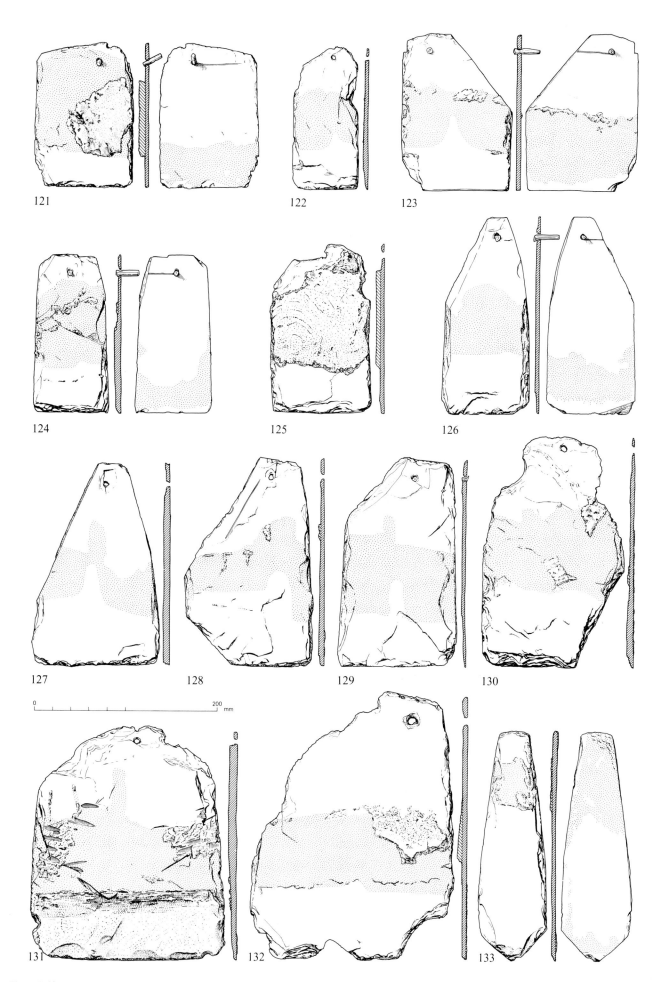

Figure 9.19
Roofing slates, catalogue nos 121–33; scale 1:4 (line drawing by Piran Bishop).

Table 9.3 Histograms showing key measurements of roofing slates

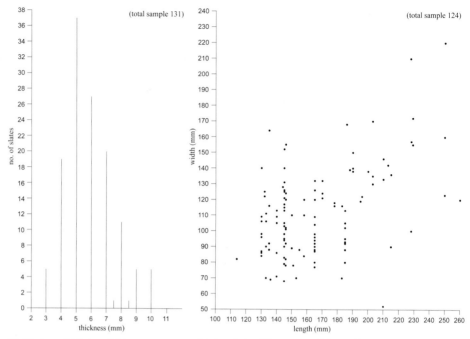

(a) Maximum thickness of slates.

(b) Length in millimetres (peg-hole to tail) plotted against width.

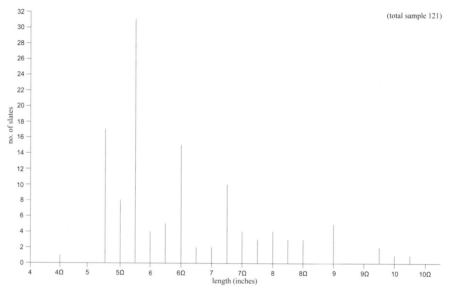

(c) Length of slates in inches, peg hole to tail; measured to nearest …".

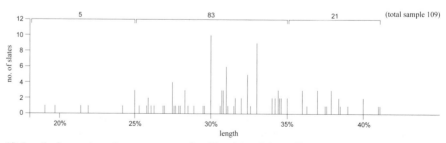

(d) Length of exposed margin as a percentage of total length (peg hole to tail).

too small to represent the composition of the roofs adequately, and that the data are misleading.

Dimensions[185]

Length is reckoned from the tail to the peg hole throughout, since this represents the effective length of the slate (when hung over the lath) and was established ancient practice.[186] Scribing lines on the lower surface of the slates (the bed) frequently mark the position of the peg holes. Slates in the sample range from 132 to 260mm in length. The measurements resolve into quarter-inch increments when converted to imperial (5¼"–10¼", 5¾" being the most common: Table 9.3b and c), indicating that the slates were laid in diminishing courses.[187] Small sizes predominate, and there are few larger slates,[188] perhaps because the deposit derived from the upper half of the roof, where the smaller-sized slates would occur (see also the pegs, below).[189] In width the slates range from 68–210mm (2¾–8¼"), the majority 70–150mm, and in thickness from 3–10mm.[190]

Shapes

Most slates are square ended, although there are occasional round-headed slates. One side is invariably smoother than the other, reflecting the limited capacity for even cleavage of the material. The smooth side, naturally, is always used as the bed. The slates are finished by retouching along their exposed edges, but often remain unshaped where they were not to be exposed to view. The most distinctive feature of shaping is to cut off a lower corner to fit a valley or possibly for use on the verge.[191] Left and right corners are treated in this way.[192] Peg holes are always close to the apex of the slate, but are often placed off-centre or even on one edge. The position of the peg hole was dictated not only by the shape of the slate, but also by the relationship of the slate to those above, where the aim was (presumably) to avoid a direct coincidence between the peg and the junction of the two overlying slates.[193] This was achieved by offsetting the join to one side if the peg hole was on the central axis of the slate. Irregularly shaped heads aid this by allowing a peg hole to be placed still further off-centre (for example no. 123). The lack of standardisation also demonstrates that holes were punched on site at the time of laying, rather than at the quarry, or prior to use.

Mortar bedding

Both surfaces frequently retain traces of mortar. Its extent is often indicated by staining where physical traces have not survived. Mortar bedding generally shows a straight lower edge on the face of the slate, but the upper limit is much less regular. The traces suggest that mortar was removed from the lower edge with a trowel to form a neat finish, but was prone to oozing upwards between the slates. The stain of the mortar bedding occasionally shows the position of the join between two overlying slates (nos 122–3 and 127–9). The mortar was sometimes applied more generously on the line of the joint in the overlying course,[194] perhaps in an effort to protect that joint (nos 127–9 and 131). On the lower surfaces (the bed) the traces of mortar were much less regular.[195] A fairly consistent feature of the lower surface is a clean (that is, free of mortar) lower edge or margin, some 5–10mm in breadth. This could show that the slates overlay the mortar bed by that amount, but more probably represents weathering under the tail of the slate, where the mortar bedding had been washed away. Some well-preserved examples (nos 121, 125 and 127) show moss or lichen growing on the edge of the mortar bed, demonstrating a limit to the extent of such weathering.

Deduction of size of exposed margin and calculation of overlap

The lower edge of the mortar bed, or the mortar staining, has been taken to indicate the length of the exposed margin of the slate. Expressing this measurement as a percentage of the length of the slate (in a sample of 109 measurable examples), the majority (83 examples/76 per cent) of slates have an exposed margin of 25–35 per cent of their length; in 21 examples the length of the margin is greater than 35 per cent of the

Figure 9.20
Selected roofing slates: (left to right) catalogue nos 131, 134, 127 and 128 (photograph by David Garner; EH B960387).

length (up to 41 per cent) and in only 5 examples is it less than 25 per cent (*see* Table 9.3d). The degree of overlap or the thickness of the slating at any given point, can thus be estimated: where the exposed margin represents 25 per cent of the full length of the slate, the roof will be at least four slates thick at any given point; where the percentage is 33 per cent the roof will be at least three slates in thickness.[196] The percentages (calculated on the basis stated above for measuring the margin) range from extremes of 19 per cent to 41 per cent,[197] but the great majority of measurements suggest an average thickness of between three and four slates (*see* Table 9.3d), concurring with evidence observed elsewhere.[198]

Torching and plastering

Many mortar fragments were recovered and examined from areas associated with the roof. Most were fragments of bedding. As there was little evidence for torching of roofs (the 'plastering' of the soffit of the slates), the evidence in the fabric in two of the three rooms of the south range (*see above*) is best interpreted as indicating plastered ceiling finishes in specific rooms, rather than as torching as a routine roofing technique. Comparative evidence suggests that torching was rarely used in combination with bedding, because of the risks of leakage through capillary action if the inner and outer mortar should come into contact with each other by accident.[199] The mortar mixes were all in the spectrum of white lime mortar with gritty inclusions characteristic of the primary building (Chapter 10, class 1).

Pointing and other repairs after construction

Traces of mortar on the exposed margins of eleven slates represent pointing or slurrying with mortar to improve water resistance when the roof had developed leaks.[200] The pointing is sometimes combined with weathering on the margin (for example, no. 131, Fig 9.19), showing that it took place long after the original construction.[201] Most of the examples of pointing show white lime mortars of primary character, but two show a dark greyish mixture containing fragments of charcoal as well as lime and sand (*see* Fig 9.20, no. 134).[202] These slates represent a later repair using a type of mortar containing charcoal, used in late (19th-century) contexts in the building (Chapter 10, class 10c).

Laths

Laths were not well represented in the collection of materials recovered from the building; but key examples were observed *in situ* in the junction of the roofs of the west and south ranges (*see* Chapter 7 and Fig 7.43). These laths were set close together, on average 20–30mm apart. The laths ran beneath the timbers associated with the abutment of the roof of the west range and may have continued across the general pitch of the roof in the same, closely spaced, fashion.[203] The failure of many laths to survive loose in the collection of roofing materials reflects the method of removal on re-roofing.[204] Fragments of original laths recorded in the roof were unusually broad in comparison with later laths in other contexts in the building, ranging between 35 and 50mm.[205] All were (by definition) riven; and all were of oak.[206] Lath nails are described above.

Catalogue of roofing slates

Most of the selected examples (*see* Fig 9.19, nos 121–29, 133 and Fig 9.20, no. 134) are from the demolition deposit associated with the removal of the west gable wall (context 376); no. 132 was from the eaves of the south range, bay 9 (south); and nos 130 and 131 are unprovenanced. The length from tail to peg hole and the length of the margin (the exposed portion of the slate) are given in inches (to the nearest quarter of an inch), as well as mm, in view of the evidence that the slates were originally graduated in this way. Archive catalogue numbers relate to the list of the full collection in the site archive.

121. Slate with bedding mortar on face (with mortar stain extending over the peg), and mortar stain on the bed (W 42mm). Peg in position (L 21mm); scribing line for peg hole on bed. L (tail to peg hole) 129mm (5"); L of margin (exposed portion of the slate, from the tail to the lower limit of the mortar bedding) 38mm (1½"). Overall dimensions: L 147mm; W 107mm; Th 4mm. Archive catalogue 103.

122. Small slate with mortar stain in a lateral band on face; bed clean. Trace of scribing line for peg hole on bed. L (tail to peg hole) 140mm (5½"); L (margin) 33mm (?1¼"). Overall dimensions: L 149mm; W 71mm; Th 4mm. Archive catalogue 64.

123. Slate with a clear mortar stain on face, the lower edge showing a joint in the overlying course. Clear mortar stain on bed, with

clean bottom edge (from the weathering out of mortar). Peg surviving in position (L 29mm); scribing line for peg hole on bed. L (tail to peg hole) 146mm (5¾"); L (margin) 40–45mm (1½–1¾"). Overall dimensions: L 167mm; W 120mm; Th 4mm. Archive catalogue 33.

124. Narrow slate with mortar stain on face; thin band of mortar staining on bed, rising against the sides of the slate. Clean bottom edge (weathering). Peg surviving in position (L 27mm); scribing line for peg hole on bed. L (tail to peg hole) 146mm (5¾"); L (margin) c 44mm (1¾"), although indistinct. Overall dimensions: L 166mm; W 82mm; Th 3–7mm. Archive catalogue 44.

125. Slate with intact bedding mortar on face (up to the peg hole, thus possibly from a ridge, since ordinary slates display a discrete band of mortar stopping well short of the peg hole); uniform thickness of 6–8mm. Lichen growth on the lower edge of the mortar bed. Diffuse mortar stain on bed. Broken peg hole; no scribing line. L (tail to peg hole) 164mm (6½"); L (margin) c 45mm (1¾"). Overall dimensions: L 178mm; W 108mm; Th 4mm. Archive catalogue 95.

126. Tall slate tapering to a narrow head. Clear mortar staining on both surfaces (notably thin and with a clean weathered margin on the bed). Peg in position (L 28mm); scribing line for peg hole on bed. L (tail to peg hole) 184mm (7¼"); L (margin) c 60mm (2¼–2½"). Overall dimensions: L 208mm; W 97mm; Th 4mm. Archive catalogue 49.

127. Slate tapering to a narrow head. Clear mortar staining on face, showing a joint (see above, no. 123). Lichen growth on margin. Diffuse mortar traces on bed, with clear (weathered) margin. Scribing line for peg hole on bed. L (tail to peg hole) 188mm (<7½"); L (margin) 50–70mm (2¼–2¾"). Overall dimensions: L 214mm; W 138mm; Th 6–7mm. Archive catalogue 107.

128. Slate with the lower left corner cut away for a verge or valley; the upper left corner also cut off (scribing mark parallel to the edge). Clear mortar stain on face; traces of mortar on margin show repointing or slurrying of the slate. Faint scribing line for peg hole on bed. L (tail to peg hole) 201mm (?8"); L (margin) approx 46–55mm (1¾–2¼"). Overall dimensions: L 220mm; W 140mm; Th 6–7mm. Archive catalogue 17.

129. Rectangular slate with upper left corner cut off. Clear mortar stain on face, including the position of a joint. Clear trace of a thin band of mortar on the bed, rising higher on the right edge of the slate than on the left;

clean weathered margin. Fragment of peg in position (L 6mm); scribing line for the peg hole on bed (unusually this is to the *left* of the peg hole; nearly all other examples are to the right of the hole). L (tail to peg hole) 199mm (7¾"?); L (margin) 45–55mm (1¾–2¼"). Overall dimensions: L 222mm; W 130mm; Th 5mm. Archive catalogue 2.

130. Slate with the lower right corner cut away for a verge or valley, shaped head. Broad mortar stain on face, with traces of mortar *in situ*; extensive traces of mortar on lower surface, with a narrow weathered margin on the lower edge. No scribing line. L (tail to peg hole) 229mm (9"); L (margin) 81mm (3¼"). Overall dimensions: L 245; W 156; Th 7mm. Archive catalogue 122.

131. Large slate with traces of reuse: two peg holes (one fragmentary on the top edge, the second in the conventional position) and chisel marks from the removal of primary mortar. The bedding mortar on the face is in two layers (although of uniform composition); a third layer of mortar on the margin represents repointing or slurrying of the roof. The bed retains mortar staining on its lower edge without a weathered margin. Scribing line for secondary (lower) peg hole. L (tail to peg hole) 241mm (9¼"), primary; 231mm (9⅛"), secondary. Overall dimensions: L 247mm; W 210mm; Th 10mm. Archive catalogue 138.

132. Large slate, with the peg hole towards the right side. Broad band of bedding mortar/staining on face; mortar *in situ* tapering in thickness (*see* section drawing). Regular band of mortar stain on the bed, no weathered margin. Faint scribing line for the peg hole. L (tail to peg hole) 255mm (10"); L (margin) 77mm (3"). Overall dimensions: L 285mm; W 220mm; Th 4mm. Archive catalogue 127.

133. Long narrow slate, carefully shaped and without a peg hole, thus probably for wall hanging. Pointed tail, square head, gently tapering form. Unconventional pattern of mortar staining: traces on both faces at the head; slight traces at the tail on the bed. Presumably set in mortar without pegging or nailing. L 245; max W 77mm; W at head 34mm; Th 4mm. Archive catalogue 56.

134. Slate not drawn here, illustrated in Fig 9.20, with traces of secondary mortar bedding or pointing in a distinctive grey mortar (containing charcoal fragments). Peg survives in position (L 23mm), no scribing line. Traces of mortar on bed. L (tail to peg hole) 147mm (5¾"); L (margin) 55mm (2⅛"). Overall dimensions: 166mm; W 127mm; Th 5–6mm. Archive catalogue 93.

Slating pegs

Approximately 450 oak slating pegs (sometimes called slating pins or helling pins)[207] were recovered from the standing building, of which 423 were complete (391 loose pegs and thirty-two slates with pegs *in situ*). As far as can be seen, without individual identification of each peg, all are of oak. The pegs are generally tapering in profile and square or polygonal in section (an angular section aids the gripping of the slate). Both ends are generally cut; some of the thicker examples were cut around the circumference and then snapped apart. The pegs frequently show a nick in the profile caused by the compression of the wood fibres at the narrowest point of the hole (Fig 9.19, nos 123–4). The pegs have not been drawn, but one group is illustrated in a photograph (Fig 9.21). The sizes of pegs are presented in Table 9.4. Lengths range from 16mm to 80mm, with 96 per cent between 20 and 70mm in length. Measurement in millimetres shows an even distribution through the range rather than fixed increments in imperial measurements. Pegs were grouped into three categories: small (20–35mm: 45 per cent), medium (35–50mm: 24 per cent) and large (50–70mm: 31 per cent).[208] Most of the pegs fall within the range of 5–10mm in overall maximum diameter, although individual examples frequently exceed this limit.

Nearly all the pegs were recovered from the controlled clearance of cavities in the roof during the dismantling of timbers for repair, the majority from wall-top beam filling (since this area of the roof provided many cavities in which waste material could lodge). It is clear that the roofing materials (including nails, slates, mortar fragments, laths and other waste materials in addition to pegs) were deposited during a phase of stripping and re-covering of the roof, most probably in the reorganisation of phase 8 (Chapter 7). Several general observations have been made from this material:[209]

1. When the smaller sub-sample of pegs *in situ* in slates is compared to the loose collection, it is clear that these fall into the small category as defined here (18–33mm), although this includes some of the largest slates to have been recovered.[210] This, again, suggests that the slates deposited in context 376 probably came from the upper part of the roof.
2. A group of forty-four pegs from the fill of slot 120 on the south side of bay 6 (*see* Fig 6.22) were distinctively longer than average, ranging from 47 to 80mm. This may reflect an origin in slates of the lower part of the roof and suggests that this context was filled as the stripping of the slates moved towards the eaves.
3. The collection from the wall top on the south side of bay 9 (above the oriel window, *see* Fig 6.22) contained the largest single group of pegs: 146 from general contexts in this bay, and a further twenty once the wall plate was removed. The removal of the oriel window and the patching up of the resultant scars in new brickwork (*see* Fig 5.8, 50) is one of the key events of phase 8 in this part of the building. Such quantities of surviving roofing materials on top of fabric of phase 8 suggests that the re-roofing took place at a late stage in the refurbishment.
4. The good condition of many of the pegs in this sample, notwithstanding their age, suggests that the failure of pegs cannot have been a key factor in the decay of the original slate roof.[211] The function of the peg in securing the slate over the lath was partly temporary anyway since, in a roof that was bedded in mortar, the slates would acquire a rigidity and solidity as a mass once the mortar had gone off. Once this had happened the need for securing individual slates over laths was diminished.

Other wooden artefacts

Two further categories of wooden peg were found, large oak carpentry pegs and small barbed pegs of obscure purpose. Nearly all were recovered in the course of the examination of bays 5–11 of the roof of the south range, with a few additional finds elsewhere in the south and west ranges.[212]

Carpenters' pegs

The collection of miscellaneous building materials from the site includes twenty-three whole or fragmentary pegs of the type used to

Figure 9.21
A selection of slating pegs recovered from the roof of the south range (photograph by David Garner; EH B960386).

Table 9.4 Histogram showing measurements of slating pegs

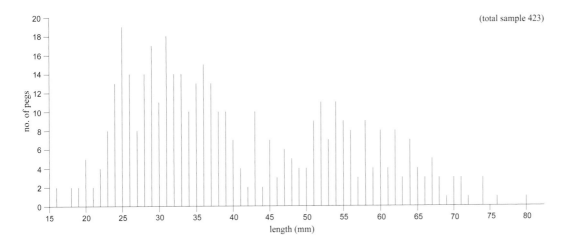

(total sample 423)

secure joints in carpentry.[213] Many more such pegs were observed in the course of repairs.[214] Sixteen of the twenty-three were complete ranging from 80–280mm in length, although most pegs from contexts in the roof were 95–120mm long. The average maximum thickness was 20–22mm. Most pegs were slightly tapered and those with pointed tips (below) showed a more pronounced taper (from 7–24mm). Few pegs are worthy of attention individually as finds, but the collection does allow important points about the pegs to be demonstrated.

Two distinct types of peg are represented:

1. A short peg of uniform diameter. The ends of pegs of this type are cut straight across, or slightly slanted and were presumably trimmed off flush with the face of the timbers after assembly. The length of the peg is thus more or less the same as the thickness of the timber.
2. The second type consists of pegs with long tapering profiles, which appear to have been left projecting from both sides of the assembled joint (*see below*). One complete specimen of this type is 280mm long. Several pegs in the collection, although broken, represent examples of the protruding ends of such pegs. The extent of protrusion is often shown by discolouration by limewash or staining (depending on the context).

Both types of peg are facetted in section. Some have a circular or sub-circular section that is roughly chamfered; others are more regularly octagonal or heptagonal. No peg is fully circular. The uniform angular sections demonstrate an important aspect of the function of pegs – one of grip. As pegs are hammered into joints they provide secure fixing by friction between the angular section of the peg and the edges of the drilled holes in mortice and tenon (circular-sectioned pegs function as dowels by simply retaining the tenon in the mortice). While this function is demonstrated in all the pegs in the collection, whether tapering or cylindrical in section, the former type would, by its form, provide a still tighter joint. The second type could have functioned as draw-bore pegs, in which the holes in the timbers to be joined are deliberately misaligned, thereby providing a tighter joint when the pointed peg is hammered home.[215]

Protruding pegs survived particularly in the upper stages of the western half of the roofs of the south and west ranges, especially in timbers such as the collars, where the pegs would have been fully visible (*see* Fig 7.1, showing protruding pointed ends of pegs in trusses X and XI of the roof of the south range and Fig 7.39, showing the same from the assembly side (face) in truss II of the roof of the west range). Photographs of the roofs of the hall and great chamber before the timbers were dismantled show that the pegs were cut off neatly flush with the faces of the timber throughout the more ornamented parts of the building (*see* Figs 7.10 and 7.11). There can be little doubt that where the technique was used it was deliberate and decorative in intent. It is probably correct to see this as a decorative effect used only in the plainer parts of the roof. Protruding pegs are frequently seen as a feature of some timber framing constructions, where they are too prominent and ubiquitous not to have been intended for decoration.[216]

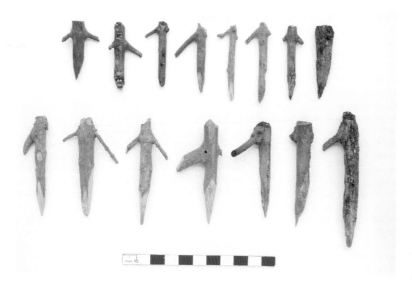

Figure 9.22
Spurred pegs of unknown
purpose, but possibly for use
in vermin traps (photo-
graph by David Garner;
EH B960390).

Spurred pegs

Thirty-nine spurred (or barbed) pegs were found in three caches at the west end of the building: twenty from the deposit of building materials in the stump of the west gable wall (376) which also yielded slates, lead cames and window glass (*see above*); seven from a deposit in the eaves at the north-west corner of bay 11; and twelve from packing around the west end of the inserted floor beam of the west range (*see* Fig 6.45, 243). All three contexts are associated with phase 8 alterations.

The pegs vary in dimensions and in appearance (illustrated by the fifteen complete examples from context 376; Fig 9.22); most appear to be of elder (*Sambucus nigra*). A feature common to all is that twigs with one or two side shoots were selected which, when cut, provided the barb(s).[217] Typically the upper ends of the pegs are cut either in one stroke or cut around the circumference and snapped. The lower ends are sharpened to a point. Most were made from the full diameter of the twig. Some were split from thicker twigs, but this type has only one barb. The pegs range in length from 15–93mm[218] and from 4–14mm in thickness; some of the longer pegs are still very slender.

When these pegs were first found it was assumed that they had some structural purpose. The lack of a clear function, however, and the absence of any parallels led to a review of other possible functions. It has been concluded that the most probable function is that the pegs served to secure wire snares for vermin. The finds of pegs in

groups might represent caches deriving from their manufacture rather than their use. Boyle observes that slating pegs were made by boys in their spare time; perhaps this job, too, was the preserve of boys.[219]

Loose timbers

Loose timbers in considerable numbers were collected as a result of the conservation work at Bowhill. Some salvaged from earlier demolition work were already on the site,[220] but the bulk of the material accumulated during the repairs, by the removal of timber from the building that (for one reason or another) was not subsequently replaced. A good deal of late softwood was removed and discarded during the work, but all hard-wood timber was retained. There were various reasons why timbers were removed and not replaced. Replacement with reconstructed timber took place frequently in the earlier years of the programme.[221] Removal of ancient features that were out of position was another factor (for instance the partitions of the inner chamber on the first floor of the south range, which were removed and not replaced, Chapter 6). Timbers judged to be structurally unsound were also removed from the building and added to the collection. One common situation was that a timber would be repaired, by scarfing in new pieces of oak and then be condemned on structural grounds. Thus the collection contains a number of whole timbers with scarfed repairs, which provide useful examples of repair techniques. Remnants of timber imported to the site for reuse form another class in this category of material.[222]

A selection of the most important timbers is described and illustrated here; more have been referred to in the main text above (for example in the discussion of the development of the parlour ceiling). All the loose timbers were listed in an archive catalogue totalling 228 items (some containing more than one timber), now deposited in the site archive.[223] The collection was weeded using the following criteria: all primary timbers and all timbers with features (mouldings, traces of joints and so on) were kept, as were representative examples of some later carpentry (softwood shutters, doors and so forth); any remaining softwood, featureless oak (decayed fragments and complete timbers) and a number of groups of plain oak studs from the filling of partitions were discarded, reducing the collection to 141 items.

Window 409, catalogue no.135

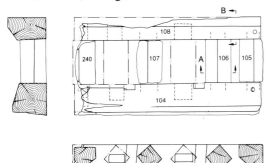

A

B

Loose window, catalogue no.136

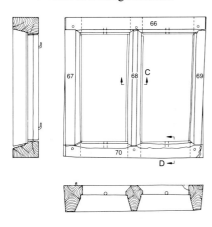

C

D

Loose window, catalogue no.137

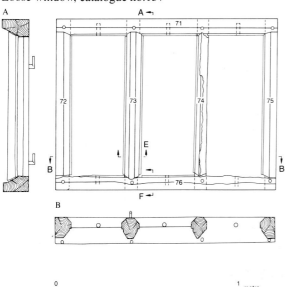

E

F

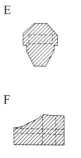

0   200
                      mm

0   1 metre

Figure 9.23
Loose timber windows,
catalogue nos 135-7; scale
1:20 (line drawing by Tony
Ives).

Catalogue of illustrated timbers

135. Five-light window with close-spaced, diagonally set mullions (Figs 9.23 and 9.24), from the north wall of the storeroom to the north of the hall (*see* Fig 6.1, embrasure 409). Squat form and massive scantling; two mullions were missing, but otherwise the window was complete, although decayed. The window was discovered and removed during works in 1985 and an entirely new copy was subsequently replaced in the embrasure. For discussion of the form of and parallels for this window, *see* Chapter 8. Archive catalogue nos 104–8.

136. Two-light window, with plain chamfered lights, rebated for glazing and with sockets for iron glazing bars (*see* Fig 9.23). Provenance unknown, but probably salvaged from the barn on its demolition in 1972 and retained loose in the building. A photograph in the NMR of the barn from the west in 1969 (*see* Fig 2.14) shows a two-light timber window that may be this frame. This window is of the same type as a fragmentary window surviving *in situ* in the west wall of the west range (*see* Fig 6.45, 238, and detail in Fig 6.53). Probably not an original window form, but representing re-fenestration sometime in the 16th century. For full discussion of the form of and parallels for these windows, *see* Chapter 8. Archive catalogue nos 66–70.

137. Three-light window with plain chamfered lights (*see* Fig 9.23), very similar in form to no. 136. An NMR photograph of the east elevation of the barn in 1969 (*see* Fig 2.75) shows this window frame *in situ* (and supports the suggested provenance for no. 136). Archive catalogue nos 71–6.

138. Frame of a screen, comprising sill and headbeams, two posts forming a doorway plus a door head (Fig 9.25) and a third post forming the far end of the partition (not illustrated). The doorway was ornamented with a double chamfer (that is, a broad chamfer interrupted by a fillet) and diagonal-cut stops (*see* those of doorways in the great chamber, Fig 6.28, no. 99, and parlour, Fig 8.29, no. 6). The screen stood beneath truss VI in the inner chamber when the building was stripped in 1978 (visible in photographs of 1969 and 1978; *see* Figs 2.28, 6.61 and 6.62) and had previously been sited beneath truss VII (Chapter 6). It was dismantled in the 1980s and never reinstated. The similarity of the decoration to other primary carpentry, the technique of infill whereby studs were fitted into mortices at one end and sprung into a groove at the other (paralleled throughout the primary phase), together with the massive scantling of the timbers, suggest that the screen belongs to the primary phase of the building or the immediately following phase in the early or mid-16th century. Archive catalogue nos 26 (headbeam), 28 (sill beam), 45 (N post) and 77–9 (door jambs and head).

139. Frame of a screen, comprising a door-frame fitted into a headbeam above. The door is ornamented with an ovolo moulding and scroll stops (*see* Fig 9.25). Probably on an east–west alignment in the inner chamber in the 1950s and 60s, although there is no photographic evidence for this. A tenon at the end of the headbeam is at the same height as a mortice in the southernmost post of screen 138 and may have fitted into it (as suggested in the discussion of the inner chamber partitions in Chapter 6). The ovolo moulding, stop, smaller scantling and similarity to other later 16th- or 17th-century carpentry (for instance the doorway in the 17th-century screen 108, forming the west wall of the great chamber, *see* Fig 6.15) all suggest a 17th-century date for this screen. Archive catalogue nos 37–9 (door-frame) and 40 (headbeam).

140. Doorframe, plain chamfered surround, scroll stops (*see* Fig 9.25). From the eastern of two later doorways that gave access through the north wall of the great chamber into the hall at first-floor level (*see* Fig 6.25, 113). Since the flooring of the hall was very late, it is presumed that this frame was reused in this position. Removed in 1987 and not replaced. Archive catalogue nos 119–21.

141. A timber plank with a pierced quatrefoil opening was recorded during the RCHME photographic survey in 1969 (Fig 9.26). This small feature is something of a puzzle. It presumably represents a window, but its provenance is unknown, nothing similar survives in the building and the fragment

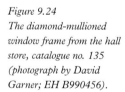

Figure 9.24
The diamond-mullioned window frame from the hall store, catalogue no. 135 (photograph by David Garner; EH B990456).

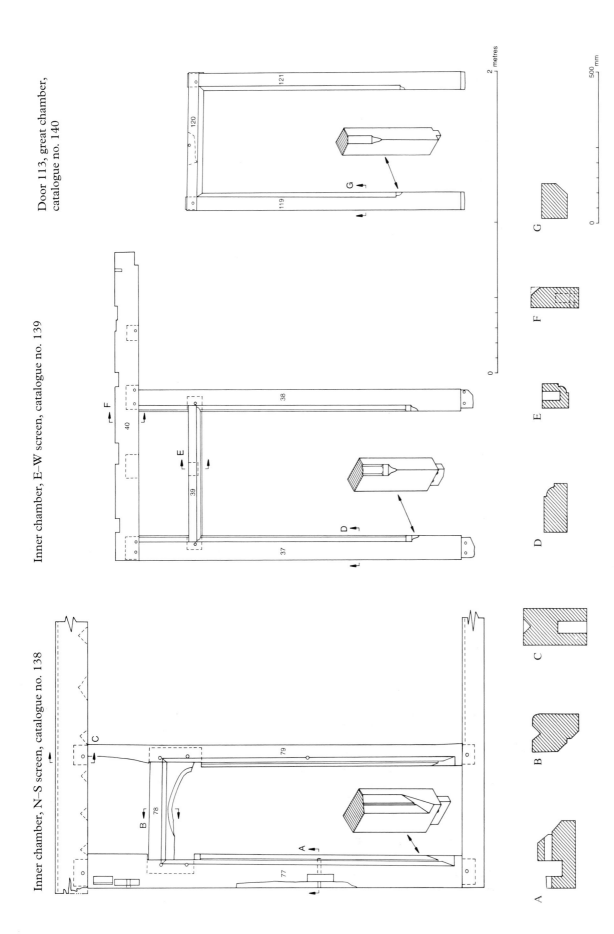

Inner chamber, N–S screen, catalogue no. 138

Inner chamber, E–W screen, catalogue no. 139

Door 113, great chamber, catalogue no. 140

Figure 9.25
Loose timber screens and a doorframe, catalogue nos 138–40; scale 1:25 (line drawing by Tony Ives).

Figure 9.26
Catalogue no. 141, loose timber with pierced quatrefoil ?window photographed at Bowhill by the RCHME in 1969 and subsequently lost (RCHME BB69/5033).

The chapel provides a possible context, especially if it was in the room over the porch (Chapter 8). Another possible context might be the partition between the great chamber and the hall. A squint is provided in this position at Higher Harestone, Brixton.[224] Otherwise, one of the few parallels for the object is from Badlake, West Anstey, where a small, single-light lancet window was constructed by piercing through a block of oak and used to light the porch.[225]

142. A fragment of plank with painted decoration in red, black and white (Fig 9.27), comprising an area of red colour surrounded by a circular line in black and a

Figure 9.27
Catalogue no. 142, architectural fragment of timber (line drawing by Tony Ives)

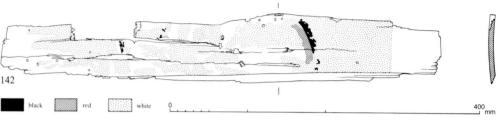

142

| ▇ black | ▨ red | ▢ white | 0   400 mm |

Figure 9.28
Catalogue no. 143, metal casement with foliate catch plate photographed at Bowhill by the RCHME in 1969 and subsequently lost (RCHME BB69/5021).

white ground beyond. The white paint stops in a straight edge some 65mm from the end of the plank, implying that this section was obscured when the piece was painted. L 566mm; W 87mm; Th 3–8mm. The piece was found reused as packing material above softwood panels of the parlour ceiling between beams 4 and 5, that is, in the extended western bay of the ceiling.[226] Although much thinner than the rest of the boards, this may represent a fragment of the original decoration of the parlour ceiling, superseded by the later softwood panelling (Chapter 6). The one surviving edge is chamfered where it fitted into a groove on the adjacent plank, a 'tongue and groove' arrangement similar to the planks of the later ceiling (*see* Fig 6.29 and Fig 10.4).

Metal window casement

143. A metal window casement with an ornate foliate catch plate was also recorded in the building by the RCHME photographic survey of 1969 (as with the timber quatrefoil window above, no. 141), with the implication that it came from the building (Fig 9.28). The object has been lost since 1969. Dimensions: approximately 420 × 925mm (based on the matchbox scale in the photograph). The frame is of a type common in buildings in Devon from the 17th to the 19th century.[227] The wrought iron frame, catch and metal glazing bars all suggest that this might be a fairly late example.

itself is lost. Measurement from the photograph suggests that the timber was *c* 610 × 645mm, and that the circle in which the quatrefoil was set was *c* 255mm in diameter. The piece could have been an exterior window; possibly connected somehow to the quatrefoil windows shown by the Buck brothers in their view of the building (*see* Fig 2.1 and Chapter 2). Equally it could have been a squint somewhere inside the building.

10
Dendrochronology and mortar analysis

Dendrochronological analysis of timbers from Bowhill

by Cathy Groves[1]

Summary

Dendrochronological analysis was carried out on various *in situ* and *ex situ* timbers at Bowhill, in a series of discrete phases over a period of 20 years. This coincides with a major period of development in the application of dendrochronology to standing buildings and serves to emphasise the value of the current approach, particularly the sampling methods and strategies now employed.

The results from the structural timbers are somewhat disappointing as only six samples have been dated against reference data from southern and western England to produce a tree-ring chronology spanning the period AD 1292–1468. The use of these dates in understanding the building is problematic as none of the six timbers can be irrefutably provenanced within the building, and it is (sadly) possible that they are from an entirely different building and thus have no association with Bowhill. This clearly highlights the importance of ensuring that detailed records are made as timbers are removed and that some form of permanent labelling is used. The results from this assemblage of structural timbers also emphasise the problems of obtaining dates for locally derived timbers in standing medieval and post-medieval buildings in the county of Devon.

Fifty-four boards and six sub-ribs from the ceiling of the parlour matched and dated to produce a tree-ring chronology spanning the period AD 1161–1483. These were all probably felled and initially used in the late 15th or very early 16th century. The oak boards and sub-ribs were derived from timbers imported from the Baltic region. They are not only the largest single-phase Baltic assemblage analysed from an archaeological or historic building context, but are also the furthest point west in England that a group of dendrochronologically proven Baltic origin timbers have been found.

Introduction

This section is based on a technical archive report on the dendrochronological analysis of timbers from Bowhill prepared for the English Heritage Centre for Archaeology.[2]

Aims and analysis

Dendrochronological analysis was originally requested by the Department of the Environment in 1979 in order to provide precise independent dating evidence for as many of the building phases as possible, to help place the development of the structure into a local and national context and to assist repair decisions. During the repair works undertaken in the 1980s and early 1990s, many timbers were removed but remained in storage at Bowhill. Between 1993 and 1995 these were catalogued, recorded and provenanced within the building where possible, though this was hampered by the lack of detailed records from the early 1980s and the introduction of historic timbers foreign to the site for use in the repair works.[3] This timber catalogue will remain in the archive. By the end of 1995 three small batches of samples, including some duplicates, had been analysed at Sheffield with somewhat limited success:

1. In 1980 three samples and three photographs of timbers were analysed but not dated.[4]
2. In 1990 three timbers were measured *in situ*, one loose timber measured on site and three slices provided from the collection of loose timbers in storage at the site. Four of these were dated.[5]
3. In 1995 fourteen slices from the collection of loose timbers in storage at the site were analysed but only two were dated.[6]

In 1996 Francis Kelly, English Heritage Inspector, South-West Regional Team, and Stuart Blaylock, Exeter Archaeology Unit, requested that all the remaining loose timbers stored at Bowhill be assessed by a dendrochronologist prior to their removal to an English Heritage store in Gloucestershire. The author, then involved in the pilot stage of a research project, funded by English Heritage, that was attempting to understand and resolve the problems of undertaking dendrochronological dating in Devon,[7] took over the dendrochronological analysis at this site. This assessment was carried out in September 1996 by the author and Stuart Blaylock in order to identify any timbers that had retained sufficient numbers of rings for dendrochronological dating purposes. The usual minimum requirement applied to a group of single phase timbers is fifty annual growth rings. A handful of borderline timbers (that is, containing forty–fifty rings) were found but further analysis was not recommended. It was not felt that these few samples could significantly aid the interpretation of the building as they potentially represented various building phases. In addition, the lack of success with longer ring sequences indicated it was unlikely that tree-ring dates would be successfully obtained. A large group of boards from the ceiling of the parlour were, however, identified. These clearly contained sufficient numbers of rings for analysis. They were also considered potentially useful to the interpretation of the building as, although they were thought to be a later 16th-century insertion, they could have included boards reused from the primary ceiling. These boards and one additional structural sample were delivered to Sheffield in 1997. Following further discussions, it was agreed that the previously analysed timbers should be reviewed as more local reference data had become available since their original analysis.[8] Finally, in August 1999 a detailed dendrochronological assessment was carried out in order to identify any further potential in the remaining *in situ* structural timbers. This report is, therefore, concerned with the analysis of the ceiling boards, sub-ribs, the newly obtained samples from structural elements, the reworking of the previously analysed structural elements and the 1996 and 1999 assessments.

Methodology

The methodology presented in this report is that in current use at the Sheffield Dendrochronology Laboratory and has been used for the analysis of the ceiling boards, sub-ribs, the newly available structural timber samples and the reworking of the previously analysed samples. Any variations due to the analysis having occurred over an extended period during which the subject has made a series of technical advancements are discussed as necessary. Professional practice at the Sheffield Dendrochronology Laboratory follows, where appropriate, the English Heritage guidelines.[9]

Oak (*Quercus* spp) is currently the only species used for routine dating purposes in the British Isles, though research on other species is being undertaken.[10] Timbers with less than fifty annual growth rings are generally considered unsuitable for analysis as their ring patterns may not be unique.[11] Thus oak timbers which have at least fifty rings are generally sought and, if possible, either with bark/bark edge or some sapwood surviving (*see* below).

In standing buildings samples are generally removed from selected timbers in the form of either cross-sectional slices or cores. Slices are taken from timbers that are either wholly or partially replaced during repair, whereas cores are removed from timbers that will remain *in situ*. The cores are taken, using a corer 15mm in diameter attached to an electric drill, in a position and direction most suitable for maximising the number of rings in the sample, while ensuring the presence of sapwood and bark edge whenever possible. Alternatively if the removal of samples is inappropriate, *in situ* measurement, high resolution photography or the taking of an imprint of the wood structure using Fimo[12] can, in instances where the end-grain is visible, accessible and cleaned sufficiently to reveal the ring sequence clearly, replace the need for the physical removal of a sample.

The ring sequence of each sample is revealed by sanding until the annual growth rings are clearly defined. Any samples that fail to contain the minimum number of rings or have unclear ring sequences are rejected. The sequence of growth rings in the samples selected for dating purposes were measured to an accuracy of 0.1mm, 0.02mm or 0.01mm depending on when and how the measurement took place; samples 1–4 were measured by hand lens in units of 0.1mm; 5–7 in units of 0.02mm using a travelling stage attached to an Apple IIe-based measuring system; 22–24, originally measured in units of 0.1mm, were remeasured in 1990 in units of 0.02mm on the Apple IIe system; 8–21 and 25–28 and all the ceiling boards were measured in units of 0.01mm using a purpose-built travelling stage attached to a PC Windows-based measuring system.[13] All old-system measurements were multiplied by the relevant factor in order to make them compatible with the current system, measuring to an accuracy of 0.01mm. The ceiling boards were kept intact and, therefore, were mounted in a cradle attached to the travelling stage. The ring sequences were plotted onto semi-logarithmic graph paper to enable visual comparisons to be made between them. In addition cross-correlation algorithms were employed to search for positions where the ring sequences were highly correlated.[14] The Student's *t*-test is then used as a significance test on the correlation coefficient and those quoted below are derived from the original CROS algorithm.[15] A *t*-value of 3.5 or over is usually indicative of a good match,[16] provided that high *t*-values are obtained at the same relative or absolute position with a range of independent sequences, and that the visual match is satisfactory.

Dating is usually achieved by cross-correlating or cross-matching ring sequences within a phase or structure and combining the matching patterns to form a phase or site master curve. This master curve and any remaining unmatched ring sequences are then tested against a range of reference chronologies, using the same matching criteria as above. The position at which all the criteria are met provides the calendar dates for the ring sequence. A master curve is used for absolute dating purposes whenever possible, as it enhances the common climatic signal and reduces the background 'noise' resulting from the local growth conditions of individual trees.

During the cross-matching stage of the analysis, an additional important element of tree-ring analysis is the identification of 'same-tree' timber groups. The identification of same-tree groups is based on very high levels of similarity in both year-to-year variation and longer-term growth trends and anatomical anomalies. Such information should ideally be used to support possible same-tree groups identified from similarities in the patterns of knots/branches during detailed recording of timbers for technological and woodland characterisation studies. Timbers originally derived from the same parent log generally have *t*-values of greater than 10.0, though lower *t*-values do not necessarily exclude the possibility. It is a balance of the range of information available that provides the same-tree link.

The cross-dating process provides precise calendar dates only for the rings present in the timber. The nature of the final ring in the sequence determines whether the date of this ring also represents the year the timber was felled. Oak consists of inner inert heartwood and an outer band of active sapwood. If the sample ends in the heartwood of the original tree, a *terminus post quem* for the felling of the tree is indicated by the date of the last ring plus the addition of the minimum expected number of sapwood rings which may be missing. This is the date after which the timber was felled, but the actual felling date may be many decades later, depending on the number of outer rings removed during timber conversion. Where some of the outer sapwood or the heartwood/sapwood boundary survives on the sample, a felling date range can be calculated using the maximum and minimum number of sapwood rings likely to have been present. Alternatively, if bark-edge survives, then a felling date can be directly obtained from the date of the last surviving ring. In some instances it may be possible to determine the season of felling according to whether the ring immediately below the bark is complete or incomplete. The onset of growth can, however, vary within and between trees and this, combined with the natural variation in actual ring width, means that the determination of felling season must be treated cautiously. The sapwood estimate applied must be appropriate to the source of the timber, as there is a geographical variation in the number of sapwood rings present which increases from east to west across north-west Europe.[17]

The dates obtained by the technique do not by themselves necessarily indicate the date of the structure from which they are derived. Evidence indicates that seasoning of timber for structural purposes was a fairly rare occurrence until relatively recent times and medieval timber was generally felled as required and used while green.[18] Physical evidence for the rapid use of trees is widespread in buildings, as many show clear evidence of warping or splitting after undergoing conversion. It is necessary, however, to incorporate other specialist evidence concerning the reuse of timbers and the repairs or modifications of structures, as well as factors such as stockpiling, seasoning and transport, before the dendrochronological dates given here can be reliably interpreted as reflecting the construction date of phases within the structure.

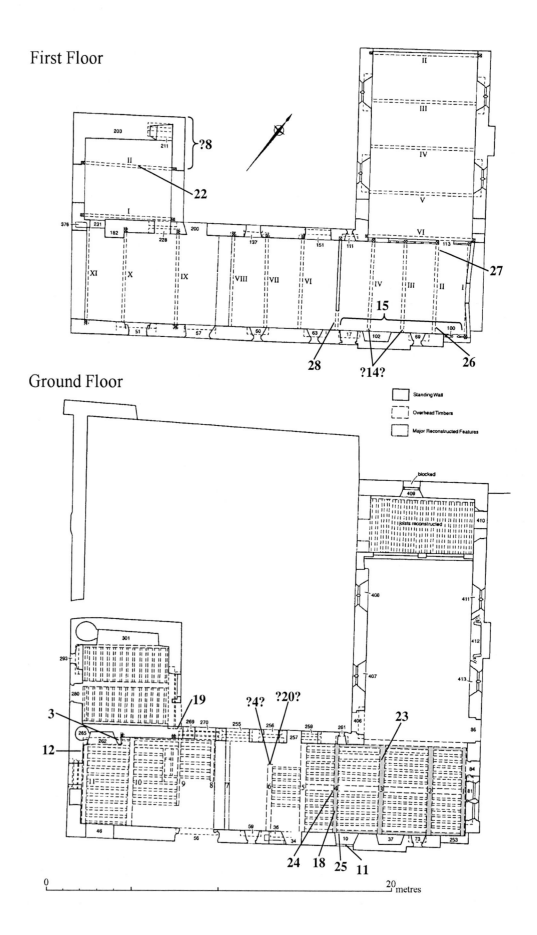

Figure 10.1
Plans showing the approximate location of the samples of the structural elements, where known, and highlighting the heavily moulded beams of the parlour ceiling (not to scale) (line drawing by Cathy Groves and Tony Ives).

Results

The results are presented in three sections: the first summarises the August 1999 'post-analysis' assessment; the second is concerned with the previously analysed structural elements and the four newly analysed samples; the third concerns the boards and sub-ribs from the parlour ceiling. Details of all samples are presented in Tables 10.1 and 10.2. Sample locations, where known, are indicated on plan (Fig 10.1).

Assessment 1999

The problematic nature of dendrochronology in Devon is well recognised, hence the undertaking of the project 'Dendrochronological Research in Devon' for English Heritage.[19] In the light of the author's experience in the assessment of over seventy buildings in the county during the last few years and in view of the results presented below, particularly the uncertain provenance of key timbers, it was felt that a post-analysis assessment of the extant *in situ* medieval timbers at Bowhill would prove valuable. This was undertaken during August 1999 with the aim of determining whether there was any further dendrochronological potential in timbers associated with the primary construction phase or whether the building could finally be 'laid to rest' dendrochronologically.

In order to facilitate detailed assessment of the roofs of the south range, a scaffold tower was hired to complement ladder access to just below collar height. Each individual element of the main and intermediate trusses was assessed at close proximity up to collar level, as were all longitudinal elements. Those above collar level were also assessed but not at such close quarters. The vast majority of the timbers in the roofs of the south range contained *c* thirty–forty rings, though some clearly had even less. Only three of the numerous timber elements forming the roofs of the south range were considered likely to have *c* fifty rings. These three were sampled in an attempt to provide at least some dated timbers of precisely known provenance within the building. At ground-floor level in the south range, all exposed timbers were also assessed but further sampling was not considered worthwhile.

The roof of the west range could not be accessed but some joists in the kitchen thought possibly to be associated with the primary phase, though not necessarily *in situ*, were also examined and rejected. Finally the hall roof was assessed. Close-up detailed assessment was not possible without a much higher tower. The timbers appeared to be very similar in nature to those in the roofs of the south range, however, and were, therefore, also considered to have no potential for further dendrochronological analysis. This assessment very strongly supported the findings of the *ex situ* timber assessment undertaken in 1996.

Structural elements

A total of twenty-eight timbers were incorporated in the analysis (*see* Table 10.1).[20] Duplicate samples were obtained from timbers 3, 5, 9, 16 and 24; 4 and 20 were also thought to be possible duplicate samples from the same beam. All of the timbers are oak (*Quercus* spp) apart from 11 and 25 that were identified as ash (*Fraxinus excelsior* L) using reference material in the form of permanent slides and an identification key.[21]

The majority of the timbers submitted for analysis were thought to be associated with the initial construction phase, although the precise location and provenance of some of the timbers within the building cannot be ascertained. As indicated earlier, some may possibly be historic timbers brought onto the site. The three exceptions are 11 and 25, the ash samples from lintels thought to date to the 17th century, and 19, a door jamb of 18th- or 19th-century date. Eleven timbers were rejected as unsuitable for analysis: 12, 15, 16, 17, 19, 23 and 24 contained less than fifty annual growth rings; 26 had fragmented; the ring pattern of 14 was severely distorted, probably by the close proximity of knots; and 11 and 25, the ash samples.

Twenty ring sequences representing a maximum of seventeen timbers were measured. The ring sequences from known duplicate samples (3A, 3B; 5A, 5B; 9A, 9B) were compared to ensure that they cross-matched (*t*-values of 4.34, 26.58, 5.75 produced respectively) and then were combined to form the individual timber sequences 3, 5 and 9. Since no match was identified between 4 and 20, these were analysed individually. All seventeen timber sequences were then compared and six (4, 5, 6, 7, 10 and 13) were found to cross-match (Table 10.3 and *see* Table 10.12). The high *t*-values and excellent visual matches produced between 7, 10 and 13 suggest that they were derived from the same tree.

Table 10.1 Details of the samples from the structural elements from Bowhill, Exeter

timber	cat no.	timber function/provenance	type	no. of rings	sap rings	AGR	cross-section size	cross-section type	date	comment
1	78	door jamb/head, part of screen	oak	73	13	2.62	unknown	unknown	–	hand lens measurement of *in situ* timber at Bowhill in 1990
2		principal rafter	oak	97	hs	2.88	unknown	unknown	–	hand lens measurement of *in situ* timber at Bowhill in 1990
3		lintel of fireplace in western room, south range, ground floor	oak	85	22b	–	unknown	quartered	–	includes measurements from two duplicate samples: hand lens measurement of photo in 1980; hand lens measurement of *in situ* timber measured at Bowhill in 1990
4		not located	oak	81	–	2.37	unknown	quartered	1341–1421	hand lens measurement of loose timber measured at Bowhill in 1990
5	97	floor beam/headbeam of screen	oak	124	–	1.90	235 × 155	quartered	1345–1468	includes measurements from two duplicate samples: cross-sectional slice measured 1990; cross-sectional slice measured 1996
6		not located	oak	136	–	1.81	250 × 120	quartered	1323–1458	cross-sectional slice measured 1990
7		not located	oak	109	–	1.81	250 × 235	whole	1292–1400	cross-sectional slice measured 1990
8	81	common rafter (tagged KIT E 17) east side of west range, primary to the roof	oak	77+	hs+ 18b	1.43	110 × 95	quartered	–	cross-sectional slice measured 1996
9	144	common rafter, roof of south range	oak	94+	20 + 11b	1.28	100 × 90	quartered	–	includes measurements from two duplicate samples: cross-sectional slices both measured 1996
10	172	beam, not located	oak	101	–	1.88	250 × 210	whole	1293–1393	cross-sectional slice measured 1996
11	215	external lintel from window 10, south-west window of parlour	ash	76	–	2.10	235 × 75	plank: tangential	–	cross-sectional slice rejected 1996
12	222	south range kitchen, west wall under lintel	oak	32	16bw	5.46	350 × 45	plank: tangential	–	cross-sectional slice rejected 1996
13	226	main beam, not located	oak	125	–	2.18	255 × 240	halved	1301–1425	cross-sectional slice measured 1996
14	59	post head, truss III(S) or IV(S) of south range roof	oak	49	–	2.91	285 × 165	halved	–	cross-sectional slice rejected 1996
15	146	wall plate, south side of chamber roof	oak	35	–	5.00	175 × 170	quartered	–	cross-sectional slice rejected 1996
16	200	not located	oak	46	7	2.55	235 × 60	plank: tangential	–	includes two duplicate samples: cross-sectional slices both rejected 1996
17	164	common rafter, south range roof	oak	38	14bw	2.63	100 × 100	quartered	–	cross-sectional slice rejected 1996
18	58	beam 4, south range floor frame, westernmost beam of moulded ceiling in parlour	oak	60	–	4.95	410 × 230	quartered	–	cross-sectional slice measured 1996
19	173	south jamb, kitchen door-frame	oak	39+	hs+ ??	3.33	175 × 130	halved	–	cross-sectional slice rejected 1996; number of additional rings unknown
20		beam 6, south range floor frame, north end	oak	73	?hs	2.15	310 × 300	whole	–	cross-sectional slice remeasured in 1990, ?duplicate of 20
21	408	north-west window of hall	oak	78	–	3.36	unknown	unknown	–	cross-sectional slice remeasured in 1990
22		west range, truss II	oak	53	–	4.45	unknown	unknown	–	cross-sectional slice remeasured in 1990
23		beam 3, south range floor frame	oak	33	–	–	unknown	whole	–	photo rejected in 1980
24		screen stud, south range between parlour and service rooms	oak	34	–	–	unknown	halved	–	includes two duplicate photos of opposing ends: both rejected in 1980
25		lintel of window 10 (18)	ash	56	–	1.79	100 × 55	quartered	–	cross-sectional slice rejected 1998
26		south range, truss II, south upper arch brace	oak	+39	–	2.92	210 × 160	quartered	–	core rejected 1999; inner section fragmented
27		south range, truss II, north upper arch brace	oak	64	–	2.88	205 × 160	quartered	–	core measured 1999
28		south range, truss V, south principal	oak	51	hs	3.49	220 × ??	halved	–	core measured 1999

Cat. no. – number assigned in 1993 for the loose timber catalogue in the site archive.

No. of rings – total number of measured rings including both heartwood and sapwood.

Sap rings – number of sapwood rings only.

date – date of measured ring sequence (AD).

+ – unmeasured rings; hs – heartwood/sapwood boundary; b – bark edge present; bw – bark edge present, felled winter.

AGR – average growth rate in millimetres per year; this is not given when measurements are from a photograph at unknown scale.

cross-section size – maximum dimensions of the cross-section in millimetres.

cross-section type – guide to conversion type.

Table 10.2 Details of the ceiling boards (AA–CE) and sub-ribs (CF–CK) from Bowhill, Exeter

board	chalk no.	type	no. of rings	AGR	cross-section size	length of board	date	comment
AA		oak	211	0.83	172 × 10	680	1244–1454	same tree group as AB, AG, AZ, AP, BE, BM, BX, and CA
AB	?6 or ?9	oak	167	0.78	133 × 9	739	1276–1442	same tree group as AA, AG, AZ, AP, BE, BM, BX, and CA
AC	29	oak	114	2.08	238 × 12	724	1338–1451	same board group as AL
AD		oak	185	1.23	232 × 12	740	1282–1466	same board group as AF and AK
AE	5	oak	278	0.92	258 × 11	650	not dated	
AF	14	oak	209	1.19	251 × 10	690	1256–1464	same board group as AD and AK
AG		oak	194	1.28	251 × 9	741	1271–1464	same tree group as AA, AB, AZ, AP, BE, BM, BX, and CA
AH		oak	193	1.25	248 × 10	738	1278–1470	same tree group as AJ/BJ, BD, and BZ
AI		oak	194	0.99	195 × 9	738	1207–1400	same board group as AQ, BC, BG, and BU
AJ		oak	106	1.57	168 × 9	737	1274–1379	same tree group as AH, BD, BZ, and inner part of BJ
AK		oak	+180+	1.16	234 × 10	736	1260–1439	same board group as AD and AF; +8 inner and +4 outer unmeasured rings
AL	24	oak	105	2.13	228 × 9	688	1350–1454	same board group as AC
AM		oak	221	1.10	250 × 10	729	1239–1459	same tree group as AO
AN	18	oak	194	1.11	217 × 10	694	1278–1471	same board group as AU and BN
AO 1	31	oak	55	1.46	251 × 11	726	1246–1300	same tree group as AM; inner part of board AO
AO 2	as above	oak	87	0.93	as above	as above	1388–1474	same tree group as AM; outer part of board AO
AP		oak	+207	1.06	255 × 11	697	1255–1461	same board group as BE, BM, BX, and CA; same tree group as AA, AB, AG, and AZ; +30 unmeasured rings
AQ	17	oak	241	1.02	240 × 10	693	1173–1413	same board group as AI, BC, BG, and BU
AR	15	oak	149	1.46	217 × 11	691	1172–1320	
AS	19	oak	161	1.05	171 × 12	697	1312–1472	same board group as AV, BA, BO, and BP
AT	16	oak	149	0.95	151 × 11	693	1334–1482	same tree group as AX
AU	11	oak	196	1.11	219 × 11	735	1274–1469	same board group as AN and BN
AV	8?	oak	173	1.06	185 × 11	738	1306–1478	same board group as AS, BA, BO, and BP
AW		oak	101	1.38	140 × 9	697	1360–1460	same board group as CB and outer part of CD
AX		oak	86	0.92	143 × 10	737	1386–1471	same tree group as AT
AY		oak	64	1.60	103 × 9	698	1265–1328	same tree group as BF, CC, CH, and CJ
AZ		oak	131	0.81	107 × 10	734	1344–1474	same tree group as AA, AB, AG, AP, BE, BM, BX, and CA
BA		oak	97+	1.04	100 × 9	731	1370–1466	same board group as AS, AV, BO, and BP; +9 unmeasured rings
BB		oak	76	0.90	79 × 8	730	1280–1355	
BC	10	oak	234	1.00	240 × 10	739	1171–1404	same board group as AI, AQ, BG, and BU
BD		oak	188	1.27	242 × 10	735	1272–1459	same tree group as AH, AJ/BJ, and BZ
BE	1?	oak	251	1.04	266 × 11	662	1211–1461	same board group as AP, BM, BX, and CA; same tree group as AA, AB, AG, and AZ
BF	2	oak	201	1.24	252 × 12	661	1270–1470	same tree group as AY, CC, CH, and CJ
BG		oak	221	0.98	205 × 10	732	1176–1396	same board group as AI, AQ, BC, and BU
BH		oak	+149	0.80	204 × 12	728	1322–1470	same tree group as BW; +50 unmeasured rings
BI	25	oak	142	1.50	222 × 11	686	1294–1435	same tree group as BK, BS, and CF
BJ		oak	78	0.94	73 × 9	737	1380–1457	same tree group as AH, BD, BZ, and outer part of AJ
BK	28	oak	190	1.13	217 × 11	714	1286–1475	same tree group as BI, BS, and CF
BL	22	oak	222	0.97	230 × 10	688	1256–1477	
BM		oak	216	1.08	235 × 11	689	1246–1461	same board group as AP, BE, BX, and CA; same tree group as AA, AB, AG, and AZ
BN	21	oak	+195	1.04	280 × 10	685	1270–1464	same board group as AN and BN; +85 unmeasured rings beyond a knot
BO	12	oak	232	1.19	272 × 11	739	1244–1475	same board group as AS, AV, BA, and BP
BP	27	oak	161	0.99	162 × 10	711	1323–1483	same board group as AS, AV, BA, and BO
BQ		oak	177	1.17	194 × 10	740	1284–1460	
BR	7	oak	197	1.13	217 × 11	641	1276–1472	same tree group as BT
BS		oak	179	1.30	245 × 12	730	1297–1475	same tree group as BI, BK, and CF
BT		oak	+80	1.02	244 × 10	739	1383–1462	same tree group as BR; +115 unmeasured rings
BU		oak	231	1.05	247 × 11	738	1161–1391	same board group as AI, AQ, BC, and BG
BV	?6 or ?9	oak	225	1.02	240 × 11	648	1243–1467	
BW	23	oak	146	1.15	173 × 11	689	1259–1404	same tree group as BH; paint analysis board 2
BX		oak	123	1.30	152 × 10	730	1222–1344	same board group as AP, BE, BM, and CA; same tree group as AA, AB, AG, and AZ; paint analysis board 7
BY		oak	+194	1.03	226 ×10	742	1279–1472	+13 unmeasured rings; paint analysis board 4
BZ		oak	189	1.26	242 × 10	690	1283–1471	same tree group as AH, AJ/BJ, and BD; paint analysis board 3
CA		oak	249	1.06	271 × 10	741	1212–1460	same board group as AP, BE, BM, and B×; same tree group as AA, AB, AG, and AZ; paint analysis board 1
CB	3	oak	178	1.50	270 × 11	659	1284–1461	same board group as AW/CD
CC		oak	142	1.05	155 × 10	697	1331–1472	same tree group as AY, BF, CH, and CJ
CD		oak	58	1.91	112 × 10	696	1302–1359	same board group as CB and inner part of AW; paint analysis board 5
CE	20	oak	222	1.33	300 × 11	692	1238–1459	paint analysis board 6
CF		oak	60	1.07	66 × 10	668	1420–1479	same tree group as BI, BK, and BS
CG		oak	66	0.98	65 × 12	714	1384–1449	
CH		oak	76	1.18	90 × 11	783	1289–1364	same tree group as AY, BF, CC, and CJ
CI		oak	72	0.76	56 × 29	922	1388–1459	
CJ		oak	68	1.31	90 × 13	706	1286–1353	same tree group as AY, BF, CC, and CH
CK		oak	68	0.81	55 × 30	741	1389–1456	

No. of rings – total number of measured rings; none had any sapwood.   AGR – average growth rate in millimetres per year.
date – date of measured ring sequence (AD).   cross-section size – maximum dimensions of the cross-section in millimetres.
+ – unmeasured rings.   length of board – maximum length in millimetres.

Table 10.3 Matrix showing the *t*-values obtained between the ring sequences from the matching structural elements

sample	5	6	7	10	13
4	–	3.87	3.58	–	3.59
5	★	4.51	4.40	4.76	6.08
6		★	3.40	3.02	4.14
7			★	18.65	13.81
10				★	15.25

– = *t*-values <3.00

In fact from the loose timber catalogue descriptions it appears possible that they are slices from the same timber, a main beam, that may have been cut into sections when removed during the repair works.[22] Their data were combined to produce a single sequence (BOW/S3) which was then combined with 4, 5 and 6 to produce a 177-year master curve, BOWHILL-A (Table 10.4). BOW/S3 was formed so that the master chronology was weighted correctly and not biased towards an individual timber or tree.

BOWHILL-A and the unmatched individual ring sequences were tested against an extensive range of dated reference chronologies spanning the last two millennia from the British Isles, including a series of recently available chronologies from central Devon.[23] It was immediately apparent that BOWHILL-A dated to the period AD 1292–1468 inclusive (Table 10.5). No consistent results were, however, obtained for any of the other unmatched sequences so these remain undated.

Parlour ceiling

The parlour ceiling was divided into large rectangular sections by heavily moulded beams, forming three bays (six half bays); each half bay was further subdivided by moulded ribs and ceiled with boards (*see* Figs 6.29, 6.20 and 6.21). The description above (Chapter 6) suggests that each half of bay 1 consisted of a two by three grid, probably with eighteen boards, while each half of bays 2 and 3 were on a three by three grid probably with twenty-seven boards. As it survived in 1985, bay 1 of the ceiling was the only one that consisted of medieval oak boards *in situ*. The four main moulded beams are clearly integral to the construction of the hall and great chamber roofs; the basic frame of the ceiling is consequently thought to date to *c* AD 1500. The ceiling was clearly designed to be panelled, but there are two forms of provision in the fabric for the insertion of boards (Chapter 6). Prior to dendrochronological analysis, the boards and sub-ribs extant in 1985 were consequently considered likely to be later insertions, perhaps from the later 16th century.

Fifty-seven lengths of oak board and six sub-ribs were available for analysis; this included the thirty or so boards that were *in situ* in bay 1 in 1985 (*see* Fig 6.32). The additional boards are presumed to have been retained from other bays, perhaps mixed in with the softwood boarding, but there is no direct evidence for this. Twenty-seven of the boards had been labelled using a chalk numbering system. This ranges from 1–31, though numbers 4, 13, 26 and 30 are absent, probably due to the chalk wearing off, and the system is thought most likely to relate to those boards from bay 1. As this numbering system was incomplete, however, each board was allocated a unique code in the form of sequential lettering, starting with AA and ending with CE. The chalk number was also recorded where present. The sub-ribs were allocated sequential letters starting with CF and ending with CK. Details of the boards and sub-ribs are given in Table 10.2.

The boards are clearly all sawn rather than radially split from the parent trunks, as the resultant striations are still apparent on some areas on the back surface (Fig 10.2). Although the tendency is for the boards to be radially sawn, the variation in angle from radial to tangential is shown in Fig 10.3. The backs of the boards have been crudely dressed, leaving adzed or rough planed surfaces (*see* Fig 10.2), while the face was finished off to a higher quality. The boards are jointed in the standard medieval fashion for panelling in an early, perhaps cruder version of tongue-and-groove, termed vee-edged by Milne.[24] The thin edge of each

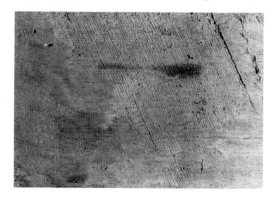

Figure 10.2

The rear face of a ceiling board, showing saw and adze/plane marks (photograph by Cathy Groves).

Table 10.4 The ring width data from the site master chronology, BOWHILL-A, dated AD 1292–1468 inclusive

date	ring widths (units of 0.01mm)	number of samples
AD 1292	176 153 225 180 317 185 125 137 107	1 1 1 1 1 1 1 1 1
AD 1301	183 198 139 215 174 193 261 231 221 270	1 1 1 1 1 1 1 1 1 1
	229 343 284 360 342 222 252 224 229 205	1 1 1 1 1 1 1 1 1 1
	201 178 366 346 218 186 261 289 319 344	1 1 2 2 2 2 2 2 2 2
	232 265 217 272 318 229 227 226 246 230	2 2 2 2 2 2 2 2 2 2
	232 272 235 204 254 210 199 264 257 172	3 3 3 3 4 4 4 4 4 4
AD 1351	170 181 230 210 210 216 223 228 220 142	4 4 4 4 4 4 4 4 4 4
	183 237 244 255 195 199 180 158 220 220	4 4 4 4 4 4 4 4 4 4
	194 212 237 236 224 275 209 212 276 237	4 4 4 4 4 4 4 4 4 4
	175 196 191 194 181 246 222 224 256 165	4 4 4 4 4 4 4 4 4 4
	208 182 205 161 215 255 189 246 253 224	4 4 4 4 4 4 4 4 4 4
AD 1401	276 164 217 204 162 208 159 220 239 173	4 4 4 4 4 4 4 4 4 4
	149 161 143 147 126 122 146 128 93 129	4 4 4 4 4 4 4 4 4 4
	142 140 222 164 194 101 136 201 177 151	4 3 3 3 3 2 2 2 2 2
	134 150 120 133 152 106 126 132 91 134	2 2 2 2 2 2 2 2 2 2
	117 98 125 153 135 119 133 161 123 98	2 2 2 2 2 2 2 2 2 2
AD 1451	145 135 127 140 114 153 136 168 108 192	2 2 2 2 2 2 2 2 1 1
	120 154 131 73 116 116 132 106	1 1 1 1 1 1 1 1

Table 10.5 Dating the site master chronology, BOWHILL-A. Results of comparisons between some relevant reference chronologies and BOWHILL-A at AD 1292–1468 inclusive. All reference chronologies are independent

region	reference chronology	t-value
Devon	Broomham (Groves forthcoming a)	5.51
	Lower Chilverton (Groves forthcoming a)	5.14
	Prowse Barn (Groves forthcoming a)	4.70
	South Yard (Groves and Hillam 1993a)	4.82
	West Hele (Groves forthcoming a)	5.32
Dorset	Sherborne Abbey Church nave (Bridge 1993)	5.76
Gloucestershire	Gloucester Mercers Hall (Howard et al 1996)	7.82
Herefordshire	Hereford Cathedral Barn 2 (Tyers 1996b)	8.00
	Hereford Farmers Club (Tyers 1996b)	8.29
	Hereford Booth Hall/High Town (Boswijk and Tyers 1997)	9.28
	Kings Pyon (Groves and Hillam 1993b)	11.01
	Staplow (Tyers pers comm)	7.36
Shropshire	Upton Cressett (Miles and Haddon-Reece 1994)	7.05
	Easthope (Miles and Haddon-Reece 1994)	6.18
	Much Wenlock 4 (Miles and Haddon-Reece 1994)	6.95
	Shrewsbury Nags Head (Miles and Haddon-Reece 1994)	7.44
Somerset	Bruton 16–18 High Street (Miles and Worthington 1997)	5.08
Worcestershire	Lower Sapey (Tyers 1995)	7.60
	Warndon St Nicholas church roof (Tyers 1998c)	8.57
Wales	Hafoty (Hillam unpublished)	5.91
	Welsh Border (Siebenlist-Kerner 1978)	7.12
Northern Ireland	Belfast (Baillie 1977a)	5.24
Ireland	Dublin (Baillie 1977b)	4.40
France	Brittany (Guibal pers comm)	3.66

Table 10.6 Matrix showing the *t*-values obtained between the ring sequences from the matching ceiling boards. Numbers in *italics* highlight those *t*-values over 10 suggesting 'same-tree' groups, while those in bold highlight *t*-values over 20 suggesting 'same-board' groups

_15.55_	4.65	4.91	4.12	8.96	–	6.01	–	5.61	4.63	–	5.42	–	5.59	_10.64_	5.69	6.43	4.49	4.33	4.40	4.67	5.50	4.97	–	9.60	3.29	3.04	6.56
*	5.32	4.64	4.85	7.61	–	6.46	–	4.61	5.57	5.00	4.76	–	3.48	9.35	6.26	3.59	3.82	4.43	4.11	4.61	4.37	3.93	–	_10.60_	–	–	7.00
	*	6.30	7.34	4.40	3.54	3.82	–	6.74	**22.28**	4.97	6.66	\	5.70	8.33	3.18		4.48	4.92	6.86	4.12	–	4.67	\	6.17	–	3.74	3.26
		*	**29.07**	5.49	6.96	4.23	4.82	_19.92_	6.74	7.42	5.72	3.13	5.57	5.98	4.31	–	7.40	5.03	5.19	7.37	4.62	4.21	5.57	8.01	5.80	4.67	–
			*	5.86	5.90	5.05	5.10	**21.63**	7.11	8.94	6.23	4.86	6.15	7.12	5.41	–	7.97	5.67	5.26	8.23	4.00	5.15	5.46	7.93	6.50	5.54	3.93
				*	–	7.46	–	5.08	4.68	3.80	4.70	–	4.53	_10.55_	7.54	3.58	–	4.29	4.72	–	5.39	–	–	9.35	–	–	8.04
					*	3.26	_17.39_	7.03	4.00	5.69	–	–	3.04	4.39	–	–	3.25	–	3.05	3.07	3.04	–	–	3.54	3.58	3.14	–
						*	–	6.78	3.32	5.35	5.00	–	\	8.59	**24.57**	8.23	–	3.33	4.87	3.12	–	–	–	6.37	–	3.72	**27.83**
							*	4.02	–	–	–	–	\	–	–	–	–	–	–	–	\	–	–	\		3.01	–
								*	8.25	6.54	4.71	–	4.99	6.44	6.21	–	4.88	4.50	4.35	4.58	3.96	4.42	5.03	6.10	3.71	4.49	4.87
									*	6.05	5.58	\	6.18	6.94	–	\	4.20	4.23	5.58	3.97	–	4.87	\	5.18	3.02	\	–
										*	5.57	_17.07_	_17.16_	5.90	5.79	–	5.66	4.02	4.92	5.51	3.99	6.69	3.39	5.16	5.43	–	4.98
											*	–	6.48	7.26	4.21	–	5.01	5.35	**34.03**	4.88	–	4.34	–	5.88	3.66	3.20	4.22
												*	\	3.09	–	–	\	\	–	\	\	\	3.31	\	\	–	–
													*	6.08	–	\	6.76	6.01	5.48	6.82	4.72	7.13	\	5.85	5.94	\	3.18
														*	7.42	4.27	4.49	5.96	7.08	5.30	5.10	4.07	–	_15.05_	4.43	–	8.74
															*	8.06	–	–	4.20	–	–	–	–	5.99	–	3.40	**32.79**
																*	\	\	–	–	\	\	–	\	\	\	8.04
																	*	7.21	4.86	**25.50**	–	7.88	–		4.43	_19.35_	–
																		*	4.48	6.57	4.04	_11.40_	\	4.57	6.15	4.35	–
																			*	4.20	–	3.32	–	5.36	–	3.12	4.46
																				*	–	6.75	–	5.25	**22.51**		–
																					*	3.27	\	5.22	–	\	3.50
																						*	\	4.12	6.22	\	–
																							*	\	\	3.23	–
																								*	4.41	\	7.74
																									*	\	–
																										*	–

1	2	3	4	5	6	7	8	9	10	11	12	13	14	15	16	17	18	19	20	21	22	23	24	25	26	27	28
–	10.47	3.35	5.14	3.12	–	–	3.81	–	9.39	4.94	3.30	4.17	6.82	8.75	4.18	7.91	5.04	6.99	5.36	5.70	6.42	–	9.06	6.22	4.65	3.38	5.96
–	9.39	4.13	5.30	–	–	–	3.41	–	8.39	4.58	4.15	4.02	7.49	8.05	3.57	6.44	6.53	7.05	7.16	5.10	4.34	–	7.63	5.39	4.01	4.12	6.65
3.20	6.73	5.04	–	–	–	5.43	3.06	7.71	6.90	4.04	4.04	7.24	5.41	4.03	3.61	–	4.56	–	\	–	–	6.97	3.49	4.06	–	5.07	
5.37	6.45	8.88	4.24	3.94	4.18	–	6.16	8.16	6.07	5.27	8.11	7.25	6.05	6.37	4.97	3.71	3.24	6.28	3.57	–	5.24	4.25	5.79	5.44	7.59	–	4.81
5.14	6.93	9.26	5.40	4.66	4.89	–	6.82	8.44	6.67	5.97	10.73	7.70	6.50	7.10	5.83	4.81	4.47	6.59	4.51	–	5.22	3.70	6.42	5.78	8.06	3.30	5.39
–	12.85	3.81	7.02	–	–	3.24	3.47	12.15	4.96	3.26	–	4.15	9.45	–	5.42	6.48	4.75	5.41	7.45	5.39	–	11.91	5.66	4.34	–	6.57	
16.35	4.04	4.67	–	–	6.01	9.06	5.88	5.59	4.44	3.23	3.62	3.22	–	5.05	5.86	–	–	–	–	4.38	17.92	3.97	3.58	3.18	–	3.15	
3.14	11.25	–	26.09	4.23	–	3.63	–	7.73	5.19	4.09	–	5.17	10.11	3.23	3.85	22.79	5.05	6.99	7.87	3.82	–	10.08	–	3.93	3.44	5.03	
19.21	–	3.56	–	–	5.75	\	5.42	5.13	–	–	–	–	–	3.71	4.53	\	–	–	–	–	10.74	–	–	–	–	–	
4.95	6.63	7.18	6.68	3.99	4.69	3.55	5.93	5.50	6.36	4.87	6.54	4.75	6.65	7.18	5.46	4.44	5.39	5.65	4.64	3.37	4.99	4.01	6.03	5.23	5.58	3.03	4.16
3.36	5.12	4.71	–	–	3.46	3.29	5.73	–	6.23	5.33	4.23	4.01	7.68	5.52	3.72	4.09	–	3.85	–	\	–	3.33	5.65	3.92	4.13	\	5.94
4.01	5.05	6.65	6.18	4.92	3.54	3.93	4.06	6.56	4.96	5.54	6.99	5.40	5.03	5.10	4.10	7.06	4.89	3.39	5.03	–	3.56	3.73	4.55	4.24	6.42	–	6.37
3.02	7.06	4.36	3.95	5.70	3.50	–	4.01	3.69	6.43	32.57	5.26	4.58	6.60	5.07	–	3.35	3.86	3.77	5.84	3.76	4.04	–	6.44	3.77	4.97	–	4.40
–	–	–	3.58	\	\	\	–	3.34	3.41	–	3.31	\	–	–	\	\	3.13	–	3.27	3.27	–	–	3.17	–	\	\	4.14
3.10	5.83	7.50	\	5.13	4.40	4.46	7.42	5.70	5.56	7.00	7.19	6.40	4.01	6.02	5.79	6.27	\	–	4.40	\	4.85	3.36	4.09	4.55	8.09	–	5.54
–	22.51	4.40	7.11	–	3.32	–	4.21	4.24	21.58	6.79	5.49	4.93	6.99	10.15	4.69	6.19	6.77	6.08	5.99	14.90	6.63	–	21.95	6.98	5.86	5.28	8.26
–	9.75	3.10	29.69	3.96	–	–	3.01	–	7.10	4.55	3.98	–	5.06	9.04	3.68	4.42	25.31	5.07	5.55	6.67	4.82	–	9.13	3.58	–	3.20	5.91
–	8.41	–	8.93	\	–	\	–	4.10	–	–	\	–	3.96	4.21	\	8.93	4.85	–	7.57	–	9.53	–	\	–	–	4.22	
–	3.35	9.06	–	4.47	4.06	–	7.30	8.55	3.05	5.03	23.65	22.12	3.52	5.57	6.27	3.15	–	4.19	–	–	4.78	–	–	3.68	10.27	3.07	5.21
–	4.14	9.90	–	3.69	4.07	–	7.66	5.24	4.20	5.21	5.11	5.72	5.22	5.51	4.42	3.86	–	5.42	4.92	\	4.45	–	4.23	5.36	9.43	3.97	4.64
–	6.62	4.44	3.82	4.99	–	3.00	3.03	6.48	31.26	4.94	4.30	6.26	4.35	–	–	3.72	–	5.72	3.86	–	6.63	–	4.65	–	4.58		
–	4.22	8.84	3.10	5.45	4.31	–	6.95	7.77	3.74	4.75	23.94	29.64	3.56	6.14	7.14	3.23	3.45	4.62	3.93	–	4.69	–	3.71	3.84	9.42	3.95	5.13
–	4.39	3.89	3.73	–	–	3.60	–	4.41	–	–	–	4.93	6.88	–	4.90	–	5.42	3.92	\	8.66	–	5.28	16.35	3.06	–	5.29	
–	–	7.60	\	4.31	3.94	7.44	5.20	–	4.88	6.42	5.82	4.78	4.85	4.22	4.10	\	3.61	7.63	\	–	–	–	4.34	7.85	–		
–	–	12.89	3.04	\	–	\	–	3.79	–	–	5.06	\	–	3.84	3.80	\	–	–	\	–	3.76	\	–	–			
–	16.25	5.75	5.47	3.45	–	3.48	4.33	18.07	5.69	4.82	4.81	5.59	9.70	3.57	5.67	4.68	6.33	3.75	\	5.01	–	14.75	5.82	5.57	3.62	6.85	
–	3.70	6.85	–	4.10	3.15	–	6.84	5.27	–	3.80	20.07	25.98	–	4.60	8.09	3.55	–	3.10	–	\	3.89	4.16	3.49	–	8.58	\	3.53
4.00	–	4.96	3.43	–	3.88	\	4.09	–	–	–	4.57	3.47	–	4.30	5.23	\	–	–	–	–	3.64	–	–	–	3.15	–	
–	11.06	–	24.40	3.97	–	–	–	7.69	4.55	3.78	–	4.85	7.86	–	5.77	26.49	4.44	5.98	7.25	4.40	–	9.45	3.32	–	3.03	5.55	
*	–	4.40	–	6.14	9.48	5.18	4.98	–	3.50	–	–	4.07	3.83	–	–	–	–	–	13.96	–	3.71	–	–				
	*	4.54	10.82	–	3.45	3.07	24.90	6.78	4.21	4.09	5.95	10.52	3.87	6.17	10.15	6.65	6.32	21.09	6.30	–	27.74	6.86	4.82	5.53	8.54		
		*	3.88	3.98	5.09	–	7.07	8.20	4.21	4.92	10.17	7.88	4.57	6.60	5.92	4.07	–	4.59	3.87	–	5.40	–	4.73	4.96	15.50	–	4.24
			*	3.11	3.13	–	4.18	–	6.94	4.52	4.60	–	4.74	9.73	3.81	–	24.59	5.15	5.98	7.69	5.00	–	9.98	4.40	–	3.78	4.97
				*	–	4.38	3.08	–	5.60	4.85	4.22	7.78	3.70	–	5.58	4.95	12.59	–	3.02	–	–	4.43					
					*	16.71	6.78	–	3.07	5.56	3.72	3.67	5.60	11.99	–	–	–	–	6.22	4.84	3.12	4.83	3.69	4.12	–		
						*	–	–	3.58	–	–	–	–	\	–	4.65	\	–	9.41	–	–	\	–				
							*	7.33	–	4.05	8.54	7.39	5.03	6.80	13.15	3.90	–	–	–	6.76	4.88	3.17	5.02	8.20	3.32	–	
								*	4.04	3.32	7.93	7.43	–	3.59	6.37	–	–	3.91	–	–	4.46	3.77	4.24	3.81	7.38	–	5.23
									*	6.22	4.69	3.28	4.71	9.44	3.90	5.29	6.54	6.64	6.12	21.61	5.44	–	26.05	6.97	4.83	5.04	9.17
										*	5.49	4.25	6.50	5.24	–	3.08	3.73	–	6.73	–	3.22	3.62	6.84	–	5.26	–	4.06
											*	25.79	5.07	7.13	9.14	3.06	4.73	4.29	3.56	–	5.01	3.01	4.68	5.72	9.09	5.22	6.51
												*	3.25	5.41	7.39	–	–	3.41	–	–	4.50	–	3.53	3.57	10.06	3.40	4.63
													*	5.65	3.66	3.98	5.49	4.82	8.32	–	3.37	–	4.68	5.99	4.27	3.09	3.63
														*	6.42	13.24	8.03	6.99	5.95	4.62	8.17	3.20	8.90	7.37	5.62	5.74	7.38
															*	3.68	–	–	–	6.30	5.03	4.06	4.37	5.17	3.93	3.86	
																*	\	5.97	4.08	\	6.91	–	4.14	4.07	4.88	\	5.95
																	*	5.02	7.04	8.63	4.06	–	9.17	4.20	–	3.86	6.19
																		*	5.36	4.00	5.42	–	6.15	5.90	4.92	3.04	4.63
																			*	5.25	–	–	5.27	3.40	4.02	–	3.53
																				*	–	–	22.91	4.34	\	4.01	5.91
																					*	–	5.36	7.54	4.33	4.84	5.09
																						*	–	–	3.30	–	
																							*	6.83	3.92	3.78	8.98
																								*	4.65	26.36	6.79
																									*	3.30	4.43
																										*	4.63

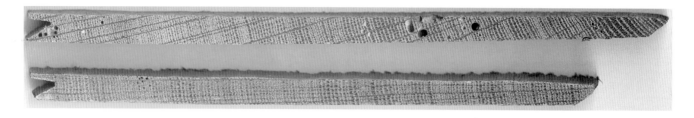

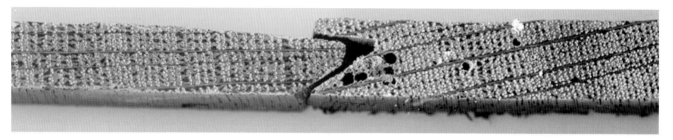

Figure 10.3
Scanned images of boards
AN and BU, showing the
variation from radial to
tangential sawn. Note the
rays in the lower board,
AN, are virtually parallel
to the long edges of the
board, whereas those in the
upper board, BU, are at an
angle of up to 45°. The face
of each board is in each
case the lower surface
(photograph by Cathy
Groves).

Figure 10.4
Enlarged image of the
jointing between two
boards. Again, the face is
the lower surface (photo-
graph by Cathy Groves).

board is bevelled to form a tongue which slots into an offset V-shaped groove cut along the length of the thicker edge of the adjacent board (Fig 10.4). The V was cut so that one edge was parallel with the back of the board and the other at an angle to the face of the board (Fig 10.4). Although sawn, the boards all taper in the direction of growth towards the pith as though they were radially split: the V-cut in the thick edge is always towards the outermost part of the tree and the tongue always towards the innermost part of the tree. The extant length of the boards varies from 641mm to 742 mm (*see* Table 10.15); the width of the boards varies from 79mm to 300mm (*see* Table 10.16), the maximum thickness of the boards from 9mm to 12mm, upper sub-ribs from 10mm to 13mm and the two lower sub-ribs 29mm and 30mm thick.

All were suitable for analysis and the decision was taken to measure all of them for the two key reasons: that they were a potentially valuable source of data for ongoing dendrochronological research on imported timbers; and in order to ensure that the aims of this part of the analysis, including reuse and possible multiple sourcing, could be adequately addressed.

The ring sequences from fifty-six of the board lengths cross-matched (Table 10.6 and *see* Tables 10.12 and 10.13); AO had to be measured in two parts as the cross-sectional surface of the board was badly degraded. It should also be noted that during the analysis it became clear that AJ and BJ were butting halves of a single board that had broken at some stage either during or since their removal. Boards AW and CD were also clearly butting sections of a single board. Thus it appears that the fifty-seven

board lengths, some of which are clearly only part-width boards, represent a maximum of fifty-five boards. Work on panel paintings suggests that *t*-values of over 20 are usual for two measurements of the same radius of a section of timber, that is at opposite ends of a single board.[25] Very high *t*-values of over 20 and superb visual matches imply that there are a number of groups of ceiling boards that are probably derived from a single originally longer length of board or boards from an immediately adjacent radius in the parent log. The level of *t*-values produced also suggests that there are probably various boards derived from different radial sections of the same tree where *t*-values of over 10 are produced, supported by excellent visual matches.

Seven 'same-board' groups were identified (*see* Tables 10.6 and 10.13):

AC AL
AD AF AK
AI AQ BC BG BU
AN AU BN
AP BE BM BX CA
AS AV BA BO BP
CB CD/AW

Eight same-tree groups were identified (Tables 10.7, 10.8; *see also* Table 10.12):

AA AB AG AZ (plus same-board group AP
  BE BM BX CA)
AH AJ/BJ BD BZ
AM AO
AT AX
AY BF CC CH CJ
BH BW
BI BK BS CF
BR BT

Table 10.9 gives an example of the *t*-values obtained for a same-board group and a same-tree group. Same-board or same-tree groups were combined to produce single board or tree sequences before being incorporated into the 323-year master curve, Bowhill-B (Table 10.10), so as to ensure that the master chronology was not biased towards an individual timber or tree.

As the ring sequence from board AE was the only unmatched one, the measurements were checked and a second set of measurements from the other end of the board were taken to ensure the accuracy of the first set. The *t*-value produced between these was in excess of 20 and the visual match showed no unexpected variation. Consequently this remains unlinked dendrochronologically with the other boards.

Bowhill-B and the unmatched sequence from board AE were compared with a wide range of European master chronologies. These comprise data-sets dating on average from AD 400 to the present and ranging between Russia and Ireland on an east–west axis and Norway and southern France on a north–south axis. Bowhill-B was dated to the period AD 1161–1483 against chronologies derived from material of eastern Baltic origin (Table 10.11). No reliable results could be obtained for board AE and so this remains undated.

Interpretation

Structural elements

None of the six dated samples showed any trace of sapwood. Although Hillam indicated that the outer edge of 4 could possibly have been the heartwood/sapwood boundary, re-examination shows no clear evidence for this.[26] It is, therefore, only possible to provide a *terminus post quem* for felling for each sample by adding the minimum expected number of missing sapwood rings to the date of the outermost measured heartwood ring (Table 10.12). The relevant sapwood estimate is a minimum of ten and maximum of forty-six annual rings, where these figures indicate the 95 per cent confidence limits of the range and are applicable to oak trees from England and Wales.[27] Samples 7, 10 and 13 are probably from the same tree and possibly actually duplicate samples from the same timber. They are, therefore, all likely to have been felled after AD 1435. If all six dated samples are contemporary, the analysis would indicate that they

Table 10.7 Matrix showing the *t*-values obtained between the ring sequences from the ceiling boards (AA–CE) and the subribs (CF–CK). Numbers in *italics* highlight those *t*-values over 10 suggesting 'same-tree' groups. No *t*-values over 20, suggesting 'same-board' groups, were obtained

	CF	CG	CH	CI	CJ	CK
AA	3.07	4.34	–	4.41	–	3.02
AB	–	–	–	3.19	–	–
AC	–	–	3.22	3.71	–	–
AD	–	–	5.06	4.13	6.08	–
AF	–	3.83	5.57	5.02	6.38	–
AG	–	–	–	3.24	–	–
AH	3.29	–	–	4.08	–	–
AI	\	–	–	\	–	\
AJ	\	\	–	\	3.49	\
AK	–	4.65	4.17	5.24	4.67	–
AL	–	–	–	4.56	\	–
AM	–	4.08	3.40	4.80	3.15	3.91
AN	–	–	3.90	4.13	–	3.20
AO1	\	\	\	\	\	\
AO2	3.79	4.43	\	4.63	\	3.72
AP	3.29	3.35	–	3.50	–	–
AQ	\	–	–	–	–	3.19
AR	\	\	–	\	4.26	\
AS	6.78	5.44	3.94	3.15	3.41	–
AT	4.04	4.93	3.67	6.50	4.12	–
AU	–	–	4.08	3.07	–	–
AV	6.48	4.13	5.21	–	5.54	–
AW	–	–	\	–	\	–
AX	3.15	5.11	\	5.74	\	3.67
AY	\	\	5.96	\	8.91	\
AZ	3.15	3.87	–	3.43	\	–
BA	7.54	4.37	\	4.14	\	3.31
BB	\	\	3.98	\	5.14	\
BC	\	3.44	–	3.54	–	–
BD	–	–	–	–	–	–
BE	–	3.59	–	3.05	–	–
BF	3.61	4.34	*11.35*	3.42	*14.00*	–
BG	\	\	3.66	\	3.43	\
BH	–	–	3.40	5.07	–	4.53
BI	–	4.45	3.09	3.89	5.05	–
BJ	–	–	\	–	\	–
BK	7.74	6.99	3.13	6.09	4.73	4.65
BL	4.31	3.87	3.74	3.36	3.75	–
BM	–	–	–	–	–	–
BN	–	–	3.81	3.84	–	3.10
BO	5.87	4.51	6.79	–	8.57	–
BP	6.46	4.21	3.40	3.01	3.60	–
BQ	–	4.46	4.76	6.44	4.60	4.90
BR	–	4.78	3.36	4.20	4.40	3.18
BS	*12.44*	5.68	3.37	4.32	5.78	4.87
BT	–	4.26	\	4.63	\	3.26
BU	\	\	–	\	–	\
BV	–	3.48	3.62	3.83	–	–
BW	\	–	3.54	6.10	–	3.77
BX	\	\	–	\	–	\
BY	–	4.17	–	3.75	–	–
BZ	3.66	–	–	3.16	–	–
CA	3.19	–	3.19	–	3.23	–
CB	–	–	3.33	3.18	4.15	3.18
CC	4.63	3.93	6.46	4.88	8.46	–
CD	\	\	–	\	3.69	\
CE	–	–	–	–	–	–

\ = overlap <15 years   – = *t*-values <3.00

Table 10.8 Matrix showing the *t*-values obtained between the ring sequences from the sub-ribs. Numbers in *italics* highlight those *t*-values over 10 suggesting 'same-tree' groups. No *t*-values over 20, suggesting 'same-board' groups, were obtained

	CG	CH	CI	CJ	CK
CF	3.28	\	3.19	\	3.48
CG	★	\	5.48	\	–
CH		★	\	*11.46*	\
CI			★	\	8.18
CJ				★	\

\ = overlap <15 years
– = *t*-values <3.00

Table 10.9 Matrix showing the *t*-values obtained between the ring sequences from a group of 'same-board' samples and a group of 'same-tree samples'

	BE	BM	BX	CA	AA	AB	AG	AZ
AP	22.51	21.58	14.90	21.95	10.64	9.35	10.55	15.05
BE	★	24.90	21.09	27.74	10.47	9.39	12.85	16.25
BM		★	21.61	26.05	9.39	8.39	12.15	18.07
BX			★	22.91	5.70	5.10	7.45	\
CA				★	9.06	7.63	11.91	14.75
AA					★	15.55	8.96	9.60
AB						★	7.61	10.60
AG							★	9.35

\ = overlap <15 years
– = *t*-values <3.00

were all felled and subsequently used in construction after AD 1478. The dubious provenance of these samples is such, however, that this *terminus post quem* for felling may or may not relate to the primary phase of construction at Bowhill.

Parlour ceiling boards

The sapwood estimates available for the likely geographical source of the timbers range from eight to thirty-eight (95 per cent confidence limits), fourteen to thirty-four (90 per cent confidence limits), nine to twenty-three (90 per cent confidence limits), eight to twenty-two (95 per cent confidence limits).[28] A sapwood estimate of eight to twenty-four at 95 per cent confidence limits has recently been produced from a large group of boards imported, again probably from the eastern Baltic region, and used in coffins excavated in Hull dating to the mid-14th century.[29] Clearly this estimate is very similar to the nine to twenty-three (90 per cent confidence limits) produced from historic oaks in Poland.[30] It is the recently produced sapwood estimate of eight to twenty-four (95 per cent confidence limits) from another imported assemblage that is

considered the most appropriate to apply to the ceiling boards at Bowhill, though clearly the coffin assemblage consists of boards over a century older than the ceiling boards.

No traces of sapwood were present on any of the ceiling boards. The lowest minimum expected number of sapwood rings is eight and it is this value that has been used to produce a *terminus post quem* for felling for each board (Tables 10.12 and 10.13). The majority of the assemblage is clearly broadly contemporary but examination of Table 10.13 does raise the possibility that the same-board group AI AQ BC BG BU is of a slightly earlier date. The quality of the intra-site cross-matching, however, as well as the visual characteristics, suggests that all of the boards form a single coherent group. It seems more probable that the timbers in this same-board group (AI AQ BC BG BU) were slightly more heavily trimmed on the outer edge. The boards appear likely to be missing in the region of fifty outer heartwood rings which, when taking into account the average ring widths, is only approximately 50mm of wood. It seems likely that all of the boards are contemporaneous and were all therefore probably felled and primarily used after AD 1491.

Table 10.10 The ring-width data from the site master chronology, BOWHILL-B, dated AD 1161–1483 inclusive

date	ring widths (units of 0.01mm)	number of trees
AD 1161	173 247 173 152 85 147 139 242 197 225	1 1 1 1 1 1 1 1 1 1
	225 175 171 155 138 163 120 136 72 98	1 2 2 2 2 2 2 2 2 2
	124 111 149 119 139 94 134 94 92 152	2 2 2 2 2 2 2 2 2 2
	107 86 102 114 113 141 167 197 156 147	2 2 2 2 2 2 2 2 2 2
AD 1201	149 118 88 97 111 131 137 107 102 106	2 2 2 2 2 2 2 2 2 2
	90 113 89 113 114 106 70 63 133 82	3 3 3 3 3 3 3 3 3 3
	132 128 91 78 111 101 156 146 149 158	3 3 3 3 3 3 3 3 3 3
	151 85 91 126 94 97 66 55 103 132	3 3 3 3 3 3 3 4 5 5
	116 156 140 140 153 166 164 149 193 157	5 5 6 7 7 7 7 7 7 7
AD 1251	151 149 167 146 182 192 134 110 155 165	7 7 7 7 9 9 9 9 10 10
	130 166 117 143 150 147 129 107 137 127	10 10 10 10 11 11 11 11 11 12
	173 133 168 156 161 135 127 121 146 168	12 13 13 13 13 14 14 14 15 16
	152 133 159 157 163 157 163 169 170 139	16 16 16 18 18 19 19 19 19 19
	142 104 107 119 142 160 160 149 144 148	19 19 19 19 19 19 19 19 19 19
AD 1301	146 165 140 108 102 100 70 104 108 116	19 19 19 19 19 19 19 19 19 19
	127 156 125 123 121 143 133 126 116 105	19 19 19 19 19 19 19 19 19 19
	111 92 100 104 124 122 108 110 103 94	18 18 18 18 18 18 18 18 18 18
	118 112 104 115 117 137 114 118 144 123	18 18 18 19 19 19 19 20 20 20
	128 107 100 107 120 123 146 114 122 134	20 20 20 20 20 20 20 20 20 20
AD 1351	124 132 129 108 100 98 73 91 131 124	20 20 20 20 20 19 19 19 19 19
	109 129 133 139 126 135 138 119 103 92	19 19 19 19 19 19 19 19 19 19
	110 83 108 101 103 116 121 133 114 127	19 19 19 19 19 19 19 19 19 19
	139 115 124 116 100 113 126 103 107 104	19 19 19 20 20 20 20 21 22 22
	102 111 111 116 98 116 73 93 103 125	22 22 22 22 22 22 22 22 22 22
AD 1401	95 121 100 94 116 115 108 115 105 102	22 22 22 22 22 22 22 22 22 22
	115 114 105 95 116 118 105 99 84 85	22 22 22 21 21 21 21 21 21 21
	94 93 72 89 99 90 78 73 86 89	21 21 21 21 21 21 21 21 21 21
	82 92 83 86 77 104 106 102 101 95	21 21 21 21 21 21 21 21 21 21
	117 106 124 113 120 95 98 105 86 96	21 21 21 21 21 21 21 21 21 20
AD 1451	99 98 86 99 100 105 113 86 92 111	20 20 20 20 19 19 18 18 18 16
	79 68 61 87 85 77 88 95 95 86	15 14 14 14 14 14 13 12 12 12
	93 106 84 101 110 100 96 104 62 85	11 9 6 6 4 4 4 3 3 2
	97 116 123	2 2 1

Table 10.11 Dating the site master chronology, BOWHILL-B. Results of comparisons between some relevant reference chronologies and BOWHILL-B at AD 1161–1483 inclusive. All reference chronologies are independent

region/group	reference chronology	t-value
Germany	South (Becker 1981)	3.97
Poland	North (Wazny 1990)	5.83
Sweden	Lund (Bartholin pers comm)	4.71
Imported	Baltic area 1: panel paintings (Hillam and Tyers 1995)	12.72
	Flemish 3: panel paintings (Lavier and Lambert 1996)	11.75
	OS020 Prince Arthur: panel painting (Tyers 1993b)	6.68
	Sutton House, Hackney, London: panels (Tyers 1991)	11.20
	171 Church Street, Stoke Newington: panels (Tyers pers comm)	7.03
	Guthrie Aisle, Tayside, Scotland: ceiling panels (Crone 1998)	6.05
	Winchester College, Winchester: ceiling panels (Lewis 1995)	17.45
	Copper Wreck: cargo planks group 1 (Wazny and Bonde pers comm 1994)	5.97
	Blaydes Staithe, Hull: vat (Hillam 1991b)	9.00
	Albion Place, Clerkenwell, London: barrel (Tyers 1994b)	7.77

Table 10.12 Bar diagram showing the relative positions of the dated ring sequences from the structural elements and the parlour ceiling boards (AA–CE) and sub-ribs (CF–CK) with their associated felling dates

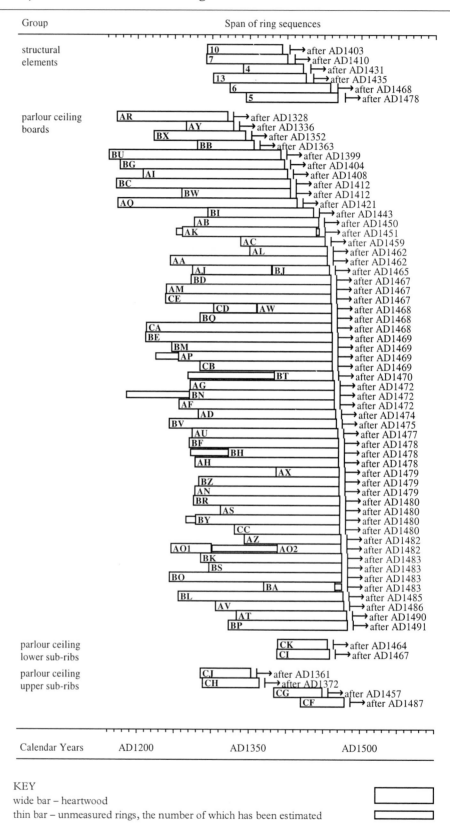

Table 10.13 Bar diagram showing the relative positions of the dated ring sequences from the parlour ceiling boards (AA–CE) and sub-ribs (CF–CK – highlighted by shading) sorted by 'same-board' groups, or 'same-tree' groups, or ungrouped individuals

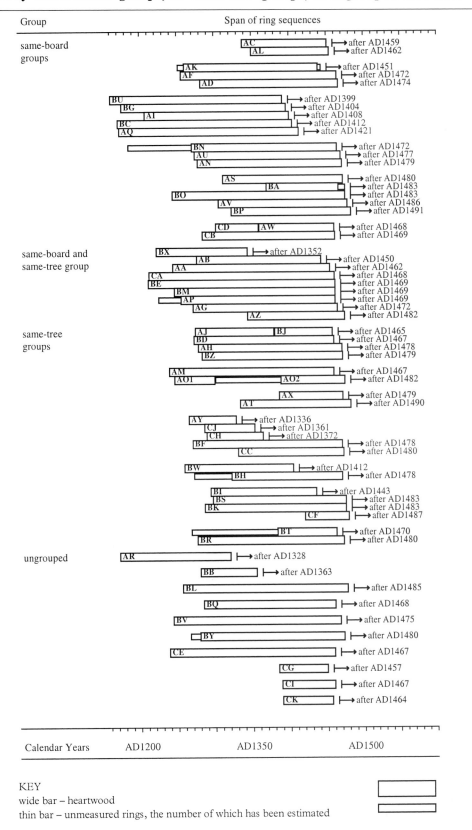

KEY

wide bar – heartwood

thin bar – unmeasured rings, the number of which has been estimated

Table 10.14 Bar diagram showing the variation in date of the heartwood/sapwood boundary of a group of timbers all known to have been felled within a year of each other (after Tyers 1998c). These are not of Baltic origin

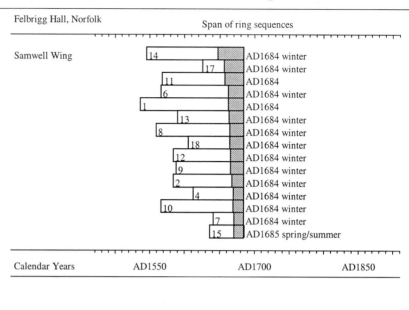

Although the *terminus post quem* of AD 1491 for felling is the strict dendrochronological interpretation, by taking into account various other factors it is possible to suggest a felling-date range. The dates of the outermost heartwood rings of forty-one boards and four sub-ribs are within 34 years of each other (*see* Tables 10.2 and 10.12). This suggests the possibility that a relatively small but variable number of heartwood rings and the sapwood band are missing (Table 10.14).[31] The expected maximum number of sapwood rings missing is twenty-four. Consequently it is suggested that the trees from which these boards and sub-ribs were derived were felled after AD 1491 but probably before *c* AD 1507. This range has been calculated simply by applying the eight to twenty-four sapwood estimate to the latest date obtained for a heartwood ring in the entire assemblage. It is possible that this estimated felling-date range could be narrowed down further by the statistical analysis of the variation in end date of the boards. As no trace of sapwood can be found on any of the boards, however, it is felt that this may not be appropriate and could introduce a false precision to the felling-date range.

Discussion[32]

Structural: dating evidence

Whether or not this analysis has provided any useful dating evidence for the structural timbers is open to question. The *terminus post quem* for felling of AD 1478 produced by the few dated structural timbers appears compatible with the *c* AD 1500 date indicated by other evidence for the primary construction phase of Bowhill (Chapter 12). Although the tree-ring evidence indicates that the timbers are broadly contemporary, the lack of bark edge and sapwood prevents the analysis from demonstrating that they are precisely coeval. Combined with the questionable provenance of the dated timbers and the possibility that the structure may contain reused timbers from an earlier building, this means that the tree-ring evidence from the structural timbers should be treated with great caution. Unfortunately the recent assessment of the extant timbers *in situ* indicates that it is simply not possible to improve this aspect of the analysis because of the unsuitability of the remaining timbers.

Structural: reuse

It has been suggested that these ranges may include reused remnants of an earlier building. None of the dated timber elements shows signs of reuse and, perhaps more importantly, no obvious signs of reuse were detected on the extant *in situ* medieval timbers during the 1999 assessment. The lack of precision as far as the production of felling dates is concerned prevents the dendrochronological evidence from unequivocally demonstrating that the dated group is from a single felling phase. The presence of a mixture of primary and reused material could also contribute to the scant intra-site cross-matching. The analysis itself can, therefore, neither confirm nor refute the possible presence of reused material, but the visual examination of the extant timbers indicates that this is unlikely.

Structural: building provenance

The other potentially complicating factor is the concern over the provenance of the dated timbers within the building. In the early 1990s the possibility was raised that the loose timbers stored on site may have included historic timbers brought in from the Greyfriars, at Gloucester. These introduced timbers are thought to be of either immediately pre-Dissolution or late 16th- to early 17th-century date.[33] Since clearly the lack of precise felling dates means that the dated timbers could feasibly represent the pre-Dissolution phase, this possibility cannot be discounted. The site master chronology, BOWHILL-A, matches particularly well with reference chronologies from the mid-west area of England (*see* Table 10.5). This similarity has, however, been noted before with chronologies from Gloucestershire, Herefordshire and Worcestershire, which have proved invaluable for dating purposes in Devon.[34] Detailed examination of the results produced by each dated individual timber (when compared with the entire suite of reference chronologies available from the British Isles) failed to highlight any obvious variation in source that might be taken to suggest that the timbers represented different buildings. Since the visual characteristics of all six dated timbers were also very similar, while the analysis certainly cannot prove that the timbers are all from Bowhill, it implies that they are more likely to represent a single building source than forming a mixture of Bowhill and Gloucester Greyfriars.

Structural: dating difficulties

Since the local network of reference chronologies has been extended significantly over the last few years, the re-analysis of the structural timbers was disappointing in that no additional samples were dated, even though the majority are almost certainly of local origin. This was, however, not particularly surprising, given the lack of intra-site cross-matching identified between all but the dated group and the low *t*-values produced between some known duplicate samples. The undated samples all have relatively short ring sequences, probably dominated by local environmental factors, natural or anthropogenic, which effectively mask the general climatic signal required for successful dating. These problems are not uncommon in Devon, but the pilot phase of the project 'Dendrochronological Research in Devon' has shown that it may be possible to address these difficulties through comprehensive sampling programmes and the production of an extensive highly localised chronological network.[35] A similar approach has certainly started to become increasingly productive in southern and western parts of Essex[36] and also proved vital in Kent.[37]

Ceiling: chalk versus non-chalk

The chalk-labelled boards are assumed to be those still *in situ* in bay 1 in 1985. Bays 2–4 were ceiled with replacement softwood boards with some oak boards surviving among them.[38] The twenty-five or so boards with no chalk label presumably came from the remaining bays of the ceiling and had been reused in secondary positions. The same-board and same-tree matches obtained between the chalk-label and no-chalk-label boards indicates that they are all part of the same group. In addition there are no obvious differences apparent when examining the board sizes (Tables 10.15b and 10.16b).

Ceiling: source

Unlike all the structural elements that appear likely to be of local origin, the analysis has shown that the parlour ceiling boards and sub-ribs are made from imported timber. The degree of similarity as indicated by *t*-values of the ring sequences from the boards and sub-ribs is remarkably high and implies that the trees used to produce the boards were derived from a single common woodland. The reference chronologies that this coherent group of

Table 10.15 Diagrams showing the variation in board length: a) all boards; b) boards split by chalk labelled and no chalk number groups

Table 10.16 Diagrams showing the variation in board width: a) all boards; b) boards split by chalk labelled and no chalk number groups. Note that the smaller widths are usually from boards which appear to be sections of boards that have been broken lengthwise

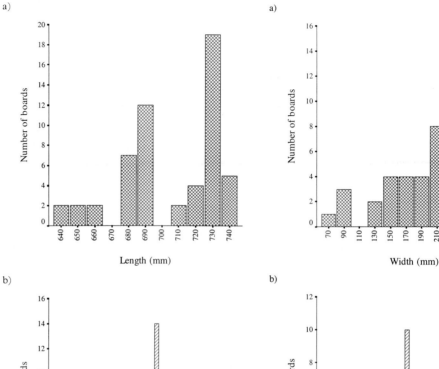

timbers matches particularly well are all produced from other groups of timbers imported into various parts of north-west Europe from the eastern Baltic region (*see* Table 10.11). These include the panels from Sutton House, London,[39] the ceiling/frieze boards from Winchester[40] and the planks from tanks at Blaydes Staithe, Hull,[41] all of which were initially used a few decades either side of *c* AD 1500 and are therefore of a similar date to the Bowhill ceiling. The match with the chronology produced from the Winchester College boards is

particularly good ($t = 17.45$), and raises the question whether the Bowhill ceiling boards and sub-ribs were part of the same consignment as the Winchester College phase 1 boards which were felled during the period AD 1498–1505. The results of comparison of the individual board and sub-rib ring sequences from the two assemblages does not indicate any obvious same-tree or same-board links. It is certainly possible, however, that given the comparable felling dates of both assemblages, they may well be derived from a similar source.

Timber in the form of oak planking was extensively exported from the eastern Baltic region from the early 14th century until around AD 1650, primarily through the German Hanse. Extensive documentary evidence in customs accounts,[42] buildings accounts[43] and the detailed records from the Danish Books of the Sound Dues[44] indicates its importance as a raw material. The timbers appear to have arrived exclusively in plank form and are referred to in customs accounts using a variety of names such as wainscot boards, clapboard, estriche-boards, rigold-boards and rigaboard.[45] The advances in dendrochronology over the last decade have seen the development and exchange of a large network of oak chronologies covering northern Europe. This has allowed imported oak timbers to be dated, with the added bonus of identifying the geographical region from which they were derived.[46] In England eastern Baltic timbers have kept appearing in various guises during dendrochronological studies throughout the 1990s. Dendrochronology has identified eastern Baltic boards used for panel paintings, coffins, boat planking, barrel staves, wall and ceiling panelling, doors, altars and decorative screens. Documentary evidence indicates its importation all down the eastern seaboard of both England and Scotland and around the south and west coast of England as far as Bristol.[47] Dendrochronological evidence has demonstrated the presence of such imports at various locations in England and Scotland. These include ports on the east coast of England, such as Grimsby,[48] Hull,[49] and London,[50] towns further inland, such as Abingdon,[51] Colchester,[52] Ely,[53] St Albans,[54] Salisbury,[55] Winchester,[56] and York,[57] as far north as Midhope, Stirling, St Andrews, Guthrie and Aberdeen in Scotland,[58] and now as far west as Exeter.

Major exporting ports during the latter part of the 16th century were Gdansk/Danzig in Poland, Konigsberg (now a Russian enclave between Poland and Lithuania) and Klaipeda/Courland in Lithuania.[59] The focus of the trade shifted in response to forest clearance, changing local political situations, upgrading of facilities offered to traders in competing ports and natural misfortune in the form of silting. The timber exported was likely to have been derived from extensive areas reaching far inland (as much as 500–1000km inland is thought possible),[60] employing major river systems to facilitate logging movement.

Information concerning the precise areas of origin and their changing location are still subject to clarification through ongoing documentary and dendrochronological research. This may also address issues such as whether the import trade was driven by the inability of the local woodlands to produce quality boarding or whether the availability of cheap imports prompted the production of alternative products in local woodlands.

The Bowhill ceiling boards and sub-ribs show a good match with the northern Poland chronology (see Table 10.11), although this is not necessarily at a sufficiently high level to indicate that the source of the timber is northern Poland. Further east, towards potentially important known export areas such as Lithuania, the current lack of a well-defined extensive network of regional master chronologies prevents the provision of more precise information concerning the location of the source of the timbers. Consequently the most that can be said regarding the origin of the trees used to produce the Bowhill ceiling boards and sub-ribs is that they grew in the eastern Baltic region.

Ceiling: dating evidence

Although there is no sapwood on any of the ceiling boards or sub-ribs it has been possible to provide a probable felling date range of AD 1491–c 1507 rather than just a *terminus post quem* (see above). The absence of sapwood on the boards is typical of panelling and panel paintings. This is because its more friable nature created problems where panels were jointed together and could cause severe damage to a painting if the sapwood rotted and was lost, thereby making it inappropriate for such purposes. Previous studies of panels and panel paintings of known date imply that very little heartwood would be removed during the manufacture of the panel from the raw timber.[61] This is supported by the very close coincidence of the end dates of the same-tree board groups (see Tables 10.2 and 10.13) and hence substantiates the evidence which suggests that very little heartwood is missing from the edge of most of the boards. This means that the date of the outermost ring of the majority of the boards is likely to be within relatively few years of the date of the heartwood/sapwood boundary.

The relationship of the felling date to the initial use of the boards also relies on evidence from previous studies of panels and panel paintings of known date. The period of time taken for transport, storage and manufacture, either before or after importation, appears to be minimal.[62] Consequently the date of use of the boards is likely to be within the same range as the felling-date range quoted, with the slight possibility that if the boards had the maximum expected number of sapwood rings the usage date could be a few years after the latest possible felling year. It is, therefore, possible that the boards and sub-ribs were associated with the initial building phase at Bowhill of c AD 1500. As Roger Holand died in 1506 and his estate was probably not settled until c 1518 (Chapter 3), it seems most likely that the ceiling timbers are associated with his building activities rather than those of his heirs. Evidence from the structural details of the ceiling suggests, however, that the boards and sub-ribs were a later insertion, as there are two forms of provision for the ceiling in the fabric (Chapter 6). The felling-date range would allow for this possibility if they were inserted shortly after the completion of the primary building phase or they could quite simply be reused. There is no evidence from the dendrochronological analysis to indicate reuse as they are clearly a coherent single-phase, single-source group of timbers. It is of course possible that they were reused en masse from another ceiling either at Bowhill or perhaps another building. This was the case at Sutton House, London, where the linenfold panelling was thought to pre-date the house. Further support was provided for this supposition by the dendrochronological analysis.[63] At Bowhill an alternative explanation in the form of a change of plan in the detailed construction of the ceiling during the primary building phase is proposed by Blaylock (Chapter 6). This is based on both the dendrochronological results and the fact that the sequence of paint layers on the main ceiling beams, which are integral to the primary build, is the same as on the boards and sub-ribs. If the boards and sub-ribs are primary timbers associated with the primary building phase at Bowhill, they at least provide support for the c 1500 construction date proposed from other archaeological evidence and perhaps hinted at by the dated structural timbers.

Ceiling: anomalous board

The successful dating of fifty-four of the boards makes the failure of the fifty-fifth board (AE) all the more frustrating. It does not prove that this board is of a different date or source, as it may simply be one of a percentage of timbers that do not date. The success rate for providing dates for individual timbers that meet the minimum criteria for analysis ranges from around 50 per cent on large complex urban sites to nearly 100 per cent on rural sites of similar size, perhaps reflecting the higher likelihood of source variation on urban sites. A tentative match was noted which, if it could be proven, would indicate that AE is contemporary with the rest of the boards. No differences in appearance could be distinguished by visual examination of board AE, such as in the way it had been worked. It seems most likely that the general climatic signal, so important for absolute dating purposes, has been masked in the ring sequence of AE by the influence of specific local environmental conditions.

Ceiling: board size

The extant length of the boards shows that the majority of the boards are between 680mm and 750mm, although there appear to be two possible groups within this (Table 10.15a). The width of the boards is relatively constant, particularly when bearing in mind that the smaller boards are often clearly fragmented lengthwise and so do not represent a true board width (Table 10.16a). The majority of the boards seem to range from 210mm to 270mm wide. The maximum thickness of the boards hardly varies (9–12mm) but is approximately 35 per cent of that of the lower sub-ribs (29mm; 30mm). The relationship of the board size to the raw material imported is somewhat more difficult to determine. Documentary evidence is of little help and the only original-sized raw planks known comprise the cargo from the Copper Wreck. These planks had dimensions of: length 2.2–2.3m; width 240–300mm; thickness 40–65mm.[64] Planks such as these could easily be converted into perhaps nine, twelve or more boards of the size found at Bowhill and would certainly explain the high number of same-board or same-tree matches produced.

Structural/ceiling: woodland type

The two groups of dated material from Bowhill are broadly contemporary but are very different in visual characteristics. These reflect the nature of the woodlands or landscape from which they were derived, as well as traditional management techniques.

The timbers selected for dendrochronological analysis are by their nature those from the longer-lived trees and, therefore, not truly representative of the overall structural assemblage. The assessments undertaken in 1996 and 1999, however, provided the opportunity to see many of the other structural elements. The overall impression is that they were generally derived from fast-grown young trees. The trees used to provide the majority of structural elements were probably well under 100 years old when felled and are more likely to have been about 40–60 years old. There are some exceptions that may have been up to about 150 years old at felling. The average ring widths suggest a relatively open environment for tree growth and the sudden growth suppressions in some may suggest anthropogenic influences, possibly in the form of woodland management. In contrast the ceiling boards were derived from slow-grown, long-lived, straight-grained trees. These appear to be derived from trees over 200 years old that have grown in a closed high-canopy environment. The differences are highlighted in Table 10.17, although it should be noted that the ring-sequence length is generally an underestimate of tree age.

Table 10.17 Diagram comparing the ring sequence length and average growth rates of the structural elements and parlour ceiling boards and sub-ribs. Note that the shorter ring sequence lengths in the ceiling board group are usually from boards which appear to be sections of originally wider, but now broken, boards

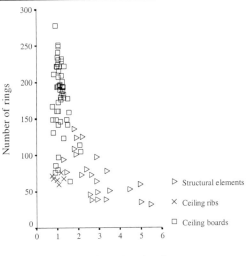

Average growth rate (mm/year)

These differences are at least in part due to the English forestry traditions that appear to have resulted in the production of trees of a very different nature to those in the eastern Baltic region. Some areas in England, however, such as Devon and East Anglia, are particularly noticeable within the dendrochronological field for producing fast-grown and apparently short, stocky trees.[65]

Work on similar buildings

As indicated above, Bowhill is one of a group of six high-status buildings with a series of distinctive features. The group is thus considered of great importance to the architectural history of the area. The other five buildings were the subject of a dendrochronological request made to English Heritage in November 1998. Cadhay House was rejected at assessment stage, but the results from the analysis of the remaining four buildings suggest that construction of this group took place over a period spanning the early to mid-15th century to the late 15th century,[66] with Bowhill clearly falling at the end of this period. The extensive sampling programmes deliberately employed at these other buildings, and the results, highlight the problems associated with dendrochronological analysis in Devon. This and a number of other points raised by these analyses, such as variation in timber source according to whether a building is within or outside the medieval city wall, could be addressed in the future when more buildings in Exeter have been successfully analysed.

Methodological implications

The application of dendrochronology to historic buildings changed and developed to a great extent during the 1980s and early 1990s. The approach to the dendrochronological analysis of Bowhill would, therefore, have been somewhat different if the request had been made now, as indeed would that of the general archaeological approach.

It is now standard practice for a dendrochronologist to undertake an assessment of a building prior to sampling, in order to identify the presence of timbers suitable for analysis and to allow a suitable sampling strategy to be formulated. Alternatively, if the timbers are considered unsuitable for dendrochronological analysis, the building is rejected and this aspect of the survey abandoned. An assessment of the building was undertaken in 1990, but by then many of the timbers associated with the phases of interest had been removed or partially replaced or were inaccessible at the time of the site visit. In addition the problems of the successful application of dendrochronological analysis in Devon were only really recognised in the mid-1990s. Reassessment of both *ex situ* (1996) and *in situ* (1999) timbers was the only way to ensure that Bowhill had been adequately assessed using current criteria and with the benefit of knowledge gained from numerous other building assessments in Devon.

The original request for the dendrochronological analysis at Bowhill was made at a stage when it was usual for one or two slices obtained during repair or a couple of photographs to be considered adequate. The removal of samples in the form of cores from historic buildings only became widely used after the early 1980s. The results produced by the structural elements serve as an example of the value of the more extensive sampling strategies currently applied and also show the need for these strategies to remain flexible. The recently published guidelines[67] indicate that a minimum of eight to ten samples per phase should be obtained. It could be argued that the sampling of the structural elements associated with the primary construction phase at Bowhill has achieved this. These few samples are spread throughout three different ranges of the building, however, and such an extensive single phase of construction may well utilise different, though nevertheless probably local, sources of timber. The sampling strategy applied now would be more extensive. It would ensure that samples of known location and function within the building were taken throughout the three ranges from the phases of interest. Wholly unprovenanced timbers would be ignored. The quantity of samples taken would be partially dependent on how relatively well dated the ranges were, the dendrochronological quality of the timbers and the aims of the project. The removal of eight to ten samples per phase is sufficient if the dendrochronological analysis is only required to provide a date, there are no additional complications such as reuse of timbers, and the timbers are dating material of high quality in an area for which plenty of reference data are available. Devon is, however, a notorious black-spot for successful dendrochronological dating. The majority of timbers at Bowhill clearly contain inadequate numbers of rings, while most of the rest are borderline with respect to the number of rings present. Consequently a far more extensive sampling strategy would have been drawn up for Bowhill in order to attempt to address the aims of the analysis adequately. A more rigorous approach to the sampling of the structural timbers (as is now widely practised), rather than the ad hoc approach used at Bowhill, is likely to have been more successful in dating the timbers, especially in the light of the results from the other roofs of the Exeter group (discussed in Howard's report that follows).

The ceiling boards have also provided valuable information supporting the evidence from panel paintings that a *t*-value of greater than 20 can be expected from boards derived from the same, or perhaps an adjacent, radius of a single timber. This aspect will be further investigated as part of the ongoing research when a larger body of data has been acquired.

Conclusion

The production of precise felling dates has not been possible for either of the groups of timbers analysed from Bowhill. The dated structural elements were all probably felled and used after AD 1478. It cannot be over-stressed, however, that the six dated structural timbers are of uncertain provenance and must, therefore, be regarded with suspicion. The results produced for the parlour ceiling boards and sub-ribs are significantly more valuable. They were probably felled and initially used during the period AD 1491–*c* 1507, during the life of Roger Holand. The tree-ring evidence cannot determine whether the boards were inserted during or shortly after the primary construction phase or whether they may have been reused from elsewhere, although other information discussed above (Chapter 6) indicates that they were more likely to be part of the primary construction. Assuming this to be the case, they certainly provide supporting evidence for the construction date of *c* 1500 indicated by other archaeological evidence. No dating evidence was provided for any other phases of repair or modification.

The structural timbers assemblage appears likely to be of local origin but the boards and sub-ribs were derived from timber imported from the eastern Baltic region and are the largest single-phase Baltic assemblage yet analysed from an archaeological

---

or historic building context. The utilisation of timbers imported from the Baltic for high quality panelling has been presumed to occur throughout the country, but this is the most westerly group of dendrochronologically proven timber of Baltic origin to be found and analysed. The boards are thus an important data-set for ongoing research into the historic timber trade from a dendrochronological perspective.

Although the reworking of the data from timbers analysed previously and the analysis of the few new samples proved disappointing in that no additional timbers could be dated, it has been useful to incorporate all of the analyses now undertaken on both groups of timbers from Bowhill into a single report. It has allowed comments to be made on various aspects of the way in which dendrochronological techniques are now applied to historic buildings and the value of the current approach and its need to remain flexible. It also highlights the need for careful recording and labelling of timbers removed during repair, so that these can if required be incorporated into an analysis at a later date. The opportunity to carry out a detailed post-analysis assessment of extant *in situ* timbers has shown quite clearly that Bowhill can finally be 'laid to rest' as far as dendrochronological analysis is concerned.

The results from Bowhill and those from the other buildings within this locally characteristic group (below) serve to emphasise the difficulties of dendrochronological analysis in Devon and hence the importance of the English Heritage research project aimed at addressing these problems.[68]

Tree-ring analysis of timbers from four of the Exeter group of medieval roofs

by Robert Howard, Robert Laxton and Cliff Litton[69]

Summary

The five other roofs of the Exeter group were inspected and four were sampled for dendrochronological dating in 1998–9. Analysis of fourteen samples from the roof of the Archdeacon of Exeter's House resulted in the production of a single-site chronology of 219 rings spanning the period AD 1186–1404 and an estimated felling date in the range AD 1415–40. Analysis of thirty samples from the floor and roof of the great chamber of the Deanery in the Cathedral Close produced four site chronologies of which two dated: one (six samples/171 rings) dated to the period AD 1233–1403; the other (two samples/85 rings) spanning the period AD 1322–1406. A further single sample dated to AD 1314–99. Interpretation of the sapwood suggests two phases of felling: the timbers of the floor have an estimated felling date range of AD 1400–35, those of the roof an estimated felling date range of AD 1418–53. It is also possible that all the timbers were felled at the same time in the period AD 1413–48. Sampling of the roof of the open hall (the Law Library) in a rear range of nos 8–9 The Close produced no datable samples. Analysis of fourteen samples from the roof of the adjacent front range produced two site chronologies (of two samples/143 rings and three samples/83 rings). Unfortunately neither cross-matched with reference chronologies and the site must remain undated for the moment. Analysis of twenty-six samples from the roof of Exeter Guildhall produced three site chronologies. The first (eight samples/143 rings) spans the period AD 1314–1456, with a felling date in the range AD 1463–98. The second and third site chronologies failed to date.

Introduction

This section describes the results of a programme of sampling of the Exeter group of roofs for tree-ring analysis. The project was initiated by English Heritage at the suggestion of Dr N W Alcock, one of the referees of this monograph. After reading an early draft of Chapter 8, Alcock suggested that such a project could refine the rather imprecise dating of the other roofs in the group, could thus improve the overall discussion of these buildings and set their chronology on a firmer basis than was possible with the dating evidence available from other sources. The roof of Cadhay, Ottery St Mary, was inspected in the initial stages of the project, but the timber was judged unsuitable for sampling (too fast-grown and with too few rings for any chance of success).[70] Sampling of the other roofs took place between December 1998 and August 1999. The Law Library roof was sampled, but the samples were not measured or analysed, as they proved to have too few rings. The adjacent range of no. 9 The Close was sampled and yielded tentative results. Although this range may be contemporary with the Law Library, the relationship is far from certain. Summary results from the four roofs that yielded results are described individually below. A series of archive reports has been prepared for the Ancient Monuments Laboratory, in which the detailed results are presented.[71]

The Archdeacon of Exeter's House, Palace Gate, Exeter

Sampling

A total of fourteen different oak timbers within the roof were sampled by coring. No timbers were available from the lower walls or floors of the building. Each sample was given the code EXT-A (for Exeter site A) and numbered 01–14. The positions of the cores were recorded at the time of sampling

on drawings provided by Stuart Blaylock.[72] The trusses were numbered from site-south to site-north (in reality south-west to north-east). Where members were made up of more than one piece (the arch braces, for example) they were further described, that is, upper or lower sections. Details of the samples are given in Table 10.18.

Analysis and dating

The samples were prepared by sanding and polishing and their growth-ring widths measured. All fourteen samples were compared with each other and at a value of $t = 4.5$ a single group composed of twelve samples formed. The ring widths from these twelve samples were combined at their suggested relative offsets to form EXTASQ01, a site chronology of 219 rings.

Table 10.18 Details of tree-ring samples from the Archdeacon of Exeter's House, Exeter

sample number	sample location	total rings	sapwood rings*	first measured ring date	last heartwood ring date	last measured ring date
EXT-A01	East arch brace (upper part), truss I	88	h/s	–	–	–
EXT-A02	East arch brace (lower part), truss I	100	h/s	AD 1300	1399	1399
EXT-A03	East arch brace (lower part), truss II	148	no h/s	AD 1202	–	1349
EXT-A04	West mid-rib (lower part), bay V	158	no h/s	AD 1186	–	1343
EXT-A05	West arch brace (lower part), truss VI	143	h/s	AD 1257	1399	1399
EXT-A06	West mid-rib (lower part), bay VI	130	h/s	AD 1269	1398	1398
EXT-A07	West lower purlin, truss VI–VII	138	no h/s	–	–	–
EXT-A08	West principal rafter, truss VI	141	no h/s	AD 1253	–	1393
EXT-A09	West mid-rib (upper part), bay V	200	h/s	AD 1203	1400	1400
EXT-A10	West arch brace (upper part), truss V	155	no h/s	AD 1240	–	1394
EXT-A11	West principal rafter, truss IV	133	h/s	AD 1271	1404	1404
EXT-A12	East arch brace (upper part), truss IV	104	no h/s	AD 1244	–	1347
EXT-A13	East upper purlin, truss V–VI	75	no h/s	AD 1315	–	1389
EXT-A14	East arch brace (lower part), truss VI	82	h/s	AD 1323	1404	1404

*h/s = the heartwood/sapwood boundary is the last ring on sample.

Table 10.19 Results of cross-matching site chronology EXTASQ01 and relevant reference chronologies when first ring date is AD 1186 and last measured ring date is AD 1404

reference chronology	span of chronology	t-value
East Midlands	AD 882–1981	4.8
MGB-E01	AD 401–1981	8.1
Southern England	AD 1083–589	6.8
Worcester Cathedral, Worcester, Worcs	AD 1181–1291	7.1
Chichester Cathedral, Sussex	AD 1173–1295	6.1
Reading, Berks	AD 1160–1407	5.2
Mercers Hall, Gloucester	AD 1289–1541	5.6
Ware Priory, Herts	AD 1223–1416	6.3

Site chronology EXTASQ01 was successfully cross-matched with a series of relevant reference chronologies for oak, giving it a first ring date of AD 1186 and a last measured ring date of AD 1404. Evidence for this date is given in the *t*-values of Table 10.19.

Taking the heartwood/sapwood boundary on those samples in the site chronology where it exists, the average last heartwood ring date is AD 1400. The usual 95 per cent confidence limits for sapwood on mature oaks from this part of England is in the range fifteen to forty rings. This would give the timbers represented by these samples an estimated felling date in the range AD 1415–40.

Site chronology EXTASQ01 was compared with the two remaining ungrouped samples, but there was no further satisfactory cross-matching. Each of the two remaining ungrouped samples was compared individually with the reference chronologies. There was, however, no satisfactory cross-matching and these samples must therefore remain undated.

Conclusion

From the tree-ring dating it would appear that the roof of the Archdeacon's House dates from the early to mid-15th century. It is, therefore, slightly earlier than expected and its dating helps to refine the relative dating of other similar buildings in and around Exeter.

The Deanery, Cathedral Close, Exeter

Sampling

A total of thirty different oak timbers was sampled by coring or, in one case, by slicing. Each sample was given the code EXT-B (for Exeter, site B) and numbered 01–30. Thirteen samples, EXT-B01–13, were obtained from timbers of the roof; the remaining seventeen samples, EXT-B14–30, were taken from the floor by Cathy Groves of the University of Sheffield Dendrochronology Laboratory, in August 1998.

The locations of samples were recorded on plans provided by Exeter Archaeology.[73] The trusses were numbered from east to west. Only a small portion of the roof between trusses 1 and 2 (bay 1) was uncovered and was accessible from an inserted floor (without the use of a scaffolding tower). From this inserted floor, however,

a substantial number of timbers were available. The height of the roof timbers elsewhere in the great chamber would have required access from a scaffolding tower for fully accessible sampling, but this could not be arranged at the time of coring. Furthermore, the underside of the roof elsewhere, beyond bay 1, had been boarded and plastered so that only the timbers of the main trusses were visible. A close inspection of these timbers from a ladder showed that most of them had very wide rings, making them unsuitable for analysis by dendrochronology; only two of these were sampled.

The floor frame was divided up into bays formed by the main north–south cross beams. The bays were numbered 1–5 from east to west. Bay 1 was taken up with the modern stairs and lobbies and was not exposed. The individual joists were numbered from south to north, including the larger east–west timbers at the southern edge of the floor that may have been part of the frame. Access for sampling at this time was made difficult by floorboards being re-laid as coring was in progress. Access to the northern end of bay 5 and all but the southern edge of bay 2 was not possible. Nor was it possible to sample the lower layer of reused joists beneath those in bays 2–4, as the upper layer of joists prevented access at suitable angles for coring.

A sliced sample, EXT-B30, was also provided by John Allan of the RAM Museum, Exeter; this was obtained from contractors working on site. Its position was not recorded and the exact location of the timber from which it came is unknown. Details of all the samples are given in Table 10.20.

Analysis

Each sample was prepared by sanding and polishing. One sample, EXT-B29, was found to have too few rings for satisfactory analysis and was not measured. The growth-ring widths of all remaining twenty-nine samples were measured and compared with each other by the Litton/Zainodin grouping procedure.[74] At a minimum *t*-value of 4.5 four groups of samples formed.

The six samples of the first group cross-matched with each other to form EXTBSQ01, a site chronology of 171 rings. Site chronology EXTBSQ01 was compared with a series of relevant reference chronologies for oak, giving it a first ring date of AD 1233 and a last measured ring date of AD 1403. Evidence for this dating is given in the *t*-values of Table 10.21.

Table 10.20 Details of samples from floor and roof of the great chamber, The Deanery

sample number	sample location	total rings	sapwood rings*	first measured ring date	last heartwood ring date	last measured ring date
	great chamber roof					
EXT-B01	south principal rafter, truss 2	144	h/s	AD 1260	1403	1403
EXT-B02	south arch brace, truss 2	100	no h/s	–	–	–
EXT-B03	south cove rafter, frame 5, bay 1	54	no h/s	–	–	–
EXT-B04	south intermediate rib, bay 1 (midrib)	104	no h/s	AD 1279	–	1382
EXT-B05	south common rafter 1, bay 1	75	no h/s	–	–	–
EXT-B06	north common rafter 1, bay 1	75	no h/s	–	–	–
EXT-B07	north mid-rib frame 3	57	no h/s	–	–	–
EXT-B08	north common rafter, frame 3, bay 1	62	no h/s	–	–	–
EXT-B09	collar, frame 2	71	no h/s	–	–	–
EXT-B10	north arch brace, truss 2	85	h/s	AD 1316	1400	1400
EXT-B11	south principal rafter, truss 6	84	h/s	AD 1322	1405	1405
EXT-B12	south principal rafter, truss 4	83	h/s	AD 1324	1406	1406
EXT-B13	north post, truss 2	55	h/s	AD 1348	1402	1402
	great chamber floor					
EXT-B14	joist 5, bay 5	95	h/s	–	–	–
EXT-B15	joist 6, bay 5	77	h/s	–	–	–
EXT-B16	joist 4, bay 5	72	6	–	–	–
EXT-B17	joist 3, bay 5	76	2	–	–	–
EXT-B18	joist 2, bay 5	70	h/s	–	–	–
EXT-B19	joist 1, bay 5	65	h/s?	–	–	–
EXT-B20	cross beam 4	86	h/s?	AD 1314	1399	1399
EXT-B21	joist 4, bay 4	110	no h/s	–	–	–
EXT-B22	joist 2, bay 4	97	no h/s	–	–	–
EXT-B23	joist 1, bay 4	152	6c	AD 1233	1378	1384
EXT-B24	joist 1, bay 3	106	h/sc	AD 1287	1392	1392
EXT-B25	joist 2, bay 3	85	no h/s	–	–	–
EXT-B26	joist 9, bay 3	95	4	–	–	–
EXT-B27	joist 12, bay 3	60	h/s	–	–	–
EXT-B28	cross beam 3	74	3	–	–	–
EXT-B29	joist 1, bay 4	nm	–	–	–	–
EXT-B30	not known	76	h/s	–	–	–

*h/s = the heartwood/sapwood boundary is the last ring on the sample.
c = complete sapwood on timber, all or part lost on sampling.
nm = not measured.

Table 10.21 Results of cross-matching site chronology EXTBSQ01 and relevant reference chronologies when first ring date is AD 1233 and last ring date is AD 1403

reference chronology	span of chronology	t-value
East Midlands	AD 882–1981	5.6
England	AD 401–1981	5.1
Southern England	AD 1083–1589	7.2
Kent-88	AD 1158–1540	3.8
Reading waterfront, Berks	AD 1160–1407	5.6
Chichester Cathedral, Sussex	AD 1173–1295	5.2
Ware Priory, Ware, Herts	AD 1223–1416	5.6
Chicksands Priory, Beds	AD 1200–1541	4.3
Daneway House, Sapperton, Glos	AD 1201–1315	5.1

Table 10.22 Results of cross-matching site chronology EXTBSQ04 and relevant reference chronologies when first ring date is AD 1322 and last ring date is AD 1406

reference chronology	span of chronology	t-value
England, mid-west	AD 860–1753	5.4
England, south-east	AD 435–1790	4.6
England, south-west	AD 770–1798	5.3
Harmondsworth, Middx	AD 1262–1426	4.5
St Mary's Guildhall, Coventry, W Mids	AD 1316–1422	4.6
Hereford City	AD 915–1617	5.9
St Cuthbert's, Wick, Worcs	AD 1257–1496	5.0
Mercers Hall, Gloucester	AD 1289–1541	4.8
Lower Chilverton, Devon	AD 1315–1488	5.3
Archdeacon's House, Exeter	AD 1186–1404	5.8

Table 10.23 Results of cross-matching sample EXT-B20 and relevant reference chronologies when first ring date is AD 1314 and last ring date is AD 1399

reference chronology	span of chronology	t-value
England, East Anglia	AD 781–1899	6.4
England, south-east	AD 435–1790	7.1
England, south-west	AD 770–1798	6.9
England, London	AD 413–1728	5.1
Upminster, Greater London	AD 1276–1414	6.5
Netteswellbury, Essex	AD 1245–1439	7.2
St Aylotts, Essex	AD 1281–1500	5.0
High Halden, Kent	AD 1299–1462	6.2
Reading waterfront, Berks	AD 1168–1407	5.9

The eight samples of the second group cross-matched with each other to form EXTBSQ02, a site chronology of 120 rings. Site chronology EXTBSQ02 was compared with a series of relevant reference chronologies for oak, but there was no satisfactory cross-matching.

The three samples of the third group cross-matched with each other to form EXTBSQ03, a site chronology of 121 rings. Site chronology EXTBSQ03 was compared with a series of relevant reference chronologies for oak, but again there was no satisfactory cross-matching.

The two samples of the fourth and final group cross-matched with each other to form EXTBSQ04, a site chronology of eighty-five rings. Site chronology EXTBSQ04 was compared with a series of relevant reference chronologies for oak, giving it a first ring date of AD 1322 and a last measured ring date of AD 1406. Evidence for this dating is given in the t-values of Table 10.22.

The four site chronologies thus created, EXTBSQ01–04, were then compared with each other. There was, however, no further truly satisfactory cross-matching between them. Each of the four site chronologies was then compared with the remaining eleven ungrouped samples. Again there was no satisfactory cross-matching.

Each of the eleven ungrouped samples was then compared individually with a full range of reference chronologies. This indicated a cross-match for sample EXT-B20 only with a first ring date of AD 1314 and a last measured ring date of AD 1399. Evidence for this date is given in the t-values of Table 10.23.

Interpretation

The relative positions of the heartwood/sapwood boundaries on the six samples in site chronology EXTBSQ01 are not particularly consistent with a group of timbers having a single felling date. Rather, the relative positions of the heartwood/sapwood bound-aries are indicative of timbers with two distinct felling phases, as they are much earlier on samples EXT-B23 and B24, from the great chamber floor, than on samples EXT-B01, B04, B10 and B13, from the great chamber roof.

The average last heartwood ring date of only those samples from the great chamber floor is AD 1385, while the average on those from the roof only is AD 1402. The variation in the average is slightly larger than might be found in a group of timbers with a single felling date, though this is not an impossi-bility. Using fifteen to fifty rings as the 95 per cent confidence limit for the amount of sapwood would give the timbers of the floor an estimated felling date in the range AD 1400–35 and those of the roof an estimated felling date in the range AD 1417–52.

Taking the other dated samples from the roof into account (EXT-B11 and B12 in site chronology EXTBSQ04 with heartwood/sapwood transition dates of AD 1405 and 1406 respectively) would push the average last heartwood ring date of the timbers from the roof up to AD 1403. The estimated felling date would then be in the range AD 1418–53. It is probable that these two samples represent timbers from the same tree, as they cross-match with each other with a t-value of 16.7.

The relative position of the heartwood/sapwood boundaries on the samples in site chronology EXTBSQ02 appears to be consistent with a group of timbers having a single felling date. The exception to this is possibly sample EXT-B18, although the relative position of the heartwood/sapwood boundary on this sample is not unduly at odds with the others. It would appear from the cross-matching between the individual samples of this group that the timbers they represent are from trees which were all growing close to each other, with some timbers possibly being from the same tree (for example, samples EXT-B14, B17 and B18). This observation might strengthen the supposition that the timbers used were all felled at the same time.

Because none of the three samples in site chronology EXTBSQ03 have a heartwood/sapwood boundary, it is not possible to say whether or not they are of the same felling date as each other. Each could have been felled at quite a different time.

Sample EXT-B20, from cross beam 4 of the great chamber floor, has a heartwood/sapwood transition date of AD 1399.

Using the same sapwood estimate of fifteen–fifty rings would give this timber an esti-mated felling date in the range AD 1414–49.

Conclusion

It would appear possible that two of the more substantial joists from bays 3 and 4 are of one felling phase (samples EXT-B23 and B24), while those of the great chamber roof and beam 4 (samples EXT-B01, B04, B10, B11, B12, B13 and B20) are slightly later. Beam 4 is the smaller scantling cross beam. Both fellings took place in the early 15th century and as their felling date ranges overlap it remains a possibility that they could be the product of a single felling phase.

Tree-ring analysis has shown that the construction date of the great chamber is somewhat earlier than thought hitherto, being early to mid-15th century rather than early to mid-16th century. Its construction can no longer be associated with John Veysey, Dean from AD 1509–1519 and Bishop thereafter.[75]

Many joists from the great chamber floor cannot be dated, though those of larger scantling in bay 5 have been shown to be contemporary with those of smaller scantling in bays 3 and 4 that have clearly been reset at some point. Those joists in bay 2, also of small scantling but thought to be in situ, could not be sampled due to access difficulties so it has not been possible to demonstrate that they are part of the same group of joists used in bays 3–5.

Nos 8–9 The Close, Exeter

Sampling

The roofs and other timbers of the front range and open hall were viewed and initially assessed for their accessibility and their suitability for tree-ring dating. While the timbers of the front range were both relatively easily accessible and suitable, those of the hall were not particularly so. Thus initial sampling was confined to the roof of the front range. From here a total of four-teen different oak timbers was sampled by coring. Each sample was given the code EXT-D (for Exeter, site D) and numbered 01–14. The positions of these cores were recorded at the time of sampling on plans provided by Exeter Archaeology.[76] On these plans the trusses have been numbered from east to west. Details of the samples are given in Table 10.24. Sampling of timbers in the

Table 10.24 Details of samples from 8–9 The Close, Exeter

sample number	sample location	total rings	sapwood rings*	first measured ring date	last heartwood ring date	last measured ring date
EXT-D01	South principal rafter, truss IV	54	no h/s	–	–	–
EXT-D02	Collar, truss IV	54	no h/s	–	–	–
EXT-D03	South principal rafter, truss V	103	h/s	–	–	–
EXT-D04	North principal rafter, truss V	99	no h/s	–	–	–
EXT-D05	South principal rafter, truss VI	146	h/s	–	–	–
EXT-D06	North principal rafter, truss VI	122	no h/s	–	–	–
EXT-D07	Collar, truss VI	54	h/s	–	–	–
EXT-D08	South purlin, truss V–VI	54	h/s	–	–	–
EXT-D09	North purlin, truss V–VI	80	h/s	–	–	–
EXT-D10	South common rafter 1, truss V–VI	56	no h/s	–	–	–
EXT-D11	North common rafter 3, truss V–VI	80	h/s	–	–	–
EXT-D12	South purlin, truss VIII–IX	118	h/s	–	–	–
EXT-D13	South purlin, truss IX–X	98	h/s	–	–	–
EXT-D14	North purlin, truss IX–X	54	no h/s	–	–	–

*h/s = the heartwood/sapwood boundary is the last ring on the sample.

Table 10.25 Results of cross-matching site chronology EXTDSQ01 and relevant reference chronologies when first ring date is AD 1324 and last ring date is AD 1466

reference chronology	span of chronology	t-value
England, Midlands	AD 882–1981	3.2
Southern England	AD 1083–1589	3.5
Kent-88	AD 1158–1540	3.9
LOND1175	AD 413–1728	3.3
Rectory Park, Horsmonden, Kent	AD 1313–1442	3.5
Ware Priory, Herts	AD 1223–1416	4.3

north-western bay of the hall roof yielded seven cored samples, although subsequent inspection showed that the samples had too few growth rings for successful dating. Analysis was therefore not attempted on these samples.

Analysis

The growth-ring widths of the samples were compared with each other, and at a minimum t-value of 4.5 two groups of samples formed. The two samples of the first group cross-matched with each other to form EXTDSQ01, a site chronology of 143 rings. Site chronology EXTDSQ01 was compared with a series of relevant reference chronologies for oak, suggesting a first ring date of AD 1324 and a last measured ring date of AD 1466. Evidence for this possible dating is given in the t-values of Table 10.25. It will be seen from this table that the t-values are rather low. Given that

there are only two samples in this site chronology, some caution must be expressed as to its reliability. Also, even if correct, it might not represent the felling date of the rest of the timber used in the building as a whole, as it represents only two timbers. The three samples of the second group cross-matched with each other to form EXTDSQ02, a site chronology of eighty-three rings. Site chronology EXTDSQ02 was compared with a series of relevant reference chronologies for oak but there was no satisfactory cross-matching.

The two site chronologies were compared with each other and with the remaining ungrouped samples. In neither case was there any satisfactory cross-matching. Each of the nine remaining ungrouped samples was compared individually with a full range of reference chronologies, but again there was no satisfactory cross-matching.

Conclusion

Due to the lack of satisfactory cross-matching, this site must remain undated for the moment. Encouragingly there are a number of timbers with over 100 rings and so it is possible that it might date against the other material from Exeter in due course.

Exeter Guildhall, High Street

Sampling

A total of twenty-six different oak timbers was sampled by coring. Each sample was given the code EXT-E (for Exeter, site E) and numbered 01–26. The positions of the samples were recorded on elevations provided by Exeter Archaeology.[77] For the sake of clarity in identifying sample locations, the trusses have been numbered from north to south (from the rear of the building to the street frontage); in reality this is north-west to south-east. Details of the

samples are given in Table 10.26. Sampling of the timbers was undertaken after discussion with Stuart Blaylock of Exeter Archaeology. The carpentry within the roof strongly suggests that it is a single-phase construction and sampling was conducted under this interpretation.

Sampling was made difficult by the height of the roof, the lowest available timbers being some 7m from the floor and many of the others being 9–10m above floor level. Access to these timbers was gained from a mobile scaffolding tower, although the curved nature of the arch braces and the height of the upper protective rails of the tower caused difficulties in safely reaching some members.

It will be seen from Table 10.26 that relatively few of the samples have sapwood or the heartwood/sapwood boundary. This is due to the highly moulded, carved and curved nature of many of the timbers, in that there were few places where sapwood, or the heartwood/sapwood boundary, was present.

Table 10.26 Details of samples from Exeter Guildhall

sample number	sample location	total rings	sapwood rings*	first measured ring date	last heartwood ring date	last measured ring date
EXT-E01	south lower purlin, bay 1	54	20C	–	–	–
EXT-E02	south lower purlin, bay 2	75	no h/s	–	–	–
EXT-E03	east upper windbrace, south side, bay 2	75	no h/s	–	–	–
EXT-E04	south principal rafter, truss 2	55	no h/s	–	–	–
EXT-E05	south lower purlin, bay 3	106	no h/s	AD 1314	–	1419
EXT-E06	west upper windbrace, south bay 3	54	no h/s	–	–	–
EXT-E07	south upper arch brace, truss 3	66	no h/s	–	–	–
EXT-E08	south intermediate rafter, bay 3	94	no h/s	AD 1343	–	1436
EXT-E09	south principal rafter, truss 5	77	no h/s	–	–	–
EXT-E10	south lower arch brace, truss 5	87	no h/s	AD 1339	–	1425
EXT-E11	north lower purlin, bay 4	65	h/s	–	–	–
EXT-E12	east lower windbrace, south bay 4	54	no h/s	–	–	–
EXT-E13	west lower windbrace, south bay 4	54	no h/s	–	–	–
EXT-E14	east upper windbrace, north bay 5	71	h/s	–	–	–
EXT-E15	collar, truss 6	52	no h/s	–	–	–
EXT-E16	collar truss 5	72	no h/s	–	–	–
EXT-E17	north upper arch brace, truss 5	54	no h/s	–	–	–
EXT-E18	north intermediate rafter, bay 5	59	10	–	–	–
EXT-E19	south principal rafter, truss 7	77	no h/s	–	–	–
EXT-E20	north principal rafter, truss 6	72	12	AD 1385	1444	1456
EXT-E21	north principal rafter, truss 7	102	h/s	AD 1348	1449	1449
EXT-E22	south principal rafter, truss 4	106	h/s	AD 1344	1449	1449
EXT-E23	west upper windbrace, north bay 6	58	no h/s	–	–	–
EXT-E24	south principal rafter, truss 6	125	no h/s	AD 1315	–	1439
EXT-E25	north principal rafter, truss 4	101	no h/s	AD 1339	–	1439
EXT-E26	north upper arch brace, truss 6	56	no h/s	–	–	–

*h/s = the heartwood/sapwood boundary is the last ring on the sample.
C = complete sapwood retained on sample.

Given that one of the purposes of sampling was to obtain tree-rings with local data, many of the timbers were sampled to obtain maximum number of rings, even if they had no sapwood or the heartwood/sapwood boundary.

Analysis

Each sample was prepared by sanding and polishing and the growth-ring widths of all samples measured. The growth-ring widths of all twenty-six samples were compared with each other and at a minimum *t*-value of 4.5 three groups of samples formed.

The eight samples of the first group cross-matched with each other to form EXTESQ01, a site chronology of 143 rings. Site chronology EXTESQ01 was compared with a series of relevant reference chronologies for oak, giving it a first ring date of AD 1314 and a last measured ring date of AD 1456. Evidence for this dating is given in the *t*-values of Table 10.27.

The average last heartwood ring date on site chronology EXTESQ01 is AD 1448. The usual 95 per cent confidence limits for the amount of sapwood on mature oaks from this part of England is taken to be in the range fifteen to fifty rings. This would give the timbers represented by these samples an estimated felling date in the range AD 1463–98.

The two samples of the second group cross-matched with each other to form EXTESQ02, a site chronology of seventy-seven rings. Site chronology EXTESQ02 was compared with a series of relevant reference chronologies for oak, but there was no satisfactory cross-matching.

The two samples of the third and final group cross-matched to form EXTESQ03, a site chronology of seventy-seven rings. Site chronology EXTESQ03 was also compared with a series of relevant reference chronologies for oak, but again there was no satisfactory cross-matching.

The three site chronologies thus created, EXTESQ01, EXTESQ02 and EXTESQ03 were compared with each other, but there was, however, no further cross-matching. Each of the three site chronologies was then compared with all the remaining ungrouped samples. Again, there was no satisfactory cross-matching.

Each of the fourteen remaining ungrouped samples was compared with a full series of relevant reference chronologies. While this indicated some tentative cross-matches for some individual samples the *t*-values were rather low and tended to be with non-relevant chronologies, for example, those in Staffordshire, Nottinghamshire and Leicestershire. There appeared to be no consistency to this individual tentative dating and as these samples cannot, therefore, be quoted with confidence, they must remain undated.

Conclusion

It would appear that, as expected, the roof of Exeter Guildhall is of a single phase of construction. The majority of the timbers have an estimated felling date in the range AD 1463–98. Thus dating by dendrochronology supports the date expected on documentary and stylistic grounds.[78]

General conclusions

The application of analysis by tree-ring dating to this group of four buildings in Exeter raises a number of general points for discussion. First (in line with the original objective of the project) it has provided precise and reliable dates for a number of similar buildings within a small geographical area. Some of these dates are at odds with dating previously suggested on stylistic or other grounds.[79] Tree-ring dating has thus helped to place these buildings in their local and national context and permitted a more informative and accurate comparative study of the Exeter group of roofs to be made.

Table 10.27 Results of cross-matching site chronology EXTESQ01 and relevant reference chronologies when first ring date is AD 1314 and last ring date is AD 1456

reference chronology	span of chronology	t-value
East Midlands	AD 882–1981	7.0
England	AD 401–1981	6.4
Southern England	AD 1083–1589	6.3
Reading waterfront, Berks	AD 1160–1407	4.4
Lodge Park, Aldsworth, Glos	AD 1324–1587	4.6
Lacock Abbey, Wilts	AD 1314–1448	5.1

The use of dendrochronology on this group of buildings in Exeter has again clearly shown the problems faced by this science in Devon, in that dating is more difficult in south-west England than elsewhere in the country. This difficulty is generally assumed to be linked to the short growth-ring sequences commonly found on samples in this region. As is indicated by the English Heritage guidelines and in the Nottingham University monograph,[80] samples should have a minimum of fifty-five to sixty rings for satisfactory analysis. It will be seen from the various tables giving details of the analysis (Tables 10.18, 10.20, 10.24 and 10.26) that only nineteen of the samples have less than this minimum. Many of them have more than the minimum (though sometimes only just) and in theory, therefore, are suitable, with between 60 and 100 rings. Only twenty-five samples have 100 rings or more. Even where samples might be considered slightly short site chronologies have been created, although some remain undated. Thus of the eighty-four samples analysed from the four buildings, only twenty-nine (some 34 per cent) have been dated. A further seven samples were obtained from the rear range of nos 8–9 The Close (above), but these had too few rings to make analysis worthwhile.

Almost anywhere else in the country, dendrochronology might usually expect to date 60–70 per cent of samples. It appears, therefore, that while short growth-ring sequences are a problem, there may be fewer such samples from urban buildings in this area than from rural ones. Furthermore, in addition to the shortness of the growth-ring sequences, the difficulty in dating may be linked to other factors, such as the complacency, or lack of distinct annual variations, of the growth rings. This problem may only be overcome when sufficient local material has been obtained by further sampling in the region. It will be seen that very few of the reference chronologies used are from south-west England, some being made up of material from Kent, Hertfordshire and Bedfordshire.

A final point worth noting is that the analysis of these buildings in Exeter has shown the importance of sampling in conjunction with other survey techniques (especially in buildings undergoing alteration or other building work). Building survey to determine the phasing of a structure is particularly important and useful as a prelude to dendrochronological sampling, especially as an aid to determining sampling strategy, and in the provision of plans and other drawings on which the samples' locations can be recorded.

Classification of mortars and plasters

by Stuart Blaylock

Introduction

This classification is based on the visual inspection of mortar and plaster finishes *in situ* and on the description and grouping of approximately 260 samples of mortar, plaster, cob and other bonding materials from the building. Physical analysis of the mortar was not carried out on a routine basis.[81] As a result the classification is heavily dependent on visual analysis of the samples and the comparison of one sample with another. It cannot pretend to be supported by objective evidence. It will be seen, however, that the classes of mortar are quite clearly defined and support the phasing of the building derived from excavation and recording. Further analysis would certainly increase the knowledge of mortar types and refine the classes described here, although it may not affect the overall phasing very much. The bulk of the samples (c 215 examples) were collected in a concerted campaign during the first analysis of the building by EMAFU in 1987. Of the remainder some were recovered by excavation (among which were several samples from the earlier, phase 2, building on the site), while others were recovered during dismantling of the roof or by the stripping of other features of the building during the works.[82]

For practical purposes there is little by which to distinguish mortar from plaster for much of the period spanned by the structural history of Bowhill; in some instances the same mixture, or 'recipe', was employed for bonding masonry and for surface rendering. In other cases differences can be detected between mixes for mortar and plaster, especially in contexts where hair or other binding agents was used. These were, however, often relatively minor differences related to practical constraints. Hair was used in greater quantities for rendering purposes, where its qualities as a binder were most needed, than in adjacent 'core mortars' of the same date, which would often display traces of hair in a very similar matrix.

This might be interpreted as the use of a single common recipe, with the admixture of hair (or extra hair) when it was intended to be used for rendering. Similarly, the lime mortars of class 1 (below) contained variable gauges of grit inclusions according to the intended use – coarse grit in core mortars, very fine inclusions for bonding ashlar or for the surface skim of plaster.

The general experience of medieval lime mortar in Exeter and its area is that very little change can be detected between the 12th and the 16th centuries and, visually at least, all medieval lime mortars are very similar in composition. Given the limited range of materials in mortar and thus the uniformity of good-quality mixtures, it is perhaps not surprising that so little variety can be detected. There is a much greater variety in post-medieval mortars (mainly due to the use of variant materials, especially earth or earth-derived sand). When a good-quality mix of lime and sand (or grit) is required, however, the product is still very similar in appearance in, for example, the 19th century as it was in the 12th-century towers of the Norman Cathedral. Further, where the optimum mixture was required, there was very little variation through time until the introduction of the use of cements which, in Devon, seems to have not become widespread until the mid to late 19th century. As a further example, a section of the city wall in Southernhay, Exeter, can be quoted, where breccia ashlar masonry and good-quality lime mortar are employed in a build dated by an inscribed datestone to 1743. Without the evidence of the inscription, this section could easily have been dated to the 16th century or even earlier.[83] The uniformity emphasises a problem in this analysis and highlights the limitations of mortar used in isolation as an indicator of date. Despite this it has been possible to construct for Bowhill a sequence of mortars with broad chronological limits, although with the general qualification that individual samples are prone to error or misplacing in the absence of independent evidence of their date by context or stratigraphic relationship.

Later plasters, relating to the later 19th and 20th centuries, have not been examined in detail in this analysis and are classed together in a miscellaneous category. This is partly because of the reduced emphasis given to the later structural history of the building in general, but also because the stripping of the building of modern accretions that took place in the early phases of the repair programme (in the late 1970s) included finishes of this period and, therefore, had removed much of the evidence for the latest stage(s) in the sequence.

Classes of mortar[84]

Class 1

Primary lime mortars and plasters, used throughout phase 3 (and in phase 2). Everywhere the primary masonry was mortar bonded and wherever primary plaster survived on interior surfaces, whether of masonry or cob, the bonding/rendering material belonged to the spectrum of medieval-type mortars (above). The few samples recovered from the excavated remains of the phase 2 building beneath the south range also fell within the same spectrum. These mortars were hard, white or off-white (or occasionally pinkish) lime mortars with moderate to frequent fine/medium grit inclusions, possibly derived from river sand. There was considerable variation in the size of aggregate – demonstrated by samples from the reveal of window 63 (large) and the splay of the oriel window 51 (smaller). Samples:

a. Mortars: 49, 61, 70, 71, 79, 98, 185, 203, 248, 254, 258, 275/283, 294, 303.
b. Plasters on stone: 63, 98, 102.
c. Plasters on cob: 51, 110, 112, 118, 124/128, 139/140, 210, 214.
d. Samples derived from the fabric and destruction deposits of the phase 2 building beneath the south range: 653, 658, 693.
e. Fallen plaster from an excavated deposit of phase 6, presumably phase 3 wall plaster: 688.
f. Occasionally, where fine masonry was employed, the coarse element in the mortar is reduced to the point where the mixture appears almost as unadulterated lime; an example of this is found in the mortar bonding the joggled joints of the fireplace of the great chamber: 102.

Class 2

Clay bonding materials were used in the footings and lowest courses of some of the interior facework of the primary (phase 3) masonry, although never in quoins (which were always bonded in lime mortar); this material was shown to be primary by overlying primary plaster in several places. Samples: 248, 254, 267.

Class 3

A class of pink(ish) lime mortars not far removed from the spectrum of class 1, but distinguished by their association with early alterations to the building, either during construction or within the 16th century (phase 4, and possibly also phase 5): the mid-16th-century construction of a door on the site of the decommissioned garderobe in the south elevation; the ?stair door in the parlour; the inserted door in the west wall of the kitchen. The mortar is good-quality hard lime mortar, sometimes white, but with a tendency to be pink and otherwise very similar in composition to class 1. Samples: 12, 13, 21, 84?, 249, 262, 278.

Class 4

An isolated use of a very distinctive soft mortar, varying in colour from yellow ochre to pink, with flecks of white lime and fine grit, but largely silty or sandy in texture and yellow in colour. The mixture occurs in the facework and associated plasters of the inserted fireplace and chimney stack in the west service room of the south range (which also shows a mortar of class 3 and is assigned to phase 4 or 5); it is probably unique, although there was one possible further instance in the blocking of the chase for a stair in that room (342: not sampled). Samples: 182, 235.

Class 5

White lime mortar and plaster mix within the spectrum of the primary mortars, but with the admixture of white hair binding. This is most notably associated with the pair of windows in the south-west corner of the parlour, constructed during the enlargement of the parlour in the later 17th or early 18th century (phase 7). Samples: 23 (but unhaired), 26/31, 27, 31, 32. Note that red lime(/earth) mortars are also associated with work of this phase. Samples: 5, 26, 259.

The inclusion of hair in mortars, but especially in plasters, is particularly associated with post-medieval dating in Exeter; no examples of medieval mixes that include hair are known, but the use of hair in mortar and plaster is well documented in the later 16th century and onwards. Several grades of hair were used, for instance, in plastering in the Elizabethan front block of Exeter Guildhall in the 1590s.[85] Haired plasters and mortars are frequent thereafter up to the 19th century.

Class 5a

An associated type seen only in the vicinity of the north-western window of the inner chamber (exterior elevation), 137. This window comprised a late 16th- to early 17th-century frame (of phase 5) inserted here in a modified form at some later date (possibly late 17th century (phase 7) if the association between the frame and a sample of plaster of class 6 (below) is correct). The sill was a still later insertion, with mortar of class 7 (thus phase 8). The insertion led to the enlargement of the window embrasure, especially on the outside and the exterior render around the original window was disturbed. The damage was repaired and the new embrasure plastered with a white lime mortar with frequent medium grit inclusions, not dissimilar in appearance to that of class 1, but distinguished from it by the heavy use of distinctive red and red-brown hair. Thus this mortar is similar to class 5, but differs in the use of coloured as opposed to white hair. Sample: 137.

Class 6

A dark red earth/heavily haired plaster, the use of which was centred on the inner chamber. Composed of very fine-grained earth, dark or strong red in colour, occasional very fine lime and grit inclusions, held together by a dense mat of dark-coloured hair; up to 16mm in thickness (measured from samples of 151). On the surface was a skim of three or four layers of limewash. The material was used as the primary rendering on both sides of the partition dividing the great chamber and inner chamber; the frame of this structure is of a post-medieval type, most probably late 17th century in date and this indicates the probable date of the plaster. The material was also used for a secondary plastering of the north and south walls of the inner chamber (the west wall did not survive). Although the later finishes had been stripped from the walls, traces survived throughout the inner chamber, mainly where the primary plaster was hacked to key in the new coat. The later plaster was preserved in the cavities. The reveals of the windows in the north wall of the inner chamber showed class 6 plaster adhering to bare cob, suggesting that both windows had been enlarged at the same time.[86] Samples: 38 (but out of context), 109 (several samples), 137, 139/140 (a sample of primary lime plaster with traces of re-rendering with plaster of class 6 on its surface); 139 (178? different colour), 151.

Class 7

A very large class comprising mortars and plasters composed of red-coloured earths and lime, characteristically mixed so that the lime appears as white flecks or inclusions in the mixture. A range of colours is represented, from pale pink-red through to the dark red imparted by the raw material deriving from the Permian sandstones or breccias and their associated subsoils, on which the site stands.[87] A variety of mixtures is seen – some have hair, some have straw or chaff as a binder, rarely neither is present. Although the immediately local character of the materials suggests a wide bracket for this class, the evidence of context shows that the majority of mixes of this type are associated with the major alterations of phase 8. Samples:

a. Mortars: 4, 6, 9, 18, 25, 48, 50, 55, 62, 74, 86 (repair?), 89, 95, 96, 106, 137?, 138, 166, 177, 179, 180, 183, 186, 196/349, 198, 201, 219, 220, 221, 222, 223, 229, 232, 234, 236, 243, 245, 247, 253, 266, 269, 284, 285, 286, 296, 306, 309, 406.
b. Plasters with hair: 10, 33, 51, 404 (external render from the west wall of the south range).
c. Plasters with chaff: loose (unprovenanced) sample.
d. Plasters with both hair and chaff: 226.
e. Misc related mixes: 24, 100, 114, 175, 200, 239, 240.
f. Misc unrelated mixes; probably of the same phase by association: 273.

Class 8

White lime mortars and/or plasters are also associated with the work of phase 8. These are distinguished from the mortars of class 1 only by context. The reasons for using mortar of this type as well as the near-ubiquitous earth and lime mixes of class 7 are obscure; a chronological distinction is unlikely, if only because the white mortars are associated with repair of fabric after demolition, demonstrably integral to phase 7. White, off-white or cream lime mortars with plentiful grit, sometimes with distinguishable white lime inclusions. Samples: 19, 75, 78, 83, 85a, 85b, 87, 92 (×2), 104 (with hair), 200 (hair plaster), 229, 276, 289.

Class 9

A spectrum of brown mortars, ranging from buff (ish) lime mortars to soft brown earth mortars. All are from contexts that have been assigned to phase 9 (19th-century date); many are associated with the insertion of sash windows. Buff/pale brown/mixed white and brown, moderate medium-sized grit, lime flecks common; hair occasional–moderate; charcoal and chaff occasional (charcoal is characteristic of 19th-century mortars elsewhere). Samples: 7, 8, 10, 11, 16, 67, 80, 102, 103, 107, 126?, 151, 155, 157, 241, 288, 290.

Class 10

A variety of later mortars and cement-and-sand mixes from later 19th- and 20th-century contexts (phases 9, 10 and 11). This class is a miscellany of late types, with no common thread. Samples:

a. Pink, sandy mortars: 46, 57, 160, 188, 299, 305.
b. Cement mixes: 22, 77, 105, 189, 300.
c. Lime and ashes, grey: 76, 241, 264?, 301?, 302, 1502.[88]

(The hard cement-based roughcast applied throughout in the 1960s or 1970s was not sampled, although specimens of this appear adhering to other samples.)

Class 11

A class of pure lime composition, mainly used for surface skims on plasters of other composition/classes. A pretty standard mix for surface skim; often as insubstantial as a coat or two of limewash. Samples: 92/1, 102.

Class 12

Cob samples: mainly primary cob, of which at least two varieties occur: the standard mix for mass walls, a redder mix filling the wall-top cavities and roof-truss chases in the south range (note that the nature of primary cob in the east range is unknown). No attempt has been made to subdivide the secondary cobs. Samples:

a. Primary cobs: 39, 53, 88, 110, 112, 127, 131, 132, 139, 202, 206, 209, 212, 218, 230, 237, 263, 277.
b. Wall-top infills: 117, 118, 121, 124/158, 134, 136, 143, 162, 164, 173, 181, 184, 190?, 192, 193, 199.
c. Secondary cobs and earth infills (undifferentiated as far as date or phase): 30, 91, 97, 109, 119, 122, 129, 137, 149, 171, 172, 195, 197, 220, 224, 244, 246, 282.
d. Burnt daub fragments: 688, 719.

A stratigraphic sequence of mortar rendering

Surviving sequences of plasters were very rare in the building. This was, no doubt, partly because the building had endured phase after phase of stripping and re-rendering (culminating in the most recent one of ubiquitous cement roughcast), but is also attributable to losses occasioned by the stripping of the building in the first stages of examination. Other than the stratification in the inner chamber, described already (above, class 6), only one area was found to retain a sequence of mortars – the first floor of the north exterior elevation of the south range around window 137. This sequence was observed when the window was removed for repair in August 1993 (*see* Figs 5.20 and 5.21).[89] All of the renders were on cob walling; the later types (3 and 4) have also been seen on stone:

1. At the top of the wall, where the cob was protected from weathering and possibly also from the various past episodes of stripping, there were quite extensive areas of rendering in white lime mortar of class 1, representing the primary rendering of the cob. In places this seemed to overlie a finer and rather greyer mixture, a lime mortar with very fine to fine grit inclusions, which was probably a make-up coat.
2. On the west reveal and above and around the lintel of the inserted moulded window (137) were areas of the heavily haired lime mortar of class 5a. The window was fitted into an original embrasure (presumably with some enlargement of the same), probably in phase 7; the plaster represents the finishing off of this insertion.
3. The familiar plaster of class 7: lime, red sand and dark-red earth, giving a white-speckled mixture that occurred all over the elevation below the eaves and elsewhere throughout the building. Here it ran over the class 1 rendering and abutted the upper edge of the stage 2 rendering (of class 5a).
4. A skim of modern hard wash was seen over the old render (1–3) where that survived; this was continuous with the ubiquitous cement roughcast of the later 20th century, applied wherever earlier rendering had not survived.

Fragments of moulded plasterwork

A number of fragments of moulded plaster were recovered from the excavation of the eastern courtyard in 1992.[90] Seventeen fragments came from unit 964,[91] one fragment came from unit 1026[92] and one fragment from unit 1022.[93] The collection contains fragments of three different moulded sections (although, since the individual fragments are small, these elements could have joined into a more complex moulding). The collection from unit 964 is made up of seven fragments of plaster without moulding, but with one plain surface; several of these have a considerably coarser composition than the average, with frequent fine and medium grit inclusions. The standard composition is considerably finer than that of class 1 mortars and plasters, above. It is a pure white fine lime plaster, with occasional fine grit inclusions. Hair binding is present although very sparse in most examples, being most distinctively visible on the surface. Although one example (that from 1026) shows a surface skim, 1 to 1.5mm thick, this is exceptional. The surfaces are finished with a clean and smooth plaster surface, but this is very thin indeed and rarely visible in section.

Three sections of moulding are represented: a quarter-round (ovolo) moulding with a projecting square fillet above (six examples from 964, one example from 1026); a broad fillet (four examples from 964; one fragment has a concave curve at the end of the fillet, possibly this should be 'read' the other way up as a corona-like moulding); a single fragment of a larger plaster element, possibly without a finished surface, in which case the fragment was either the backing of a larger element (that is, its plaster core) or represents a very crude and unidentifiable shape.

Although the excavated fragments represent a very small collection they are enough to show the former existence in the building of moulded plasterwork. Since no figural work is present, the surviving fragments represent a minimum of a moulded cornice to a ceiling, perhaps part of an over-mantel.[94] It is not possible on the surviving evidence to suggest that the fragments came from a larger feature, such as a ceiling, although this might have been demonstrable had the collection been larger. The occurrence of these fragments in the late

17th- to 18th-century fills of the large ditch (along with architectural fragments, Chapter 9) and cultivation soils associated with the 19th-century nursery gardening in the eastern courtyard is of interest in that it represents another aspect of the interior decoration of the building that has now vanished. On the basis of comparison with the incidence of architectural fragments and tiles in this part of the site (Chapter 9) it can be assumed that the fragments were derived from the building, and were removed from it at one of the phases of sustained demolition (most probably that of phase 8, c 1800, although conceivably a slightly earlier phase, as might be suggested by the single fragment from 1026). The presence of hair in plaster, and the general (although admittedly vague) 'renaissance' character of the mouldings both indicate a date after the mid-16th century.[95] This would seem to show that at least one room of the building was updated with some form of ornamental plaster work sometime in the later 16th or 17th century. Since no trace of such plastering survived in the standing building, the most probable position for the ceiling is one of the rooms of the vanished south-east range.

Physical analysis of a sample of an excavated mortar floor

This analysis was carried out on a sample of a mortar floor from the western room of the south range, exposed on the lifting of a modern concrete floor in 1993 (Chapter 4, 1502). The floor was dated to the 19th century and ascribed to phase 9 on the basis of its stratigraphic position and the fact that it sealed various earlier features.[96] The sample was analysed by Geoffrey Teychenné who writes:

> This was a firm well-compacted mortar as one might expect from a floor. ...The proportions of lime to aggregate worked out as close to three parts by volume of lime to four parts of aggregate. I am interpreting this as a mix made from equal volumes as it would seem most unlikely that the more complicated mix would have been adhered to and this would be well within the variation that one must expect using only one sample. The aggregate is a water-worn mix of sandstone and decayed granite type particles (and a few charcoal fragments)....[97]

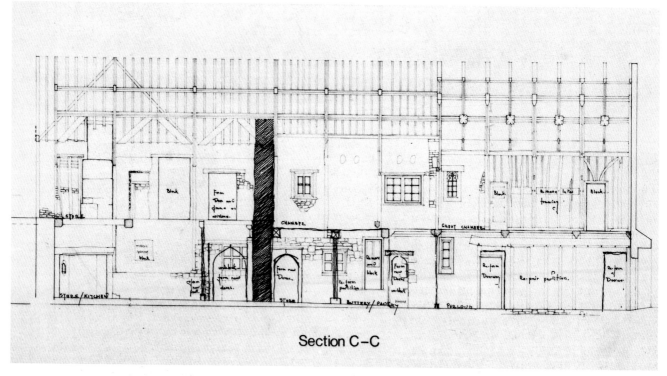

Section C-C

Figure 11.1

Longitudinal section through the south range. One of Chris Gray's survey drawings of May 1979 with freehand annotations by H G Slade identifying the following for reintroduction (ground floor, from the left): partition between west service room and through passage; (unblocking of) doorway to north end of passage; stone cross wall; new surround to existing doorway from store to courtyard; partition between store and buttery; blocking of part of existing north elevation door; door to courtyard (from existing window); moving of parlour west wall; (first floor, from the left): block doorway; form door to proposed access gallery in courtyard; cob cross wall; blocking of doors in partition to hall. Almost all these proposals were implemented (not to scale) (EH A980217).

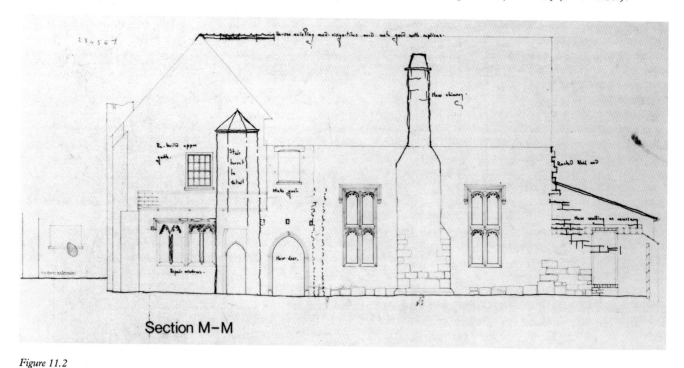

Section M-M

Figure 11.2

The east elevation of the east range by Chris Gray, 1979, annotated by H G Slade, with proposed external stair turret from parlour to great chamber and reintroduction of upper part of hall chimney stack. Note the retention, at this stage, of the existing roof form to the north extension (not to scale) (EH A980216).

11
The development of the conservation programme

by J R Harrison and F P Kelly

Objectives

The period spanned by the consolidation and display works at Bowhill (1976–95) saw various changes in the role of the professionals who had until then been pivotal to the consolidation, management and development of the historic sites and buildings in state guardianship or ownership (in addition to the changes in the government department responsible for ancient monuments, Chapter 1). These were Inspectors of Ancient Monuments with a special remit for Guardianship monuments.[1] Until 1984 the Guardianship Inspector, working within what is now called the Historic Properties arm of the organisation, had a degree of freedom of decision not possible for the private owner of a 'monument'.[2] The ground rules for the works at Bowhill were put in place before 1984 and it is their effect on the conservation and presentation of the building that is examined in what follows. What is described (phase 12 in the overall phasing of the site) is not of course the final stage in its history. Pressures for change to the fabric, as well as the demands of maintenance, will continue for as long as the building is put to practical use.

An account of the works undertaken in phase 12 is included here in part to explain what was done where and why but in large measure because of the significance of the works themselves. They exemplify changing approaches to conservation on one site between the 1970s and 1990s and the dilemma of a monument being repaired without a clear understanding of its future use. The works also shed light on the changing roles of professionals and craft teams involved with the site. Importantly this was a site where the presumption in favour of historic authenticity, particularly in the matching and use of traditional materials and techniques, led to key historical and technical research, particularly in respect of cob, but also in relation to mortars and slating.

The working drawings reproduced here as specimens are not intended to be legible in every detail, but to show the types of drawings used in the works. They especially show how the survey drawings were adapted for works purposes and how supplementary sketches and similar material were used by engineers to support works requisitions.

Acquisition and chronology of repair campaigns

Bowhill was acquired for its own protection at a time when the DoE was actively looking for suitable sites, mostly to illustrate building types – in this case a medieval house of high status. It was seen as a pendant to Kirkham House in Paignton. At the same time the DoE considered taking on a yeoman's longhouse, such as Sanders, Lettaford (now conserved by the Landmark Trust). Lower-status houses were illustrated by Hound Tor, already in Guardianship. It was considered that Bowhill contained enough evidence for considerable reconstruction (*see below*, pp 284–6).

At acquisition in 1976 the building had suffered major recent damage and the fabric was already in serious decline, the roof structures were in poor condition (*see* Figs 6.16 and 6.17) and the house had no safe, demonstrable future in private hands. It was initially intended that it would remain in public care following repair, open to the public with a permanent, on-site custodian. By 1987 circumstances had changed, however, and from this time Bowhill was treated as a 'building at risk'. It was to be repaired for 'recycling' to the private sector, ideally for semi-public use with a high degree of public access. The rehabilitation process was envisaged from the outset to be a long one. In the event it lasted from 1976 to 1995.[3] In 1983 H G Slade estimated, with remarkable prescience, the completion date of the project at April 1995.[4] Stripping out works and other alterations had already begun under private ownership in the 1960s and 1970s. The south range stone and cob cross wall was removed during this period.[5]

The investigation and repair programme can with hindsight be divided into three stages (referred to hereafter as 'Pre-works', 'Stage 1', and 'Stage 2' as appropriate):

Pre-works, 1976–80: Initial emergency stabilisation works; visual building exploration and record; stripping of later accretions and the first phase excavation and record. These were managed by Beric Morley (Inspector), Stephen Dunmore (Assistant Inspector to 1979; Inspector to 1983) and Harry Gordon Slade (Architect).

Works Stage 1, 1980–7: Ian Stuart succeeded Morley as monuments Inspector in the south-west in 1981. The site was now managed by Slade and Dunmore. The first campaign covered the hall in the east range, the junction with the south range and the south range parlour ceiling and west partition. From 1984 until his retirement in 1986, Slade became Inspector with Donal MacGarry as architect. Works were implemented by the DEL.

Works Stage 2, 1987–95: The second works campaign dealt with the rest of the building. The Inspector was Francis Kelly, initially with MacGarry and later John How as Architects, and Arthur McCallum as Engineer. This ran concurrently with the EMAFU's archaeological contract (Chapter 1). On How's retirement in 1993, further management restructuring followed with Richard Baker reporting to project manager Tim Steene, acting as Supervising Officer. (Other design consultants involved during the latter part of this stage were Douglas Evans and Messrs Samwell Locke.) The works continued to be carried out by the DEL organisation, who from 1993 became a contracting arm of English Heritage, under the new name of Historic Property Restoration (HPR), which was privatised in 1996 (in

the South West now part of Quadron Services Ltd). Thus from 1993 more conventional contractual arrangements were introduced, albeit as a 'test-bed' contract to accustom DEL/HPR to outside working practice.

Inspectorate proposals 1979–92

The 1981 programme of consolidation

In 1976, under the Pre-works stage, the building first underwent emergency stabilisation works to make it safe and was then stripped of 'its internal non-original plaster and partitions'.[6] Post-medieval material was regarded as being of secondary interest to the period to which the house was being restored and therefore sacrificial.[7] Regrettable as this was, it helped the understanding of the fabric so exposed. By February 1979 Morley was able set out in his 'Preliminary Inspectorate Report': '… observations by myself and conclusions drawn during discussion with colleagues on site over the past two years'.[8] Chris Gray's drawn survey was also begun at this time (Figs 11.1 and 11.2; *see also* Chapter 1). This excellent record was undertaken before the fabric was stripped out; invaluable further observations were added by Dunmore to his copy during stripping. At the same time documentary research was undertaken and excavation of the guardianship area was begun in 1977–8 in order to understand the archaeological context of the house, which was clearly truncated (Chapter 4).

By May 1981, with the dismantling and repair of the great hall roof already under way, a programme for the repair and display of the building had been developed by Slade

Figure 11.3
Proposed site layout, sketch plan by Chris Gray/H G Slade (not to scale). Note the removal of the west annexe (shown in outline only) and the arrow pointing to the proposed public entrance in the through passage. The public were to reach this via a hedged pathway from the car park. The car park for five cars was separated from the building by a proposed orchard. The eastern courtyard is shown as a herb garden (line drawing by Chris Gray, April 1980; AK/1).

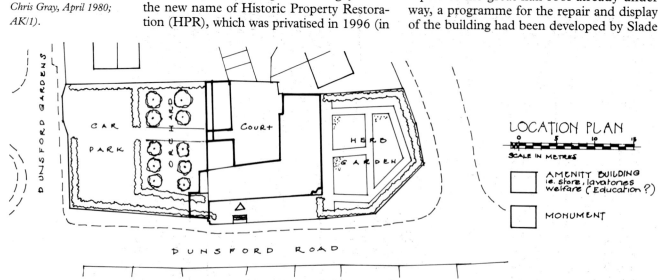

and Dunmore from the findings and conclusions of the Morley Report.[9] Proposals were also marked up and annotated by Slade on copies of Gray's survey drawings. Despite some initial reservations, there was from the start a strong view that Bowhill was not just a case of repair but also one of reconstruction.[10] The approach to the works was to be one of restoration, wherever possible 'after the original', seeking to reinstate missing elements (for instance the hall fireplace), to restore damaged fabric (for example, the hall roof) and to correct inappropriately altered elements (for example, the north gable of the hall or the west partition of the parlour). Later interventions 'of no historic interest' or degrading to the original were to be removed. Where fabric was needed for support or for interpretation, these elements were replaced in as accurate a reinstatement of the original as possible, as far as that was understood in the absence of detailed records. Some works were undertaken on the basis of assumption. One example of this is the cob floor in the hall. It is now of considerable interest in its own right, but there is no evidence for it and the hall probably had a flagged or tiled floor more appropriate to the status of the room.[11]

At that time the approach to conservation for a Guardianship Ancient Monument was very much to consolidate and display under Inspectorate advice. Apart from some superb records by the Ancient Monuments Drawing Office between the wars, there was little in the way of archaeological recording of standing buildings. The building and the works done to it would form their own record. Thus there are few detailed 'before' and no detailed 'after' architect's drawings of the works done at this period at Bowhill. This mode of operation was possible because of the involvement of the DEL force, dedicated to the maintenance and repair of national monuments.[12]

The advantages of reinstatement and restoration for display and interpretation were developed in the draft 1981 programme for the Ancient Monuments Board of the DAMHB, which concluded:

> The proposals seek to return the building to its earliest phases of construction, and include an element of reconstruction ... Broadly speaking the recreation is limited to those elements which are essential to recreate the pattern of circulation and the overall plan of the building in the medieval phase ... Some individual features are also reconstructed, where both direct and circumstantial evidence are sufficient ... [13]

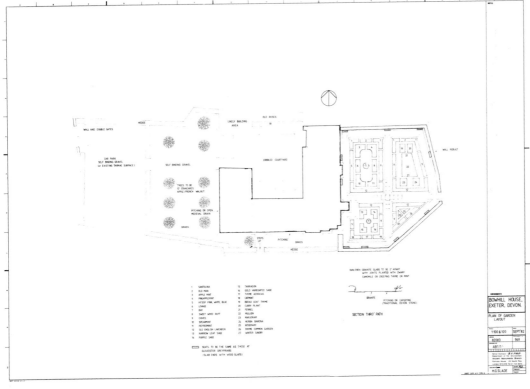

Figure 11.4
Site plan showing planting scheme as proposed by Richmond Park in 1982 (not to scale) (line drawing by Chris Gray, September 1982; AB1/1a).

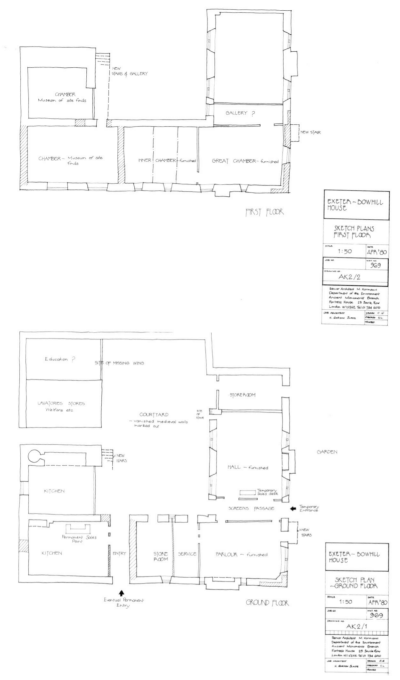

The following labels appear within the floor plans:

FIRST FLOOR plan:
NEW STAIRS & GALLERY
CHAMBER Museum of site finds
GALLERY ?
NEW STAIR
CHAMBER – Museum of site finds
INNER CHAMBER – furnished
GREAT CHAMBER – furnished
FIRST FLOOR

EXETER – BOWHILL HOUSE
SKETCH PLANS FIRST FLOOR
SCALE 1:50 DATE APR '80
JOB NO 969
DRAWING NO AK2/2
Senior Architect: M. Kormann
Department of the Environment
Ancient Monuments Branch
Fortress House 23 Savile Row
London W1X1AB Tel 01 734 6010
JOB ARCHITECT
H. Gordon Slade

GROUND FLOOR plan:
Education ?
SITE OF MISSING WING
LAVATORIES STORES Welfare etc
STOREROOM
COURTYARD – vanished medieval walls marked out
SITE OF STAIR
NEW STAIRS
GARDEN
KITCHEN
HALL – furnished
Temporary Sales desk
Permanent Sales Point
SCREENS PASSAGE
Temporary Entrance
KITCHEN
ENTRY
STORE ROOM
SERVICE
PARLOUR – furnished
NEW STAIRS
Eventual Permanent Entry
GROUND FLOOR

EXETER – BOWHILL HOUSE
SKETCH PLAN – GROUND FLOOR
SCALE 1:50 DATE APR '80
JOB NO 969
DRAWING NO AK2/1
Senior Architect: M. Kormann
Department of the Environment
Ancient Monuments Branch
Fortress House 23 Savile Row
London W1X1AB Tel 01 734 6010
JOB ARCHITECT
H. Gordon Slade

Figure 11.5
Sketch ground- and first-floor plans of the building, showing proposed uses and areas to be furnished, as well as new toilets and education room in the north-west corner of the courtyard and new access to the first floor adjacent to the east wall of the kitchen (not to scale) (line drawing by Chris Gray, April 1980; AK2/1 and AK2/2).

Where the evidence was insufficient, for example, for the hall dais and screen, other elements were not proposed for reconstruction.

One key but understated proposal bearing on circulation was the reintroduction of an external stair and short first-floor access gallery from the courtyard to the oriel and kitchen chambers. A new external stair tower on the east elevation was also considered, to provide a direct link from the parlour to the great chamber above (*see* Fig 11.2).[14] Proposals for the reinstatement of major internal features included: the cob east and west end gables, the stone and cob cross wall and two post and plank partitions in the south range (*see* Fig 11.1); one post and plank partition in the hall; and the removal of the extant partition in the parlour to its original position. A separate proposal of visual significance was the demolition of the annexe at the south-west corner to reveal the original form of the west gable and to open up a route from the western car park to the proposed main visitor entrance via the south doorway of the through passage of the south range (Fig 11.3).

Wider proposals were also tabled at this time, involving improvements to the existing site car park and reduction in its size, with new landscaping, public lavatories, sales point, welfare facilities and education room.[15] Later on there were interesting plans for the planting of a formal garden in the east courtyard and an orchard in the west by staff of Richmond Park (Fig 11.4).[16] Some new building on the footprint of part of the missing west and north ranges was proposed to accommodate some of these functions (Fig 11.5). Lastly it was intended to furnish some of the rooms with modern craft furniture and textiles, to augment the educational aspect of the project by suggesting (without slavishly copying) the level of furnishing to be expected in a building of the date and status of Bowhill.[17]

A programme largely based on the 1981 proposals was agreed in 1983 with modifications by the then Chief Inspector of Ancient Monuments, A D Saunders, and Principal Inspector for England, C J Young. The proposed stair tower on the east elevation was not supported nor was the formal garden in the east courtyard. The resulting approved strategy, managed by the architects of the regional team and implemented by the DEL, remained in place until 1993, well into Stage 2.

For the detail of the Stage 1 repairs traditional approaches prevailed, but 20th-century technology was embraced where considered appropriate. Occasional recourse was had to simulation of original materials to achieve the desired effect.[18] This contrasted with the Stage 2 approach in which the search for authentic historic solutions and methods was axiomatic, although not always successfully achieved.

The 1992 Inspectorate guidelines

Stage 2 followed under Francis Kelly (Inspector) and John How (Architect). The change in management personnel in 1987 entailed a review of the philosophical approach to the works. Additionally, declining funding meant that the employment of a custodian in the finished building was no longer envisaged. This was to have serious implications for the nature of the final 'product'. Between September 1991 and March 1992 the 1981 programme was updated to take these factors into account. The resulting *Inspectorate Guidelines for Conservation and Display* of 1992 were more open-ended than those of 1981, reflecting the uncertain nature of the times as far as English Heritage's operations were concerned[19] and were predicated on the amended aim of conserving and recycling a 'building at risk'. Meanwhile, works continued to follow the strategies set down in the 1981 programme.[20]

Although the possibility of retaining the house 'in care' remained until 1994, it was now effectively accepted that on completion it would, in some form or other, return to the private sector.[21] The plans for public lavatories, sales point and so on were, therefore, set aside and the concept of the external stair and gallery to the oriel and kitchen chambers, although briefly resurrected, was also eventually dropped for reasons of economy and shortage of time. In 1993–4 revised proposals for access to the first-floor relocated stairs to the south-west annexe building, now to be retained rather than demolished.[22] One area of the east gable framing was reconstructed (so that it could be broken out without affecting the structure) to make provision for a fire escape from the first floor of the south range, should this one day be required.

Within the revised Stage 2 context, significant missing features such as plastering and partitions were proposed for reintroduction so as to ensure a basic level of convenience for the building's eventual user. Internal doors, however, were not provided.[23] One new major reintroduction was now proposed, a courtyard pentice to provide a covered link between all parts of the building, essential to any future user. Following Stage 1 practice, for the implementation of most of these features 'restoration after the original, rather than the potentially more contrasting "modern" equivalent, was deliberately chosen'.[24] Finally, new external works were reduced to a minimum and (in a departure from the 1981 and 1992 proposals) a second car park was added occupying the east courtyard (Fig 11.6). [25] In detail:

> The basic concept behind all the second stage repairs ... was conservative repair and the use, as far as possible, of the minimal, reversible, repairs, fitting new to old rather than cutting old to fit new, replacing like with like and, where possible, avoiding synthetic materials, but not rejecting them where their use would entail the retention of more of the original: hence the continued use of resin for beam-end repair.[26]

'Authenticity' in repair and reinstatement became a paramount concern. This meant continuing the previous policy of reinstatement but trying to 'do it right' for the sake of compatibility (with fabric) and also researching lost/dying craft skills in order to understand and reproduce original techniques as found in the building and to promote their wider appreciation.

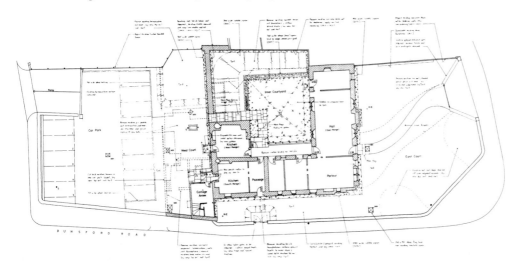

Figure 11.6
Layout of the site and ground-floor plan of the house at the penultimate stage to completion, before the east car park was added. The west car park, with its double row of parking spaces, encroaches more on the building than the car park in Slade's original proposal (Fig 11.3). With the addition of the later eastern car park the building is surrounded. The main public entrance is now via the west service room from the west car park. The stairs in the south-west annexe are now the only means of access to the first floor. Note the lines of the missing north and west sections of the building set out in the inner court-yard (not to scale) (April 1994; AL/5K/03/A).

287

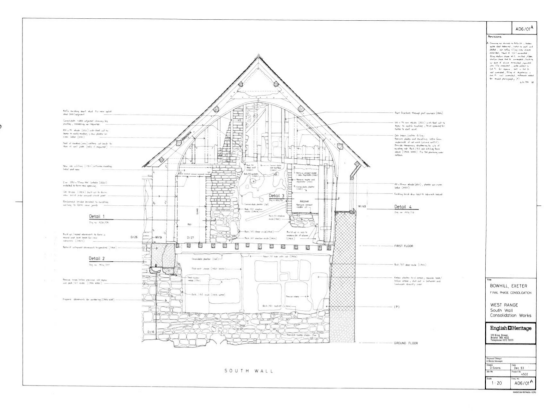

Figure 11.7
Cross section through the
west range, looking south.
Later working drawing by
consultant Douglas Evans
using the archaeological
record drawings as a base
(see Fig 5.17), marked up
with repair proposals and
references to standard
descriptions in the spec-
ification (not to scale)
(December 1993;
AD6/01/A).

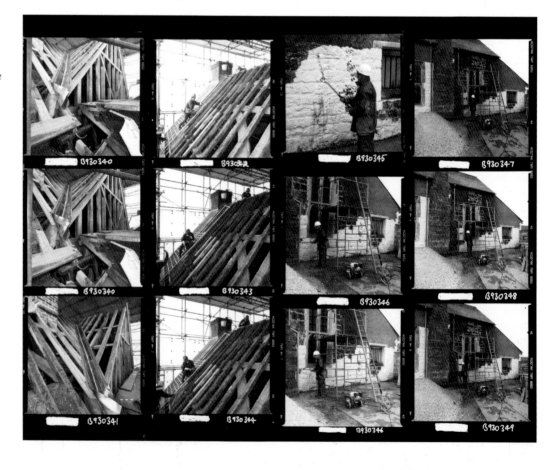

Figure 11.8
A typical example of the
photographic works record
commissioned from David
Garner in Stage 2 (contact
strips, March 1993; EH
B930340–49).

Archaeology, works information and recording from 1987

A feature of MoW, DoE and EH consolidation works is the reliance on controlled excavation to inform decisions. Detailed archaeological records were made by Dunmore and subsequently by EMAFU. A second level of recording, via the workers of the DEL, was also used on the site (above, n 12). In terms of both works and archaeological records there was a long-established understanding within English Heritage between the Inspectorate and the labour force. Individual craftsmen were aware of the need to record, the importance of 'provenance' and the function of the 'finds' room. A good example of a Stage 1 'after' record made by DEL craftsmen, on the instructions of Stephen Dunmore,[27] is the 'marked up' drawings of the timber repairs to the great hall roof structure (partially reproduced in Fig 11.56 below). No other record of the detail of this work exists.

As part of the 1987 personnel change ' ... greater emphasis than before was placed on achieving certainty about original, missing, arrangements (and techniques) prior to the implementation of repair and reconstruction ... '.[28]

In 1987 the Exeter Museums Archaeological Field Unit (EMAFU) was commissioned to provide a locally based archaeological service (Chapters 1 and 4). From this point the Unit's work was integrated with the conservation process. Although EMAFU surveys did not come into full use as the basis of architects' working drawings until 1992–3, its findings were informing the design process before this (Fig 11.7). The introduction of working drawings backed up by detailed specifications represented another late development arising from changes in the relationship between the DEL and English Heritage; this was greatly assisted by the availability of the EMAFU record survey.

Experimental site working coupled with recording related specifically to the earth repair and reconstruction works at the site was introduced from 1990. This was a controlled extension of similar work already undertaken during Stage 1, as well as at another English Heritage site, Leigh Barton, Churchstow, Devon. An in-depth photographic recording project was developed (Figs 11.8 and 11.9) and works staff were involved in the process of experiment, observation and feedback. The building

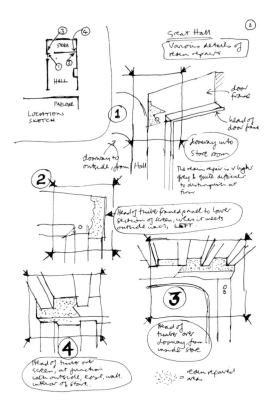

Figure 11.9
A typical example of sketches for the requisitioning of views and angles for the photographic record in Stage 2 (line drawing by Ray Harrison, March 1994).

thus became, briefly and in a limited way, a test bed. The resulting illustrative material with an accompanying explanatory text has been published separately by English Heritage as a contribution to the growing debate on the conservation and repair of earth structures in the United Kingdom and further afield.[29]

The works

The project broke down into three main works sections. The first section, the east range, was largely completed under works Stage 1 (1980–7). The second and third sections, works on the south and west range, continued under works Stage 2 (1987–95) including the changes in philosophical approach described above. In order to structure this (necessarily limited and selective) review, works are considered under the following headings:[30]

- Changes or introductions, both structural and decorative having a material effect on the character of the building (that is, those changes for which Listed Building Consent would normally apply) as it was when taken into care.
- Types of repair, considered by material.
- Completed works (illustrations of the building after repair).

Changes having a material effect on the character of the building

Stage 1: Major items of removal and 'heroic' reconstruction

Stage 1 saw the reconstruction of the dilapidated lean-to north extension to the hall (*see* Figs 2.7 and 2.9) with new cob placed wet in shutters. The plentiful use of dung and lime (on the advice of the internal research and technical advisory service led by the architect John Ashurst) emphasises the tentative use of cob at that time. For the west wall the cob was mixed 1:3 subsoil:French hydraulic lime. This set rock hard. Gradually the amount of lime was reduced until it was omitted completely for the east wall.[31] A modest reinstatement of the hall store was first intended (Fig 11.10). Later this developed into a virtually complete rebuild, with raised side walls in cob/lime under a new, steeper-pitched slated roof. The entirely new west wall, replacing a modern partition, followed the original foundation line. A loft floor was constructed to an heroic scale dictated by the original mortices in the hall screen headbeam (*see* below). The 'unhistorical' as-built roof and elevations reflect the 'improving' of a mutilated structure, employing 'matching traditional' (vernacular) wall and roof forms (Figs 11.11 and 11.12).

The timber-framed north gable of the hall was reinforced and re-displayed, inside and out. Lath and plaster external cladding and inserted windows of *c* 1800 (Fig 11.13; *see also* Fig 2.7) were removed from the upper part of the frame, which was repaired; the failed studwork at the apex was secured by stainless-steel plating. Both faces were clad with new split-oak horizontal lath and the cavity packed with daub. This was composed of cob and dung and was added in successive lifts one shutter board (scaffold plank) high.[32] The shuttering was placed slightly proud of the laths, so that the daub squeezed through to form an exterior coating, as observed in original work in the great chamber. The shutters were struck the following day, the surface made good[33] and then lime plastered and limewashed up to the main timbers, which were left exposed (*see* Fig 11.113). The exterior gable was hung with Delabole slates (*see* Fig 6.6).[34]

At ground-floor level, the later brick underpinning was removed and a new post and plank partition reinstated on the evidence of mortices in the headbeam (Fig 11.14; *see also* Figs 6.2, 11.13 and 11.113). The mortices indicated a doorway, the head and jambs of which were based on those of the parlour partitions (jamb stops conjectural). The new sole plate with conjectural chamfer on a Fletton brick sleeper wall,

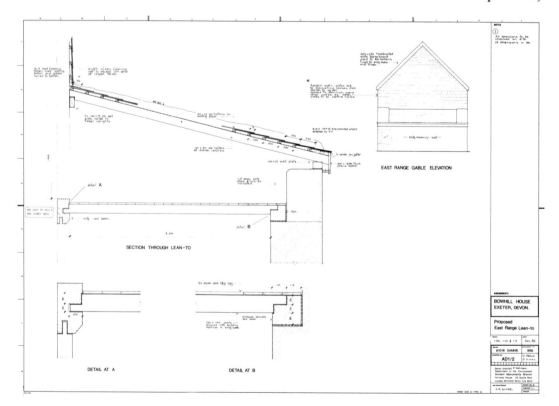

Figure 11.10
Details of the original proposal for the roof of the hall store; slating laid at such a slack pitch is liable to leak (not to scale) (line drawing by 'G S', December 1982; AS1/2).

was based on one surviving at the lower end of the hall.[35] Such a reconstruction, based only on the evidence of mortices, is clearly less reliable than that of the west wall of the parlour where much original fabric survived. Nevertheless, the effect was achieved and the process was repeated in Stage 2 (following the 1981 programme) in the service room and the through passage of the south range.

At the south end of the hall, the damaged ground-floor partition was largely dismantled, repaired and reassembled as the first stage in the reconstruction of the whole of this two-storey screen (Figs 6.17, 6.18; *see also* Fig 11.115; continued in Stage 2, below). The studs were repaired and reinstated on the evidence of mortices. The jambs of the paired doorways (which had been displaced) were replaced in their original position at the west end, again on the basis of evidence, and new heads added on the pattern of the parlour partition (although rebates for doors were omitted). The filling of the framing, of daub packed around bulbous oak pegs, may have been a unique system.[36] One original peg survived (Chapter 6, n 19) as a model for the replacement (*see* Fig 6.18). The panels were refilled with new daub containing dung as in the north gable (above). The daub required much 'aftercare' to sag-shaped cracks at intervals in each panel, possibly caused by the pegs impeding downward drying shrinkage in the daub.

The 1981 programme called for the reinstatement of the first-floor structure in the south range where sections were missing (*see* extent of original timbers in Fig 6.1). A section of beam 6 (which had also formed the head of a partition) and many joists had been removed for a new stair in the 1970s. Large-scale repairs were made to the north and south ends of the beam and new joists were fitted to bays 5 and 6. In the process the north end of the beam was replaced slightly too far to the east (probably because joints between joists and beams were closed up tight, where previously there had been some play).[37] At that time the floor below remained unexcavated and the presence of the sleeper wall of the partition, revealed by excavation in 1989 (Chapter 4), was unknown. The result in the restored fabric is that the slot for the dividing timber in the window embrasure appears to be misaligned in relation to the beam and the reinstated partition. Originally the relationship of slot and partition was axial (Chapter 6). Missing portions of beams 8 and 9 in the through passage were also replaced, with joists in the

Figure 11.11
The east elevation of the completed hall store; much of the cob walling above the window lintel is new (photograph by David Garner, April 1993; EH B931122).

Figure 11.12
The west elevation of the completed hall store; almost all the rendered walling is new (photograph by David Garner, July 1991; EH B917152).

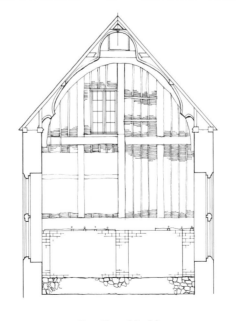

Section N–N

Figure 11.13
Chris Gray's record of the internal elevation of the north wall of the hall, showing the brick blocking on a stone plinth (later replaced by a new stud and plank partition) and later windows at high level, afterwards removed (not to scale) (line drawing by Chris Gray, May 1979; AS2/4). See Fig 11.113 for the same view after completion of works.

Figure 11.14
Working drawings for the
new partition shown in Fig
11.113 (not to scale) (line
drawing by 'G S',
December 1982; AS1/3).

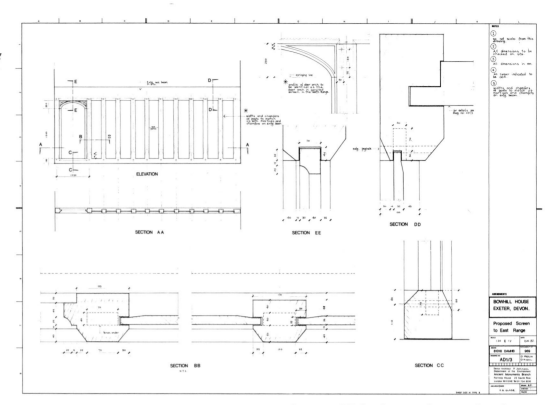

southern half of bay 8 removed where a stair had been introduced. The reconstruction of the stone cross wall (below) included a concealed horizontal stainless-steel angle to give additional support to beam 8 (which had split along the line of its joist mortices).[38]

A major item was the repair and moving of the west post and plank partition of the parlour. This returned it to its original position and relationship with the parlour ceiling structure – a good example of structural advantages deriving from a decision taken for 'display' reasons. There was much reconstruction, including the formation of one new door head with decorated spandrels (*see* Fig 11.117) and the sill and sleeper wall are modern. The exercise necessitated, however, the removal of the applied mouldings in the extended bay 4 of the ceiling (Chapter 6). A knock-on effect of moving the parlour partition was the need to block the opening in the south wall of the service room (*see* Fig 6.22, 34), a later feature that most recently had contained a doorway of phase 11 (*see* Fig 5.16). This was done in new stone in 1987, its coursing, stone type and size differentiated from the adjacent original stonework. Later still (in 1993) the blocking was finished by creating a new east reveal to represent the entry to the garderobe, along with a thin brick blocking of the area of the garderobe itself (*see* Fig 6.41).

Stage 2: Major items of renewal and reconstruction

The reintroduction of the cross wall east of the through passage in the south range was undertaken in Stage 2 (Fig 11.15). The stone for the ground-floor stage was Carboniferous sandstone from Hayne quarry, Zeal Monachorum, Devon. The reconstruction of the first-floor stage of cob rising into the roof was a key element of Stage 2 (Fig 11.16; the evidence is summarised in Chapter 6; *see also* Fig 6.22, 127, and Fig 6.25, 131). The wall was rebuilt in cob (without dung) and included a doorway (from evidence). Cob blocks, which were easier to lay and consolidate in this position than cob, were used at the apex. The whole was subsequently lime plastered.[39] The policy of reconstruction using 'original' materials and techniques, even when these were to be hidden, was an important aspect of Stage 2.[40]

In the south range, at first-floor level, the daub-filled partition between great chamber and hall (called the 'daub screen') was reconstructed (Fig 11.17; *see also* Figs 6.19, 6.57, 6.59, and Fig 6.25). By 1989 only a very small area of original daub infilling in this partition remained from what had been a considerable survival in 1976. Conventional repair to the main timbers, entailing the loss of original lath, daub, later doors and 17th-century door-framing, had taken place early in Stage 2.[41]

Figure 11.15 (top, left)
The east elevation of the
reconstructed stone cross
wall in the south range in
1993 before plastering
(photograph by David
Garner, July 1993; EH
B933548).

Figure 11.16 (top, right)
The completed new cob
cross wall between the inner
and oriel chambers, looking
east. The thickness of the
wall was reduced on this
side as it rose, in accord-
ance with the archaeolog-
ical evidence. The top was
finished with cob bricks to
manage potential shrinkage
problems in this area
(photograph by David
Garner, December 1992;
EH B926342).

Figure 11.17 (below, left)
The framed wall panel
('daub screen') between the
great chamber and hall
with most oak lathing rein-
stated in the early stages of
being daubed, looking north
(photograph by David
Garner, October 1990;
EH B906970).

Figure 11.18 (below, right)
The framed wall panel
('daub partition') between
the great and inner cham-
bers with timber, plaster
and daub repairs complete
and awaiting a section of
new daub-plaster finish,
looking west (photograph
by David Garner,
November 1992; EH
B925482).

The lost armatures, consisting of vertical timber staves with horizontal gapped oak lathing nailed to each side were reinstated in the late 1980s around the fragment of original armature and daub, which survives to serve as a model for the new daub infilling work that followed in the early 1990s.[42] The framed west partition of the great chamber survived (called the 'daub partition'), but the upper area into the arch braces of truss v was missing (Figs 11.18, and 11.19; *see also* Figs 6.15 and 6.58). This was reformed with modern framing and lathed and plastered on both sides. There was inadequate evidence for its earlier form and the arrangement was chosen as being traditional and aesthetically satisfactory. The 17th-century lower section with daub infill, to be described later, needed less attention. It was stiffened by the reinstatement of its lathing and daub and the door-frame at the south end of the partition was reinstated (*below*). Repairs and new work using cob and daub were to become an important aspect of the programme of experiment and record at Bowhill. From 1990 the reinstatement of daub to these partitions formed part of these trials.

The 1981 programme had envisaged that the south-west annexe would eventually be demolished. In the early 1990s, when Stage 2 had progressed to the west end of the south range, it was decided to retain the external form of the structure (above). The late 20th-century accretions containing modern stairs and kitchen facilities (*see* Fig 12.2) were removed because of their inconvenient location and poor architectural quality and in order to manage and display the building better (Figs 11.20, and 11.21; *see also* Fig 11.109). Unavoidable structural work involved the demolition of much of the side walls, although the south wall was retained and followed the original in general

Figure 11.19
Working drawing (with site annotations), showing proposed repairs and reconstruction of the framed daub partition between great and inner chambers (not to scale) (line drawing by Richard Baker, April 1992; AD1/1).

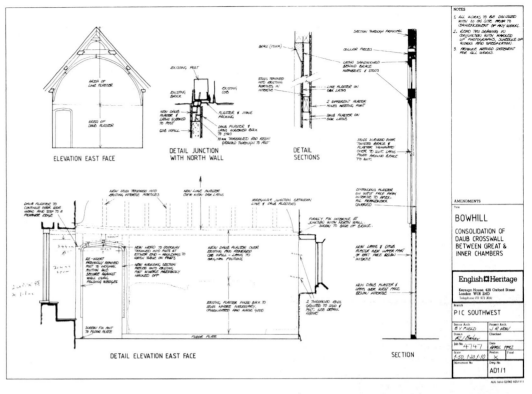

Figure 11.20 (left)
The completed works to the south-west annexe and kitchen, prior to the post-completion addition of a porch (photograph by David Garner, May 1995; EH B953003).

Figure 11.21 (right)
Detail of the reproduction of the early 19th-century framing of the annexe (photograph by David Garner, September 1994; EH B945326).

form and detail. Its plan was extended by a foot at the north end. Swanage bricks surplus from another English Heritage site (Lulworth Castle in Dorset) and modern softwood framing following the original pattern were used. The rebuilt shell accommodates a staircase to the first floor, WCs (including one for disabled visitors/users) and a small kitchen. The roof reused the original Devon slates and the exterior was rendered on lath (or brick) as before.

It was originally intended to rebuild the west gable wall in cob. This was abandoned. The ground-floor was rebuilt to the north of

the central door to the original wall thickness with random rubble set in lime mortar (replacing concrete blockwork; *see* Fig 11.89). To the south a new electrical intake cupboard was constructed of double-lathed daub framing within a void in the wall (formerly housing a phase 11 dumb waiter).[43] Above, the gable was replaced in new softwood framing (Fig 11.22) clad both sides in lath and lime plaster and limewashed. The plaster leaked, partly because it was exposed and west facing. The apex of the gable was, therefore, slate-hung, a common West-Country arrangement (*see* Fig 11.20),

following the precedent of the north gable of the hall. A small external lobby was added at a later phase and the opportunity used to re-render the lower section of gable over a membrane and to insert insulation.

Other structural interventions in the ground floor of the south range included the reintroduction, from the evidence of the headbeam, of the missing timber post and plank partition between the service room and the store (Fig 11.23; see also Fig 6.35). Mortices in beam 6 gave the positions of studs (see Fig 5.30), although those in the replaced northern section of the beam are conjectural (this area could have accommo-dated a doorway originally, although the separate doorways from the pentice to the two service rooms argues against this). The sole plate detail is conjectural. This was the first case of partition reinstatement to use unchamfered studs and sole plate and cut

pegs rather than dowels.[44] Chamfers were omitted because the original details were unknown and also because as the room had functioned as a store its joinery was unlikely to have been complex. The sole plate was supported by modern brickwork on a slate damp-proof course (ironically in the process destroying the original foundation, which was the evidence for the original position of the partition; Chapter 4).

Reconstruction of the partition beneath beam 9 between the through passage and west service room (see Fig 11.118) again followed the evidence of mortices in the surviving headbeam, including in this case the form of chamfers to the studs. Details of the paired doorways were based on the original examples in the parlour (see Fig 5.27). The new sole plate rested on a brick sill on a slate damp-proof course built off the level left by archaeological excavation.

The 1970s (phase 11) service hatch between the kitchen and the west service room, which had been cut through the cob wall without lintels (see Figs 5.17 and 6.25), was blocked. This was filled with new cob that, with much 'aftercare', hardened satisfactorily.

To make sense of the internal re-ordering of the south range, ground- and first-floor plans proposed in the 1981 programme and 1992 guidelines (which justified restoration by proposed use), three external ground-floor openings in the north wall were returned to their original forms or were blocked (see Fig 5.17, 259/257 and 270/271; cf Figs 5.18 and 5.19 for the effect of the changes). Two of these alterations were related to the replacing of the west parlour

Figure 11.22 (top, left) Modern softwood framing to the rebuilt west gable of the south range. Note the rafter and main truss repairs and the new rafters to the left of the valley gutter in an area where most of the originals had been lost (photograph by David Garner, February 1993; EH B930200).

Figure 11.23 (below, left) 'Trying' the posts of the new post and plank parti-tion in the service room, south range, ground floor (photograph by David Garner, July 1994; EH B943797).

Figure 11.24 (top, right) View of the completed pentice (photograph by David Garner, February 1995; EH B950961).

Figure 11.25 (above) Design proposals for the reinstatement of first-floor access via a partially reinstated gallery; key points are the roof pitches and the relationship between pentice and gallery, which was lost in the completed work (see Fig 11.24) where the open bay of the pentice is too wide (drawings by Mark Samwell, c January 1994).

Figure 11.26 Part of a working drawing showing the proposed reconstruction of the pentice in cross section. Note the provision for glazing in the design, although this was not installed (and relegated to future fitting out) (not to scale) (line drawing by Mark Samwell, November 1993).

partition (*above*). The original north door to the service room was re-opened (*see* Fig 6.25, 259) and the adjacent opening of phase 11 was blocked in stone. Further west, the north doorway of the through passage (*see* Fig 6.25, 270; Chapter 6) was brought back into use by removing blocking inserted in phase 11 (271). Above, the external doorway in the north wall of the oriel chamber (200) had been redundant for some years. As the external stair to the first floor at this point (proposed in 1981) was not built, the doorway was filled in Stage 2 by a timber-framed panel rendered externally and plastered inside and slightly set back from the wall faces to 'read' as a blocked opening.

Finally the lost pentice, along the external, north wall of the south range was reconstructed as a new proposal of Stage 2 (*above*; Figs 11.24 and 11.26–11.28; *see also* Fig 5.18 for 'before' condition and Fig 11.25 for alternative designs not implemented). The sockets for the ends of the roof timbers of the original pentice, exposed in the cob following stripping of recent cement-based finishes (*see* Chapter 5 and Fig 5.17), determined the general design of the new structure. It projects slightly further into the courtyard than the original. The design was derived from the jointed-cruck system, in line with the overall strategy to fit in with the pattern of the house and in view of the evidence for a hierarchy of trussing.[45]

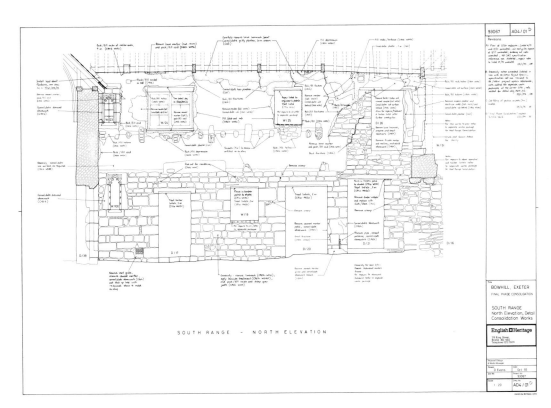

SOUTH RANGE — NORTH ELEVATION

Figure 11.27
Drawing for preparatory works prior to the reconstruction of the pentice, showing filling of sockets and consolidation of surfaces (not to scale) (line drawing by Douglas Evans, based on EMAFU record, October 1993; AD4/01d).

Figure 11.28 (below)
Details of the main framing of the pentice. The structure is designed to transfer its load onto the head of the stonework (at first-floor level via existing beam slots) rather than into the cob walling. The timbers are sized for softwood, but were executed in oak by the DEL to a very high level of craftsmanship (not to scale) (line drawing by Mark Samwell, February 1994; AK6/02b)

Construction in painted softwood was intended, to leave no doubt as to its newness. In the end, by double irony, softwood of appropriate scantling could not be obtained and oak was used, but of an heroic scantling which had been insisted upon for the proposed softwood construction! The result is very beefy. The roof framing was fitted against the cob wall using cantilever construction up from the stonework of the ground floor to avoid cutting into the cob (Fig 11.28). The roof was slated to match the main roofs. At the west end, where the original had carried a gallery above, the pitch of the new roof was slackened to give better headroom for those emerging into the courtyard. By an oversight in the design, the opening formed here was made wider than the original. Apart from this entry, the spaces between the pentice wall posts were infilled with low, conjectural, timber-framed and lime-rendered panels on slate sleepers.

There were no changes to the west range in plan and only one major change to the fabric 'as found' – the reinstatement of a substantial section of cob wall at first-floor level (Figs 11.29, 5.27, 389 and 6.47, 225). The large gap (created for access in phase 8) was initially intended to be rebuilt in cob, after the 'reinstate like with like' philosophy of Stage 2. Cob block was eventually preferred, because of advantages in speed of

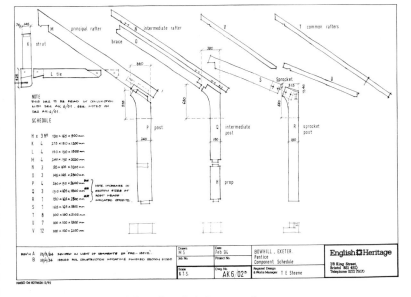

work and in minimising the shrinkage problems that arise with cob. A hollow-cored, double-skin wall of blocks was built to minimise load and as an experiment.[46] Two minor extensions to internal walling were carried out. The first, both an aesthetic and a structural exercise, reduced the width of the 1970s breakthrough into the oriel chamber (*see* Fig 5.17, 228) by reintroducing an eastern reveal abutting the end of the hollow-block wall described above. This was also (for reasons of time) carried out in

Figure 11.29
Completed cob block rein-
statement to the east wall of
the kitchen chamber,
including the new window.
The window had no historic
precedent and was intro-
duced to bring extra light
into the room (photograph
by David Garner, July
1994; EH B943806).

solid walling of cob block, where mass cob might have been used earlier. The second operation involved building back in cob block a section of missing cob wall around the jointed-cruck post of truss I in the south-west corner of the room (*see* Fig 5.17).[47]

All Stage 2 works described above were included in principle in the 1981 programme, except for the retention of the south-west annexe and the introduction of the pentice. Respect for the integrity of the historic fabric was reflected in the detailed nature of matching repairs. The re-slating of the building would normally have needed Listed Building Consent, but is dealt with below in the section on types of repair.

Smaller-scale new enhancements and alterations: Stages 1 and 2

A degree of architectural integrity can be regained by the reintroduction of smaller-scale features based on recorded evidence and this was seen from the first as a means of enhancing the character of the building for the visitor.[48]

Features in the hall proposed for reproduction in the 1981 programme and introduced during the Stage 1 works included:

1. The hall fireplace was fully reintroduced (Figs 11.30–11.31; *see also* Fig 6.12), the design based on the surviving keystone and moulded cornice stone (Chapter 6) and on extant fireplaces in the parlour and great chamber (*see* proposal drawing, Fig 11.30 and Fig 6.23). The new lintel and relieving arch are supported by a concealed reinforced concrete lintel (*see* Fig 6.14). Stone from Raddon, near Thorverton, was used as the nearest matching material obtainable to the

original volcanic trap from Pocombe or Barley. The appearance is shown by comparison of old and new blocks (Figs 11.30 and 11.31; *see also* Fig 6.2, inset).[49] A concrete hearth was laid in place of hearth slabs (which could still be installed).

2. The north-west doorway of the hall was opened up (*see* Fig 6.15, 417). The southern jamb had survived. The northern jamb and part of the head were reconstructed in coloured concrete to match Permian breccia. The use of cast concrete was enforced, as the original breccia is now only available in second-hand form and rarely in suitable blocks. The substitute was a deliberate choice. Although the use here of modern materials to express the fact of reinstatement is not consistent with the use of natural stone in the fireplace, the critical points were matching and availability of materials.

3. New carved detail was produced for the hall, with themes and general design based on extant carvings in the great chamber. Bosses and cusps for the intermediate trusses were carved in oak by the DEL carpenters. Wholly missing details, such as the small bosses at the intersections of the intermediate trusses and cove purlins and corbels at the feet of the main trusses (that is, those without surviving precedents in the fabric), were not replaced, although both are partially recorded in the engraving of 1843 (*see* Figs 1.2 and 7.7).[50]

4. New door heads were carved to complete missing panelling in the hall and parlour (Fig 11.32). Like the bosses, these were carved by the DEL carpenters. Most took as their model the surviving door head in the parlour partition, although the spandrels of the partition of the west service room were more elaborate than most. At least one carpenter involved in this work experimented with carving from life.

5. New external doors were fitted to each end of the screens passage, hung in the original rebates (*see* Fig 11.107). Their design of overlapping planks was based on an unprovenanced late medieval door found in a fish-pond at Leigh Barton, Churchstow, Devon. The original worn and redundant pintles were removed and replaced with copies (based on Fig 9.8, no. 55). Similar doors were hung in the north-west doorway and the west door of the hall store.

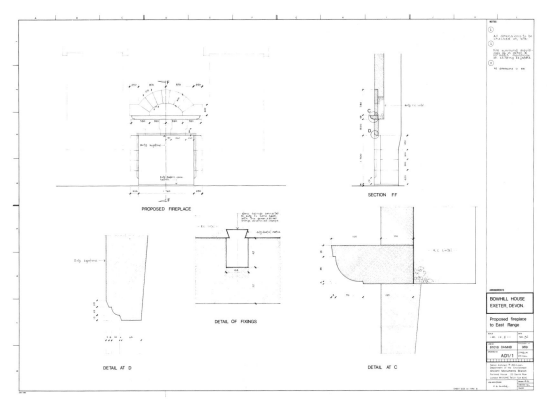

Figure 11.30
Working drawing showing
elevation, section, and
details of the proposed hall
fireplace (not to scale)
(line drawing by 'G S',
December 1982; AD1/1).

Figure 11.31 (left)
The new hall fireplace as
completed (photograph by
David Garner, June 1995;
EH B953011).

Figure 11.32 (right)
New carved spandrel to the
door-frame in the north
partition of the hall (photo-
graph by David Garner,
May 1994; EH B942050).

6. New oak shutters, replacing 19th-century softwood shutters, were fitted to the lower (but not to the upper) lights of the hall windows (Fig 11.33). Evidence for shutters in the lower halves of the windows is described above, Chapter 6. In restoring them in this way, a didactic point was made about the expense of glass in the late 15th century and the nature of life in the primary building. By 1969 (the date of the earliest reliable photographic evidence) the original ferramenta had all gone. New steel ferramenta, halved over non-ferrous tips,

were replaced in the hall windows (Fig 11.34), following the evidence of sockets in the stonework and general historic patterns. 'Reemy antique' glazing in lead cames was added to the ironwork of the upper and lower sections of each window.

The 1981 programme called for the reinstatement of the upper part of the hall chimney stack (Figs 11.35; *see also* Fig 2.9). The shouldered junction of the new stack with the original masonry build below was formed in moulded and coloured cast

Figure 11.33 (top, left)
The north-east window of
the hall, showing new
diamond-paned glazing
and timber shutters to the
lower lights (photograph by
David Garner, June 1995;
EH B953008).

Figure 11.34 (top, right)
Detail of a new saddle bar
and glazing in the hall
windows, installed in the
mid-1980s. The end of the
saddle bar has a bronze tip
halved and screwed to the
bar. This is to obviate
rusting, so potentially
damaging to the masonry
into which the bar is bedded
at each end, a common
failure in historic fabric
(photograph by David
Garner, June 1995; EH
B953010).

Figure 11.35 (centre)
The east elevation after the
reinstatement of the top
section of the hall chimney
stack (to an assumed design
and height). The modern
brickwork was subsequently
limewashed to make the
contrast between original
and new less obvious
(photograph by David
Garner, June 1993; EH
B933141).

concrete imitating Permian breccia. The new stack was of red hand-made brick, the top weathered by a sheet of Georgian wired glass (though vented, condensation still falls onto the hearth). Brick and concrete confirm the work as low-key reconstruction, in which detailed form and height are indicative only. The use of brick also echoes the historic secondary brickwork of the other chimney stacks. In Stage 2 both brick and stone sections were lime rendered and limewashed, as with the rest of the walls. Colour from the concrete offsets is now 'bleeding' through this render.

Lastly, two new windows and a loft doorway were added to the hall store (*see* Figs 11.11 and 11.12). The intact late medieval timber window uncovered in the north wall was stored and replaced *in situ* by

a direct copy (Chapter 9, no. 135). The design was used for a new and taller window in the east elevation, on the evidence of a mid-wall chase (Chapter 6). The new loft space above was fitted with an access hatch in the west wall, whose design of paired lintels flanking a mid-wall door-frame was based on original door and window openings of the cob-walled parts of the building. The new doorway on the ground floor follows that of the hall cross-passage doors (above). Some of these items were practical necessities; their significance lies in their style.

The revised philosophy of Stage 2 gave fewer opportunities for the introduction of such features. While the approach changed to 'treat as found', precedents set under Stage 1 were respected and work already

Figure 11.36 (top, left) The new stone arch to the through passage after external re-rendering. This shows limewash carried over wall plaster and stone mouldings to ensure the mouldings 'read' and following evidence of historic arrangements (photograph by David Garner, April 1996; EH B960560).

Figure 11.37 (top, right) The reinstated doorway between the great and inner chambers. The jambs are original, the head modern. Note the recently conserved lathed and daub-filled wall panel with heavily haired daub plaster intact and conserved (below) and new lath and plaster above (photograph by David Garner, October 1992; EH B926250).

Figure 11.38 (below, right) Original fragment of a 16th-century window frame from the kitchen (scale: 300mm rule) (photograph by David Garner, July 1994; EH B943789).

approved and begun was continued as started, thereby retaining some aesthetic continuity in the finished building. A number of new external doors were installed, the patterns varying according to context.[51] Windows, however, were generally repaired to their existing, always secondary, form (see Fig 11.20 for repaired doors and windows in the west elevation and Fig 11.24 for the same in the north wall of the south range). A new window in the north wall of the south range (replacing a modern window) followed the pattern of the close-set mullioned window from the hall store (above), although there was no archaeological evidence that the window was of this type (see Fig 11.84). Fixed glazing was set behind the mullions.

By contrast the large opening in the south elevation forming the south door of the through passage presented a number of repair and reconstruction problems. In the early 1980s the phase 8 blocking of this door had been removed (see Fig 5.8, 56). Recording of the reveals and sill showed evidence for the blocks of the original jambs. Options for treatment were:

1. To leave exposed the raw edges resulting from the robbing of the moulded arch stones.
2. To render these edges over.
3. To reconstruct the missing arch in some other material.
4. To put back unmoulded stone.
5. To put back moulded stone.

By the early 1990s options being seriously considered were a plain, square-headed door with a plain rendered panel around it, possibly set back slightly (in accordance with the didactic spirit of the 1992 guidelines) or a new stone surround with moulding profiles and stops based on scaled-up versions of those of the hall doorways (Fig 11.36; see also Fig 8.30), with a medieval-style door. The latter arrangement was chosen reflecting the view that such work should be in the same vein as earlier 'enhancements' so as not to clash with them, aesthetically or didactically. Volcanic stone, said to be from a quarry at North Tawton, was used for the new surround.[52]

Figure 11.39
Initial proposal for the
reconstruction of the 16th-
century window frame from
the kitchen (not to scale)
(line drawing by Douglas
Evans, January 1994;
AD6/08).

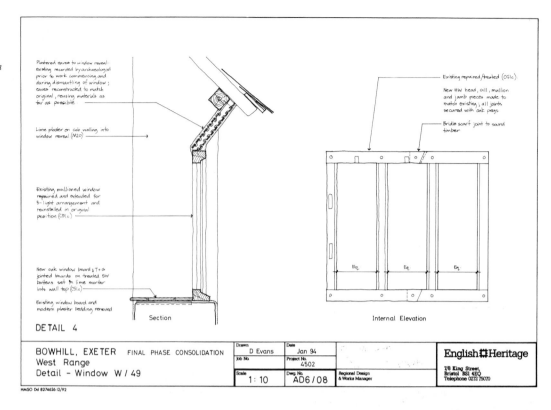

Plastered eaves to window reveal; existing recorded by archaeologist prior to work commencing and during dismantling of window; eaves reconstructed to match original, reusing materials as far as possible.

Lime plaster on cob walling into window reveal (M20)

Existing mullioned window repaired and extended for 3-light arrangement and reinstalled in original position (C51c)

New oak window board; T+G jointed boards on treated SW battens set in lime mortar into wall top (C51c)

Existing window board and modern plaster bedding removed

Existing repaired/treated (C51c)

New HW head, cill, mullion and jamb pieces made to match existing; all joints secured with oak pegs

Bridle scarf joint to sound timber

Section

Internal Elevation

DETAIL 4

BOWHILL, EXETER FINAL PHASE CONSOLIDATION West Range Detail – Window W/49	Drawn D Evans	Date Jan 94		English Heritage
	Job No	Project No. 4502		2/8 King Street,
	Scale 1:10	Dwg. No. AD6/08	Regional Design & Works Manager	Bristol BS1 4EQ Telephone 0272 75070

HMSO Dd 8274626 12/92

Figure 11.40
The same window as in
Fig 11.39, as finally
reconstructed from all the
evidence and from deduc-
tion (photograph by David
Garner, June 1995; EH
B953007).

Carved spandrels to partition doorways were reinstated, as in the Stage 1 works in the hall (above). An anachronistic arched head (to an earlier historic pattern) was introduced to the doorway in the west partition of the great chamber (Fig 11.37; *see also* Fig 6.15, 108), in part to improve headroom. The early door-frame in the southeast corner of the great chamber is also potentially confusing (*see* Fig 6.22, 99, and Fig 6.55). Although this was not the original location of the frame, it has been in this position since phase 8 or earlier; its presentation with recessed blocking was intended to indicate the former connection into the lost south-east range.

Controlled opening up and recording of the secondary (16th-century) timber window in the west wall of the first-floor room in the west range led to its repair and reinstatement to its full dimensions (Figs 11.38 and 11.39; *see also* Fig 6.45, 238). This opening was occupied by a 20th-century two-light timber window cutting into one-and-a-half lights of a 16th-century timber window (Chapter 6; *see* Fig 5.22, 242 and 238) of the same type as two loose windows in store (Chapter 9, nos 136–7). It was decided to repair the historic fragment of frame. On the basis of evidence described above (Chapter 6), the modern window was omitted altogether and the

window reconstructed to five lights as far as the nearby cruck post (Fig 11.40). The new window was glazed with fixed panes; red ochre paint identified on the historic frame was not repeated in the new work.

New floor finishes

The 1981 programme included new floors of lime concrete and charcoal in all public ground-floor rooms and pitched-stone floors in the service rooms, passages and kitchen. One architect's drawing of the period suggests that a tile pavement was considered in the great hall. The floor of the great hall, the only floor to be laid during Stage 1, was constructed of a mix of 'lime and earth', the latter comprising clay and aggregates (Fig 11.41). The choice was made for didactic reasons, rather than on structural evidence; archaeological investigations have since determined that 'earth' was unlikely to have been used for flooring in the building.[53] The floor was composed of a relatively dry rammed-cob and French hydraulic and hydrated lime mix.[54]

A lime concrete floor was also proposed in the parlour. In Stage 2 it was decided to retain the 19th-century character of this room, as far as it then remained, in accordance with less-interventionist policies. New suspended timber flooring was used, built off modern sleeper walls on slate damp-proof courses (Fig 11.42). The cavity beneath this floor (the result of the archaeological excavation of the parlour) was used to conceal services and the garderobe pit of the phase 2 building to house electrical gear. The floor of the adjoining service room was of earth, as in the great hall, formed in a cob/putty lime mix.

An experimental floor, consisting of a number of panels in various cob and cob/lime recipes, was laid in the store of the south range, late in Stage 2.[55] This took place too late in the contract for its full experimental value to be realised through a long period of monitoring; the panels survive beneath the modern floor.

Archaeological evidence suggests that the through passage and west service room of the south range were floored with volcanic trap slabs (Chapter 4), justifying the reintroduction

Figure 11.41 (above, left) Section through the cob/lime hall floor, when cut back to accommodate new floor finishes in the screens passage (see Fig 11.43) (photograph by David Garner, June 1991; EH B917139).

Figure 11.42 (above, right) The new timber suspended floor of the parlour under construction (photograph by David Garner, June 1994; EH B943757).

Figure 11.43 (below, left) Laying the floor in the screens passage: cobbles in a cob mix (photograph by David Garner, July 1991; EH B917144).

Figure 11.44 (below, right) Extending the surviving stone cobbling to the kitchen floor. Note the trial panels of daub on the cob wall in the background (photograph by David Garner, July 1994; EH B943801).

Figure 11.45
Working drawing showing
ground-floor finishes. Note
the new staircase in the
annexe serving the first
floors of the south and west
ranges (not to scale) (line
drawing by Mark Samwell,
November 1993; unnum-
bered).

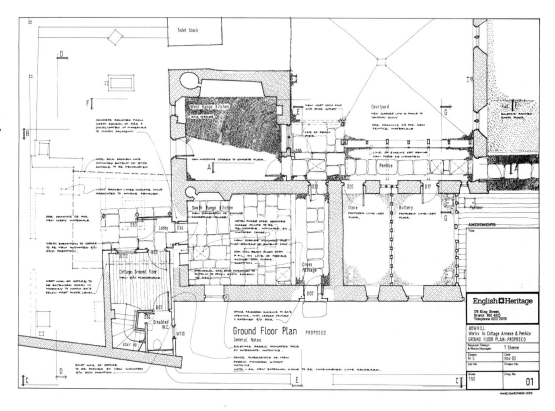

of stone slabbing in these rooms. Since trap is now unavailable, second-hand slate – discarded churchyard memorials – was obtained for this purpose.[56] The slabs were bedded face-down on lime mortar laid on the excavated sub-floor levels (*see* Fig 11.118).[57]

The flooring of the screens passage comprises a central run of stone flagging with bands of cobbles on each side, based on 19th-century evidence excavated in 1989 (Fig 11.43). The level is some millimetres below that of the lime/cob floor of the hall. Thresholds to the cross passage doorways were replaced in Devonian limestone ('Ashburton stone'). In the kitchen approximately half of a 19th-century cobbled floor survived running into the fireplace (*see* Fig 4.19). The missing section was re-laid in new cobbles to match (Fig 11.44).

Hearths were all lost, although some evidence for reconstruction often survived. In Stage 1 a concrete hearth slab was cast in the hall fireplace level with the new floor, with no attempt at reconstruction. In Stage 2 a hearth detail of pitched herringbone slates, set on edge, was created in the great chamber fireplace, with a slate hearth slab projecting into the room. The same was done in the parlour, although the projecting slab was omitted. In the west service room the new floor slabs (above) were carried into the fireplace opening.

A working drawing of the ground floor (Fig 11.45) records the variety of new floor finishes, as well as the other interventions in this part of the building, namely the pentice, the new timber partitions and stone wall and the internal rearrangement of the annexe.

Nothing remained of the original first floorboards in the south range. New oak floorboards were installed throughout. These were rebated and laid in random widths. After the building had been leased, a false floor was inserted in the first-floor room of the west range to level its irregular floor to allow its use as an office (Chapter 6).

Fabric presentation

Many of the 'enhancing' features described earlier might also be described as presentational features, in that they contribute to an understanding of the building. The change in conservation philosophy in Stage 2 entailed the retention of certain later features that exemplify development and that are relevant to the educational presentation of the building's history (for example, later inserted windows and other features and the outline form of the south-west annexe).

In 1981, early in Stage 1, the external render of the west range was partially stripped and walls were re-rendered on expanded metal lathing. During these works the scar of the lost east wall of the remainder

Figure 11.46
View of the courtyard. Note the examples of 'didactic' display in the north gable of the kitchen (the scar of the wall of the west range and the chase of a door frame above) set into the modern render. In the foreground, the laying of stone pitching on the lines of the demolished walls is in progress, again didactic in purpose (photograph by David Garner, February 1995; EH B950948).

of the west range (*see* Fig 5.27, 427), was consolidated in DoE 'racked' form to show where lost fabric has been broken away (Fig 11.46; *see also* Fig 11.111). This was a classic 'didactic' repair, as were the consolidation of the sunk imprint of a former doorframe in the face of the cob wall above (425) and the racked wall scars of the lost porch on the east elevation (*see* Fig 5.1, 85 and 87). An early 19th-century window above the western door of the screens passage was removed in order to return the hall interior to its original form (*see* Figs 5.30, 2.22 and 6.7). The stone blocking shows clearly from outside confirming that there has been an alteration, although it is uncertain if the didactic element is intentional or a chance result of the blocking process. These items represent the most important presentational features of Stage 1.

In Stage 2 the following features assist presentation:

1. The scar of the parlour fireplace shelf. The lintel was strengthened by a concealed steel within the flue wall, and one failed joggle-joint was repaired. The new single-coat plaster to the surrounding wall was made to die out on the dressed stonework of the surround and the whole was limewashed (an 'authentic' finish). The stonework, especially its damaged surfaces, is thus visible through the finished wall face (as also in the great chamber fireplace, Fig. 11.47).
2. The ground plan of the excavated walls of the west and north ranges laid out in stone pitching in the central courtyard (*see* Fig 11.46).
3. The wall scars at the junctions with the lost south-east range. These were clear prior to re-rendering (*see* Fig 5.1, 78, Fig 5.8, 75, and Fig 5.10), but they are now less obvious under the external finish (that is, less of a manifesto of theatrical

Figure 11.47
The fireplace of the great
chamber on completion of
conservation. Limewash is
carried indiscriminately
over all materials in the
wall, as originally (note the
effect in comparison to the
exposed stonework in Fig
6.23) (photograph by
David Garner, February
1995; EH B950947).

Figure 11.48
A didactic display –
conserved window embra-
sure and lintel in the great
chamber. The original lintel
is intact, with reduced
bearing on the right exposed
when the embrasure was
widened in the 19th
century. Sockets for iron-
work or timber of uncertain
date survive in its under-
side. The lintel was
preserved by the insertion of
steelwork into the wall
above (photograph by
David Garner, February
1995; EH B950940).

Figure 11.49
Protective hinged panels
over the surviving area of
original lath and daub in
the great chamber/hall
partition, subsequently
painted (photograph by
David Garner, September
1992; EH B925481).

display than the 'didactic racking' of wall scars in Stage 1). Normandy floor tiles patching the face of one scar (Chapter 5) were consolidated *in situ* rather than being removed for storage as 'finds'.

4. Lintels of the south windows of the great chamber were decayed (Fig 6.22, 17 and 69). They were conserved *in situ* by taking down the masonry over the lintels and incorporating hidden stainless-steel supports in the rebuilding, thus retaining the evidence for window bars in the two lintels and allowing the evidence for two phases of opening to be displayed in the conserved work (Fig 11.48).

5. The internal cob and daub reinstatement work on the first floor. Because much of this last work was innovative and unusual, limited areas of the interior wall faces were left unplastered to demonstrate key details of structural and super-ficial treatment. These were eventually covered over, although they were recorded before obliteration (*see* Figs 11.125–11.130).[58] They comprised:

a. An area of new cob, pared down before plastering,[59] adjacent to the doorway through the new cross wall to show the natural texture and compos-ition of the material (*see* Fig 11.128).

b. A small section of original cob wall adjoining a first-floor jointed-cruck post to show: the wide chase left in the wall to permit the post to move to allow purlin assembly during con-struction; the rough-and-ready way in which the post had been wedged into the chase after its erection; the way the post had originally been plastered over; and the modern repair to the chase to make it sound (*see* Fig 11.126).

c. In the south elevation of the oriel chamber adjacent to the oriel window showing repair of the cob work using cob blocks and truss x bearing on the extended window lintel (*see* Fig 6.22 and Fig 11.127).

d. One panel of the north wall of the great chamber was left unplastered to display new and original daub side by side. This was protected by a hinged plywood cover board and, uniquely, remains accessible (Fig 11.49, *see also* Fig 11.125).

e. Aside from these limited 'exhibits', the main area chosen for interior didactic 'display' of unplastered walling was the interior of the kitchen at first-floor level (north of truss II). This comprised the original cob walling to each side of the massive stone chimney flue, on which a series of repair types and solutions could be 'read' (Fig 11.50, and Figs 11.129–30).

6. Finally, continuing the long-established works tradition of marking new material to identify it as repair or reinstatement, the English Heritage logo was cut into a stop at the base of the stone mouldings to the new archway in the south range (Fig 11.51), cast into brackets for rainwater goods and deployed elsewhere where appropriate.

Services

Under Stage 2, basic services were installed in order to make the building usable and with the hope of pre-empting any possibly damaging action by a future owner or occupier.[60] Little thought had been given to services at the outset, because the approach to conservation of the 1981 programme was derived from a tradition of working with 'monuments' that were not expected to provide practical inside comfort levels.[61]

Water was kept to the south-west annexe only, as were WCs (under the revised Stage 2 arrangements). A connection for foul drainage was made directly to the sewer under the road. Surface-water disposal was a long-standing problem. At one point during the works, flash flooding put the screens-passage area of the hall and the parlour under water. New surface-water drainage to the central courtyard and other external areas included a 'relief' drain under the screens passage to alleviate this problem. Manhole covers were concealed by slate paviours (with small key slots at their edges to facilitate lifting).

Electricity supply was rated for use at higher loadings than were finally required. The main was brought in at the west end of the south range, formed within new work in the west gable (Fig 11.52). Ducts for wiring were run beneath ground floors through excavated areas (Figs 11.53 and 11.54). The edge of the hall floor was trenched for the ring main. Rising trunking was concealed within existing voids, where possible, or fixed to the walls in galvanised conduit (Fig 11.55). Historic work was treated as sacrosanct as far as possible, new work as sacrificial. Ring main trunking was laid in boxed-out timber skirtings on the first floor (as there were no floor voids; see Fig 11.119). Lighting wiring was placed so as not to be

Figure 11.50
The north wall of the kitchen (first-floor chamber) showing the display of repairs: various daubed wall surface repairs and cob/lime wall face rebuilding to the left; cob brick pieced in to the niche on the right; lime-mortar repointing to the stonework (photograph by David Garner, February 1995; EH B950937).

Figure 11.51
English Heritage logo cut into the stop of the new doorway to the through passage (photograph by David Garner, April 1996; EH B960561).

Figure 11.52
Electrical intake cupboard in the west wall of the west service room (photograph by David Garner, July 1994; EH B943796).

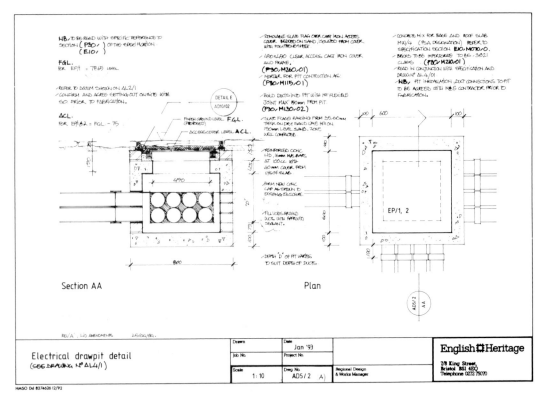

seen by a standing individual. Lighting was by means of simple pendant bulbs and reflectors hung from the roof or floor structures. Heating by electric storage heaters set against walls was chosen as cheap and simple to install (*see* Figs 11.119 and 11.120).[62]

Types of repair

Roof structures and associated works

In both stages, the full enveloping of the roof structure in a free-standing scaffold frame clad in galvanised corrugated iron and plastic sheet allowed the works to go on unhindered by the weather.[63] On acquisition the hall was still roofed in galvanised iron (the saviour of many an historic structure; *see* Figs 2.9 and 2.19). The roof framing and common rafters were in very variable condition, but the worst of all were the intermediate trusses, where the missing decorative bosses had been (perhaps because of the number of joints at those points; Fig 6.8). In the early 1980s, under what became the 1981 programme, the roof was dismantled, removed and repaired, inappropriate timbers were replaced and missing timbers reintroduced (Fig 11.56). Dismantling included the removal for repair of the jointed-cruck posts as well as the principal rafters. Reused timber from the roof of the Gloucester Greyfriars, also in guardianship, was imported to the site to supplement the supply of new oak (as a source of seasoned oak). Failed members were reformed using traditional timber repair techniques, with the aim of reinstating the roof to its original structural condition and dispensing with later ties and props (Figs 11.57 and 7.7). Repairs thus routinely involved cutting away sound areas of original timber to obtain a good bearing for scarfing new timber. This work followed 'traditional' Ancient Monuments DEL practice. All the roof works of Stage 1 (that is,

Figure 11.55
Left, *electrical socket outlets face-fixed to walls and* right, *conduit rising from within ground floors (photographs by David Garner, March 1994; EH B940993 and EH B940972).*

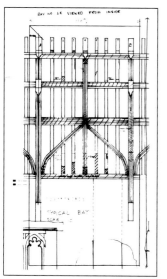
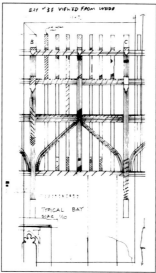
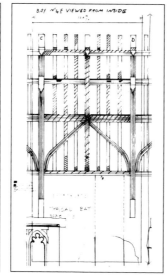
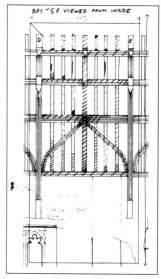

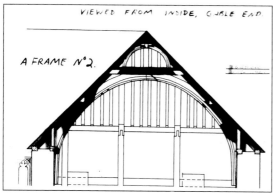
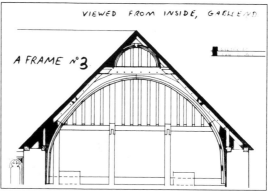

the roofs of the hall and chamber) included beetle treatment of timbers by immersion in tanks of liquid insecticide.[64] Most of the cob wall-topping was missing and was then replaced (*see* further below, cob repairs).

The roofs of the south range tackled in Stage 2 presented different problems from that of the great hall. The main trusses in the south range were generally in better condition than those of the hall roof. Common rafters and purlins required most attention, but were mostly repaired (Fig 11.58), in contrast to the near-universal replacement of

common rafters in the hall roof. Repairs to trusses and rafters were individually specified and recorded on drawings (Fig 11.59).[65] Work commenced on the great chamber roof in 1986, as before, with full disassembly (Fig 11.60, showing re-assembly). The north daub screen incorporated the jointed-cruck posts of the roof structure and supported it against racking or spreading (Fig 11.17). Thus, much had to be repaired *in situ*, but there was also a general realisation that *in situ* structural stabilisation was the only course because: the roof trusses were intimately tied into the wall

Figure 11.56
Record drawings of hall roof repairs by DEL carpenter Paul May, March/April 1987 (photograph by David Garner, September 1998; EH B980885-97).

Figure 11.57 (left)
The hall roof structure after
repair (photograph by David
Garner, October 1993; EH
B935851)

Figure 11.58 (right)
Detail of the underside of
the great chamber roof
before application of
torching, showing a repair
to the purlin, the underside
of new laths and the ends of
slate pegs (photograph by
David Garner, July 1993;
EH B933546).

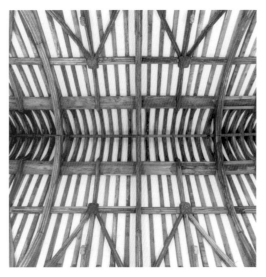

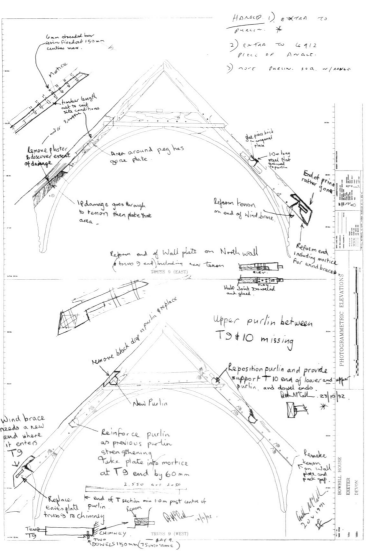

Figure 11.59
Works copy of a record drawing showing the repair proposals agreed by the engineer and
inspector (south range, Main Truss 9).

structure by the long jointed-cruck posts embedded in the daub screen (*see* Figs 6.25 and 6.57); much greater disruption to the fabric of the roof was caused by dismantling (that is, the 'heroic' repair philosophy that had guided the earlier roof repairs was now unacceptable);[66] and a repaired truss had failed during strain-testing. This led to detailed specification of individual repairs and the deployment of a variety of non-intrusive engineering repair techniques, involving stainless-steel reinforcements between the roof timbers to reintroduce structural continuity (*see* typical patterns illustrated in Fig 11.61). Hidden splints of this kind were also used to support and thus retain original fabric which would traditionally have been lost to accommodate repairs (Figs 11.61 and 11.62), although small-scale traditional repairs continued to be used where appropriate (*see* Fig 11.58). Stainless-steel straps were also used to extend failed structure inconspicuously, for example, the extended purlins of the half bay over the west gable. Such structural expedients also demonstrate a significant difference in repair philosophy between Stages 1 and 2 – propping rather than replacement. Lastly the resin-bar method was generally employed for the splicing of new to old in rafter repair: resin-fixed bars take the place of and simplify otherwise complex traditional scarfing repairs or those involving bolted flitch-plating (Fig 11.63).[67]

Methods devised for the repair of the roof of the south range were continued in the reinstatement of the roof of the west range combined, as before, with traditional timber repairs (*see* Fig 6.49). An elm prop had been inserted to support the principal of truss I of the west range, the post of which had been lost

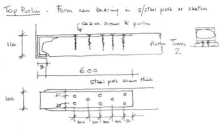

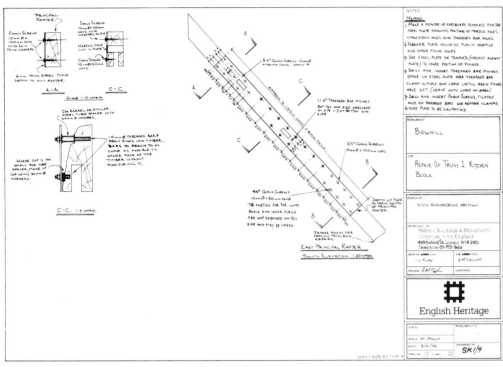

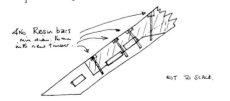

BOWHILL

ROOF TO WEST RANGE.

TRUSS 1 - EAST SIDE.

Reform end of Truss Principle Rafter as previous repairs.

4No Resin bars
min diam. 16mm
into new timber.

NOT TO SCALE.

Figure 11.60 (left)
The great chamber roof,
bays 1 and 2 after repair,
during the re-erection of
trusses I and II, looking
north-east (January 1988;
EMAFU 1412/18).

Figure 11.61 (right)
Patterns for small-scale
structural engineering inter-
ventions using steelwork
and resin in the repair of
the roofs of the south and
west ranges, designed by
EH engineering section
(MS specification for the
repair of a purlin in Bay 2
of the west range roof by
John How and Arthur
McCallum, August 1992).

Figure 11.62 (centre)
Example of a larger-scale
structural intervention to
roof truss I of the west range
(not to scale) (line drawing
by Arthur McCallum,
April 1992; SK1/9).

Figure 11.63 (left)
Architect's drawing
showing the use of resin
bars to repair the end of a
rafter (MS specification by
John How and Arthur
McCallum, August 1992).

Figure 11.64 (right)
Rafter and purlin reinstate-
ment in the roof of the west
range. Note the replacement
jointed-cruck post
supporting the original
principal rafter on the right
(photograph by David
Garner, March 1993; EH
B930332).

in phase 11 alterations (*see* Fig 5.17, unnumbered). This was replaced by an oak post with a curved head, bringing the structure into working order again (Fig 11.64). Because the roof timbers were in better condition in the west range, less rafter and purlin repair was needed here than elsewhere (Fig 11.65).

Figure 11.65
Rafter repairs in the roof of
the west range (photograph
by David Garner, March
1993; EH B930344).

Figure 11.65
Rafter repairs in the roof of
the west range (photograph
by David Garner, March
1993; EH B930344).

Figure 11.66
The underside of the rein-
stated ceiling triangle over
the great chamber at the
junction of the south and
east ranges, before re-
daubing (photograph by
David Garner, January
1991; EH B910523).

Figure 11.67
Ceiling daubing in progress
in the great chamber
(photograph by David
Garner, May 1991; EH
B916284).

Roof coverings and ceilings

The hall was re-roofed under Stage 1 with random Delabole slate, dry-laid to diminishing courses according to the 'Delabole system' on sawn softwood battens over felt on counter battens.[68] A proprietary gypsum (Sno-plast) ceiling was applied to expanded metal lathing fixed over the rafters, under felt, without insulation.[69] The visual intention was for effect, combining superficial traditional appearance with perceived ease of future maintenance.[70]

Where the roofs of the east and west ranges overlay that of the south range, evidence of original ceiling remained – a composite construction of clay daub on laths. This used a similar technique to that of the daub screen (*see* Fig 8.28). The ceilings were formed on laths on the backs of the rafters with a continuously plastered top surface and were interrupted by rafters on the soffit. That over the great chamber (that is, east) was reinstated in Stage 2, as intended in the Stage 1 programme. This introduced experimental working with daub, using a mixture of the original daub taken from the ceiling during the stripping and stored for reuse and new material (Figs 11.66 and 11.67).[71] The tiny area of original daub at the west end of the range was recorded but then removed during roof repairs (*see* Fig 7.43; Chapter 7).

The Welsh slate roofs of the south and west ranges were removed to allow repairs to roof structures and wall heads in Stage 2 and were re-laid in Delabole slates. In keeping with the aim of historical authenticity, they were wet-laid. The stated objectives here were first to perpetuate a dying tradition, secondly to provide an exemplar and thirdly as an illustration for a mooted advisory leaflet to encourage the preservation and restoration of such roofs in Devon. In practical terms the costs and the uncertainties attendant on rekindling a vernacular craft[72] made the last objective unrealistic. Bowhill remains a relatively isolated, if significant, example of the revived tradition. The research and the promotion of the subject has, however, led to a wider interest in understanding the vernacular of the craft.[73]

Based on the results of historical research commissioned from Keystone Historic Buildings Consultants,[74] the architect was asked to explore the possibility of roofing with random slates laid to diminishing courses, wet-laid in lime mortar and hung on hardwood pegs over riven hardwood laths.

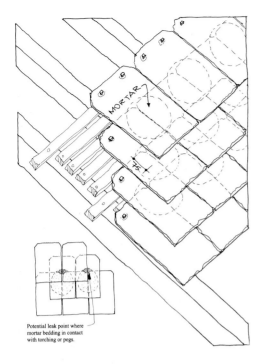
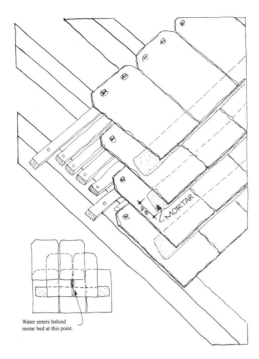

Potential leak point where mortar bedding in contact with torching or pegs.

Water enters behind mortar bed at this point.

Figure 11.68
Sketches illustrating the different treatment of mortar bedding:
(left) *the first showing mortar 'dobs' as employed in the first south range slating contract over the great chamber;* (right) *the second showing mortar strips used on the remainder of the south range and the west range (line drawings by Richard Baker and Philip Hughes).*

The underside of the same laths was to be used to carry plaster ('torching') to form a ceiling.[75] The projecting slating pegs were snipped off to ease plastering. Keystone's brief had been to seek out and examine surviving evidence – physical, documentary and oral – and to establish, if possible, what local slating traditions might have been when Bowhill was built. The aim, unrealised in the event and probably unrealisable, was to recreate what the specification for the slating of Bowhill might have been *c* 1500, as well as in the mid-18th century and in the mid-19th century (had craftsmen needed such aides memoires!).

The roofs were slated in two contracts with outside firms, the first, over the great chamber, employing mortar 'dobs' on each slate (Fig 11.68 left), the second mortar strips, more closely matching the evidence of historic roofing slates found on the site (Fig 11.68 right). Torching was applied by HPR later as a separate operation to all the roofs. It was done in a continuous exercise after completion of the roofing. The specification for both roofing contracts was based on the 'Delabole System'. Subsequent observation, research and trials suggests that the lap was greater on surviving historic examples of the technique, with a cover of three rather than two slates at the pin (or peg), which is how present-day wet-laid roofs in Cornwall are set out.[76] The roof over the annexe was not wet-laid and a proportion of the existing Devon slates was reused interspersed with Delabole.

Figure 11.69
The ceiling/first floor structure in the south range service room, with reinstated beam 6 doubling as headbeam to a new partition. Note the original (left) *and reinstated* (right) *floor joists. The diamond-shaped timber pellets conceal the heads of bolts connecting a concealed metal flitch plate to the timber, a standard modern 'traditional' solution. The profile of the new timbers matches that of the originals (photograph by David Garner, April 1994; EH B942043).*

Figure 11.70
The south end of beam 4 reinstated (south-west corner of the parlour). Here the profile of the new work is deliberately left unmoulded to confirm the repair by more than just its newness. The lamination of timbers facing the repair suggests that it is in situ shuttering for a mass resin repair (photograph by David Garner, April 1994; EH B942038).

Figure 11.71
Mass-resin reinstatement of the east end of a beam in the north gable of the hall, looking south-east within hall store (photograph by David Garner, May 1994; EH B942053).

Figure 11.72
The east gable of the great chamber with the secondary timber frame re-erected and stainless-steel bracing in place (photograph by David Garner, November 1990; EH B906962).

Figure 11.73
Internal view of the east gable of the great chamber, with lathing for lime plaster and with repaired window reinstated (photograph by David Garner, August 1991; EH B917212).

Other general timber repairs

No records of the timber repairs undertaken in Stage 1 were made other than that for the hall roof (*above*, p 289). Repairs seem to have followed traditional practice for the most part (Figs 11.69 and 11.70). One exception was the use of resin in the reinstatement of the post-and-plank partition at the north end of the hall and to consolidate and reform decayed ends of the headbeam at the external walls (Fig 11.71). Resin was again used in repairs to the beams 1–3 of the parlour ceiling, also carried out during Stage 1. The failed south ends of the beams (*see* Fig 6.28) were made up in resin to allow proper bearing on supporting elements (a new post for beam 1, seating in the walls for beams 2 and 3 and additional support from a new stone corbel for beam 3; *see* Fig 6.22, 22).[77] The beam-end repairs were reinforced with resin rods, drilled and resin-grouted in (typically where the timber had separated along a horizontal shake) and then concealed by continuous resin grouting set back within the shake. Practice in both cases followed that conventionally recommended – avoiding the use of resin in timber joints.[78] With regard to the ceiling boarding taken down at the stripping stage, the 1981 programme proposed replacing the moulded inner orders in the east bay (where original timber survived),[79] but plain boarding elsewhere. In the event the ceiling boards were not reinstated and remain in store.

In 1976 the upper part of the east gable of the south range was a timber structure of *c* 1800, lathed and plastered externally and internally. The 1981 programme had proposed its reconstruction in cob. By 1987 the lath and plaster finishes had been stripped and the timber framing of phase 8 dismantled and stored. In 1990, reinstatement of the timbers rather than reconstruction in cob was decided upon. The timber-framed structure was to be retained in the form in which it had survived until it was taken down and stored, although many of the historic timbers were very rough and ready. This was the first major departure from the 1981 programme. A frame of stainless-steel plating was made to hold the internal timbers together and to fix them to blades of the jointed-cruck truss I (Figs 11.72 and 11.73). The gable, incorporating the potential fire escape trap (*above*, p 287), was then (hardwood) lathed and plastered inside and out (without insulation) and lime rendered and limewashed.[80] Reinstatement included a

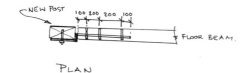

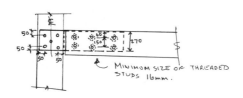

Figure 11.74 (top, left) The jointed-cruck post of west range truss I, seen from the south. The repair was designed to slide into place from the side and was fixed to the original by three oak pegs; the engineer's recommendation was '1) prop post from cruck down to floor to allow post to shrink upwards and 2) pack to make good any shrinkage' (MS specification by Arthur McCallum, December 1992) (photograph by David Garner, March 1994; EH B940979).

Figure 11.75 (top, right) Detail of the upper part of the timber shown in Fig 11.74. Note the new vertical post picking up the end of the extended eaves purlin (replacing secondary support introduced after the cob gable was demolished). The horizontal scarf joint is a traditional solution. The use of stainless-steel angles fixed with coach screws greatly simplify the construction of the three-way junction at the top of the post. The new framing to the left of the plate is part of the reconstructed west gable (photograph by David Garner, April 1993; EH B931145).

Figure 11.76 (centre, right) Engineer's sketches for the stainless-steel flitch plate to the south beam of the inserted phase 8 floor to the kitchen (MS specification by Arthur McCallum, December 1992).

Figure 11.77 (below, right) As in Fig 11.76, showing the slot in the beam completed and the flitch plate awaiting insertion (photograph by David Garner, April 1993; EH B931143).

plank string and a sash window, early 19th-century features lost at restoration from the equivalent north gable of the hall.

In the west range, Stage 2 timber repairs included the repair and extension of the partition within the tympanum of truss I, hiding the chimney stack, and the lathed and plastered niche in the south-west corner of the first-floor room (*see* Fig 5.17, 231). This work was mainly in new lath and plaster; some historic, secondary, plaster was consolidated in the niche. In the same area a new lower section was scarfed on to the west post of truss I (Figs 11.74 and 11.75). In addition the southern and central inserted (phase 8) first-floor beams needed repair. The failed west terminal of the southern beam (and its junction with the west jointed-cruck post of truss I) was repaired by inserting a stainless-steel flitch plate on the central axis of the beam, extended and turned around the side of the post (Figs 11.76 and 11.77). The central beam also had a flitch plate, resin bonded into the badly decayed core of the beam, with staggered horizontal metal studs passing through both timber and flitch. The end of the flitch plate was bolted to a vertical metal hanger to carry the load up the inside wall face and, in turn, fixed to the centre of a horizontal metal spreader plate on the window sill above.[81] Load was thus taken off the lower level of the wall and redistributed at a higher level, removing it from the immediate vicinity of a crack in the cob wall below the beam terminal.[82]

Figure 11.78
A decayed original timber
lintel to the north doorway
of the through passage in
the south range, stabilised
by a steel strap carrying its
load into the stonework
beyond the jamb (photo-
graph by David Garner,
September 1994; EH
B945310).

Figure 11.79
A small timber 'cleat' used
to pick up the end of a lintel
in the inner chamber, where
its bearing had been
removed (by widening the
window). The heads of the
fixing screws have been
'pelleted' to produce a tidy
appearance. It is impossible
to mistake this detail for
anything other than a
repair (photograph by
David Garner, October
1993; EH B935838).

Figure 11.80
Larger-scale timber cleats
used for the same purpose
as in Fig 11.79. Here the
cleats support the ends of
replacement lintels, span-
ning the modern opening
between the oriel and
kitchen chambers (photo-
graph by David Garner,
December 1993; EH
B926343).

Repairs to timber lintels and windows

No repairs were recorded to the hall window lintels. Elsewhere some timber lintels had deteriorated badly, requiring repair, support or replacement. The approach under Stage 2 was for retention wherever possible (Fig 11.78). Examples are: the lintel to the south-west window of the great chamber, where the outline of the medieval window reveals and laths from the plaster soffit of *c* 1800 were retained; and the inadequate lintel to a widened window opening in the north wall of the inner chamber, where a lining-board set against the interior window reveal was used to prop the lintel-end (Fig 6.25, 137). In the adjoining window, a cleat was used for the same purpose (Fig 11.79), similar in principle to historic (?phase 8) repairs to the roof to support the purlins. The original lintel of the north-west window of the great chamber was scarfed new to old, a classic timber repair. Lastly the later lintel of the south window of the west service room (*see* Fig 5.8, 332) was replaced by 'needling' with metal rods through the cob wall above the lintel, removing it and sliding in a replacement. The process was repeated for the replacement in new oak of crude 1970s lintels over the doorway from oriel chamber to kitchen chamber (Fig 11.80; Fig *see also* Fig 6.25, 228).

Concealed support was given to the external lintel (one of two set abreast in the wall) over the hatch and door in the east wall of the kitchen. In places only the exterior surface of this beam survived (*see* Fig 5.28). A stainless-steel inverted T angle, cut and welded to follow the deformation of the timber (designed by Arthur McCallum), was inserted in the cavity behind it to pick up the wall load from the lintel (Figs 11.81 and 11.82).[83]

Timber windows were replaced in the hall store (above). Following the Stage 2 policy of 'treat as found', existing, invariably later, timber windows in the south and west ranges were mostly repaired and reinstated (Figs 11.83 and 11.84). Thus 19th-century timber casements were retained in the medieval cinquefoil-headed lancets. In the west range late 19th- to 20th-century windows in the east and west elevations were repaired as found and a new first-floor east window was provided to a modest design. Timber frames, sashes and casements were generally taken out and repaired on the bench (Fig 11.85).

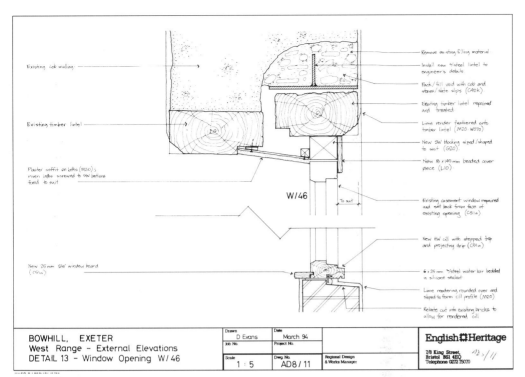

Figure 11.81
Section through the lintels and wall in Fig 5.28b, showing the proposed inverted stainless-steel T angle to relieve the load on the original lintel (not to scale) (line drawing by Douglas Evans, March 1994; AD8/11).

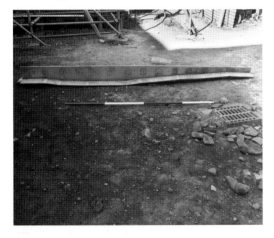

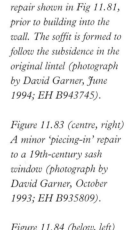

Figure 11.82 (centre, left)
Stainless-steel lintel for the repair shown in Fig 11.81, prior to building into the wall. The soffit is formed to follow the subsidence in the original lintel (photograph by David Garner, June 1994; EH B943745).

Figure 11.83 (centre, right)
A minor 'piecing-in' repair to a 19th-century sash window (photograph by David Garner, October 1993; EH B935809).

Figure 11.84 (below, left)
Fitting a new oak frame to the window serving the service room and store in the south range. Glazing set behind the bars was added to this window – pragmatic but anachronistic (photograph by David Garner, September 1993; EH B934872).

Figure 11.85 (below, right)
Repairing the sill of a 19th-century box-sash window on the bench. Sills and the lower sections of boxes are the commonest points at which repair is needed (photograph by David Garner, October 1993; EH B935811).

317

masonry, the southern bay (below) and upper courses of the wall further north were rebuilt (Fig 11.86). A major intervention made to the appearance of the hall as part of the 1981 programme was the piecing-in of missing sections of tracery and moulding using Beer stone to return the hall windows to something like their original form (*see* Figs 11.86 and 6.9; Chapter 6).[85] The windows were reinstated with glazing grooves throughout.

Masonry elsewhere was generally in good condition. Other than occasional prepara- tion by raking out loose mortar or dubbing out, little attention was needed. The repair of an oven surround in the kitchen, though of interest, is thus atypical (Fig 11.87). Where minor stabilisation of volcanic trap (original window surrounds) was needed, experiments were made with ground-up trap as a pozzolan in a lime grout, for injection into the fissures in the stone (Fig 11.88). This appears to have been successful. The existing, very exposed weatherings to the south range chimney stack were in poor condition and were consolidated where possible with some new Devonian limestone additions where necessary. Minor rebuilding of lost or poor modern walling for subse- quent plastering was done in such a way to prevent mistaken identification in the future (Fig 11.89).

Figure 11.86 (above) The west elevation of the hall; the window tracery has been fully reinstated and the secondary window removed and blocked (high- lighted by the distinctively sized, coursed and pointed masonry at the upper right- hand side). Notice in the roof the 'pig'-course (sudden diminution) near the ridge. This mistake in laying out had to be perpet- uated in the Stage 2 roofing of the south range (photo- graph by David Garner, April 1992; EH A920553).

This gave the opportunity for close study and record of the construction of the inserted moulded window (*see* Fig 5.17, 137; Chapter 5).

Stone repairs

The masonry of the east elevation of the hall remains partly 'as found', but with a little DEL pointing, beneath render of 1992.[84] The west elevation was patch repointed in 1987–8 and some sections of

Figure 11.87 Detailed drawing of stonework support and repair to the oven in the rear of the kitchen fireplace based on engineer's advice and on survey by EMAFU (not to scale) (line drawing by Douglas Evans, January 1994; AD6/09).

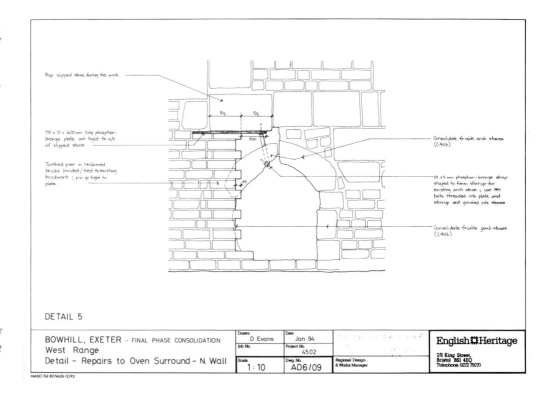

DETAIL 5

BOWHILL, EXETER - FINAL PHASE CONSOLIDATION West Range Detail - Repairs to Oven Surround - N. Wall	Drawn D Evans	Date Jan 94		English Heritage
	Job No.	Project No. 4502		7/8 King Street, Bristol BS1 4EQ Telephone 0272 750700
	Scale 1:10	Dwg. No. AD6/09	Regional Design & Works Manager	

HMSO Dd 8274626 12/92

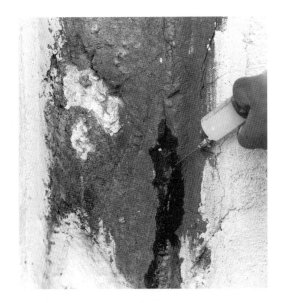

Brick repairs

During Stage 2 the top section of the brick chimney stack of the oriel chamber proved beyond repair (Fig 11.90; *see also* Fig 6.25, 183 and 198). It was taken down and rebuilt exactly, reusing the original bricks externally laid in lime mortar. New bricks were used in the annexe and hall chimney stack (above), in finishing the blocking of the garderobe in the south elevation (*see* Fig 6.41) and mixed with stone in blocking at the south-east corner of the south range. This fills the entrance into the lost south-east range and is designed to be easily distinguished under the plaster from the original. Note the modern post supporting the end of the ceiling beam (Fig 11.91).

Cob repairs

The western wall head of the hall was reinstated with new cob beam filling by the DEL (Chapter 6; shuttered and containing dung and hydraulic lime). This work set the initial pattern for the new cob of the hall store (above). There were also some repairs to original cob in the exterior of the east elevation of the hall, in one place at least. This had been reinforced with expanded metal lath, although there is no record of what was done.

In Stage 2, the reconstruction of the cross wall in the south range was the main new cob project (*see* Fig 11.16); the material was traditionally prepared (without dung or lime). Other new cob-work was restricted to the filling of voids and cavities in existing walls on various scales and using various methods of 'placing' (*see* for example, the specimen requisition in Fig 11.92). Inappropriate earlier repairs in brick or concrete

Figure 11.88 (top, left) Injection of ground trap as pozzolan in a lime grout into the stonework of the east window of the parlour (photograph by David Garner, October 1993; EH B935830).

Figure 11.89 (centre, left) The interior of the west wall of the west service room, showing (left to right): a remnant of original cob; lathing exposed at the back of the 19th-century annexe; modern concrete blockwork; the former west doorway with original lintel; Stage 2 rebuilding in lime-mortared rubble; return in wall to historic, secondary fireplace. Subsequently the remaining concrete block was replaced with daub-filled studwork (see Fig 11.52) and the door opening was reinstated (photograph by David Garner, January 1994; EH B940372).

Figure 11.90 (below, left) Brick chimney stack between the south and west ranges, subsequently taken down and rebuilt. Note the condition of the rafters in this area; valleys between roof slopes and against other features are always vulnerable to water penetration and failure (photograph by David Garner, July 1992; EH B924246).

Figure 11.91 (top, right) Rubble masonry blocking replacing inferior modern blocking at the south-east corner of the parlour (photograph by David Garner, July 1993; EH B933521).

Figure 11.92 (top, left)
Specimen of a cob repair
requisition to the DEL (line
drawing by Ray Harrison,
September 1991).

Figure 11.93 (top, right)
Reinstating cob in the north
wall of the great chamber
(photograph by David
Garner, January 1991;
EH B910505).

Figure 11.94
Surface repairs to cob
around the embrasure of the
former oriel window,
carried out in new cob
(photograph by David
Garner, March 1993;
EH B930328).

Figure 11.95
Completed, dry and pared-
back cob beam fill to the
south wallhead of the south
range and the integration
into the rafters of the top of
the new cob cross wall
(photograph by David
Garner, November 1992;
EH B926265).

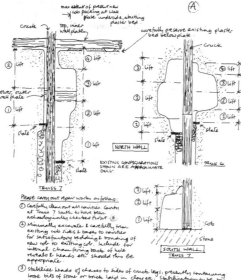

block were also removed and replaced in cob or cob brick. Some of this work was 'reinstatement' (Fig 11.93), some 'making good' (Fig 11.94). All the cob (and daub) repairs were intended to bring the walls back into their original condition (Figs 11.16 and 11.93–11.95), broadly repairing like with like to ensure compatibility.[86] Some small-scale, monitored experiments with cob/lime mixes were deliberately made in order to compare performance with straight cob mixes. Study of the archaeological record will identify numerous areas of cob wall, especially internally, where minor reinstatement was needed. New cob was placed in deeper or shallower beds, through the width of the wall or through part of its width, as circumstance demanded. Occasional use was made of pre-formed cob blocks as time became short (Fig 11.96; *see also* Fig 11.29).[87] Once the rafters had been repaired, continuous reinstatement went on at the wall heads between the rafters, where the original cob beam filling was eroded (*see* Fig 11.95). Eventually all exposed cob, inside and out, new and old, was given a coating of lime plaster or render.[88]

In the west range the new stainless-steel window lintel described earlier had to be inserted beneath a fragment of cob walling containing a beam socket of the lost gallery structure. The exercise to preserve

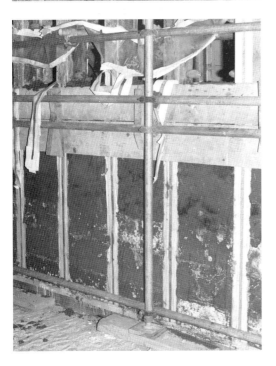

this fragment while inserting the lintel is examined elsewhere.[89] The socket was temporarily filled with polyurethane foam, needled below (Fig 11.97), then (under-built) rubble was removed, the lintel slid in and the wall 'stoned up' again under the cob.

The west boundary wall of the court-yard, essentially of cob but heavily patched and faced, was repaired using slate stitching to pack up voids and particularly to build up under the coping.[90] The Bridgwater-tile coping was replaced with Delabole slate.

Daub repairs

The filling with daub of the timber-framed panels of the north and south ends of the hall in Stage 1 has already been discussed. Nothing was recorded about this work. The bull's dung and subsoil used to fill the framed, double-lathed, north gable wall was free of lime as a result of experience with the new cob for the walls of the north extension.[91] Both were filled in stages using climbing shutters (above and Fig 11.98).

Stage 2 works related to the infilling with daub of the two partitions in the great chamber (briefly discussed above, pp 292–3). Philosophically this was a matter of repairing and reconstructing 'like with like'. Filling the frame of the great hall/great chamber screen also made the wall suffi-ciently rigid to take the strain of the repaired roof once again. Framing and oak lathing were reintroduced where missing (see Fig 11.17) – in most of the panels in the case of the daub screen, the daub had originally extruded through the laths to form an inte-gral exterior finish. This detail was repeated in the new work (Fig 11.99). All placing was by hand without shuttering. The reinstated

Figure 11.96 (top, left) Cob block 'blocking-up' around the repair area shown in Figs 11.74–75 (photograph by David Garner, May 1994; EH B942058).

Figure 11.97 (centre, left) 'Needling' to a remnant of cob wall surviving in the east wall of the west range, in order to allow the steel shown in Fig 11.82 to be slid into place (photograph by David Garner, June 1994; EH B943742).

Figure 11.98 (below, left) Method of shuttering the cob infill to the ground-floor partition at the south end of the hall (undated photo-graph, c 1987) (reproduced courtesy of Larry Keefe; © Larry Keefe).

Figure 11.99 (top, right) The daub screen between the great chamber and the hall, looking north, showing lathed studs in the process of being filled and covered with daub (photo-graph by David Garner, November 1990; EH B906973).

*Figure 11.100 (top, left)
The daub-filled and lathed
partition between the great
and inner chambers. Here a
separate finish was applied
to the laths, of which an
original section survives on
the lower half of the wall.
Above are three trial areas
of new daub. The wall
behind has been made solid
by packing with new daub
(see Fig 11.99) (photo-
graph by David Garner,
September 1992; EH
B925506).*

*Figure 11.101 (below, left)
Original plaster on the
south wall of the oriel
chamber; the edges of such
areas were all filleted before
new plaster was applied
around them. Note the cob
wall repair to the top of the
window reveal* (left)
*(photograph by David
Garner, March 1994;
EH B940989).*

*Figure 11.102 (top, right)
Applying new plaster to
daub using a wooden float,
great chamber (photograph
by David Garner, August
1992; EH B925531).*

*Figure 11.103 (below, right)
Original and new plaster
side by side, great chamber
(photograph by David
Garner, September 1992;
EH B925480).*

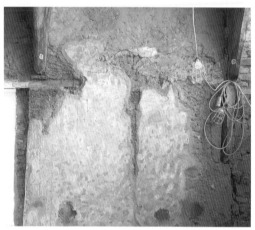

daub panels were either plastered (great chamber side) or limewashed direct (hall side), all following historical evidence. The daub partition comprised closely spaced lathing, the core filled with daub (*see* Fig 11.18). In this case, the laths had been separately daub-plastered (rather than worked up from extruded daub) and the same technique was applied to the repairs, followed by limewash.[92]

Wall finishes

Following stripping in 1978 nothing remained of the original internal wall finishes of the hall. Experiments designed to find appropriate renders for cob and stone were then made *in situ* on the kitchen walls.[93] New internal finishes chosen and used in the hall during Stage 1 comprised lime/sand plasters for masonry and lime/cob plasters for cob. Application followed the contours of the walling rather than being 'squared up'.[94] Plasters were generally finished with coarsely sieved limewash.

Some later, heavily haired, red cob and lime plaster was repaired and reinstated during Stage 2 on the daub partition (Fig 11.100; *see also* Fig 6.15, 109) and on an adjacent window reveal. Otherwise the internal finishes in the south and west ranges are of medieval lime plaster made good and extended with matching new single-coat lime plaster of Stage 2, both covered with new, well-sieved limewash (Figs 11.101–11.103). In some places, such as to the north, hall, face of the daub screen and to the plaster of the daub partition, limewash has been applied directly onto daub. This follows evidence of early, possibly original, historic practice observed in the building.

By Stage 2 no historic external render remained on the east elevation of the hall. In 1987–8 the whole façade was limewashed as a temporary measure to its varying exposed backgrounds (stone or cob) after repair.[95] In Stage 2 this limewash was hosed off and replaced with single-coat lime render (*see*

below), as prescribed by the 1992 guidelines. Though the west elevation of the hall is known also to have been rendered originally,[96] in 1992 it was decided to leave the fair-faced masonry exposed (as it had been at acquisition).[97] It thus became the only example of the didactic exposure of a substrate at Bowhill (*see* Fig 11.86), displaying the quality of the stone, the workmanship (which retains some evidence of original 'struck' pointing) and evidence of alterations made over time (including the replacement of the original wall-top cob beam filling with rubble stone, and the post-1987 repairs and window blocking).

Elsewhere the building was stripped of sprayed-on 1970s roughcast cement render during Stage 2. The limited surviving evidence suggested the original external render, like the interior plaster, was single-coat work.[98] The irregular outer edges of dressed masonry around windows (*see*

above, n 96) suggested that the original render died out over the dressed work, leading to the conclusion that this had been the original finish over all materials including timber lintels and stone dressings (inside and out). This overall finish had not been applied inside the hall in Stage 1; timber lintels, for instance, were left exposed in the wall face, rather than whitened-over with the rest of the walling as intended originally. This provides another contrast between the approaches followed under Stages 1 and 2.

Re-rendering was generally applied to the east, south and west ranges (Figs 11.104 and 11.105); the only exceptions were the west wall of the east range (above) and the north wall and east return of the west range. On the latter areas cementitious render on an armature of chicken wire stapled to the cob (applied in 1980) was retained. Similarly, the west elevation of the courtyard

Figure 11.104 (top, left) Dubbing out of exterior stone-work, south range (photograph by David Garner, April 1993; EH B931136).

Figure 11.105 (below, left) Single-coat lime rendering in progress, south range (photograph by David Garner, September 1993; EH B934850).

Figure 11.106 (top, right) Completed external rendering to the south range (photograph by David Garner, October 1993; EH B935843).

323

Figure 11.107 (top)
The east elevation after the
completion of works (photo-
graph by David Garner,
May 1995; EH A950712).

Figure 11.108 (below, left)
The view from the south-
east in May 1995 (photo-
graph by David Garner;
EH B952999).

Figure 11.109 (below, right)
The west elevation after the
completion of works,
including the new porch
against the west gable (see
Fig 11.20) (photograph by
David Garner, February
2000; EH B000014).

boundary wall retains an earlier 20th-century two-coat cementitious render. All exterior render was limewashed, with yellow-ochre tint (also carried over carved detail; Fig 11.106). The limewash has been carried over all features, as inside, including the mouldings. This creates a different aesthetic from the standard 'truth to materials' one derived from the 19th-century approach of stripping and (to some extent) from 'Arts and Crafts' practice. The justification for such extensive external use of limewash lies in its aesthetic effect (providing, at least temporarily, an element of visual continuity) and in the general record and evidence of medieval practice.[99]

Finished external and internal works

The series of photographs of the finished building (Figs 11.107–11.130) is intended to provide a record of the building at the completion of repairs and to act as a counterpoint to the photographs in Chapter 2 showing the building before repairs (*see* Figs 2.8–2.28).

Figure 11.110
The central courtyard after
the completion of works,
looking south-west (photo-
graph by David Garner,
May 1995; EH A950711).

Figure 11.111
The central courtyard with
final laying-out works in
progress, looking south-east
(photograph by David
Garner, February 1995;
EH B950954).

Figure 11.112
The restored arch of the
through passage in the
south elevation during
insertion. For the final
appearance see *Fig 11.36*
(photograph by David
Garner, January 1995;
EH B950929).

Figure 11.113
The hall, looking north,
showing the restored
northern partition and the
roof (photograph by David
Garner, May 1994; EH
B942049).

Figure 11.114 (left)
The hall looking north-east,
showing the restored fire-
place and windows (photo-
graph by David Garner,
October 1996; EH
B961857).

Figure 11.115 (right)
The hall, looking south,
showing the completed daub
screen (photograph by
David Garner, July 1991;
EH B917125).

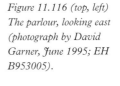

Figure 11.116 (top, left) The parlour, looking east (photograph by David Garner, June 1995; EH B953005).

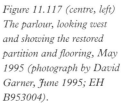

Figure 11.117 (centre, left) The parlour, looking west and showing the restored partition and flooring, May 1995 (photograph by David Garner, June 1995; EH B953004).

Figure 11.118 (below, left) The through passage, looking south, showing the restored partition to the west service room, arched doorway and slate paving (photograph by David Garner, April 1996; EH B960563).

Figure 11.119 (top, right) The great chamber looking east. Note the skirting trunking for electrical services and electrical storage heater (photograph by David Garner, February 1995; EH B950946).

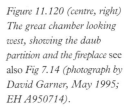

Figure 11.120 (centre, right) The great chamber looking west, showing the daub partition and the fireplace see also Fig 7.14 (photograph by David Garner, May 1995; EH A950714).

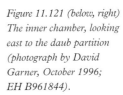

Figure 11.121 (below, right) The inner chamber, looking east to the daub partition (photograph by David Garner, October 1996; EH B961844).

Figure 11.122 (top, left) The inner chamber, looking west to new cob wall (photograph by David Garner, June 1995; EH B953006).

Figure 11.123 (centre, left) The oriel chamber, looking east, showing 'didactic window', October 1996 (photograph by David Garner; EH B961849).

Figure 11.124 (below, left) The oriel chamber, looking west to the modern gable, October 1996 (photograph by David Garner; EH B961846).

Figure 11.125 (top, right) A 'didactic window' in the north wall of the great chamber, showing the surviving section of the daub screen and repairs (photograph by David Garner, February 2000; EH B000019).

Figure 11.126 (below, right) A 'didactic window' in the north wall of the inner chamber showing a section of the north post of truss V of the roof of the south range, the broad cut in the cob for the insertion of the truss and the stone packing of the cut. Primary plaster survives partly over the cut up to and onto the roof truss; now plastered over (photograph by David Garner, February 1995; EH B950943).

*Figure 11.127 (top, left)
A 'didactic window' in the south wall of the oriel chamber, showing the foot of truss X bearing on a window lintel and associated cob; now plastered over (photograph by David Garner, October 1996; EH B961847).*

*Figure 11.128 (top, right)
A 'didactic window' in the east wall of the oriel chamber, with a section of the new cob cross wall exposed to show its composition and shrinkage, now plastered over (photograph by David Garner, October 1996; EH B961850).*

*Figure 11.129 (left)
The kitchen chamber, looking north-west and showing walling left unplastered, subsequently plastered over (photograph by David Garner, February 1995; EH B950936).*

*Figure 11.130 (right)
The kitchen chamber, looking north-east and showing walling left unplastered, subsequently plastered over (photograph by David Garner, February 1995; EH B950938).*

Phase 1, medieval

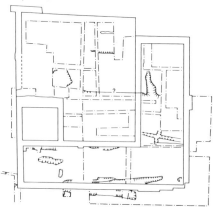

Phase 2, 15th century

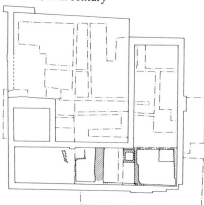

Phase 3, late 15th/early 16th century

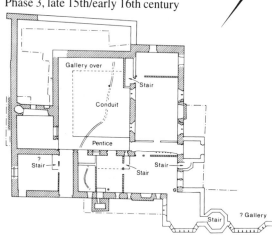

Gallery over

Stair

Conduit

Pentice

? Stair

Stair

Stair

Stair ? Gallery

Phase 4, mid 16th century

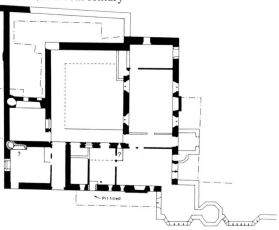

?

?

Pit filled

Phase 5, late 16th/early 17th century

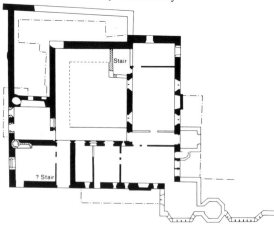

Stair

? Stair

Phase 6, mid 17th century

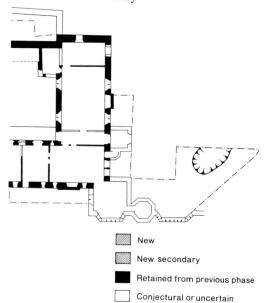

New

New secondary

Retained from previous phase

Conjectural or uncertain

Edge of excavation trenches

0 _____ 25 metres

12
Concluding discussion

The development of the site

This chapter is intended to provide a short overview of the phasing and chronology of the site, to draw attention to the most significant events and architectural features and, in conjunction with Chapter 3 and the tables of ownership/tenancy, phasing, and genealogy (*see* Tables 3.1–3.3), to provide a link between archaeological observations and the historical sequence. To some extent this is a commentary on the series of phase plans (Figs 12.1–12.4) that illustrate the development of the building at a small scale. The small phased elevation drawings (*see* Figs 5.1, 5.8 and others in Chapters 5 and 6) will also be of use.

Period I: medieval agricultural use

Pre-building, phase 1

Since the early phases of activity at Bowhill pre-dating the construction of the building that we see today are represented only by excavated remains, little can be said for certain of the nature of the earliest phases in the sequence. The few stray finds of Roman material show that there was activity of some sort in the vicinity of Bowhill in the 1st and 2nd centuries AD (Chapter 9), although no associated features were identified. There then followed a hiatus until the sequence of early ditches and other intrusive features in the central courtyard, beneath the hall and the south range, and to the south of the standing building, here described as phase 1 (*see* Fig 12.1). These clearly represent use over a period of time, as there are sequences of features cutting and recutting on different alignments in similar positions. Comparable features may have been terraced away by later activity in the eastern and western courtyards, as surviving ground levels were relatively lower outside the core of the building. No structural remains of this phase had survived. It is uncertain whether any of the intrusive features related to structures on the site (which had otherwise been destroyed) or were dug in the course of agricultural or horticultural activity. Traces of mortar and slate in the fills at least testify to the presence of buildings somewhere nearby. Dating of this activity is generally 'medieval', the datable pottery is of the 11th–14th century, with some or all of that likely to be residual. In view of the evidence for the building of phase 2, phase 1 features are likely to antedate the late 14th- to early 15th-century bracket assigned to the construction of the phase 2 building.

Period II: gentry houses, construction and occupation

Phase 2: construction of the first house

In phase 2 a building of at least three rooms was constructed on the southern edge of the site (beneath the later south range). This may well have been larger than it appears from the surviving plan (*see* Figs 4.4 and 12.1), as later truncation could have removed parts of its plan beyond the limits of the south range. If the possibility that the phase 3 house had been influenced by the extent and/or layout of this building (discussed in Chapter 4) is correct, then this, too, would argue for a more extensive plan than that represented by the three contiguous rooms which survived. Similarly, since the phase 3 plan showed every sign of having been slotted into a predetermined area, the limits of the site (especially the road to the south and the property boundary to the north) may also have been established in the course of phase 2. Preservation of the structure was poor throughout. Although only the bases of the walls had survived, there was a stone-lined garderobe pit in one room, while fragments of building materials in the fill of the rooms demonstrate that the building was roofed with slate and clay ridge tiles and had some glazed windows. These elements clearly suggest a building of more than vernacular size and status. There is no specific documentary evidence for the owners and/or tenants of

Figure 12.1 (facing page) Phased plans to illustrate the development of the site: ground floor, phases 1–6 (scale 1:500) (line drawing by Tony Ives).

Phase 7, late 17th/early 18th century

Phase 8, late 18th/early 19th century

Phase 9, 19th century

Phase 10, 20th century: up to 1969

Phase 11, 1969-1976

Phase 12, 1976-1995

Phase 3, late 15th/early 16th century

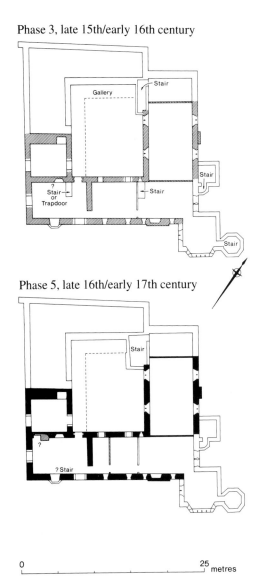

Phase 4, mid 16th century

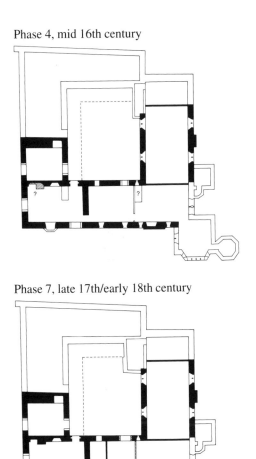

Phase 5, late 16th/early 17th century

Phase 7, late 17th/early 18th century

New

New secondary

Retained from previous phase

Conjectural or uncertain

0   25 metres

Figure 12.2 (facing page) Phased plans to illustrate the development of the site: ground floor, phases 7–12 (scale 1:500) (line drawing by Tony Ives).

Figure 12.3 Phased plans to illustrate the development of the site: first floor, phases 3–7 (scale 1:500) (line drawing by Tony Ives).

the building at this time. The pattern of acquisition of property by Richard Holand in the early 15th century, however (Chapter 3), coupled with the apparently rapid rebuilding of the house after the fire, probably as Roger Holand's main residence, argue that the house was already in Holand ownership earlier in the 15th century. Their main residence in the parish was probably elsewhere, however, in the main built-up area around the parish church of St Thomas. Sherds from the fill of the building, which may have derived from collapsed cob walling, were of 13th- to 14th-century date and suggest a late 14th- or early 15th-century date for the construction of phase 2 (context 601).

That the building was destroyed by fire is shown by extensive layers of burnt material within the rooms and the demolition debris and charred timbers that filled the garderobe pit. There was every sign that the rebuilding (phase 3) followed directly after the fire, as well as some independent dating evidence from the fill of the garderobe. This was filled with a destruction deposit containing late 15th- to early 16th-century material (Chapter 9, context 685). Carbonised timbers within this fill unfortunately proved to have too few rings for successful dendrochronological dating. Also in a destruction deposit (the fill of a post pipe of the phase 2 building) was a coin of Edward IV (*see* Shiel, Chapter 9). Minted in 1461–4, the coin was in a worn condition by the time of its deposition, suggesting a *terminus post quem* for the destruction of the building towards the end of the 15th century. These various items of dating evidence coincide with the date proposed for the construction of the standing building (*below*) and also

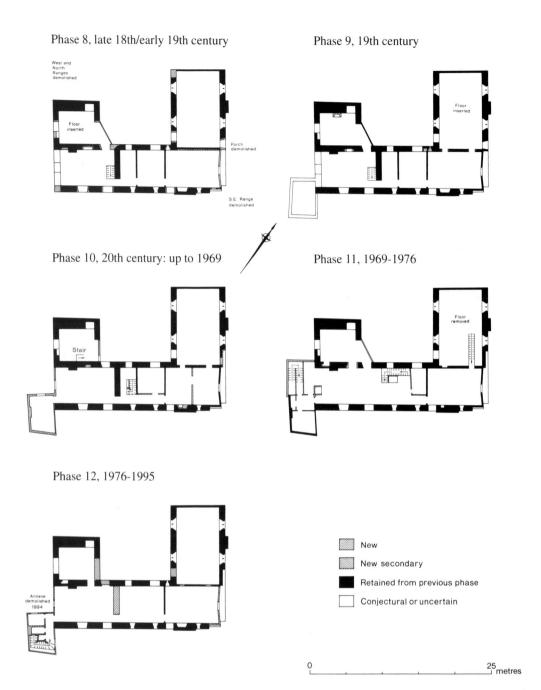

Figure 12.4
Phased plans to illustrate
the development of the site:
first floor, phases 8–12
(scale 1:500) (line drawing
by Tony Ives).

Phase 8, late 18th/early 19th century

Phase 9, 19th century

Phase 10, 20th century: up to 1969

Phase 11, 1969-1976

Phase 12, 1976-1995

New

New secondary

Retained from previous phase

Conjectural or uncertain

support the suggestion that the fire, demolition and rebuilding occurred within a limited span of time.

Construction of the standing building, phase 3

The rebuilding after the fire was probably on a much larger scale than the earlier building, using newly acquired materials – there is no sign of the reuse of materials on any scale from an earlier building. The preceding building had been largely of cob (the clay from which, of course, could have been recycled without trace), but no traces of

reuse were noted in the vast numbers of timbers inspected in the roofs of the phase 3 building.[1] Walls were generally built in foundation trenches (about 0.50–0.65m deep), with footings projecting beyond the faces of the standing walls.

The overall layout of the buildings survives from this phase, although much reduced (*see* discussion of the plan in Chapter 8). Details have fared rather worse, because of later rearrangement of the interior and truncation of archaeological strata, but excavation and fabric recording have provided glimpses of the original fittings and finishes of the building. Few original floor surfaces survived within the building, although several instances of mortar bedding and traces of later paved floors suggest that most of the internal floors were flagged or paved originally. Finds of ceramic floor tiles and a few small Beer-stone paviours suggest a floor of these materials in at least one room of the building, perhaps in one of the ground-floor rooms at the south-east corner (Chapter 9). A sequence of external surfaces was recorded in the central courtyard, including construction, primary and secondary pebbled surfaces. A stone conduit for a drain or water pipe ran across this area. Architectural fragments recovered by excavation or observed in the fabric show Beer-stone window forms of high quality, string courses and other details which have not survived *in situ*. One fragment of architectural sculpture hints at sophisticated ornament. Many windows in the principal rooms were glazed although, even in an important room such as the hall, windows could be shuttered rather than glazed (as is shown by the combination of glazed upper lights and shuttered lower lights). The primary fenestration of many lesser rooms was probably unglazed, employing a variety of window types (Chapter 8). This was replaced with glazed timber-framed windows, partly in a concerted programme of re-fenestration in the later 16th century (below, phase 4), but also on a more piece-meal basis.

The sequence of construction

The numbering and orientation (that is, the direction of the faces of the timbers) of roof trusses form a consistent pattern and sequence, which shows that the east range was constructed from north to south, the south range from east to west and the west range from south to north. This suggests an overall sequence of construction in which the east range was commenced first. Construction then proceeded clockwise through the south, west and north ranges. Stone foundations and footings were constructed first throughout, although in those parts of the building where the stone rose to a higher level no structural breaks have been observed between footings and walls proper. It is thus concluded that the construction of stone walling was continuous to the intended full height. In a given wall or range, this presumably took place first (before the raising of any cob walling). In the south range, the cob walling was then added to wall-top/cornice level and the roof trusses inserted thereafter. Complications arose towards the west end of the range, where structural timbers (floor beams and lintels) were sometimes supported differentially on stone at one end and cob at the other.[2] Clearly cob and stone must have been built up in tandem in such instances. The sequence in the east and west ranges was more conventional, in that the roof trusses were mainly raised onto the top of the stone walling[3] and the cob was subsequently built up around the timber (and simpler in the sense that neither range had first floors). This suggests that the south range was further advanced than the east and west ranges by the time the roof was ready and a delay in the construction process has emerged as the preferred explanation of the curious means of fitting the roof of the south range.

The date of the building

Architectural dating

The generally late medieval character of the architecture of the standing building is combined with features integral to the primary construction that indicate an advance on late 15th-century domestic architecture in the area. The parlour element in the plan, the oriel windows and the intersecting-beam ceiling might all fit more comfortably into a date bracket after rather than before 1500.

The separation of public and private functions in different rooms, the consequent tendency for great halls to decline in favour of larger and more private 'withdrawing' rooms and the increasing importance of more private parlours and other living rooms over the traditional hall and solar is a well-documented aspect of architecture and interior arrangement in the early 16th century.[4] Holcombe Court, Holcombe Rogus, perhaps of the 1520s, is the most prominent surviving local example of this in Devon.[5] Although few parallels for the placing of such rooms at the lower end of the hall have been traced (Chapter 8), this aspect of the planning of Bowhill is probably to be attributed to the particular constraints of the site and specifically in this instance the need to arrange the principal rooms along the road frontage.

Detailed parallels for architectural features are discussed in Chapter 8. Here attention is drawn only to (reasonably) closely dated examples that provide a context for the features of Bowhill itself.

The buildings of Henry VII's court provide the most spectacular example of the taste for elaborate projecting fenestration. Some, such as Richmond (largely complete by 1501), could have provided generic (rather than specific) parallels for primary features at Bowhill. Others, such as Thornbury Castle (before 1521), Hengrave Hall, Suffolk (1525–38),[6] are too late for direct inspiration, although they belong to a similar architectural milieu. Projecting oriel and bay windows were particularly fashionable in the years 1500–25 and so provide a particular aid to dating. Closely dated examples include Elyott's house, Exeter (directly coeval with Bowhill, built in 1500), Cerne Abbey, Dorset (1497–1509), Athelhampton Hall, Dorset (*c* 1498), Southam Delabere, Gloucestershire (*c* 1512), Horham Hall, Essex (1500–10), Lytes Cary, Somerset (1515–20) and Forde Abbey, Dorset (formerly Devon), *c* 1528).[7]

Intersecting-beam ceilings

Discussion of intersecting moulded beamed ceilings in Chapter 8 identified early domestic examples at Great Chalfield, Wiltshire, and Cothay, Somerset, both of *c* 1480. There are many parallel (and slightly earlier) examples in churches, but in Devon moulded beamed ceilings of this sort are unlikely to date much earlier than 1500 (and this is consistent with the dendrochronological dating of the planks of the Bowhill ceiling, Chapter 10). This is really the key piece of architectural dating evidence, since the frame of the ceiling is demonstrably integral to the primary construction (supporting the roofs of both south and east ranges) and displays a range of mouldings consistent with the other primary carpentry.

Dendrochronological dating

The dendrochronological dating of Bowhill is described in detail elsewhere (Groves in Chapter 10). The structural timbers sampled offered a felling date after 1478 (although with many qualifications and even doubt that the dated samples can be associated with the building). The timbers used for the boards and ribs of the parlour ceiling gave a felling-date range of 1491–*c* 1507. As the boarded ceiling is probably an integral component of the primary parlour design (since it is difficult to envisage the crude unfinished joists being tolerated in this room; *see* discussion in Chapter 6), the dendrochronological dating of the boards assists in the establishment of a date for the building as a whole.

Dendrochronological analysis has also provided refinement of the comparative stylistic and documentary dating of the Exeter group of roofs (Howard in Chapter 10).

Dating of the roofs

Stylistic grouping within the local group of roofs allows some connections to be made, especially by comparison of moulding details. The hall roof at the Archdeacon of Exeter's House, Palace Gate, which dendrochronology has shown to be the earliest roof (Howard in Chapter 10), has some connections with the roofs at the Deanery and the Law Library, both in the Cathedral Close, but is largely *sui generis*. There are many similarities between the Deanery and the Law Library, also probably close in date, according to the dendrochronology; Cadhay, near Ottery St Mary, has connections with the Law Library, although this roof is not closely dated and the similarities may be more to do with common structural traits deriving from their hammer-beam construction. The hall roof at Bowhill is closest in its mouldings to Exeter Guildhall, probably of the late 1460s. Although they are separated in date by possibly 30 years or more, these two roofs still form the latest members of the Exeter group.[8] Outside the Exeter group itself, well-dated parallels for the roofs are scarce. The refectory at Cleeve Abbey, Somerset (perhaps of the ?1480s), Athelhampton Hall, Dorset (after 1493) and Milton Abbey, Dorset (1498), offer the nearest closely dated West-Country roofs.

Archaeological dating evidence

Several key points from Chapter 9 are worth reiterating here. The ceramic finds from construction deposits of the phase 3 building give as close a date for its construction as could be expected from any source of evidence (the group from context 1559, particularly the sherd of Coarse Sandy Ware, which comes into use *c* 1500, *see* Allan, Chapter 9). The dating of finds from the destruction deposits of the phase 2 building is also of importance in establishing a precise date, particularly the find of a Normandy floor tile from the phase 2 garderobe pit (context 685, probably dating after 1490). The dating of this material is almost indistinguishable from the groups retrieved from phase 3 deposits and indicate that the phase 2 building was in use until close to 1500 (as does the coin already mentioned from a demolition context of phase 2 (*above*, p 333)).

Summary

The discussion of the dynastic history of the Holands (Chapter 3) shows that Roger Holand as a man of substantial means was in a position to contemplate building on the necessary scale. The documentary evidence shows that he was involved in building activity in the upper reaches of the parish, if the licence to lay water pipes can be taken as evidence for primary building work, rather than for additions or improvements. Furthermore Roger was associated with the site (if not specifically with the standing building) by the time of his death in 1506. The architectural and archaeological dating evidence now discussed suggests a date of *c* 1500 for the standing building at Bowhill (*see also* Table 3.3), although certain features (such as the moulded ceiling of the parlour) might suggest an even later date. This dating is consistent with the dendrochronological dating, especially the felling-date range of 1491–*c* 1507 for the superficial timbers of the parlour ceiling. The coincidence of these various types of evidence, all pointing to a date within, say, ten years of 1500, is surely enough to identify Roger Holand as the builder of Bowhill, in the period between 1491 and his death in 1506. Although the proviso that aspects of the building may have remained unfinished at Roger's death remains, major construction work in the years immediately following seems to be ruled out by the prolonged disputes over his estate (which does not seem to have finally been settled until late in the second decade of the century; Chapter 3).

The coincidence of the position of the earlier building with the new south range of phase 3, shown by excavation, suggests that the one was still visible when the other was planned. The possibilities that the earlier building influenced the later or even of some structural continuity from phase 2 to phase 3 are discussed elsewhere (Chapter 4). Whatever the details, the fire probably provided the context for a building project to provide a new house in keeping with Roger Holand's rising status and with up-to-date architectural features. Given the dating evidence just discussed, the destruction of the phase 2 building perhaps occurred somewhere in the early 1490s, when Roger was at the height of his powers and influence. An alternative possibility is that Bowhill was built for one of Roger's daughters on her marriage although, since the house passed into the ownership of the elder

daughter, Thomasina, wife of John Carew, who had already inherited Antony House in Cornwall[9] (and John and Thomasina were married before 1498[10]), rather than the younger Joan, this seems unlikely.

Reconstruction drawings

The surviving fabric and excavated plan have been used in combination with the various pieces of evidence provided by architectural fragments and pictorial sources, to produce the accompanying isometric drawings (Figs 12.5 and 12.6). These represent conjectural reconstructions of the structural core of Bowhill (the ranges around the central courtyard) as they might originally have appeared in the early 16th century (that is, on the completion of construction, but before any of the alterations of subsequent phases). There is some evidence (archaeological, structural, artefactual or pictorial) for all the major elements of the core structure shown here (although plenty of potential for more than one interpretation of individual items of evidence). The drawings are cut off to east and west to avoid the addition of wholly conjectural elements and so any buildings in the outer courtyards remain unrepresented here. Some details require comment or qualification, especially the vanished ranges to the north and west and their chimneys and fenestration (*see* Fig 12.6). The two missing ranges have been reconstructed with two storeys throughout, although there is no unequivocal evidence for an upper floor in the north range. Fenestration in these ranges is conjectural (in the west range spaced according to bay divisions extrapolated from the south) and employs simple plain-mullioned timber window frames as standard (other more complex or variable solutions are, of course, also possible). Fireplaces (represented by chimneys in the drawings) are also conjectural in the north, west and south-east ranges, although some at least of these rooms must have been heated and (allowing for individual flues having served either one or two fireplaces) the number is consistent with the twelve hearths for which the house was taxed in the late 17th century (Chapter 3). With the exception of the chimneys, the view from the south-east (*see* Fig 12.5) is perhaps more reliable (in the sense that there are fewer conjectural features shown in it). The gallery around the west and north sides of the courtyard is based on the surviving section of gallery carpentry at Leigh Barton, Churchstow, Devon (Chapter 8).

Figure 12.5
Conjectural reconstruction
drawing of the central core
of the building in its
primary form; isometric
drawing looking north-west
(scale 1:400) (line drawing
by Tony Ives).

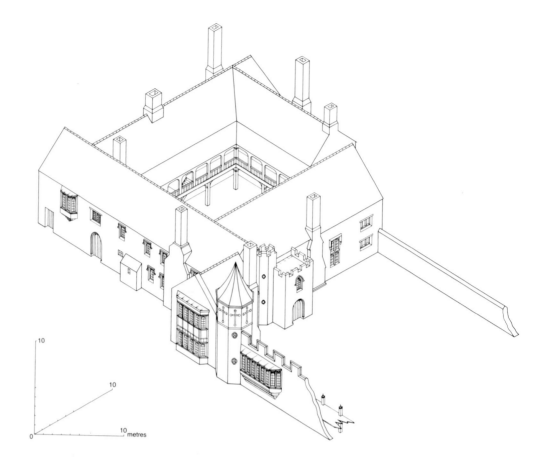

Figure 12.6
Conjectural reconstruction
drawing of the central core
of the building in its
primary form; isometric
drawing looking south-east
(scale 1:400) (line drawing
by Tony Ives).

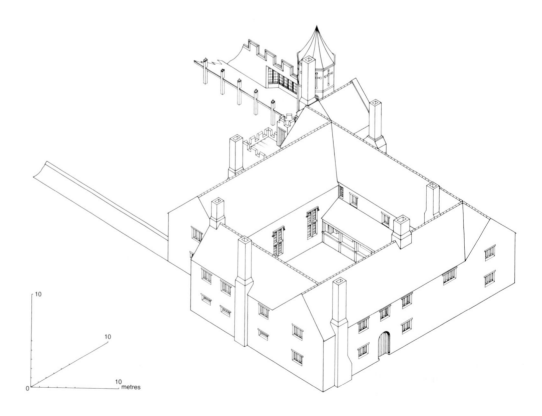

In both drawings the south-east range is based on the Bucks' view and the evidence in the surviving fabric.

Early phases of alteration to the building, phases 4 and 5

These phases are characterised by relatively minor alterations and improvements to the fabric during the period when the building was in its heyday of occupation through the 16th and into the early 17th century (Fig 12.1). Perhaps the most widespread change of this period has left very little trace in the fabric: original and probably unglazed timber windows in the cob-walled parts of the building were replaced. Most windows in the stone-walled parts of the building were retained (although with some limited new glazing work, for example, in the lower lights of the hall windows). If the three timber windows described above (Chapter 9) are survivals from this programme of re-fenestration (and not themselves original windows altered for glazing), this work should probably be assigned to phase 4 (mid-16th century), that is, before c 1580, by which date ovolo-moulded window frames might be expected in a building of this calibre. The garderobe in the south wall of the south range was decommissioned at about the same time. One of the few good groups of stratified material from the site was recovered from its fill, dated with some precision to c 1550 (context 2307, Chapter 9). Perhaps rather later than this, the stair in the north-west corner of the central courtyard was rebuilt on larger footings, in a move to improve access from the high end of the hall to the north range and adjacent buildings. Since a larger stairwell implies a framed timber stair, which is likely to be rather later, this has been assigned to phase 5, probably late 16th or early 17th century. The west service room of the south range was improved in one of these phases, probably the later, by the addition of a fireplace and oven. A moulded window frame in the first floor of the south range (Fig 5.17, 137), was also introduced in phase 5, although in its surviving form it was the product of later alteration.

Too little is known of the documentary history of the house under Carew ownership in the 16th century to be able to say much about how the house may have been used at this time. The main family seat was at Antony throughout the 16th century, as it was thereafter, and Bowhill can, therefore, never have been the main residence. Nor is there evidence for permanent residence by other family members, however, and the house remains among the property of the eldest Carew sons until well into the 17th century. No doubt it provided a convenient base for the household in Exeter. The alterations of this period, especially the re-fenestration, show that the house was improved and updated. This would suggest that it functioned as a main family dwelling, if only on an occasional basis. The provision of a fireplace and oven in the west service room suggests that this might have been intended to provide living and cooking facilities for an establishment independent of the rest of the household, perhaps for the accommodation of a steward or a bailiff? Although this doubling-up of facilities could be interpreted as a retrenchment to provide for times when the household was absent, the second kitchen, supplementary to the main kitchen in the west range, could equally be seen simply as an enlargement of food-preparation facilities to meet new needs. In the early 17th century, with the division of the Antony and Bowhill properties on the second marriage of Sir Richard Carew (Chapter 3), the house may have been used more frequently as a family residence, although it was still one among a number of properties held by this branch of the Carew family.

Phase 6: mid-17th-century events

This phase was only represented in the below-ground deposits and had left no trace in the standing building. The terminal of a deep ditch was located in the eastern courtyard, some 12–15m east of the building. This was similar in form to the ditches of other Civil War fortifications revealed by excavations in Exeter in recent years. Contemporary reports name Bowhill as one of the sites to the west of Exeter fortified by Parliamentary troops in 1645–6 prior to the final siege of the city (Chapter 3). The feature provides a glimpse of this event. Inside the building, deposits on the floors of the service rooms yielded material of early to mid-17th-century date, among numerous lead fragments, including window cames and a number of musket balls. This is in accordance with the use of the building for military purposes and may represent Civil War activity inside the building (corresponding levels failed to survive in other rooms). When the ditch began to be filled, a number of architectural fragments were deposited in the lowest layers, indicating that the demolition of structures of good quality was taking place in the vicinity later in the 17th century.

Later 17th-century alterations, phase 7

The main event of this phase was the enlargement of the parlour and the rearrangement of the service rooms to the west. The partition forming the west wall of the parlour was moved one bay to the west. The extra bay of the ceiling was adapted with applied timbers to reflect the moulded beams of the original parlour and the planked ceiling, which was of oak, was replaced with a pastiche in softwood in all but the first bay (see Fig 2.25). This represents a remarkable example of sympathetic addition and repair to this ceiling which, by then, was more than 150 years old. A pair of new windows was inserted in the south wall of the parlour at the same time.[11] The paired openings may have contained high cross-transomed windows in late 17th-century style; the initial phase, at least would appear to be rather too early for sash windows. Also in the parlour, the alterations to the screen conflicted with the position of the door in the north wall that formerly gave access from the service room to the pentice. This was now blocked. On the first floor the west wall of the great chamber was reconstructed with a new partition of framing in contemporary style. This was filled and plastered with a distinctive type of heavily haired mud plaster (daub), which was used at the same time to re-plaster the inner chamber. The incidence of this plaster on window reveals in cob walling shows that there was also some re-fenestration of the inner chamber at this phase. Several doorways and screens (now in the collection of loose timbers from the building) compare closely with the door-frame in the great chamber/inner chamber partition and may also belong to this phase (or a slightly earlier one). The pottery and stratigraphic dating evidence suggests that the enlargement of the parlour took place in the late 17th century. The operation cut layers of phase 6 containing Civil War detritus and clay pipes of 1610–50 (contexts 688 and 725). The Bucks' engraving of 1736 shows that alterations to the parlour area had taken place before this date.

Sir Thomas Carew probably lived at Bowhill, but from his marriage to Elizabeth Cupper in 1661 and the uniting of his estate with Barley the latter house gradually took over. Perhaps understandably the (by now) archaic fabric of Bowhill, with its small and poorly lit rooms, was outclassed by the attractions of a newer house more suitable as a gentleman's residence. Fascinating glimpses of life in both houses, their furnishing and of the running of the estate are provided in the accounts of the executors of Sir Thomas quoted at the end of Chapter 3.

Period III: decline and contraction of the house

The evidence of 17th- and 18th-century leases

Some members of the Carew family continued to live in the house, well into the 18th century, after Barley had become the main residence, but the decline had begun and gradually parts of the house began to be leased off. Three surviving leases provide a valuable picture of the house at this time (Table 12.1; see also Chapter 3).[12] The two earlier leases represent similar (but not identical) portions of the north and west ranges. That of 1711 has more clues to the layout and position of rooms. The 'chamber over the cellar at the end of the hall' must equate to bay 1 of the east range, next to the medieval great hall. The 'little kitchen next to the hall' must then have been in the east end of the north range or perhaps in the angle of the two ranges (in the structure originally built to contain a stair in phase 5).[13] Assuming that the description is arranged sequentially, the 'great cellar and chamber over' would then occupy much of the rest of the north range, and the 'dye house and chamber over' the remainder of the north or (since it is 'next to' the old kitchen) the west range. The 'old kitchen' may be the surviving medieval kitchen, although there are problems with the chamber 'over the old kitchen' in 1711, because the kitchen was not floored over until phase 8 c 1800).[14] The 'old kitchen' could as easily have been a room further north in the west range (where further food-preparation rooms are indicated by the access to the ovens of the main kitchen from the north; Chapter 6).

With the information so established, the details of the 1696 lease suggest that it applies to slightly more of the building, including the dye house itself (only the chamber over this room is mentioned in 1711), and a buttery (possibly to be equated with the 'cellar at the end of the hall' of 1711,

Table 12.1 Comparison of leases and agreements to rent Bowhill House (abstracts)

reference	CF2/463/1	CF2581	CF2605
date	14 Sept 1696	25 June 1711	19 Sept 1740
tenant	William Bickford of Denbury, yeoman	Robert Wadling of St Thomas, serge-weaver	William Lucombe of Powderham, gardener
period/rent	7 years, £80	6 years, £35	Life, £35
rooms	Inner kitchen Buttery Old kitchen Dye house Great celler and chamber over the same Chamber over dye house Chamber over inner kitchen Two little chambers & chamber over buttery Apple chamber over pound house	Little kitchen next to the hall Chamber over the little kitchen Chamber over the cellar at the end of the hall Great cellar and chamber over Dye house and chamber over it Chamber over old kitchen next to dye house Apple chamber over pound house	That part of Bowhill now in poss. of William Grafton, lying in the front range: Kitchen Dayry room Large parlour Four chambers over
land etc	Orchard, back court linneys, stable Little drang against the road Little nursery opposite house Hill Parke, Bolleys, Will Mead, Little Orchard, Will Parke, Four Acres Total: 19½ acres	Little pigsty next to orchard gate Little stable at end of linney adjoining dye house Access through court and use of pump Orchard Little garden next to the barn, ¼ acre	Green court adjoining the end of Bowhill Lane Stable adjoining the pound house Use of Great Court and of the pump Apple orchard and field lately a pear orchard, known as Bowhill Orchard and walled round

although the name 'great cellar' implies the existence of at least one other cellar in 1696). The 'inner kitchen' may be the same as the 'little kitchen' of 1711, but equally could refer to another room. Despite some ambiguity, the two leases give a consistent picture of peripheral (and mostly demolished) parts of the building at the turn of the 18th century.

The 1740 lease to Lucombe is less problematic, since it specifically concerned the 'front range' and the rooms described can be equated (more or less) with those of the south range as they survived in phase 7 (see the plans, Figs 12.2 and 12.3). The 'kitchen' was the west service room, the 'dayry room' the service room to the east of the through passage and the 'parlour' the enlarged parlour. The 'four chambers over' are the first-floor rooms as planned (or with the great chamber divided into two or possibly with the first-floor room of the south-east range counted as the fourth chamber).[15]

The three leases together also provide interesting information about the curtilage at this time. The 'pound house' (not included in the lease, although available for the tenant to use) with its 'apple chamber' over, common to 1696 and 1711, was probably in the west courtyard, which in view of the water supply and the well still there could be identified as the 'great court' of 1740.

The 'Green court, adjoining the end of Bowhill Lane', in Lucombe's lease must be the eastern courtyard, presumably used as a garden by this date. The 'little drang against the road'[16] in 1696 could be the strip along the south side of the building. A pound house would be expected on any large Devon farm[17] and both the first two tenants seem to have been involved in commercial cider production, because Richard Carew agreed to provide twenty hogsheads, well-repaired and well-hooped, which the tenant would return at the end of the lease. The first two leases unexpectedly also included the dye house; as the 1711 tenant was a serge-weaver, this part of the house may have been in use for cloth finishing.

Phase 8, c 1800: widespread demolition and alteration

Phase 8 represents a substantial period of activity that took place around the turn of the 19th century and comprised a series of episodes of demolition, repair and refurbishment representing a retrenchment from the extensive site of the early 16th century to a smaller (but more manageable) residual core. The context of this work was probably the period when the Barley estate recovered the house after the long tenancy of William Lucombe ended in the 1790s (Chapters 3 and 4). Excavated pottery provides a date bracket of 1780–1820; the house had probably attained its reduced plan by 1801 (Chapter 2). Major events of phase 8 include: the demolition of the north and most of the west ranges; the demolition of the south-east range; the demolition of both east and west gables of the south range (and their replacement with timber-framed structures); the removal of the porch; the removal of the pentice and gallery in the central courtyard; the insertion of a floor in the kitchen in the remaining portion of the west range; the creation of modified gallery access into the first-floor room so created, reusing the southern remnant of the gallery; the construction of a new kitchen/bakehouse building in the north-east corner of the courtyard, adjoining the north-west door of the hall; and new cobbled surfaces in the courtyard and elsewhere, including some interior surfaces. The south range (and the remnant of the west range) were re-roofed at this time, although the east (hall) range appears to have been left until the following phase. Minor alterations include: the removal of the oriel window in the first floor of the south range; alterations to windows at the west end of the south range; the narrowing of the through passage in the south range (and the insertion of a stair in ground-floor bay 8); and many other lesser alterations. Work of phase 8 is readily identifiable by its materials, since it employed brick on a large scale, a distinctive mortar type (Chapter 10) and incorporated many architectural fragments (many probably *spolia* from the south-east range) and reused building materials in its fabric. Especially noteworthy in this context are numerous late 15th- to early 16th-century floor tiles from Normandy, representing a tile pavement in some part of the building demolished at this phase.

The new kitchen, coexistent with the original kitchen, appears to indicate that the house was formally split into two dwellings at this point[18] and documentary and cartographic evidence confirm this rather later in the 19th century. As the building appears to have had only one stair at this time, the division would seem to have involved an unequal split with a flying tenancy over much of the south range, perhaps divided up approximately as: 'House A', comprising the hall, the ground floor of the south range up to the cross wall and the new kitchen; 'House B', comprising the old kitchen, the ground floor of the south range beyond the cross wall and all the first-floor rooms of the south and west ranges.

Nineteenth-century alterations: phase 9

The latest phases of the building contain evidence for many small changes. The new kitchen does not appear to have lasted for very long and had probably been demolished by 1841 (the date of the tithe map; by this time the Kerswill nursery was well-established at the house, Chapter 3). Thereafter the former central and eastern courtyards were given over to horticultural uses (as shown by the many pits in the central courtyard and the parallel cultivation trenches in the eastern courtyard). Minor structures were built on the site of the west range (a boiler house) and at the west end of the south range (the building that came to be known as the 'annexe'). In the hall there was a series of new floor surfaces, interspersed by intrusions and pit digging (it is known that the hall was used as a barn in the early 20th century and this usage may extend back into this phase). The thatched roof of the hall was probably added at this time, replacing one of slate. A first floor was inserted into the hall for about three-quarters of its length. The blocking and reduction of windows was widespread and new window frames (initially glazing-bar sashes of early 19th-century type, but subsequently casement windows) were widely added to existing embrasures.

Twentieth-century alterations: phases 10–12

Minor alterations continued in the period 1900–69, when the building continued to be used as the headquarters of a nursery garden (Figs 12.2 and 12.4; phase 10). These included some repartitioning of interior spaces, the addition of porches to doorways in the south elevation and further rebuilding of and additions to the annexe. Concrete (and in the hall, tarmac) floors were laid and there was some disturbance from drainage and other services. The few years between the sale of the building in 1968–9 and its purchase by DoE in 1976 saw the most widespread and destructive alterations since those of phase 8, *c* 1800, mostly concentrated in the years 1969 to 1972 (phase 11). These included: the demolition of the cross wall; the cutting of a door through a medieval fireplace in the north wall of the oriel chamber; the replanning of the ground floor of the south range to accommodate lavatories and kitchens; construction of new stairs in the south range (involving the removal of ceiling beams and joists); further demolition of the west gable of the south range (to make space for kitchen facilities and a dumb waiter); and further additions to the annexe. In the western courtyard the barn was demolished, and the ground surface bulldozed to make a car park.

The phase of DoE/English Heritage exploration and repair of the building of 1976–95 (phase 12) is more fully described in Chapter 11. It fell into three sub-phases: the initial exploration of the building, the stripping of later 'accretions' and the first phase of excavation (1976–80); the first phase of repair – mostly of the east (hall) range, but also working on the north gable of the west range and the parlour (1980–87), in which the principal aim was to reinstate the building to the appearance of its early phases; and the later phase in which the principle of repair as found was predominant on the remainder of the south and west ranges (1987–95). Major additions and alterations of this phase are shown on Figs 12.2 and 12.4. With the completion of the repair work and sale of the lease in 1997, Bowhill has entered into a new phase of its history, an ancient monument with a practical use as the headquarters of the Devonshire Association.

Appendix: the archive

The archive of the archaeological recording project at Bowhill, along with the excavated finds and much of the material recovered archaeologically from the standing building, is deposited in the RAM Museum, Exeter. The remainder of the Bowhill archive has been dispersed to a number of places. The large architectural finds, comprising mainly the timbers recovered from the building or removed from it during the repairs and not reinstated are deposited in the English Heritage Regional store at Toddington, near Winchcombe (Gloucestershire). A few further early finds are in the English Heritage Regional store at Salisbury. The archive of works drawings and paperwork is split between the English Heritage Historic Plans Room, now at the National Monuments Record Centre at Swindon, and the Public Record Office, where material formerly at the English Heritage Regional Office at Bristol has been deposited.

The paper archive alone forms a substantial body of material and thus an outline of its contents seems desirable for the benefit of anyone thinking of consulting it in the future. The bulk of the archive is stored in ring binders and box files where possible, although much of the drawn material is too large for such storage and is hung in a drawing file (Vertifile); colour slides are sorted thematically in polyethylene hangers for filing cabinet storage; black and white photography is represented by contact prints, which should enable prints to be identified and obtained from the holder of the negative(s) (normally Exeter Archaeology or the English Heritage Photo Library). One ring binder contains all the typescript indexes to the archive and should enable the location of specific items to be found. Material is organised in the following categories:

Records of EMAFU observations prior to 1987
Manuscript notes by J R L Thorp (copies stored with the Bowhill project archive); black and white negatives (refs EMAFU 177; 231; 255); colour transparencies stored under ref no. 238.

Records of preliminary work in 1987
Annotated AMDO drawings from the author's preliminary assessment of the building in June and July 1987.

Correspondence files
A series of ring binders containing correspondence and other general matters in chronological order; individual files for the years 1987–91, 1992–3, 1994–5, 1996–7, 1998–2000 and 2001–03.

Miscellaneous manuscript notes on the fabric
Ring binders containing MS notes on various matters to do with the fabric, observations and interpretative material; material of significance subsumed into archive reports and finally into the text of this report, although some accompanying sketches and other background material make the retention of these notes worthwhile.

Documentary research archive
Box file of copies of the archive reports prepared by Norma Parfitt, Jean Manco and Nat Alcock, plus notes and copies of relevant documents.

Excavation archive
Comprising field notes, context sheets, plans and sections, are stored by phase of work in A4 ring binders. There are also files of notes compiled during the preparation of the archive reports (for example, preliminary flow charts, indexes and so on).

Drawings
Field drawings on A4 sectional paper or plastic drawing film are stored in a large lever arch file with index. Many drawings were inked up into an interim stage for use in archive reports; these, along with pencil drafts and so on are stored flat in a Vertifile; final drawings of larger than A4 size (in practice all drawings except those done by computer graphics) are also hung in a Vertifile, identified by their final figure number. Copies of many working drawings for the works are included in the paper archive, although the primary drawings (and key copies with manuscript additions) are stored elsewhere (*see above*).

Roof survey drawings
The site archive contains drawings of all of the principal trusses (both faces and plan views) and all of the rafter trusses of the chamber roof produced by the AMDO, to whom we are indebted for working copies. For bays 5–10 (trusses VI–XI) of the south range and the roof of the west range, photogrammetric drawings were employed, checked and corrected on site by EMAFU. For the hall the coverage is confined to standardised drawings of rafters and trusses, produced for the purpose of marking up the treated, repaired and replaced timbers; plus a specimen drawing of one main and one intermediate truss of the hall roof produced by EMAFU, which forms the basis of the drawings used in Figs 7.2 and 7.6.

Photographic archives
The photographic archive comprises prints from the RCHME and DoE coverage of the building; negatives and contact prints (plus some enlargements) from the EMAFU recording; contact prints of the EH/David Garner photographic record (patchy coverage in the early years 1990–3; reasonably complete from 1994 to 1997); and colour-print recording of aspects of the works (some with negatives). At the time of writing the full archive existed only as print material, with the negatives spread between several different locations: English Heritage's photographic division; EMAFU, RAM Museum; works photographs with the archive itself; the NMR and other institutions. The intended aim of eventually uniting this material in one location now looks too optimistic, but the copies of prints should (at the least) enable the location of a given photograph to be identified and enable prints to be obtained.[1]

Digital data

Disc and hard copy of the text of the present report, along with significant earlier draft material and the texts of the archive reports, correspondence and so on. Also copies of the few illustrations to have been produced on disc.

Duplicate material

In addition to a set of the archive reports with the archive in the RAM Museum, Exeter,[2] further sets are deposited with English Heritage, the National Monuments Record, the Devon County Sites and Monuments Register, the West Country Studies Library Exeter, the Exeter University Library, the Devon and Exeter Institution and the Devonshire Association at Bowhill. A set of colour slides for lecture purposes is retained by the author at Exeter Archaeology.

Project design

The work on this report was planned, as far as was possible, according to principles recommended by English Heritage's *Management of Archaeological Projects* (MAP2; that is, according to the 'Updated Project Design' of section A5.1).[3] Given that most of the work forming the subject of the report was carried out before the publication of that document, certain aspects of the corpus of material could not be made to conform to the framework of MAP2. A copy of the project design is deposited in the archive.[4] The section of the proposal in which the importance of the work at Bowhill was established and the elements required of a publication of the site were defined[5] is quoted here as it represents a convenient summary of the aims of the report:

2.1.1 The importance of the work at Bowhill:

The fabric of Bowhill is important in the study of local architectural styles in a number of ways: the building is planned on a large scale, with grand and fashionable appointments, yet the construction shows a combination of high-quality and vernacular techniques and materials that is unusual in the surviving stock of comparable buildings. The carpentry of the building belongs to a small group of work in high-status buildings in Exeter and its vicinity; centred on the houses of the Cathedral clergy in the close (the Deanery, the Law Library, and the house of the Archdeacon of Exeter), but also encompassing a municipal building (Exeter Guildhall) and substantial country houses (Bowhill and Cadhay). Of this group Bowhill is the only building where it has been possible to study the fabric in detail, including much of the carpentry when it was dismantled for repair. Excavation and fabric recording have provided material for the analysis of the history of the building, and objects which fill out the picture of its appearance and fittings; such an opportunity, to examine the construction of a building in detail from a variety of perspectives, is unusual if not unique.

As the excavation of a standing building, the work provides a control on the effectiveness of excavation: i.e. some aspects of the structural history of the building, as derived from an analysis of the fabric, are reflected in the finds of the excavation; others are absent. Similarly the excavated evidence is of great value and interest as a control on the fabric analysis.

The work also provides a model for the recording of standing fabric, and the integration of this work with conservation works. Although commenced at a late stage in the repair process, and beset by other less-than-ideal impediments, the product can be promoted as an ideal level of recording for a large and complex historic building and as an optimum approach for general application elsewhere. The work will also use innovative forms of drawing, especially in the illustration of the roofs, but also in the presentation of other observations.

2.1.2 The principal requirements of a publication of the site:

- To provide a record of the fabric of the building now concealed (or, on occasion, removed) by the repair works, and a record of the archaeological deposits removed by excavation: local importance.
- To present evidence for the establishment and refinement of the known history of an important Exeter house, whose history (as promulgated to date) has been fraught with misconceptions and errors: regional importance.
- To present the detailed study of the fabric, especially the carpentry, of one of the group of six late-medieval buildings in Exeter; of which Bowhill is the only one to be so studied: national importance.
- To present the lessons learned from the simultaneous (or consecutive) excavation and fabric survey of a medieval site; a case study that will be of general interest to archaeologists and architectural historians.
- To present the techniques of recording, the forms of drawing, etc. as employed at Bowhill as suggestions for others engaged upon similar work.
- To present those of the excavated finds which are judged by specialists in the appropriate fields to be worthy of publication for their inherent interest or, in the case of pottery and coins, for their value as dating evidence.
- To present the collection of architectural fragments and building materials from the site which inform the reconstruction of the original fittings of the building or of the form and ornament of its vanished portions.

Notes

Chapter 1

1 Cresswell 1908, 168–70. The church was originally dedicated to St Thomas of Canterbury, but this lapsed under the orders of Henry VIII. When it was rebuilt, yet again, after the Civil War, it was dedicated to St Thomas the Apostle (Orme 1996, 151).

2 Excavation of a site in this area suggested that the earliest building flanking the street was erected after 1400 (Henderson 1984b, 28–30).

3 Amery *et al* 1911, 240; Ravenhill 1965.

4 Gover *et al* 1932, 438.

5 Sale plan of 1887, DRO 62/9/2/Box 11/58; illustrated by Harvey 1989, 33.

6 Yeo 1986, 322 ff.

7 Worthy 1892, 164; *see also* Chapter 2.

8 Franklin House, Cleeve House (Cherry and Pevsner 1989, 439); Barley House (Harvey 1989, 39) and Lower Bowhill (Chapter 3). Cowick Barton, although an older house, also ranks among the large houses of the parish (Cresswell 1935, 242–6). An account of a journey through St Thomas by the Revd John Swete of Oxton in 1797 gives a view of these houses and their residents (one which, significantly, mentions Bowhill only in passing as an adjunct to Barley; DRO 564M/F11, vol 13, 179–88).

9 Geological Survey of Great Britain (England and Wales), Drift Geology, Sheet 325 (1:63 360), 1965; Ussher 1902, 18–23. The latest mapping shows Quaternary 'head' and 'river terrace' deposits immediately around the site, with Permian rocks of the Alphington Breccia and the Whipton Formation lying to the west (and presumably underlying the gravels; British Geological Survey, 1:50 000 series, England and Wales Sheet 325, Solid and Drift Geology, 1995; Bristow *et al* 1985, 67–9).

10 Built-up areas were not surveyed by the Soil Survey of England and Wales, (Clayden 1971, 46–7 and map), but these soils are mapped to the west and south-west.

11 Bristow *et al* 1985, 21–2; *see also* below, p 9; Scrivener 1993.

12 Since it was recorded, when examined in 1982, as being lined with granite.

13 The problems of drainage were demonstrated on several occasions during the repair programme, when the building flooded during heavy rain. This was exacerbated by two factors not present in the past: the large areas of tarmac to the west of the site and a doorway in the west wall of the courtyard (inserted in the 1970s) at the point where the flow concentrated.

14 Risdon 1811, 117. Risdon died in 1640; the first published edition of his manuscript was in 1714 and contained further notes on topographical material (Brockett 1977, 373).

15 Pole 1791, 238; Polwhele 1797, II, 98.

16 DRO 564M/F11, vol 13, fol 186; *see also* Chapter 2, n 1.

17 Jenkins 1806, 435.

18 Lysons and Lysons 1822, 498.

19 *Transactions of the Exeter Diocesan Architectural Society*1843.

20 Chapter 3; the misconception derives from the earliest accounts of the building.

21 Worthy 1892, 163, which states that the chapel was 'long used as a barn'; Worthy may have been referring to the hall, by this time resembling a barn (*see* Harding 1849, 172, where the 'fine wooden open roof'of the 'private chapel' is clearly describing the hall). Other reports of the 1840s also state that the chapel had become a barn (Devon and Exeter Institution, Exeter: Stockdale papers vol G, fol 374); in the 1880s the hall is

descibed as a 'storehouse for the nurseryman's stock' (Attwood 1886, 51).

22 Anon 1913, an account full of period detail, for example, ' ... the party took trams along the Dunsford road to Bowhill'. The description of Bowhill is on page 514.

23 Ibid; one of the best published photographs of the Law Library roof is in this source (facing page 517).

24 Lega-Weekes 1935; Everett 1935.

25 Radford and Radford 1937, 1938 and 1939. This was a familiar occurrence in Exeter, as elsewhere, at the time; the surviving wing of the Benedictine nunnery of St Katherine at Polsloe, to the east of the city, was also threatened by a development in the 1930s (Lega-Weekes 1934, 182).

26 Everett 1958. Everett's original survey drawings of Bowhill are held by the Devon Record Office (DRO 3116Z/Z11/5).

27 Anon 1957.

28 Portman 1966, 61–2.

29 Typescript notes of the 1930s–1950s by Copeland held by Plymouth Local Studies Library (ref LS 728.8).

30 Article *Express and Echo* 26 June 1982; letter subtitled 'Two Bowhills' *Express and Echo*, 22 July 1969, in which the parallel histories of Bowhill and the 18th-century speculator's house called Lower Bowhill are charted. Both can be found in the WSL cuttings file: B/Exeter Buildings A–B.

31 A copy is deposited in the project archive.

32 DoE file AA 75549/2 pt1; earliest entries are dated October to December 1976.

33 From 1997 the Department of Culture, Media and Sport.

34 Formerly Grade II*, DoE 1974, 68; amended listing by the Department of National Heritage, dated 21 February 1996.

35 DoE file AA 75549/2B, concerning proposals for the display and presentation of the site 1978–83. It is clear that the original intention was to display the site to the public as an ancient monument: 'This large medieval house on the outskirts of Exeter will open gradually over the next six years' (ibid, 7 March 1980). For an interim guide leaflet prepared in 1994 for visitors to the building during repairs, *see* English Heritage nd.

36 Morley 1979.

37 Drawing numbers 969/AS2/1-6 by Chris Gray, mostly dated May 1979. Subsequently augmented as additional detail became available.

38 Slade and Dunmore 1981.

39 Harrison 1999.

40 For a survey of contemporary practice in this area *see* Wood *et al* 1994.

41 In the late 1970s 'modern' was deemed to include finishes that would probably have been retained as of interest in later years; thus post-medieval plasters and renders of 17th- to 19th-century dates were removed at this time.

42 An example can be drawn from Area 3, to the south-east of the south range. When first excavated in 1978, a number of small ditches were found and correctly interpreted as the earliest features in the sequence. These were, quite reasonably, apportioned to an early phase (Blaylock 1991a, 21). Excavation on a wider scale in 1992 showed that the features were a part of a system of cultivation trenches relating to the 19th-century nursery. They were indeed the earliest features in the sequence, but what was overlooked (for want of any datable finds or characteristic exposure) was that the sequence did not begin until a late date.

43 Barker 1977, 196–9; Harris 1975, 119.

44 Morley 1979. In addition to attempting an analysis of the building, this report is now valuable for what it records of the configuration of the interior at that time, before the alterations of the first half of the 1980s. The sketches of screens, mouldings and other features have also proved particularly valuable.

45 Especially by Stephen Dunmore.

46 By Francis Kelly, then newly appointed as Inspector for the building.

47 This was done by means of marking up copies of the elevation drawings with observations of additional material then visible and notes (Appendix).

48 For a recent description of the methodology, *see* Brown 1996, 2–4.

49 Although there are no detailed drawings of the hall after stripping.

50 The illustrations here and those in the report on the cob (Harrison 1999) bear testimony to the quality of David Garner's work at Bowhill.

51 Blaylock 1991a.

52 Hall and Blaylock 1994.

53 Blaylock 1991b.

54 Hall and Blaylock 1995.

55 English Heritage 1991 and the earlier reports cited in Chapter 1.

56 The project design is deposited with the project archive; a key section summarising the aims of this report is quoted in the Appendix.

57 An example may be drawn from the central courtyard: post-medieval structures of phase 8 are presented in plan (*see* Fig 4.19) and discussed. Succeeding phases comprised of layers of garden soils and debris, pockmarked with postholes and irregular cultivation trenches, have been omitted from the present account and are consigned to the archive report (Blaylock 1991a, fig 6).

58 The term 'cross passage' is deliberately avoided due to its established usage in vernacular terminology (for example, Beacham 1990, 35).

59 Barley 1963, 496–7; but *see* Alcock 1993, 5, for the parlour as a sleeping room in Warwickshire at this time.

60 Barley 1963, 485; Pantin 1962–3, 207–8; Wood 1965, 193.

61 Schofield 1995, 66.

62 Ibid, 67; Pantin 1962–3, 208.

63 Scrivener 1993, 1; *see also* Ussher 1902, 60; Tidmarsh 1932, 719. Stone with the typical visual characteristics of 'Pocombe' stone can also be seen at a number of other sources around Exeter.

64 Allan 1991, 15.

65 Blaylock 1995, 13, 34.

66 Gale 1992, 14; Blaylock 1990, 129, 145.

67 Scrivener 1993, plate 3. Examples of vesicular trap bearing carving or moulding can be found in the Roman legionary baths at Exeter (Bidwell 1979, 135), in Norman church detailing, such as zigzag ornament of the south doorway of the church at Loxbeare, near Tiverton (Stabb 1911, plate 103), or scalloped capitals at Upton Hellions, near Crediton, as well as in numerous later medieval contexts.

68 As is suggested by Scrivener (1993, 2).

69 Specifically vesicular stone was used for the filling of the high vault of Exeter Cathedral. In this case the stone was from Silverton (Allan 1991, 10–11), but stone could have been employed from Barley, the other immediately local quarry.

70 Notably in the reconstructed fireplace in the great hall.

71 The reasons for this may be more to do with the processes of cob construction, than with any inherent distrust of the material. All cob will shrink, because of the moisture content necessary for its mixing; the initial shrinkage after construction thus prevented the direct support of structural timbers and encouraged a system of roof support independent of the cob walling

(jointed-cruck trusses with long posts). The one example of cob supporting timber in a primary context is the short posts of truss XI of the roof of the south range that were both originally supported on cob walling. Presumably here the cob was 'pre-shrunk', that is, it was dry enough before the roof truss was erected to minimise further movement. In secondary contexts there were no such problems, for the shrinkage had taken place and the risks of movement in structural timber bearing on cob were correspondingly much reduced.

72 *See* discussion in Chapter 4.

73 For the composition of cob samples *see* Harrison 1999, 16.

74 The use of narrow beds may have been determined by the inter-relationship of cob and masonry, as the beds seemed to match the depth of adjacent masonry courses to the east (*see* Fig 5.8). The speed of drying of cob is also expedited by building in narrow beds and this may also have dictated the use of the technique here (Harrison 1999, 17).

75 Elm is not mentioned, for instance in the fabric rolls of the Cathedral of the late 13th and 14th centuries (Erskine 1983, xv–xvi and 334), but was used for scaffolding boards and possibly for floorboards in the reconstruction of the front of Exeter Guildhall in the 1590s (Blaylock 1990, 146). Salzman records the occasional use of elm as a structural timber in the Middle Ages (1952, 250), as well as its frequent use for inferior boarding purposes (ibid, 249–50).

76 The position traditionally occupied by the 'solar' (or principal private living room) on the first floor at the high end of the hall. The function of this room may not have been related to this traditional arrangement, however, because the main living rooms at Bowhill were placed at the opposite end of the hall, in the south and south-east ranges. The first-floor room has vanished; the little surviving structural evidence argues against any special emphasis or importance for this room: the hall roof continued over the northernmost bay, but in a plain form, without moulding or other ornament. In addition to the concept and function the very term 'solar' was disappearing at this time: the term was obsolete in London as early as 1400 (Schofield 1995, 66); it does seem to have continued in use elsewhere in the early 16th century, although increasingly supplanted by the terms 'parlour' and 'great chamber' (Howard 1987, 112–13; Mercer 1975, 20 and 231); its use in 16th- and 17th-century contexts is rare, regional and increasingly vernacular (Barley 1963, 498–9).

77 At a minimum the gallery provided access to the southernmost first-floor room in the west range; but there is some evidence that the gallery continued around the north side of the courtyard and was also reached via the stair at the junction of the east and north ranges.

78 The second doorway between the screens passage and the parlour could also have provided screened access to the service rooms to the west. 'Movable' partitions or screens in late medieval contexts include the screen at Rufford Old Hall, Lancashire (Beard 1990, 15; Pevsner 1969, 213), and one at Wortham Manor, Lifton, Devon (Oswald 1956, 1228–9; Cherry and Pevsner 1989, 922, although there is some doubt as to the provenance of this piece according to Bridget Cherry, pers comm). Another example is at Place House, Ware, Hertfordshire (Smith 1992, 39–40, plate 67). The evidence of inventories in the West Midlands suggests that non-structural partitions and sub-divisions were widely used in the late medieval and post-medieval periods and that such structures rarely left tangible traces in the fabric of a building (Francis Kelly and N A D Molyneaux, pers comm). Interior porches also contribute a possible parallel, such as one of the 1530s in the great chamber at Lytes Cary, Somerset (Dodd 1990, 12 and 20),

79 The ?secondary framing and small doorway now placed in the first-floor opening shows one way of closing such a gap (*see* Fig 6.22, 99). The evidence in the fabric was so slight that the original partitions in these openings could have been free-standing.

80 The problem had not been thought of in these terms when the roof was dismantled in 1987 and so the opportunity to search for surviving details (such as patterns in the positions of lath nails) was lost.

81 This structure is best placed for the view towards Exeter, dominated, of course, by the Cathedral. *See* the belvedere of the 1530s at Melbury House, Dorset (Girouard 1978, 78–9), Sharington's tower at Lacock (Howard 1987, 118 and fig 17) or the stair turret of St Catherine's Chapel, Abbotsbury, Dorset (RCHME 1952, 3 and plate 60).

82 Similar quatrefoil windows light the turret stair of the parish church of St Thomas the Apostle (Cresswell 1908, 168).

83 As no depth is shown in the rear ranges, its absence in a vanished portion of the building is unsurprising.

84 With parallels in structures at Thornbury Castle in Gloucestershire (Verey 1970, 381), the Privy Garden and Privy Orchard at Richmond Palace (Colvin *et al* 1982, 17 and 227–8) and other examples quoted by Coope 1986, 45–8.

Chapter 2

1 DRO 564M/F11, vol 13, fol 186, 'Picturesque Sketches of Devon, Thirteenth Volume (with twenty-seven views taken 1797 AD)'. The fact that Swete failed to pay any attention to Bowhill or to mention that it contained any historical fabric can be taken to be some indication of the decline of the building by this time. Swete was particularly interested in gentleman's seats and the omission supports the suggestion that the building cannot have ranked as an eligible residence for a gentleman at this time (Chapter 3).

2 Produced between 1728 and 1753, the two Exeter views are dated 1736 (Somers Cocks 1977, nos 925, SW view and 926, W view).

3 Forming a group with the two other large houses of the area: Lower Bowhill (the other 'Bowhill House', here labelled as 'Chilcott Syms Esqrs House') and Franklyn House.

4 Hyde's discussion of the preliminary drafts is of interest in this respect, especially the example illustrated of Richmond, Yorkshire (Hyde 1994, 25–6 and fig 19). In the first draft of the Richmond view the buildings of the town were drawn in ink, but the foreground and peripheral areas were more simply and sketchily drawn in pencil. The difference is not detectable in the engraving (ibid, plate 62; *see also* the finished drawing of a second view of Richmond that shows that the peripheral areas were completed at this stage, ibid, fig 20). Tree growth could well have been used to disguise a deficiency in observation or recording. For further discussion of the careful nature of Samuel Buck's preliminary work *see* Hall 1979, viii–ix.

5 Hyde 1994, 30.

6 Ibid, 25. No such sketches have been discovered, although some Devon material is preserved in the Bodleian Library, Oxford (Gough Maps, vol 5).

7 Depending on whether the separate sketches were worked up directly onto the plate, or on a preliminary draft of the 'prospect'.

8 An alternative interpretation of the Bucks' view has been put forward that the view is the artists' convention for showing two ranges in one; that the south-east range as shown here is, in fact, the hall range twisted through 90°, and that the turret represents something attached to this, perhaps to the porch (Slade 1990, 94). This interpretation is rejected in view of: the physical evidence of the wall scars at the south-east corner of the surviving fabric; the architectural fragments recovered by excavation; the demonstrable accuracy of the Bucks' work (or the sketches upon which it was based); the lack of projecting bay and oriel windows in the hall range (or evidence for their existence) to match those of the structure shown by the Bucks; and the lack of an explanation for the absence of the remaining rear ranges in the alternative thesis.

9 Chapter 9, catalogue nos 104–6, 110–12 and possibly others.

10 Drawing no. 40, part III; coloured original in British Library and monochrome photograph in WSL, Exeter.

11 Chapter 3, n 114.

12 DRO ECA 'Plan of St Thomas the Apostle, Devon, showing the present and proposed sewers and watercourses, by S. R. Southwood, Archt & Engineering Surveyor, Exeter, 1850'.

13 There is a very similar drawing of the view of the interior of the courtyard (Fig 2.5) in the Devon and Exeter Institution, Exeter, ref D81. Although this is not attributed to Stockdale, it is so similar that it must represent a copy by him.

14 WSL B/Exeter Houses, Bowhill House, St Thomas *c* 1840 (but has 'B/Exeter 728.3, Bowhill House St Thomas 1855' pencilled on the rear), P & D 40,103; B/Exeter Houses, Bowhill House St Thomas *c* 1860 (by G Townsend), P & D 6471. If clarity and accuracy are the criteria, the first would appear to be the original, the second to be the copy.

15 I am grateful to Dr Todd Gray of the Centre for Maritime Historical Studies, University of Exeter, for bringing these drawings to my attention and for the loan of photographs of the drawings. The second drawing has also been published by Dr Gray in an account of Stockdale's work (Gray 1996, 28).

16 Above a position in the north wall of the inner chamber, where a brick flue was recorded in the standing fabric (*see* Fig 6.25, 155).

17 Otherwise unknown; the painting is in the possession of Mr and Mrs W Trump of Whimple, who kindly provided a colour photocopy for the archive.

18 Everett 1935, opposite p 305: a general view from the east and a detail of the west elevation of the hall (the former was republished by Thomas and Warren 1980, 314).

Chapter 3

1 Typescript reports on documentary research by Mrs Norma Parfitt, Ms Jean Manco, and Dr N W Alcock are stored in the project archive, with copies of relevant documents.

2 There is considerable confusion over the relationships of different branches of the Holand family; attempts to disentangle them were made in the 1930s by Alexander (1934, especially the Appendix 'Note on the Holand Families', pp 98–104) and Lega-Weekes (1935) with considerable success, but certain errors and false traditions persist. The relationship to Robert, Lord Holand (d. 1328), is indicated in the 1564 Visitation of Devon (Colby 1881, 133–4). It is supported by the use of an identical coat of arms by the Holands of Weare (now Countess Wear, Topsham, near Exeter) and of Cowick (Manco 1991, 4). The lion rampant of Lord Holand appears on the seal of Roger, last of the Holands of Cowick (DRO W1258 M, G4/52/3).

3 No relationship has been established between the fourth family, the Holands of Dartmouth, and the other families.

4 Two deeds show the progression of ownership to John Holand, clerk, in August 1400 (DRO ED/M/555; 564); Holand then disposed of the premises in October 1404 (ED/M/580). The property was ' ... situate in Cowykstret between the highway

from Exeter to Ide on the south and a park called Brodepark de la Heghes on the north' (ED/M/555). The name suggests that the properties in question lay towards the east end of Cowick Street, since this is the area occupied by the lands of the Prebend of Hayes, alongside the Okehampton Road (*see* Henderson 1985, fig 3). For John Holand's career *see* Orme 1980, 60, and Manco 1991, 6.

5 Cresswell 1908, 168–9; Hingeston-Randolph 1886, 132 (vol II, fol 287); *see also* Alexander 1934, 94.

6 Alexander 1914, 490; a list of Richard's offices, with references, is given in Alexander 1934, 94–5.

7 Dunstan 1963, 220.

8 For example, Alexander 1934, 94, and Harvey 1989, 8.

9 Eton College 63/69. This is a rental for the Manor of Cowick, of 30 Henry VI (1451–2), recorded immediately after Cowick Priory was granted to the college (29 May 1451). Although the heading is damaged and the precise date is lost, as the rental covers four quarter days, it must start with Michaelmas (29 Sept) 1451 and continue to 24th June 1452 (all falling within 30 Henry VI). It includes eleven paper membranes, sewn head-to-head, of which the first three membranes list the rents payable by Richard Holand at each of the quarter days. He owed £3 3s 11d at Michaelmas, £1 14s 2½d at Christmas, £1 14s at Easter and £1 10s 5½ on 24 June, a total of £8 2s 7d. Most entries give the nature of the property (land or tenement, *ten*), the recent (*nuper*) and a former (*quondam*) tenant, sometimes an intermediate tenant (*antea*) and sometimes the name of the property.

10 *Puteus*, a well or pit (Latham 1980, 384).

11 A persistent tradition gives John Holand, first Duke of Exeter (the half-brother of Richard II) a mansion in Cowick Street (Jenkins 1806, 435; Worthy 1892, 164). The Duke's inquisition post mortem shows that he held no property in St Thomas (WSL, bound typescripts of inquisitions post mortem). Much more likely is that the building used as the Bridewell prison originated as a house of the Holands of St Thomas and acquired its association with the Duke of Exeter through a confusion of this family with their more eminent (and royally connected) namesakes (a suggestion by Jean Manco 1991, 7). The old Bridewell was put up for sale in 1809 (WSL Cuttings file B/Exeter/Districts/St Thomas/A49, cutting from the *Star*, 3 May 1809; Cherry and Pevsner 1989, 409). A new brick house, called Beaufort House, was built on the site soon after (Torr 1921, 14).

12 Alexander 1934, 96, and appendix, 102–3.

13 On 30 January 1448–9 (Dunstan 1968, 21).

14 PRO E364/90, Foreign Accounts Enrolled.

15 Wedgwood 1936, 461–2.

16 Mayor's Court Roll 12/13 Edw. IV, MS XVII, 25 January 1472–3; typescript transcript in WSL, Exeter; *see also* Alexander 1934, 97.

17 DRO W1258, G50/1. This also includes quite a large group of later court rolls which provide very little evidence for Bowhill.

18 Professor C Dyer informs us (pers comm) that he is not aware of any precisely similar court roll entries, but he interprets it as confirming the high standing of Roger Holand.

19 Wedgwood 1936, 462; and the records of attendances in Wedgwood 1938, vol 2, 553 (for 1491–2); 577 (for 1495); 592 (for 1497); and 608 (for 1504).

20 *Calendar of Patent Rolls, vol II, 1494–1509*, 22 Henry VII (16 December 1506).

21 Oliver 1861b, 236. Roger Holand's arms appear on one of the shields in the frieze of the late16th-century panelling around the main hall in the Guildhall (Blaylock 1990, 172). The charge is described by Oliver as 'Azure, a lion salient guardant, between five lilies argent [now within a border argent]' (Oliver 1861b, 210).

A variant description of the arms of Holand of Weare (/Cowick) is given by Benson as 'Azure semée de lys, a lion rampant guardant argent'. (Benson *c* 1959, 3).

22 *Calendar of Patent Rolls, vol II, 1494–1509*, 22 Henry VII (16 December 1506).

23 DRO W1258 M/G4/39.

24 DRO W1258 M/G4/52/3.

25 DRO Exeter, St Thomas Tithe Map and Apportionment. A survey of the Manor of Cowick of 1619 refers to Lower and Higher Barley Parks respectively of 14 and 16 acres (DRO W1258/G4/49). These fields were eventually incorporated in the Bowhill estate after the marriage of Thomas Carew and Elizabeth Cupper.

26 PRO PROB 11/15 fol 137v – will of Roger Holand, transcribed by Jean Manco in an appendix to her report (Manco 1991, 17).

27 This provides strong prima facie evidence for the existence of a domestic chapel or oratory in the building, as it implies that Holand was maintaining a priest at home (*see also* discussion of the chapel, Chapter 8).

28 The aisle was used as a Carew family pew in the 17th century (*see* Lega-Weekes 1935, 303–4) and payments for glazing the 'Isle' appear in the late 17th-century accounts quoted in the appendix to this chapter.

29 PRO E150/149/4 IPM Roger Holand, 1510. Hayes was a prebendal 'manor' in the parish of St Thomas; it is extensively documented in the Buller records (DRO D2065M/E1/9: 1787 map and survey) and also in the Petre archives (summary in DRO Exeter St Thomas binder). It was located near the Exe, north of the Old Okehampton Road (Fig 3.1), but Hayes Barton itself was destroyed in the Civil War (Ponsford 1992, 115–16).

30 Dyer 1989, especially 31–3 and 36.

31 DRO W1258 G4/53/1. The valor [value] of the manor prepared before it was granted to Lord John Russell in 1549 (PRO E315/48, fol 10) gives the total free rent from the manor as £16 13s 5½d (compared to £24 18s 3¾d in 1451–2), but lacks further details; *see also* Youings 1955, 5. Cowick Priory was owned by Eton College for just over 10 years (1451–62). In 1462 the priory and its possessions were granted by Edward IV to Tavistock Abbey (Finberg 1969, 28, 263–4).

32 DRO W1258 G4/49. The most detailed surveys of the Bedford Cowick estate (1619 and 1634) describe the leaseholds and copyholds, but only give the total free rent (£11 4s 2¾d in 1619).

33 The inconsistency between the total of £4 18s 4d and the sum of these two payments (£5 1s) is not commented on by the surveyor. He had presumably obtained the first figure from a Cowick *compotus* (either that for 1488–9 or another similar one) although the true sum in 1489 was unlikely to have been precisely the same as in 1452.

34 In the 17th-century surveys, all the farms at Barley formed part of the demesne land of the manor.

35 An undated rental of *c* 1680 is particularly informative (DRO D2065M/SS5/27). This seems to have been drawn up with reference to an earlier rental, the same as or very similar to the surviving Bedford rental of 1586, because the corresponding earlier owner is noted for each of the 1680 entries. The Courtenay portion of the rent had been split into two and the former Holand entries are given as:

Thomas Carewe Esq for Bowell Barton   £2 9s 8d
Nicholas Trosse Esq for close called [blank]   £1 5s 8d
John Gidley for the moyety of Gooc [Goose?] Closes
    called Exweek Meadowe and Greenaway Head,
    now Glydes formerly Courtenayes land   £1 5s 8d

36 He was probably the third son of Sir Thomas Fulford of Fulford (Vivian 1895, 378).

37 PRO E150/149/4.

38 PRO C1/393/5, dated from the name of the Chancellor. Walter Courtenay is otherwise unidentified, but he may well have been related to the Philip Courtenay recorded as owning property in St Thomas in the 15th century.

39 Halliday 1953, 69.

40 DRO Z1/48/22/4, dated 8 October 1577. It is interesting to note that the distinction between Bowhill and other property in St Thomas was still maintained at this date, since the latter follows as a separate entry after 'Bowell'.

41 Lega-Weekes 1934, 196.

42 Carew-Pole CD/AT/13; Manco 1991, 10.

43 PRO WARD7/10/14 (IPM Thomas Carew, 1564); DRO Z1/48/22/4; Carew-Pole CS/II/5.

44 Carew-Pole CS/II/11.

45 DRO Z1/48/22/4. Manco notes that, in the regrant of 1662, 'Bowhill was to be held of the King "in free socage as of the manor of East Greenwich" (DRO DD 36996)', (Manco 1991, 10); this was the usual formula for smaller grants, in contrast to complete manors which were held by knight service.

46 Stoyle 1992, v.

47 Ibid, x–xiv.

48 Stoyle 1995, 29–30.

49 Stoyle 1990, 27, quoting British Library (BL), Thomason Tracts (TT), E.322.14 and 'The Weekly Account', 4–11 February 1646.

50 Ibid, quoting BL, TT, E.332.23; 'Sir Thomas Fairfax's Further Proceedings', 22 April 1646; see also the map in Stoyle 1995, fig 40.

51 Ibid, quoting WSL SB/EXE/1645/FAI.

52 Ibid, quoting St Thomas Parish Church Wardens' Accounts, WSL; BL, Burney Collection, 'Special and Remarkable Passages', 6–13 February 1646; and Sprigg 1854, 313–14.

53 Ibid, quoting BL, TT, E.322.8; 'The Kingdoms Weekly Intelligencer', 3–12 February 1646.

54 Ibid, 3, where Stoyle makes the point that the lack of information is ' … chiefly because the Parliamentarian pamphleteers and correspondents (who are our main source of information at this stage of the war) were far more interested in the exploits of Fairfax's army than in the slow progress of the siege at Exeter'.

55 Chapters 4 and 9.

56 Stoyle 1990, 36, quoting BL, TT, E.332.23, 'Sir Thomas Fairfax's Further Proceedings', 22 April 1646.

57 Chapter 4.

58 The Dictionary of National Biography, III, 963. Carew's entry in the DNB shows that he was a man of principle and took his punishment as a regicide with courage and composure:

> … he was afforded many opportunities to escape, but he refused to avail himself of them. His trial took place at the Old Bailey on 12 Oct. 1660.... He endeavoured to prove that his acts were done under the authority of parliament, and asserted that he did his part 'in the fear of the holy and righteous Lord, the judge of the earth' … Carew was a republican without guile and reproach.

Although he suffered a criminal's death, an exception was made when it came to the display of his quartered remains and his body was granted to Thomas for burial. The exception was noted as a 'great favour' by Pepys in his note on the execution (15 October 1660; Latham and Matthews 1995, 266).

59 Calendar of State Papers Domestic 1661, May, p 604.

60 DRO DD/36996 (transcript).

61 Oliver 1861b, 236; Henning 1983, 15.

62 PRO PROB 11/277, fol 287v.

63 Recited in CRO CF2486 (regrant of the estate to Richard Carew). It also appears that he received the £800 after all, as this sum is included in a list of legacies to be paid after the death of Thomas Carew (Carew-Pole CW/H/23/9). Thomas had presumably been paying interest on the debt but had not paid off the principal.

64 CF4407; CF3488; tithe composition, DRO 2065M/add4/E1. It is very possible that Thomas Carew was unable to provide the necessary cash for Thomas Cupper and so had to transfer the farms instead.

65 CF3091–2; PRO PROB 11/481, fol 85; CF4108.

66 CF4112b.

67 DRO DD 36997, transcript of 1792 purchase by John Graves from Bridget Sawle (below).

68 CF3096; Exeter Flying Post, Friday 15 April 1774.

69 CF2500.

70 Exeter Flying Post, 8 September 1791, 2d.

71 The estate was sold on the death of Sir Charles Graves-Sawle, fourth baronet, in 1932, when the baronetcy became extinct (Burke and Burke 1937, 2120).

72 Of Bowhill in April 1661, CF2523; of Barley in 1664, CF2525.

73 Thomas 1974, 246; we are indebted to Peter Weddell for this reference.

74 Polwhele 1797, II, 98–9.

75 The accounts include payments for twenty-four hearths in May 1682 and later, which are seen from the half-year payment in May 1686 to relate to the same number of hearths in each house. The only surviving Devon Hearth Tax account lists twelve hearths for Thomas Carew, but must have omitted his second twelve hearths in error (Stoate 1982, 59).

76 Carew-Pole CA/H/1, 1 and 31 March 1687.

77 Peter West, the glazier, received a salary of 16s a year to maintain the windows both in the house and in the Barley Bowhill aisle in St Thomas' Church.

78 It is notable, however, that very few original title deeds have come to light, suggesting that these were kept separately and have either been passed on to purchasers or have been lost. For example, the 1661 Letters Patent restoring Bowhill was in the possession of Coode and Gifford, solicitors, when it was transcribed in 1935, but is not in the big collection deposited by them in Cornwall Record Office (CF).

79 PRO WARD7/10/41.

80 Carew-Pole CW/H/23/9.

81 They can be identified particularly from the abstract of title prepared for the whole estate in 1782 (CF2500) and from a 1753 list of deeds relating to the lands of John Penneck.

82 CF2500; CF3096.

83 The attorney preparing the 1782 abstract of title (CF2500) noted in the margin 'This is the first Particular Description of the Premises'.

84 For those parts of the estate sold in 1791, the Exeter St Thomas Land Tax assessments have been used to follow their ownership up to 1841.

85 CF2564; CF2511; PRO CP43/762, MS122, enrolment of deed to disentail the estate. Lower Barley House may have been situated in the field later called Green Field (TM).

86 CF2/463/1; CF2581; CF 2605.

87 Surprisingly, neither the 1773 deed (CP43/762, MS122) nor the 1774 sale particulars give much evidence of the cottages. The latter distinguishes only half a dozen houses, but notes 'and other occupiers', probably implying blocks of property.

88 DRO D36997; TM 433–4.

89 CF2552; CF2541, 2544. The group of five fields known as The Cleaves or Western Cleave can be identified with the westernmost block of lands belonging to Bowhill (Figs 3.1 and 3.2).

90 CF2528, 2546, 2594. Lugg's house, part of Great Barley in 1774 (TM 557); a garden near St Thomas' Workhouse is also listed in 1779 (Drew's).

91 CF2572; CF2559.

92 CF2521.

93 For example, CF2512–16 (1648–50); 2521 (1658); 2524 (1664).

94 CF2496; Pearse Box 57; TM 142 and 143. The name of Cuckold's Bridge is preserved in the adjacent court, called Cockell's Court on the 1876 1:500 OS map; this property is included in an 1820 deed (DRO 48/28/16/7), when it was known as Hamlyn's and was bounded on the east by a public drain or watercourse.

95 CF2555.

96 CF2542; the reserved rent was 10s.

97 CF2605; other agreements of 1748 and 1770, possibly involving renegotiation of the original terms, are referred to in the 1792 conveyance (DRO DD/36997), but have not survived. Lucombe occupied 'the manor house of Bowhill & walled garden belonging together with three fields or closes called Hill Park, Great Gore, & Little Gore' and the three fields immediately north of the house named as 'Lucombe's Garden' and 'part of Lucombe's' in the tithe apportionment. The lease of another field to William Ford, gardener, in 1748 (CF2608), was also made for an exceptional period of 60 years.

98 Lysons and Lysons 1822 II, 498.

99 William Lucombe was buried on 17 September 1794; his wife, Elizabeth Lucombe, on 10 May 1798 ('St Thomas Parish Registers, vol 3, 1743–1812, Transcribed and Indexed by Thomas Lane Ormiston, 1933', Devon and Cornwall Record Society Library, WSL, Exeter).

100 *Exeter Flying Post*, 8 September 1791.

101 Hadfield 1960, 288; Harvey 1974, 104; Heriz-Smith 1988a and 1988b; Rogers 1989, 18–19.

102 Hadfield 1960, 236; 287–8; Harvey 1974, 72; Le Lievre 1995, 88; Rogers 1989, 17. For general accounts of both Lucombe and Veitch nurseries, *see also* typescript notes entitled 'The Early Nurseries of Exeter' prepared by John Harvey for the Garden History Society conference in Exeter in 1981.

103 Caldwell and Wilkinson, 1953; Nicholson and Clapham 1975, 159. Several specimens may be seen in the grounds of Exeter University, said to be descendants of Lucombe's originals (Caldwell and Proctor 1969, 29–30; 53, 62 and maps, 63–9). There is also a specimen in the gardens of Killerton House at Broadclyst.

104 As early as October 1794 John Lucombe was advertising the sale of trees growing on the Bowhill nursery at reduced prices (*Exeter Flying Post*, 23 October 1794).

105 A name that it retained into the time of the Sclater ownership in the 20th century (*see below*).

106 Trewman 1839, 60; *Exeter Flying Post*, 9 July 1835, 2d; 17 March 1836, 2c. The street names Pince's Gardens and Pince's Road to the west of Alphington Road (and towards Cowick Lane) preserve the connection; *see* Harvey 1989, 23–4.

107 Trewman 1827, 55; later called Dunsford Road. The evidence of the tithe apportionment shows that the land and property in question was Bowhill and the fields adjacent to the north-west, previously occupied by Lucombe.

108 DRO St Thomas Tithe Apportionment (TA), no. 431a (House & garden); the western half was occupied by Mary Gibbs, TA no. 431 ('House yard, garden & barn'). Kerswill also occupied two-thirds of the large field to the north of Bowhill, now split into three parts and described as 'part of Lucombe's garden' (TA 430, 430a) the remaining (southernmost) third being occupied by Mary Gibbs (TA 430b). All of this land and the large fields to the south-west were still in the ownership of Sir Joseph Sawle (TA 427–9, 'Eight Acres', 'Five Acres', and 'Great Barley Park' respectively). The archaeological evidence for the division

of the house into two dwellings is the construction of a separate kitchen block to serve the eastern half of the building, perhaps in the early 19th century (Chapter 4); additionally Southwood's sewerage map of the parish of 1850 shows the building divided into two halves (Chapter 2).

109 John Kerswill is listed in directories in 'Moreton Road' until 1839 (Trewman 1839, 59); then, perhaps on his death, a Harriet Kerswill appears (Trewman 1844, 61; Besley 1853 [230], not paginated). From 1881 George Kerswill, 'nurseryman and florist' is listed in Dunsford Road in the directories (Besley 1881, 28 and later editions *passim*). The evidence of the occupation of Bowhill by the Kerswills at the time of the tithe map must indicate that the house formed the core of this nursery garden, although the name is nowhere used in this context through the later 19th century.

110 Exeter *Express and Echo*, 8 October 1917: 'all those well known gardens known as the Bowhill nurseries for many years part in the occupation of the late Mr Geo. Kerswill … The buildings consist of an historically interesting and commodious Dwelling House with ample accommodation for storing and packing fruit etc.'.

111 Besley 1919, 26, 183; 1920, 27. The Sclaters were already established in the nursery business in St Thomas parish, and were running the former Lucombe nurseries in Alphington Road (DRO Pearse 62/9/2 box 1164, 'part of the well known "Exeter Nursery" long occupied by Messr Lucombe Pince and Co. and more recently by Mrs W. H. Sclater, 9A, 1R, 25P' (25 April 1912); note that this is *not* the Bowhill premises). Sclater continued in occupation until the sale of the building in 1968 (Everett 1935, 307, and *see below*).

112 Burke and Burke 1937, 2120. Barley House was finally sold in 1938 to become the headquarters of the County Library (*WMN* 9 ix.1938; WSL Cuttings Files Exeter Buildings/A–B/6), in whose occupation it remains.

113 *WMN*, 28 May 1937, 15 and 29 May 1937, 5; Radford and Radford 1937, 73, and 1938, 57: 'We regret to have to report that Bowhill, the fine fifteenth century manor house mentioned in our last Report, is not to be preserved, though it will not be demolished immediately'; possibly the outbreak of war in September 1939 ensured its survival (Radford and Radford 1939, 67).

114 RAF 106G/UK865, 30 September 1945.

115 Comparison of the OS 1:1250 map sheet SX9091 NE, editions of 1951 and 1967 (surveyed 1950, revised 1966), shows that all of this area had been developed by 1966. The south-east corner of the enclosure wall of the property had also been rebuilt, presumably in order to create a 'traffic splay' at the corner of Bowhay Lane. This resulted in the loss of a distinctive kink in the boundary wall (*see* the detail from the map of 1951 shown on Fig 1.1, and the aerial photograph of 1945 (Fig 3.4), which may have perpetuated an element in the lost south-eastern range of the building (Chapter 8).

116 Advertisement for sale in *Express and Echo*, 24 June 1967; 'Half acre grounds and three acres Market garden (1½ miles distant), as a going concern … '.

117 In March 1968 (*Express and Echo*, 24 August 1968); the new owners were said to have burned 2,000 square feet of floor boards from the great hall in the previous winter.

118 Exeter City Council Planning files, ref 952/68, 31 October 1968, and various additional applications in 1969 – 23/69, 131/69 and LBC/2/69. Plans for the conversion of the building, involving the removal of the cross wall in the south range and other radical alterations, were drawn up in late 1968 and early 1969 and presumably relate to this application. These works involved more damage to the fabric of the building than had

been sustained during most of the 19th and 20th centuries. Copies of the plans are held in the site archive.

119 *Express and Echo*, 22 July 1969.

120 Exeter City Council Planning file, ref 29/72.

121 *Express and Echo*, 17 July 1972, that also claimed that 'old [*sic*] ancient timbers from the barn' had been used to restore some of the passages of the old house.

122 Photographs in EMAFU files, ref 231/1–7 and 255/1–4, dated June 1976.

123 Inspectorate memo dated June 1979, ref AA75549/2; also a letter dated 15 February 1979, giving the date of acquisition as 22 November 1976. The price paid was £25,000.

124 DRO Exeter St Thomas Overseers Accounts 1741–4.

125 DRO Land Tax Assessment, St Thomas, 1780.

126 As the assessment for that year lists the owner of Bowhill as 'The heirs of Chilcot Syms Esqr.' (DRO Land Tax Assessment, St Thomas, 1782).

127 *Exeter Flying Post* for 31 March 1791, 3d.

128 Both this document and the Exeter St Thomas Land Tax assessment for 1791 confirm that William Augustus Gordon (1739–1809), the grandfather of General 'Chinese' Gordon, lived at Lower Bowhill in the 1790s and dispose of the erroneous association of the Gordon family with the ancient Bowhill (Bulloch 1933, 93; Harvey 1989, 30; Slade 1990, 93; Pollock 1993, 319).

129 CF 2504; the lunatic asylum was owned by Sir Joseph Sawle; TM 436.

130 Jenkins's *History of Exeter* provides the background: ' ... subscriptions were begun about the year 1795, and in 1800, a neat mansion, called *Bowhill-house*, was purchased, just without the *Moreton* turnpike, and converted into an *Asylum for Lunatics*' (Jenkins 1806, 434).

131 Ibid; a drawing of the building is in the Devon and Exeter Institution (Hervey 1980, cover illustration; Harvey 1989, 13). Hervey states that the building was further enlarged in 1824 and 1848 (1980, 14–15). The suggestion that the ancient house of Bowhill was also used by the asylum (ibid,14; Harvey 1989, 30) cannot be supported in the light of Jenkins's account on the location of the first asylum '*just without the Moreton turnpike*', which was situated on the downhill side of the crossroads at the bottom of Dunsford Road. The gate is shown on Hayman's map of Exeter, engraved to illustrate Jenkins's *History* (Fig 2.2).

132 Russell 1976, 86; Hervey 1980, 15.

133 DRO Pearse 62/9/2/Box 11/58, 10 October 1887; illustrated by Harvey 1989, 33.

134 Russell 1976, 84; Hervey 1980, 14; Harvey 1989, 30; Slade 1990, 93.

135 Other items in CW/H/23 include legacy receipts and memoranda.

136 The accountant in volume 1 is identified by such items as 'paid for my nephews Richard, Henry and Joseph Carew'; although, strictly, Richard was their cousin, no other candidate appears. The cover of the volume has a partly illegible inscription ' ... Richard Carew, esq. Deceased ... '; the hand of the entries changes somewhat in style around the beginning of 1685 and it may be that a second accountant had taken over. On volume 2, the accountant's name is written on the front cover but is smudged. Henry Stephens is identified by his signature against the final calculations on the last page of volume 3.

Chapter 4

1 The details of the archaeological record are presented in a series of archive reports, prepared as the first stage in the post-excavation and publication process and cited here as: Blaylock 1991a; Blaylock 1991b; Hall and Blaylock 1991; Blaylock and Norton

1991; Hall and Blaylock 1994; Stead *et al* 1994; and Hall and Blaylock 1995.

2 Blaylock 1991a.

3 Jefferies 1977, for a summary of the procedures and specimens of recording forms.

4 Blaylock 1991a, figs 2–16.

5 It has not been possible to use the original context numbers of the 1977–8 excavations in this report, because EMAFU had already commenced working at Bowhill before the DoE archive was taken on. All DoE context numbers have been increased by 2000 to avoid duplication of the sequence in the standing building (thus the number 244 in the original excavation becomes 2244 here and 150 becomes 2150). Knowledge of the dual numbering will be necessary for users of the archive; numeration in the present account is internally consistent.

6 For instance, at the time it was thought that the corner turret, now interpreted as a stair turret, might have contained a garderobe. If this had been so, a cess pit perhaps penetrating more deeply than the wall footings could have been expected.

7 This small area proved to have a complex stratigraphic sequence of thirteen phases (Blaylock and Norton 1991, 4–11), which are here integrated with the overall phasing of the site.

8 Up to 1m of deposits on the Dunsford Hill frontage had been cut away in a wide foundation trench when the boundary wall was rebuilt in 1985. This is shown on a photograph in the archive, negative ref C850070.

9 The grid appears throughout the series of plans.

10 All this material is stored in the project archive (*see* Appendix for details).

11 Hall and Blaylock 1994, 6, and fig 3.

12 Although (as with the ditches found within the building) the precise relationship of these separate lengths of ditch remains uncertain.

13 *See* summary of dating evidence, Chapter 9.

14 Fig 4.18, section 13, otherwise illustrated only as a cut out along the south edge of the area (Fig 4.3, cutting 2244); *see also* Blaylock and Norton 1991, fig 2, 'Phase 3'.

15 The fill layers of ditches 621, 1736, 2244, 2386 and 2398 contained slate fragments; 1522, 1524 and 1736 also contained mortar and 2244 contained plaster fragments.

16 Compare the incidence of foundation trenches inside the building, especially the south range, with the tendency for the wall footings to be built directly onto the ground when viewed from the exterior.

17 Not illustrated (Hall and Blaylock 1994, fig 3).

18 Blaylock and Norton 1991, fig 2, phases 4 and 5.

19 Hall and Blaylock 1991, 32–3 (two sherds of 12th- to 13th-century date).

20 Henderson 1984a, 36.

21 In the Cowick Street house, a floor was subsequently formed with a layer of waste mould from the bronze foundry and thus the initial lowering cannot be explained by wear to the floor. At Bowhill, where the floors appear to have been of trodden earth, lowering of the floor by wear during the life of the building must represent an alternative explanation.

22 For instance, a very well-preserved wholly cob-walled building in the ditch of Wallingford Castle, Berkshire (Carr 1976; *see also* Webster and Cherry 1973, 159–61). I am grateful to Ray Harrison for this reference and to him and John Thorp for discussion of cob buildings without stone footings.

23 It is assumed that the road to the south prevented much expansion of buildings in that direction.

24 *See* Beacham 1989, 67.

25 Hall and Blaylock 1991, 10; contexts 646, 685 and 686 for the cess pit and contexts 601, 692, 719 for the room fills. These

details illustrate the cumulative value of small individual observations.

26 The charred timbers from the pit were considered for dendrochronology, but were uniformly fast-grown and although of substantial scantling (up to 140 × 160mm) had too few rings for successful dating.

27 Equally possible is that the factors conditioning the design of the two buildings remained the same through the period of the rebuilding. For example, the proximity of an adjacent farmyard, the road to the south, other fixed topographical features, boundaries or even other pre-existing ranges of buildings could all have conditioned the position, plan and extent of the building (in addition to the wishes of the owners and builders).

28 Chapter 9, Appendix 1, phase 3, context 1559.

29 Not published (*see* Blaylock 1991a, fig 12, section 120, 233). This layer may have been, at least in part, equivalent to the deposits of phases 1 and 2 recorded in the screens passage (870, 883, 886), in which case it should be presumed that the walls, in fact, cut this layer, but the relationship was not recorded (perhaps because the wall footings completely filled the foundation trenches in the manner described above). Against this is the observed relationship of the footings to the natural subsoil and the depth of the footings, just described, which seem to follow the natural ground surface in rising from south to north.

30 Blaylock and Norton 1991, 7 and fig 2, phase 7.

31 Two shallow pits in the underlying deposits also belong in this phase in the western room, but are of unknown purpose (Hall and Blaylock 1991, 20, and fig 4, 711 and 740).

32 Although the sill of the screen is replaced, its original level was established by the height of extant original studs (*see* Fig 6.15).

33 The evidence for the eastern room comprised the threshold of the blocked doorway, 259 (*see* Fig 6.25), at 21.30m OD (the same level as the timber threshold of the doors to the parlour). The floor is unlikely to have been higher than this. Levels on natural subsoil (on the line of the wall base of the phase 2 building) were as high as 21.20m OD, giving a lower limit and a margin of only 0.1m for variation in the floor level.

34 Paul Drury has suggested (pers comm) that the unusual configuration here should be interpreted as evidence that the chimney stack is earlier in date, pre-existed the present fabric of the hall, had survived from a predecessor of the east range (presumably of phase 2) and was constructed wholly of cob. A chimney stack of breccia (of primary or secondary construction) could have survived the demolition of adjacent cob walls and been reused in the phase 3 building. Although persuasive thus far, this hypothesis fails to account for the wide seams to either side of the stack and the crude rubble filling between the stack and the masonry beyond. Thus the interpretation outlined in the text (to this author at least) still seems preferable.

35 Chapter 9, catalogue no. 20.

36 Also seen by S L Dunmore beneath the east window of the kitchen in 1982, trench 5a; *see* Fig 4.7, 2441, and Blaylock 1991, 29–30 and fig 16.

37 In the 19th century, phases 7 and 8, *see* below.

38 The case for a north range is discussed in Chapter 1.

39 An area of scorched clay was recorded in the central part of the courtyard, towards the wall of the north range (Fig 4.7, 2176). This may have represented a hearth on the primary surface, although the soil was judged to be probably of natural origin; a second similar area within the junction of the west and north ranges (2209) showed very little signs of burning, on the basis of examination by a soil scientist (Keeley 1988, 2; samples 176 and 209).

40 Not illustrated (*see* Blaylock 1991a, fig 9, section 102, layers 67/70). Seen again in the same area in 1993–4 (Hall and Blaylock 1995, fig 4, section 1, layer 1752).

41 Perhaps a part of the piping referred to in the licence from the Abbot of Tavistock in 1499 (Chapter 3). A comparable example of a lead water pipe in a culvert (in this case on a bed of clay) was excavated at King William Street, Exeter, in 1983 (Youngs *et al* 1984, 213; Stoyle 1994, 8). This formed a part of the earliest aqueduct to carry water into the city, perhaps of the late 12th century (ibid, 13).

42 I am grateful to Paul Drury for observing this and for discussion of the possible phasing of this feature.

43 Not illustrated (*see* Blaylock 1991a, fig 9, section 102, 150 and so on). The level of the projecting footings acts as a guide to the intended ground levels throughout, as it is unlikely that the crude masonry of the foundations protruded above ground level.

44 Figure 4.7, partly represented in plan by the dashed lines of a later cut out (cutting through the drain 2150); elsewhere (to the east) a baulk was left on the line of the known disturbance.

45 The lack of data regarding floor levels, treatments and finishes also affected the conservation and reinstatement work. There was perhaps more conjecture in this than in any other aspect of the work (Chapter 11).

46 I am grateful to Paul Drury for suggesting this line of enquiry and for discussion of this example in particular.

47 An early instance of such materials being reused. Many more examples occur in later phases, especially phase 8.

48 Not illustrated (*see* Hall and Blaylock 1991, 15–16, and fig 5, phase 5).

49 Other deposits and features were assigned to this phase, on the grounds of intermediate status between phases 3 and 8 (not illustrated; Blaylock 1991a, 8).

50 The layer was also cut by the construction cut for the repositioned western partition of the parlour. A sub-square pit in the south-western corner of Area 8 was also placed in this phase on the basis of late 16th- to early 17th-century sherds in its fill (not illustrated, but *see* Hall and Blaylock 1989, fig 5).

51 For other finds of lead shot *see* Chapter 9.

52 Egan 1990, 161–3;

53 Egan 1989, 29–32; Stoyle 1995, 31.

54 Chapter 9; Stead *et al* 1994, 21.

55 Stoyle 1990, 27; *see also* Chapter 3.

56 John Allan, pers comm; *see also* finds listings in the archive reports by John Allan and Graham Langman.

57 Originals in the British Library; monochrome photographs in Westcountry Studies Library, Exeter.

58 I am grateful to Nat Alcock for pointing this out.

59 Not illustrated, Hall and Blaylock 1991, fig 6, section 4, 627.

60 Ibid, 628 and 642. Probably post-medieval as granite is an uncommon material in medieval buildings in Exeter (and other materials available locally provided alternatives in the primary phases).

61 Hall and Blaylock 1991, 16 and 21.

62 Figure 4.19, 1526, 1555, 1556, 1568.

63 The full sequence is described in Blaylock 1991a (17–21; fig 11); evidence for two later floor surfaces is here conflated into one plan (Fig 4.19).

64 Such as similar poorly preserved paved floors in the screens passage and the west service room.

65 The only unequivocal dating evidence was a note of late 17th- and 18th-century material from layers beneath the cobbled surface 2133 in MS notes in S L Dunmore's finds file in the site archive.

66 Blaylock and Norton 1991, fig 2, phases 11 and 12.

67 Possibly indicating that the fireplace was no longer in use. The flagged area to the east may represent a smaller hearth area at this phase (Fig 4.19, 1665).

68 The demolition must have included the stair in the angle of the north and east ranges, as the new kitchen occupied its site. The removal of the stair provides additional evidence that the north range and the first-floor room in the northern bay of the east range were removed as a part of the demolition of this phase, since the stairs and gallery access were now redundant.

69 The bulk of the deposit was clay and small stones, as would be expected of demolished cob walls. The incidence of building stone in the deposits was low and there was other evidence of the reuse of stone in the shape of robber trenches removing stone from the footings of the east wall of the west range (Fig 4.7, 2432).

70 The house was divided into two dwellings in the 1840s, for example, in the tithe apportionment for St Thomas parish, as well as other early and mid-19th-century sources (Chapter 2).

71 The representation of the cobbled surfaces on the plan (Fig 4.19) needs explanation. Only specimen areas were drawn in detail in 1977–8, the full extent is shown by dotted lines, for example, 2103. Cobbling was denser than is implied by the plan in the northern half of the courtyard. To the south the pavement was heavily disturbed and only isolated patches survived (for example, 2049–51; *see also* Fig 4.22).

72 The building had gone when the sketch of the interior of the courtyard was drawn in the mid-19th century (Fig 2.5). The building was occupied by two tenants at the time of the tithe apportionment, yet Southwood's map (of 1850), shows a dividing wall, but not the kitchen building (Chapter 2). Unlike the tithe map, this survey is at a sufficiently large scale to show such a detail of the plan had it been extant. A date bracket of 1841–1850 is, therefore, suggested for the re-amalgamation of the building into one unit.

73 Best seen on an unpublished section (Blaylock 1991a, fig 9, section 107, layer 37). The deposit was thought to be derived from the roof of the phase 8 kitchen building, as the slates lay above the cobbled surfaces of that phase. Evidence in the standing fabric suggested that the south and west ranges were completely re-roofed, probably during the major demolitions and alterations of phase 8. This process left no trace in the archaeology of the central courtyard, perhaps because the slates were removed from the site in a controlled manner rather than being dumped within the courtyard. An alternative possibility is that the slate deposit was related to the re-roofing of the hall, which is seen to have been thatched from the mid-19th century and thus was probably stripped of its slate at a different (and later) date from the south and west ranges.

74 Architect's' 'as existing' plan. Mr Tony Abraham of Oakfield Road, Exeter, recalls that a 'shed' in this position was used for boiling beetroot as a sideline in the time of the Sclaters' nursery (pers comm to F P Kelly, letter of April 1996).

75 Stead *et al* 1994, 6, and listings 19–21.

76 Not illustrated (Hall and Blaylock 1994, fig 3, 1502); *see also* Fig 4.18, section 6. Analysis of a sample of mortar from this floor is described in Chapter 10.

77 Chapter 2, for references; the west view of the building by Stockdale (Fig 2.17) of approximately the same date gives additional information on this structure (if it is reliable on this point). The first 'annexe' building was of a single storey, with its roof on an east–west orientation. Later views show a two-storey building roofed on a north–south axis.

78 Not illustrated (Blaylock 1991a, fig 6). A substantial tree bole is visible on a photograph of the courtyard by A W Everett of the 1950s, Fig 2.17.

79 Not individually illustrated (Stead *et al* 1994, fig 3, 996, 998 and 1000).

80 Blaylock 1991a, 23–7 and figs 14–15.

81 The cobbled floor is still visible in an NMR photograph of 1957 (NMR/AA/57/150), but one of 1969 shows the cement floor laid over the cobbles (NMR/BB/69/5036).

82 The function of the second phase of the structure, as well as the modern replacement, was partly to accommodate stairs. Late 19th- or early 20th-century alterations made new stairs necessary.

83 The temptation (when apportioning phases to recorded works) to combine elements from the two classes of evidence whose association is unproven or not demonstrable should be noted as a constraint, as should the tendency to simplify the sequence in order to 'tidy up' or 'rationalise' it into as small a number of phases as possible.

84 The absence of the early phases (1 and 2) is obvious inasmuch as these represent vanished features and buildings. Had there been no excavation within the south range, these phases would have remained largely unknown.

85 Many additional fragments might well have been included in the below-ground archaeology of the site, if the imaginary situation had come to pass and Bowhill was being examined as a long-demolished building.

86 Brown and Laithwaite 1993, 181.

87 Brown 1991.

88 Blaylock and Henderson 1987, 1–21.

89 Higham *et al* 1982.

90 Brown 1988.

91 Gaskell Brown *et al* 1995.

92 Blaylock 1991c; excavation work by J P Allan (Webster and Cherry 1979, 250 and fig 4).

93 Heighway 1980, especially for its innovative (at the time) approach to the recording and interpretation of standing fabric.

94 Rahtz and Watts 1997, especially for its presentation of recorded fabric and the balance of primary data with synthesis.

95 Lindley 1991, especially the chapters on the excavation and standing fabric analysis of the west range, respectively by Naomi Field (34–42) and M V Clark (43–56).

96 Sutherland 1990, especially as an example of the level of information that can be obtained from detailed drawing and examination of multi-phased masonry.

97 *See* further the overviews presented by Morris (especially 14–17) and Meeson (especially 249–53) in Wood *et al* 1994; or the lucid account of church archaeology by Rodwell (1989, especially with regard to techniques, 85–113, and the investigation of standing fabric, 134–42). The preceding list of work testifies that the Exeter Museums Archaeological Field Unit has been involved in this since the 1970s.

98 As is shown by a number of the other contributions to the publication of the Chester conference just cited (Wood *et al* 1994).

99 Brown and Laithwaite 1993, 161.

100 In fact stripping of renders provided a constantly changing picture, which necessitated continual updating of drawings.

101 An almost inconceivable prospect, given the political and administrative changes than have intervened since the work at Bowhill was begun.

Chapter 5

1 The figure is a composite of EMAFU hand survey and outline detail added from the earlier AMDO survey where no new hand survey was possible.

2 The south elevation was also a 'show front' in the sense that it was built of good-quality materials, had showy features and was visible from the road; perhaps this functioned as the everyday entrance.

3 Recorded in a detail drawing, AMDO no. AS 4/2, May 1984 (incorporated in Fig 5.1).

4   Described in 1849 thus: ' ... about one third of the north end was taken down, not many years since, and the materials used in building stables at Barley' (Harding 1849, 172).

5   The impression and the massive interior quoin suggest that the north wall of the south-east range was of stone up to first-floor level. Above this the walls were probably of cob, as in the first floor of the east gable of the south range, although this would have entailed another cob corner (Chapter 8, n 57).

6   Recorded by Francis Kelly.

7   At Bowhill the cob cross wall within the building survived until the 1970s, although both gables (with the same overall dimensions, but more uniform thickness) had failed by c 1800. Ray Harrison has observed (pers comm) that cob gables are more vulnerable to decay than half or fully hipped gables, on account of their height. The gable walls were not load bearing, and it is not surprising to find cob used in this position (on the basis of the arguments advanced in Chapter 1 for the relative incidence of cob and stone). I am grateful to Ray Harrison for discussion of these matters.

8   The present wall top, when cleaned up and examined in 1990, showed good-quality white lime mortar and no sign of cob staining; some masonry, if only one course, must have been removed from the wall top (projection of the top of stone from further north suggests that this was the case, see Fig 5.1).

9   Partly bearing on beam 1 of the parlour ceiling and partly obscuring the carved capitals of the wall posts.

10 The frame was dismantled by 1987 and was not recorded in detail. It was replaced in 1991 (Chapter 11).

11 In reconstructing the porch (Figs 1.1, 12.1 and 12.5) a square plan has been assumed, that is, that the width gives a clue to the projection. The same line (that is, the front wall of the porch resulting from this exercise) was also used to reconstruct the eastern limit of the south-east range. The assumption has thus exerted a considerable influence on the conjectural reconstruction of the building.

12 Certain evidence of the wall scar was seen no higher than this; a cob face of the east wall across the line of the porch wall was all that had survived in the early 1980s, according to the AMDO drawing of the east elevation (AS 2/3, Section M–M, dated May 1979 and repeated in outline in Fig 5.1) and pre-works photographs. This suggests that the consolidated return wall, in new stone up to eaves level, may be spurious.

13 Beacham 1989, 74.

14 There is a similar arrangement at West Challacombe, Combe Martin, Devon (Richardson 1993, 4).

15 Otherwise the window could have been placed centrally, and aligned with the central axis of the interior of the room (as shown by the ceiling beam; see Figs 6.2, 6.20 and 6.24).

16 There are cases of isolated attached stair turrets in domestic architecture (and the device is common in ecclesiastical architecture for rood stairs and sometimes for tower stair turrets). The stair in the centre of the east wing at Cadhay is a local example (anon c1957, 14 and 24).

17 RCHME photographs of 1957 for example, AA/57/144). The recent DoE/EH restoration has seen the rebuilding of the southern jamb of the window (Fig 5.1, 93) and the upper part of the northern wall scar of the porch (rather against the evidence of the fabric; see above, n 12). Morley drew a sketch of the oak lintel of this window, with a moulded lower edge (apparently a double-roll moulding) and run-out stops; Dunmore noted additionally that the timber was reused in this position (Morley 1979, 'window 37' and sketch, fig 3; the timber is also recorded on the AMDO drawing of the east elevation as 'lintel removed'). The timber has not survived at Bowhill.

18 For repairs see Chapter 11.

19 On the interior straight joins are less clear, although the record photographs of January 1981 suggest that a join was observed here (see Fig 6.12 and archive photographs J11/6–8/81).

20 MS record by Stephen Dunmore.

21 The record is less specific on this point, but photographs of the wall top of the east wall (see Fig 6.8) seem to show that the cob butted up to the roof trusses. This implies a sequence in which the stone sections of wall were constructed, the roof raised and then the top of the wall (and the end bays to north and south, see Figs 6.2 and 6.15) were completed in cob. I am grateful to Adam Mackenzie for advice on this point.

22 With cob superstructure above, the standard pattern for the west end of the south range and the west range.

23 The reasons for this are obscure, although Ray Harrison has pointed out (pers comm; see also Harrison 1999, 17) that the thin beds would have a greater surface area, dry more quickly and, therefore, shrink less after the wall was complete. The greater-than-usual mixture of cob and stone and the need to accommodate the projecting oriel in the cob wall were the critical factors in this elevation. It may be that the parallel construction in cob and stone proceeded smoothly at this point.

24 It is possible that this elevation was rendered in two-coat work that looked smart initially, but soon fell off. Alfred Howard has observed that cob will slough over-heavy render (pers comm to Francis Kelly).

25 The struck-pointing technique was observed elsewhere in the building (for example, on the west elevation of the hall), but it only survived where primary joints had been protected from weathering and from repointing.

26 Similar incised joints below render have been observed at Kirkham House, Paignton, Devon (where the rear wall is enclosed by the gallery; 16th century) and also on the merlons of the north side of the wall walk at Restormel Castle, Cornwall (13th century). I owe these observations to Francis Kelly.

27 Harrison 1999, 58.

28 The eastern room may have been provided with the larger window type because of its closer relationship to the parlour.

29 Contra Slade 1990, 96.

30 No parallels are known to the author of such an elaborate stone structure set in a cob wall. Stone window and door-frames appear in cob walls in Cumberland (Harrison 1989, 117–20) and Bowhill itself provides an example in the lancet window in the north wall of the great chamber (see Fig 6.25, 111). The oriel window is the most striking example of the confidence of the builders in integrating the two materials: here they were imitating a stone construction in cob and presumably expecting it to behave in the same way.

31 Unless the feature had been shored up or underbuilt by the early 18th century.

32 At a height appropriate for paper or a lamp (Wood 1965, 384).

33 A stone arch was restored within the opening in 1995 (Chapter 11).

34 Removed by the time of recording in 1987 and thus not shown on the main elevation drawings. It has, however, been added to the smaller-scale interpretation drawings (Figs 5.8 and see Fig 6.22).

35 A deeply splayed sill is described by Morley (1979, opening 6). This did not survive at the time of the survey and is not shown on early photographs.

36 See EH photographs F850039/3 and 5 (colour prints) dated August 1985.

37 Associated work of phase 8 replaced the arches (Fig 5.8, 9). The blocking of the windows contained voussoirs and so on (above). Arches are also shown on the Bucks' engraving, surmounting large rectangular windows.

38 It has been suggested that the twin-window arrangement might have been intended to minimise window tax. The tax (introduced in 1696) was not, however, levied heavily until 1784 (Woodward 1994, 4), too late for these windows and it is more likely that the technique was used to provide support for the floor beam at this point.

39 Rather narrower than the reconstructed version (Chapter 11).

40 No beam was provided against the wall of the east range. This suggests that the sockets represented two tiers of timbers in which the beams supported another longitudinal timber that, in turn, supported the rafters, rather than a closed truss assembly. The misalignment of sockets would matter less in such an arrangement.

41 The straight stops to the chamfers also suggest a door rather than a window, but this assumes that the lintel was reused in its original position. The modification to the opening took place in phase 8 after the removal of the gallery (below).

42 All the variant elements of the roof of the west range, the type and placing of purlins and the bearing of the common rafters may have been conditioned by the need to accommodate a gallery roof.

43 The feature is attested in 1945. By 1969 (Fig 2.17) only the roof remained (this is represented in the fabric by a weathering scar of the roof, Fig 5.17, 362), that is, the structure itself had been dismantled. Further traces were to be seen in the form of the doorway openings at first-floor level. Doorway 200 was now apparently filled with a fixed timber partition, but that in the west range (now void, Fig 5.22, 389) appears to have retained its door (Fig 2.20). The bridge was rebuilt in the reorganisation that took place in 1969 (Fig 2.18) and served as a bar during the restaurant period (*see* the interior photograph Fig 2.28, *inter alia*).

44 The product of setting the frame in position while building the wall, rather than a deliberately constructed chase.

45 The technique may have been used elsewhere, although this was the only example to survive.

46 Or possibly partitioned-off areas of these rooms (Chapter 6).

47 Labels were redundant because the heads of the windows were hidden by the pentice and the eaves of the roof.

48 Three-, four- and five-light windows survived at the time of a survey in 1979 (Blaylock 1991c, 9; figs 6 and 9).

49 Portman 1966, 49.

50 Probably also because the roof carpentry was available at the necessary stage of construction (Chapter 7).

51 Although there were glimpses of the later builds recorded on the south elevation at this corner (Fig 5.8), it was not possible to disentangle these behind the rendering (which was not removed).

52 A feature of obscure function (Chapter 6).

53 A common arrangement in farmhouses in Devon and occasionally seen in larger buildings, for example, the smaller of two ovens in the kitchen at Okehampton Castle (Higham *et al* 1982, fig 21).

54 The breccia is unusual, with irregular inclusions and some of it would be better described as Permian sandstone, that is, it has few coarse inclusions.

55 The section in Fig 6.47 also shows a section of cob walling at first-floor level (400) in which several lifts and the shrinkage crack against the post of the roof truss were seen.

56 The drawing shows the elevation as it was in 1987, with some details from the AMDO drawing of 1979 (*see* Figs 6.2 and 2.19).

57 Prior to the repair works in 1980–2 the interior face of the wall was missing above the level of the window lintels (*see* Fig 7.9 of *c* 1981, which shows the rear of the exterior facework and the step in at window-head level). The exterior face of masonry of

phase 8 originally refaced the cob wall top, which later was itself removed, exposing the rear of the refacing and creating the 'half-thickness' wall described here. The wall was restored to its full thickness in new masonry in 1981.

58 Not represented in the below-ground archaeology (Chapter 4, pp 56–7).

59 The archaeological evidence for the stair plus the socket for the first-floor doorway in truss II of the hall (Chapter 6) both strongly support a primary stair at this point.

60 Wood 1965, 333.

61 Such as the stair at South Yard, Rose Ash, Devon (Wood 1965, 194–5; Beacham 1989, 73).

62 This tallies with the cob walling in the adjacent north wall of the south range (the top of masonry is 0.4m lower than that above the hall door; *see* Figs 6.15 and 6.25) and with the long posts of truss VI of the hall roof, which must have been set in cob from the first.

Chapter 6

1 This part of the building was repaired in the early 1980s, before the author was involved in the study of Bowhill; this description is from photographs, drawings and the repaired fabric, rather than from personal observation of the building when stripped.

2 By analogy with the partition at the south end of the hall, the original character of the infilling is not known.

3 Also the basis for the reconstructions of the screen and floor frame to the north in 1985 (*see* Fig 6.5).

4 The north wall was not drawn. The repair and re-plastering of the interior was complete prior to the beginning of the EMAFU recording programme, and the exterior has never been accessible for drawing.

5 This evidence could apply as equally to windows of the type seen in the north wall of the south range as to the surviving window in this room. It is uncertain whether the primitive close-set diagonal-mullioned window was as widespread in the building as is implied by the use of the one surviving example as a model for reconstruction elsewhere.

6 Unfortunately no record has survived of the relationship of the roof trusses to the cob walling. A trace, including a ragged cut into cob from which a roof truss has been removed, is visible at the very edge of an archive photograph showing work in progress on the hall roof (ref DoE J8/1/82). Since the cob of the wall top was recorded as overlying the fabric of the chimney stack, it is likely that the stone and the cob, as well as the roof, belonged to one building phase.

7 Morley 1979, openings 40 and 41; the lower lights and the eastern windows were obscured by modern frames for glazing and shutters at the time of Morley's observations (ibid, openings 35 and 36), but the evidence can be extrapolated from one pair to the other. Photographs of the exteriors of the windows after the removal of later accretions show the positions of saddle bars in upper and lower lights – three horizontal and one vertical bar to each light (Fig 6.9). Another archive photograph (ref NMR BB/69/586) shows a glazing slot in the lower light of the NW hall window, although this could, of course, be secondary. Original glazing in the upper lights only is supported by Portman's observations in the 1960s (Portman 1966, 13).

8 MS addition to Morley 1979, 'Great Hall, East Wall' by S L Dunmore.

9 Compare John Aubrey's comments: 'Heretofore (before Henry VIII) glasse windowes were very rare, only used in churches, and the best roomes of gentlemen's howses. Even in my remembrance, before the Civil Warres, copy holders and ordinary people had none. Now, the poorest people that are upon almes,

have it' (Powell 1949, 7–8). Windows in which upper lights are glazed and lower lights shuttered appear frequently in the domestic interiors of Netherlandish paintings of the 15th century (see works by Hans Memling in the Memlingmuseum, Bruges, and the Metropolitan Museum of Art, New York (Pächt 1997, plates 26–27; McFarlane 1971, plate 39), by Robert Campin in New York and elsewhere (Davies 1972, 258–60, plate 141; Panofsky 1953, figs 203–4 and 211–13), by Roger van der Weyden (ibid, figs 309–10, 340 and 343), and Jan van Eyck's *Giovanni Arnolfini and Giovanna Cenami* (1434) in the National Gallery, London (ibid, 211–13 and fig 247).

10 The site finds book records the finding of the keystone in 'the edge of opening 21', the north door of the through passage (Fig 6.25, 270; presumably from the blocking, 271) on 28 February 1980) and the section of the mantelshelf on 16 June 1981, above the lintel of the kitchen doorway (Fig 5.27, 423).

11 S L Dunmore, MS notes in project archive.

12 At 2.2–2.4m north of the south wall of the hall, they were too far north to have been related to the screen represented by the excavated features.

13 Secondary because the mortices are not parallel to the beam. Their lower edges, between 115 and 145mm above the lower edge of the beam, represent an interim stage in the subsidence of the timber.

14 Everett's first note on the building implies that it was floored by 1935 (Everett 1935, 306).

15 The floor was 'standing on upright poles with no anchorage to the walls' (*Express and Echo*, 24 August 1968).

16 Ibid; the claim that 2,000 square feet of boards from this floor had been burnt is exaggerated, as the full area of the hall amounts to only some 60m² (or about 645 square feet).

17 Morley 1979, 'screen at south end of hall'.

18 *See*, for instance, Portman 1966, fig xv, 6.

19 Dunmore recorded, in a MS note, that two studs survived *in situ*, that the daub infill was originally 'pegged' to this studding and that one peg survived (I am also grateful to Roger Scobie for discussion of this point). This evidence formed the basis for the reconstruction in 1987 (Figs 5.17 and 6.18; Chapter 11).

20 A sash is shown in the painting of that date by A D Horne, Chapter 2.

21 Visible on the extreme right of Fig 6.20; Morley 1979, fig 1 and text, 'window 2'.

22 Hall and Blaylock 1991, 4.

23 Morley 1979; Dunmore 1979–87.

24 By the RCHME (refs AA/57/170–173); and by the DoE (Figs 6.20–6.21); *see also* Figs 2.24–2.26.

25 A survey of the condition of the first-floor timbers made by Arthur McCallum of English Heritage (Civil Engineering Section) in 1985 provides a valuable record before dismantling. A copy is in the project archive (drawing numbers X S1/1 and /2).

26 Replaced with one of volcanic stone in c 1987–8.

27 In bay 1 (east) the marks ran from north to south and all joists were numbered consecutively (including the main joists). The first three and the last two marks were obscured, but between them the timbers were numbered IIII; V; VI; VI[I]; VIII (the axial joist); VIIII; X; XI; XII; XIII. In bay 2 (central) the joists were numbered from south to north and followed the same pattern distinguished by a compass arc through the first or last stroke of the numeral. In this bay the first, sixth, eleventh and twelfth and fourteenth and fifteenth joists retained no markings. In bay 3 (west) traces of marks were noted on joists 3–5, numbering from the south, but (if the vestiges were interpreted correctly) seemed to represent the marks V–VII, thus arguing for some displacement in bay 3. Here the marks were distinguished

by a semicircular arc against the first stroke of the numeral. (Based on notes by Keith Westcott.)

28 Morley 1979, 'Beam 1'.

29 Photographed during dismantling in 1985; Fig 6.32 (archive refs EH F850039/10-12).

30 Recorded by Morley 1979, fig 6, 'Beam 2' and 'Beam 4'.

31 While there are general views of the room, such as the one reproduced here (Fig 6.21), no detailed photographs survive to show the enlarged ceiling with its planking and subsidiary mouldings or the applied timbers after the removal of the panelling.

32 MS addition to Morley 1979, 'Beam 4'.

33 Morley 1979, 'Beam 5' (and sketch in fig 8).

34 Ruth McNeilage, wall paintings and polychrome conservator, McNeilage Conservation, Bristol.

35 As these timbers were cleaned and stripped when they were dismantled for repair in the mid-1980s, the paint survives poorly in relation to that on the planks and ribs.

36 It is unfortunate that none of the later softwood timbers was kept on the demolition of the ceiling in 1979, as these would have provided (by comparison with the earlier boards and ribs) the means to establish a closer integration of the paint sequence and the overall chronology of the ceiling.

37 In October 1979, recorded in the site finds book.

38 It could equally have been inspired by antiquarianism, conservatism or parsimony.

39 Although the two rooms could have functioned as a single grand room, an interpretation as two interconnected rooms seems much more plausible.

40 A chimney might account for the anomalies in the roof in the Bucks' engraving (Chapter 2).

41 No frame survived; an unglazed mullioned frame has been placed in the embrasure (Chapter 11).

42 Presumably a new sleeper wall was needed below beam 5 and the floor of the parlour was extended westwards, but no evidence for either survived.

43 Although the blocking was removed, again too rapidly to appear on the phased elevations (Fig 5.17, 117).

44 As has been suggested by various commentators (Morley 1979, 1A) or that it was an insertion (Everett 1958, fig 1).

45 Everett 1958, 204 (fig 1).

46 Recorded on a field drawing (no. 56, in archive), but not published.

47 Taking into account the levels of later floors, surviving subsoil and wall footings, the original floors of the passage and the storeroom probably lay at c 21.45–21.50m above OD (Figs 4.7 and 4.19).

48 Mortices for joists spanned the opening, but it seems that they were never used. The existing joists were inscribed with assembly marks at their junction with the trimmer and the whole assembly was closed (recorded in an undated memorandum by H G Slade to S L Dunmore in the project archive).

49 The opening could also have functioned as a trap door, although this would discount the evidence of the narrower doorway.

50 Recorded by Morley 1979, 'opening 7', from which it is clear that the work was of the same phase as the narrowing of the northern doorway. The arch was first noted by Everett (1958, 205, n 1).

51 Morley 1979, 'Beam 9'.

52 An exploratory trench in 1983 found a layer of mortar on the footings of the west wall (more or less in the centre), possibly a threshold to an inserted doorway replacing the primary window, but pre-dating the late 19th- to 20th-century alterations (Blaylock 1991a, 30–31, 422; trench 5c). This itself is likely to have been a late feature, as a window is shown in this position on

Stockdale's view of the west elevation of the building (Fig 2.6); thus it is assigned to phase 9 (*see* Fig 12.2).

53 Architect's plans 'as existing' in 1969; copies in project archive.

54 In a variation on the pattern of the fireplaces in parlour and chamber, in which joggled joints were used to compose a straight lintel. Here, in an arched head, they were not strictly necessary.

55 A sketch by A W Everett of January 1936 shows unstopped chamfers descending to ground level (sketchbook in St Katherine's Priory, Polsloe, file held in fabric recording archive, RAM Museum).

56 A finish produced by axe dressing. I am grateful to Andrew French for discussing this technique and for a practical demonstration of how the result is achieved.

57 Like the arrangement in the kitchen at Cotehele, Cornwall, illustrated in 19th-century drawings (Gotch 1928, plate 7; I am grateful to Ray Harrison for this reference); *see also* discussion of smoking chambers in Brown 1998, 65–6.

58 Wood 1965, plate 39b; Thurley 1990, 8–16.

59 Cherry and Pevsner 1989, 287 (illustrated in Trinick 1989, 12).

60 Although rebuilt by Weir the fireplaces are of similarly large proportions (Emery 1970, 172).

61 On the use of ovens in farmhouses *see* Brain and Brain nd, 47–50; *see also* Hartley 1969, 39–41.

62 NMR AA/57/150, for example (not illustrated, copy in project archive).

63 Known from a trial trench by Dunmore in 1983 (Area 5a, Fig 4.1).

64 The differential stops are difficult to explain. The timbers almost look like oversized gateposts (that is, with pyramidal stops at the base and the return of the chamfer onto a lintel at the 'top'), but this interpretation is ruled out by the absence of mortices for a 'lintel'.

65 There are two deeper joists in each bay, one to each side of a joist of normal scantling on the central axis (Fig 6.47).

66 This was necessary because the post of the roof truss prevented the beam from being dropped in from above in this position.

67 Indeed the circulation from parlour to great chamber was dependent on stairs in the south-east range (unless the stair by the porch gave access to the chamber as well as the porch room).

68 The evidence for the secondary nature of the fragment in this position comprised:

1. The open assembly of the fixing of the screen in its present position. The upper ends of the studs were rebated and nailed (with flat-headed nails) to the rear face of the cornice, a crude device when compared to the assembly of equivalents elsewhere. The halving of the studs was also crude. The joints were cut larger than necessary and so voids were visible at the top of the studs and planking. The plank panels above the doorway were fitted into chases in the studs, in the same manner as those of the other primary screens. The plank filling the gap between the doorway and the post of truss I (although fitted into a chase in the post), was, however, fitted in a rebate cut on the outer edge of the eastern stud. Thus this plank was set in a vertical plane further north than those of the regular panels. This assembly too was crudely nailed together.

2. The quoin of the adjacent return wall retained primary plaster around the angle and across the position of the screen. While this is not, in itself, proof of anything more than the sequence of the original construction (that is, that the plastering took place before the installation of a door-frame), it strengthens the assertion that this timberwork was not intended in the primary arrangement. Observations elsewhere in the south range show that the building was not plastered until the roof was in position.

3. The proportions of the doorway were smaller than would be expected for a communicating door between the two principal rooms of the first floor. The deep area of plank infill above the door, the failure to provide neat returns at the top of the panels (although this was also a feature of the western screen of the parlour) and the irregular level of the stops in the frame also contributed to the impression of reuse and haphazard assembly.

4. The frame was probably originally intended to fill an opening of the same width as the door-frame. Neither of the long studs forming the jambs of the door had original chases for plank infilling on their *outer* edges and thus it is unlikely that the frame was any wider than this originally. The eastern plank was an addition (above) and the rebate was not deep enough to have cut away an earlier chase in the centre of the stud.

69 Harrison 1999, 78–80.

70 The combination is to be seen in a number of Exeter buildings of the period *c* 1660–80. Extensive works carried out on Exeter Quay by the city authorities *c* 1680–81 employed pine extensively for major structural timbers, but still used oak for some purposes (Ponsford 1993, 225). Post-Restoration alterations to the Bishop's Palace, probably of the 1660s, used very similar designs for roof trusses and partitions, but largely in oak (Blaylock 1987, 12). The two examples illustrate stages in the adoption of other timber for structural use in Exeter.

71 Medieval plaster rarely contains hair, but the use of this material is documented in the 1590s at the Guildhall in Exeter (Blaylock 1990, 146) and is ubiquitous locally in plasters of the 17th century. For a technical appraisal of this partition *see* Harrison, 1999, 82–3.

72 Recorded after repair and re-erection (Figs 5.1 and 6.2).

73 Everett 1958, fig 1 and RCHME photographs of 1957.

74 Shown on the architect's 'as existing' plans of December 1968 (Barry M Woodford, drawing 969/AS1/4).

75 The door may have been for occasional rather than regular use, since the lintel was rather low in relation to the floor level of the oriel chamber – 2.0m clearance from the floor of the inner chamber, but only 1.76m from that of the oriel chamber.

76 Unless one can be suggested in an axial position in the demolished cross wall (below). This is unlikely since the wall survived until the 1970s without traces of a fireplace or flue being recorded (Everett 1958, fig 1). The west face of the cob wall narrowed in the apex of the roof and the roof structure was continuous over the cross wall, leaving no space for a flue. The room could have been heated by a portable brazier.

77 The same technique as seen in the large-framed partitions forming the north and south walls of the hall.

78 The position at this stage is shown in the first AMDO plans of 1979 (ref 969 AS2/2) and in a photograph after stripping in 1978 (Fig 6.61).

79 Everett 1958, fig 1; also the 'as existing' architect's plan of 1968 (as n 74, *see above*).

80 It is also possible that the screen could have been placed here in 1972. Since this would involve three moves of timberwork, however, as opposed to the two moves required by the first suggested sequence, the former is to be preferred as an abstract reconstruction of events. Everett's evidence, quoted below, n 82, suggests that remnants of this timberwork were visible in his time. This would rule out a later origin for the timbers.

81 Morley 1979, fig 12.

82 Everett 1958, 206.

83 Shown by Everett (1958, fig 1).

84 Its removal is not proposed on the architect's plans of that year, but evidently took place in the course of the alterations nonetheless.

85 There may have been others in the vanished ranges, of course.

86 Unusually in the building where the other examples are of volcanic stone; but there are parallels elsewhere in Exeter (Chapter 8).

87 The conjectural extent of the original fireplace is shown in dashed lines on Fig 6.25.

88 A socket at first-floor level is possibly related to the stairs (Fig 6.22, 178). Although early, the stairs cannot have been primary since they rise beneath the site of the oriel window.

89 The northern brick facing (Fig 6.25, 179) was associated with a substantial deposit of roofing and other materials deriving from the demolition and alteration of this phase (discussed in Chapter 9).

90 Implying that the northern post of truss XI was originally supported on cob alone, like its southern counterpart

91 Something of this sort could have existed before, although all of the materials associated with this splay were apparently of phase 8 origin.

92 Possibly the combination of stone on top of cob (if that was in fact what had been used) contributed to this event, as well as the leakage of water inferred from the rotten area of the principal truss, discussed above.

93 The fireplace was known to the architect who planned the alterations of 1969 and onwards, since it was marked on his 'as existing' plans and it presented an obstruction to a doorway in bay 9 as it had done to earlier phases. The insertion of the crude doorway lined with breeze-blocks in this position entailed hacking through the breccia lintel and jamb and is a still later addition in phase 11, between 1970 and 1976.

94 Probably in phase 11 (early 1970s). The feature does not appear on plans of 1968 and employs gypsum plaster and other modern materials.

Chapter 7

1 Anomalies occur in the common rafters that are occasionally out of order within a bay, but this can be attributed to disturbance by re-roofing in the past.

2 Many scribing lines for the setting out of joints, marking of central axes, positions of pegs and so on were recorded (for example, those on truss IX shown in Fig 7.29; also visible on Fig 7.36).

3 Interpretation of discrepancies of this sort as 'misalignments' is founded on modern preoccupation with symmetry. It is unlikely that this was a critical factor in the views of the builders or of the clients. Discrepancies between ground- and first-floor bays are preconditioned by the need for the cruck posts to descend to the masonry plinth that in many cases was also supporting the floor beams.

4 If the position and amount of trimming had been known in advance, these timbers would have been better designed as arch braces rather than posts providing the essential functions (at least in decorative terms) of bracing the principal and of providing a seating for the tenons of the cornice (lowest purlins) of the roof.

5 The details of the sequence in the east range remain uncertain. No cob survived on the top of the west wall and no explicit record was made of the relationship of the cob filling and the roof timbers on the east wall top. The photographic record seems to suggest that the cob abutted the posts of the roof trusses here, implying that it was built around the roof timbers once they were in position (Fig 6.8).

6 The southern posts of trusses IX, X and XI (although the last two bear on cob or timber, above) and the northern posts of trusses IV–XI inclusive (the post of XI is surrounded by later infill). The longest post is that of truss X (N); this measures 4.5m from stone plinth to wall top (the height of the cob wall in this position).

7 As happened when the cob was laid up to the side of the post and then shrank back from it. Again, the trusses of the west range show this.

8 The degree of shrinkage in the new cob used at Bowhill has been much less, averaging c 20–30mm in masses of similar size (see Harrison 1984, 156–57; 1999, 13–18).

9 Observation made originally by Arthur McCallum of English Heritage.

10 Salzman (1952, 157, 192, 431, 478 and 570). For examples relating specifically to the filling of the space between the wall top and the soffit of the rafters see the OED under 'Beamfill', and Neve's definition (1969, 33; I am grateful to Ray Harrison for this reference). The term is used hereafter. Examples of the technique of filling the wall head with cob or rubble are plentiful in local late medieval buildings. A good extant example can still be seen in the roofless Hall of the Vicars Choral (Kalenderhay) in South Street, Exeter (Chanter 1933, 7–8), where the rubble beam filling survives complete with impressions of the common rafters in the top of the north-east wall. Another local example was in the hall of no. 38 North Street, Exeter (c 1500–50; records by John Thorp/EMAFU archives). Early examples in churches with wall paintings (where the beam filling and plastering are therefore unequivocally authentic and early) occur, inter alia, at Kempley (12th century) and Hailes (13th–14th century) in Gloucestershire (Verey 1970, 279–80; 1979, 265) and at Edingthorpe in Norfolk (c 1400; Pevsner and Wilson 1997, 455).

11 Cob was trusted as a load-bearing material, supporting the feet of roof trusses (sometimes with a template) and being used for chimney flues (Harrison 1984, 164), although it was still standard practice to seek the firm support of stone or timber for roof timbers where possible. The evidence of Bowhill argues that this was the one exception (in the minds of the builders) to the equal treatment of the two materials.

12 In bays 5–7 the wall is of stone to its full height on the south, but only to first-floor level on the north. In bays 8–10 the stone steps down progressively on the south, but (originally) formed only a footing c 1m high on the north (Figs 6.22 and 6.25).

13 As are those of the hall roof, although these posts are much shorter (compare Figs 2.22 and 2.23).

14 Truss I was presumably a plain jointed-cruck truss as in the inner chamber of the south range. Further evidence for the northernmost bay was recorded in the shape of sawn-off tenons for the lower purlins of bay 1 surviving in mortices on the north side of truss II; MS additions to Morley 1979 by S L Dunmore.

15 Presumably caused by a poor fit between builders and carpenters or by cutting the posts to the wrong length?

16 Although it is possible that they were pegged from the rear and not detected in the limited photographic evidence available.

17 Anon 1843.

18 Blaylock 1990, 126, or similar details on the terminals of hammer beams at, for example, Weare Giffard Hall, Devon (Cherry and Pevsner 1989, 892 and plate 60) or Orleigh Court, Buckland Brewer, Devon (ibid, 614).

19 Everett (1935, 306–7) does not mention bosses in his account published in 1935 and implies that the carved cusp terminals and the corbels at the base of the main trusses were also missing at this date.

20 A collection of ancient ridge tiles had survived on this section of roof (Chapter 9). The slates, like those of the south range, were modern Welsh slates (19th to 20th century).

21 Parallels for variation of the level of ornament in the roof of a single range exist in the south range at Cleeve Abbey, Somerset

(of the 1460s), where the highly ornamented refectory roof is continued in simpler form in the adjacent upper chamber, and at Cadhay, Ottery St Mary, Devon, where the roof of the hall is continued in plain form over the screens-passage bay to the west.

22 In contrast to the hall where they had vanished.

23 Tenons of the purlins of adjacent bays are accommodated in one mortice in the principal rafter, thus permitting purlins at the same height in adjacent bays (Fig 7.13, lower and upper purlins). The joint is used throughout the roof for the purlins; both tenons are generally secured by pegs, a detail visible in Fig 7.19.

24 Something of the sort did survive in the hall in the mid-19th century (above, see also Anon 1843).

25 Although this detail is sometimes omitted.

26 These timbers are strictly purlins, although in supporting the common rafters and ashlar pieces they also fulfil some of the conventional function of a wall plate. Definitions vary. Some imply that any timber set square (as opposed to diagonally in the plane of a roof) should be termed a plate (Alcock et al 1996, 13). Others restrict the term to timbers carrying or spreading the load of the roof (Brunskill 1994, 161). The Bowhill timbers are hybrids in that they support ashlar pieces and common rafters, but not the principals.

27 Cob dust was observed staining the east (blind) face of truss I (Chapter 5).

28 Three unnumbered and unprovenanced colour print photographs are reproduced here in black and white. The evidence for an earlier ceiling was noted by Dunmore: 'Solar roof originally laths on the back of rafters, smoothed/torched on inside – present solar ceiling is placed beneath this' (MS note adding to Morley 1979). This evidence did not survive the further stripping and cleaning that the timbers received in the course of repair.

29 According to the distinction drawn above, n 26.

30 The timbers of the partition are in the collection of loose timbers from Bowhill now stored at the English Heritage store at Toddington, Gloucestershire (Chapter 9, catalogue no. 138).

31 Archive photographs, EMAFU 1815/18–36.

32 Examples drawn from the south side of the roof. Marks were on the upper surface of the timber, normally at the east end.

33 This ceiling was of modern material (plasterboard?) supported on laths or battens that have left very fine nail holes in the common rafters (visible on close inspection). It was added after the demolition of the cross wall (when the inner and oriel chambers were amalgamated in the first restaurant period) to provide a ceiling at a uniform height with that of the oriel chamber (below).

34 As has been remarked elsewhere, it is unlikely that the craftsmen of the roof would have allowed their own work to be mutilated during fitting in this way. Perhaps this indicates that the carpenters had departed and that the fitting and beam filling had been left to lesser workmen. At the least this argues for a hiatus between preparation and assembly to account for the incongruities.

35 Probably an effect of standardised production of the roof timbers rather than an error as such.

36 The technique of continuing timbers over solid walling has been described as 'common practice' in cases where slate was used (instead of a bargeboard) to finish gables (Cox and Thorp 1991, 7). It is seen at the Exeter Inn, Ashburton, Devon (Francis Kelly, pers comm).

37 The roof timbers were stripped of paint and varnish (as a part of the process of removal of 'modern' finishes). Although the second ceiling line is still visible on the timbers, much of the evidence formerly visible has gone or is obscured by the torching of the reinstated roof. The process also accounts for the rough surfaces now seen on some timbers. The physical remains of the ceiling that were removed prior to recording could have represented an 18th-century finish to the oriel chamber.

38 A point first observed by Rebecca Child and reported to the author by Francis Kelly.

39 Although the need to provide for a gallery does not explain the same change in design on the west side. Alternatively the pegging of common rafters to purlins could be seen as the normal practice (one certainly widespread in vernacular contexts) and the treatment in the south range the variant practice.

40 Recorded in an archive photograph (not illustrated, ref EMAFU 3010/18).

41 Photographs in the site archive NMR BB 69/595 and 596 (dated September 1956). The phase 11 ceiling is shown in archive photographs DoE J10/19/78 and 20/78 (dated January 1978); the roof is seen after the removal of this ceiling (with the main timbers painted below ceiling level) in Figs 6.48 and 6.73 (dated July 1978).

42 This area was observed as it was dismantled for repair in 1992. Much of the fabric was not replaced.

43 Two other areas of surviving lathing represented introductions around the inserted (?16th-century) chimney.

44 Archive drawing 835 (not illustrated).

45 The lay board had been cut in order to provide a firm seating for the end of the purlin (archive photograph EMAFU 3033/11).

46 The original middle purlin of the east side had survived, with peg holes for common rafters. The timber had been repositioned, as it had failed to bear squarely on the lay board and its position clashed with the primary chimney stack of the oriel chamber fireplace (see above).

47 This evidence is crucial in assessing the sequence and dating of roof coverings of the east range. MS notes by S L Dunmore record that medieval slates and pegs were recovered from the top of the east wall of the hall ('stratified below straw'), but that the wall top of the west wall, which had been comprehensively rebuilt in masonry bonded with phase 8 mortar (Chapter 6) showed only traces of thatching (straw) and no slate fragments. This would suggest that the hall roof was thatched in the alterations of phase 8. It was certainly so covered by the time of the mid-19th-century drawings of Townsend and Stockdale (Figs 2.4–2.6). In view of the limited lifespan of thatch, there must have been some re-thatching between this date and the 1930s.

48 The account of roofing materials, as with that of the roofs in general, is skewed towards the south range, because the majority of physical evidence was recovered from that part of the building. Bays 5–10 of this roof were monitored intensively when they were dismantled in 1991–2. The evidence is also confined to loose finds, as the roof had long been stripped of its modern covering (and with it any vestiges of earlier roof covering which might have survived in situ). This emphasises the importance of observation and recording during stripping even of apparently modern roofs in the recovery of such evidence.

49 Cox and Thorp 1991, 5.

50 The evidence of ridge tiles suggests work on the roof in the 17th and 18th centuries, although care must be taken to distinguish maintenance and repair from wholesale re-roofing (Chapter 9).

51 For details of the geology see Chapter 9.

52 Slates of the Nordon Formation were especially prone to decay (Chapter 9).

53 Cox and Thorp 1991, 5; Salzman 1952, 234.

Chapter 8

1 The possible influence of the phase 2 building on the new building of phase 3 is discussed in Chapter 4.

2 Pantin 1962–3, 202.

3 Portman 1966, fig 9.

4 Bridget Cherry's introduction to the Devon volume of *The Buildings of England* gives further examples of courtyard plans (Saltram and Youlston), but also observes that 'This arrangement is sometimes described as typical of the south-west, but it is not universal, especially in larger houses: at Compton, Old Newnham, and North Wyke, the kitchen is in a range adjacent to the hall (at Newnham very oddly at the high rather than the low end), while at Dartington and Powderham it is in line with the hall' (Cherry and Pevsner 1989, 57).

5 Brown 1996, 160–2.

6 Hussey 1933, fig 12 (plan).

7 A rare survival of a farmhouse with a detached kitchen opposite the hall (Cherry and Pevsner 1989, 793).

8 RCHME 1970a, 206–8 and plan, 207; *see also* plan and discussion in Smith 1951, fig 48 and 187–99.

9 Elrington 1992, 82 (plan).

10 Ibid; Haslam 1992, 86 (photograph).

11 Wood 1965, 336. In addition to Wood's examples (ibid, 335–7), pentice walks connecting service and living rooms have been recorded at Acton Court, Iron Acton, South Gloucestershire (Rodwell and Bell forthcoming, 196); Okehampton Castle, Devon (Higham 1984, 20); and at Windsor Castle, Berkshire (Jo Cox, pers comm).

12 As is suggested by Howard 1987, 88.

13 Wood, 1965, 335.

14 Ibid, 193; Howard 1987, 82–3.

15 Cherry and Pevsner 1989, 841; plan in HBMCE guide leaflet, 1985; Oswald 1956, 1177 (remodelled in the early 16th century).

16 Schofield 1995, 66; *see also* Pantin 1962–3, 209.

17 I am grateful to John Thorp for useful discussion of this point.

18 Morley 1983, 92–3 and fig 6; *see also* Brown (1998, plates 3–4). Leigh is one of a number of similar manor houses in the South Hams area of Devon in which vestiges of lodging ranges served by galleries survive (*see* Keynedon, Sherford; Waterhouse 2000; Cherry and Pevsner 1989, 727).

19 Coope 1986, 44–5.

20 Wood 1965, 337, and HBMCE guide leaflet, 1985.

21 Also known as the Prysten House (Barber 1973; Cherry and Pevsner 1989, 661); although the present arrangement (a balcony) is a 20th-century restoration, several extant first-floor doorways demonstrate that there was a gallery originally.

22 Laithwaite 1990, 108; Portman 1966, 34; in Exeter there are (or were) examples of such galleries at nos 41–2 High Street (EMAFU observations), 45–6 High Street (Portman 1966, 80), 18 North Street (ibid, 85), 36 North Street (ibid, 87), 38 North Street (ibid, 88).

23 Wood 1965, 337; Radford 1960, 36 and plate 8 and folding plan of first floor.

24 RCHME 1970a, 206–7.

25 Pantin 1961, 172, figs 9.2–3 and plate 18.

26 Pantin 1961, 180, fig 9.6 and plate 17.

27 Ibid, 183–4.

28 Howard 1987, 90.

29 Trinick 1990, 41, and plan on end-paper. A similar arrangement, although again only in plan, is found at The Old Rectory, Walton, Somerset (Wood 1965, 200 and plan, fig 63).

30 Portman 1966, 70 and plan, fig 17.

31 Wood 1965, 103–4, especially examples quoted of oriels containing staircases at Penshurst Place, Northborough Manor (Northants), Minster Lovell (Oxon) and West Coker Manor (Somerset; I am grateful to Francis Kelly for the last reference).

32 Ibid, 105, 107–110; Goodall 1996, 40, for Gainsborough Old Hall.

33 *See* Hawkyard on Thornbury Castle (1977, 54).

34 In the first inventory of Lulworth Castle, *c* 1640 (Manco *et al* 1990, 36); I am grateful to Francis Kelly for this reference.

35 Howard 1987, 118, for the tower room of Sir William Sharington at Lacock, which combined the functions of viewing place with an emphasis on privacy.

36 The open space surviving to the east (in the direction of the main approach) presumably represents continuity of the eastern courtyard in the modern topography of the site.

37 Howard 1987, 61–3 and fig 31.

38 Cherry and Pevsner 1989, 727; DoE 1990a, 42; Waterhouse 2000. I am grateful to Robert Waterhouse for information about this house.

39 Chesher and Chesher 1968, 88; Francis Kelly (pers comm).

40 Orme 1992, 1, and plate 4.

41 Where a crenellated wall and gatehouse were added to the east side of the plan in the late 15th century; this structure was ' ... designed for show, for reasons of prestige, rather than defence' (Radford 1960, 45; *see also* plates 3 and 4).

42 Emery 1996, 380–2 and plate 188 (Mortham); 405–7 and plate 203 (Walburn).

43 Howard 1987, 69, 72 and colour plate 3.

44 Harris 1979, 16

45 Ibid, 203, also with a crenellated wall, although this is said to be later.

46 Webb 1956, 203–4.

47 In much the same way as the long galleries of later 16th-century houses acted as places of indoor recreation (Coope 1986, 51).

48 Colvin *et al* 1982, 18–19, 224; Coope 1986, 46, says '... the layout which once existed has suggested to those familiar with the fabric an almost "theatre-like" relationship between the upper galleries and the enclosed space below ... A common feature of these garden corridors was that they were invariably open on at least one side so that those using them would look out on to the garden. It can therefore be assumed that their function was partly recreative as well as functional' (Howard 1987, 88–9).

49 Colvin *et al* 1982, 17–18, 227–8 and fig 22.

50 Ibid, 224; Thurley 1993, 31.

51 Colvin *et al* 1982, plate 19; identified as a 'Banquet House' by Thurley, 1993, plan 11.

52 Coope 1986, figs 5 and 6.

53 Webb 1956, 202–3; Verey 1970, 381; Hawkyard 1977, 52–5.

54 Colvin *et al* 1982, 18.

55 Slade 1990, 95–6.

56 Ibid, 93.

57 Although the best construction in cob is where adjacent walls are built continuously as one, corners still represent a weak point in cob structures, perhaps because shrinkage causes separation of the walls and thus a crack at the corner. This weakness may account for the loss of cob walls elsewhere in the building, such as the east and west gables (certainly the latter was bonded to cob north and south walls), although the greater height of the gable walls could equally be to blame. I am grateful to Francis Kelly and Ray Harrison for discussion of this point.

58 This relationship was the source of suggestions in the past that the cross wall was an insertion to the building (it is shown as such on Everett's plan, 1958, fig 1) or (curiously) that the western bays of the south range were a later addition. Despite the fact that the correct interpretation of the building as of one build was established in the first sentence of Morley's report of 1979, interpretations involving multiple phases of construction were still being propounded as late as 1990 (Slade 1990, 93 and 96).

59 The oversailing sections are not strictly necessary to the roofing of the building, since the three ranges could have been roofed

separately (with framed filling of the gables). No evidence for such framing was recorded, however, and no trace of slating (or other evidence of primary roofing) was recovered from the roof of the south range in the areas abutted by those of the east and west ranges. It follows that, while the possibility remains, the evidence of the fabric makes the solution of independent roofing unlikely.

60 Slade 1990, 93.

61 Such as a piscina, image niche, other fittings of a liturgical nature or elaborated window heads/tracery. Any one of these would be sufficient to identify a chapel (see Copeland 1949, 104).

62 Above, Chapter 3; Lysons and Lysons 1822, 498, and later authors following them.

63 The evidence of Roger Holand's will could still indicate no more than the use of normal domestic rooms for the saying of divine service, as is suggested for London houses by Schofield (1995, 69).

64 Examples of domestic chapels exist in Devon houses from the 12th century. Occasionally they are free-standing structures, for example, Bickleigh Castle (12th century; Cherry and Pevsner 1989, 171–2) or Bury Barton, Lapford (15th century; ibid, 533). More often they are attached to domestic ranges, as at Membury Court (late 13th century; ibid, 567; Copeland 1957, 310; also unpublished work by Dr Joanna Cox and John Thorp), Higher Harestone, Brixton (14th century, ibid, 482), Uplowman Court (14th century, ibid, 881–2; Cox and Thorp, as above), Edge Barton Branscombe (Clifford 1962, 464–5) and Bradley Manor (15th century, ibid, 587–9). Clergy houses in Exeter tend to have first-floor chapels, such as the Bishop's Palace, the Deanery and no. 10 The Close (Cherry and Pevsner 1989, 57). Chapels above porches occur at Orleigh Court (Rogers 1926, 191), Place Court, Colaton Raleigh (Richards 1917), and Dunsland (Copeland 1949, 109). For full lists of domestic chapels in Devon see ibid, 108–11).

65 Parallels are wall paintings of prominently sacred character in domestic contexts at the Old Manor, Littlehempston, Devon (Hussey 1933, 124 and fig 3) and Cothay, Somerset (Hussey 1927a, 603–4; 1927b, 628). The painting by Campin quoted below in Chapter 9 (p 226, n 176) provides an example of sculpture in a domestic setting.

66 For example, chapels at Bickleigh Castle, Bury Barton, Lapford, and Ayshford, Burlescombe, in Devon (Cherry and Pevsner 1989, 57). A fuller list is given by Copeland (1949, 108–9). In Cornwall chapels are often a considerable distance from the property they served (Adams 1957, 61–2). Tinten, near St Tudy, is an example of a detached chapel in a domestic context (Pevsner 1970, 221).

67 Wood 1965, 239; although a chapel could be formed in a part of a room with a secular use, it was often placed in a room adjoining the hall, parlour or great chamber; see also Oldham 1906, 393.

68 Small size was no impediment to the proper functioning of a chapel (see Copeland 1949, 105) and the evidence of Cothay and Place Court, Colaton Raleigh (below), where the chapel measures 9' × 7'6" (Richards 1917, 335).

69 Wood 1965, 239; Lower Marsh Manor, Dunster, is another close parallel in which the room above the porch is small (about 8' × 10'), but completely furnished as a chapel, with wagon roof, statue niche and piscina (Pevsner 1958, 223).

70 Ibid, 235; Delderfield 1970, 29–31.

71 Hussey 1927a, 602, plan, fig 16 and fig 9 for the gallery. Although the evidence for a similar gallery at Bowhill is very slender (and is best interpreted as a ceiled passage, rather than a floored gallery, Chapter 6), such an arrangement remains a

possible element in the plan (and would, at the least, have increased the directions from which this room was visible). As the survival of original cob on the inside elevation shows that there can never have been a door into the room from this direction, the most that this area could have accommodated is a squint or window-like opening (Fig 6.2).

72 I am grateful to Jeanne James of the Department of History, Exeter University, and John Thorp for useful discussion of aspects of domestic chapels and their interpretation.

73 The terms and conditions of such licences varied widely. Occasionally a blanket licence would be issued to an individual, such as that of 1408 to John and Joan Butte for 'all their mansions in the Diocese' (Hingeston-Randolph 1886, 272). Some conditions were normal, however. Often other parishioners were excluded, sometimes wholly, such as in the licence of 1318 to Sir William de Feraris and his wife Matilda (Hingeston-Randolph 1892, 299), or on Sundays and festivals, such as in the licence to John and Joan Beauchamp of 1414–15 at Binnerton (Hingeston-Randolph 1886, 271). The licensee was sometimes required to attend their parish church on Sundays and/or festivals (such as in the licence to Elizabeth Credy of Orleigh Court quoted below). This condition was sometimes relaxed to allow licensees to attend the parish church when convenient (as in Bishop Stafford's licence to John Rynsy of Godolphin, in 1398, ibid, 280). The saying of mass is rarely specifically mentioned, but one instance, a licence of 1320–1 to Master William Wolleghe of Yarnscombe, is illuminating on the limitations placed even on a priest in his own domestic chapel, as he was permitted to say mass, but not to administer the sacraments of the church to anyone (Hingeston-Randolph 1892, 302). For further discussion of the terms and conditions of episcopal licences see Copeland 1949, 106–8 and Oldham 1906, 394–99.

74 Adams 1957, 59.

75 Ibid, 107.

76 As in a licence of 1408 for Newnham, Plympton, which specifies matins, mass and evensong (Copeland 1949, 107).

77 Or, more strictly, rediscovery. The group comprised five examples (six if hall and chamber at Bowhill are counted separately) when its collective characteristics were previously described by Everett (1958, 206), Wood (1965, 317–8) and Blaylock (1990, 131–4). Since 1990 the roof of the Archdeaconry of Exeter has come to light and drawings of it have been prepared (Bishop et al 1994; Henderson et al 1995). Accurate drawings have also been made of the Guildhall roof (when it was scaffolded for redecoration in 1996). The previous account and drawings having depended on the drawings of James Crocker (1875). It is possible that the roof of the Chantry in Deanery Square/Palace Gate, Exeter (immediately south of the Cathedral cloisters) was of this type. The building was demolished in 1870 and no illustration of its interior is known. The roof is described in a contemporary newspaper article as: 'a panelled wagon roof with moulded hoops and great bosses at the intersections' (Woolmer's Exeter and Plymouth Gazette 1.xi.1867, supplement).

78 The roof at Cadhay is strictly a false hammer-beam construction, since the hammer posts rose only to the arch brace rather than the principal/upper purlin. There are many variant definitions of true and false hammer-beam roofs. Cadhay has hammer posts bearing on the beams and thus would be counted a 'true' hammer-beam roof according to Brunskill's definition (1994, 133). Margaret Wood counted a roof 'false' if the posts were morticed into the hammer beams rather than standing on them (Wood 1965, 319), an even stricter definition. Here the term 'false' hammer beam will be used to define the form of extended sole piece that may support an arch brace, but not a

post (*see* Alcock *et al* 1996, 8; Pevsner 1958, 128, in the context of the Cleeve Abbey refectory, or Cherry and Pevsner 1989, 804, in the context of Traymill, Thorverton). By this definition the Cadhay roof is a 'true' hammer-beam structure.

79 Cherry and Pevsner 1989, 55.

80 Alcock and Barley 1972, 133–4; the principal rafters rise only to the level of the collar, with a separate structure above (*see* Alcock *et al* 1996, 5).

81 Alcock and Barley 1972, 142. Roofs with base crucks or short principals tend to occur in the buildings of a higher social class than the range of other rafter/arch brace roofs and the factor of status may play a part in the equation, independently of size (ibid, 135–7).

82 Wood 1965, 313–4; Alcock and Barley 1972, 142.

83 Blaylock 1990, 126 and 129.

84 Registration of bays and windows is also poor in the Law Library (MoW plan). Traces of windows recently recorded in the Archdeacon of Exeter's house were not centred on the bays of the roof (Richard Parker, pers comm). At Cadhay the evidence for ancient fenestration broadly follows the bays of the roof. The Deanery is exceptional in that the elevations of the great chamber are perfectly in accord with the bays of the roof (Blaylock 1993, figs 5 and 6).

85 Providing further support for the contemporaneity of the roof and other carpentry (above, pp 173–4).

86 Normally the ogee/cavetto combination adapted to the individual dimensions of the timber. Similar treatments appear elsewhere, for example, on window lintels and door-frames.

87 The upper purlin at the Guildhall has a similar, but not identical moulding to those of the Deanery and of the Law Library.

88 A full set of mouldings is illustrated in the MoW drawing (Fox 1957, 139).

89 Compare Fig 8.5 with Fox 1957, 139, fig 2.

90 Compare Henderson *et al* 1995, figs 5 and 7, with Fox 1957, fig 2.

91 Alcock and Barley 1972, 134 ff.

92 Cherry and Pevsner 1989, 414–5; Allan and Thorp 1990, 46.

93 Oliver 1861a, 120–5.

94 Bishop and Prideaux 1922, 55–6 and plate opposite 56 (the chair may incorporate or be crowned with a mitre – *see* the sub-triangular object in the top foil of the design; Allan and Thorp 1990, 45).

95 Blaylock 1993, 4–8.

96 Blaylock 1990, 129 and 133–4.

97 Early 15th century (Fox 1957, 138); *c*1450 (Portman, 1966, 67); several 15th-century dates (Lega-Weekes 1915, 166–71).

98 Linehan 1975, 4.

99 Risdon 1811, 47.

100 Anon nd, 18–20.

101 I am grateful to Mr O N W William-Powlett for showing me this block, as well as for his assistance during visits to Cadhay.

102 Cherry and Pevsner 1989, 242; Thorp 1990c, 101; the reason for pushing the date as late as the 1540s is the report of ecclesiastical (or more strictly monastic) *spolia* reused in the fabric of the new house. These are attributed to the dissolved collegiate buildings at Ottery, of which John Haydon was one of four governors, or to Dunkeswell Abbey, where Haydon purchased materials (Linehan 1975, 4). No such fragments can now be seen *in situ* (although a large quantity of material has been recovered from the site in the past).

103 Thorp 1990c, 101.

104 Whetham 1913, 178.

105 Ibid, 178; the house has traditionally been dated to the last years of the 15th century (Baldwin and Spittle 1957, 162).

106 Cherry and Pevsner 1989, 46.

107 For example, the roofs of nave and aisles of St Andrew's, Cullompton (variation on the wagon-roof theme and flat intersecting-beam ceilings respectively; Delagarde 1849, 58, plates 3 and 11).

108 Alcock and Hulland 1972, 53–5.

109 Youings 1968, 15–16; *see also* Portman 1966, 9.

110 Ibid, 9 and 67.

111 Tipping 1915, 20–1; Cherry and Pevsner 1989, 893 (and plate 60). The dating by heraldic supporters of Henry VII, which are said to appear among the carvings in the roof (Tipping 1915, 22; Cherry and Pevsner 1989, 892), does not stand up to detailed scrutiny. All these carvings are different and none convincingly represents either a greyhound or a dragon.

112 Brunskill 1994, 133 and above, n 78.

113 Ashworth 1861, unnumbered plates showing scale drawings of a principal truss and a bay elevation.

114 Youings 1968, 226; the cusped braces were restored in the late 1980s.

115 This is a product of the panelled arrangement of the purlins, sub-principals, intermediate trusses and windbraces; *see* the 19th-century engraved drawings, with two sets of mouldings placed together at the apex (Ashworth 1861, unnumbered plates).

116 Cherry and Pevsner 1989, 614; the carvings ornament the feet of the intermediate trusses at Orleigh, whereas at Weare Giffard they are attached to the main trusses.

117 Description based on the 1956 NMR photograph, Fig 8.24.

118 Groves forthcoming b.

119 Richardson 1993, 4–6; I am very grateful to Isabel Richardson and Shirley Blaylock for the opportunity to examine this roof.

120 Hulland 1980, 149–50, fig 16 and plate 2c; Hillam and Groves 1993, 47.

121 Anon 1903, 928; Hayward 1867, unnumbered plate. Other variants in this roof are the vestigial (very short) hammer posts and king posts in the main trusses. The unusual traceried windbraces of the Bradfield roof are echoed still further to the east at Whitestaunton Manor House, Somerset (Anon 1883, 40–1; Pevsner 1958, 344).

122 Cherry and Pevsner 1989, 804; Richardson 1993, 6; I am very grateful to John Thorp for discussion of the roof of Traymill and for copies of his drawings.

123 I am grateful to Richard Parker for information about this roof.

124 Prideaux 1915, 168.

125 Blaylock 1985, 122 and fig 9.

126 Hussey 1933, 121.

127 Haslam 1992, 260, for a photograph; Cherry and Pevsner (1989, 922) date the hall roof to the earlier, 15th-century phase rather than the early 16th-century remodelling, which also saw the moulded beamed ceiling inserted into the hall.

128 Cherry and Pevsner 1989, 529.

129 Parker 1996 14–15.

130 Child 1990, 40; continuing much later than this in vernacular contexts; *see also below*, pp 190–1 and notes 183–9.

131 Slader 1968, 57–8 and 62.

132 Cherry and Pevsner 1989, 47–9; Slader 1968, 79, 92–6; *see also* the list of 16th-century bench ends, ibid, 130.

133 Thorp 1990b, 47–50.

134 DoE 1990b, 4; I am grateful to Peter Child and John Thorp for information about this roof.

135 Cherry and Pevsner 1989, 515.

136 Alcock 1966a, 110–11; Hulland 1980, 134; dendrochronological dating of *c* 1328–39: Tyers *et al* 1997, 139.

137 Jope 1961, 200.

138 Smith 1958, 126 (and fig 12); Cherry and Pevsner 1989, 899.

139 Blaylock 1985, 122 and fig 9.

140 Where such research has taken place, for instance in the study of 16th- and 17th-century plasterwork, close links between Devon and Somerset and Dorset have been demonstrated (Penoyre and Penoyre 1994, 53).

141 RCHME 1970b, 11–13.

142 Ibid, 9.

143 Ibid, 12 (drawings). The link in the shape of upper coving was first recognised by Margaret Wood, although she did not identify the use of the square-set plate (Wood 1965, 317).

144 RCHME 1980, 103–4 and plate 83; the transomed windows with cinquefoil heads provide another useful parallel for Bowhill, ibid, plate 59.

145 Wood 1965, 319 and plate 46B.

146 RCHME 1970b, 191.

147 Ibid, 194.

148 Especially Bradfield, which may have links further east in Somerset (see above, n 121).

149 RCHME 1970b, plates 172–3.

150 Gilyard-Beer 1992, 47; dendrochronological sampling of this roof is under consideration at the time of writing.

151 Ibid, 32–6.

152 Hulland 1980, 150–1; Wood 1965, plate 47c; similar decoration was recorded in a 19th-century drawing of Colston's house, Small Street, Bristol, now demolished; ibid, 319; Pantin 1963, 4758 and plate 24.

153 Newman 1995, 44; similar timbers appear in a roof at St Donat's Castle, ibid, 556.

154 Wood 1965, 318.

155 Ibid, 319.

156 Chanter 1932, 30, quoting Charles Tucker's report of its demolition in 1845 (Archaeol J 5 (1848), 225).

157 Alexander and Binski 1987, 464 (three bosses in the V&A Museum); one further example is in the RAM Museum, Exeter (accession number 122.65).

158 Portman 1966, 69; Beacham 1990, plate 18; the ceiling may have been altered in the 19th century (Cherry and Pevsner 1989, 411) and the colouring is later still (Thorp 1990a, 130).

159 Cherry and Pevsner 1989, 812; Blaylock 1988, 3 and 6–7.

160 RCHME 1970b, 105–7 and plate 21.

161 Delagarde 1849, plates 3 and 11; Cherry and Pevsner 1989, 303–4; the aisles probably c 1500, Chalk 1910, 192.

162 Pevsner 1958, 93 and plate 19; Wickham 1952, 52 and plate 62; Pevsner 1958, 44, 232 and plate 18a.

163 RCHME 1970b, 151 and plate 151.

164 Ibid, 111 and plate 142.

165 The date given to Cothay (below) and to Great Chalfield, Wiltshire, with a cranked or shallow-pitched profile, thereby perhaps owing more to church roofs (Pevsner 1975, 257–8; illustrated in Wood 1965, plate 26).

166 Of many possible examples, see early 16th-century buildings in Essex (Paycock's House, Great Coggeshall, RCHME 1922, 117–9, and others at Colchester and Earl's Colne, ibid, 61 and 90, respectively).

167 RCHME 1959, 33–4; Shipley 1916. Ceilings subdivided by moulded ribs in the first-floor oratory, drawing room and state bedroom and an unceiled intersecting-beam ceiling with heavily moulded joists in the ground-floor Master's Study (ibid, 382, 383, 408 and 379/383 respectively).

168 Oswald 1932, 412.

169 Ibid, 1230.

170 Hussey 1927b, 629 and 632.

171 With later plaster ornament applied over the moulded beams (Cherry and Pevsner 1989, 488–90; Phillips 1915, 50–2). There is also an elaborate intersecting-beam ceiling reused in a 19th-century wing, with multiple mouldings, a carved inner order and composite bosses, as at Cullompton and Exeter Deanery.

172 RCHME 1952, 245 and plate 188.

173 Gotch 1901, 175–6 and plate 67; presumably before Wolsey's fall in 1529 (see Colvin et al 1982, 127).

174 Dated 1627 (Trinick 1990, 30–1). For Poole see Smith (1951, 204 and fig 61); I am grateful to John Thorp for this reference.

175 Cherry and Pevsner 1989, 415; Allan and Thorp 1990, 46; the composite bosses, where a small central boss on the beams is combined with additional elements in the corners of the adjacent panels also appears in the Cullompton roof (above).

176 Cherry and Pevsner 1989, 424; Portman 1966, 12.

177 Thorp 1990a, 130.

178 Beacham 1990, fig 7.1.

179 Pantin 1957, 139–40 and plate 17d.

180 Cherry and Pevsner 1989, 205 and 285.

181 Alcock 1966b, 145 and fig 5.

182 Cherry and Pevsner 1989, 399; Blaylock 1991c, 1 and fig 9.

183 Hulland 1980, 147–8; Cherry and Pevsner 1989, 704.

184 Alcock and Laithwaite 1973, 104–5 and figs 42–43.

185 The Church House Inn at Holne has moulded joists as well as beams (Copeland 1962, 433).

186 Alcock and Laithwaite 1973, 102.

187 Cherry and Pevsner 1989, 922; Oswald 1956, 1228–30.

188 Hulland 1980, 163; Child 1990, fig 2.4; see also inserted ceilings at Pilliven, Witheridge (Alcock and Hulland 1972, 39 and fig 2); at West Clatworthy, Filleigh (Alcock and Laithwaite 1973, 119 and fig 43); and a primary construction at Higher Thornham, Romansleigh (Blaylock 1998, 5).

189 For this reason the term girding beam has been avoided here.

190 Beacham 1989, 76.

191 Alcock and Hulland 1972, 52 and fig 6; Hulland 1980, 161 and fig 24.

192 Chapter 6; similar, though not identical techniques occur in other Exeter buildings (Thorp 1998, 86).

193 No trace of plastering or any surface skim was detected on either face of the screen, although there were scorch marks from candles or rush lights in many places on the surviving timbers (these, of course, could have been later). Perhaps this wall of the room was hung with tapestry?

194 Alcock and Hall 1994, 58 and fig 36.

195 Portman 1966, 58; sometimes described as a trussed partition (Brunskill 1994, 80, 156 and 161) and as platform framing (for the technique of constructing partitions over flooring).

196 Now removed, but visible in a 1930s photograph (Hussey 1933, 123, fig 7).

197 Pantin 1957, 128 and fig 24.

198 Lega-Weekes 1900, 201 and plate facing 204; see also Cherry and Pevsner 1989, 606; it is not known whether this partition is in situ or reused from elsewhere in the building.

199 Alcock and Hulland 1972, 51–3 and fig 6.

200 Peirce House, Charing, Kent (Pearson 1994, fig 115); Shieling Hall, Langley, Kent (Barnwell and Adams 1994, fig 19a); Dukes Place, West Peckham (ibid, fig 116c), inter alia. These have been chosen because of the quality of the published evidence; other areas are, as yet, less well served by modern survey work.

201 Alcock et al 1996, fig 31i.

202 The relieving arches are not unlike the smaller versions used in the stone windows of the south range and thus represent one of the distinctive traits of Bowhill's architectural style (Figs 5.8 and 6.22).

203 Portman 1966, 14.

204 Including examples at: the Deanery (see above, p 183); one formerly at the Hall of the Vicars Choral (Lega-Weekes 1915, opposite 53); at no. 5 The Close (Parker 1997a, 30 and plate 23);

an example from the Precentor's House in the Close, now on display in the RAM Museum (Wood 1965, plate 43c); and, above all, Bishop Courtenay's monumental fireplace in the Bishop's Palace (Chanter 1932, opposite 32).

205 Blaylock 1991c, figs 7 and 9 (detail). Despite infelicities in its construction, examination of the fireplace and its surrounding fabric in 1979 revealed no signs of later insertion or alteration to the arch and lintel (ibid, 5); its association with the building of *c* 1300 at Polsloe seems secure.

206 Ibid, fig 6, 1827. A good illustration of the properties of breccia and the extremely large blocks in which it could be obtained.

207 Portman 1966, 74–5 and fig 11.

208 Laithwaite 1990, 106 and fig 5.10.

209 Portman 1966, 77, and records made by John Thorp for EMAFU. The fireplace now has the remains of a timber lintel, probably replacing an original stone lintel. The hooded form of fireplace was a later development. Another example (with volcanic jambs and a Beer-stone lintel) was recorded in a later 16th-century phase at 198 High Street before its demolition in 1975 (again by John Thorp for EMAFU).

210 Blaylock 1990, 163 and fig 10. The lintel was replaced by William Weir in 1900.

211 Beard 1990, 60; Portman 1966, 47; Thorp 1990a, 130.

212 Thorp 1982, 175–7.

213 Polsloe Priory has two examples of early or mid-17th-century date (Blaylock 1991c, fig 7, 1813 and 1814).

214 Exposed by bombing in 1942 (photograph of 7 April 1944, English Heritage Photo. Library, ref E1284).

215 Lloyd Parry and Brakspear 1917, 40–1.

216 A house erroneously called the Annuellars' College (Lega-Weekes 1915, 60 ff; Cherry and Pevsner 1989, 413). Canon Stevens was the founder of the adjacent St Catherine's Almshouses (Lega-Weekes 1915, 62; I am grateful to A G Collings for discussion of this property).

217 Now reconstructed (Chapter 11).

218 Portman 1966, 12.

219 Beacham 1990, plate 12.

220 Creswell 1908, plate opposite 168.

221 Alcock 1968, 21 and plate 2.

222 Parker 1997b, fig 11.

223 Pevsner 1958, 228–9 and plate 38a; with three forward-facing lights, as opposed to (probably) two in the Bowhill window.

224 RCHME 1970b, plate 195; with two forward-facing lights and a panelled lower tier with shields in relief (as suggested for the bay window in the south-east range, below); *see also* examples in West Dorset, for example, Parnham, Beaminster (RCHME 1952, plate 74).

225 Cherry and Pevsner 1989, plate 61; one forward-facing light.

226 Elyott was Collector of Customs for Exeter and Dartmouth in the reign of Henry VII and was a contemporary of Roger Holand (Chanter 1932, 119). He received a licence to construct the window over Dean and Chapter property on 20 July 1500 (Lega-Weekes 1915, 92). For the location of the house *see* Lega-Weekes 1921, 253–4 and Dymond 1889, 23–4.

227 'A valuable ancient gothic stone window' advertised for sale, *Exeter Flying Post*, 30 June 1842, 3g.

228 Reduced to two storeys and with deepened lights subdivided by transoms, added to the Palace for Bishop Philpotts in 1845–6 (Blaylock 1987, 14); the architect was Ewan Christian according to Chanter (1932, 119), but the Torquay architect Edward Gribble, according to Musson (1998, 46).

229 The sources are: a lithograph published by Oliver 1839, vol 1, plate 2 (opposite 80); a watercolour drawing in the possession of The Devon and Exeter Institution (Fig 8.31); a pencil drawing in a sketchbook by Edward Ashworth (also in The Devon and

Exeter Institution, no. 5); a drawing in the collection of the Exeter Pictorial Record Society at the Westcountry Studies Library (B/Exeter Houses, Elyott's House, The Close; P&D D7243, EPRS 321).

230 Cherry and Pevsner 1989, 487–8 and plate 62.

231 RCHME 1952, 77 and plate 105.

232 Ibid, 244 and plate 186; much the most heavily ornamented example. A full two-storey bay window, with 1+4+1 lights divided by a transom and king mullion, survives in the west elevation of Melbury House, Melbury Sampford, Dorset, although this is said by the Royal Commission to be 'reconstructed' and is thus not reliable (ibid, 165 and plate 144). Although perhaps somewhat later and dated before 1540 (ibid, 164; note the uncusped lights), this provides a close parallel for the Bowhill window.

233 Tipping 1907; Howard 1987, 206 and plate 108; Cooke 1957, 58–9.

234 Oswald 1959, plate 35.

235 Pevsner 1958, 294 and plate 41.

236 Airs, 1995, 54–5; RCHME 1916, 308–10; anon 1905, 18 and 19.

237 For Cadhay *see* anon, nd, frontispiece; a detail of the turret is given by Weaver 1913, 91; for Wortham *see* Oswald 1956, 1175, 1228 and fig 3.

238 Wood 1965, 364; to which could be added windows at The Vicarage, Congresbury, Somerset, and Rectory Farm, Stanton Drew, Somerset (Pantin 1957, figs 25 and 26); the hall windows at Truthall, Sithny, Cornwall, (Chesher and Chesher 1968, 30 and plates on pp 66 and 76, I); plus variations with ogee-headed lights at Tickenham Court, Somerset (Wood 1965, plate 56f); and an ornate four-light window at Doverhay Manor House, Porlock, Somerset (Pevsner 1958, plate 42a).

239 Portman 1966, 12–13 (for Exeter).

240 Cherry and Pevsner 1989, 587–9; Woolner 1989, 33; traces of foiled heads removed from several windows in the ante-chapel and great chamber are visible on close inspection. All the windows may have had foiled heads originally.

241 Hussey 1933, 122 and fig 6.

242 Tipping 1915, fig 15; Weare Giffard has a lot of imported material incorporated in its fabric. Some individual features may, therefore, be unreliable; ibid, 16; Cherry and Pevsner 1989, 891–3.

243 Trinick 1989, 13; although these may be restorations (*see* photos on pp 14 and 16 and Everett 1956).

244 Cherry and Pevsner 1989, 804; NMR photograph of 1967, ref AA 68/44.

245 RCHME 1939, 29 and plate 82; Howard 1987, plate 34 for a detail.

246 Woolner 1989, 33–5; some have been replaced.

247 Tipping 1915, fig 15.

248 On the basis of the Buck engraving and surviving architectural fragments.

249 Portman 1966, 12.

250 Ibid, 91; Henderson 1985, 36–8; Hussey 1933, fig 6.

251 Higham *et al* 1982, 84 and fig 40, 6; Pevsner 1958, 134; Trinick 1989, 12–13.

252 Slade 1990, 94.

253 Harris 1979, 25 and *passim*; Lloyd 1951, 333, fig 506; and examples (drawn almost at random) from Essex (Forrester 1975, 52), Hertfordshire (Smith 1992, 95) and Kent (Barnwell and Adams 1994, 103–4).

254 Fox and Raglan 1951, 55 ('dozens' of examples recorded by the RCHME in Herefordshire are also mentioned, but the Commission's *Inventory* volumes record very few such windows). One possible plain mullioned window is visible in a

house at Weobley (RCHME 1934, plate 28); *see also* Fox and Raglan 1953, 62, where the possibility that the narrow lights of these windows had been closed with horn is considered and rejected.

255 RCAHMW 1988, 82, 86 and map 24.
256 Smith 1988, 658–61; also a sparse distribution in North Wales.
257 Fox and Raglan 1953, figs 5, 19, 24, 25 and others.
258 Fox and Raglan 1951, 90–95, fig 53 and plate 18b.
259 Hussey 1933, fig 4; 1950, fig 7.
260 Also dated to *c*1500; unpublished archive report by John Thorp, EMAFU.
261 Richardson 1993, 4.
262 Alcock and Laithwaite 1973, 116 and fig 47.
263 Cherry and Pevsner 1989, 793.
264 Alcock and Laithwaite 1973, 112; Chalk 1934, plate facing p 35, for illustration.
265 Alcock and Hulland 1972, 41 and plate 6.
266 Sheldon 1932, fig 11 (now destroyed).
267 Lloyd 1951, 70–71; Kenyon 1967, 82–4; Schofield 1995,106; Airs 1995, 127. *See also* above, Chapter 6, n 9.
268 In Glamorgan (RCAHMW 1988, 82 and 90) and Monmouthshire (Fox and Raglan 1954, 21–2); *see also* Smith 1988, 487 and map 36. For ovolo-moulded windows *see* Barley 1961, 106 and 112, and Alcock *et al* 1996, 11–12. Fox and Raglan (1954, 40–2 and fig 48f) identified a type of window in Monmouthshire with plain eight-sided mullions, but this seems to be coeval with the ovolo-moulded windows, although (apparently) unglazed.
269 Alcock 1966a, 121–2 and fig 11.
270 Alcock 1962, 224 and fig 9 – Great Moor detail D; Middle Moor detail A.
271 Williams 1974, 225 and fig 9.
272 Copeland 1961, 261 and plate 24, 264 and plate 26.
273 Pevsner 1970, 145.
274 The Old Manor and Church House are both houses with late medieval origins (Cherry and Pevsner 1989, 778 and 487); author's photographs of the windows in the project archive. Some of the Holcombe Rogus windows are visible in the photograph published by Copeland 1960, plate 25. For Hele Manor *see* photographs in the National Monuments Record by R F Wills of 1954 (refs AA64/3524; AA 73/902).
275 Copeland 1960, 125 and plate 40. The church house at Silverton also has a 'rectangular oak-framed two-light window with segmental heads to the lights and chamfer moulds' (Copeland 1963, 151).

Chapter 9

1 Sections of this chapter not otherwise attributed are by Stuart Blaylock.
2 John Allan, Curator of Antiquities, RAM Museum, Queen Street, Exeter EX4 3RX.
3 Allan 1984a.
4 I am grateful to Mr Graham Langman of Exeter Archaeology for compiling the site archive.
5 For example, Exeter Museums accessions A1372–7, a hoard from Freehold Society land, St Thomas 1874; single coin finds from Plymouth Inn, Alphington Road 1909; St Thomas Gasworks 1882; King's Hall, Okehampton St 1912; Cowick Fields 1927 and various St Thomas finds without specific locations. Goodchild's unpublished list of Roman coin finds from Exeter (MS in Westcountry Studies Library, Exeter) includes a coin of Postumus found in 1850 at the Lunatic (Hospital), that is, the junction of Cowick Street and Buddle Lane, *c* 100m from Bowhill.
6 Allan 1984a, 31 and 71–9.
7 Ibid, 133, 166–73, where nearly 3,000 sherds from at least 1,187 different vessels in contexts of *c*1550–80 are presented.
8 Ibid, 100–53.
9 Ibid, 103–4.
10 Unpublished.
11 Unpublished.
12 Allan 1984a, 167–71.
13 Ibid, 131–5.
14 For example, Hurst *et al* 1986, 48–53.
15 Hurst 1986, 48.
16 In Allan 1995, 309, no. 27.
17 1995, 287 and 290.
18 Allan 1995, 309.
19 I am grateful to John Hurst for his comments on this sherd.
20 Hurst *et al* 1986, 216, no. 333, Plain Narrow Globular Jug type.
21 Allan 1984a, 149.
22 Ibid, 149.
23 Ibid.
24 Ibid, 153.
25 Ibid, nos 1711, 1802.
26 Coleman-Smith and Pearson 1988, 130–43; publication of site 13 forthcoming by R Coleman-Smith.
27 For example, Hurst *et al* 1986, 194–7 and 214–16.
28 Ibid, 102–3, 110.
29 For example, Allan 1984a, 159, 163–4.
30 Ibid, 6.
31 Ibid, 6, 90–3.
32 Coleman-Smith and Pearson 1988, 162–3.
33 Allan 1984a, 6.
34 For possible reconstructions of the general form *see* Archer 1997, 274–7 (water bottles); Austin 1994, 254, no. 608 (flower bottles).
35 Austin 1994, 267–71.
36 For example, ibid, p 46, plate18 and p 144, nos 199–200.
37 *See* Pearce 1992, 73, nos 403–13, 'small rounded jars'.
38 For example, Allan 1984a, nos 1531 and 1832.
39 Jennings 1981, fig 51, no. 843.
40 Allan 1984a, fig 125, no. 2811.
41 Jennings 1981, 125.
42 Reineking-von Bock 1971, no. 545.
43 Allan 1984a, 240–1.
44 Ibid.
45 Ibid, 91–3.
46 Ibid, 227–30.
47 Cherry 1991, 195.
48 Pers comm; for the house *see* Weddell 1991, 26.
49 I am grateful to Mr M L Corney of Bull Hill for drawing these to my attention.
50 Hanham 1970.
51 Watkin 1935, 334–46.
52 *See* Staniforth n d, *passim*.
53 Salzman 1952, 229–34.
54 Welch 1967, 24 and 27.
55 Gregory 1950, 6.
56 Erskine 1981; 1983.
57 Alcock 1965; 1966.
58 Erskine 1981, 76, 101, 106, 151 and 154; 1983, 240, 260 and 289.
59 Alcock 1966b, 149; 1965, 150.
60 Allan 1984a, no. 2964.
61 Ibid, no. 2958.
62 Ibid, no. 2957.
63 Polsloe Priory.
64 Polsloe Priory.
65 Salzman 1952, 230–1.

66 Fox and Radford 1933, 119–20; Jope 1951; *see* Cherry 1991, 195 for reference to other studies.

67 Dating quoted in Allan 1984a, 234.

68 Brown 1988.

69 Higham *et al* 1982, 38–77.

70 Emery 1970.

71 Higham *et al* 1982, 52–4.

72 Brown 1996.

73 Allan 1984a, no. 2951.

74 Allan 1984b, 79–81.

75 Huge numbers from the ranges of *c* 1600: Brown 1996, the tiles unpublished.

76 Platt 1962; the finds from his excavation have recently been transferred to Exeter City Museums.

77 Brown 1998, 56.

78 Intact tile in Exeter Museum.

79 Allan 1985.

80 Allan 1988, 85–6.

81 Allan and Perry 1982, fabric 9.

82 Excavations by Exeter Archaeology, unpublished.

83 Dunning 1974, 112–19.

84 This tile escaped Dunning's notice. It consists of the trunk of an animal (a ?horse).

85 Miles and Miles 1975, 281, no. 48.

86 Allan 1984b, 79–91.

87 Allan 1984a, 227, no. 2956.

88 Ibid, no. 2964.

89 *See* Brown and Vince 1984 and other petrological work presented in Allan 1984a, 32–7.

90 Allan 1984a, 135–6.

91 Vince and Brown 1982, 101–3.

92 For Hants and Dorset finds *see* Keen 1992, 134; for Plymouth *see* Gaskell Brown 1986, 70, where such tiles are described but not identified, and various more recent discoveries, notably from Vauxhall Street 1990. For various Exeter finds *see* Allan and Keen 1984, 240–1, series 4.

93 Polsloe finds from the excavations of 1976–8 are in Exeter City Museums; Plympton finds from the excavations of the early 1960s are at Plymouth City Museums; Haccombe tiles are *in situ*; Torre Abbey tiles from excavations by Exeter Archaeology are currently being studied by Dr L Keen; Fore Street, Totnes, finds from excavation by Exeter Archaeology in 1985 are now at Exeter City Museums; for Exmouth, *see* Allan 1986, 135–6.

94 Allan and Keen 1984, 240–1.

95 Norton 1983.

96 Oswald 1984.

97 Reference CX 235; X-ray photographs are stored in the main conservation archive of the RAM Museum, Exeter, rather than the site archive. I am grateful to Alison Hopper-Bishop for advice on the interpretation of the X-ray photographs.

98 Ref CX 208.

99 Ref CX 204.

100 Ref CX 466.

101 Several similar knives were found at Basing House, Hampshire (Moorhouse 1971, 36 and fig 17). *See also* Biddle 1990, 839.

102 Ibid, 565, for changes in pin manufacture in the 19th century. The range of pins is consistent with those published by Allan (1984a, 345); *qv* for discussion of pins.

103 For example, Egan and Pritchard 1991, 299.

104 The remaining unpublished objects comprise rings, wire twists, two amorphous lead objects and several modern objects including a spoon handle and buttons. These are listed in the archive reports.

105 Indicating a post-medieval type (Allan 1984a, 345).

106 Holmes n d, 2–3.

107 Allan 1984a, fig 194, nos 211–17.

108 Blanche M A Ellis, Candlespur, Acrise, Folkestone, Kent CT18 8LW.

109 A curvilinear gully in the eastern half of the hall (Fig 12.2, phase 8; *see also* Blaylock 1991a, 18 and fig 11); the fill is of mid-18th-century or later date.

110 National Maritime Museum, London.

111 Sotheby Parke Bernet and Co, London sale, 10 February 1977, Lot 177.

112 The fill of a shallow pit, 1526 (Fig 4.19), containing structural debris of the late 18th- and 19th-century demolition (that is, phase 8); also the fragment of sculpture, catalogue no. 103 (below).

113 Mynard 1969, 80–1 and fig 11.

114 Bridgewater 1969, 454 and 453, fig 6, where despite its context and its typically 16th-century form, it was described as 'residual'.

115 Stoyle 1995, 19 and figs 25–7; Ponsford 1992, 115–6.

116 For example, the variation in relationship of weight to diameter here and elsewhere; *see* Winchester, where the standard diameter appears to be 17mm (Biddle 1990, 1070); also Sandal Castle, Yorkshire (Mayes and Butler 1983, 261); and Beeston Castle, Cheshire (Ellis 1993, 159).

117 Courtney 1988, 3, which suggests that a shot mould was a part of general equipment, to produce shot when central supplies ran out; *see also* finds from Beeston Castle (Ellis 1993, 158–9).

118 Glynis Edwards, Centre for Archaeology, English Heritage, Fort Cumberland, Eastney, Hants PO4 9LD (formerly the Ancient Monuments Laboratory).

119 Thornton 1973.

120 Alison Hopper-Bishop, Keeper of Conservation, RAM Museum, Exeter EX4 3RX.

121 Crowfoot *et al* 1992, 80.

122 Norman Shiel, Exeter School, Manston Terrace, Exeter EX2 4NS.

123 From the fill of post-pipe 680 associated with the phase 2 building beneath the south range (Fig 4.4), therefore, relating to the removal of the post and probably to the destruction phase of the building.

124 North 1991, 84.

125 One cent, Netherlands, 1916; small find no. 87; from context 2007, a feature in the topsoil of the central courtyard (Blaylock 1991a, fig 6). Copper-alloy disc, ?modern coin, totally illegible; small find no. 118; from context 2117, topsoil layer in the central courtyard (ibid, 14). Farthing 1875; small find no. 282; from context 2279, modern pipe trench (ibid, fig 14). Small find no. 94 is recorded as a coin but without context, description or identification.

126 Allan 1984a, 263.

127 Archive plan 818, Blaylock 1991a, fig 14.

128 Diamond cutting replaced grozing in the late 16th century according to Knight (1996, 271).

129 Rather than, for instance, being interpreted as a sign of limited literacy. Stone (1969, 109–12) estimates that the literacy rate for artisans and tradesmen in the mid-18th century was in the region of 85 per cent and Lucombe added a firm and confident signature to his lease of 1740 (CRO CF2605).

130 Barry Knight, Collections Conservation Team, English Heritage, 23 Savile Row, London W1X 1AB.

131 The typology is that used by Knight 1983–4, 49–51.

132 Egan *et al* 1986, 303–9.

133 Geoff Egan, pers comm.

134 Similarly massive pintles observed in 'Bishop Brewer's' doorway at Exeter Cathedral (late 12th century) on their removal in 1992 had barbs cut into the arrises of the shank, presumably for the same purpose (EMAFU archive photographs: B&W 3041/7–28).

135 A possible provenance is from one of the hall windows, although no pintles were recorded by Morley (1979) or in the site finds book.

136 Note that nos 58–60 are not pintles, as the vertical sections are rectangular in section rather than round; *see also* the pintles and fixed hooks published from London, Egan 1998, 43–6 and 52–5.

137 Formerly on display in the great hall, recovered from there 16 February 1995.

138 The flattened and splayed vertical of this example is paralleled by a holdfast from Preston Street, Exeter, dated 1550–1600 (Allan 1984a, 337 and fig 189, 14).

139 A further seventy-eight hand-made nails were recovered from the excavations of 1977–8, but these were discarded and are not considered here (*see* Blaylock 1991a, 44, Appendix VI by J P Allan).

140 As with some other classes of material, the distribution was skewed in favour of the south and west ranges; the east range and east end of the south range, dismantled under a different regime, remain poorly represented in the collection.

141 From the fill of a pit of phase 5 (741, Fig 4.18, section 9).

142 From an occupation layer of phase 6 (Fig 4.15, 688, and Fig 4.18, section 9).

143 From a soil layer of phase 8 in the eastern courtyard (Fig 4.17, 1028, section 4).

144 Jenkins 1972, 111–12; Bodey 1983, 12–14.

145 Salzman 1952, 306–7.

146 Sometimes called a rose head (Noël Hume 1991, 252 and fig 81).

147 Sometimes called a chisel point, used to avoid splitting of the timber (Tomlinson 1852–4, 308; Mercer 1929, 235).

148 Salzman 1952, 305–6.

149 According to Bodey (1983, 21), cut nails were pioneered in the early 19th century.

150 Hall 1996, 330–1; Friedmann 1946.

151 Ferguson 1961, 19.

152 Friedmann 1946, 1.

153 Ibid, 3.

154 For example, the early 14th-century De Lisle Psalter, Alexander and Binski 1987, 452.

155 Cheetham 1984, 191–3.

156 Stone 1955, 225 and plate 184.

157 Cave 1948, 41–2; illustrated at Chester and Worcester, plates 72 and 284.

158 Radford 1907, 147 and 152; Cherry and Pevsner 1989, 280.

159 I am very grateful to Jane Harcourt for information about this fragment and its context at Muchelney.

160 Shelmerdine 1879, 1078; 1881, 833.

161 Ibid.

162 Ibid.

163 Cheetham 1984, 42 and 296.

164 Ibid, 296–310.

165 Cave 1948, 23; plates 71 and 118.

166 *Inter alia*, Clayton 1968, 139 and plates 31, 40 and 55.

167 Drake 1913, plate 5; Cave 1948, plate 165.

168 Cave 1948, plate 180.

169 Ibid, 24 and plate 272.

170 Cherry and Pevsner 1989, 803.

171 Orme 1986, 30 ff; Erskine, Hope and Lloyd 1988, 51.

172 For other ornament of the period, *see* Blaylock 1986, 102–4 and Rose-Troup 1932–3, opposite 152; it has to be admitted that these sculptors were more at ease with low-relief architectural decoration than with figure sculpture in the round.

173 Blaylock 1990, 137–9.

174 Cox 1957, 172.

175 Cheetham 1984, 18 and 28.

176 Ibid, 30 and fig 18; Panofsky 1953, fig 213.

177 The site finds book records several architectural fragments and their provenances, but the general descriptions ('moulded/carved stone' and such like) are now insufficient for identification: 23 April 1980; 28 May 1980 (× 2); 16 June 1981 (× 2).

178 The piece was extracted in February 1980, according to the DoE finds register in the site archive. It is possible that the two string-course fragments, nos 104 and 105 (otherwise unprovenanced), also came from this blocking. The secondary usage/limewashing might support this interpretation.

179 Unfortunately this block was mislaid during finds processing before it could be drawn or photographed. Despite extensive searches it has not been relocated and thus cannot be illustrated here. It is hoped that the piece will eventually be rediscovered (the most likely explanation of its loss is that it was inadvertently stored with material from another site).

180 The deposit contained 116 (109 intact) of the total sample of 138 slates; seventeen oak 'helling' pins; twenty barbed pegs (of uncertain function, below); seven iron nails; 295g of lead run molten out of a crucible and solidified into amorphous shapes; a mass of tangled window cames, 1735g in weight (above); c180 sherds of window glass varying in size from splinters to nearly whole quarries (including some with graffiti, above); and various other finds.

181 Chapter 4 and Chapter 7 n 47.

182 I am very grateful to Dr Brian Selwood for examining the slates and providing the identifications.

183 Allan 1984a, fig 169; Durrance and Laming 1982, fig 4.3.

184 Samples were not kept from the large deposits of smashed slates in the courtyard (above).

185 One or more complete measurement was obtainable from 131 slates, although key elements were often missing.

186 Cox and Thorp 1991, 7.

187 These increments may be too small and intervals of half an inch are more likely. Boyle indicated that slates in a given size range should not vary by more than half an inch in length (1955, 12).

188 A range of 7" to 18" (175–455mm) is quoted by Boyle (1955, 12), although this is the *full* length of the slate, rather than the length tail to peg hole. *See also* Jope and Dunning 1954, 211–12 and Allan 1984a, 301–2.

189 Possibly because larger slates from the lower part of the roof were more easily reused.

190 The most common thickness was 5mm (37 examples); the majority were 4–7mm (103 examples).

191 I am grateful to Philip Hughes for the latter suggestion.

192 Two examples are published (nos 128 and 130); four more remain in the archive. The opposite effect, of shaping for a hip, was not noted.

193 Cox and Thorp 1991, 5.

194 The perpend or 'perp' in practical terminology.

195 Suggesting that the mortar was applied to the lower course of slate and the upper course laid onto it (rather than being applied to the bed of the slate prior to placing it in position).

196 Since the portion of the slate above the peg hole is ignored, the thicknesses will always be rather greater than this.

197 As much as five, or as little as two-and-a-half slates thick; weathering of the mortar bedding will tend to exaggerate these measurements and the true range is likely to be smaller.

198 Thorp 1996, 292.

199 Cox and Thorp 1991, 6 (quoting Holden 1989, 80); English Heritage 1998b, 10.

200 Boyle 1955, 14; Cox and Thorp 1991, 6. It is possible that Stockdale's view of the west range (Fig 2.6) shows the slate roof slurried in this way.

201 Although examples without weathering could support the opposite contention, that pointing was used as an initial weather-proofing device as much as for repair.

202 The second example not illustrated.

203 Such close-set laths are unnecessary simply for hanging the slates. They may have been set in this way to support the earth plaster sealing the roof in the oversail of the west range.

204 The laths would have been snapped into short sections, between common rafters.

205 The modern riven oak laths used in repairs were 30–45mm in width.

206 For a practical account of the manufacture and use of cleft laths *see* Boyle 1955, 38–9.

207 Salzman 1952, 234–5; Erskine 1983, 225–6 and *passim*; Cox and Thorp 1991, 4 and 5–6. Payments for 'helling pins' are widespread, along with the purchase of other roofing materials in the Exeter City Receivers' accounts in the late 15th and 16th centuries (transcripts by P R Staniforth for EMAFU).

208 Other factors are also significant (diameter, for instance), but this division gives a rough idea of the requirements for different sizes in an average roof. Boyle's account of the practice of slating describes pegs of a standard length of 2"/51mm (Boyle 1955, 14).

209 Detailed lists are lodged in the site archive.

210 Among which a slate of 9¾" length has a peg of only 30mm length, two of 9" pegs of 23 and 25mm and one of 8½" a peg of 28mm length.

211 Contra Cox and Thorp 1991, 5, who imply that pegs are unlikely to last for more than 100–150 years.

212 There were no finds of this nature from the roof of the east range and from bays 1–4 of the roof of the south range, dismantled in 1980 and 1985–6 respectively, presumably because the detritus filling cavities in the roof in these areas of the building was discarded without inspection.

213 Plus one specimen of a modern peg as used in the repairs.

214 Where timbers were dismantled for repair the pegs were invariably replaced on reassembly. This practice means that relatively few original pegs survive in the building.

215 Brunskill 1994, 127.

216 Rufford Old Hall, Lancashire provides good examples of this in both exterior and interior contexts (Wood 1965, plate 25d). Although the timber framing has been repaired extensively, the distinctive projecting pegs are shown in a sketch by Buckler of 1817, which antedates any repairs (Dean 1991, 51). The group of three early 14th-century roofs at Bury Barton, Lapford, Rudge, Morchard Bishop, and Thorne, Clannaborough, also illustrates the use of long (untrimmed) pegs left projecting from the principal trusses (Hulland 1980, 133–4; *see also* Beacham 1990, 18).

217 Some of these side shoots seem incapable of supporting any weight (even when green).

218 Less than 45mm, four examples; 45–60mm, twenty-seven; 66–75mm, nine; plus one exceptionally long peg: 93mm.

219 Boyle 1955, 14.

220 Two loose window frames (nos 136 and 137), for instance, can be assigned a provenance in the demolished barn.

221 Chapters 1 and 11; *see also* Harrison 1995a, 24.

222 In the early years of the repair programme a quantity of ancient timber was brought into the site for reuse in the Bowhill repairs (Chapter 10). Appreciable quantities of medieval and 18th- to 19th-century oak from elsewhere in the country have found their way into the building by this means. When planed down, this timber appears very similar to the new oak and the record drawings of the carpenters in the middle 1980s (when the bulk of this timber was used) are thus a crucial part of the site

archive. This factor also has implications for the integrity of the site in relation to any future dendrochronological analysis (*see also* Chapter 11).

223 A window (no. 136; Fig 9.23) and a door-frame (no. 140; Fig 9.25) are now in the collections of the RAM Museum, Exeter; otherwise all this material is stored at the EH regional store at Toddington, Gloucestershire.

224 Lomas 1974, 136.

225 Alcock and Hulland 1972, plate 5.

226 MS note by Stephen Dunmore added to the archive copy of Morley 1979, 'beam 4'.

227 Alcock and Hall 1994, figs 32–3; for example, in the Manor House Hotel, Cullompton, presumably early 17th century, or in buildings in Fore Street, Silverton, of a variety of dates.

Chapter 10

1 Cathy Groves, Sheffield Dendrochronology Laboratory, Research School of Archaeology and Archaeological Science, Department of Archaeology and Prehistory, University of Sheffield, West Court, 2 Mappin Street, Sheffield S1 4DT.

2 Groves 2002a.

3 Blaylock, pers comm.

4 Hillam, pers comm 1982; Hillam 1991a.

5 Ibid.

6 Hillam, pers comm 1996.

7 Groves forthcoming a.

8 *See* in particular, Groves forthcoming a.

9 English Heritage 1998a; details of dendrochronological principles and techniques are also discussed in, for example, Baillie 1982 and 1995; Eckstein *et al* 1984; Schweingruber 1988.

10 Tyers 1997a; Groves 1997.

11 Hillam *et al* 1987.

12 Leuschner and Leuschner 1996; Groves 2000.

13 Tyers 1997b.

14 Baillie and Pilcher 1973; Munro 1984.

15 Baillie and Pilcher 1973.

16 Baillie 1982, 82–5.

17 Baillie *et al* 1985; Hillam *et al* 1987; Wazny and Eckstein 1991.

18 For example, Rackham 1990.

19 Groves forthcoming a.

20 Where possible sample numbers are linked to the timber archive catalogue numbers (Table 10.1).

21 Schweingruber 1990.

22 Blaylock, pers comm.

23 Tyers *et al* 1997; Groves forthcoming a.

24 Milne 1992, 15.

25 Tyers, pers comm.

26 Hillam 1991a.

27 Tyers 1998a.

28 For example, Baillie *et al* 1985; Eckstein *et al* 1986; Hillam *et al* 1987; Klein and Wazny 1991; Wazny and Eckstein 1991; Wrobel, pers comm 1993.

29 Tyers 1998a.

30 Wazny and Eckstein 1991.

31 Baillie 1982, 56–7.

32 The discussion addresses a series of points raised during the analysis or in response to comments from Stuart Blaylock, Francis Kelly and Nat Alcock.

33 Francis Kelly, pers comm.

34 Groves forthcoming a.

35 Tyers *et al* 1997; Groves forthcoming a.

36 Tyers 1993a; 1997c.

37 Laxton *et al* 1989; Pearson 1994.

38 MS addition by Stephen Dunmore to Morley 1979.

39 Tyers 1991.
40 Lewis 1995; Miles and Haddon-Reece 1996.
41 Hillam 1991b.
42 Dollinger 1970; Fedorowicz 1980; Clarke 1992.
43 Salzman 1952, 206.
44 For example, Bonde *et al* 1997.
45 Salzman 1952, 245.
46 Bonde and Jensen 1995; Bonde *et al* 1997.
47 G Simpson, pers comm, 1999.
48 Groves 1992.
49 Hillam 1991b; Tyers 1998a.
50 Tyers 1991; 1994a; 1996a.
51 Howard *et al* 1992; Miles and Haddon-Reece 1995.
52 Tyers 1998b.
53 Esling *et al* 1990; Howard *et al* 1993.
54 Howard *et al* 1995.
55 Howard *et al* 1991; Miles, pers comm, 1998.
56 Lewis 1995.
57 Fletcher and Morgan 1981; Groves 2002b.
58 Crone 1998; Crone and Fawcett 1998; Mills and Crone 1998.
59 Bonde *et al* 1997.
60 Zunde 1998.
61 For example, Fletcher 1980; Lavier and Lambert 1996; Tyers 1998b.
62 For example, Fletcher 1980; Lavier and Lambert 1996; Tyers 1998b.
63 Tyers 1991.
64 Heymanowski 1979.
65 Groves forthcoming a; Tyers 1993a and pers comm.
66 *See below*, Howard, this chapter.
67 English Heritage 1998a.
68 Groves forthcoming a.
69 Robert Howard, Robert Laxton and Cliff Litton, Nottingham University Tree-Ring Dating Laboratory, University Park, Nottingham NG7 2RD.
70 Howard, R E, Laxton, R R and Litton, C D *Cadhay House, Ottery St Mary, Devon: A Brief Report on the Assessment of the Timbers as to their suitability for Tree-Ring Dating*, typescript report to AML, dated July 1999; copy in project archive.
71 Howard *et al* 1999a; 1999b; 2000a; 2000b.
72 Howard *et al* 1999a, fig 7.
73 Howard *et al* 2000a, figs 5–6.
74 Litton and Zainodin 1991.
75 *See*, for instance, Blaylock 1990, 131.
76 Howard *et al* 2000b, fig 7.
77 Howard *et al* 1999b, figs 5a and 5b.
78 Blaylock 1990, 129–34.
79 *See* Blaylock 1990, 131–4, for an earlier discussion of the dating and sequence of the group.
80 English Heritage 1998a; Laxton and Litton 1988.
81 The one exception is described separately below.
82 A parallel collection of sixty-two samples of mortar, plaster and cob was taken in 1980 by Stephen Dunmore and John Evans (of the then North-East London Polytechnic); the present collection duplicates and enlarges the range of this early collection, although it was not able to cover the fabric of the east range, where conservation work was completed in 1987, before the collection of the later series of samples began. Enquiries in 1997 led to the conclusion that the 1980 samples had been discarded some time prior to 1990.
83 Blaylock 1995, 88.
84 Based on initial sampling and sorting of mortar samples by Keith Westcott in 1987, augmented and refined by further sampling during the later works. Twelve classes of material have been identified, of which the first nine can be specifically related to phases of work in the building. Some subdivision is attempted for the larger classes (1, 7, 10 and 12); individual samples are identified by the feature number (*see* the elevation drawings). No attempt has been made to subdivide the cob samples on the basis of composition. Although there is some variation in colour and visible composition, much of the cob is visually indistinguishable. Full lists and descriptions of the mortar samples are deposited in the project archive; *see also* Harrison 1999 for cob.
85 Blaylock 1990, 146. The purchase of hair for plaster and daub is recorded by Salzman (1952, 190–2), but apparently only in 16th-century sources; it would be interesting to establish if this date for the introduction of the use of hair extends beyond Devon.
86 This distinctive plaster was also seen over the scar at the base of the northern arch brace of roof truss VII, which was crudely hacked away at this time, perhaps for a ceiling.
87 This type of red sandy mortar was ubiquitous in the Exeter region as late as the end of the 19th century.
88 This was a bulk sample from an excavated mortar floor; *see* the brief report on its analysis, p 281.
89 The area is illustrated in a series of detailed photographs taken when this was observed in July 1993: refs EH 933522–933527 (in archive).
90 Stead *et al* 1994, 22.
91 Not illustrated, *see* archive section 67, fig 5.
92 The fill of the large defensive ditch of phase 6 (Fig 4.15, 1024) filled in phases 7–8 (Fig 4.17, section 4).
93 Not illustrated, *see* archive section 72; Stead *et al* 1994, fig 5.
94 *See* the late 16th- and early 17th-century examples described and illustrated by Thorp (1990a, 134–7 and ff).
95 *See* the comment on hair in plaster, above, class 5.
96 Hall and Blaylock 1994, 2, 19, and fig 3 for plan of extent.
97 Letter and report dated 23 September 1996. Mr Teychenné also comments that the aggregate was 'virtually the same in colour, type, particles and fines' as a sample of medieval mortar recently analysed from the Exeter city wall. This provides an interesting hint of objective support for the similarity of good-quality lime mortars in Exeter, whatever their date, outlined above. I am grateful to Geoffrey Teychenné and to M J Baldwin (Architect for Exeter City Council) for information about these analyses.

Chapter 11

1 Until 1984 the Inspectorate reported, via the Chief Inspector, to the (internal) Ancient Monuments Board; this was replaced by the Ancient Monuments Advisory Committee, responsible to the Commissioners of English Heritage.
2 There was debate as to whether or not the ground around the building should be scheduled. When the DoE bought the building in 1976, guardianship or ownership by the State was the highest accolade and form of protection, superseding listing and scheduling. The intervention of the DAMHB, with its full panoply of cultural and technical advice and its dedicated work force, was taken to mean that Bowhill would be preserved and displayed in an exemplary manner as one of the nation's museum pieces. This lies behind the apparently nonchalant lack of concern to obtain Planning Permission for the remodelling of the lean-to extension to the north. While Crown Exemption was clearly a relevant factor, in fact the architects and inspectors, as curators of the nation's heritage, pursued an independent line as it were in the best interests of the site. Scheduling procedures in train at the site were discontinued to allow marketing in 1995. In the light of PPGs 15 and 16 it is now considered that normal Listed Building procedures are sufficient to control matters at Bowhill.

3 The reason stems from the 'Office of Works' management practice for Directly Employed Labour employed at the site. Bowhill was one among a number of buildings in the area worked on concurrently by small teams of craftsmen and labourers. It was not considered a priority site. Fabric was repaired and conserved in discrete sections starting with the east range, moving next to the south range and lastly to the west range and south-west annexe (Harrison 1995a, 21ff).

4 The file note of February 1983 containing this estimate is interesting for the light it sheds on Ancient Monument job management practice of the time:

...In the absence of any guidance on the likely number of D.E.L. that will be made available to work on the site it has been assumed that the work will be continued with staff at the present level, together with some back up from contractors where this is suitable. Because of the complex nature of the building and the peculiarities of its construction this is essentially a D.E.L. site. Should however it be handed over to a contractor there would be a need for daily site supervision by someone well versed and experienced in A.M. techniques and methods (DoE file AA 75549/2B).

5 The plans, elevations and sections of the building submitted to the Local Authority as part of a Planning Application *c* 1968 (the only drawn documentation from this period), show the cross wall as retained. Its subsequent removal thus took place without the consent of the Local Authority or of the DoE.

6 Morley 1979.

7 The philosophical background to this fundamental intervention is examined elsewhere (Harrison 1995a, 16–19); twenty years on, of course, the decision would have been different.

8 Speaking of these observations and conclusions Morley noted: 'It is hoped that they will help towards formulating a policy for the display of the building to the general public by indicating what evidence remains in the structure for the planning of the building as originally built' (Morley 1979, introduction). The production of such an explicit written assessment of a monument was itself an unusual step at the time.

9 Slade and Dunmore 1981.

10 Morley argued that partition replacement should be done in a clearly modern way (Harrison 1995a, 19). Reconstruction, both in spatial terms and in construction detail, can of course be carried out in a number of different ways. For instance (as first proposed by Morley), by the use of 'modern' design and where appropriate 'modern' materials in 'contrast' with the historic fabric. Alternatively traditional precedent may be followed, 'in sympathy' with the historic spaces, both in design and materials. The latter course was quickly settled on. The pattern, once set, was generally maintained (for the arguments behind this choice, *see* Harrison 1995a). Justification of reinstatement on the grounds of structural need and didactic intelligibility was (and sometimes is still) promoted by those charged with conservation (Brereton 1995, 5–6; *see* below, n 48). This approach was at the root of the 1981 programme and, while the academic justification of some of the results might be questioned in detail, the proposals were based on close observation and experience. Inevitably some aspects were conjectural and therefore remain questionable.

11 Given the large amount of alteration over the years before acquisition and the more cavalier approach to conservation then prevalent, it was inevitable that some works were based on assumption. This approach was in part influenced by contemporary *Monuments Historiques* practice in France. Its elevation of the presentation of the finished product through restoration and reinstatement above its preservation (that is, the 'theatre of display') was by then in contrast with mainstream British conservation philosophy that puts preservation above presentation. The DEL had a long history of working in this way and the best among them were expert in 'displaying the evidence' in consolidation works.

12 Members of the DEL, generally familiar with the techniques of repair 'display', were regularly entrusted with the detailed management of this aspect of the works. A significant disadvantage of the 'repair forms its own record' approach, which at Bowhill extended from 1983 to 1987, is that information about items of importance coming to light during works and subsequently destroyed, damaged, amended or concealed may only survive in the memory of those who dealt with them at the time. For this reason the DEL site managers, either the Superintendents of Works or the Chargehands, would arrange professional photographic records of work in progress, often with advice from the Inspectorate. Valuable informal photographs have also survived, taken by the DEL and others. It was for the same reason that, at the start of the Stage 2 works in 1987, professional archaeological investigation and reporting were formally integrated into the conservation process at Bowhill, to a level not usual before that on Guardianship sites.

13 Slade and Dunmore 1981. They go on to state:

In summary, both the medieval emphasis and the policy of reconstruction seem to us to be essential if this particular building is to be properly consolidated and displayed. This is largely because the depredations of the 1960s stripped the interior of both its medieval and sixteenth/seventeenth century details and layouts. What is left of sixteenth/seventeenth century modifications makes so little sense, that it seems reasonable to return to an almost exclusively medieval interpretation.

There was a history to this particular approach; other Guardianship examples of the time were works to the churches of the Greyfriars and the Blackfriars in Gloucester. Inevitably, the attempt to return to an earlier stage of development by removal of later alterations frequently led to difficulties and contradictions, whose resolution was neither academically correct nor satisfactory in practical terms.

14 Based on a misunderstanding of the evidence in the Buck drawing of Bowhill. There had originally been a stair in a vice at this point, serving the first-floor room over the porch.

15 DoE file AA 75549/2B, 21 May 1981.

16 Ibid, November/December 1982, including a plan.

17 As had recently been done at Kirkham House, Paignton, Devon, and can still be seen there.

18 Examples are: the use of a modern 'patent' slating system with the new Delabole slates of the hall roof; plaster on Expamet instead of riven lath, to form the hall ceiling between the rafters; and lime/cob instead of cob for some of the works to the hall store. Also of interest are the use of concrete to simulate Permian breccia (now unobtainable) in the hall chimney and in the surround to the north-west doorway of the hall.

19 Kelly 1992. The guidelines note that the complexity of the house was reflected

....not only in the diversity of its building materials but also in the number and type of conservation problems posed by them, by the condition of the house, alterations to it over time and the need to adapt it to fit with late 20th century requirements. There are also still a number of unsolved academic problems, such as the medieval stair arrangements, which will have an effect on use and display (ibid, 2).

On works progress to date it commented that the 'hall range is complete bar the screens passage and doors. It has been "restored", partly from evidence, partly to demonstrate 1970s views on medieval buildings and partly from assumption ...

Partial access to the site is now possible but the details have yet to be finalised'. The dropping of the idea of the site as a custodial operation on completion was reflected in the comment on access: 'Long-term access has yet to be addressed, particularly as the site will not be a custodial one ... Little thought has yet been given to the retention/ adaptation/rebuilding of the South West block which is the 'safety valve' in terms of access, stairs and administration'(ibid).

20 *See below*, notes 24 and 26.

21 During the early 1990s various possible users came forward or were canvassed. For a time, until the Registry Bill (which would have placed family history records under local Registries) was dropped, there was a possibility that the Exeter Register Office might move to the building; the Landmark Trust briefly considered taking it. While funding for the repairs and recording of Bowhill continued, there was by 1996 an increased emphasis on disposal. On completion of the works, the house was marketed and leased to the Devonshire Association in 1997.

22 Alternative stair sites at the east end and south-east corner of the south range were also investigated at this time. The interior of the annexe was in the end preferred as the least visually intrusive and the least historically compromising place for the new stair, its structure being late in date and internally altered.

23 Fitting out was only partially considered in the haste to complete the works. Surface finishes and services were provided to minimise future interventions. In relation to the doors, the Devonshire Association has introduced heavy curtains over doorways; aesthetically a very successful solution.

24 Harrison commented (1995a, 20) that:

> This was an attempt to grasp the nettle of continuing the work in sympathy with the reconstruction already done in the Great Hall in parts of the building where evidence was on the face of it harder to come by. This choice ... perpetuated ... the first-stage approach but in a more cautious and self-consciously managed way. It was applied to most of the south and all the west range works commencing in 1987...

> It reflected a decision to try to present the building as a whole, rather than allowing differing approaches to conservation and restoration to show in different stages of the works. In the case of the pentice, though its overall form was deduced, it can only approximate to the original in materials and detail. In addition, difficulties over obtaining appropriate materials during its fabrication further affected its character.

25 This was considered essential for the sale of the building; the treatment of these spaces will probably eventually need reconsideration to improve the setting of the Grade I building.

26 Harrison 1995a, 25. A key statement on the new approach is given in the 1992 guidelines:

> Current philosophy is to repair conservatively but comprehensively as an Historic Building using traditional materials and techniques both in order to demonstrate the skills of our Directly Employed Labour and to set standards. Some of the earlier restoration proposals will be kept for the sake of consistency but emphasis is now on treat as found and adapt as necessary, sensitively, for beneficial re-use and maximum public access (Kelly 1992, 2).

27 Memo of 14 November 1980.

28 Harrison 1995a, 20.

29 Harrison 1999 plus interim reports of work in progress: Harrison 1992; Harrison 1994 and Harrison 1995b.

30 Francis Kelly's technical notes are deposited with the site archive.

31 Roger Scobie, pers comm.

32 The use of dung in daub had been developed at Leigh Barton, another Devon guardianship site, where a slurry of fresh dung was used to wet the raw soil for the daub.

33 Adam Mackenzie, pers comm.

34 Replacing the former external plaster, plank string, verge boards and windows of *c* 1800 (Fig 2.7). This splendid restoration epitomises the approach of Stage 1 repairs: workaday, historical fabric representing the genuine Exeter vernacular of *c* 1800 (and incorporating reused material, perhaps from demolished elements of the site) was replaced with a high-quality and 'improved' restoration. The slate-hanging reflecting, more than a little, an Arts-and-Crafts-derived pride in natural materials, in this case justifiable for practical weathering purposes, but wholly without precedent. It is interesting that this was done also at the end of the works, on the west gable of the south range (but for different reasons).

35 The brick sleeper wall was raised as at that stage a hall dais was envisaged.

36 The loss of evidence of the panel infilling confirms the hierarchy of value placed on different materials at the time (below, n 41; although this was not consistent, *see* the retention of daub from the oversail of the hall roof over the great chamber).

37 Has there ever been a building contract without mistakes? John 8: 7.

38 During the fixing of the new first-floor boards in the oriel chamber, the original floor hatch was also boarded over (Fig 6.42). Its display as a hatch (originally for a stair or 'coffin hatch') had been envisaged under Stage 1.

39 Harrison 1999, chapter 4.

40 *See* Harrison 1995a, 18.

41 As there was no interruption of the works planned in 1983, the changing conservation strategy could only be adopted piecemeal. The unwritten MoW hierarchy of historic materials (and what was regarded as 'sacrificial') was followed: (from least to most sacrificial) ashlar, rubble, timber, brick, plaster if medieval, painting and bonding agents, vernacular infill materials and armatures. The cultural significance of the last is now accepted.

42 Harrison, 1999, 75–80; and below.

43 The cupboard was a late 20th-century requirement. The archaic method of construction was drawn from reconstruction experience of such original fabric elsewhere at Bowhill and its use was no more or less philosophically justifiable than the use of modern stud and plasterboard would have been.

44 The use of tapered and facetted pegs in the traditional manner was long resisted by the DEL in the South-West Region in the 1980s. It had not always been so, as the remarkable repairs to the roof of the refectory of Cleeve Abbey in Somerset undertaken by MoW in the 1950s demonstrate. An alternative works 'tradition' of the manufacture and use of cylindrical dowels had developed. These were made by preparing oak roughly to a size at which it could be forced through a former – a cast block with holes of various sizes, from which cylindrical dowels of excellent quality would emerge. Sometimes these were soaked in buckets of watered-down Cuprinol. The manufacturing process took longer than making traditional pegs and so was regarded as superior (*see* Rose 1946, 64). Amazingly, at one site, rather than whittle facetted and tapering pegs, subterfuge was resorted to whereby dowels were used with one end left square and the other end worked! This small detail illustrates the relationship of the trusted DEL with their colleagues in Regional management: they had their ways of doing things and they stuck to them. By and large the results were superb; sometimes, one feels, a trick was missed. When they responded to a challenge, as with the cob and daub exercise, the results were undoubtedly superior than would have been possible in the private sector, given universal financial constraints.

45 Another survival of jointed-cruck posts in a lean-to can be seen in the gallery of Kirkham House, Paignton.

46 Harrison 1999, 66–8.

47 Ibid, fig 157.

48 Brereton comments (1995, 5–6) that

> Some elements of a building or monument which are important to its design, for example balustrades, pinnacles, cornices, hoodmoulds, window tracery, and members of a timber frame or roof truss, may have been lost in the past. Where these are of structural significance, they will normally be replaced anyway in the course of repair; but a programme of repair may also offer the opportunity for the reinstatement of missing non-structural elements, provided that sufficient evidence exists for accurate replacement, no loss of historic fabric occurs, and the necessary statutory consents are obtained in advance. Speculative reconstruction is hardly ever justified.

The debate on this issue goes on. It is not uncommon to grant Listed Building Consent for the reintroduction of such features into altered 18th- and early 19th-century houses. Recent Conservation Area Partnership practice agreed between EH and Local Authorities has involved the reintroduction, subject to evidence, of substantial missing original elevational elements such as bay windows to both unlisted and listed buildings receiving public sector grant aid.

49 There is uncertainty about the accuracy of the stops, which may have had forward-facing chamfers rather than run-out stops. As installed, the fireplace was not humoured to the plane of the wall but stands proudly vertical; this vertical misalignment was not disguised.

50 The carving was undertaken by DEL carpenters. It is of good quality and captures some of the spirit of the surviving originals in the great chamber. This is in part due to Harry Slade's encouragement and exhortation.

51 New 'medieval'-style planked doors were made where the medieval idiom was being restored (the instances in the east range already mentioned; the service room and store leading onto the pentice; the south through passage door). Three surviving historic doors (two in the kitchen and one in the parlour, all of 19th-century date) were repaired. Flush-panel doors were used elsewhere.

52 In the event, certain details of this stonework proved inadequate, in failing to follow drawings exactly and the omission of rebates for the door.

53 For the flooring of the hall, see Chapter 4.

54 The wearing capability of this floor may have been acceptable for the museum use originally intended, but it has not proved robust enough for the heavier use to which it is now being put and is to be replaced.

55 A small area of original, cobbled threshold survived here (Fig 4.7, 755), but was not reinstated.

56 The use of these slabs was allowed by the Diocesan registry; they would otherwise have been broken up.

57 The contractors were persuaded to tighten the joints between slabs only after the floor of the west service room had been laid; those in the through passage were more successful.

58 These 'didactic windows' were plastered when the building was marketed and were thus only visible for a short time. Their history illustrates the differences that can sometimes exist between valuer and professional building historian, even within a body such as English Heritage, as well as the uncertainty about the final use of the building that prevailed in the later stages of the work.

59 Harrison 1999, 37–8.

60 In the event, perhaps inevitably, the current user has wanted to do other things, including installing new kitchen services to the west of the parlour and replacing the hall floor; see n 54.

61 It was considered that their omission simplified things and reduced the clutter of 'mod cons'. With the introduction of services two important conservation philosophies come into conflict. One view is that service supply routes, appliances and so on are best hidden so as not to disrupt spatial quality; the other is that historic fabric should not be damaged by chasing for hidden services. In the end, as so often, actual solutions tended to be a compromise of the two views.

62 Storage heaters cannot be claimed as visually unobtrusive in empty room spaces; they will attract less attention in rooms cluttered by use.

63 This scaffold protection was an eyesore for several years and was very unpopular with neighbours.

64 Cuprinol, Wykhamol Plus or similar (Roger Scobie and Adam Mackenzie, pers comm). By the time the timbers of the parlour ceiling were repaired in 1987, changing approaches to the indiscriminate use of pesticides (for environmental and health reasons) entailed a change to the use of Deep Kill (paste) application on completion of repairs. With time, this became more targeted and was abandoned altogether after the completion of works to the great chamber (Ridout 2000, 50–3; 2001; Coleman 2001).

65 The AMDO survey for trusses I–V; photogrammetric survey drawings (with field correction by EMAFU) for trusses VI–XI.

66 Harrison 1995a, 19.

67 With the advantages of allowing retention of the maximum amount of original fabric and of concealing the means of support, while not ruling out full carpentry repairs in the long term (Ashurst and Ashurst 1988, 21). As with other repair systems using resin, the method remains unproven. The evidence shows that it works well in engineering terms, but it is a relatively recent innovation and national long-term, controlled, performance trials being undertaken do not appear to be drawing to a conclusion (DoE 1995).

68 Setchell and Setchell c 1938.

69 Insulation was debated. In Stage 1 the intended quasi-museum use meant it was unnecessary. In Stage 2, it was not possible to include it on account of the quasi-authentic specification.

70 In contrast to the concern with the use of 'original' materials and techniques in the structural roof repairs described above, an inconsistency typical of some aspects of most 'conservation' projects where roofed buildings are involved.

71 The historic daub, when reworked, gave off a haunting smell of hay.

72 Wet-laying had had a bad press as not conforming with 'good building practice' (that bane, indeed too often the death-knell of authenticity) since the mid-20th century on account of costs, the impracticalities of maintenance and concerns about guaranteeing such work (another death-knell to traditional practice).

73 There are other, more recent, examples, such as the Old Library at Dartington. There is now more information available, for example, Green 1995; Bosence 1996. An internal report by Philip Hughes to EH on slating trials at Bowhill is deposited in the archive. Importantly, the EH technical advice note on stone slate roofing (English Heritage 1998b) makes the point that all roofs should be carefully recorded before and during stripping, in such a manner as to ensure that their vernacular is understood, if not necessarily slavishly matched.

74 Cox and Thorp 1991.

75 The word is probably from the French torchis (cob or earth mortar). It and 'torching' are used indiscriminately to mean various more or less patchy vernacular finishes or ceiling applied directly to the underside of the roof covering.

76 Thorp 1996; Philip Hughes's report (above n 73); Chapter 9. This is in contrast to the 'stretched' gauge of the Delabole system which was designed for slating random-slate roofs with

the minimum of dry-laid, centre-nailed slates on sawn battens (as opposed to wet-laid, top-hung slates on split lath with three slates to the pin (or more) to provide a second line of defence if moisture did penetrate).

77 At acquisition beams 2–4 had been supported on temporary props (Fig 6.20); these repairs allowed the beams a clear span again.

78 Ashurst and Ashurst 1988, 19–21.

79 Chapter 6.

80 The render was applied by masons from Berry Pomeroy Castle. There was concern at using their usual 1:3 (putty:sand) mortar mix without adding water and they found the work difficult. Later rendering inside and out was made using a pan-mixer to ensure plasticity.

81 Harrison 1999, 70–2, and fig 181.

82 Ibid, 70–2.

83 Ibid, 73.

84 *See below*, n 95.

85 Tracery reinstatement may relate to the practical need to protect fabric from weather or to the reintroduction of 'enhancing' features. Here, under Stage 1, both concerns played a part. Morley had recorded that originally the upper lights were glazed and the lower lights unglazed (Chapter 6).

86 In this the work differed from that done under Stage 1 where, because of inexperience in the use and uncertainty about the performance of unadulterated cob, it was initially mixed with a liberal amount of hydraulic lime. This approach was partly the result of technical advice. It also reflects the commonly held but erroneous belief that new should be stronger than the original.

87 The variety of techniques and experiment is described in Harrison 1999.

88 Harrison, 1999, 90–3.

89 Ibid, 72–3.

90 Ibid, 73–4.

91 Adam Mackenzie, pers comm.

92 Harrison, 1999, 82. The same, later process was observed and repaired at Leigh Barton, Churchstow, Devon.

93 Ibid, 86 (fig 219).

94 This was, according to the then Regional Superintendent Adam Mackenzie, a new departure for the DEL. It is sound practice for walling of the sort found at Bowhill.

95 On the advice of John Ashurst and as part of a lime day held at Bowhill jointly by EH and The Society for the Protection of Ancient Buildings.

96 Demonstrated by the uneven outer edges of the window dressings.

97 Justification was originally to allow sight of the masonry fabric of the building, but eventually it was decided to leave as found because the masonry was sound and little needed doing to it.

98 Harrison 1999, 84; although there is a hint of two-coat work in a surviving patch on the north wall (described in Chapter 10).

99 Ibid, 93–4.

Chapter 12

1 *See*, for example, the evidence discussed by Groves in Chapter 10.

2 Examples are beam 9 of the south range and the lintels of doorways 270 and 423 (Figs 5.27 and 6.25).

3 For exceptions *see* Chapters 6 and 7.

4 Howard 1987, 108ff; *see also* above, Chapter 8.

5 Cherry and Pevsner 1989, 57 and 487–8.

6 Howard 1987, 37–8.

7 Although the reliability of these dates is variable; for references, *see* above, Chapter 8.

8 The late position of the Bowhill roofs in the chronology of the group suggests the remote possibility that their design might have been influenced by roof carpentry of the earlier, phase 2 house, which was destroyed by fire (it is suggested in the last decade of the 15th century). The 'old-fashioned' nature of the roofs of the phase 3 house might thus have been the result of Roger Holand's wish to replicate features of the earlier house. I owe this suggestion to Francis Kelly.

9 On the death of his father Alexander, in 1493 (Halliday 1953, 311).

10 Date of birth of their son Wymond Carew (Garnett 1992, 5 and 48).

11 Incorporating a post for the support of the ceiling beam (previously supported by the screen; Chapter 6).

12 The table and preliminary discussion of the leases are the work of Nat Alcock; further discussion is by Stuart Blaylock.

13 This was rebuilt as a kitchen/bakehouse in phase 8, representing possible continuity of function. The ceramic dating evidence is unequivocally late 18th century (Chapter 9) and rules out the possibility that the 'new' kitchen structure could have been earlier.

14 Either 'over' in this case is used loosely to mean 'above and next to' or some of the earlier beam sockets in the north half of the kitchen represent a floored chamber (Chapter 6).

15 It is also possible that the south-east range was excluded from this lease, if these rooms were not counted as one with the parlour and chamber (by this time they may have been beyond habitation).

16 Drang is a West-Country dialect word for a narrow alley or passage (Wright 1898, vol 2, 155).

17 Laycock 1920, 165, 189; 1924, 163; Pearse Chope 1918, 269.

18 Informal divisions had been in play for some time, as the evidence of the leases discussed above shows.

Appendix

1 The photographic archive up to 1991 was indexed in the EMAFU archive report on the standing building (Blaylock 1991b, 49–72); this included earlier material from the NMR and the Ancient Monuments Branch. At the time of writing work remained to be done on drawing together of the material from 1991 to 1995 into a consolidated index.

2 *See above*, Chapter 4, n 1.

3 English Heritage 1991.

4 S R Blaylock 'Bowhill, Exeter: Updated Project Design for the Publication of Excavation and Building Recording Work 1977–80 and 1987–95', Exeter Archaeology, for English Heritage, May 1995. This contains a detailed proposal for the plan of this report, proposals for illustrations, as well as planning of time and cost.

5 The 'research objectives' of MAP2.

Glossary

In general I have followed the Council for British Archaeology's *Recording Timber-framed Buildings: An Illustrated Glossary* (Alcock *et al* 1996) for terms for timber framing, joints and so on. The reader is referred to this for standard terminology. For slating terms, *see* Cox and Thorp 1991 (especially p 5). Otherwise a variety of sources is required to cover the material presented here. Works especially relevant are Brunskill 1994, Clifton-Taylor and Ireson 1994, the OED and a variety of specialist publications.

beam filling: Infill of earth or rubble between the top of a wall and the soffit of the roof above (*see* Chapter 7, n 10 for examples).
bed: The lower surface of a roofing slate.
bedding: The mortar in which slates are laid.

came: Lead strip joining individual glass panes of a window.
cob: Earth building material used for mass walling; in contrast to daub (*below*).
cove purlin: Longitudinal timber at the crown of a roof assembly, in this case (in the hall and great chamber roofs) forming the apex of the coving above the collar (*see* Figs 7.6 and 7.13).

daub: Earth building material, especially where laid on laths or timber armatures, in contrast to cob which is used for mass walling.
dovetail: In a halved joint, a wedge-shaped tenon which prevents the joint from pulling apart; the windbraces of the south and west range roofs employ dovetail joints (*see* Figs 7.29, 7.31 and 7.41). For the term bare-faced dovetail, *see* Alcock *et al* 1996, G9 and fig 28j.
dowel: See 'peg'.
draw-bore peg: A technique used to ensure a tight joint in carpentry, in which the holes in the tenon and receiving timber are deliberately misaligned, so that the joint is tightened when the peg is driven home.
dubbing out: The infilling of major irregularities in a wall face before the application of plaster, cognate to daubing (*see* Harrison 1999, 105).

face: The upper surface of a roofing slate.
face halved tenon: Used here for the technique of halving the tenons of adjacent purlins, so that they can be accommodated in a single mortice in a principal rafter (the method of jointing the purlins of the roofs of the south and east ranges; Figs 7.6 and 7.13; *see* Brunskill 1994, 143, and fig d150, and Alcock *et al* 1996, 10).
false hammer beam: Discussed in Chapter 8, n 78.
ferramentum (pl **ferramenta**): Iron grillage on windows to support glass and shutters andprevent entry; ironwork in general.

heavitree stone: Popular local term for Permian breccia, some of which was quarried at Heavitree (Chapter 1, materials).

jointed cruck: Roof truss composed of two timbers: a lower *post* with a curved head (often, as at Bowhill, incorporating a moulded or chamfered termination of an arch brace) jointed into and supporting a *principal rafter* (Figs 7.6 and 7.13). The constructional techniques dispense with a wall plate. The jointed cruck is restricted to the West Country and South Wales (Alcock *et al* 1996, 5–6).

lay board: At the junction of two roofs, a plank laid on top of the common rafters of the first roof to support jack rafters of the overlying roof (which, in turn, support valley boards).

margin: The exposed portion of the slate in a roof.

paviour: A paving stone.
peg: A timber fixing which is facetted and sometimes tapered or pointed in order to secure a joint by gripping the sides of the drilled hole. This is unlike a dowel, which is perfectly cylindrical and designed to hold a mortice and tenon joint together without additional tension.
perpend ('perp'): In slating, the vertical joint between two roofing slates, taken from the common term for vertical joints in masonry (Clifton-Taylor and Ireson 1994, 77).
pozzolan: A setting agent (rather than its strict definition of a volcanic-ash additive to lime mortar. Thus pozzolana or pozzuolana is avoided).

rainwater goods: Guttering, down pipes and so on.
reemy antique: A commercial name for modern reemed glass, usually machine made.
robber trench: Archaeological term for the trench (or other less regular excavation) made by the removal (hence 'robbing') of the stone of wall footings for reuse.

slip tenon: A tenon formed of a loose piece of timber fixed into adjacent mortices in two adjacent timbers, often indicated by two juxtaposed pegs in separate timbers. The technique was widely used in the intermediate trusses at Bowhill (*see* Figs 7.6 and 7.13).
soffit tenon: A form of tenon used for fixing joists to beams throughout the original floor framing of Bowhill, in which the projecting tenon is positioned at the base of the joist level with its soffit. When *housed*, the whole depth of the joist is set into a deepened mortice in the beam (Alcock *et al* 1996, fig 30, l).
stud and panel: Form of partition with planks infilling the gaps between vertical posts, normally set in grooves in the sides of the posts (*see* Fig 8.28); also called plank and muntin (or post and panel) screen, terms avoided as they are less readily intelligible than stud and panel.

tail: The lower edge of a slate.

template: Horizontal timber set in a mass wall (of stone or cob) to support and spread the weight of a vertical timber, often the post of a cruck roof truss (Alcock *et al* 1996, 18).

torching: The ceiling of the soffit of a roof with mortar or plaster to create a flush surface between the rafters and also to secure the slates/laths from below (Chapter 11, n 75).

trimmer: A short timber framing a gap in, for example, joists. Often (as at Bowhill) used for stair openings and trap doors.

vice: Winding stair in a structure attached to a wall or other structure, in this case in the angle of the porch and the east wall of the south range.

References

Three especially relevant works have appeared since work on this book was completed, and it has not been possible to make reference to them within the text: Nicholas Cooper's *The Houses of the Gentry, 1480–1680* (Yale, 1999); Anthony Emery's *Greater Medieval Houses of England and Wales 1300–1500, Volume II: East Anglia, Central England and Wales* (Cambridge, 2000; volume III, dealing with the south and south-west of England, is forthcoming); and Jane Penoyre's 'Medieval Somerset Roofs', *Somerset Archaeol Natur Hist* **141** (1998), 77–89.

Adams, J H 1957 'The Medieval Chapels of Cornwall'. *J Roy Inst Cornwall* New Ser **3**, part 1, 48–65

Airs, M 1995 *The Tudor and Jacobean Country House: A Building History*. Stroud: Alan Sutton

Airs, M (ed) 1994 *The Tudor and Jacobean Great House*. The proceedings of a conference [...] held at the Department for Continuing Education, The University of Oxford, 14–16 January 1994

Alcock, N W 1962 'Houses in an East Devon Parish'. *Rep Trans Devonshire Ass* **94**, 185–232

— 1965 'The Medieval Cottages of Bishop's Clyst, Devon'. *Medieval Archaeol* **9**, 146–53

— 1966a 'Bury Barton, Lapford'. *Rep Trans Devonshire Ass* **98**, 105–31

— 1966b 'The Medieval Buildings of Bishop's Clyst'. *Rep Trans Devonshire Ass* **98**, 132–53

— 1968 'Devon Farmhouses, Part I'. *Rep Trans Devonshire Ass* **100**, 13–28

— 1993 *People at Home, Living in a Warwickshire Village, 1500–1800*. Chichester: Phillimore

Alcock, N W and Barley, M W 1972 'Medieval Roofs with Base-Crucks and Short Principals'. *Antiq J* **52**, 132–68

Alcock, N W, Barley, M W, Dixon, P W and Meeson, R A 1996 *Recording Timber-Framed Buildings: An Illustrated Glossary*. Council for British Archaeology, Practical Handbook in Archaeology **5**: York

Alcock, N W and Hall, L 1994 *Fixtures and Fittings in Dated Houses 1567–1763*. Council for British Archaeology, Practical Handbook in Archaeology **11**: York

Alcock, N W and Hulland, C 1972 'Devonshire Farmhouses, Part IV: Some Medieval Houses in East and North Devon'. *Rep Trans Devonshire Ass* **104**, 35–56

Alcock, N W and Laithwaite, M 1973 'Medieval Houses in Devon and their Modernization'. *Medieval Archaeol* **17**, 100–125

Alexander, J J 1914 'Devon County Members of Parliament, Part III: The Later Plantagenet Period (1399–1485)'. *Rep Trans Devonshire Ass* **46**, 478–96

— 1934 'Third Report on the Parliamentary Representation of Devon'. *Rep Trans Devonshire Ass* **66**, 93–104

Alexander, J and Binski, P (eds) 1987 *Age of Chivalry, Art in Plantagenet England 1200–1400*. London: Royal Academy of Arts

Allan, J P 1984a *Medieval and Post-Medieval Finds from Exeter, 1971–1980*. Exeter Archaeol Rep **3**. Exeter: Exeter City Council and University of Exeter

— 1984b 'The Pottery', in Griffiths, D M and Griffith, F M, 'An Excavation at 39 Fore Street, Totnes'. *Proc Devon Archaeol Soc* **42**, 77–100

— 1985 'The Pottery', in Weddell, P J, 'The Excavation of Medieval and Later Houses at Wolborough Street, Newton Abbot'. *Proc Devon Archaeol Soc* **43**, 102–5

— 1986 'The Pottery, Floor Tiles and Brick', in Weddell, P J, 'The Excavations of Medieval and Later Houses at St Margaret's Chapel, Exmouth'. *Proc Devon Archaeol Soc* **44**, 131–6

— 1988 'The Pottery', in Brown, S W 1988, 80–86

— 1991 'A Note on the Building Stones of the Cathedral', in Kelly, F P (ed) 1991, 10–18

— 1994 *Exeter's Underground Passages*, guidebook. Exeter: Exeter City Museums and Art Gallery

— 1995 'Iberian Pottery Imported into South-West England, *c* 1250–1600', in Gerrard, C M *et al* (eds) 1995, 299–314

Allan, J P and Keen, L 1984 'The Medieval Floor-tiles', in Allan, J P 1984a, 232–47

Allan, J P and Perry, I 1982 'Pottery and Tiles', in Higham, R A *et al* 1982, 86–101

Allan, J P and Thorp, J R L 1990 'The Deanery', in Cooper, N (ed) 1990, 45–7

Amery, J S, Adams, M, Windeatt, E and Tapley Soper, H 1911 'Rocque's Plan of Exeter'. *Devon and Cornwall Notes and Queries* **6**, 240

Anon 1843 'Roof of a Hall or Chapel at Bowhill, in the Parish of St Thomas, Exeter', engraved plate of sections and details of the hall roof, with no accompanying text. *Trans Exeter Diocesan Architectural Soc* **1**, plate 11

Anon 1883 'Proceedings of the Somersetshire Archaeological and Natural History Society during the Year 1882: Thirty-Fourth Annual Meeting'. *Proc Somerset Archaeol and Nat Hist Soc* **28**, 1883, 1–66

Anon 1903 'Bradfield, Devon'. *Country Life* **14**, 26 December 1903, 926–34

Anon 1905 'Horham Hall, Essex'. *Country Life* **18**, 8 July 1905, 18–25

Anon 1913 'The Summer Meeting at Exeter' (Royal Archaeological Institute). *Archaeol J* **70**, 495–557

Anon 1957 'Report on the Summer Meeting of the Royal Archaeological Institute at Exeter in 1957'. *Archaeol J* **114**, 126–84

Anon nd [*c* 1957] *Cadhay*, guidebook. Privately printed, Ottery St Mary, Devon

Archer, M 1997 *Delftware: the Tin-glazed Earthenware of the British Isles*. London: The Stationery Office

Ashurst, J and Ashurst, N 1988 *Practical Building Conservation: English Heritage Technical Handbook, Vol 5: Wood, Glass and Resins and Technical Bibliography*. Aldershot: Gower Technical Press

Ashworth, E 1861 'The Ancient Manor House of Weare Giffard'. *Trans Exeter Diocesan Architectural Soc* **6**, 151–7

Attwood, J S 1886 'Bowhill, near Exeter'. *The Western Antiquary* **6**, 51

Austin, J C 1994 *British Delft at Williamsburg*. Williamsburg, USA: Colonial Williamsburg Foundation

Baillie, M G L 1977a 'The Belfast Oak Chronology to AD 1001'. *Tree Ring Bulletin* **37**, 1–12

— 1977b 'Dublin Medieval Dendrochronology'. *Tree Ring Bulletin* **37**, 13–20

— 1982 *Tree-Ring Dating and Archaeology*. London: Croom Helm

— 1995 *A Slice Through Time*. London: Batsford

Baillie, M G L, Hillam, J, Briffa, K R and Brown, D M 1985 'Re-dating the English Art-historical Tree-ring Chronologies'. *Nature* **315**, 317–19

Baillie, M G L and Pilcher, J R 1973 'A Simple Crossdating Program for Tree-ring Research'. *Tree Ring Bulletin* **33**, 7–14

Baldwin, M and Spittle, S D T 1957 'Architectural Note' [to Coate 1957, qv]. *Archaeol J* **114**, 162–3

Barber, J 1973 'Yogge's House or Prysten House'. *Rep Trans Devonshire Ass* **105**, 75–86

Barker, P A 1977 *Techniques of Archaeological Excavation*. London: Batsford

Barley, M W 1961 *The English Farmhouse and Cottage*. London: Routledge and Kegan Paul

— 1963 'A Glossary of Names for Rooms in Houses of the Sixteenth and Seventeenth Centuries', in Foster, I L L and Alcock, L (eds) 1963, 479–501

Barnwell, P S and Adams, A T 1994 *The House Within: Interpreting Medieval Houses in Kent*. London: RCHME

Beacham, P 1989 'Rural Building 1400–1800', in Cherry, B and Pevsner, N 1989, 62–78

Beacham, P (ed) 1990 *Devon Building, an Introduction to Local Traditions*. Exeter: Devon Books

Beard, G 1990 *The National Trust Book of the English House Interior*. London: The National Trust

Becker, B 1981 'Fällungsdaten Römischer Bauhölzer'. *Fundberichte aus Baden-Wurtemberg* **6**, 369–86

Benson, J W *c* 1959 'A Devon Armoury'. Unpublished ms in Devon and Cornwall Record Society Library, WSL, Exeter

Besley 1853 *West of England Pocket Book or Gentleman's Diary with an Almanack, 1853*. Exeter: Henry Besley

Besley 1881 *Besleys Post Office Directory of Exeter and Suburbs for 1881*. Exeter: Henry Besley

Besley 1919 *Besleys Directory of Exeter and Suburbs 1919*. Exeter: Besley & Copp

Besley 1920 *Besleys Directory of Exeter and Suburbs 1920*. Exeter: Besley & Copp

Biddle, M 1990 *Object and Economy in Medieval Winchester, Artefacts from Medieval Winchester*, 2 vols. Winchester Studies 7 **ii**. Oxford: Oxford University Press

Bidwell, P T 1979 *The Legionary Bath-House and Basilica and Forum at Exeter*. Exeter Archaeol Rep **1**. Exeter: Exeter City Council and University of Exeter

Bishop, H C, Collings, A G and Henderson, C G 1994 *An Archaeo-Historical Assessment of The Presentation of Mary Convent School Buildings and Grounds, Palace Gate, Exeter*. EMAFU Rep **94.01**

Bishop, H E and Prideaux, E K 1922 *The Building of the Cathedral Church of St Peter in Exeter*. Exeter: James G Commin

Blaylock, S R 1985 'An Architectural Survey of the Late Medieval Hall at Plymouth Gin Distillery'. *Proc Devon Archaeol Soc* **43**, 121–5

— 1986 'A Survey of Greenway's Porch at St Peter's Church, Tiverton'. *Proc Devon Archaeol Soc* **44**, 85–105

— 1987 *Observations in the Bishop's Palace, Exeter, 1985*. EMAFU Rep **87.03**

— 1988 *Tiverton Castle: Observations in the Gatehouse Tower, 1988*. EMAFU Rep **88.10**

— 1990 'Exeter Guildhall'. *Proc Devon Archaeol Soc* **48**, 123–78

— 1991a *Bowhill, Exeter: Archive Report II, The Excavation of 1977–78*. EMAFU Rep **91.06**

— 1991b *Bowhill, Exeter: Archive Report III, The Building Recording 1987–90*. EMAFU Rep **91.07**

— 1991c *St Katherine's Priory, Polsloe: Fabric Survey of the West Range, 1979–80*. EMAFU Rep **91.57**

— 1993 *Archaeological Observations at the Deanery, Exeter, 1993*. EMAFU Rep **93.72**

— 1995 *Exeter City Wall Survey, 1994*. EA Rep

— 1998 *Observations During Rebuilding Work at Higher Thornham, Romansleigh, Devon, 1997*. EA Rep **98.07**

Blaylock, S R and Henderson, C G (eds) 1987 *Archaeology in Exeter 1985/6*. Exeter: EMAFU

Blaylock, S R and Norton, J 1991 *Bowhill, Exeter: Archive Report IV, The Screens-Passage Excavation of 1989*. EMAFU Rep **91.08**

Bodey, H 1983 *Nailmaking*. Princes Risborough: Shire Album **87**

Bonde, N and Jensen, J S 1995 'The Dating of a Hanseatic Cog-find in Denmark' *in* Olsen, O, Madsen, J S and Riech S (eds) *Shipshape, Essays for Ole Crumlin-Pederson*. Roskilde, 103–22

Bonde, N, Tyers, I and Wazny, T 1997 'Where Does the Timber Come From? Dendrochronological Evidence of the Timber Trade in Northern Europe' *in* Sinclair, A *et al* (eds) 1997, 201–4

Bosence, O 1996 'Report on Leigh Barton Slate Exemplar'. Unpublished typescript report to English Heritage. Totnes: Bosence and Forrester

Boswijk, G and Tyers, I 1997 *Tree-ring Analysis of Booth Hall and 16–18 High Town, Hereford*. AML Rep **101/97**

Boyle, V C 1955 'Scantle Roofs'. *Devon and Cornwall Notes and Queries* **26**, 10–15 and 37–40

Brain, P and Brain, R nd [*c* 1985] *Disappearing Devon*. Instow, Devon: Roundabout Devon Books

Brereton, C 1995 *The Repair of Historic Buildings: Advice on Principles and Methods*, 2nd edn. London: English Heritage

Bridge, M 1993 'List 52 – London Guildhall University Tree-ring Dates'. *Vernacular Architect* **24**, 48–50

Bridgewater, N P 1969 'The Manor of Tretire'. *Trans Woolhope Naturalists' Field Club* **39**, part 3, 447–55

Bristow, C R, Edwards, R A, Scrivener, R C and Williams, B J 1985 *Geology of Exeter and its Environs* (Geological Report for DoE). Exeter: British Geological Survey

Brockett, A 1977 *The Devon Union List, a Collection of Written Material relating to the County of Devon*. Exeter: Exeter University Library

Brown, D H and Vince, A G 1984 'Petrological Aspects; the Pottery of Exeter under the Microscope' *in* Allan, J P 1984a, 32–4

Brown, S W 1988 'Excavations and Building Recording at Buckfast Abbey, Devon'. *Proc Devon Archaeol Soc* **46**, 13–89

— 1991 *Excavations on the Medieval Exe Bridge, St Edmund's Church and Frog Street Tenements, Exeter 1975–9*. EMAFU Rep **91.52**

— 1996 'Berry Pomeroy Castle'. *Proc Devon Archaeol Soc* **54**, 1–335

— 1998 'Recent Building Recording and Excavations at Leigh Barton, Churchstow, Devon' *Proc Devon Archaeol Soc* **56**, 5–108

Brown, S W and Laithwaite, J M W 1993 'Northwood Farm, Christow: An Abandoned Farmstead on the Eastern Fringe of Dartmoor'. *Proc Devon Archaeol Soc* **51**, 161–84

Brunskill, R W 1994 *Timber Building in Britain*, revised edn. London: Gollancz

Bulloch, J M 1933 'The Ancestors of Chinese Gordon'. *Notes and Queries* **164**, February 11 1933, 93–5; plus further comment by anonymous author in same volume, February 25 1933, 140–41

Burke, B and Burke, A P 1937 *Burke's Peerage and Baronetage*, 95th edn. London: Burke's Peerage

Caldwell, J and Proctor, M 1969 *Grounds and Gardens of the University of Exeter*. Exeter: University of Exeter

Caldwell, J and Wilkinson, J 1953 'The Exeter Oak-Quercus Lucombeana Sw'. *Rep Trans Devonshire Ass* **85**, 35–40

Carr, R D 1976 'Wallingford Castle Excavations 1972: An Interim Report'. Unpublished typescript report

Cave, C J P 1948 *Roof Bosses in Medieval Churches: An Aspect of Gothic Sculpture*. Cambridge: Cambridge University Press

Chalk, E S 1910 'The Church of St Andrew, Cullompton'. *Rep Trans Devonshire Ass* **42**, 182–205

— 1934 *Kentisbeare*. Devonshire Association, Parochial Histories of Devon **3**. Exeter

Chanter, J F 1932 *The Bishop's Palace, Exeter, and its Story*. London: SPCK

— 1933 'The Custos and College of the Vicars Choral of the Choir of the Cathedral Church of St Peter, Exeter'. *Trans Exeter Diocesan Architectural Archaeol Soc* **16**, part 1

Cheetham, F 1984 *English Medieval Alabasters, with a Catalogue of the Collection in the Victoria and Albert Museum*. Oxford: Phaidon/Christies

Cherry, B and Pevsner, N 1989 *The Buildings of England: Devon*, revised edn. London: Penguin

Cherry, J 1991 'Pottery and Tile' *in* Blair, J and Ramsay, N (eds) *English Medieval Industries*, 189–209

Chesher, V M and Chesher, F J 1968 *The Cornishman's House, an Introduction to the History of Traditional Domestic Architecture in Cornwall*. Truro: D Bradford Barton

Child, P 1990 'Farmhouse Building Traditions' *in* Beacham, P (ed) 1990, 33–45

Clarke, H 1992 'The Hanse and England: a Survey of the Evidence for Contacts between England and the Baltic in the Middle Ages'. *Archaeologia Elbingensis* **1**, 135–8

Clayden, B 1971 *Soils of the Exeter District*. Harpenden: Memoirs of the Soil Survey of England and Wales, Sheets **325** and **339**

Clayton, M 1968 *Victoria and Albert Museum: Catalogue of Rubbings of Brasses and Incised Slabs*. London: HMSO

Clifford, H D 1962 'A Manor House Restored'. *Country Life* **132**, 30 August 1962, 464–5

Clifton-Taylor, A and Ireson, A S 1994 *English Stone Building*, new edn. London: Gollancz

Coate, M 1957 'Cadhay'. *Archaeol J* **114**, 159–62

Colby, F T (ed) 1881 *The Visitation of the County of Devon in the Year 1564*. Exeter: Pollard

Coleman, G R 2001 'The Chemical Control of Deathwatch Beetle' *in* Ridout B V (ed) 2001, 51–3

Coleman-Smith, R and Pearson, T 1988 *Excavations in the Donyatt Potteries*. Chichester: Phillimore

Colvin, H M, Summerson, J, Biddle, M, Hale, J R and Merriman, M 1982 *The History of the King's Works, Volume IV: 1485–1660 (Part II)*. London: HMSO

Cooke, R 1957 *West Country Houses, an Illustrated Account of some Country Houses and their Owners, in the Counties of Bristol, Gloucester, Somerset and Wiltshire*. London: Batsford

Coope, R 1986 'The "Long Gallery": Its Origins, Development, Use and Decoration'. *Architectural History* **29**, 43–84

Cooper, N (ed) 1990 *The Exeter Area*. Proceedings of the Summer Meeting of the Royal Archaeological Institute at Exeter, July 1990. Supplement to *Archaeol J* **147**

Copeland, G W 1949 'Presidential Address, 1948–49. Ancient Chapels and Oratories in Devon'. *Trans Plymouth Institution* **21**, 99–123

— 1957 'Chapel into Barn' (correspondence). *Country Life* **122**, 15 August 1957, 310

— 1960 'Devonshire Church Houses'. *Rep Trans Devonshire Ass* **92**, 116–41

— 1961 'Devonshire Church Houses: Part II'. *Rep Trans Devonshire Ass* **93**, 250–65

— 1962 'Devonshire Church Houses: Part III' *Rep Trans Devonshire Ass* **94**, 427–39

— 1963 'Devonshire Church Houses: Part IV'. *Rep Trans Devonshire Ass* **95**, 135–55

Courtney, P 1988 *Small Arms Accessories of the Mid-Seventeenth Century*. Finds Research Group 700–1700, Datasheet **11**

Cox, J and Thorp, J R L 1991 'Authentic Slating in Devon'. *Association for Studies in the Conservation of Historic Buildings* **16**, 3–12

Cox, M D 1957 'The Kirkham Chantry' (Report of the Summer Meeting of the Royal Archaeological Institute at Exeter in 1957). *Archaeol J* **114**, 172–4

Cresswell, B F 1908 *Exeter Churches: Notes on the History, Fabrics and Features of Interest in the Churches of the Deanery of Christianity, Devon*. Exeter: James G Commin

— 1935 'Cowick Barton'. *Devon and Cornwall Notes and Queries* **18**, 242–6

Crocker, J 1875 *Sketches of Old Exeter*. London: published for the author

Crone, A and Fawcett, R 1998 'Dendrochronology, Documents, and the Timber Trade: New Evidence for the Building History of Stirling Castle, Scotland'. *Medieval Archaeol* **42**, 68–87

Crone, B A 1998 *The Dendrochronological Analysis of Panels from the Painted Ceiling of Guthrie Aisle*. AOC Archaeology Group Rep **1773**

Crowfoot, E, Pritchard, F and Staniland, K 1992 *Textiles and Clothing c 1150 – c 1450*. Medieval Finds from Excavations in London **4**: London: HMSO

Davies, M 1972 *Rogier van der Weyden: An Essay, with a Critical Catalogue of Paintings Assigned to him and to Robert Campin*. London: Phaidon

Dean, R 1991 *Rufford Old Hall, Lancashire* (guidebook), revised edn, 1997. London: The National Trust

Delagarde, P C 1849 'An Account of the Church of St Andrew Cullumpton'. *Trans Exeter Diocesan Architectural Soc* **3**, 52–61

Delderfield, E R 1970 *West Country Historic Houses and Their Families, Volume Two: Dorset, Wiltshire and North Somerset*. Newton Abbot: David and Charles

Dodd, D 1990 *Lytes Cary, Somerset* (guidebook). London: The National Trust

DoE 1974 *List of Buildings of Special Architectural or Historic Interest. District of Exeter, Devon (Exeter Area)*. London: DoE

— 1990a *List of Buildings of Special Architectural or Historic Interest. District of South Hams (Parishes of Charlton, Chivelstone, East Portlemouth, Malborough, Sherford, South Huish, South Milton, South Pool, Thurlestone, West Alvington)*. London: DoE

— 1990b *List of Buildings of Special Architectural or Historic Interest. District of Torridge, Devon (Parishes of Bradworthy, Bridgerule, Bulkworthy, East Putford, Holsworthy, Holsworthy Hamlets, Pancrasweek, Pyworthy, and West Putford)*. London: DoE

— 1995 *TRADA Wood Information: Section 4, Sheet 22* (Construction Sponsorship Directorate). London: DoE

Dollinger, P 1970 *The German Hansa*. London: Macmillan

Drake, F M 1913 'The Painted Glass of Exeter Cathedral and other Devon Churches'. *Archaeol J* **70**, 163–74

Dunmore, S L 1979–1987 ms additions to Morley 1979, recording observations in the fabric.

Dunning, G C 1974 'The Horse and Knight Roof-Finial, with a Discussion of Knight Finials and Rider Finials in England and on the Continent' *in* Baker, D, 'Excavations in the Area of Mill Street, Bedford, 1971'. *Bedfordshire Archaeol J* **9**, 112–28

Dunstan, G L 1963 *The Register of Edmund Lacy, Bishop of Exeter, 1420–1455*, Registrum Commune *Vol I*. Devon and Cornwall Record Society, New Series 7. Exeter

— 1968 *The Register of Edmund Lacy, Bishop of Exeter, 1420–1455*, Registrum Commune *Vol III*. Devon and Cornwall Record Society, New Series 13. Exeter

Durrance, E M and Laming, D J C (eds) 1982 *The Geology of Devon*. Exeter: University of Exeter

Dyer, C 1989 *Standards of Living in the Later Middle Ages*. Cambridge: Cambridge University Press

Dymond, R 1889 *Parish of St Petrock, Exeter. Calendar of the Deeds and Documents belonging to the Feoffees of the Parish Property*. Exeter: Pollard

Eckstein, D, Baillie, M G L and Egger, H 1984 *Handbooks for Archaeologists No 2 Dendrochronological Dating*. Strasbourg: European Science Foundation

Eckstein, D, Wazny, T, Bauch, J and Klein, P 1986 'New Evidence for the Dendrochronological Dating of Netherlandish Paintings'. *Nature* **320**, 465–6

Egan, G 1989 'Post-Medieval Britain in 1988'. *Post-Medieval Archaeol* **23**, 25–67

— 1990 'Post-Medieval Britain in 1989'. *Post-Medieval Archaeol* **24**, 159–211

— 1998 *The Medieval Household: Daily Living c 1150 – c 1450*. Medieval Finds from Excavations in London **6**. London: The Stationery Office

Egan, G, Hanna, S D and Knight, B 1986 'Marks on Milled Window Leads'. *Post-Medieval Archaeol* **20**, 303–9

Egan, G and Pritchard, F 1991 *Dress Accessories c 1150 – c 1450*. Medieval Finds from Excavations in London **3**. London: HMSO

Ellis, P (ed) 1993 *Beeston Castle, Cheshire: A Report on Excavations by Laurence Keen and Peter Hough 1968–85*. English Heritage Archaeological Report, Old Series **23**. London: English Heritage

Elrington, C R 1992 *The Victoria History of the County of Somerset, Volume VI: Bridgwater and Neighbouring Parishes*. Oxford: The University of London Institute of Historical Research/Oxford University Press

Emery, A 1970 *Dartington Hall*. Oxford: Oxford University Press

Emery, A 1996 *Greater Medieval Houses of England and Wales 1300–1500, Volume I: Northern England*. Cambridge: Cambridge University Press

English Heritage 1991 *Management of Archaeological Projects (MAP2)*. London: English Heritage

— nd (1994) *Bowhill Exeter* (guide leaflet). London: English Heritage

— 1998a *Dendrochronology – Guidelines on Producing and Interpreting Dendrochronological Dates*. London: English Heritage

— 1998b *Stone Slate Roofing: Technical Advice Note*. London: English Heritage

Erskine, A M 1981 *The Accounts of the Fabric of Exeter Cathedral, 1279–1353, Part 1: 1279–1326*. Devon and Cornwall Record Society, New Series **24**. Exeter

— 1983 *The Accounts of the Fabric of Exeter Cathedral, 1279–1353, Part 2: 1328–1353*. Devon and Cornwall Record Society, New Series **26**. Exeter

Erskine, A M, Hope, V and Lloyd, J 1988 *Exeter Cathedral, A Short History and Description*. Exeter: Exeter Cathedral

Esling, J, Howard, R E, Laxton, R R, Litton, C D and Simpson, W G 1990 'List 33 – Nottingham University Tree-Ring Dating Laboratory Results'. *Vernacular Architect* **21**, 37–40

Everett, A W 1935 'Bowhill House, Exeter'. *Devon and Cornwall Notes and Queries* **18**, 305–7

— 1956 'The Rebuilding of the Hall of Compton Castle'. *Rep Trans Devonshire Ass* **88**, 75–85

— 1958 'A Note on Bowhill, Exeter'. *Archaeol J* **115**, 203–6

Fedorowicz, J K 1980 *England's Baltic Trade in the Early Seventeenth Century*. Cambridge: Cambridge University Press

Ferguson, G 1961 *Signs and Symbols in Christian Art*, 1st edn, 1954. New York: Oxford University Press

Finberg, H P R 1969 *Tavistock Abbey: A Study in the Social and Economic History of Devon*, 2nd edn. Newton Abbot: David and Charles

Fletcher, J 1980 'Tree-ring Dating of Tudor Portraits'. *Proc Roy Inst Gr Brit* **52**, 81–104

Fletcher, J M and Morgan, R A 1981 'The Dating of Doors and Cupboards in the Zouche Chapel, York Minster'. *Yorkshire Archaeol J* **53**, 429–36

Forrester, H 1975 *The Timber Framed Houses of Essex*. London: Regency Press

Foster, I L L and Alcock, L (eds) 1963 *Culture and Environment: Essays in Honour of Sir Cyril Fox*. London: Routledge & Kegan Paul

Fox, C and Radford, C A R 1933 'Kidwelly Castle, Carmarthenshire, Including a Survey of the Polychrome Pottery Found There and Elsewhere in Britain'. *Archaeologia* **83**, 93–138

Fox, Sir C 1957 'The Law Library: No. 8, The Close, Exeter'. *Archaeol J* **114**, 138–9

Fox, Sir C and Lord Raglan 1951 *Monmouthshire Houses, Part I: Medieval Houses*. Cardiff: National Museum of Wales

— 1953 *Monmouthshire Houses, Part II: Sub-Medieval Houses*, c *1550–1610*. Cardiff: National Museum of Wales

— 1954 *Monmouthshire Houses, Part III: Renaissance Houses*, c *1590–1714*. Cardiff: National Museum of Wales

Friedmann, H 1946 *The Symbolic Goldfinch: Its History and Significance in European Devotional Art*. Washington DC: The Bollingen Foundation/Pantheon Books

Gale, A W *et al* 1992 *The Building Stones of Devon*. Exeter: The Devonshire Association

Garnett, O 1992 *Antony, Cornwall* (guidebook). London: The National Trust

Gaskell Brown, C 1986 *Plymouth Excavations: The Medieval Waterfront, Woolster Street. The Finds, Castle Street*. Plymouth Archaeol Soc **3**

Gaskell Brown, C *et al* 1995 'Buckland Abbey, Devon: Surveys and Excavations, 1983–1995'. *Proc Devon Archaeol Soc* **53**, 25–82

Gerrard, C M, Gutiérrez, A and Vince, A G (eds) 1995 *Spanish Medieval Ceramics in Spain and the British Isles*. Brit Archaeol Rep, Int Ser **610**. Oxford

Gilyard-Beer, R 1992 *Cleeve Abbey, Somerset* (guidebook). London: English Heritage

Girouard, M 1978 *Life in the English Country House: A Social and Architectural History*. New Haven and London: Yale University Press

Goodall, J 1996 'Gainsborough Old Hall, Lincs'. *Country Life* **190/3**, 18 January 1996, 38–41

Gotch, J A 1901 *Early Renaissance Architecture in England: A Historical & Descriptive Account of the Tudor, Elizabethan & Jacobean Periods, 1500–1625*. London: Batsford

Gotch, J A 1928 *The Growth of the English House*, 2nd revised edn. London: Batsford

Gover, J E B, Mawer, A and Stenton, F M 1932 *The Place Names of Devon, Part II*. Cambridge: Cambridge University Press

Gray, T 1996 'Stockdale's Drawings of Early Nineteenth-century Devon'. *The Devon Historian* 53, 24–9

Gray, T, Rowe, M and Erskine, A (eds) 1992 *Tudor and Stuart Devon: The Common Estate and Government*. Exeter: University of Exeter

Green, R J 1995 'Common Rag and Scantle: Traditional Methods of Slate Roofing in Cornwall'. Unpublished MA dissertation, School of Architecture, University of Plymouth

Gregory, I L (ed) 1950 *Hartland Church Accounts, 1597–1706*, privately printed

Groves, C 1992 *Dendrochronological Analysis of Timbers from New Baxtergate, Grimsby, Humberside, 1986*. AML Rep **08/92**

— 1997 'The Dating and Provenancing of Imported Conifer Timbers in England: the Initiation of a Research Project' *in* Sinclair, A *et al* (eds) 1997, 205–11

— 2000 *Tree-ring Analysis of Oak Timbers from Peterborough Cathedral, Peterborough, Cambridgeshire: Timbers from the Painted Nave Ceiling*. Centre for Archaeol Rep **10/2000**

— 2002a *Dendrochronological Analysis of Bowhill, Exeter, Devon*. Centre for Archaeol Rep **23/2002**

— 2002b 'Tree-ring Analysis of Imported Medieval Timbers from 16–22 Coppergate' *in* Hall, R A and Hunter-Mann, K, *Later Medieval Urbanism in Coppergate: Refining a Townscape*. The Archaeology of York **10/6**, 853–8. York: Council for British Archaeology

— forthcoming (a) *Dendrochronological Research in Devon. Phase 1 – the Pilot Study*. Centre for Archaeol Rep

— forthcoming (b) *Tree-ring Analysis of the Roof of West Challacombe, Combe Martin, Devon*. Centre for Archaeol Rep

Groves, C and Hillam, J 1993a *Tree-ring Analysis of Oak Timbers from South Yarde, Rose Ash, Devon, 1992*. AML Rep **36/93**

— 1993b *Tree-ring Analysis of Oak Timbers from the Medieval Barn, King's Pyon, near Leominster, Hereford and Worcester, 1992 – Interim report*. AML Rep **24/93**

Hadfield, M 1960 *Gardening in Britain*. London: Hutchinson

Hall, I (ed) 1979 *Samuel Buck's Yorkshire Sketchbook: Reproduced in Facsimile from Lansdowne MS 914 in the British Library, with an Introduction by Ivan Hall*. Wakefield: Wakefield Historical Publications

Hall, J 1996 *Dictionary of Subjects and Symbols in Art*, revised edn. London: John Murray

Hall, M E P and Blaylock, S R 1991 *Bowhill, Exeter: Archive Report I, The Excavation of 1989*. EMAFU Rep **91.05**

— 1994 *Bowhill, Exeter, Archive Report V: The Excavations of 1993 in the South and West Ranges*. EMAFU Rep **94.106**

— 1995 *Bowhill, Exeter Archive Report VII: Excavations and Observations 1993–95*. EMAFU Rep **95.22**

Halliday, F E (ed) 1953 *Richard Carew of Antony: The Survey of Cornwall*. London: Andrew Melrose

Hanham, A (ed) 1970 *Churchwardens' Accounts of Ashburton, 1479–1580*. Devon and Cornwall Record Society, New Series **15**. Exeter

Harding, W 1849 'A Paper on the Church and Chantry on the Ancient Exe-Bridge'. *Trans Exeter Diocesan Architectural Soc* **3**, 165–72

Harris, E C 1975 'The Stratigraphic Sequence: a Question of Time'. *World Archaeol* **7/1**, 109–21

Harris, J 1979 *The Artist and the Country House, a History of Country House and Garden View Painting in Britain, 1540–1870*. London: Sotheby Parke Bernet

Harris, R 1979 *Discovering Timber Framed Buildings*, 2nd revised edn. Princes Risborough: Shire Publications

Harrison, J R 1984 'The Mud Wall in England at the Close of the Vernacular Era'. *Trans Ancient Monuments Soc* **28**, 154–74

— 1989 'Some Clay Dabbins in Cumberland: their Construction and Form, Part I. *Trans Ancient Monuments Soc* **33**, 97–151

— 1992 'The Devon Earth Building Initiative'. *English Heritage Conservation Bulletin* **16**, 10–11

— 1994 'The Conservation of Bow Hill (*sic*), Exeter, Devon' *in* Watson, L L and Harding, S (eds) 1994, 26

— 1995a 'Changing Perceptions of Architectural-Historic Value, A Case History: Bowhill, Devon'. *Association for Studies in the Conservation of Historic Buildings* **20**, 14–29

— 1995b 'The Bowhill Cob Report' *in* Watson, L and Harries, R (eds) 1995, 208–11

— 1999 *Earth. The Conservation and Repair of Bowhill, Exeter: Working with Cob* (Research and Case Studies in Architectural Conservation). English Heritage Research Transactions **3**. London: James and James/English Heritage

Hartley, D 1969 *Food in England*, 5th impression. London: Macdonald

Harvey, H 1989 *Discovering Exeter, 6: West of the River*. Exeter: Exeter Civic Society

Harvey, J H 1974 *Early Nurserymen*. Chichester: Phillimore

Haslam, C (ed) 1992 *The Landmark Handbook, 1992*. Maidenhead: The Landmark Trust

Hawkyard, A D K 1977 'Thornbury Castle'. *Trans Bristol and Gloucestershire Archaeol Soc* **95**, 51–8

Hayward, J 1867 'A Paper on Bradfield House'. *Trans Exeter Diocesan Architectural Soc*, 2nd ser **1**, 79–84

Heighway, C M 1980 'Excavations at Gloucester, Fifth Interim Report: St Oswald's Priory 1977–8'. *Antiq J* **60**, 207–26

Henderson, C G (ed) 1984a *Archaeology in Exeter 1983/4*. Exeter: EMAFU

— 1984b 'Albany Road Excavation, St Thomas' *in* Henderson, C G (ed) 1984a, 28–36

— 1985 *Archaeology in Exeter 1984/5*. Exeter: EMAFU

Henderson, C G, Matthews, A J and Parker, R W 1995 *Archaeological Evaluation of The Presentation of Mary Convent School Buildings, Palace Gate, Exeter*. EMAFU Rep **95.05**

Henning, B D 1983 *The History of Parliament: The House of Commons 1660–1690*. London: Secker and Warburg/The History of Parliament Trust

Heriz-Smith, S 1988a 'The Veitch Nurseries of Killerton and Exeter *c* 1780 to 1863, Part I'. *Garden History* **16**, no. 1, 41–57

— 1988b 'The Veitch Nurseries of Killerton and Exeter *c* 1780 to 1863, Part II'. *Garden History* **16**, no. 2, 174–88

Hervey, N 1980 *Bowhill House: St Thomas's Hospital for Lunatics: Asylum for the Four Western Counties, 1801–1869*. Exeter: University of Exeter

Heymanowski, K 1979 'Niektore sortymenty drzewne w Polsce w XV w w swiete materialow z "miedziowca"'. *Kwartalnik Hostorii Kultury Materialnej* **27**, 345–51

Higham, R A 1984 *Okehampton Castle, Devon* (official handbook). London: HMSO

Higham, R A, Allan, J P and Blaylock, S R 1982 'Excavations at Okehampton Castle, Devon: Part 2: the Bailey'. *Proc Devon Archaeol Soc* **40**, 19–151

Hillam, J 1991a *Tree-ring Analysis of Timbers from Bowhill House, Exeter, Devon*. AML Rep **4/91**

— 1991b *Tree-ring Analysis of Native and Baltic Timbers from Blaydes Staithe, Hull, Humberside*. AML Rep **108/91**

Hillam, J and Groves, C 1993 'Tree-ring Dates from Sheffield University'. *Vernacular Architect* **24**, 46–8

Hillam, J, Morgan, R A and Tyers, I 1987 'Sapwood Estimates and the Dating of Short Ring Sequences' *in* *Applications of Tree-ring Studies: Current Research in Dendrochronology and Related Areas* (ed R G W Ward). Brit Archaeol Rep, Int Ser **333**, 165–85

Hillam, J and Tyers, I 1995 'Reliability and Repeatability in Dendrochronological Analysis: Tests Using the Fletcher Archive of Panel-painting Data'. *Archaeometry* **37**, part 2, 395–405

Hingeston-Randolph, F C 1886 *The Register of Edmund Stafford (AD 1395–1419), An Index and Abstract of its Contents*. London: George Bell and Exeter: Henry Eland

— 1892 *The Register of Walter de Stapledon, Bishop of Exeter (AD 1307–1326)*. London: George Bell and Exeter: Henry Eland

Holden, E W 1989 'Slate Roofing in Medieval Sussex'. *Sussex Archaeol Coll* **127**, 73–88

Holmes, E F nd (1988) *Sewing Thimbles*. Finds Research Group 700–1700, Datasheet **9**

Howard, M 1987 *The Early Tudor Country House*. London: George Philip

Howard, R E, Laxton, R R and Litton, C D 1996 *Tree-ring Analysis of Timbers from Mercer's Hall, Mercer's Lane, Gloucester*. AML Rep **13/96**

Howard, R E, Laxton, R R and Litton, C D 1999a *Tree-Ring Analysis of Timbers from the Archdeacon of Exeter's House, Palace Gate, Exeter*. AML Rep **41/99**

— 1999b *Tree-Ring Analysis of Timbers from Exeter Guildhall, High Street, Exeter, Devon*. AML Rep **56/99**

— 2000a *Tree-Ring Analysis of Timbers from the Floor and Roof of the Great Chamber, The Deanery, Cathedral Close, Exeter, Devon*. AML Rep **1/2000**

— 2000b *Tree-Ring Analysis of Timbers from The Law Library, and 8/9 The Close, Exeter, Devon*. AML Rep **47/2000**

Howard, R E, Laxton, R R, Litton, C D and Simpson, W G 1991 'List 39 – Nottingham University Tree-Ring Dating Laboratory Results'. *Vernacular Architect* **22**, 40–43

— 1992 'List 44 – Nottingham University Tree-Ring Dating Laboratory Results'. *Vernacular Architect* **23**, 51–6

— 1993 'List 48 – Nottingham University Tree-Ring Dating Laboratory Results: General List'. *Vernacular Architect* **24**, 40–42

— 1995 'List 60 – Nottingham University Tree-Ring Dating Laboratory Results: General List'. *Vernacular Architect* **26**, 47–53

Hulland, C 1980 'Devonshire Farmhouses, Part V: Some Medieval Houses in North and Mid-Devon'. *Rep Trans Devonshire Ass* **112**, 127–70

Hurst, J G 1986 'Late Medieval Iberian Pottery Imported into the Low Countries'. Madrid: *Segundo Coloquio Internacional de Cerámica Medieval en el Mediterráneo Occidental, Toledo, 1981*, 347–53

Hurst, J G, Neal, D and van Beuningen, H J E 1986 *Pottery Produced and Traded in North-West Europe, 1350–1650*. Rotterdam Papers **VI**

Hussey, C 1927a 'Cothay-I, Somerset'. *Country Life* **62**, 22 October 1927, 596–604

— 1927b 'Cothay-II, Somerset'. *Country Life* **62**, 29 October 1927; 626–33

— 1933 'The Old Manor, Little Hempston, Devon'. *Country Life* **74**, 5 August 1933, 120–26

— 1950 'Knightstone, Devon-I and -II'. *Country Life* **108**, 8 and 15 September 1950, 754–8 and 836–9

Hyde, R 1994 *Prospect of Britain: Town Panoramas of Samuel and Nathaniel Buck*. London: Pavilion Books

Jefferies, J S 1977 *Excavation Records: Techniques in use by the Central Excavation Unit*. DAMHB (DoE), Occasional Paper **1**

Jenkins, A 1806 *A History and Description of the City of Exeter*. Exeter: P Hedgeland

Jenkins, G 1972 *The Craft Industries*. London: Longman

Jennings, S 1981 *Eighteen Centuries of Pottery from Norwich*. East Anglian Archaeol Rep **13**

Jope, E M 1951 'The Development of Pottery Ridge Tiles in the Oxford Region'. *Oxoniensia* **16**, 86–8

— 1961 'Cornish Houses, 1400–1700', *in* Jope, E M (ed) 1961, 192–222

Jope, E M (ed) 1961 *Studies in Building History, Essays in Recognition of the Work of B H St J O'Neil*. London: Odhams

Jope, E M and Dunning, G C 1954 'The Use of Blue Slate for Roofing in Medieval England'. *Antiq J* **34**, 201–17

Keeley, H C M 1988 *A Report on Some Soil Samples from Bowhill, Exeter, Devon*. AML Rep **198/88**

Keen, L 1992 'The Floor-tiles' *in* Horsey, I P *Excavations in Poole 1973–1983*. Dorset Natur Hist Archaeol Soc Monogr Ser **10**, 133–4

Kelly, F P (ed) 1991 *Medieval Art & Architecture at Exeter Cathedral*. Brit Archaeol Ass Conference Trans **XI**, 1985

Kelly, F P 1992 'Inspectorate Guidelines for Conservation and Display', unpublished typescript. Bristol: English Heritage

Kenyon, G H 1967 *The Glass Industry of the Weald*. Leicester: Leicester University Press

Klein, P and Wazny, T 1991 'Dendrochronological Analyses of Paintings of Gdansk Painters of the 15th to the 17th Century'. *Dendrochronologia* **9**, 181–91

Knight, B 1983–1984 'Researches on Medieval Window Lead'. *J Brit Soc Master Glass Paint* **18**, 49–51

Knight, B 1996 'Appendix 7: Window Lead and Glazing History' *in* Brown, S W 1996, 271–74.

Laithwaite, J M W 1990 'Town Houses up to 1660' *in* Beacham, P (ed) 1990, 95–115

Latham, R and Matthews, W (eds) 1995 *The Diary of Samuel Pepys, A New and Complete Transcription: Volume 1, 1660*. London: G Bell & Sons

Latham, R E 1980 *Revised Medieval Latin Word-List from British and Irish Sources*. London: The British Academy/Oxford University Press

Lavier, C and Lambert, G 1996 'Dendrochronology and Works of Art' *in* *Tree Rings, Environment and Humanity: Proceedings of the*

International Conference Tucson, Arizona, 17–21 May 1994 (eds J S Dean, D M Meko and T W Swetnam). Department of Geosciences, The University of Arizona, Tucson, Arizona, 543–56

Laxton, R R and Litton, C D 1988 *An East Midlands Master Tree-ring Chronology and its Use for Dating Vernacular Buildings*. University of Nottingham, Department of Archaeology Publication, Monogr Ser **3**

Laxton, R R, Litton, C D and Howard, R E 1989 'Construction of a Kent Master Dendrochronological Sequence for Oak AD 1158–1540'. *Medieval Archaeol* **33**, 90–98

Laycock, C H 1920 'The Old Devon Farmhouse, Part I: Its Exterior Aspect and General Construction'. *Rep Trans Devonshire Ass* **52**, 158–91

— 1924 'The Old Devon Farmhouse, Part II (continued): Its Interior Arrangement and Domestic Economy'. *Rep Trans Devonshire Ass* **55**, 154–81

Le Lievre, A 1995 'Westward Grow'. *Country Life* **189/18**, 4 May, 1995, 88–9

Lega-Weekes, E 1900 'The Old Mansion of North Wyke'. *Rep Trans Devonshire Ass* **32**, 195–205

— 1915 *Some Studies in the Topography of the Cathedral Close, Exeter*. Exeter: James G Commin

— 1921 'Bokerel or Elyot's House'. *Devon and Cornwall Notes and Queries* **11**, 253–4.

— 1934 'The Pre-Reformation History of St Katherine's Priory, Polsloe'. *Rep Trans Devonshire Ass* **66**, 181–99

— 1935 'The Hollands of Bowhill in St Thomas's, Exeter'. *Devon and Cornwall Notes and Queries* **18**, 300–305

Leuschner, B and Leuschner, H H 1996 'Plasticine Imprints for Recording Tree Rings'. *Dendrochronologia* **14**, 287–9

Lewis, E 1995 'A Sixteenth Century Painted Ceiling from Winchester College'. *Proc Hampshire Field Club Archaeol Soc* **51**, 137–65

Lindley, P (ed) 1991 *Gainsborough Old Hall*. Occasional Papers in Lincolnshire History and Archaeology **8**

Linehan, C D 1975 *Cadhay and the Whetham Family*, privately printed. Dorchester

Litton, C D and Zainodin, H J 1991 'Statistical Models of Dendrochronology'. *J Archaeol Sci* **18**, 429–40

Lloyd, N 1951 *A History of the English House*, 3rd edn. London: The Architectural Press

Lloyd Parry, H and Brakspear, H 1917 *St Nicholas Priory, Exeter*. Exeter: W J Southwood

Lomas, J 1974 'Restoration of Higher Harestone Manor-Brixton (1972–1973)'. *Rep Trans Devonshire Ass* **106**, 119–40

Lysons, D and Lysons, S 1822 *Magna Britannia, VI: Devonshire*. London: Cadell

McFarlane, K B 1971 *Hans Memling*. Oxford: Oxford University Press

Manco, J 1991 'Bowhill, Exeter: The Documentary Evidence', unpublished typescript. English Heritage

Manco, J, Greenhalf, D and Girouard, M 1990 'Lulworth Castle in the Seventeenth Century'. *Architectural History* **33**, 29–59

Mayes, P and Butler, L A S 1983 *Sandal Castle Excavations 1964–1973: A Detailed Archaeological Report*. Wakefield: Wakefield Historical Publications

Mercer, E 1975 *English Vernacular Houses: A Study of Traditional Farmhouses and Cottages*. London: RCHME

Mercer, H C 1929 *Ancient Carpenters' Tools*, reprinted 5th edn, 1975. Doylestown, Pennsylvania

Miles, D H and Haddon-Reece, D 1994 'List 56 – Tree-ring Dates'. *Vernacular Architect* **25**, 28–30

— 1995 'List 64 – Tree-ring Dates: Part II. *Vernacular Architect* **26**, 62–8

— 1996 'List 72 – Hampshire Dendrochronology Project Phase 2'. *Vernacular Architect* **27**, 97–102

Miles, D H and Worthington, M J 1997 'List 84 – Somerset Dendrochronology Project Phase 1'. *Vernacular Architect* **28**, 172–4

Miles, H and Miles, T J 1975 'Pilton, North Devon. Excavation within a Medieval Village'. *Proc Devon Archaeol Soc* **33**, 267–96

Mills, C and Crone, A 1998 'Tree-ring Evidence for the Historic Timber Trade and Woodland Exploitation in Scotland' *in* Stravinskiene, V and Juknys, R (eds) 1998, 45–55.

Milne, G 1992 *Timber Building Techniques in London c 900–1400*. London: London and Middlesex Archaeological Society

Moorhouse, S, 1971 'Finds from Basing House, Hampshire (c 1540–1645): Part Two'. *Post-Medieval Archaeol* **5**, 35–76

Morley, B M 1979 'Bowhill House, Exeter: Preliminary Inspectorate Report', unpublished typescript. London: DoE

— 1983 'Leigh Barton, Churchstow, South Devon'. *Proc Devon Archaeol Soc* **41**, 81–106

Munro, M A R 1984 'An Improved Algorithm for Crossdating Tree-ring Series'. *Tree Ring Bulletin* **44**, 17–27

Musson, J 1998 'The Palace, Exeter'. *Country Life* **192/12**, 19 March 1998, 44–7

Mynard, D C 1969 'Excavations at Somerby, Lincs, 1957'. *Lincolnshire Hist Archaeol* **1**, no. 4, 61–91

Neve, R 1969 *The City and Country Purchaser and Builder's Dictionary*, reprint of 1726 edn. New York: Augustus M Kelley

Newman, J 1995 *The Buildings of Wales: Glamorgan*. London: Penguin

Nicholson, B E and Clapham, A R 1975 *The Oxford Book of Trees*. Oxford: Oxford University Press

Noël Hume, I 1991 *A Guide to Artifacts of Colonial America*. New York: Vintage Books

North, J J 1991 *English Hammered Coinage II: Edward I to Charles II, 1272–1662*, 3rd revised edn. London: Spink & Son

Norton, E C 1983 'The Medieval Tile Pavements of Winchester' *in Medieval Art and Architecture at Winchester Cathedral* (eds T A Heslop and V A Sekules). Brit Archaeol Ass Conference Trans **VI**, 1980, 78–93

Oldham, D'O W 1906 'The Private Chapels of Devon: Ancient and Modern'. *Rep Trans Devonshire Ass* **38**, 391–403

Oliver, G 1839 *Ecclesiastical Antiquities in Devon*, 3 vols. Exeter: W C Featherstone

— 1861a *Lives of the Bishops of Exeter and a History of the Cathedral*. Exeter: William Roberts

— 1861b *The History of the City of Exeter*. Exeter: Roberts

Orme, N 1980 *The Minor Clergy of Exeter Cathedral, 1300–1548*. Exeter: University of Exeter

— 1986 'Sir John Speke and his Chapel in Exeter Cathedral'. *Rep Trans Devonshire Ass* **118**, 21–41

Orme, N (ed) 1992 *Nicholas Roscarrock's Lives of the Saints: Cornwall and Devon*. Devon and Cornwall Record Society, New Series **35**. Exeter

Orme, N 1996 *English Church Dedications, with a Survey of Devon and Cornwall*. Exeter: University of Exeter

Oswald, A 1932 'Baddesley Clinton, Warwickshire – I and II'. *Country Life* **71**, 9 and 16 April 1932, 408–14 and 434–40

— 1956 'Wortham Manor, Devon – I and II'. *Country Life* **119**, 31 May and 7 June 1956, 1174–7 and 1228–31

— 1959 *The Country Houses of Dorset*, 2nd revised edn. London: Reed International

Oswald, A 1984 'The Clay Pipes' *in* Allan, J P 1984a, 279–93.

Pächt, O 1997 *Early Netherlandish Painting from Rogier van der Weyden to Gerard David*. London: Harvey Miller

Panofsky, E 1953 *Early Netherlandish Painting, its Origins and Character*, 2 vols. Cambridge, Massachusetts: Harvard University Press

Pantin, W A 1957 'Medieval Priests' Houses in South-West England'. *Medieval Archaeol* **1**, 118–46

— 1961 'Medieval Inns' *in* Jope, E M (ed) 1961, 166–91.

— 1962–3 'Medieval English Town-House Plans' *Medieval Archaeol* **6–7**, 202–39.

— 1963 'Some Medieval English Town Houses: A Study in Adaptation', *in* Foster, I L L and Alcock, L (eds) 1963, 445–78

Parfitt, N 1981 'Summary of Evidence Relating to Bowhill House', unpublished typescript. English Heritage

Parker, R W 1996 *Archaeological Assessment of 21 The Mint, Exeter*. EA Rep **96.39**

— 1997a *Archaeo-Historical Assessment of No 5 The Close, Exeter*. EA Rep **97.30**

— 1997b *Archaeological Recording at No 2 Broadgate, Exeter*. EA Rep **97.73**

Parsons, D (ed) 1990 *Stone: Quarrying and Building in England AD 43–1525*. Chichester: Phillimore

Pearce, J 1992 *Post-Medieval Pottery in London, 1500-1700. Volume I: Border Wares*. London: HMSO

Pearse Chope, R 1918 'Some Old Farm Implements and Operations'. *Rep Trans Devonshire Ass* **50**, 268–92

Pearson, S 1994 *The Medieval Houses of Kent: An Historical Analysis*. London: RCHME

Penoyre, J and Penoyre, J 1994 *Decorative Plasterwork in the Houses of Somerset, 1500–1700: A Regional Survey*. Taunton: Somerset County Council

Pevsner, N 1958 *The Buildings of England: South and West Somerset*. Harmondsworth: Penguin

— 1969 *The Buildings of England: Lancashire 2, The Rural North*. Harmondsworth: Penguin

— 1970 *The Buildings of England: Cornwall*, 2nd revised edn by Enid Radcliffe. Harmondsworth: Penguin

— 1975 *The Buildings of England: Wiltshire*, 2nd revised edn by Bridget Cherry. Harmondsworth: Penguin

Pevsner, N and Wilson, B 1997 *The Buildings of England: Norfolk 1: Norwich and North East*, 2nd revised edn. London: Penguin

Phillips, E March 1915 'Holcombe Court, Devonshire'. *Country Life* **37**, 9 January 1915, 48–53

Platt, C P S 1962 'Excavations at Dartington Hall 1962'. *Archaeol J* **119**, 208–24

Pole, Sir W 1791 *Collections Towards a Description of the County of Devon, [now first printed from the Autograph in the possession of his lineal descendant Sir John William de la Pole, Bart, of Shute, etc in Devonshire]*. London: J Nichols

Pollock, J 1993 *Gordon, The Man Behind the Legend*. London: Constable

Polwhele, R. 1797 *The History of Devonshire*, 3 vols, reprinted 1977. Dorking: Kohler and Coombes

Ponsford, M 1992 'Post-Medieval Britain in 1991'. *Post-Medieval Archaeol* **26**, 95–156

— 1993 'Post-Medieval Britain in 1992'. *Post-Medieval Archaeol* **27**, 205–96

Portman, D 1966 *Exeter Houses, 1400–1700*. Exeter: University of Exeter

Powell, A 1949 *Brief Lives, and Other Selected Writings by John Aubrey*. London: The Cresset Press

Prideaux, E K 1915 'Remains of an Ancient Building in Exeter'. *Devon and Cornwall Notes and Queries* **8**, 161–70

Rackham, O 1990 *Trees and Woodland in the British Landscape*, 2nd edn. London: J M Dent & Sons

Radford, C A R 1960 'Tretower: The Castle and the Court'. *Brycheiniog* **6**, 1–50

Radford, C and Radford, R 1937 'Sixteenth Report on Ancient Monuments'. *Rep Trans Devonshire Ass* **69**, 73

— 1938 'Seventeenth Report on Ancient Monuments'. *Rep Trans Devonshire Ass* **70**, 57

— 1939 'Eighteenth Report on Ancient Monuments'. *Rep Trans Devonshire Ass* **71**, 67–8

Radford, G H 1907 'The Courtenay Monument in Colyton Church'. *Rep Trans Devonshire Ass* **39**, 144–55

Rahtz, P A and Watts, L 1997 *St Mary's Church, Deerhurst, Gloucestershire: Fieldwork, Excavations and Structural Analysis, 1971–1984*. Woodbridge, Suffolk: The Boydell Press

Royal Archaeological Institute 1913 'The Summer Meeting at Exeter'. *Archaeol J* **70**, 495–557

Ravenhill, W L D 1965 *Benjamin Donn. A Map of the County of Devon, 1765*. Devon and Cornwall Record Society, New Series **9**. Exeter

RCAHMW 1988 *An Inventory of the Ancient Monuments in Glamorgan, Vol IV: Domestic Architecture from the Reformation to the Industrial Revolution, Part II: Farmhouses and Cottages*. London: HMSO

RCHME 1916 *An Inventory of the Historical Monuments in Essex, Vol I: North West*. London: HMSO

— 1922 *An Inventory of the Historical Monuments in Essex, Vol III: North East*. London: HMSO

— 1934 *An Inventory of the Historical Monuments in Herefordshire, Vol III: North West*. London: HMSO

— 1939 *An Inventory of the Historical Monuments in the City of Oxford*. London: HMSO

— 1952 *An Inventory of the Historical Monuments in Dorset Vol I: West*. London: HMSO

— 1959 *An Inventory of the Historical Monuments in the City of Cambridge*. London: HMSO

— 1970a *An Inventory of the Historical Monuments in Dorset Vol II: South East Dorset*. London: HMSO

— 1970b *An Inventory of the Historical Monuments in Dorset Vol III: Central Dorset*. London: HMSO

— 1980 *An Inventory of the Historical Monuments in the City of Salisbury Vol I*. London: HMSO

Reineking-von Bock, G 1971 *Steinzeug*. Cologne: Catalogue of the Cologne Kunstgewerbemuseum

Richards, A E 1917 'England's First Potato: Where It Was Planted' (correspondence). *Country Life* **42**, 6 October 1917, 334–5

Richardson, I J 1993 'West Challacombe Manor' in *Annual Archaeology Abstracts, Selected Papers from National Trust Archaeological Staff on Projects Undertaken in 1993*, 3–8. London: The National Trust

Ridout, B 2000 *Timber Decay in Buildings: The Conservation Approach to Treatment*. London: E & F N Spon

— 2001 'Deathwatch Beetle and its Treatment: Conclusions and some Practical Results from the Woodcare Research Programme', in Ridout B V (ed) 2001, 3–5

Ridout, B V (ed) 2001 *Timber: The EC Woodcare Project: Studies of the Behaviour, Interrelationships and Management of Deathwatch Beetles in Historic Buildings* (Research and Case Studies in Architectural Conservation). English Heritage Research Transactions **4**. London: James and James/English Heritage

Risdon, T 1811 *The Chorographical Description or Survey of the County of Devon*. London: Rees and Curtis

Rodwell, K and Bell, R forthcoming *Acton Court: The Evolution of an Early Tudor Courtier's House*. Swindon: English Heritage

Rodwell, W J 1989 *Church Archaeology*. London: English Heritage/Batsford

Rogers, C 1989 'The Historical Background' in Anon *The Magic Tree: Devon Garden Plants, History and Conservation*, 16–28. Exeter: National Council for the Conservation of Plants and Gardens, Devon Group

Rogers, W H 1926 'Orleigh: An Ancient House'. *Rep Trans Devonshire Ass* **58**, 185–92

Rose, W 1946 *The Village Carpenter*. Cambridge: Cambridge University Press

Rose-Troup, F 1932–1933 'Bishop Oldham and Ottery St Mary'. *Devon and Cornwall Notes and Queries* **17**, 152–7

Russell, P M G 1976 *A History of the Exeter Hospitals, 1170–1948*. Exeter: Exeter Medical Post-graduate Institute

Salzman L F 1952 *Building in England, Down to 1540. A Documentary History*, new edn, 1967. Oxford: Oxford University Press

Schofield, J 1995 *Medieval London Houses*. New Haven and London: Yale University Press

Schweingruber, F H 1988 *Tree Rings*. Dordrecht: Reidel

— 1990 *Anatomy of European Woods*. Berne and Stuttgart

Scrivener, R C 1993 'Report to English Heritage on Bowhill House, Exeter'. Exeter: British Geological Survey

Setchell, G T and Setchell, J c 1938 *The Delabole System of Random Slating in Diminishing Courses* (later reprinted with amendments), privately printed. Cornwall: Delabole Slate Company

Sheldon, L 1932 'Devon Barns'. *Rep Trans Devonshire Ass* **64**, 389–95

Shelmerdine, T 1879 'Muchelney Abbey, Somerset'. *The Builder* **37**, 27 September 1879, 1075–8

— 1881 'Emblems of the Trinity'. *The Builder* **41**, 31 December 1881, 833

Shipley, A E 1916 'The Master's Lodgings, Christ's College, Cambridge – I and II'. *Country Life* **40**, 30 September and 7 October 1916, 378–85 and 402–12

Siebenlist-Kerner, V 1978 'The Chronology, 1341–1636, for Certain Hillside Oaks from Western England and Wales' *in* Fletcher, J M (ed) *Dendrochronology in Europe*. Brit Archaeol Rep Int Ser **51**, 157–61. Oxford

Sinclair, A, Slater, E and Gowlett, J (eds) 1997 *Archaeological Sciences 1995: Proceedings of a Conference on the Application of Scientific Methods to Archaeology*. Oxbow Books Monograph Series **64**. Oxford: Oxbow Books

Slade, H G 1990 'Bowhill, Exeter' *in* Cooper, N (ed) 1990, 93–7

Slade, H G and Dunmore, S L 1981 'Bowhill House, Exeter: A Programme of Consolidation', 2nd revised draft, May 1981. London: DAMHB

Slader, J M 1968 *The Churches of Devon*. Newton Abbot: David & Charles

Smith, H P 1951 *The History of the Borough and County of the Town of Poole, Vol II: County Corporate Status*. Poole: J Looker

Smith, J T 1958 'Medieval Roofs: A Classification'. *Archaeol J* **115**, 111–49

— 1992 *English Houses 1200–1800, The Hertfordshire Evidence*. London: RCHME

Smith, P 1988 *Houses of the Welsh Countryside: A Study in Historical Geography*, RCAHMW. London: HMSO

Somers Cocks, J V 1977 *Devon Topographical Prints, 1660–1870, A Catalogue and Guide*. Exeter: Devon Library Services

Sprigg, J 1854 *Anglia Rediviva; England's Recovery: Being the History of the [...] Army under the [...] Conduct of [...] Sir Thomas Fairfax*, new edn of 1647 edn. Oxford: Oxford University Press

Stabb, J 1911 *Some Old Devon Churches: Their Rood Screens, Pulpits, Fonts, etc: Volume II*. London: Simpkin, Marshall, Hamilton, Kent & Co

Staniforth, P R nd Unpublished Transcripts of Exeter City Receivers' Accounts, held at Exeter Archaeology, Exeter

Stead, P M, Manning, P and Blaylock, S R 1994 *Bowhill, Exeter, Archive Report VI: The Excavation of the Eastern Courtyard, 1992*. EMAFU Rep **94.107**

Stenning, D F and Andrews, D D (eds) 1998 *Regional Variation in Timber-Framed Building in England and Wales Down to 1550* (The Proceedings of the 1994 Cressing Conference). Chelmsford: Essex County Council

Stoate, T L (ed) 1982 *Devon Hearth Tax Return: Lady Day, 1674*, privately printed. Bristol

Stone, L 1955 *Sculpture in Britain: The Middle Ages*. Harmondsworth: Pelican History of Art/Penguin

— 1969 'Literacy and Education in England 1640–1900'. *Past and Present* **42**, 69–139

Stoyle, M J 1990 *The Civil-War Defences of Exeter and the Great Parliamentary Siege of 1645–46*. EMAFU Rep **90.26**

— 1992 *Documentary Evidence for the Civil-War Defences of Exeter, 1642–43*. EMAFU Rep **92.10**

— 1995 *Exeter in the Civil War*. Devon Archaeol **6**

Stravinskiene, V and Juknys, R (eds) 1998 *Dendrochronology and Environmental Trends*. Kaunas, Lithuania: Vytautas Magnus University, Department of Environmental Sciences

Sutherland, D S 1990 'Burnt Stone in a Saxon Church and its Implications' *in* Parsons (ed) 1990, 102–13

Thomas, P and Warren, J 1980 *Aspects of Exeter*. Plymouth: Baron Jay

Thomas, R G 1974 'An Unknown Devon County Poll Book'. *Rep Trans Devonshire Ass* **106**, 231–58

Thornton, J H 1973 'Excavated Shoes to 1600'. *Trans Mus Assistants Group* **12**, 11

Thorp, J R L 1982 'Two Hall Houses in a Late-Medieval Terrace: 8–12 Fore Street, Silverton'. *Proc Devon Archaeol Soc* **40**, 171–80

— 1990a 'Wall Painting and Lime-Plaster Decoration' *in* Beacham, P (ed) 1990, 129–49

— 1990b '10 The Close, Exeter' *in* Cooper, N (ed) 1990, 47–50

— 1990c 'Cadhay' *in* Cooper, N (ed) 1990, 101–2

— 1996 'The Excavated Slate and Slate Hanging' *in* Brown 1996, 291–4

— 1998 'Carpentry and Framing Techniques in Devon Buildings up to 1550' *in* Stenning, D F and Andrews, D D (eds) 1998, 79–87

Thurley, S 1990 'The Sixteenth-Century Kitchens at Hampton Court'. *J Brit Archaeol Ass* **143**, 1–28

— 1993 *The Royal Palaces of Tudor England: Architecture and Court Life 1460–1547*. New Haven and London: Yale University Press

Tidmarsh, W G 1932 'The Permian Lavas of Devon'. *Quart J Geol Soc* **88**, part 4, 712–75

Tipping, H A 1907 'Southam Delabere, Gloucestershire'. *Country Life* **22**, 26 October 1907, 594–601

— 1915 'Weare Giffard, Devonshire'. *Country Life* **37**, 2 January 1915, 16–25

Tomlinson, C 1852–54 *Cyclopaedia of Useful Arts*, 2 vols. London: J S Virtue

Torr, C 1921 *Small Talk at Wreyland, Second Series*. Cambridge: Cambridge University Press

Trewman 1827 *The Exeter Journal or Gentleman's, Merchant's and Tradesman's complete Annual Account Book*. Exeter: Trewman & Co

Trewman 1839 *The Exeter Journal and Annual Companion or Complete Book of Reference for the West of England*. Exeter: R J Trewman

Trewman 1844 *The Exeter Journal or Complete Book of Reference for the West of England [...] for the year 1844*. Exeter: R J Trewman

Trinick, M 1989 *Compton Castle, Devon* (guidebook). London: The National Trust

— 1990 *Cotehele House, Cornwall* (guidebook). London: The National Trust

Tyers, I 1991 *Dendrochronology Report on Building Timbers and Wooden Panelling from Sutton House, Hackney, London*. MoLAS Dendro Rep **02/91**

— 1993a 'Tree-ring Dating at Cressing Temple and the Essex Curve' *in Cressing Temple: a Templar and Hospitaller Manor in Essex* (ed D Andrews), 77–83. Chelmsford: Essex County Council

— 1993b *Tree-ring Analysis of a Panel Painting: Prince Arthur*. MoLAS Dendro Rep **05/93**

— 1994a *Tree-ring Analysis of the ABB87 Door and Barrel*. MoLAS Dendro Rep **6/94**

— 1994b *Tree-ring Analysis and Artefact Identification for the St John's Clerkenwell Project*. MoLAS Dendro Rep **05/94**

— 1995 *The Tree-ring Analysis of St Bartholomew's Church, Lower Sapey, Hereford and Worcester*. AML Rep **14/95**

— 1996a 'Appendix 1: Dendrochronology of Shipping from London, Twelfth to Seventeenth Centuries' *in* Marsden P *Shipping and the Port of London: Twelfth to Seventeenth Centuries*. English Heritage Archaeol Rep **5**, 193–7

— 1996b *The Tree-ring Analysis of Six Secular Buildings from the City of Hereford*. AML Rep **17/96**

— 1997a *Dendrochronological Analysis of Beech Timbers from the Magor Pill I Wreck, Gwent*. ARCUS Rep **261**

— 1997b *Dendro for Windows Program Guide*. ARCUS Rep **340**

— 1997c *Tree-ring Analysis of Seven Buildings from Essex*. ARCUS Rep **292**

— 1998a *Tree-ring Analysis and Wood Identification on Timbers Excavated on the Magistrates Court Site, Kingston upon Hull, East Yorkshire*. ARCUS Rep **410**

— 1998b *Tree-ring Analysis of St Martins Church, Colchester, Essex*. ARCUS Rep **366**

— 1998c *Tree-ring Analysis of the Samwell Wing, Felbrigg Hall, Norfolk*. AML Rep **65/98**

Tyers, I, Groves, C, Hillam, J and Boswijk, G 1997 'List 80 – Tree-ring Dates from Sheffield University'. *Vernacular Architect* **28**, 138–58

Ussher, W A E 1902 *The Geology of the Country Around Exeter*. London: Memoirs of the Geological Survey of England and Wales, Sheet **325**. HMSO

Verey, D 1970 *The Buildings of England, Gloucestershire 2: The Vale and the Forest of Dean*. Harmondsworth: Penguin

Verey, D 1979 *The Buildings of England, Gloucestershire 1: The Cotswolds*, 2nd edn. Harmondsworth: Penguin

Vince, A G and Brown, D H 1982 'The Petrology of Some Pottery from Okehampton' *in* Higham, R A *et al* 1982, 101–3

Vivian, J L 1895 *The Visitations of the County of Devon, Comprising the Heralds' Visitations of 1531, 1564, & 1620*. Exeter: Eland

Waterhouse, R 2000 'Keynedon Barton, Sherford, Kingsbridge'. *Proc Devon Archaeol Soc* **58**, 127–200

Watkin, H R 1935 *Dartmouth: Volume 1, Pre-Reformation*. Devonshire Association, Parochial Histories of Devon **5**

Watson, L and Harries, R (eds) 1995 *Out of Earth II, National Conference on Earth Buildings*. Plymouth: Centre for Earthen Architecture, University of Plymouth

Watson, L L and Harding, S (eds) 1994 *Out of Earth: First National Conference on Earth Buildings*. Plymouth: Centre for Earthen Architecture, University of Plymouth

Wazny, T 1990 'Aufbau und Anwendung der Dendrochronologie für Eichenholz in Polen'. Unpublished PhD dissertation, University of Hamburg

Wazny, T and Eckstein, D 1991 'The Dendrochronological Signal of Oak (*Quercus* spp) in Poland'. *Dendrochronologia* **9**, 35–49

Weaver, L 1913 'Cadhay, Devon'. *Country Life* **33**, 18 January 1913, 90–97

Webb, G 1956 *Architecture in Britain: The Middle Ages*. Harmondsworth: Pelican History of Art/Penguin

Webster, L E and Cherry, J 1973 'Medieval Britain in 1972'. *Medieval Archaeol* **17**, 138–88

— 1979 'Medieval Britain in 1978'. *Medieval Archaeol* **23**, 234–78

Weddell, P J 1991 'The Origins of Newton Abbot'. *Devon Archaeol* **4**, 19–28

Wedgwood, J 1936 *A History of Parliament: Biographies of Members of the Commons House 1439–1509*. London: HMSO

— 1938 *A History of Parliament: Register of the Ministers and of the Members of Both Houses, 1439–1509*. London: HMSO

Welch, E (ed) 1967 *Plymouth Building Accounts of the Sixteenth and Seventeenth Centuries*. Devon and Cornwall Record Society, New Series **23**. Exeter

Whetham, C D (ed) 1913 *A Manor Book of Ottery Saint Mary*. London: Longmans Green

Wickham, A K 1952 *Churches of Somerset*. London: Phoenix House

Williams, E H D 1974 'Poltimore Farmhouse, Farway'. *Rep Trans Devonshire Ass* **106**, 215–29

Wood, J, Chitty, G, Daniels, R, Grenville, J, Hook, R and Stocker, D (eds) 1994 *Buildings Archaeology: Applications in Practice*. Oxford: Oxbow Books

Wood, M 1965 *The English Mediaeval House*. London: Phoenix House

Woolner, D 1989 *Bradley, Devon* (guidebook). London: The National Trust

Woodward, C 1994 *Windows*, no. 2 in a series of advisory booklets. Bath: The Building of Bath Museum and Bath City Council

Worthy, C 1892 *The History of the Suburbs of Exeter*. London: Henry Gray and Exeter: S Drayton & Sons

Wright, J (ed) 1898 *The English Dialect Dictionary*. London: Frowde

Yeo, G 1986 'Where Was Cowick Priory'. *Devon and Cornwall Notes and Queries* **35**, 321–6

Youings, J 1955 *Devon Monastic Lands: Calendar of Particulars for Grants 1536–1558*. Exeter: Devon and Cornwall Record Society, New Series **1**. Exeter

— 1968 *Tuckers Hall, Exeter: The History of a Provincial City Company Through Five Centuries*. Exeter: The University of Exeter and The Incorporation of Weavers, Fullers and Shearmen

Youngs, S M, Clark, J and Barry, T B 1984 'Medieval Britain and Ireland in 1983'. *Medieval Archaeol* **28**, 203–65

Zunde, M 1998 'Wood Export from Medieval Riga and Possibilities for Dendrochronological Dating' *in* Stravinskiene and Juknys (eds) 1998, 67–74

Index

Illustrations are denoted by page numbers in *italics*. The following abbreviations have been used in this index: C – century; d – died; fl – *floruit*; m – married.